TALES FROM
SACRED WIND

CONTRIBUTIONS TO SOUTHERN APPALACHIAN STUDIES

TALES FROM SACRED WIND

Coming of Age in Appalachia

◆ The Cratis Williams Chronicles ◆

CRATIS D. WILLIAMS

Edited by David Cratis Williams
and Patricia D. Beaver

CONTRIBUTIONS TO SOUTHERN APPALACHIAN STUDIES, 8

McFarland & Company, Inc., Publishers
Jefferson, North Carolina, and London

This volume is part of the Cratis Williams Chronicles, the first installment of which was published as *The Cratis Williams Chronicles: I Come to Boone*, also edited by David Cratis Williams and Patricia Beaver (Boone, N.C.: Appalachian Consortium Press, 1999).

LIBRARY OF CONGRESS CATALOGUING-IN-PUBLICATION DATA

Williams, Cratis D.
     Tales from sacred wind : coming of age in Appalachia. The Cratis Williams chronicles / edited by David Cratis Williams and Patricia D. Beaver.
          p.   cm.—(Contributions to southern Appalachian studies ; 8)
     Includes bibliographical references and index.

     ISBN 0-7864-1490-1 (softcover : 50# alkaline paper) ∞

     1. Williams, Cratis D.   2. Mountain life—Appalachian Region, Southern.   3. Appalachian Region, Southern—Social life and customs. 4. Appalachian Region, Southern—Biography.   5. Educators—Kentucky—Biography.   I. Title.   II. Series.
CT275.W565A3   2003
976.9'26043'092—dc21   2002155764

British Library cataloguing data are available

Front cover: Cratis Williams on the day after his fourteenth birthday; background photograph by Marty McGee

Manufactured in the United States of America

McFarland & Company, Inc., Publishers
Box 611, Jefferson, North Carolina 28640

Acknowledgments

The personal memoirs, family stories, folktales, and commentaries on Appalachian culture, history, and folkways that comprise this collection are drawn from the writings of Cratis D. Williams (1911–1985). A native of Lawrence County, Kentucky, he gained renown as a leading authority on the southern Appalachian culture "in fact and fiction," as the title of his award-winning dissertation at New York University phrased it, as well as an influential educator in a career that began in a one-room country schoolhouse in eastern Kentucky and concluded as a professor, dean, and acting chancellor at what is now Appalachian State University in Boone, North Carolina. This rich assortment of his writings focuses on life as experienced growing up on an Appalachian farm during the first third of the twentieth century.

In 1986, following the death of Cratis Williams in 1985, Carl Ross, director of the Center for Appalachian Studies, and Cratis's son David Williams began working on the publication of this collection of memoirs from Cratis Williams's boyhood. However, Carl Ross's untimely death in 1988 saw this project laid aside.

In 1997 Patricia Beaver returned to the position of director of the Center for Appalachian Studies which she had held from 1978 to 1983, and learning of the work that Carl and David had begun, contacted David about the possibility of again undertaking this project for the university's centennial celebration during the 1999–2000 academic year. David responded enthusiastically, but suggested that a more appropriate memoir for the centennial would be Cratis's account of his first year in Boone, 1942–1943, when he was hired to teach at the Appalachian Demonstration High School associated with Appalachian State Teachers College. As coeditors we pursued that publication, resulting in *The Cratis Williams Chronicles: I Come to Boone* (1999).

Soon after publication of *I Come to Boone*, we picked up the work that Carl and David had begun on the eastern Kentucky boyhood stories. Cratis Williams left behind an abundance of memoirs, genealogical records, and notes on language, essays, speeches, and letters. Our task has been to choose the materials to be included in this work, to organize these various documents into a text that will be meaningful to readers and true to Cratis's intent, and to complement the text with appropriate photographs and other documentation that will be beneficial to the reader or researcher. We have selected as many of Cratis's writings as conceivably fit, and organized them in a way that was meaningful to us. Some of these memoirs had titles that appear in the text; Cratis left no guidance as to the organization of these materials into chapters, so we have combined these into the six chapters and appendices that follow and developed titles derived from the text. Some pieces have been combined to eliminate duplication, especially in the genealogical accounts, family histories, and the folkways segments.

Chapter One closes with Cratis's telling the story of Mutts Mag, learned from his grandmother Amanda Griffith, who learned it from her mother Elzina See. This account of the trio Mutts Mag, Poll, and Nance is the only female variant of the more widely known Jack Tales with their triad of Jack, Tom and Will. We thank Charlotte Ross who transcribed the Mutts Mag story. In addition to Carl Ross, who worked with David to begin this project, we wish to thank Elizabeth Bordeaux for her assistance in the organization of this project and for her careful proofreading, Kinny Baughman for his computer wizardry, and Matthew Mellon for assisting Jon Hill in scanning photographs. While Jon Hill worked extensively on the completion of the text and compilation of materials, fellow graduate students in the MA program in Appalachian studies Donavan Cain, Jessica Wrye, and Cassie Robinson worked on this manuscript in its various forms. Dean Williams assisted with photographs of artifacts, and Fred Hay, director of the W.L. Eury Appalachian Collection, and Kathy Staley, archivist for the collection, who ably manage the Cratis Williams archival materials, assisted us in myriad ways, for which we are grateful. Kathy Starks assisted in developing the genealogy.

Richard Miller, chair of the Department of Philosophy and Liberal Arts at the University of Missouri at Rolla, provided computer expertise in Missouri, and Alec Arnold, student assistant at UMR, assisted in background research and checking footnotes. Our thanks as well go to the staff of the Louisa [Kentucky] Public Library for their assistance in locating information. We are very appreciative of the suggestions provided at our request by Loyal Jones, who offered sound advice that we didn't always follow.

Photographs and stories were generously shared by many in Cratis's family, including his wife, Libby Williams, daughter Sophie Williams, sister

Ruth Williams Lester, brother-in-law Woodrow Barber, and nephews Jim Lester, Jack Lester, and Tony Williams. Bobbi Lynn Williams Fugate, Cratis's niece, deserves special recognition for digging through musty records and moldy boxes and producing some gems. Barbara Lingerfelt had the foresight many years ago to transcribe one of her brother-in-law's speeches on Appalachian culture, and for that we can all be grateful. James Guy Riley deserves thanks in ways that cannot be expressed.

These are, of course, Cratis Williams's writings, and we are very grateful that he left them for us to read. Cratis said many times that he did not write his memoirs with publication specifically in mind. We believe that through his memoirs he was keeping alive within himself and making available to his descendents his memories of a life and a people now far more removed than their mere distance in years would suggest. In these pages Cratis reanimates his own unique voice, and through it we can follow along as he comes of age in the culturally rich community that once was known as Sacred Wind.

David Cratis Williams
Rolla, Missouri

Patricia Beaver
Boone, North Carolina

February 2003

Contents

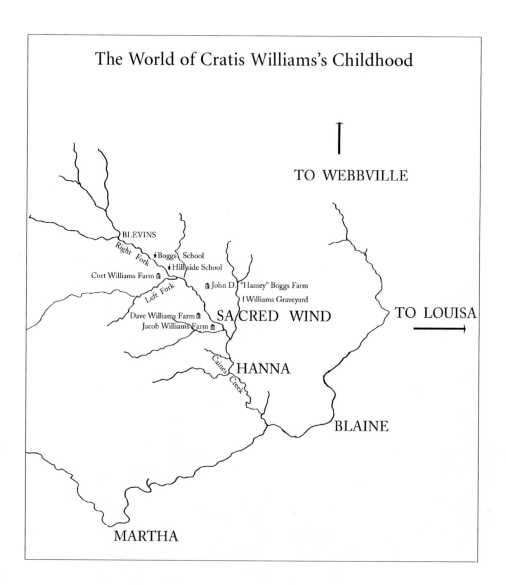

The World of Cratis Williams's Childhood

TO WEBBVILLE

BLEVINS

Right Fork

Boggs School

Hillside School

Curt Williams Farm

Left Fork

John D. "Hamey" Boggs Farm

Williams Graveyard

Dave Williams Farm

SACRED WIND

TO LOUISA

Jacob Williams Farm

Caines Creek

HANNA

BLAINE

MARTHA

Introduction

Cratis Williams is widely recognized as a pioneer in the Appalachian Studies movement. He was a nationally recognized spokesperson for Appalachian culture through his documentation and interpretation of its ballads, folk tales, language, historical traditions, religions and customs, and his advocacy for Appalachian youth and cultural grounding. He was frequently called "a complete mountaineer." Born on Caines Creek, in Lawrence County, Kentucky, in 1911, he drew lifelong inspiration from his rural family and the culture of the community.

The first child of Curtis and Mona (Whitt) Williams, Williams was educated in the one-room Hillside Elementary School on Caines Creek. He then boarded with relatives in the county seat, Louisa, in order to attend Louisa High School, from which he graduated in 1928. His interest in ballads was sparked in high school, when he began a lifelong pursuit of the historical traditions of the community into which he was born. He attended Cumberland College (1928–29), then taught in one-room schools on Caines Creek (1929–1933) while taking classes for his BA at the University of Kentucky (1933). He then taught science and English at Blaine High School (1933–1938). In 1937 he married fellow teacher Sylvia Graham, and that same year received the MA in English from the University of Kentucky with a thesis entitled "Ballads and Songs." This thesis, analyzing 471 ballads and songs from eastern Kentucky, was reproduced on microcard for use by folklore scholars. Williams served as principal of Louisa High School (1938–1941) and ran unsuccessfully for Superintendent of Schools; following his defeat, he and his wife Sylvia were unable to find work locally as teachers. Employed by New Idea, Inc., in Coldwater, Ohio, he next found work as the instructor at the Apprentice School for International Nickel Company in Huntington, West

Virginia. In 1942 Williams was hired as critic teacher at the Appalachian Demonstration High School, Appalachian State Teachers College, in Boone, North Carolina. During that first year in Boone, his wife Sylvia succumbed to tuberculosis, a disease with which he had also been diagnosed. Recovering from that illness, Williams served the high school until 1949 as critic teacher, assistant principal, director of drama, and director of the first schoolwide counseling program in North Carolina. In 1946 he was named assistant professor of English and speech at Appalachian State Teachers College. He earned his Ph.D. at New York University in 1961, with a dissertation "The Southern Mountaineer in Fact and Fiction" (abstracted in *Appalachian Journal* 1975–1976), a work which is unparalleled in the field of Appalachian literature.

Williams married Elizabeth Lingerfelt in 1949, with whom he had two children, Sophie (born 1953) and David Cratis (born 1955). At Appalachian State University he was named professor of English in 1950, then served as dean of the Graduate School from 1958 to 1975. During his term as dean, the Graduate School of Appalachian State University became a member of the Council of Graduate Schools in the United States and experienced a dramatic increase in graduate enrollment, and Williams became a nationally recognized authority on graduate programs in education. He also served as acting vice chancellor for academic affairs (1974) and acting chancellor (1975), before his retirement in 1976.

By the late 1940s Williams had developed curricula on traditional ballads and songs and worked with associates in a Saturday afternoon folk festival in Boone. In 1956 he developed with Beulah Campbell one of the first senior level college curricula in Appalachian studies, a summer workshop on the "Living Folk Arts of Southern Mountain People," offering students the opportunity to participate in Saturday folk festivals and home visits to document local speech, songs, tales, folk remedies, traditional crafts, and to study Appalachian literature, history, and sociology. In addition to offering ballads and songs and Appalachian literature in the English department, he sparked the development of new courses among his colleagues throughout the region, and among his students in their teaching positions in secondary schools, colleges, and universities.

His abiding interest in mountain speech led to the publication of a series of articles between 1961 and 1967 in *Mountain Life and Work,* and reprinted as *Southern Mountain Speech* (1992). His approach to linguistics was based in his lived experience, native ear, and keen memory. His devotion to the nuances and rich subtlety of mountain speech was matched by his meticulous knowledge of ballads and his artful capacity for telling tales learned in childhood. He both treasured and taught ballads as literature and as a key to the mountain aesthetics. He lectured widely and entertained diverse audiences with his perspective on the Scotch-Irish heritage as manifest in cultural values and speech. He played a role in the decision to create the Appalachian Collection of Belk Library, named the W.L. Eury Appalachian Collection in 1971, which was composed initially of materials the library had purchased to support his dissertation research.

The 1970s saw many of Williams's interests bear fruit in the formation of new curricula, outreach, and collaboration, including preparation of teachers and supervisors for instruction in rural Appalachia. In 1972 the *Appalachian Journal* was launched on the Appalachian State University campus, with Jerry Williamson as editor and Williams as advising editor. He was a founding member of the Appalachian Consortium, and the Appalachian Consortium Press was established in 1972 with Williams as a member of the editorial board. He was the major catalyst behind the creation of the Center for Appalachian Studies in 1979 and the MA degree in Appalachian studies in 1980 at Appalachian State University.

Following his retirement in 1976 from a distinguished career as a teacher and administrator at Appalachian, Williams began to write memoirs of his life. His published memoirs, two published posthumously, include *William H. Vaughan: A Better Man Than I Ever Wanted to Be* (1983), *I Become a Teacher* (1995) and *The Cratis Williams Chronicles: I Come to Boone* (1999), which includes a biography, chronology, and bibliography of Williams's writings and videos. Video treatment includes *Cratis Williams: Living the Divided Life* (1998). The Cratis Dearl Williams Collection, containing his personal library and papers, is housed in the W.L. Eury Appalachian Collection, Belk Library, Appalachian State University.

A retirement symposium held in Williams's honor (1976) featured an array of regional scholars; selected papers were published in *An Appalachian Symposium: Essays Written in Honor of Cratis D. Williams* (Williamson 1977). This symposium also sparked the organization of the Appalachian Studies Association the following year in Berea, Kentucky, and in 1992 the highest award of the association, given annually to an outstanding regional scholar, was designated the Cratis Williams Award.

Though his achievements were recognized throughout his professional life, many awards came nearer the end of it. He was awarded the Founders Day Certificate for Excellence, New York University (1962), North Carolina Historical Society's Achievement Award (1972), O. Max Gardner Award, University of North Carolina (1973), Honorary Citizen of Harlan County, Kentucky (1973), Brown-Hudson Award, North Carolina Folklore Society (1975), Laurel Leaves Award, Appalachian Consortium (1976), and W.D. Weatherford Award, Berea College (1979), and received honorary degrees from Berea College (1977), from Cumberland College, Morehead State University, College of Idaho (1984), and from Marshall University and Appalachian State University (1985).

The Legacy of Caines Creek

By the end of his career Cratis Williams was a nationally recognized scholar and educator who moved easily in the cultural circles typically associated with higher education. Yet he began life in cultural circumstances far removed from the rarefied air of universities. He never detached himself from his cultural roots, although it did take him many years and no doubt much agonizing before he was able to embrace with pride his Appalachian heritage, even as he ascended through the academic ranks. In many respects, the memoirs, tales, and accounts of Appalachian folkways compiled in this volume tell the tale of that struggle to come to terms with his Appalachian self while at the same time prospering in a cultural and intellectual milieu far removed from his home community. In the absence of that community's gentle corrections, which he himself came to provide, he was all too often inclined to look down upon his native culture, a culture shared with the millions of other Appalachian Americans.

Cratis Williams was born on April 5, 1911, in his grandfather's log house along the "main waters" of Caines Creek, about six miles from the town of Blaine, in Lawrence County, Kentucky, in the heart of the Big Sandy Valley. Founded in 1822, Lawrence County was named for Capt. James Lawrence, the famed sea commander who was fatally injured in the fight between the U.S. frigate *Chesapeake* and the British frigate *Shannon*. His immortalized last words were, "Don't give up the ship" (Chaffin 1991, 4). Prior to the founding of Lawrence County, the area of the Mouth of Hood that was later to become Blaine "had already become a trading center for the pioneer families who had settled in that part of what was then Floyd County": "Tanners, shoemakers, saddlers, blacksmiths, coopers, distillers, sawyers, carpenters, masons, traders, and doctors had followed fast upon the heels of the first hunters and trappers who came there, certainly as early as 1796 and possibly earlier." And trade "had been brisk. The main source of bearskins for the headgear of Napoleon's armies had been the Big Sandy Valley (Williams 1991)." Although the destruction of the old Floyd County courthouse by fire in 1808 makes impossible precise dating of the arrival of Richard and Margaret Caines to the hollows surrounding the creek that came to bear their name, available evidence suggests that they had settled in as early as 1796 (Williams 1991). A direct descendant of Richard Caines and others among the first settlers of "the Big Sandy Valley, referred to frequently as 'Kentucky's Last Frontier,'" Cratis Williams was also descended from "Indian fighters, 'long hunters,' veterans of the American Revolution, Tories escaped to the backwoods, refugees from the Whiskey Rebellion, and Kentucky mountain feudists" (Williams nda).

The first Williams in Cratis's family tree to come to America had been

John Williams, "who was kidnapped and bound out in Virginia for a three year period to pay for his passage over" (Williams, C.A. 1991, 737–738). He never fulfilled the terms of that involuntary obligation, joining in the Revolution against British authority and gaining his freedom with the birth of the new nation.[1] According to one account, John fathered Lewis Haney Williams, born in Virginia in 1809 (Williams, C.A. 1991, 737), but Cratis Williams believed that the original John had a son, also named John, who fathered Lewis Haney. Lewis Haney was Cratis's great-great-grandfather, who brought his family to Caines Creek in 1839; Cratis's great-grandfather Jacob Peters Williams was eight years old at the time. Jacob Peter's son David married Martha Boggs, and they had three children together: Grace, Blanche, and Cratis's father Curtis Williams, who was born in 1890. Two of Martha's sisters married brothers of David Williams, and among the three couples "there were 29 children, according to all reports, all of whom would have been double first cousins" (Carson 1979, 32–33). David Williams and his young family attempted to improve their fortunes in the late eighteen-nineties by moving west to Missouri along with David's brothers and Martha's sisters.

But David missed Kentucky, and after a short while they returned to Caines Creek, where David opened a distillery and moved his family into a fine house below the forks of the creek. It was in that house that Cratis was later born.

In his early childhood, Cratis began "growing up in an isolated valley relatively untouched by influences from the outside," and he began to learn "the traditions of his people, whose songs, hymns, religious attitudes, manners, customs, and speech were essentially those of the borderers of the 18th century." He came to think "of himself as a 'complete mountaineer'" (Williams nda). But even by the time of Cratis's birth in 1911, the forces of modernization had already begun to move into the mountains of eastern Kentucky, and during his youth the external pressures upon the traditional culture only increased. The relative isolation and cultural continuity within the nooks and crannies of the Big Sandy that had endured for a hundred years or so prior to "the coming of the railroad and the public high school" and other such influences had been "disturbed" by the turn of the century, and the "first quarter of the twentieth century proved to be a strategic period in the history of the Big Sandy Valley, witnessing a change in the customs and institutions of the inhabitants and a struggle between old and new" (Williams ndb). It was during this period of increasing erosion of time-honored cultural practices, that in many mountain homes and communities had endured for as long as a century (an eternity by American measurement), that Cratis Williams came of age.

Martha Boggs Williams died in December 1899. David "had a peculiar belief about preserving the bodies as long as possible." Toward that end, he

David O. Williams family, 1898, in Lamar, Missouri. Left–right: Curtis, Martha, Blanche, David O.; standing: Grace. David was not given a middle name, so he gave himself one, Oscar.

had a "heavy, awkward looking" stone tomb constructed beside his house. It took three weeks to build the stone tomb, and Martha "was placed in the tomb on January 1, 1900" (Carson 1979, 20). David later married Martelia Swann, and they produced a large family. Curt Williams had several half-brothers and half-sisters, and Cratis had an aunt younger than he.

Curt Williams (left) and Harrison Williams, half brothers, sons of David O. Williams.

Years later, in 1948, David hired Alf Matney, a black man from Louisa, to build a concrete structure encasing the original stone vault that contained Martha, which also now included space for both Martelia and David himself. When the concrete encasement was finished, David was "so proud of it that he said at the Judgement Day the devil would have such a hard time cracking this tomb open that he thought he might pass him by ("Cratis Williams: Living the Divided Life" 1998)." David posed on his tomb-to-be, and Alf Matney, who had been staying at David's house while he worked on the concrete encasement, took a photo. And in a few short years, David O. Williams, sober in his last days, found his final resting spot within his devil-proofed tomb.

The arrival of Prohibition had a tumultuous effect upon the economy of the community within which Cratis lived. Though still a child at the time, Cratis was old enough to have experienced the relatively prosperous local economy and buoyant spirits which had accompanied the three legal distilleries operated in the county prior to passage of the amendment, all three of them operated by Cratis's relatives: in addition to David O. Williams's distillery, David's brother-in-law operated one in "Stillhouse Holler" on what was to become Curt Williams's farm, and his first cousin William Henderson ("Little Hen") Boggs operated the third ("Cratis Williams: Living the

Divided Life" 1998). The art of whiskey-making had become an established and honored skill within the Williams family long before they settled in Lawrence County, perhaps even ante-dating the arrival of the first Williams in the New World as an involuntary indentured servant in Colonial Virginia in the late 1760s. In any event, at the time the "Williamses migrated from Copper Creek in Scott County [Virginia] to Kentucky in 1837," the skills and accouterments for whiskey-making accompanied them. Cratis related in an oral history interview, "the story is that when they came the ox wagons and carts had the stills, and the brandy, and the whiskey, and the family walked behind." And upon arrival in Lawrence County, "one of the first things my two-greats-grandfather did was to set his still up." Cratis recalled his "great-grandfather's still, my grandfather's still, and my father's still," emphasizing that prior to Prohibition the family distillers "were all legal distillers." "According to family legend" all of the men in Cratis Williams's lineage had a "similar history back to the Whiskey Rebellion. If that's the case, I am the first in direct lineage since the American Revolution not to have been a distiller myself, though I think I could do it" (Shackelford and Weinberg 1977, 104).

Part of Cratis's familiarity with the art of whiskey-making came from his childhood days, many of them spent in the company of his grandfather David Oscar Williams at his distillery on Caines Creek. "I was a kind of mascot in the distillery," Cratis recalled years later, "curious about how everything was done, and no doubt very much underfoot. I weighed twenty-five or thirty pounds then, but my rugged, two-hundred-and-fifty-pound grandpa indulged my whims and the workmen respected his wishes. Sometimes, when whiskey had been proofed and was ready for the barrel, Grandpa would fill my little four-ounce bottle for me and Grandma would put some brown sugar in it. The workmen enjoyed cajoling me into treating them to a swig from my bottle and making me feel that I was a very important person" (Shackelford and Weinberg 1977, 104). That status seems to have carried over into his play-time relations with other young boys in the community: "When I got some of the little boys to play games with me we played 'distilling.' We would get cans of one kind or another and make up little distilleries. Of course I knew more about that than any of the others, so I was always the leading distiller in these games" (Carson 1979, 22).

Although small by the standards of the distilling industry, David Williams's distillery was nonetheless a vital and thriving concern during the first decades of the century. The distillery was a "seven-day, twenty-four-hour-a-day concern." Consequently, he "had to have people on duty all the time. The upstairs of his house had bunks in it in which somebody was sleeping all the time. He had about fifteen people working for his distillery." But the roots of the distillery dug more deeply into the local community than is

David O. Williams poses at the mouth of his tomb, 1948. Photograph by Alf Matney. "I have a picture of my grandfather sitting on the stone that ultimately closed him up. At the time he was enjoying the drama and sentiment of the situation and was quite drunk"—Cratis Williams.

reflected in simply the number of employees. The type of whiskey made "would depend upon what happened to be in season at the time. Sometimes it was fruit whiskey. My grandfather contracted with old women who had apple orchards and needed to sell their apples. He'd [also] buy the barley and the rye and the corn that the neighbors had to sell, so that he could have the grain whiskey when the time came. A bushel of grain made about a gallon of whiskey, and the quality of the whiskey was unusually good" (Shackelford and Weinberg 1977, 105).

The whiskey that was produced was taken by wagon to Webbville then shipped by railroad to Catlettsburg, where it was marketed to distributors. Although his license permitted him to retail his whiskey directly to consumers, by law those sales had to be in quantities of five gallons or greater. The purpose of the law "was to keep the local fellows from buying half a pint and getting drunk, you see. Of course, they were skilled at getting around that. They'd simply make up a group of twelve to fifteen to buy five gallons." But if Dave Williams were to violate the five-gallon regulation, "he could be indicted, which happened to him occasionally. He would sell less than five gallons to some of his friends and sometimes he'd get caught" (Shackelford and Weinberg 1977, 106). When that happened "he was usually able to manage courts in such a way that he wasn't fined. Sometimes he would make the plea for himself in court. He understood the law quite well, though he was not really a well educated man. He was literate, he could read and write pretty well, he kept books well" (Carson 1979, 22). And he generally stayed free of legal difficulties with regard to his distillery prior to Prohibition and was never convicted of any major violations, either of selling unauthorized amounts or of violations of other regulations. Distilleries "were inspected periodically to see that they were obeying the little requirements of the law. 'Devil' John Wright was one of my grandfather's inspectors. No doubt the storekeeper and gauger and the distiller sometimes had under-the-table deals" (Shackelford and Weinberg 1977, 105).[2] Though legally "clean," Dave Williams began to earn notoriety as a bit of a mountain "bad man" prior even to the turn of the century, including through a well-publicized acquittal (along with Hige Holbrook) on charges of killing John Ferguson ("Abstract" 1893, 81).

The arrival of Prohibition, first in the form of the War-Time Prohibition Act of 1918 and then, emphatically, in the Volstead Act, changed dramatically the economy of Caines Creek. David O. Williams "might have been the last legal distiller in eastern Kentucky. His still was closed after the 'Act' became effective. I was a small boy [and] I happened to be present at the time the internal revenue officers came to close it down officially in 1918. I saw them remove the caps from the stills and carry [them] out to a sweet-potato patch to cool off" (Shackelford and Weinberg 1977, 107). At first, the "government took possession" of David Williams's "stills, but he filed an injunction and the stills were returned to him" (Williams qtd. in Wolfford 1972, 158). After the introduction of Prohibition "for a time he operated his full distillery every now and then." Indeed, for "the first three years after his legal distillery closed what he made was for market" (Carson 1979, 22), but it was for a special market that arose locally as a result of an oil boom: "The oil camp development that brought in about 5,000 outsiders in just over a year stimulated at least a resurgence of moonshining and most of that was done on this creek and so people came to buy whiskey" (Carson 1979, 2).

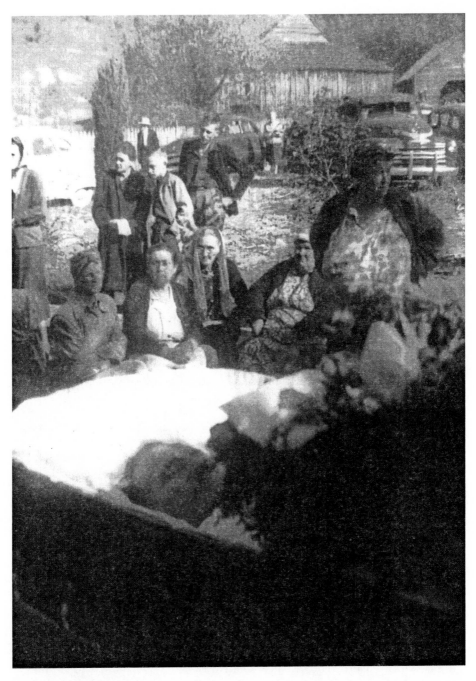

David O. Williams in his casket, 1951. Lillie Boggs seated second from left. Kate Boggs Castle seated in the middle.

According to Cratis's recollections, "Those men who worked over there around the oil wells would pay $40 a gallon for whiskey. Grandpa just made a lot of money there during that time and never did get caught." But the boom immediately after the introduction of Prohibition was short-lived, and as the oil men left so too did much of the local market for whiskey. About 1922, David Williams stopped operating his full distillery altogether. The largest of his stills, with a 300-gallon capacity, "was sold to Cap Hatfield, son of mountain feuder Devil Anse" (Williams qtd. in Wolfford 1972, 158). David Williams put a smaller still of about 100-gallon capacity "in the barn loft and kept his oats in it. I used to play in those oats. That was still there when a tornado came through and blew the barn down. Didn't hurt the still, but somebody picked it up and carried it off" (Shackelford and Weinberg 1977, 107). David O. then had a "small still" of about 90 gallons made for himself "which he kept hidden up the hollow above his house there and he would try to put off a run at least once a year to make his own whiskey" (Shackelford and Weinberg 1977, 22–23).

Although deferred somewhat by the brief oil boom, the closing of the distilleries brought not only economic ruin but also distorting influences to the traditional values and practices of the community. Cratis explained the economic impact in an oral history interview conducted in the 1970s (Shackelford and Weinberg 1977, 107–8):

> After my grandfather's still was closed officially, within three years the population of the valley had reduced 50 percent, because those three stills had sustained the economy of the valley. The apple orchards were neglected. Trees were neglected and cut down. There was no longer any market. It was eleven miles to the railhead [and] the corn was not worth carrying by wagon eleven miles to sell. Although my grandfather didn't pay these local men working in his distillery very much money—probably a dollar a day or less—he kept their family [in food]. The farmers that had white oak on their farms would cut trees for barrel staves; there was no longer any market for that.

Both the loss of the economic base provided in large measure by whiskey-making and the concurrent de-legitimating, indeed criminalizing, of the skills associated with it, skills which had been passed down within families for generations, precipitated the grinding poverty of the 1920s and 1930s and an advancement of a "culture of moonshining."

The economic devastation that followed from Prohibition is revealed rather dramatically in the out-migration and depopulation of the community which ensued. For instance, Cratis recalled, "The one-room country school had seventy-five in it [when] I attended. I went back to teach that school my first year of teaching, 1929; it had thirty-three in it. Three years later when

I left it had sixteen" (Shackelford and Weinberg 1977, 108). Indeed, it was not long after the closing of the distilleries that Curt Williams accepted a tenant farming arrangement in Ohio and in 1920 moved the family to Selma, Ohio, for a brief period of time before returning to Caines Creek. Curt Williams finally persuaded his father to sell him the section of the farm on which they had lived and worked prior to going to Ohio (indeed for all of Cratis's life), and he devoted himself to husbandry of farm and family.

By the time Cratis graduated from the one-room elementary school in 1924 and determined to attend high school in Louisa, a costly proposition involving room and board, Curt was not only farming but also trapping, collecting herbs, attending to sick and injured animals, and occasionally making moonshine whiskey, or doing virtually anything else he could to provide for his family and generate the scarce hard cash necessary to send Cratis to school. Cratis recalled of his father, "He was always doing little things to make some money. He couldn't walk through the woods without gathering the herbs that were worth something in the country store, for example." "He never wasted anything. His farm looked like a park. The fences were straight as arrows and the wires were stretched tightly. Every year he gave time to cleaning the fence rows. He mowed his meadows clean to the water's edge and to the edge of the fence, and his haystacks were neat and his barn was clean." Although Curt had little formal education, he became quite accomplished in many different vocations. "In late life he got permission of the county court to practice veterinarian medicine, while never having gone to school, in this part of the county because there was no veterinarian out here. He was also a skilled hunter and trapper and bought skins and furs and processed them and sold them to a dealer in Cincinnati who came every February to pick them up. He made enough money doing that to send each of us away to school" (Carson 1979, 14–15). It should also be noted that from time to time, Curt would also "run-off" a batch of whiskey, the sales of which also contributed toward the education of his children.

The onset of Prohibition may have forced the closure of the county's three legal distilleries, but it did not stop the practice of the traditional art of whiskey-making. Moonshining replaced legal distilling, although it did not offer the same economic benefits. Moreover, the illegality of moonshining soon created many problems for both the makers and consumers of the whiskey, and it also probably had more generalized effects upon the nature of social relations as practitioners of the art soon began to wonder about what their neighbors might know, or see, or tell. David Williams, for instance, who Cratis characterized as "a very, very independent, stubborn man" and who "did just about what he pleased," took his new, specially made still and "set up in a cave in the hollow behind his house" and made whiskey "whenever he wanted to. He was moonshining then" (Carson 1979, 108). He frequently

Casket of David O. Williams, 1951. Victor Brickey behind casket; Lloyd Castle, husband of Kate Boggs, at right.

found himself in legal snares that plagued him for years, although he still never served any jail time. He did, however, develop a notorious reputation in Lawrence county—and in large measure he did so at the time that his oldest grandson Cratis was attending school in the county seat of Louisa, trying to blend in to the more middle class mores that had developed in the town and struggling with feelings of shame for his country speech, manners, and family.

The *Big Sandy News* of July 23, 1926, trumpeted news of Cratis's grandfather on page one: "Dave Williams Convicted for Possessing Liquor" read the headline. A raid "a few weeks ago" had located "some moonshine ... concealed in the ground near his house," and the jury, "after deliberating for only a few minutes," had "returned a verdict giving him the highest penalty—$300 and 60 days." The *Big Sandy News* also reported of David Williams, "It was stated by witnesses that he bore a general reputation of not observing prohibition." In addition to the conviction of David Williams, the newspaper reported that after the trial, two of David Williams's sons "accosted" the deputy who was "instrumental in bringing their father to answer to the charge, and one of them was locked up." The paper does not give the names of the sons involved, but it does note that both "were charged with breach of the peace, but were released on bond." David Williams "appealed his case to circuit court."

In 1928, 62-year-old Dave Williams was back in the news. The front page headline of the *Big Sandy News* on June 15 announced, "Dave Williams Shoots Son, Said." Curt's half-brother Charles had been shot twice, but would recover. According to the news account,

> Returning from down the creek, young Williams stopped at his father's home where a dispute arose over some corn chop which the son wanted. After a heated argument the son started for home riding his mule by a short cut through a field of cowpeas. Reprimanded by his father for riding through the growing crop, the son, it is said, jumped off his mount and swore violently. The father turned and started into the house, the son daring him to get his guns, it is said. The father returned to the door with his revolver as the son topped the porch steps, with knife in hand, it is reported. The elder Williams then shot Charlie through the right shoulder near the apex of the lung cavity. Still advancing and cursing, Charley [sic], it is said, told his father to shoot again but suddenly turned to flee when the father shot him again in the top of the left shoulder.

The account tersely noted, "Reports say that liquor featured in the affair."

It was against this backdrop that Cratis attended Louisa High School and struggled to come to terms with the sophisticated culture of the county seat. When his father first took him to Louisa to attend school, Cratis later recalled, "I had a culture shock." Soon, however, he "was learning about the 'Yes Sir That's My Baby' jazz era with his new school friends," but it was not without tension: "I was living in two cultures. I couldn't let the people back on the creek know or they'd think I was puttin' on the dog" (Todd 1970). Many of his experiences during that time are recounted in this volume, particularly during his first years in school in Louisa, including the semester he spent in seventh grade. But he does not recount all of his academic involvement or convey fully the depth of his involvement in extra-curricular activities. Cratis left Caines Creek for Louisa to go to high school on February 10, 1924, but he was assigned to the seventh grade for the remainder of that semester. He began high school as a freshman in the fall of 1924, at the same time that the high school began publishing its own newspaper, the *Louisian*, every other week ("School Notes" 1924).

The newspaper was a harbinger of a "rounding-out" of the academic and extra-curricular program at the high school. In 1925–1926, William H. Vaughan[3] became principal amid the expansion of the school's programs, and the *Big Sandy News* proclaimed that "Louisa High School this year is rounding into a position of thoroughness and completeness equaling that of any of the larger high schools. All the outside scholastic activities that are sponsored by the larger schools are being organized here. These activities include debating, athletics, oratory, music, and editing the school paper." Among the first organized were two literary societies, the Ciceronian and the Athenian, which began sponsoring programs as early as September 1925 ("Activities Sponsored" 1925). In January 1926, Cratis tried out for the Louisa High School debating team. He was among 12 students vying for four spots on the team. The first competition for the eventual team was slated against Pikeville Academy toward the end of the month ("Students Out for School Debating Team" 1926). Evidently, Cratis was not successful in his initial debate try-out; the *Big Sandy News*'s announcement of the debate against Pikeville Academy did not include Cratis among the Louisa debaters ("Louisa to Debate Pikeville" 1926).

The growth in Louisa High School's "outside scholastic activities" during Cratis's sophomore year was matched by an explosion in enrollment during his junior year. When school opened for the term in September 1926, the enrollment in the high school was "greater than ever before": "At the beginning of the school term last year only 174 entered high school. There are 221 this year. By mid-year there will be about 240 or 250, as several usually enter at the beginning of the second semester." The curricular offerings had expanded as well, and "(b)esides the regular high school curriculum" there had "been added Solid Geometry, Trigonometry and second year Spanish." And "band and orchestra music" had been added to the assortment of "the regular music courses" ("School Opens" 1926). The faculty had expanded from seven, including Principal Vaughan, at the time of graduation, 1926 ("Graduating Class" 1926), to nine at the opening of the fall term, "all of them college graduates and with previous experience." The faculty and their subjects were as follows: William H. Vaughan, principal; N.Q. Gilmer, science; A.F. Young, mathematics; Lawrence Ellis, science; A.R. Hayden, mathematics and Latin; Miss Ellen Hughes, geography and modern languages; Miss Annie Beavers, English; Miss Katherine Logsden, English and history; and Miss Helen Lowe, home economics and home planning. In addition, a music teacher was to be added after the start of school. Four of the teachers were new: "Miss Beavers, who will be head of the English department is from Boaz, Alabama, a graduate of her State University and also of Peabody College of Nashville, Tenn. She has an M.A. degree in English and has taught in high schools three years." "Miss Logsden is from Franklin, Ky., has an A.B. degree, and has taught three years. Mr. Ellis is a graduate of the Eastern State Teachers College and comes well recommended. Miss Lowe is from the south, has an A.B. degree in Home Economics, and is a graduate student in this subject" ("Louisa Schools" 1926). These were sophisticated "outsiders" to the local community, and they exposed Cratis to influences from beyond the Big Sandy Valley.

During his final years at Louisa High School, Cratis boarded with the Wilson family in Louisa. By then, Cratis was popularly known by his school

Wilson family in Louisa, with whom Cratis boarded during his final years in high school. Nola standing behind her father, Cratis's classmate Bug standing beside Nola.

nickname, "Cricket." The Wilsons' son Richard was a classmate, and they became fast friends. Richard was popularly known by his nickname, "Bug."

As a high school junior, Cratis became increasingly involved in extracurricular activities, including the high school newspaper, the *Louisian;* the first issue of volume three rolled off the presses on September 27, 1926, with Henry Wellman as editor. A five column, four page publication scheduled to "appear each fortnight," the *Louisian* had enjoyed a circulation of approximately 400 the preceding year and was looking toward even greater circulation by adding a "new department for rural school news." Cratis was club editor for the 1926–1927 year ("First Issue" 1926). Despite having existed for only three years, the *Louisian* began to gain recognition as a stellar high school newspaper. In the competition "for the best all-round high school paper in the state, Louisa won her measure of recognition by receiving honorable mention on two different counts at the Kentucky High School Press Association." The paper "ranked fourth among high school organs of the state," with fourth place rankings in the categories of "general excellence" and "headline display" ("Louisian Given" 1926).

Bug Wilson, high school friend of Cratis.

Cratis also ascended to a more central role on Louisa High School's debate team. Although not one of Louisa's top debaters, he was nonetheless an active participant in the school's highly successful and visible debate program. Following tryouts on December 11, 1926, Cratis was selected to the out-of-state debating team; he was slated to represent Louisa along with Hubert Prichard and Henry Collinsworth at a "home" debate against Huntington High School (W.Va.) on January 17, 1927 ("Louisa Debating Team" 1926). The outcome of that scheduled debate is not known, but as a member of the "out-of-state" team, Cratis participated in competitive, public debates representing Louisa High School against nearby non–Kentucky schools. The *Big Sandy News* reported in February that Cratis and partner W.M. Crutcher lost a 3–0 decision to Huntington High School in an "unusually interesting debate" before an audience of "approximately 50 persons." The judges were area educators: "Professors M.J. Robinette and W.C. Lovely, of the Fort Gay schools" and "Prof. M.B. Geiger of Paintsville" ("Louisa Tied" 1927).

A member of the Science Club throughout high school, Cratis became one of the club's leaders by the time he was a junior. For the club's "Stunt Night" fundraiser in January 1927, Cratis delivered the opening address, "The Science Club, Its Past, Present, and Future," and then joined the cast of a one-act comedy, *A Sudden Bethrothal*, as the male lead, Wellington Whipple ("To Offer" 1927).

By his senior year, Cratis had clearly established himself among student leaders at what continued to be a growing, vibrant, and ambitious high school. Prior to the opening of the term in August 1927, the *Big Sandy News* reported expectations "that the high school enrollment this year will exceed even last year's record enrollment of 260. Increased enrollment has always followed improved conditions. In a five year period the increase has been from 60 to 260, and now that the school has been accepted in the Southern Association — a distinction that only 74 of Kentucky's more than 400 high schools enjoy — the increase will naturally continue." The faculty had been expanded again, and among its eleven teachers "Louisa high school will have three teachers with M.A. degrees. For a high school in a town the size of Louisa this is an unusual record" ("Louisa Schools" 1927).

Cratis's own activities continued to expand as well. He was selected editor of the *Louisian*, an activity upon which he elaborates in this volume. But his orbit was wider. During the fall of Cratis's senior year, Mr. Luwig, the "Y.M.C.A. worker of this district," came to Louisa to help "with the organization of a Hi Y Club at the high school." Cratis was elected secretary of the new student organization ("Hi Y Club" 1927). As a fundraiser "for the improvement of the science department," the Science Dynamic Club presented "'The Little Clodhopper,' a three-act play by the author of 'Deacon Dubbs,' and 'My Irish Rose,' which [had] proved so popular in Louisa" on December 2, 1927. In the comedy, Cratis played the male lead, "Septimus Green — A young book agent full of pep" ("Hi School Talent" 1927).

The senior class play gave Cratis another opportunity to engage his theatrical abilities. The three-act comedy *Am I Intruding*, a "thoroughly modern production written by Frederick G. Johnson," was selected as the class play, with Mrs. K.C. Elswick directing. Cratis was cast in the supporting role of Bobby. The *Big Sandy News* predicted, "based upon a plot unique and different," the production would "afford an evening of delightful entertainment which Louisians should avail themselves of enjoying" ("Seniors Present" 1928). After the production, the *News* reported that the production had indeed "afforded an evening of delightful entertainment to between three and four hundred Louisians who were present to witness the performance." Happily, the paper judged that the "parts taken by all the cast were well played, and the play as rendered speaks much praise for the senior class and Mrs. Elswick, the director." The "admission receipts totaled $113.00" ("Senior Play" 1928).

Although less active in debating during his senior year, Cratis was nonetheless active in other forensic activities. In the "interscholastic high school tournament for the eastern district of Kentucky, comprising 13 counties," that included contests "for district championships in scholarship, oratory, music, and declamation," Cratis represented Louisa High School in the declamation competition ("District Tourney" 1928). One of the ironies of Cratis's high school career is that, despite deep involvement in all sorts of extra scholastic activities — and perhaps especially those which, like drama, declamation or debate, involved performance — he was never involved with any of the music clubs or groups. As editor of the *Louisian* he did include some ballad verses in the newspaper, but the future balladeer did not participate in any of the numerous singing opportunities while in high school. As a result Cratis had little formal knowledge of music, and his voice was never formally trained ... and perhaps thus unspoiled by affectations of musical style.

Cratis was the salutatorian of his graduating class of 40 on May 25, 1928; Shirley DeBord, who had played the female lead opposite Cratis in the Science Club's production of *A Sudden Bethrothal* the previous January, was the valedictorian. William H. Vaughan, now superintendent, presented the seniors to the board of education, and the diplomas were awarded by Dr. H.H. Sparks ("40 Are Awarded" 1928). The *Big Sandy News*'s account of the graduation ran: "Cratis Williams, honor student of the class, delivered the salutatory address. 'We are intoxicated,' he said, 'with pride in that we are numbered among the privileged few who have taken advantage of the opportunities offered them and who have reached the top of high school on the road to knowledge and fame.' Painting with beautiful diction a picture of happy, restful high school life, he said, 'We bitterly lament that we have to give up these pleasures, yet our cup bubbles over with delight in that we have chosen the right course.'"

After the valedictory address by Shirley DeBord and a presentation by class president Ward Patton, "Supt. Vaughan then presented the honor student silver loving cup to Cratis Williams, the student selected as best typifying the ideals of the school" ("40 Are Awarded" 1928). According to the *Big Sandy News*, "Williams was selected as honor student on the basis of scholarship, conduct, character, influence, and participation in extra-curricular activities" ("Cratis Williams Best Typified" 1928). The article continues to summarize Cratis's accomplishments in high school:

> His standing throughout the four years of his high school career is a remarkable one. He entered high school at the age of 13 and was elected president of the freshman class. In his sophomore year he was secretary of the Athenian Literary Society. As a junior he was president of the English Club, secretary of the Hi-Y Club, president of the Science Club, member of the out-of-state debating team, and a member of the *Louisian* staff. In his senior year he was Editor-in-Chief of the *Louisian*, president of the Science Club, and salutatorian of the class. In addition to these offices he found time to serve as president of the B.Y.P.U. of the Baptist church and vice-president of the Christian Endeavor of the Christian church. Throughout his four years in high school he has maintained a high scholastic standing and has been a favorite among his classmates and the entire student body.

These accomplishments are all the more impressive given the relative uniqueness of Cratis's situation. As the article in the *Big Sandy News* noted, "Although there are 64 families on Cains' [sic] Creek young Williams is the first person from that section to graduate from high school."

After high school, Cratis accepted a workship to attend Cumberland College, a two-year institution in Williamsburg, Kentucky. The memoirs contained in this volume end during his stay at Cumberland. From there, Cratis returned to Lawrence County and taught at the Upper Caines Creek School.

He lived with his parents during the school terms, but between sessions he enrolled at the University of Kentucky and began work toward his bachelor's degree. Again, he found himself between two cultures: in Lexington, "I dressed like Joe College, and then in the summer I'd go back" to Caines Creek to teach (Todd 1970). Following his graduation in 1933, Cratis moved to the new high school in Blaine, and he began work between

Cratis Williams as a high school senior, age 17.

terms at the high school on his master's degree at the University of Kentucky. In 1934 he became principal of Blaine High School. On August 7, 1937, he married Sylvia Graham, and two weeks later, on August 20, he received his M.A. degree. In 1938 he became principal of Louisa High School, although in the ten years since he had himself graduated from the school most of the faculty had changed. Forced out of the high school following an unsuccessful campaign for superintendent in 1941, Cratis was unable to find employment teaching. Sylvia suffered from tuberculosis, and her condition continued to deteriorate. After working during the summer and fall of 1941 at a farm implements company in Ohio while Sylvia stayed with her parents in Cherokee, Kentucky, Cratis obtained a job as the instructor at the Apprentice School for International Nickel in Huntington, West Virginia, in the winter of 1942. It was there that he received the fateful call from Chapell Wilson in August 1942 inviting him to be "critic teacher" at Appalachian Demonstration High School in Boone, N.C.[4]

Although Cratis Williams's trajectory in life may, in retrospect, seem relatively clear following his blossoming forth in high school, he continued to struggle along the way, and acutely so during his early years, with the tensions between the culture in which he had come of age and the middle-class culture of the modern age. In many respects, the narratives and essays that comprise this volume show Cratis Williams at the beginning of his lifelong

Upper Caines Creek School in the early 1960s. Cratis Williams taught in this build-ing between 1929 and 1933.

odyssey toward "what he would later call his bi-culturalism" (Miller 1992, x). And Cratis Williams himself referred to "my odyssey from the happy innocence of a secure childhood in the cultural and social context of an Appalachian valley through troubling adventures of doubt, challenges to self-hood, denial, shame, and rejection, to understanding, acceptance and affirmation of self as an Appalachian person who embraces his culture, searches out its history, and is proud of his identity as an Appalachian with-out feeling that he is therefore something less as an American for being an Appalachian" (1985, 69). A poem that he wrote during his undergraduate period at the University of Kentucky seems an appropriate way to bring this introduction to a close:

"The Blood of Ancestors is Surging"
Cratis Williams
October 7, 1931

The blood of ancestors is surging in my veins—
Clutched skeleton fingers grip at my throat,
Fingers with long claws and a strong pull,
Fingers of old grandfathers reaching from the corners of the earth,

Cratis Williams (standing on a washtub, tallest in the back row) as teacher of the one-room Upper Caines Creek School. His brother Ralph, standing to Cratis's immediate left, was among his students.

Fingers of old grandmothers reaching from the dark.
Grandfathers reaching skeleton fingers:
    grandfathers stooped with burdens
    from the black hells of the Middle Ages,
    grandfathers picking grapes along the Rhine,
    grandfathers fighting in the Wars of the Roses,
    bewhiskered yellow-toothed grandfathers spilling
    dark blood on the grass to make room for sheep,
    ashen grandfathers cursing in Welsh,
    red-faced, hungerpinched grandfathers
    from the Scotch Highlands,
    slow-witted Gaelic grandfathers
    singing from the Cornish hills,
    gin-soused grandfathers from the Netherlands,
    short, keen-eyed mountaineers from Southern Europe,
    chieftan grandfathers from Scandinavia,
    grandfathers from Arya,
    grandfathers from bastard races
    corroding in corruption in virgin America,

Those grinning old grandfathers
Shake long cold skeleton fingers at my throat.

    Beggars and kings,
    Hussies and virgins,
    Fools and geniuses
    Jostle together in me;
    A taste of all things—
    Foaming wines of Italy,
    And gin from the Zuider Zee;
    The voice of humanity sings—
        Sings from gutteral Germany,
        Chants from village May-poles,
        Rises from the Baltic Sea;
    Poems on wings
        From Alfredian England
    Melodies from Grecian lyres
    Flit through me.
    Invisible strings
    Are holding me fast—Strings from dank graves
    And slimy depths of the sea.

The call of blood storms in my ears,
The curse of blood is upon my head—

    epileptic uncles gnash with skeleton teeth,
    feeble-minded aunts wriggle bony spines,
    tousle-whiskered beggars turn over in the poorhouse yard,
    and all laugh a mean hideous laugh
    because I carry their blood.

A-ha-a-a-a-a!

The curse of blood tears at my heart—
    tears with passionate pain
    of apprenticed courtesans,
    tears with blushing shame
    of pregnant unmarried lassies,
    tears with weird praises
    to a strange and hard god—
    tears with wild praises
    that have turned wiry in the grave,
    tears with rusty knives
    of drunken-eyed gamblers

spilling their lives
cutting … cutting for recognition of their own blood —
tears with loud voices of the old
shouting strange hallelujahs and wild goddamits
claiming my chaotic soul.

The blood of ancestors burns
When it passes through my heart.

REFERENCES

"Abstract for April 28, 1893." 2000. In the *Big Sandy News Abstracted by Cora Meek Newman (1885-June 1903)*. Eastern Kentucky Genealogical Society, Inc. PO Box 1544, Ashland, KY 41102-1544.

"Activities Sponsored by City Schools have been Organized Here." 1925. *Big Sandy News*. 25 September, p.5.

Carson, Marguerite E. 1979. "Interview of Cratis Williams on Trip to Caines Creek, June 9–10, 1979." Unpublished.

Chaffin, Doris. 1991. "Lawrence County." In *History of Lawrence County, Kentucky, as told by those who lived in it, and others who heard their stories*. Project coordinators Regina Tackett, Patricia Jackson, and Janice Thompson, in cooperation with the Lawrence County Public Library. Dallas, TX: Curtis Media Group.

"Cratis Williams Best Typified Ideals of Louisa High School: Awarded Loving Cup." 1928. *Big Sandy News*. 1 June, pp. 1, 4.

Cratis Williams: Living the Divided Life. 1998. Videotape. Producers Fred Johnson and Jean Donahue. Covington, KY: Media Working Group.

"Dave Williams Convicted for Possessing Liquor." 1926. *Big Sandy News*, 23 July, p.1.

"Dave Williams Shoots Son, Said." 1928. *Big Sandy News*. 15 June, p.1.

"District Tourney Here Saturday." 1928. *Big Sandy News*. 16 March, p.1.

"First Issue of 'The Louisian' Sept. 27." 1926. *Big Sandy News*. 17 September, p.1.

"40 Are Awarded Diplomas Here." 1928. *Big Sandy News*. 8 June, p.1.

"Graduating Class of Louisa High School." 1926. *Big Sandy News*. 4 June, p.2.

"Hi School Talent to Present Play." 1927. *Big Sandy News*. 25 November, p.1.

"Hi Y Club Organized in Louisa High School." 1927. *Big Sandy News*. 17 September, p.1.

"Louisa Debating Team Selected." 1926. *Big Sandy News*. 17 December, p.1.

"Louisa Schools to Open September 5 with 20 Teachers." 1927. *Big Sandy News*. 26 August, p.1.

"Louisa Schools to Open September 6." 1926. *Big Sandy News*. 27 August, p.1.

"Louisa Tied with Holy Family Trio in Debate Series." 1929. *Big Sandy News*. 25 February, p.1.

"Louisa to Debate Pikeville Friday." 1926. *Big Sandy News*. 22 January, p.1.

"Louisian Given High Ranking." 1926. *Big Sandy News*. 17 December, p.1.

Miller, Jim Wayne. 1992. "Introduction." In Cratis Williams, *Southern Mountain Speech*, eds. Jim Wayne Miller and Loyal Jones. Berea KY: Berea College Press.

"School Notes." 1924. *Big Sandy News*. 26 September, p.5.

"School Opens Auspiciously." 1926. *Big Sandy News*. 10 September, p.1.

"Senior Play Given Here Thursday." 1928. *Big Sandy News*. 28 March, p.1.

"Seniors Present Play Next Week." 1928. *Big Sandy News*. 9 March, p.1.

Shackelford, Laurel and Bill Weinberg, eds. 1977. *Our Appalachia: an Oral History*. New York: Hill and Wang.

"Students Out for School Debating Team." 1926. *Big Sandy News*. 8 January, p.1.

"To Offer Stunt Night Program." 1927. *Big Sandy News*. 14 January, p.1.

Todd, Becky, 1970. "Former Blaine Educator Teaching Appalachian Studies at Berea College." *Big Sandy News*, 3 July, p.10.

Williams, Christopher Allen. 1991. "Williams Family." In *History of Lawrence County, Kentucky, as told by those who lived in it, and others who heard their stories*. Project coordinators Regina Tackett, Patricia Jackson, and Janice Thompson, in cooperation with the Lawrence County Public Library. Dallas, TX: Curtis Media Group.

Williams, Cratis D. 1937. "Ballads and Songs." MA Thesis. University of Kentucky.

_____. 1961. "The Southern Mountaineer in Fact and Fiction." Ph.D. dissertation, New York University.

_____. 1974. "Cratis Williams on Mountain Religion." 21 January. Unpublished transcript of speech, Williams family papers.

_____. 1975. "The Southern Mountaineer in Fact and Fiction (Part I)," ed. Martha Pipes. *Appalachian Journal* 3 (1): 8–61.

_____. 1976a. "The Southern Mountaineer in Fact and Fiction (Part II)," ed. Martha Pipes. *Appalachian Journal* 3 (2): 100–162.

_____. 1976b. "The Southern Mountaineer in Fact and Fiction (Part III)," ed. Martha Pipes. *Appalachian Journal* 3 (3): 186–261.

_____. 1976c. "The Southern Mountaineer in Fact and Fiction (Part IV)," ed. Martha Pipes, *Appalachian Journal* 3 (4): 334–392.

_____.1983. *William H. Vaughan: A Better Man Than I Ever Wanted to Be*. Morehead, KY: Morehead State University.

_____.1985. "A Humanist Reviews his Life." In his *William H. Vaughan: A Better Man Than I Ever Wanted to Be*, 69–72. 2nd ed. Morehead, KY: Morehead State University.

_____. 1991. "History of the Blaine Community." In *History of Lawrence County, Kentucky, as told by those who lived in it, and others who heard their stories*. Project coordinators Regina Tackett, Patricia Jackson, and Janice Thompson, in cooperation with the Lawrence County Public Library. Dallas, TX: Curtis Media Group.

_____. 1992. *Southern Mountain Speech*, eds. Jim Wayne Miller and Loyal Jones. Berea, KY: Berea College Press.

_____. 1995. *I Become a Teacher: A Memoir of One-Room School Life in Eastern Kentucky*, ed. James M. Gifford. Ashland, KY: The Jesse Stuart Foundation.

_____. 1999. *The Cratis Williams Chronicles: I Come to Boone*, eds. David Cratis Williams and Patricia D. Beaver. Boone, NC: Appalachian Consortium Press.

_____. nda. "Cratis Williams" (autobiographical sketch). Unpublished manuscript, Williams family papers.

_____. ndb. Untitled essay (incomplete). Unpublished manuscript, Williams family papers.

Williamson, J.W., ed. 1977. *An Appalachian Symposium: Essays Written in Honor of Cratis D. Williams.* Boone, NC: Appalachian State University Press.

Wolfford, George. 1972. *Lawrence County: A Pictorial History.* Ashland, KY: WWW Co.

NOTES

1. Accounts of John's escape from servitude vary. According to Christopher Allen Williams (1991, 737) "soon" after John's arrival, the Revolution broke out, and John enlisted. The version told in Cratis's branch of the family had John running away to join in the unsuccessful revolt that terminated in the Battle of the Alamance in 1771, after which he fled toward the mountains. In a presentation entitled "Cratis Williams on Mountain Religion," Cratis pointed out that many of the "people who participated in that battle" later "came into the mountains. Two ancestors of my own were there. One on one side, one on the other" (1974, 11–12).

2. "'Devil' John Wright [was] one of the most respected — and feared — men who roamed a small part of central Appalachia in the late nineteenth century. 'Devil' John had the reputation of having killed scores of men; whether he ever killed more than a handful of people has yet to be proven. John was an enigmatic man: he protected the law by running the Ku Klux Klan out of the area; he flirted with it by taking more than one wife; and he scorned it by offering revenuers a drink of his splendid homemade whiskey." Feuding occurred in Letcher County between "Devil" John (1844–1931) and James Claybourn Jones (1826–1914), "another so-called Kentucky 'badman'" (Shackelford and Weinberg 1977, 57, 59n.). "Devil" John was the model for the character of Devil Judd Tolliver in John Fox, Jr.'s *The Trail of the Lonesome Pine.* See "'Devil John' Wright," *http://www.geocities.com/Athens/Delphi/2839/devil.html.*

3. William H. Vaughan became an influential and somewhat controversial educator in eastern Kentucky. He was to serve as president of Morehead State Teachers College and, after his dismissal at Morehead, as professor and registrar at Peabody College for Teachers in Nashville. See Williams 1983.

4. For more complete discussions of this period of Cratis's life, see Williams (1999); see also Williams (1995).

Chapter One

In the Beginning

I was born on Wednesday morning at 7:23 on April 5, 1911, in the lower front room (the telephone room) of my grandfather David Williams's log house on Caines Creek, Lawrence County, Kentucky. The oldest of the five children of Curtis and Mona (Whitt) Williams, I was, in the language of the community, a "puny and pindlin'" child, plagued with tonsillitis, colds and infections, and hives. My mother said a teacup would have fit over my head. In 1911 the closest post office to my grandfather's home was Blaine, twenty-five miles from the county-seat town of Louisa, although three post offices (Hannah, Blevins, and Sacred Wind) were subsequently established on Caines Creek. My father and mother moved soon after my birth to the Blythe cabin, which my grandfather had purchased. In this house, which was altered later and added to, I grew to maturity.

The farm on which my parents lived was until I had gone away to high school a part of my grandfather's 640-acre farm. South of my grandfather's farm was the 400-acre farm of his father and mother and on it stood the log house in which my grandfather was born shortly after the Civil War. East of my grandfather's farm was the 350-acre farm of his father-in-law and on it stood the log house in which my grandmother was born, also shortly after the Civil War. These three farms comprised largely the geographical bounds of the world of my childhood.

My childhood was generally happy and packed with hard work and exciting ventures. The oldest grandson of each of my grandfathers, I enjoyed a special place in my early years in the favor of each. My grandfather Williams led me by the hand through the mysterious arrangements of his distillery, said to have been the last legal distillery in Eastern Kentucky. He held me up for full views of the huge mash tubs, permitted me to drink "beer" from

Blythe Cabin at the forks of Caines Creek, built by Abe Blythe c. 1890. A 1953 photograph taken from a wooden bridge at the end of the lane, crossing the right fork of Caines Creek. "Later, home of Judge [son of Jesse] Boggs. Then home of Curtis and Mona Whitt Williams. I grew up in this home"— Cratis Williams.

the mash ready for the stills, explained what happened when the mash was "cooked" in the stills, why "singlins" had to be "doubled," why a barrel of "backins" was kept for establishing uniform "proof" of the whiskey. He gave me my own little bottle of whiskey so I could drink along with the workers. Grandfather Whitt, a keen "hardshell" scholar of the Bible, began talking Calvinistic theology with me before I was nine years old. By the time I was twelve we could "argy" the "scriptors" together with great skill, but more warmth was generated in our discussions when I shared with him my little bottle of whiskey.

The Sunday visits to the homes of relatives and neighbors were gala affairs. Chicken and dumplings, vegetables in season, pies and cakes all laid out on the table together were standard fare for "company" dinner. The traditional games of children, slipping away to the swimming holes, the mischievous raids on orchards, melon patches, hen houses, and cornfields, the secrets of grownups passed along from the big boys to the little ones, the squaring off of cousins in battles of one kind or another did much to add zest and excitement to the lives of farm boys who toiled in the fields with their elders six days a week during the growing and harvesting seasons. And always, there were the talk of the older folk, the "recollections of other days" from bearded elders, the swapping of yarns, hunting tales, ghost stories, the topping contests of liars, the intricate maze of kinship tracing, and, occasionally, family fights.

Once a month there was the "regular meeting" of the Baptist congregation in the old church that doubled as the school during the week. A bench full of horny-handed, chanting preachers took their turns. The singing style was close to the Gregorian chant of the Middle Ages, marked by a slow-moving tempo, curious sliding notes, thin trembles, pale nuances, and emphatic soughs. No instruments were tolerated, not even a pitch pipe, and part singing was not permitted. People came and went at will, the preachers carrying on with great solemnity and taking no notice of children romping among the benches, dogs lying under the seats, squalling infants, and "sparking" couples drawing up to each other shyly "out thar amongst the kind and attentive sinner folks." Outside the church, young men and boys lolled in the shade of the trees, or squatted on their heels, while they swapped knives, showed their six-shooters, exchanged drinks of whiskey from fruit jars (which they called "cans"), and waited for the shouting to start.

Occasionally, around a bend from the church some gay blade, all dressed up in a sailor hat, a blue serge suit with a celluloid rose in his lapel, buttoned shoes, a silk shirt, and a red necktie, would have a crowd gathered around him in admiration at the "way he could make a banjer talk." Photographers were sometimes present, and in the hot summer months, Henry J. Pack, who pitted his Big Blaine Produce Company against the world, would drive his spring wagon with the multicolored beach umbrella up from the village of Blaine and sell ice cream, soda pop, and lemonade to such of the famished and thirsty as had five cents to spend for such goodies.

As the meeting drew toward an end, the shouting began, for though men are "predestyned," they can be certain of their "election" through the "sperrit," and warmth in a meeting gives reassurance to those who are moved to shout. As the medley waxed in fervor, the sinner folk scattered about the "meetin' house grounds" converged upon the building, pushing and crowding for a place at the windows or along the walls from which to view the winding up of the "sarvice." Well-turned young women, their hair a-flying, their breasts a-bouncing, their hips a-shaking, and their dresstails a-cracking, would often vie with black-bonneted matrons waving tiny white handkerchiefs for shouting room while singing, preaching, praying, exhorting, handshaking, and joyous laughter found a "perfect union in the Lord," but the young sinners at the windows would cluck their tongues, wink lecherously, and punch one another with their elbows, knowing full well the shortcuts to hell, even from heaven's gates.

Blythe cabin in 1950, taken from the road going up the left fork.

I See a Baptism

Mama did not take us to church that Sunday. It was the fourth Sunday following the first Saturday in March, and we did not have new shoes. Papa had bought the shoes we were wearing last fall and they had seen their best days. Papa had fixed them several times, taking one night to fix everybody's shoes when one of us had worn his shoes out till they were no longer protecting his feet from the wet and the mud, but he had said the young 'ens' shoes were so far gone that they couldn't be fixed again. We would just have to make out with them the way they were until they fell off of our feet or it was time to go barefoot. We would get new shoes again just before frost time in the fall if Papa had the money by then to pay for them.

Having ragged shoes, scuffed, toe caps curling, sides cracked and patched, spurs crushed down, heels run over, and soles turning up at the edges because they had holes in them, did not bother us all that much but Mama was proud and wanted us to look nice and clean when we went anywhere. We might be able to go to church in April if it was warm enough by then for us to go barefoot.

We wanted to go to church because Hanner Ike was going to be "baptized." We had never in all of our lives seen a "baptizin'." When Hanner Ike stopped at our house, she left a bundle of clothes wrapped up in a sack towel and said she would be back after meeting to change from her Sunday clothes to those wrapped in the towel for the baptizin', which would take place in the deep hole by the big sycamore tree in the creek that flowed by our house.

The deep hole was where I was allowed to fish with a bent-pin hook when the water was clear. I could see big fish nearly as long as my hand swimming deep in the water and sometimes they would take the red worm wriggling on my pin hook and swim away with it without pulling very hard at my line, which was a piece of black sewing thread my mother had rolled from her spool. She had tied the thread a few inches from the end around a bent nail to make the hook sink. I had never been able actually to catch one of the big fish. Sometimes I could lift one out of the water, but he would always wriggle a few times and drop back into the hole before I could throw him on the bank of the creek. A few times I had been able to land enough "minners," maybe two or three inches long, for Mama to fry a minner or two apiece for us, but I had to jerk hard and throw the fish fast to get it on the bank. But even the minners would come off the hook and try to flip themselves down the bank into the hole again. I would have to throw the pole down and capture the minner in my hands before he could get down the bank to the hole.

After Hanner had warmed by the fireplace a little while and gone on toward the church house, I asked Mama whether the baptizin' might cause all of the fish to leave the hole. She didn't think so. What did they do when they baptized? Mama explained that after a person was saved, she would join the church, and that part of joining the church was the baptizin', which was done by the preacher. He'd lead the saved person into a creek deep enough for the purpose while the crowd sang and say a few things while his hand was lifted up toward the sky, and then he would souse her under all the way and help her to her feet again. She'd come out shouting and happy and everybody would know, after that, that she was a saved woman and would go to heaven when she died unless she was just pretending she had been saved and was playing the hypocrite. Baptizin' by its ownself would not save a body, but a body that had been saved had to be baptized.

I thought it would be fun to see a person baptized. If Hanner Ike was to be baptized in the sycamore hole just across the lane from our yard, maybe we could watch. Mama thought we could do that, but we would have to wash our hands and faces with soap and warm water, comb our hair, and put on clean clothes. We could stand on the bottom railing of the palings around the yard and watch if we would get ready, but we would have to be quiet and just listen and watch.

Mama brought into the living room a pan of warm water, a towel and a wash rag, and the blue soap dish with a whiskered cat's face in the bottom of it and a bar of hand soap on it. She placed the pan on the hearth and the

Blythe Cabin in 1953, taken from the barn. Left–right: cellarhouse (veterinary room on top), end of house and bedroom that Cratis added on while teaching school, smokehouse/summer kitchen.

soap dish beside it, pulled up one of the cane bottom chairs, laid the wash rag and towel on it, and invited us to begin. She would lay out clean clothes for us. After we had all washed our hands and faces and our ears and our necks, we could then take turns and wash our feet and legs, being particular to scour our knees, too. She returned to the kitchen and we began.

We were all scrubbed up, our faces looking slick and clean, and dressed in our fresh clothes a long time before the meeting at the church house on the hillside across the valley was over. We could hear the preacher chanting his sermon. Mama would not let us stay outside very long at a time, for it was a cold day, even though the sun was shining warm across our shoulders when we stood on the railing, three in a row, and clung to the paling slats as we looked at the sycamore hole, skimmed with a thin layer of ice, where the baptizin' was to take place.

Mama had put on a clean dress, combed her hair, and arranged it with side combs by the time the singing after the sermon at the church had begun.

We could hear women shouting in a chant like that the preacher had used to sing above the singing. Mama thought the meeting was almost over and the church crowd would soon be moving over to the sycamore hole for the baptizin'. She had us stand with our tails to the fire so we could get good and warm. Then she held each of our coats with the inside toward the fire for a few minutes, put them on us, and buttoned us up. We would not have to wear our caps, they were all so battered and bedraggled.

Soon we saw the crowd leaving the church house, Hanner Ike and another woman hurrying along in the lead. Young people of courting age and some old men found their horses and mules hitched to flying limbs of trees that stood above and behind the church house and rode slowly along behind the walkers. At the end of the procession a man was driving a wagon with spring seats on which he and some older men and women sat, the women wearing black coats and bonnets and white fascinators wrapped around their necks and dangling in front of them.

Hanner Ike and the woman with her hurried into our kitchen. By the time Hanner Ike had changed her clothes, the crowd had gathered around the sycamore hole, the young people on horses reined up in a row on the bank across the creek, the wagon load of people in the lane that led to our house, and others, standing along the bank between the lane and the creek. The preacher began a song in a loud voice, and everybody joined in. It was a long song and the tune was so slow that I could not understand the words by the time each of the singers had ornamented them. After that, the preacher moved into his chant and preached a sermon about Jesus being baptized too by a feller named John in the flowing "River Jurdan."

We were standing on the railing and holding to the paling slats as we peeped over the top of the fence to see what was going on. Mama stood beside us, the little diamonds on her side combs glinting in the sunshine.

After Brother Clem, the preacher, had finished his little sermon, there was singing again. Brother Clem, his powerful voice leading the song, picked up a club lying on the bank and broke the thin ice that reached with splinter fingers toward the middle of the creek. He swept the ice down stream with swipes. Then he removed his shoes and socks and stepped into the icy water, singing loudly as he did so. Wading across the creek he broke and swept away the ice on that side. He used the club like a cane as he waded into the deep water until it came almost to his straddle. Little pieces of ice danced on the waves he made while wading. He stuck the club in the bottom of the creek and waded back to the bank, where a woman was leading Hanner Ike down to the edge of the water. He took her by the hand and led her into the creek. I could see her white bare feet in the clear water. As she waded on, Brother Clem supporting her firmly by the arm, she began to shiver and shake from the shock of the icy water. Her dress tail had spread out over the

Home of Jacob Peters Williams, Sr. (Grampap Jake) and Phoebe Jane Boggs Williams, 1955 photograph. Built about 1850, the German influence is manifest in the chimney between the two houses, with the dogtrot between the original kitchen and dining room.

surface of the creek, but by the time they were in the middle of the hole where the club was standing, her skirt had sunk around her and the weight of her heavy wet clothes was pulling at her waist.

I was afraid for Hanner Ike. We liked her. She had come to cook for us and wash our clothes and make our beds and clean our house when Mama was sick back during the big snow. She had made sop bread for our dinners from leftover cornpone and meal gravy boiled in a black skillet over a bed of live coals at the edge of the ashes on the hearth, and she had told us stories about bears and panthers and hants in the graveyards and deep tree-shaded hollows through which roads and trails led. She would let us take turns sitting on her lap as she told the stories and would hug us when the stories were scary. Remembering these things, I was afraid for her to be led so firmly, while shaking and shivering, into the icy sycamore hole to be baptized. Baptizin' began to seem cruel and wicked to me. I did not understand very clearly what being saved meant and why it seemed so important to let the world know you had been saved by being dunked under ice water at the edge of winter. Spring or fall when the creek flowed warm would be better, I thought.

Brother Clem turned Hanner Ike around so she was facing the sun. Then he lifted her right hand to her face and she held it tightly over her nose and mouth. When Brother Clem lifted his left hand toward the sky and threw his head back like he was looking God in the face, the sunlight glinted in his eyes. He stopped singing and the congregation stopped with him.

He spoke a short prayer, this time not chanted as his sermon had been, but, still, kind of sung. I had not understood his words very well while he was preaching about that feller named John that had baptized Jesus in the flowing water of Jurdan, but the words of his prayer were plain. He asked that we be handed down to our graves in peace and lifted up at the Day of Rizzer Rekshun, whatever that might be, and for the Lord to save us, own us, and crown us at the right hand of power in that world that has no end, amen. People standing on the bank answered amen! amen! amen! It all sounded pretty to me but I couldn't make out what it rightly meant. I would ask Mama later.

Hanner Ike was shivering and shaking and her chin was pumping up and down pretty fast below the side of her hand when Brother Clem turned toward her after he had said the prayer. He changed his position beside her and placed his hand for a moment over her hand that was clapped over her mouth and nose. Then, all of a sudden, he spread his legs apart in the deep water so hard that the water boiled up around him, making the little pieces of ice dance again.

Bending toward her, he placed his right arm around her shoulders, tightened his grip on her left arm, and said "I baptize thee in the name of the Father" as he plunged her backward into the cold water. I saw her feet fly upward as he buried her beneath the surface. He lifted her upright as she sputtered and strangled, for her hand had slipped from over her nose and mouth. "And the Son," and he plunged her, struggling and coughing, under again. With the second plunge, I screamed. My mother grabbed me up in her arms and held me tightly while whispering to me to be quiet, but I yelled that he was trying to drown her. Mama, in a low voice was saying not to be afraid, that everything was all right. I turned my head to look again, noting that the young people sitting on their horses across the creek were laughing and looking at me and that some of the old people standing between the lane and the creek turned their heads suddenly in my direction but then snapped them back to watch the rest of the baptizin'. My brother and sister had climbed down from the palings and were weeping quietly as they clung to Mama's skirts and stretched their necks to peep through the cracks between the paling slats. The preacher was holding Hanner Ike upright again, but she was coughing and struggling and flinging her arms around wildly. He swept a powerful arm downward, pinning her arms to her body, "and the Holy Ghost," as he plunged her backward into the roiling water again.[1]

"Somebody stop him! He's a-drowndin' er!" I yelled.

The young people on the horses laughed and leaned towards one another

Home of David O. Williams in 1955. "Built in 1902. Burned down in 1974. I was born in this house"—Cratis Williams.

and talked rapidly as they looked at me. The people standing on the bank snapped their heads around suddenly and then snapped them back.

"Sh-h-h-h!" Mama hissed, as she held me more tightly than ever. My brother and sister were crying loudly now. "I'll take all of you young 'ens in the house if you don't hush. You're disturbin' meetin'."

Brother Clem had started to raise Hanner Ike from the water the third time, but he noticed that in his struggle with her he had not succeeded in immersing her completely. He repeated "and the Holy Ghost" and plunged her under again, this time surveying the situation to make sure that she was completely beneath the surface.

When he lifted her up, she bent forward and spat out a mouthful of water. She was coughing and a stream of water was pouring from her. Flailing wildly she started for the bank, the preacher beside her and slapping her hard between the shoulders with his broad hand. The water kept pouring from her as he handed her to two women waiting on the bank. They took her by the arms, and held her up while she strangled and spat.

The preacher started another song, the congregation joining at once. After a minute or two, Hanner Ike straightened up and took a deep breath without coughing. She began to shout as the brethren and sisters, many of whom joined her in a chorus of chanted shouting, gathered about her to extend to her the right hand of fellowship in the faith and order.

David O. Williams house. Martelia Swann Williams in front, doing laundry.

Hanner Ike, saved and baptized, had made her peace and assured herself of eternal bliss in that world that has no end, but she was lucky to be still alive in this world after the baptizin'.

Preacher Clem Boggs

I heard Preacher Clem Boggs preach many times since he was the "moderator" of the Caines Creek United Baptist Church during my early boyhood. He was considered a great preacher by people on Caines Creek.

Many stories are told about Clem and his preaching. I remember hearing him tell about his "conversion." He had been what he considered "a weaked man." Following a week-end drunk, he had gone to his field to plow. While singing a hymn, he fell under "conviction" for his sins. He stopped his team and began to pray among the stumps in his field. After a time he became unconscious and then a great flash of light appeared before him and he arose a "new" man with a call to preach the gospel to others. But he was unable to read. He had members of his family read the Bible to him. Once, while preaching, he found it appropriate to relate the account of Jonah and the whale, but he had heard imperfectly the account as it was read to him. He told his congregation the story of how Jonah, seeking to avoid his duty, had been swallowed by a great *quail* the Lord had prepared. At the close of the account he paused before his congregation and then thundered, "Think of it, folks, as little a thing as a patteridge [partridge] a-swallerin' a full-growed man! But this here old Bible says it, and [thumping the Bible and bellowing] I believe ever' word in it from kiver to kiver!"

I am indebted to Larry Boggs, a great-grandson of Clem's brother "Hook Jim" Boggs for another story about Clem. Clem was holding a "protracted meeting" with a better educated fellow minister in the faith who stated at the beginning of his sermon one night that God chose men with enough knowledge of the Bible to bring His message to the people and that people must not permit themselves to be led by the blind into the ditch. Clem listened attentively and with becoming respect. After the first preacher "had given way" for his fellow laborer in the Lord's vineyard, Clem rose up and began: "Brethren and sistren and kind and attentive sinner folks, you have heared how the brother has said that preachers ort to have a nough of eddication to bring the word to the people. He has let on like, mebbe, I ain't fit to preach the gospel because I'm eegorant [ignorant] and not a scholared man. But I just want to tell you, folks, that if the Lord could make Balaam's ass to speak, he can make me to preach!"

I remember one exemplum that Clem used. He was illustrating the necessity for going directly to the Bible for truth. If truth is accepted "second-handed," said Clem, a man will find himself like the carpenter that sawed each board by the one he had just sawed instead of by the first board every time. His house won't stand up straight if he builds in "sich a way."

Clem starved off his branch farm and went to live near his brother "Hook Jim" in Greenup County. He came back to Caines Creek for the annual "sakermint" meeting a time or two. The last vivid memory of the living Clem that I have is that of an aging man with a broad, red neck removing his shoes for the foot-washing ritual and singing in the Gregorian mode, "Hit's I don't want you to grieve after me." He died soon afterwards and was returned to the Clem graveyard on the ridge at the head of the Clem Branch for burial. I did not attend the "burying," but I attended the memorial funeral at the graveyard later. Hundreds of people were there. A preacher in the United Baptist Church named Nelson, whom Clem had known in his youth, rode from Wise County, Virginia ("Wes' Ole Fudginny"), to deliver the memorial sermon. The meeting lasted the better part of the day. Families had brought baskets of food.

Grampap Jake and Granny Feeb

On Caines Creek, fathers were referred to by their descendants as "pa," grandfathers as "pa" or "grampa," and great-grandfathers as "grampap." I cannot remember my "grampap" Jake Williams, though I am told that he enjoyed holding me on his short, fat lap and permitting me to play with his white whiskers, which he enjoyed combing with his fingers as he sat in meditation. Grampap Jake, by all accounts, was what local people called a "char eck'ter."

My great-grandfather, Jacob Peters Williams, was born March 5, 1829, in Scott County, Virginia, the son of Lewis Haney and Susan Peters Williams. His father, Lewis Haney, was the son of John Williams and his wife, a Lawson, said to have had a brother William Lawson and a sister Dicie, who married a Godsey. John Williams must have been the son of another John, a Revolutionary War veteran, who had been shanghaied as a boy and brought from Liverpool to America not long before the Revolution began. Jacob Peters Williams's mother, Susan Peters, was the daughter of Jacob and Catharine Hacker

Cratis Williams's earliest photograph, November 1911, 7 months old, at Grampap Jake's funeral.

Peters. Jacob Peters, born in Virginia in 1779, appears to have been a grandson of Jakob Peter and his wife Maria Stadler, religious dissenters who fled from Switzerland to Holland in 1711 and came to Pennsylvania in 1714. Catharine Hacker, also German, was born in 1783 in what was to become Tennessee. It is said that Catharine, who never learned to speak English, died at the age of 104.

When Jacob Peters Williams was eight years old, his parents moved from the Clinch River in Scott County, Virginia, to the village of Blaine in Lawrence County, Kentucky, where he grew up. He attended Sam Sparks's "blab" school in Blaine and learned carpentry, leatherworking, and the blacksmith's trade from his father, who farmed but also operated a tannery and a leathergoods shop.

Once when Grampap, a short, broad man of girth, attended a political meeting, he felt so keenly the inconvenience in a standing crowd of being short that he vowed he would marry a tall woman in order to assure his sons of height. On April 25, 1850, at the age of 21, Grampap Jake, himself only five

Jacob Peters Williams and Phoebe Jane Boggs Williams.

feet four inches tall, married Phoebe Jane Boggs, the wiry six feet tall, 18-year-old daughter of Hugh and Hannah Blevins Boggs. They first lived on Lick Fork of Cherokee Creek, but later bought the Fields farm on Caines Creek, about four miles from Blaine, where they raised their large family of eleven children, most of them as tall as Phoebe Jane. When Grampap's father became excited about the Kansas-Nebraska trouble and left along with Detroit Burton for Kansas in 1854, taking along nine of his children, Grampap and his older sister Mary Jane, who had married Dr. Hamilton Swetnam and moved to Louisa, remained behind with their own growing families. When the Civil War came, Grampap and his brother-in-law Dave Sturgill, just arrived from Ashe County, North Carolina, organized a unit of union home-guards, Company "A" of the 68th Kentucky Enrolled Militia, with David Sturgill as captain and Grampap as first lieutenant.

Following the war, Grampap worked in the charcoal furnaces in what is now Boyd County, Kentucky, to earn money to finish paying for his farm. He was an enterprising and versatile man. His farm paid for, he turned to other pursuits. He was a skilled blacksmith, a cabinet-maker, a coffin-maker, a distiller, an orchardist. He operated a successful country store, a saw mill, and a grist mill. Grampap knew how to bleed horses. He had made special instruments for clipping veins in a horse's mouth. It is said that people brought horses to him from afar for the annual spring bleeding. He also castrated farm animals, calling always for soot and cobwebs with which to stanch the bleeding. A skilled iron worker, Grampap made in his shop hinges and latches for doors and gates, tires for wagon wheels, nails, horseshoes, and fixtures. He also did such precision work as boring rifle barrels. He was a careful and skillful worker with woods. He made coffins without charge for neighbors, measures for grain, and fiddles. Also a mason, he dressed stone and built fine chimneys.

Grampap Jake's wood plane.

He was sober, well behaved, and courteous. He helped to organize the Caines Creek United Baptist Church on the third Saturday in July 1870, and attended, usually on Saturdays only, the monthly meeting at the church as long as he was able to walk. Grampap talked loud and fast, his voice a treble in his older days. An expression he used frequently was "Aye, well! Aye, well!" He was crotchety, opinionated, brutally frank, critical of others, and inclined to pass judgment readily on the conduct of members of his family and his neighbors, but he was also a strictly honest man and one who revered bare truth.

But Grampap, abrupt and frank, was extremely close and hard in business dealings. He drove hard bargains and supervised carefully those who came to work for him on the farm ten hours a day for thirty-five cents and two big meals, and he would count the biscuits each workman ate for supper. Most of the stories about Grampap that trickled down to my generation deal with this aspect of his character. Once Grampap needed to recruit work hands to "save" his wheat. He rode his gentle old horse up Trap Branch to invite old Mr. Steele, another Civil War veteran who eked out a bare living on a branchwater farm, to help "save" the wheat. Mr. Steele had just received his first veteran's pension check, but Grampap did not know this. Grampap explained that he needed work and that he would pay a bushel of shelled corn, five pounds of bacon, or 50¢ in trade at his store for a full day of work with dinner included. Mr. Steele, hearing the wages quoted, said that his family liked side hog mighty well, but "much obleege, Jakie, we are a-eatin' a little furder *back* on the hog now."

At another time Grampap was moving among his field hands on one hot afternoon in cradling time. As he passed Lafe Lester (pronounced Luster on Caines Creek), who was binding sheaves, Lafe looked up and said, "Oncle

Jake, what do you pay a man in cash for a day's work on a hot day like this one?" "Ay well, Ay well, I pay binders 35¢ and all they can eat for dinner and supper, sir; and the way you eat, I lose money, for I counted twelve biscuits that you took out today." Lafe slapped the bundle of straw in his hand against the ground and declared, "By Johnnies, I'm a-quittin'. I'd set at home and play with my pecker before I'd work for 35¢ a day!" "Ay well, Ay well, go on home and play with your nasty, stinkin' little pecker. At the end of the day you'll have nothin' to show for it but an empty gut and an achin' back."

It is said that Grampap and his tall wife, Granny Phoebe, never quarreled in their long married life. As they rode back from their wedding, Grampap asked her whether she wanted to wear skirts or breeches. When she replied "skirts," Grampap told her he would wear the breeches, then, and when he made a judgment she must remember that she wore only the skirts. Grampap was opinionated, spoke his convictions bluntly, and was given to moralizing easily. I have heard my mother relate an account of an incident in which she and her sister, who married another of Grampap's grandsons, were involved. One Sunday morning she and her sister, after walking through fields in which dew had not yet dried on the grass, stopped at Grampap's to rest before going on to church. Grampap, observing that their skirts were wet, lifted up the hem of my aunt's skirt, peeped at her wet stockings, and observed, "Young womern, if you was a datter of mine, I'd whup ever' bit of hide offen your back."

Once when Grampap was at church, he stood up in the middle of one of Clem's sermons and signaled that he wished to say something. Clem stopped and said, "Yes, Brother Jakie." Grampap held his hand toward the preacher and broke wind lustily and sat slowly on the bench in the "amen" corner. Just as his rear reached the bench, the silence was broken by half-suppressed giggles from the young women in the "sinner" section. Grampap, pulling himself forward with the help of his stout cane, turned toward the young women, his head shaking rapidly and his white beard flapping, "Titter, titter, titter! Don't you never break wind?"

Grampap loved his family and was especially fond of children. He provided each of his five sons with a farm and helped each to get started, but three of the five had sold out and migrated to the West by the time of his death. In time, Jacob was referred to as "Grampap Jake" by members of his family. A heavy, muscular man, he became bald as he grew older and wore a long white beard. He had hard gray eyes and a dark complexion, which he attributed to his "black Dutch" ancestors. He died of heart dropsy November 18, 1911, and was buried beside Phoebe Jane, with whom he boasted that he had never quarreled, in the family graveyard on the point overlooking the homeplace.

My great-grandmother, Phoebe Jane Williams, was born July 7, 1832,

The funeral of Jacob Peters Williams, Sr., son of Lewis Haney and Susan M. (Peters), born March 5, 1829, and died November 18, 1911. Cratis Williams, infant, at the back, Martelia (Swann) Williams, front right of casket, Charlie Williams (child) to right, David O. Williams, to his left, Mona (Whitt) Williams second row far left, Ulysses (Lyss) Williams, second row, fourth from left.

on Caines Creek near Blaine, Kentucky, the daughter of Hugh and Hannah Blevins Boggs. Her mother was the daughter of James and Hannah Lyon Blevins, who had migrated from Virginia, where James had served as a private in the Virginia Line during the American Revolution. Hannah Lyon Blevins, who was 102 years old when the 1860 census was taken, is said to have been the last widow of a veteran of the Revolution to receive a widow's pension in Lawrence County.

Phoebe Jane married Jacob Peters Williams, three years her senior. She was the mother of eleven children, all of whom lived to maturity and married: Margaret Susan, William Henderson, Hannah Catharine, Mary Jane, Lewis, Aurenia (Rena) Elizabeth, John Nelson, David Oscar, Jacob Peters, Phoebe Alice, and Sarah Ellen. Hannah Catharine, who married George Church, died in childbirth at the age of 22. The average life of her remaining children was 88 years.

Phoebe Jane was six feet tall and slender, a head taller than her short, muscular husband. She had brown hair, blue eyes, and a fair complexion.

She went to Andrew Woods' "blab" school on Caines Creek where she learned to read, write, and cypher.

She was a strong, resourceful woman, skilled in gardening, cooking, and cloth-making. When the Civil War came she was already the mother of five children and pregnant again. While her husband, a first lieutenant and captain of his company of militia, was away during the War, she and her children grew a garden and a patch of corn. Her oldest daughter, Margaret, ten to fourteen years old, plowed with oxen, took care of livestock hidden in a corral made with poles at the head of a hollow on the farm, and carried grist on the old black mare to the mill near the forks of Blaine.

After the Civil War was over, Jacob moved the cabin from above the well closer to the road, which ran beside the creek, and built another cabin beside the huge chimney of dressed stone he had constructed. The square dance scheduled for a housewarming in the new cabin had to be canceled because my grandfather, David, was born two weeks earlier than he was expected.

Phoebe Jane and Jacob were charter members of the Caines Creek United Baptist Church, which was constituted in 1870, after they were already old. Earlier, they had attended the Old Hood Church and the Big Blaine Church at Martha. It is said that Phoebe Jane sang hymns beautifully. Before she became a member of the church she liked to dance. Although her church frowned on secular music and singing "ballets, songs, and ditties," Granny continued to sing ballads, especially her favorite, "Lord Thomas and Fair Ellender." She also composed ballads of her own and wrote poetry in the ballad style.

As her husband's enterprises prospered, Phoebe Jane's responsibilities became heavier. Work hands for planting, cultivating, and harvesting, for operating the saw mill, grist mill, and distillery in season, and for getting in supplies of wood and coal were fed dinner and supper as a part of their compensation. Care of the house and garden, helping out in the store when her husband needed to be supervising field hands, making and mending clothing, and caring for the sick all taxed her energies. In addition to the help of her daughters, she usually had a hired girl to work in the kitchen, where she peeled heaps of potatoes, strung stacks of beans, kept the fire going, carried water from the well, and looked after pots of vegetables and bread in the oven in preparation for up to four shifts ("tables") of hungry people for each meal.

"Granny Feeb," as she came to be called, was a skilled herb doctor. She knew medicinal plants and their properties and gathered a supply each year. In her old age she became one of the most celebrated midwives in the community and responded to calls for help day and night and in fair weather and foul, sometimes riding on a side saddle on a gentle mare and with bags of herbs tied to her saddle, sometimes walking great distances, with the help of a staff, and taking with her one of her grandchildren to carry the bags of herbs for her.

Grampap, who retained a teamster for transporting chickens, eggs, butter, herbs, hides, and other items to Louisa for barter for what was needed in his store, went to town often himself. On one of his trips there during the 1880's he saw cook stoves for sale, the first he had seen, according to stories handed down in the family. He bought one, a "step stove," and brought it back with him, the first stove in the valley. Unwilling to connect the stove with his fine chimney, Grampap cut a hole between the logs above a window by the hearth and extended the stove pipe by elbows up the outside of the wall. Hearing of the newfangled contraption for cooking that Jake Williams had fetched from town, people gathered to see how the thing worked. Later, Grampap built a kitchen-dining room ("cook room") as a T to the upper side of the house. Step stoves were crude. They tended to heat too rapidly and required careful attention to prevent food in pots and pans from burning and bread from becoming too done on top while remaining raw beneath the crust. But with care in its use, a housewife could save much kitchen time, especially if black pots of beans and ham hocks, leatherbritchy beans, hominy, and dried pumpkin were cooked slowly over beds of hot coals in the fireplace, as had always been done.

As Granny Feeb became older she was revered as a matriarch in her family and became a fount of wisdom for younger women on the creek. Because of her compassion and tenderness and her wise counsels, her sons sought her advice, rather than Grampap's, in times of trouble, for Grampap, garrulous, opinionated, angular, and set in his ways, was prone to offer advice too readily and imperatively and was too quick to say "If you had done what I told you" when it had not been followed and things had gone badly. In general, he was honored, indulged, listened to politely, but ignored, both by sons and daughters, when he volunteered advice easily and at the least provocation.

Granny was ill for several months before her death on October 3, 1907. During the last days of her illness she suffered from severe pains in her legs, which were massaged frequently with a cloth soaked in whiskey kept in a graniteware pan under her bed. Her sons, sons-in-law, and grandsons consoled themselves by drinking whiskey during the wake, some of them becoming maudlin during intoxication. At the funeral services in the yard of her home women wailed out their grief and the ashen-faced men stood about as the hard-shell preacher chanted leather-lunged warnings of doom and everlasting torment in a sulphurous hell for those who were not prepared for Judgment Day.

Following the graveside services in the family cemetery, at which women wailed in a bedlam of grief, the men of the family began to suffer from withdrawal from the alcohol, all of which they had consumed. Many of them began to weep, a shame for a real man. One of Granny's sons-in-laws, remembering the graniteware pan under her bed, stole it away and shared the bathing whiskey with those who cared to drink it. On their way home he and his wife met a traveler from a neighboring valley, to whom the son-in-law reported that they were returning from his mother-in-law's funeral: he had had such a good time, he explained, that he wished his wife had a mother to die every day.

Postmark: Sacred Wind

David Sturgill, who married Rena, daughter of Hugh and Hannah Blevins Boggs, migrated from Ashe County, North Carolina, during the early years of the Civil War. It is said that he and two companions left Ashe County to escape being drafted into the Confederate Army, that they traveled at night and slept during the day as they made their way to Kentucky. When David reached Kentucky, he joined a unit of Union homeguards, in which he was captain. His brother-in-law, my great-grandfather Jacob Peters Williams, was the first lieutenant of the same company. Uncle Dave lived on the farm later owned by Noah Wells. His log house with "boxed" additions faced down the creek. The road up the Clem Branch went past his door. Late in life he lost his farm. He died in a little house up the branch from Jay Boggs's barn. My mother took me with her to see Uncle Dave as he lay dying. Uncle Dave was a farmer and a preacher in the United Baptist Church. I remember hearing him preach. His neighbors did not think he was as good a preacher as Clem Boggs. Whereas, Clem and other brethern in the faith cultivated the chanting delivery with complex melody patterns and inimitable fadeouts on high notes, Uncle Dave preached in a calm, almost conversational voice. He possessed what might be considered a noble face with a high forehead, a patrician nose, and a white beard. I have a vivid memory of Uncle Dave lying on his back as he was dying, the fine lines of his profile outlined against a dark wall and his white beard pointing upward from the covers at a 45-degree angle.

Uncle Dave's son, Dick, lived with him in his home at the mouth of the Clem Branch. Dick applied for the first post office on Caines Creek. When the office was granted, Dick, a fiddler, dancer, and great hunter and trapper, wanted an imaginative name for his office. One day, during the rest hour from labor in the fields, Uncle Dave and Dick sat in the porch following dinner (the midday meal on Caines Creek). Dick, thumbing through a list of Kentucky post offices, said that he couldn't decide what to call his new post office. Uncle Dave lifted up his leg and broke wind vigorously, like tearing new bed-ticking, and said, "Call it that!" Dick named the post office Sacred Wind in honor of the occasion.

Envelope for Curt Williams, Sacred Wind, Kentucky, from Smith and Wesson.

A Cathide Banjo Head

One winter day, when I was five years old, Grampa Dave stopped his spring wagon at the top of the bank above our yard and called. My mother went to the door. He wanted me to go along with him to his "upper store," up the valley about three miles, to keep him company. Mama, recognizing that he was quite drunk, slightly afraid of him, and unwilling to "contrary" him, explained that I had coughed all night, that it was cold, and that she was afraid being out in the weather might not be good for me.

Grampa said he could take care of me all right. I could sit between his legs on the wagon seat and he would button his big coat around me. Buttoned in and resting against his warm belly, I would not get the least bit cold.

Mama put my "sailor coat" on me, buttoned it up, warmed my mittens by the fire and pulled them on for me, pulled my cap over my ears, and carried me in her arms through the snow to the wagon, cautioning me meanwhile to stay inside the store and close to the stove all day, for if I did not I would be sure to have an earache again. She handed me up to Grampa.

Grampa already had his big heavy coat unbuttoned. Moving back on the seat, he placed me between his fat legs and pulled the coat around me and buttoned me in, leaving my face peeping out like a young 'possum peeking from the pocket on its mother's belly. Mama asked that I not be permitted to go outside the store because I would get earache again out in the cold wind.

The sunshine was bright on the snow, which blew in little puffs into our faces when the horses, moving glibly over the frozen road, reached the tops of banks over which the road passed. Grampa was happy. He sang little ditties between his shouts at the horses and his popping at their rumps from time to time with his long whip with a "blacksnake" cracker at the end of it.

When we reached the store, located on the bank of the creek, the bed of which was also the road at that point, he tied the checklines to the brake pole of the wagon, unbuttoned me, and lumbered out. Then he took me in his arms and carried me to the platform at the front of the store and stood me against the wall close enough for me not to have to stand in the snow, about two inches deep, while he found the key on a brass ring that would unlock the door. Inside the store, he set me on the counter and heaped his great coat around me so I could remain warm while he shook ashes from the pot-bellied stove, whittled kindling, built a fire, and then added lumps of coal until they caught. When the fire was far enough along for him to dump the coal from the bucket into the stove, he set me on a keg in front of the stove and put his coat back on. He then carried in from his wagon some egg crates and boxes of canned stuff.

Leaving me to mind the store, he hurried on to Ison's barn to put the horses in stables. Responding to the warming stove, I turned on the keg to keep myself warm all around while the room heated. By the time Grampa had returned, the stove was glowing between the ashbox and the door, and I was quite warm.

Grampa found a broom and swept out ashes and dirt that had collected along the floor from the stove to the door, singing his little ditties, making happy clucking sounds, and yipping out little yells of joy as he worked.

Then he went behind the counter and returned with a little bag with a yellow drawstring at the top, from which he took six blue glass marbles for me to play with on the floor between the counters. He sat in a chair near a window and watched me play, saying nothing when I flipped my taw and missed but uttering delightful sounds of encouragement when I struck.

Soon Harrison Edwards, who lived in a little house across the valley, came in to trade. He watched me shoot my taw for a few minutes, said things to me to which Grampa supplied responses together with "Tell him ..." as if I were much younger than I really was, but Grampa was so happy for me and feeling so good himself that he just had to help me find the right things to say, and I was pleased to pretend that I was younger than I really was.

After Harrison had finished with his trading, he sat down on a keg for a little visit. He reported that someone had caught his big gray tomcat in a deadfall last night, that he was a fine cat, and that he surely hated to lose him.

He had kept the rats away from the barn and the mice away from the corn-crib. Grampa wanted to know what Harrison planned to do with the dead cat. Well, he didn't want to skin him. He supposed he would either throw him in the creek or bury him somewhere after the ground thawed.

Grampa said he would like to have the cat for his hide. He had broken the head in his banjo and the hide of that big cat would make a fine banjo head. Harrison told him he could have it. He would bring it over after a while.

Later that day it clouded up again and turned warmer. Some boys came into the store and played marbles with me, and a woman with a white fascinator tied under her chin brought a basket of eggs which she bartered for things in the store. Some men riding horses stopped and warmed themselves by the stove. One of them bought Brown's Mule plug chewing tobacco, which Grampa cut with a special contraption he had on the counter just for that purpose.

When lunch time came, Grampa took a big knife from his pocket, opened it with a click, and slit open a can of sardines, which he set on a piece of wrapping paper from the roll at the end of the counter. He then took four or five crackers from the barrel and placed them on the paper, found two horseshoe nails in a rack of narrow long boxes in which nails of many sizes were kept, gave one of them to me, and invited me to eat with him. We had nothing to drink, though. Grampa was expert in spearing sardines from the can with a horseshoe nail, but I broke the sardine in two when I tried. Grampa then heaped a sardine on a cracker for me and I ate. Afterwards, he gave me two balls of candy from a wooden bucket in which lumps of all colors and shapes were mixed together. Then he took a small lump of dark brown sugar from a barrel and gave it to me to hold in my mouth until it melted.

After we had eaten, he opened the door and looked up and down the road for a minute or two, then he closed the door, walked behind the counter, where he had put his overcoat, and drew from the inside pocket a flat bottle of Sam Clay whiskey, which he turned up to his head. I could see bubbles running up the neck of the bottle from his mouth while he was drinking. When he took the bottle from his head, he smacked his lips and looked happy as he drew the sleeve of his jacket across his mouth. He handed the bottle to me, and I turned it up to my head and took a swallow. I wanted to see whether I could make bubbles run up the neck of the bottle like he had done, but the swallow of whiskey made me cough and I could feel tears coming in my eyes, too. So I smacked my lips and rubbed the sleeve of my sailor coat across my mouth and handed the bottle back to Grampa. Soon I could feel a warm glow going out from my stomach and the taste of Sam Clay blended with the brown sugar, some of which had not yet melted, in my mouth.

Grampa was pretty happy. He rattled ashes into the ash box, put some coal in the stove, and sat on a wooden box close by for a little while. He opened the stove door and punched at some of the blocks of coal with an iron poker, then he tapped out little rhythms on the floor with the poker while he recited rhymes that he knew, some of them songs, except he didn't sing them while he was tapping. I was happy, too, while Grampa was.

About the middle of the afternoon Grampa said I could mind the store again while he harnessed the horses and drove the wagon down. Nobody came while he was gone. I tried to play with the marbles on the floor, but I could not shoot very well. My head seemed to swim when I straightened up from knuckling down for the shot. So I picked the marbles up, laid them on the counter for Grampa to put them back in the little poke with a yellow drawstring, and sat on the keg by the stove, where I was warm and happy, just sitting.

After Grampa came back and had hitched the team to the brake pole on the wagon, Harrison Edwards came again. He was carrying the big gray cat by the tail. It had dried blood around its mouth and its eyes were open, though it was dead.

Grampa took the cat and measured off its length with the breadth of his big hand. Then he measured it around the middle. He said its hide would be just the thing for his banjo head. He would tan it in green wood ashes and work it up. He laid the dead cat beside the door while he and Harrison visited by the stove, but Grampa did not offer Harrison a drink of his Sam Clay. I looked at the cat. Its eyes seemed to be peeping at me, but it was dead.

After Harrison left, Grampa put his big coat on again, returned the marbles to the poke with the yellow string, pushed the ash box all the way back into the stove, and adjusted the damper. He put the dead cat in the back of the wagon, carried out a box or two of things he wanted to take to his other store, and then picked me up and carried me to the wagon. Seated himself, he put me between his legs again and buttoned me inside his big coat. A drizzle of rain fell on us as we returned, and the horses slogged through only a trace of snow on the road, now muddy and slick in places. Grampa was not as happy as he had been that morning, but he made jokes about his little 'possum when we met people along the road who stopped long enough for brief visits.

Grampa tanned the catskin. It made a good head for his banjo. Whenever I went to see Grampa after he had repaired the banjo, he would pick it for me to dance for him. He liked to play "Cripple Creek," "Shout Little Lulie," "Old Granny Hobblegobble," "The Old Hen Cackled," and "Big Cat, Little Cat." Sometimes he would begin "Cripple Creek" very slowly and then speed up to see whether I could keep up with him with my dancing.

When he was old, he told Granny that he wanted me to have his banjo. After he died, Granny gave it to me.

Grampa's banjo has an interesting story of its own. He made it himself, mostly. In 1890 he attended a minstrel show at a county fair. The black-face banjo picker broke his banjo. He threw the rim of it out into the audience and Grampa caught it on his arm. Some of the brackets had jumped off the rim. Grampa took the rim home with him, made in his blacksmith shop brackets to replace those that were gone, whittled out with his pocketknife a neck from a piece of yellow poplar and smoothed it with a piece of glass, made new keys and a bridge, and put in a head made from calfskin. It had a broad fretless neck. After about twenty years, the head was broken. Grampa replaced it with one made from the hide of Harrison Edward's tomcat. That one has been in it ever since.

I had Frank Proffitt[2] re-string the banjo for me. Disturbed by the grimy spot on the head, Frank also tried to scrape off the deposit that had built up there from Grampa's sweaty hands, but he left streaks across the dirty spot.

The banjo hangs on the wall of my home, an instrument that Grampa made, mostly, and that Frank Proffitt cleaned, nearly.[3]

David O. Williams. "He would also pick a banjo when he was drunk. He had a fairly good singing voice, which my father didn't have, and he liked to sing little ditties, especially naughty little ditties. He would do this as he worked. He loved children. Although I think most of the neighbors considered him an old rascal, the children in the family thought he was marvelous"—Cratis Williams.

My First Drunk

Monday was wash day at our house. Mama had built the fire under the big black pot set on stones and propped in place with plowshares above a pit

David O. Williams.

at the side of our wood yard, carried water from a pool in the creek and filled the pot, set her washtub on the bench close by, and was dividing the clothes into piles of white, light, and dark while the water was heating.

Estill Boggs, whom we called Jim's Estill for his father to distinguish him from two other Estill Boggses about the same age, one of whom we called Lucy's Estill for his widowed mother and the other Shine's Estill for his father,

Estill Boggs (Jim's son) center, Orville Whitt (Mona's brother) seated.

came riding into our lane. He was returning from a weekend in another valley, where he had been drinking whiskey with the boys and become so drunk that he had slept in a barn rather than returning home late at night.

He had not eaten any breakfast and did not want any, but he had a splitting headache and would like to have a drink of whiskey to pick himself up. Mama told him that he would find my father's jug behind the safe in the dining room and that he could get a glass from the safe and help himself from the jug.

He dismounted, hitched his horse to a post, and went into the house. I followed him. He found and uncorked the jug, selected a teacup rather than a glass from the safe, and poured a stiff drink. Then he drew a chair up to the table, sat down, and was in the act of raising the cup to his lips, when he stopped and looked at me leaning against the table opposite him.

"Do you want a sup?" he asked.

"Yeah, I think I would like one."

He handed the cup to me. I turned it up and emptied it before taking it from my mouth, sputtering but fighting back as best I could the urge to cough, while my eyes were filling with tears. I was ashamed of the cough and the water in my eyes.

"Won't that make you drunk?"

Left–right: Cora Lester, Estill Boggs (Jim's son), Lula Lester (Cora and Lula were daughters of Tom and Polly [Mary] Griffith Lester).

"I hadn't never been drunk yit," I responded, wiping my eyes as I returned the cup to him. I was proud that I had been able to hold my liquor throughout the five years of my life.

He then poured another cupful and drank it slowly, shuddering after each swallow. Then he poured perhaps a half a cup and dashed it down hurriedly. He put the stopper back in the jug, struck it solidly with the side of his fist, and returned the jug to its place.

I followed him to the gate. As he was swinging himself into the saddle, he thanked Mama for the drink, adding that he "was needing that," but he made no reference to my having taken a drink with him.

I stood at the gate and watched him ride out the lane toward the bridge and turn up the road past our house. By the time he had reached the top of the bank above the yard, he was beginning to look like two men, riding identical horses, one perhaps a nose ahead of the other. When I blinked, he became one man again, but by the time he had passed out of sight one horse was fully a neck ahead of the other. I was beginning to feel as if it was no longer necessary for me to be concerned about the earth. It was down there somewhere below my feet. Not only that, but my head had expanded many times over and I was tingling to my fingers and toes with a delightful sensation. I was aware of a warm titillation in my stomach that mounted to little quivers and then receded briefly. I thought I needed a drink of water.

I was aware of my zigzagging footsteps and my reeling from a porch post to the wall, and from one facing of the door to the other, as I found my way to the water bucket on the bench in the kitchen. Steadying myself against the bench, I spilled most of the water from the dipper as I lifted it unsteadily to my mouth. The water was a cooling sluice through the midst of flame. I attempted to drink several dipperfuls of it, spilling much of it down the front of my shirt and overalls, but I was not aware of any wet sensation from my soaked clothing.

It then occurred to me that I might not feel so much as if I were floating above and beyond reality if I could make my way to the rocking chair by the fireplace in the living room and sit down.

While passing through the door from the dining room to the living room, I stubbed my toe against the doorsill just as I retched. As I went down, I was aware of a sluice of white liquid squirting quite vigorously from my mouth.

It must have been a long time afterwards before consciousness dawned. I was lying in the doorway, my head across the threshold in the living room and the rest of me crumpled down in the dining room. A pool of clear liquid spread across the floor from my mouth. Apparently, no one knew that anything had happened to me. Mama and my brother and sister were in the wood yard.

It was difficult for me to get up. My legs bent like strings and did not have much feeling in them, but I wanted a drink of water very much. Attempting to pull myself up by holding to the door facing, I slipped back several times before I was able to get on my feet. Blundering from the table to the wall and from the range to the water bench, I was able to get to the water bucket again. Again, it was hard to hold the dipper steady enough to get water to my mouth. I drank slowly, if sloshingly, and found that the sips of water brought relief.

I made my way unsteadily to the rocking chair and sank into it. I do not know how long I sat there, but I did not vomit again. I still had a warm glow in my veins and whatever I looked at danced crazily before me.

Sometime later Mama came into the kitchen from the outside and my brother and sister came into the living room from the porch. My sister built up the fire, and I could hear my mother rattling pots and pans in the kitchen. No one had discovered the puddle of vomit in the floor.

The flames in the fireplace roused me. I no longer felt as lightheaded as I had felt while making my way to the rocking chair. The tags of soot dancing above the flames against the back wall of the fireplace attracted my attention. I watched them dance a long time. Then some of them would catch fire from a flame and glow for a few minutes before dropping into the grate.

I had seen my father sweep burning soot from the back wall with the broom. He had done it so quickly that the broom had never caught fire. It looked so easy that I felt confident I could do it too. After all, the house might burn down if the soot along the back wall should carry the glow into the chimney itself, set the soot on fire there, and then roar out at the top of the chimney and set the roof on fire.

A broom stood against the mantel, all decorated with a lacy paper curtain that hung eight or nine inches below it. I rose from the rocker, took the broom, and began to sweep the back wall from side to side, the glowing soot tags showering into the flames. My brother and sister stood in transfixed admiration. I believe I was not fully aware that the straw in the broom would burn, for my father had always swept away the burning soot without any thought, apparently, of the broom's catching afire.

But the broom caught fire. When I saw flames crackling at the end of it, I attempted to beat them out against the back wall. When the beating only made the flames bigger, I then withdrew the broom to stick it into the ashes below the grate, but the flames leapt upward as I drew it from the fireplace and the paper curtain around the mantel caught on fire.

My sister screamed and my brother ran to the kitchen to fetch Mama, yelling, "Cratis has set the house on fire!"

Mama came running, her sleeves rolled to her elbows. She grabbed the flaming curtain, tore it from the mantel, and flung it into the fireplace. At one end of the mantel the paper on the wall had also caught fire. She was able to rip off enough of it to bring it under control. She sent for the water bucket and dipper to have handy in case she saw any sparks, but there were none. Her arm had been burned slightly when the flaming curtain curled after she had torn it away, but she thought she had been lucky that her clothing had not caught afire.

Everything under control, she turned on me. I had burned up the broom, ruined her curtain, set the paper on fire, and come close to burning the house down.

In my assurance that I would compensate generously for all the damage I had done, that I would buy a new broom and a new curtain, better than the ones that had burned, and new paper for the wall; in the very absence of any attempt to defend myself or to make excuses for the terrible thing I had done, my mother, her own excitement by then subsiding, began to weep.

When she came close to show me compassion, she discovered that I was drunk.

"W'y, Cratis, you are drunk. How did that happen?"

I told what had happened to me. She said my father would be mad when he learned what I had done. I begged that she not tell. She told me that I would have to tell him myself and be prepared for the whipping that he was almost certain to give me.

Mama returned to the kitchen. I sat weeping in the rocking chair, but feeling that I would indeed be able to make enough money doing something to buy at least a new broom. Perhaps I could sell old rags to the ragman, or dig mayapple root, or thin somebody's corn row for a dime a day when corn came up in the spring. My brother and sister played together and left me alone in the rocking chair.

The bed in one corner of the room had been pulled forward at our request to provide us with a hiding place for our game of "whoopy-hide" on rainy days. The bedstead had a high, decorated headboard that reached almost to the ceiling. When I heard my father coming across the porch, I ran and hid behind the bed.

Mama, having heard him, came into the room ahead of him. When he entered, there was complete quiet, but I was peeping from behind the bed and could see Mama's face.

"What in the hell has happened?" my father asked.

"The mantel curtain caught on fire and the wallpaper caught from the curtain. I put it out just in time to keep the house from burning down."

"How did it happen?"

No one said anything, but I saw Mama nod her head toward the bed. I then moved quietly back into the corner and waited in fear as I heard my father walking toward the head of the bed.

He looked at me for a long time, it seemed to me. Then he smiled.

"Come out and tell me what happened."

I related what had happened. When I reached the part in the narrative that dealt with how the broom had caught fire, my brother and sister entered their comments. Then my mother related how she had fought the flames and burned her arm, but that I was sorry I had burned the broom and the curtain and was going to buy new ones.

My father in a surprisingly tender voice assured me that I would not be expected to buy a new broom and a new curtain, but I must promise never to try to clean the back wall with a broom again.

"Next time, use the shovel," he said.

Papa said nothing at all about my having been drunk, but at the dinner table he told me I might feel better if I would drink a glass of buttermilk and not eat very much. Contrite and meek and feeling that I had escaped deserved punishment, I found that buttermilk was all I wanted for dinner.

Appalachian Folkways: Food and the Country Stores

We ate well as mountain farm people. All of our food except flour and sugar was produced on the farm. Only when we felt that there was a comfortable little margin beyond absolute necessity did we use at the country store what was left beyond the price of our purchase and the worth of our eggs, chickens, or farm produce to buy knicknacks and furbelows.

Occasionally, we might be permitted to buy a can of mackerel, a bottle of syrup, a box of cereal, or a pound of rice, but these items, alternative foods to what we had at home, were considered luxuries that we could have only when there were not other things we needed more. Usually the storekeeper wrote a "due bill" for what he owed us after we had "traded." Due bills were saved as a reserve for the purchase of muslin, gingham, calico, percale, socks, overalls, work-shirts, gloves, ten-cent jimmy hats for summer wear, and the like, most of which were paid for by barter. Store-bought necessities that could not be produced on the farm included salt, baking soda, baking powder, canning acid, vinegar, black pepper, spices, kerosene ("coal oil") for the lamps and lanterns, turpentine, castor oil, camphor. We considered a nickel's worth of mixed candy, or soda crackers weighed out from a barrel, or gingersnaps, or chewing gum a special treat, for only occasionally did we indulge ourselves in such extravagancies.

Going to the store was an exciting experience that we looked forward to. Most of the time people would be gathered there, in the summer sitting on the porch, swapping news and exchanging accounts of progress of their farm work, and in the winter on kegs and boxes around the pot-bellied stove, spinning yarns, discussing the good old days, exchanging points of view about the weather and on the spirit of the times, and spitting tobacco juice into the sandbox which the merchant provided both to enhance sociability and to discourage spitting on the stove itself.

The odor of an old-time country store is unforgettable. Near the merchant's cash drawer the mellow blend of the odors of plug tobacco and "natural leaf," candies, spices, cookies, cinnamon, and other delicious things kept one lingering with watering mouth as he studied all of the goodies kept on exhibit in the showcase or in full view on the shelves behind the storekeeper himself as he stood in proprietary pride in the midst of his "stand of goods." If one followed him to his kerosene tank to watch him operate the pump that brought the kerosene tumbling into the funnel stuck in the top of the "coal oil can," he was sensitive to a different quality of the blend of odors, one in which the smells of brown sugar, leather harness, salt pork, corn meal, flour, kerosene, vinegar, wash-day soap, cases of eggs, and sundry heavy things like hoes, axes, mattocks, cast iron pots, plowshares, galvanized tubs and buckets came together, but this unique odor, pleasant in its richness and fullness, held one, too. Taken altogether, a country store stimulated one to buy, created wants that he did not know he had, motivated him to feel that his wants were also his needs, and frustrated him with desire and ambition largely through the medium of smell. The memory of a country store provides us with a measure of what we have sacrificed for the prophylaxis of the sealed container, the plastic wrapper, and the refrigerated counter. Olfactory-visual aid, if such a dimension should be achieved by public media, is not likely to recapture the power in advertising of the smell of the now vanished country store.

Breakfasts in my boyhood home were basically the same from day to day and season to season. Always there were homemade biscuits cut with a tin can from dough rolled out with a sturdy rolling-pin, gravy, bacon or smoke-cured ham, butter, and all the milk one cared to drink. Seasonal variations of what was served beyond the basics included fried white ("Arsh") potatoes, baked or fried sweet potatoes, jams, jellies, and preserves, syrup, molasses, or honey, and tomato, apple, or grape juice. During hunting and fishing seasons squirrel or fish might be served in addition to pork. A favorite breakfast sweet for cold winter months was boiled molasses to which a pinch of baking soda had been added and into which an egg had been stirred rapidly prior to pouring it into a white bowl from which one dipped ample servings to cover one of the large, rough-looking biscuits broken open across his plate and spread with butter for his "bit of sweetenin'" at the end of the meal.

Juices were not drunk prior to beginning a breakfast but along with it as was milk. One began with a biscuit broken open on his plate, a generous serving of potatoes, enough gravy to cover both, and a piece or two of thick but well done bacon or ham. He then proceeded to the sweet, which was eaten with buttered biscuit and bolstered with more bacon or ham if one wanted it. Eggs, a main source of family income, were used sparingly except at Easter time. Only when there were guests or on an occasion considered special for some reason were we served eggs for breakfast. They were fried in the bacon drippings or ham fat, some well done, some medium, and some "over quick," and all served on a platter which was passed around the table.

Breakfast, an important meal, was prepared by my mother and sisters while the men of the house did the morning chores. When we all came together at the breakfast table we were ready for the day. Generally, when we left the table we went immediately to work or school.

In the summertime, after the old potatoes had been used up, or become so dried and sprout-covered that they were not edible, and before new potatoes "came on," we ate fried apples instead of potatoes. The young green apples, sliced with the peeling left on, sweetened with molasses, and flavored with cinnamon, were fried brown. Bacon achieved a different quality when eaten with fried apples. If the apple crop failed but the hens laid well ("slammed out the store pay"), we ate rice as a cereal, sweetened with sugar when we could afford it or with molasses when we had no choice and covered with cream. By the time we were in our teens we had switched from rice to rolled oats, which had not been available at country stores in my early childhood. Sometimes, when sugar was in short supply, we dipped our oats from the bowl in which they were brought to the table, put them on our plates as we did fried potatoes, salted them, and covered them with butter. Well-done "streak of lean" bacon complemented the butter-laced oats most satisfactorily.

As we were growing up, only our mother drank coffee, our father preferring milk along with the children. I learned to drink coffee in the boarding house in which I stayed during my junior year in high school. The first of the children to become a coffee drinker, I found a considerable difference between the boarding house coffee and my mother's coffee, about which she was considered "right perticklar." She bought green coffee at the store, roasted it herself, and ground only what she needed each morning. She boiled the coffee in a large granite-ware pot, adding new coffee each morning for a week. On Sunday morning she emptied the pot, washed it in cold water, and started over. By Thursday or Friday her coffee was black and strong enough to spin the uninitiated into a St. Vitus dance. She drank it hot, saucering it carefully, blowing it lustily, and sipping it with appreciative and gratified soughs. When Grandpa and Grandma spent a night with us, watching the three of them enjoy the "sassering" and blowing of their scalding black coffee, soughing each sip joyfully, and Grandpa grunting in contentment after each swallow had made it to his stomach, was a study in culinary delight and appreciation.

While my brothers and sisters were small we came into the kitchen for mid-morning snacks, which consisted of cold ham or bacon biscuits (we did not know the word "sandwich" then), or biscuits with butter and jam or jelly in them. Biscuits left from breakfast and the "pone of biscuit bread," made from rolling all of the scraps and cuttings from the biscuit dough together into one pad and baking it in a small frying pan, were kept in the oven and the meat platter was left on the apron ("edge") of the stove. When enough heat remained in the stove to make the biscuit pone hard, we fancied it to be much like the soda crackers we were permitted occasionally to buy at the store and spread it with butter and brown sugar when we had the sugar.

The main meal of the day was "dinner," our midday meal. Like breakfast, dinner consisted of certain basic foods supplemented by others in season. Cornbread, beans, potatoes, gravy, stewed pork or fried sausage, pickles or relishes, butter, and sweet milk, skimmed milk ("blue john"), or buttermilk ("sour milk") were basic. In season, we had, in addition, "sallet" greens, mustard, turnip greens, boiled cabbage, boiled pumpkin, roasting ears (corn on the cob), radishes, green onions or sliced onions, lettuce wilted with hot bacon grease and sprinkled with vinegar, turnips, parsnips, sliced tomatoes, sliced muskmelon. For dessert there were fruit pies, cobblers ("sonkers"), stewed fruit, cakes (including "stack cakes"), gingerbread, and cookies. All that had been prepared for dinner was placed on the table together, diners being permitted to pick and choose as their taste and preference dictated. Nothing special was prepared in addition for anybody outside the family who happened to appear at meal-time, for there was always enough for two or three extra persons.

From time to time such special dishes as tomato dumplings, vegetable soup, potato cakes, or crackling bread might be included among the wide variety of foods served. In the late winter and early spring months dried, pickled, and canned foods were dominant among the supplements to the basics. Pickled beans, shucky beans ("leather britches"), or canned beans, sauerkraut, pickled corn, canned corn, dried pumpkin, and canned mustard were served along with the more enduring "side meat" and jowl, shoulder, and ham produced from the smokehouse.

Only for Sunday dinner or for guests from a distance were such "fine things" prepared as chicken and dumplings, eggs, canned meats, biscuits in addition to cornbread, special cakes coated with icings and decorated with coloring.

Before the appearance of tularemia, or "rabbit fever," among the wild rabbits of the community in the early 1930's, rabbit often supplemented the pork for dinner. It was stewed, baked, or fried, or sometimes stewed slowly, picked from the bones, minced, and baked into a pie. Woodchucks ("groundhogs"), opossums, squirrels, and quail were hunted and eaten in season. Groundhogs and 'possums were soaked overnight in cold water, parboiled, and baked, "banked with sweet potatoes," in the oven. Quail was baked slowly or stewed and worked into a pie. Squirrel was fried (the "leavings" in the frying pan made into a delicious gravy) and eaten for breakfast.

We rarely had beef, for beef cattle, purchased by "stock men" and driven away on foot by drovers, were a source of hard cash needed for paying taxes and purchasing those things that were not available at country stores. We did not raise turkeys, and the geese were raised for their feathers. I never ate turkey or goose until after I had graduated from college. We did not grow sheep, but occasionally we were sent a "mess of mutton" by a neighbor. Once or twice my father brought home wild ducks from his hunting trips. Wild ducks had tough, dark meat that was difficult to prepare.

The preparation and preservation of food for winter and early spring months took much of our time. Picking berries, gathering apples, picking, stringing, and breaking beans, chopping kraut, cleaning the silk from the corn for pickling, shelling corn to take to the mill for meal or "chop" were activities that required the help of every member of the family. Sometimes neighbors came for bean stringings, corn shuckings, corn shellings, apple peelings, or hog killings, and the shared labor became a social occasion that laid obligations on us to assist neighbors who needed help.

Supper, the simplest meal of the day, was eaten by lamplight in both summer and winter. It came after the evening chores were completed and consisted mostly of milk and cornbread and butter. If one wished, he might supplement the basic supper with a serving of dried beans ("soup beans") cooked with ham hocks or side meat, and top off his meal with a dish of stewed fruit and a cookie or a piece of gingerbread. Ours was a genuine supper in the traditional meaning of the word and was a preparation for sleep, for my father rose at 5 o'clock in the winter months and 4:30 in the summer and the whole family was "rousted out of there, their feet a-hittin' the floor a-runnin'," even when we had to sit by a roaring fire and doze between breakfast and daylight during the short days of winter.

On extremely cold winter days, when "everything was frozen as hard as a buck's horn," my mother would sometimes cook the dinner (but never the breakfast) in the fireplace and bake the cornbread for the evening meal in hot coals on the hearth. Dried beans with ham hock cooked in a black pot slowly over the coals, corn meal mush prepared in a cast iron skillet, sweet potatoes baked in the ashes, cornbread baked slowly in a mound of live coals on the hearth, pumpkin, sauerkraut dipped cold from the barrel, butter churned from the milk that had been clabbering in the stone churn, fruit juice, and all the milk one wanted to drink and all served in plates that we held on our knees and glasses that we set beside us on the floor as we arranged ourselves around the fireplace took us back to the "old days" that our grandparents remembered from their childhood when people living on Caines Creek were only two or three generations away from the pioneer ancestors who had settled there shortly after the War of 1812. We felt as if we were reliving the history of our valley and that the bears, the panthers ("painters") and the wildcats that appeared in family stories might be howling in that wind that whistled through the palings in the yard fence and groaned under the eaves of the house before rushing on to rattle the gate to the barn lot and shake the doors to the stalls of the old barn across the garden where the mules and the cows remained while the world was wrapped in snow and ice. The intimacy and reassurance of such an experience is not easily duplicated in the age of "modern conveniences" in which we now live.

Old Shep

Old Shep was a sensitive, lovable dog, but he insisted on having his rights. He had been Grampa's dog, but after Grampa, in a fit of anger, shot his ear off with a shotgun when he refused to swim the flooded creek to bring the cows in the milk gap, Shep came to our house to live. He was a large, black dog with long hair, a friendly face, a deep-throated bark.

Shep permitted us to wallow on him and loved to romp with us. We would throw chips from the woodyard for him to fetch. He was so fast and skillful that he could fetch chips for the three of us as long as we cared to play that game. When among ourselves we tossed the woolen ball our mother had made from old socks, Shep would find the ball for the one who had failed to catch it and bring it to him, barking encouragement and bouncing about in a lively fashion.

Sometimes we played doctor. Shep, an agreeable patient, took the pills, coated with bread, that we prescribed, let us hold his paw to determine his pulse rate, and would even cooperate when we wanted to open his mouth to see whether he had a coated tongue, but he would not hold in his mouth the stick we used for a thermometer.

Wherever we went Shep went, too, but if we went to Grampa's, he always stopped off before we got there and waited in the weeds and bushes by the creek until we came along.

But Shep would not suffer indignities. He left us following an insulting episode and went to live with Gord Boggs, a kind and understanding widower who was wise in the ways of animals.

I was responsible for Shep's leaving. My mother had given me a crippled biddy that had been rejected by the mother hen. I kept the biddy in a shoe box under the kitchen stove. Following each meal I would crumble some cornpone in the box and replenish the water in a can lid at one end of the box. Between times, I would take the biddy out and hold it close to me to hear it make comfortable sounds as it snuggled against my warm belly.

One evening at twilight, after the biddy was big enough to hobble about with its broken leg, I had to go. My mother went with me. She took me to the edge of the bank between the woodyard and the creek. I took the biddy along and put it down beside me while I was doing my business. After I finished and was pulling up my overalls, the biddy moved in to feed from the steaming pile, cheeping its appreciation. Fascinated, I stood in admiration.

Shep, who had been lying in the lane close by, moved in to feed from the pile also. The biddy gave way at the approach of the dog and then hobbled back to the pile. Shep snapped at it and it fell back in fear.

I scolded Shep but he ignored me. I picked up a stick of wood and threw it at him. It struck him across the shoulder. With a sharp yelp of pain he retracted toward the lane, howling piteously as he went. The chicken returned, ate all it wanted, and I picked it up and returned it to the box under the kitchen stove.

The following morning Shep was gone. We searched for him but could find no trace of him. Neighbors had not seen him. Several weeks later, Gord Boggs and some of his sons and grandsons passed down the road in a wagon. Shep, all excited and filled with energy, was trailing the wagon, but he gave no indication that he knew any of us. My father thought he would see whether he might catch Shep as the wagon returned.

As Gord resumed, Shep was racing ahead of the team and barking and rushing about as if he were much involved in affairs. My father ran around the end of our garden to be beside the road when the wagon passed. Shep, keeping well to the upper side of the road, ignored my father's entreaties and hurried on as if my father were a complete stranger to him.

My father asked Gord about the dog. Gord said he was the best dog he had ever had. One morning he had opened his door and the dog was sitting in the yard. He fed him and Shep had been with him ever since.

My father reported his conversation with Gord. Shep, he concluded, was happy where he was. In fact, he did not blame the dog for leaving. If he was living at a place where he was not considered good enough to eat decent dung he probably would leave, too. He looked at me significantly as he surrendered his claim to an excellent dog.

A Basket for My Rooster

I called it Tommy, but I did not give it that name until it was big enough for me to tell that it was a rooster. Before that, it was simply the biddy.

It had been crippled when it was only a few days old. Mama, thinking that the other chickens would kill it, had given it to me to care for and feed. At night I kept it in a shoebox under the stove in the kitchen. I kept fresh water for it in a jar lid in the shoebox and fed it crumbs.

Papa thought it would not live long away from its mother, but in time it began to grow. It always limped. While it was beginning to show that it was a rooster, it had a bald breast and showed by its cheeping that its voice was changing to that of a rooster. By the time it had grown a comb and wattles it could get around pretty well, but it still limped.

Other roosters attacked it when they came into the yard or when I let it outside with other chickens. It would call for help when it was attacked and one of us would rescue it.

It was a pretty chicken with bright eyes and healthy looking comb and wattles. It grew a proud tail, and its coat of brilliant red feathers glistened in the morning sun when it took its position at the upper yard to crow lustily in response to roosters that ran with the flocks. Sometimes angry roosters would run along the outside of the paling and ruffle their neck feathers and threaten when Tommy crowed, but he would just straighten up and crow again.

Tommy was gentle. He would follow us about as we played in the yard. He liked to be picked up and held, but he would coo little gurgling sounds as he was being lifted as if he were asking that he be handled easily. He enjoyed having the feathers on his back and breast stroked but was uneasy if we tried to rub his comb and wattles or run a hand over his tail feathers.

After he grew up, he roosted on a shelf under the shed of the smokehouse. It was my job to feed him corn and cold cornbread kitchen scraps and to see that his pan had water in it.

After frosts came Tommy developed "big craw." As his craw grew his eyes lost their lustre and his comb and wattles became dull. He crowed less, was listless, and reached the place that he did not even caution us to handle him gently when we picked him up.

My father decided that Tommy had not been getting enough grit and that our feeding him whole grains of corn had caused his craw to become packed. One rainy day Papa assembled instruments and materials needed to operate on Tommy. I held him firmly against my belly while Papa slit his craw with a razor, removed a great wad of whole-grain corn cemented together with cornbread and biscuit crumbs, cleaned the craw with warm water, and sewed it up with shoe thread in a big needle. He then put the craw back inside the rooster and sutured the slit in the skin with knots of shoe thread.

After that, I cracked corn for Tommy. I would tie eight or ten grains of corn in a piece of an old shirt-tail, place it on the hearthstone, and beat it with a hammer. I also brought sand and gravel from the creek bed and spread them under the smokehouse shed. Tommy's lame leg had prevented him from scratching for gravel. Papa thought I ought not to feed him biscuit crumbs for a while, but that some clabbered milk would be good for him if I would keep our remaining dog, old Tip, away so he could eat it.

Tommy was right droopy for a while, but soon he began to mend. Papa would examine him every day to see whether he was healing. After a few days Tommy was crowing again, but the stitches down his breast bothered him. He began to peck at them and to try to pull them out with his beak. Papa thought the healing was causing him to itch. He cut some of the sutures with a razor and pulled the threads out with tweezers, but those in the middle of the incision needed to stay there for a while.

Tommy was not pleased. He kept pecking at himself and pulling at the sutures. An opening appeared, from which pieces of grains of corn worked out. Tommy, seeing the chopped corn appear, would peck it out and eat it again.

This seemed funny to us. People who stopped for water at our well or to rest a while in our porch enjoyed watching Tommy peck the corn from the opening in his craw and swallow it again.

One bright morning following a white frost we saw an old man with a white beard and wearing a red sweater coming up the road. He was carrying a load of baskets strapped to himself. Trotting along beside him was a little boy about my age. They crossed the bridge and came out the lane to our house. Papa recognized the old man as John Cotten, an old widower who lived in a little house with a dirt floor near Blaine and supported himself by making baskets. The little boy was his orphaned grandson.

They came into the porch. The little boy and I moved away from the porch so we could feel the warmth of the sun on our backs. Tommy was sunning himself at the upper edge of the yard, his comb and wattles red again and his eyes glistening like jewels in the sunlight. He was busily engaged in pecking corn from the hole in his craw and swallowing it again. The little boy was fascinated by it all.

I noticed that the little boy was not clean. His ears were dirty, there were black scabs at the edge of his hair, and the backs of his hands had scales on them. Papa and John Cotten were talking about baskets. Papa had asked the price of a saddle-shaped bushel basket. It was worth thirty-five cents, Mr. Cotten said. After Papa expressed his opinion that the price was a little high, Mr. Cotten began to observe Tommy, engaged in feeding himself over and over the same grains of corn.

Papa gave Mr. Cotten an account of the rooster's ailment and the surgery he had performed on him. Mr. Cotten chuckled as he squinted his eyes at the rooster, threw his head back, and stuck his white beard straight out. I noticed that his ears had black rims, his neck was scaly, and his hands were rusty, but he had on a pretty red-and-yellow checked shirt under his red sweater and a straw hat pulled forward on his head, although it was late autumn.

Mr. Cotten, his beard sticking straight out in front of him, looked at the rooster a long time. Then, jerking his beard back in place, he asked how much Papa would take for the rooster.

Papa explained that the rooster belonged to me and that he would have to talk with me about that. Mr. Cotten looked at me for the first time. The little boy said, "Yeough, what'll ye take fur 'im?"

Papa remained quiet. I looked at him and he smiled encouragement. I said Tommy was a fine rooster and that he liked for us to play with him. I had never thought at all that I would ever be wanting to sell him.

Mr. Cotten said, "Would ye trade 'im for this hyur bushel basket?"

I was puzzled. I had no earthly use for a bushel basket. Papa came to my rescue.

"If you are willin' to trade, I'll give you a quarter for the basket." He reached in his pocket and drew out a quarter, which he held up for me to see.

I looked at the quarter and then at Tommy, his wattles shaking and his eyes glistening like bright beads as he pecked the corn from the hole in his craw and swallowed it again. Papa, Mr. Cotten, and the little boy studied me quietly as I made up my mind.

"I'll trade," I said.

Papa handed me the quarter. Mr. Cotten set the bushel basket on the porch floor. I caught Tommy and handed him to Mr. Cotten.

Mr. Cotten cut a piece of string from the harness he had made for himself to hold the baskets on his back, tied Tommy's feet together, laid him in an egg basket, and handed the basket to the little boy. Then, getting into his harness again, Mr. Cotten and his grandson departed. I could hear Tommy flapping his wings and cackling as they turned up the road.

At my father's death over forty years afterwards, the Tommy basket, by then dark with age and seasoned with use, was still as strong and sturdy as it had been when Mr. Cotten set it on the porch, though it had carried many a load of corn and chop from the crib to the chicken house during those forty odd years.

My Great-grandparents: Gabriel Griffith and Elzina See Griffith

Not much information was passed along about my great-grandfather Gabriel (Gabe) Griffith. He was born about 1816 in Virginia, a son of Abel Griffith and grandson of Evin and Susannah Griffith of Augusta County, Virginia. Gabe's father, Abel, who died at Blaine, Kentucky, at the age of 77 in 1860, might have been the nephew of the Abel who was listed as a 65-year-old head of a household in the 1830 census of Lawrence County, Kentucky, and who must have been the father of David (b. 1783), Robert (b. ca. 1790), and Evan (b. ca. 1795), who had arrived at Blaine as early as 1810, as well as James (b. 1801), another Abel (b. 1803), John (b. 1807), and Jesse (b. 1809). Descendants of Gabriel say that he and two of his brothers walked as small boys from Virginia to Blaine with their widowed father. One of the two brothers was Abel (b. 1817 in Va.), who married Mary Edwards. Abel lived on Hood Fork of Blaine. He had a son Edmond and at least two daughters, one of whom married Crate Slone and the other William McDowell. Gabe's other brother might have been Rice (Rece, Reece, Reice, Reason) Griffith (b. 1814 in Virginia), who married Margaret Edwards and who had at least two sons, Laban and Leander.

Gabriel Griffith, said to have been eleven or twelve years older than his wife, married Elzina See about 1846. In the 1860 census for Lawrence County, however, their ages were entered as 39 and 31 respectively, and the ages of their oldest sons Abel and Evan as 13 and 11.

Gabriel and Elzina, by all reports, were poor. They lived in a cabin on a small hillside farm between the farms of Henry Evans and Walter Osborn on Lower Laurel Creek and about three miles from the village of Blaine, called then the Mouth of Hood.

Gabe, it is said, was a tall, slender man. He was a Union soldier during the Civil War, but we have not yet determined the company to which he belonged. He was wounded in battle; a bullet lodged in his lung, and he carried it for the remainder of his life. On his way home from the war he met a group of Confederate soldiers in the road. They greeted him and passed on. Thinking they might decide to return and kill him, Gabe hid in tall weeds between the road and a stream. They returned. While they were threshing about in the weeds in their search for him, Gabe slipped into a deep pool in the creek and hid himself in the water and under a ledge of roots extending from the bank. The soldiers did not find him.

Unable to work after his return from the war, Gabe and his family remained poor. The census report for Lawrence County for 1880 lists Gabriel as 64 years old and Elzina as 53. Evan and Mary (Pol) had married. Reuben, 24, was living with them and five of their younger children.

Left–right: Elia Edwards, Nelson Sturgill, Mona Whitt.

The date of Gabriel's death was not remembered by his descendants, but it was said that he lived for twelve or fifteen years after he returned from the war. He must have died soon after the 1880 census was taken. No one remembers whether he received a soldier's pension.

He was buried near the northeastern corner of the Osborn graveyard. His and Elzina's graves, located next to the grave of their son Reuben, are marked only by field stones.

My great-grandmother Elzina Griffith was illegitimate. Her mother, also illegitimate, went by the name of Bowman, although her father was a Coffey. Elzina, born on Mill Creek near Cassville (later Fort Gay) in Wayne County, Virginia, about 1827, was the daughter Garred See, son of Garred and Flora Graham See. Flora was the daughter of Col. James and Florence Graham, whose log house, built in 1768 and located about twelve miles from Alderson, West Virginia, is still standing.

Elzina grew up in the family of Frank Pigg, who moved to Blaine when Elzina was about sixteen years old.

After she married Gabriel (Gabe) Griffith, they lived on a little farm near that of the Osborn family on Lower Laurel Creek and about three miles west of the town of Blaine. She was the mother of twelve children: Evan, Abel, Harvey, Reuben, John, William, Milton, James, Mary (Polly), Sarah, Elizabeth, and Amanda Jane. Three of her sons died young: William, Milton, and James. Milton died at about the age of four of worms, which crawled out of his mouth and anus after his death.

Life was hard for Elzina, a short plump woman with fair skin and light brown hair. During the Civil War, while Gabe was in the Union Army, she and her children almost starved. Companies of home guards representing both sides passed her cabin often. They took whatever they could find of food and quilts and blankets. She dug a pit under the lower side of her cabin in which she hid her meagre supply of provisions. Once a group of soldiers drove away a pig belonging to Henry Evans, a neighbor, and butchered it and cooked it in a hollow below her cabin, where they spent the night. They gave her what was left of the pig when they were ready to depart the following morning.

Gabe came back from the war with a bullet in his lung. Unable to work thereafter, he lived in almost constant pain before he died soon after the 1880 census. Many years after Gabe's death, Elzina went to live with her son Harvey, his second wife, Sarah, and Harvey's children. But after Harvey abandoned them and eloped with Calpurnia Wheeler, her son John took Elzina and Harvey's children into his home.

Later, Elzina lived with two of her grandchildren in a part of a 16-room house built by Baity Gambill in a bottom above the Horseshoe Bend of Lower Laurel Creek. By then, Elzina was afflicted with asthma and heart dropsy, from which she suffered intensely during stormy weather. She smoked crumpled homegrown tobacco ("chamblins") in a corncob pipe.

Late one spring, about 1900, she went to visit her daughter Sarah, who had married Frank Hellum (Helms?) and lived on Paint Creek in Johnson County. While there, she died. Her corpse was returned in a wagon to the Osborn graveyard for burial beside the grave of her husband. Both graves, next to that of their son Rube, are marked only by field stones. It was said that Elzina's corpse became so swollen on the two-day trip by jolt wagon from Paint Creek that it burst and blood was running from her coffin, which was not opened for graveside services, when it was lowered into the grave.

My grandmother, who had wanted to visit her mother during her illness

Alma Whitt Williams, date unknown (Mona's sister, married Nelse Williams).

but could not do so in peace because my grandfather "rared and staved" every time she mentioned wanting to go, refused to attend her funeral. My mother and her sister, then eight or nine years old, were not permitted to go either.

My mother remembered her grandmother's hospitality. On her way to Sprucy School my mother would stop frequently at Elzina's cabin to warm by her fire or to have a snack of cornbread and beans.

"Mutts Mag"[4]

I learned this story from my grandmother Amanda Griffith Whitt when I was a very small boy. My grandmother, in turn, had learned it from her mother Elzina. My grandmother came along after the Civil War; she never went to school a day in her life, and she spoke the prototypical Appalachian dialect. I'm going to try to tell it in her dialect. I told the story for Richard Chase[5] forty years ago nearly, and he collected it also from people in Wise County, Virginia, and put the stories together. And, I have read his story so that now I can't really be certain whether everything I'm telling you is what my grandmother remembered, but I'll try it in her dialect.

Oncet, they's a pore ole widder worman that lived in the middle of a cabbage patch. She had a little ale tumdled-down shack, and she lived on it with three girls. Two of 'em was her daughters, Poll and Nance, and one, Mutts Mag, was the daughter of her second old man that had died a year or two before and had been buried back on the back side of the cabbage patch. They's awful pore. And Poll and Nance thought they's awful fine gals, and they didn't wantta do no work. And they wouldn't work in the cabbage patch because they didn't want to get their complexions sunburnt; and they wouldn't pack in warter from th' spring because they didn't wantta get callouses on their hands handlin' th' bails of th' buckets; and they wouldn't pack out ashes or they wouldn't help warsh the dishes because they didn't want the strong lye to make their hands rough. And about all they done was just to set around and primp and fix one another.

Mutts Mag, she had to do all the work. She worked in th' cabbage patch, and she split th' wood and fetched in th' kindlin', and she packed th' warter from th' spring in th' cedar buckets, and she raked out th' ashes ever mornin' and built th' faar and done th' cookin'. Everthing uz done, Mutts Mag done it. And she never did get nothing new to wear; everything she wore uz something handed down from Poll and Nance. And they never did want her to go anywhars with 'em 'cause they's ashamed of her.

Well, one day th' pore ole wid-

Amanda Griffith Whitt.

der worman tuk sick and was like to die. And she was a-laying in th' bed, and she called th' girls to her and she says to Poll and Nance says, "now, Poll and Nance, I'm a-gonna give you 'uns th' cabbage patch and th' little house, and I want you to take good keer of it. That's all I have fur you." And then she looked at Mutts Mag, and she reched down in her apern pocket and pulled out an old case knife with th' handle broke and handed it over to Mutts Mag and says to her, says, "Mutts Mag, all I've got in this long, wide world is this here old case knife," said, "but I want you to have it. Allus have it in yore apern pocket because a body don't never know when a case knife might come in handy."

And then she turned ever and died. And they laid her out, tied her ankles together, and put pennies on her eyes and a bandage around her chin to hold it up while she's a-gettin' stiff. They invited th' neighbors in, and they had a funeralizin', and they buried her back on th' back side of th' cabbage patch betwixt th' two ole men.

Well, as soon as th' funeralizin' was over, Poll and Nance, they lit in to eatin' up them thar cabbages jist as fast as they could. And it wasn't long til they wasn't nothing left 'ceptin' a little pot likker in th' bottom o' th' pot. And Poll and Nance got to a-talkin' around th' faar, and they says, "Well, reckon it's about time we's agoin' on a journey to find our fortunes."

They looked in th' meal barrel, and they wasn't a dustin' o' meal in it. And they says to Mutts Mag, says, "You run over to th' neighbors' house and borry a cup o' meal, make us a johnnycake, and we'll go on a journey in th' mornin' to find our fortunes." Mutts Mag says, "Can I go along too?" And they said, "No, you can't go along, you dirty thang, we'd be ashamed to have you with us." She says, "I wantta go awful bad." "No, you can't go, you got to stay here and take keer of th' little house and look after th' cabbage patch."

Well she went over and got a cup o' meal and brought it back to 'em and put at 'em again to let her go, and they said, "No," she couldn't go along. Well, th' next mornin' she got up early to help 'em so they could get a soon start. And she made th' johnnycake fur 'em, and then she said, "Now, I wantta go too." They said, "No, you can't go." And she jist kept on a-ding-dongin'. And finally, they says to her, says, "Well, you can't have any of our johnnycake, and you can't walk with us. But if you wantta borry a little meal to make you a johnnycake fur your ownself, and you stay a great fur piece behind us, we'll let you go."

Well she run over to th' neighbors' house as fast as she could and made her a johnnycake and wrop it up in a towel and cleaned herself up best as she could. She's barefooted; didn't have no shoes to wear. And she shut up th' little house and tuk out down th' road atter Poll and Nance. They's already way outta sight. She hurried along jist as fast as she could, and it's a-gettin' a way up in th' day: ten o'clock, maybe, when she seed 'em way on down th' road thar ahead of her.

Well, she stepped up a little bit and got up pretty close to 'em, and they happened to look back. And they's a-talkin', and she could see 'em a-lookin' at her and a-hangin' their faces together. And she knowed something uz up. Well, they's a-talkin', and one says to th' other, says, "They lord a-mercy, thar that stankin' thang is a-trailin' right along atter us. She's about to catch up with us. We can't have her a-goin' along with us. What are we a-gonna do with her?" The other 'un said, "Yet's kill her." The first 'un said, "No yet's not kill her. Yet's stop her up in that ole holler stump over thar and put a flat rock on her. Nobody 'll know she's in thar."

Well, they stood up right straight. Mutts Mag got up fernest 'em. They rech out and grabbed her and stopped her up in that ale holler stump and laid a big flat rock on her and went on. Well, Mutts Mag, she was a-screamin' and a-swarpin' and a-stavin' around in thar, but it wasn't doin' no good. Atter while she bethought herself of that thar ole case knife she had in her apern pocket. So, she scrounged around 'til she could get it out, and begun to scratch on th' rotten wood on th' inside of th' stump. And while she's a-scratchin' away with that ole case knife, a fox come by. He heared her in thar. He says, "Who's in thar a-scratchin'?"

She says, "Hit's me." He says, "Me who?" She says, "Me, Mutts Mag."

He says, "What are you doin' in thar, Mutts Mag?" She says, "Why, Poll and Nance put me in here." He says, "What'll you gimme to let you out?" She says, "I'll take you to whar they's fat on a goose's neck."

And so's'un th' fox, he rared up on th' stump, lifted th' flat rock off with his nose, and Mutts Mag hopped out. She tuk him to whar they was fat on a goose's neck, and then, went on.

It's a-gettin' up almost in th' middle of th' day by that time when she seed Poll and Nance away on down th' road thar ahead of her. And it's about time to eat because she could step on th' head of her shadder. But she wanted to catch up with 'em first.

Well, one of 'em happened to look around and seed her a-comin', and she said, "They Lord God a-mercy, look a thar, thar that thang is a-trailin' atter us again. What are we a-gonna do with her?" And the other 'un says, "I says, 'Yet's kill her.'" And the other 'un says, "Oh, no, yet's not kill her. Let's throw her in that ole shop house thar across th' road. Th' latch jest lifts on th' outside. We get her in thar, they ain't no winder, and she never can get out. And nobody'll find her fer a long time. She'll be dead then."

"All right," said th' other 'un. So they straightened up and waited fer Mutts Mag to get up close to 'em. And she got right up fernenst 'em. They rech out and grabbed her and throwed her into th' ole shop house and shet th' door.

And, well, well, Mutts Mag began to bounce from one side of that shop house to th' other and squall and to cavort around, but hit didn't do no good. Atter while she bethought herself again of that ole case knife in her apern pocket. So, she rech down and drawed it out and begun to whittle around th' door about whar she thought th' latch was on th' outside.

Well, th' ole fox come along, and he heered that scratch, scratch, scratching in thar. And he says, "Who's in thar?" And she says, "Why, hit's me." He says, "Me who?" She says, "Mutts Mag." He says, "Why, Mutts Mag, what're you doing in thar?" She says, "Why, Poll and Nance throwed me in here, shet th' door and went on." He says, "Why don't you lift th' latch and come out?" She says, "Ain't no latch in here. Haft to lift th' latch on th' outside." He said, "What'll you gimme to lift th' latch and let you out?" She said, "I'll take you to whar they's fat on another goose's neck."

And, so, th' fox, he rech up with his nose and lifted th' latch. And Mutts Mag walked out, happiest person you ever seed. And she tuk him to whar they was fat on a goose's neck and then went on.

And she was a-hurrin' along on down th' road, and hit uz a-gettin' way long late in th' evenin'. Oh, I guess, nearly dusky dark when she catched up with Poll and Nance. She seed 'em away on down th' road thar ahead of her. Well, she stepped up as fast as she could, got up right close to 'em. One of 'em happened to look around and see her and says, "What in th' world are we gonna do with her?" "Thar she is a-trailin' along after us again." The other 'un says, "I says, 'Yet's kill her.'" Th' other 'un said, "No, yet's not kill her." Said, "I have a idea."

Said, "You know, we ain't got no money. And hit's a-gettin' late, and we'll want to stay all night somewhars right away, and we can't pay. So, yet's jest let her foller along behind us, a right smart piece behind, and we'll tell people that she's our hired girl and that she's th' best hired girl in this whole country. And maybe we can get to stay all night and let her help in th' kitchen and pay for our keep."

So, they 'lowed they'd do that, and they told Mutts Magg what they was a-aimin' to do. And then they went on. Well, th' first house they asked to stay all night — th' worman said they didn't foller keepin' people, and they went on. And hit's a-gettin' pretty dark, and they come to a little ole log house at th' mouth of th' branch. And hit didn't have no winders, but they could see a faar burning through th' cracks of th' logs, and they's a smoke — smoke coming outta th' chimley. So, they knowed somebody lived thar, and they walked up pretty close to th' door and hollered, "Hello."

And th' door opened, and thar outlined against th' faar in th' faar place was th' ugliest little ole worman you ever seed in all o' yore life. And she was wearin' a long poke bonnet and you couldn't see her face very well. And she says, "What'll ye have, gels?" And one of 'em says, "We're two ladies, and we've come a long ways today, and we're tared and hungry. We haint got no money to pay our way, but we've got with us th' best hired girl in th' whole country. And she'll help you pack in th' warter, and fetch th' wood and th' kindlin', and take keer of th' ashes, and scour th' pots and th' pans to pay for our keep, if you can keep us."

Th' little ole worman says, "Hee, hee. Well, we don't never foller turnin' nobody away. Jest come right in."

And so's'un they went in. And she put Mutts Mag to work. And th' other 'uns set down around th' faar. Well, she — after Mutts Mag had fetched in a bucket o' warter and poked up th' faar a little bit — th' little ole worman dished out some beans and cornbread and poured some buttermilk, and they set around and eat it, Poll and Nance talkin' like they was ladies. And Mutts Mag, she was a-listenin' and she knowed they's somethin' wrong here. This little ole worman looked to her plimeblank fer th' world like a witch. And she was a-gonna be keerful.

Well, after Mutts Mag got th' faarplace reddened up and everythang in its place, th' little ole worman says to 'em, says, "Well, I guess you gals is tired. Maybe you'd like to lay down. Jest climb right up th' ladder thar agin th' wall and find you a place up thar in th' straw in th' loft. Now, my own daughters are already up thar, but you'll find ye a blanket and jest make you a place and lay down and sleep."

Well, they went up th' ladder, and Mutts Mag was oneasy about all this. She got her a blanket, and she scrounged around in th' straw thar a little bit and found a knothole. So's'un she laid down so she could peek down through that knothole and see what war a-goin' on downstairs.

Well, Poll and Nance went off to sleep and begun to snore right away, and Mutts Mag was a-layin' thar a-figuring out what would happen. Well, atter while, th' door opened, and in come th' biggest, ugliest ole giant you've ever heered tell of in your life. But his head wasn't much bigger than your fist. And he had to bend away over to get into th' little house. And he says to th' little ole witch worman, says, "Ole worman, is my supper ready?"

She says, "Hesh, yore mouth you ole fool; I've got you three fat pullets in th' loft, and you're making so much noise you're goin' to get 'em all upset. Now, I'm a-gonna haft to have some more warter. So, I'll take th' buckets down to th' spring to get some more warter, and while I'm gone, you wring their necks. And when I come back, I'll cook 'em fer you. But you be keer-ful, you bumbling ole fool, and don't you wring th' necks of my own pretty daughters. They're all a-wearin' nightcaps."

Then she went out at th' door a-swingin' her cedar buckets. Well, th' ole giant, he walked over to th' ladder, and he jest had to step on th' first round. And he rech up through th' scuttle hole, and he was a'feelin' around up thar.

Well, Mutts Mag, she didn't lose no time. As soon as she heered that ole witch say her own daughters was a-wearin' nightcaps, she snatched th' nightcaps off 'n them girls and put one on her head and one on Nance's head and one on Poll's head and laid back down and went to snorin'.

Well, th' ole giant come to a head and it had a nightcap on. So, he'd pass that one by. Then he'd come to a head didn't have a nightcap on it. And with his big, ole finger and thumb, he'd mash down on th' throat and pulled it down through that scuttlehole and wrung it a time or two and throwed it over agin th' pot. Well, he'd just wrung th' neck of th' third daughter when that ole witch worman come back in with them buckets of warter in her hands. And she looked and she seed what he'd done. Well, she set them buckets down and grabbed up a skillet and lit into him. And she said, "You ole stupid fool, look what you've done. You've already wrung th' necks of my own pretty daughters."

Well, when Mutts Mag heered that commotion a-goin' on downstairs, why she ripped up her blanket and made a rope of it. Then she stood up and bumped her head against th' boards three or four times and knocked off three or four boards around a rafter and tied that blanket rope to th' rafter. And her and Poll and Nance didn't lose no time a-skinnin' down that thar rope and a-gettin' away from thar.

Well, it's awful dark, but they went on down th' road a little ways and slept in a haystack. Next mornin' they got up awful early cause they thought maybe th' ole giant and th' witch worman might be a-follerin' 'em, and went on down th' road. Didn't have nothin' to eat except some berries and thangs they picked along by th' road. Well, they traveled on all day — pretty fast — because they thought maybe th' witch worman or th' giant 'd be atter 'em. And never did have nothin' to eat except what they could find a-growin' on th' bushes and th' briars along by th' roadside.

And hit uz a-gettin' awful late, and they come to this here fine house at th' mouth of a creek. Hit uz a big white house with fine winders in it and a two-story porch with woodwork around it and a big chimley at either end of th' house. And th' winderframes and th' doors uz painted blue. And they knowed that uz a fine house; somebody fine had to live thar. And they walked up to th' gate and they hollered, "Hello." Well, th' door opened and a man with a crown on his head come out. Standin' thar at th' edge o' th' porch said, "What 'll ye have, girls?" And one of 'em says, "We're two ladies; we've come a long, long ways. We hain't got no money, but we've got th' best hired girl in th' whole country here with us. And we'd jest like to know what th' chances might be fer us to spend th' night here." He says, "Why I don't never foller turnin' nobody away. Come right on in."

And so's'un they went in. And hit's th' king, and they set down around th' faar with 'em. Th' king sent Mutts Mag on back into th' kitchen to help th' queen whip up something fer 'em to eat. But Mutts Mag, she could heer what was a-goin' on, and she knowed that Poll and Nance was jest a-makin' up a lot of stuff.

Poll and Nance they told th' king all about bein' at that thar little ole house th' night before, and about th' witch worman and th' ugly ole man. And th' king says, "Why, that little ole worman is a witch and that giant is th' biggest headache I have in my whole kingdom." Said, "He's a thief; he stole my fine white horse, my ten-mile stepper. I'd give a bushel o' gold to get that horse back. You gals could get it too, you're smart 'uns."

Well, Poll and Nance they begun to talk like they had a big plan; they'd go back and get th' ten-mile stepper for th' king and get that thar bushel of gold. Well, Mutts Mag was a-listenin' to everthang, and she knowed they wouldn't do anythang. Well, after th' queen and Mutts Mag got something fixed up fer supper and they all eat, th' king says to 'em, says, "Well, I guess you gals would like to lay down now 'cause you've had a mighty hard day." And so's'un th' queen tuk 'em upstairs and give a room to each of 'em. They never had had a room of their own before in all their lives.

Well, Mutts Mag, she laid there and thought a long, long time about how they might get that ten-mile stepper away from that thar ole giant. Then she went to sleep. Next mornin' when they got up, she went down to help th' queen fix breakfast and then went to fetch Poll and Nance, and they's gone.

They'd slipped out endurin' th' night. And nobody never did hear another word about Poll and Nance. Don't know what happened to 'em.

Well, Mutts Mag, she stayed on thar at th' king's house and worked. And him and th' queen both uz awful pleased with her work. And she was a-plannin' how she might get rid of th' ole giant and th' ole witch and get that thar ten-mile stepper back. Well, one night she said to th' king, says, "I've got a plan." Says, "I'm a-gonna go up to th' ole giant's house and see how it works." And he said, "Well, good." He said, "I'll give you a bushel o' gold if you can bring back that thar ten-mile stepper." And said, "I shore would like to git rid of that little ole witch worman and that giant too. If you can bring me th' head of ary one of 'em, I'll give you another bushel o' gold."

Well, Mutts Mag, she left next mornin' before daylight, got jest as soon a start as she could. And she had a poke o' salt under her arm. And she walked all day, and got to th' little ole house jest after dark. And she clumb up on th' roof and stood thar by th' chimley a-lookin' down, a-watchin' th' pot bile. Well, ever now and then, th' little ole witch worman ud come over and lift th' pot lid and stir what was a-bilin' in thar, and when she'd do that, Mutts Mag ud drop a handful of salt in.

Well, attar while, she didn't have no salt left in that poke; she'd put a peck o' salt in that stew. So she jest waited. Directly, th' door opened and th' ole giant come in. She could hear him down thar. And he says, to th' little ole witch worman, says, "Ole worman, is my supper ready?" She says, "Yes, I've got you a pot of mighty good stew in thar on th' hathstone. Set down and I'll dish it out fer you."

So th' ole giant seat down and th' little ole witch worman ladled him out a dishful o' that thar stew. And he tuk one bite, and he went to sputterin'. "What in th' world are you tryin' to do me? Are you tryin' to pizen me?" She said, "Why, no, what's wrong?" He said, "That's so salty I can't have it in my mouth." She said, "Why that can't be, I didn't put more than a pinch or two of salt in it." He said, "It's so salty I haft to have some warter."

She went over, looked in th' cedar bucket and says, "They ain't a drap o' warter in th' bucket." He says, "Old worman, you go down thar to that spring and bring me some warter." Said, "I can't eat this unless I have a lot o' warter to go with it." She says, "It's awful dark; it's too dark fer me to go." He says, "Why, throw out yore light ball."

Well as soon as Mutts Mag heered that, she jumped down off'n that thar little ole house and run ahead o' th' worman down th' pathway to th' spring and got on th' other side o' th' spring to wait fer her. Well, th' little ole worman uz pullin' them thar cedar buckets down toarge th' spring and she got pretty close to th' spring and set one o' th' buckets down and throwed out her light ball. Well, Mutts Mag didn't lose no time, she jest reched down in her pocket and got out her ole case knife and caught it on th' end of th' case knife. And then dipped it down in th' spring, and it went out. Well, th' little ole witch worman stubbed her toe over a root and fell right into th' spring. And when she done that, Mutts Mag grabbed her by th' hair o' th' head and cut her head off with that case knife. Left her body thar in th' spring, and traveled all night to get back down to th' king's house.

She got thar jest about th' time th' king was a-comin' out atter breakfast. And when he seed her with that thar little ole witch's head a-swingin' by th' haar, he was th' tickeledest man you ever saw. And he says, "Why, Mutts Mag, I've got this here bushel of gold fer you." And says, "Now, if you can bring me that ole giant's head, I'll give you another bushel o' gold. And if you can bring me back my ten-mile stepper, I'll give you three bushel o' gold."

Well, Mutts Mag, she got to a-thinkin about that, and she thought maybe it might be better if she tried to get th' ten-mile stepper first. And so's'un she planned and schemed and studied about it. And, finally, she decided she had a plan worked out, and she told th' king what she was a-goin' to do. He said, "Well, I'll jest be awful tickled to get that thar ten-mile stepper back."

Well, she left out before daylight one morning so's'un she could get up to that ole giant's house in plenty o' time endurin' daytime. Well, she traveled all day long and got thar jest attar dark. Now, she had with her a poke o' barley. And so's'un she saw th' ole giant in th' little house a-settin' by th' faar. She slipped into th' stable whar th' ten mile stepper was and went over to th' feed trough and put out a handful or two of th' barley. And then she tuk out her case knife and started whackin' off th' bells on th' bridle. They wasn't a-rattlin' as long as th' ten mile stepper was a-eatin' th' barley, but she didn't notice, and th' ten mile stepper eat all th' barley before she got th' bells cut off. And so, hit lifted its head, and th' bells rung. Well, when th' bells rung, th' door of th' little ole house opened and here come that giant a-chargin' down through thar with a lantern in his hand. He opened th' stable door and helt up th' lantern. Mutts Mag didn't lose no time; she hid under th' feedbox.

And, th' ole giant looked behind th' door, and he looked over in th' corner, and he looked all around under th' ten-mile stepper's belly. Didn't see nothin'. Shet th' door and went back.

Well about th' time he's all settled down before his faar, Mutts Mag put another handful or two of barley in th' feedtrough and started whackin' off more bells. But agin th' horse eat th' barley faster n' she thought he would and lifted his head and th' bells rung again — them that was left. And here come that ole giant a-chargin' down through thar again.

That time she jest barely had time to hide behind th' door. He opened th' door, held up th' lantern and looked at th' feedbox. He looked under th' horse; he looked in th' corner — didn't see nobody — turned around, shet th' door behind him and went back. And about th' time he was all settled down before th' faarplace, Mutts Mag was busy again a-feedin' th' barley to th' horse and a-whackin' off th' bells.

Well, th' horse eat all th' barley before she got all of 'em whacked off, and lifted his head. Th' bells ring again. Here come th' giant. She jest barely had time that time to hide under his tail.

Th' giant opened th' door; he held up his lantern, and he looked at th' feedbox and he looked in th' corner. He looked behind th' door. Didn't see nobody. Turned to start out, and then he says, "Now, wait a minute here! They's too many laigs back here." And so's'un he reched back under th' horse's belly and caught ole Mutts Mag by th' laig and pulled her out. Said, "I gotcha!"

She says, "What are you aimin' to do with me?" He says "Don't know yet, ain't make up my mind." She says, "Well, above all, don't put me in th' chickenhouse and lock me up thar and jest feed me bread and honey. If they's anythang in this world I can't stand to eat, it's bread and honey." He says, "That's exactly what I'm a-aiming to do."

And so's'un he threwed her in th' chickenhouse and didn't give her nothin' to eat atall 'cept bread and honey and brought her a little warter to drink ever now n' then. He kept her in thar two or three weeks. She didn't know what he's a-gonna do with her. Til finally, one evenin' he come and opened th' door and says, "Well, I've come to get you."

She said, "What're you a-aimin' to do with me?" He said, "I'm a-aimin' to kill ye!" She said, "How're you a-gonna do it?" "Don't know, hadn't made up my mind yit." She said, "Now don't you swing me up in a sheet to the rafter and beat me to death with a stick, 'cause if you do, I'll rattle like pots a-rattlin' and crackle like dishes a-breakin', and I'll meow like cats, and I'll bark like dawgs, and my blood will run like honey out of a jug."

He says, "That's exactly what I'm a-gonna do." And so, he swung her up to th' rafter in a sheet and went out to get a pole to beat her with. Well, she didn't lose no time. Soon as he went out th' door, she got out her ole case knife, ripped a hole in that sheet and let herself down and sewed it up right fast. And then she called th' cat and th' dawg and she put in th' pots and th' pans and all th' dishes and a five gallon jug of honey. And then clumb out on th' roof to wait to see what'd happen.

Well, that ole giant come back. And he rared back to swarp that thar bundle with that stick, and hit uz as big as a fence post. And he swarped it oncet, and th' cat meowed and th' dawg barked. And he says, "Oh, yes, ole Mutts Mag, I'll make you meow like cats and bark like dawgs." Then he rared way back and he swarped it agin, and th' dishes crackled. "Oh, yes, ole Mutts Mag," he says, "I'll make ye meow like a cat and bark like a dawg and crackle like dishes a-breakin'."

And then he swarped it agin and th' pots rattled. "Oh, yes, ole Mutts Mag, I'll make ye meow like a cat, bark like a dawg, and crackle like dishes a-breakin', and rattle like pots a-bein' beat." And then, he rared back and struck with ever might he had. And the honey begun to roll out.

He says, "Oh, yes, ole Mutts Mag," he says, "I'll make ye meow like cats and bark like dawgs and crackle like dishes a-breakin' and rattle like pots a-bein' beat, and yore blood a-runnin' like honey." Well, Mutts Mag, when she heared that, she hopped down off 'n that thar little ole house fast as she could, went down to th' stable, led that ten-mile stepper out, clumb on it, and tuk off down th' road fast as she could.

Well, when th' ole giant tuk th' sheet down to open it up, and found his dishes all broke up, his cat and dawg killed, his pots beat all outta shape, and his jug o' honey all a-runnin' out, he was th' maddest man you ever heared tell of in all yore life. He's so mad he went around and around in circles thar a little bit before he knowed what he was a-gonna do.

And then he thought of his ten-mile stepper, and so's'un he went off down to th' barn. Th' stable door was open, and th' ten-mile stepper was gone. He was a-lookin' in th' dirt in th' barn lot, and he could see how it'd gone— that Mutts Mag had rid off on it, down th' river road. And so's'un, he tuk out down th' river road jest as fast as he could go.

Atter while, he come to whar th' road crossed th' river at th' ford, and he looked over on th' other side a' th' river, and thar was th' ten mile stepper hitched to a flyin' limb. And Mutts Mag was a-dancin' on a flat rock. And he called across to her, and he says, "Hey, over thar Mutts Mag, how'd ya git over thar?"

She says, "Why, tied a millstone around my neck, tuk a runnin' go, and skipped across th' river." "That's what I'm a-gonna do." he says. And so's'un, he found a millstone, put a rope through it, tied it around his neck and helt it in his arms. And he backed up and tuk a big runnin' go and throwed it. Well, it jest drug him right to th' bottom of th' river. Mutts Mag stood on th' bank and watched him blubber until she knowed he's dead.

Then she hopped on that ten-mile stepper and rode off down to th' king's house fast as she could. She got thar long about th' middle of th' evenin', I guess. Th' king was a-sittin' on th' porch. When he seed her a-ridin' up on that ten-mile stepper, he was th' happiest feller you ever seed. And so's'un, he brought out three bushel o' gold and give it to Mutts Mag.

Well, Mutts Mag stayed around a little while a-thinkin' what she's a-gonna do with her gold. Til' finally, she decided she'd jest buy her a place of her own. So she went over in th' other valley and bought her a nice farm over thar and built her a house on it—looked jest like th' king's house: a big, long white house with a chimley on either end of it, and a double porch with fancy-work around it, and th' doors and th' winders painted green!

Th' last time I was over that way and a-askin' about Mutts Mag, folks tole me that she's a-livin mighty fine.

NOTES

1. Loyal Jones has noted that Triune baptisms were not the common practice in the United Baptist Churches, although they were the standard practice among the old Dunkards of Virginia. Some United Baptists may well have adopted the practice during this time period, but it has not survived as a typical practice among that congregation. Loyal Jones to Patricia Beaver, October 5, 2001. See also Loyal Jones, 1999. *Faith & Meaning in the Southern Uplands.* Urbana: Univ. of Illinois Press, especially pp. 147–150; and Deborah Vansau McCauley, 1995. *Appalachian Mountain Religion: A History.* Urbana: Univ. of Illinois Press.

2. Frank Proffitt (1913–1965) was an internationally recognized expert on the traditional Appalachian fretless banjo as well as a singer of traditional ballads and mountain songs. A native of Johnson County, Tennessee, Frank Proffitt spent most of his life in the shadow of Beech Mountain in Avery County, North Carolina. Cratis Williams first met him in 1944, when Frank Proffitt and "some of his neighbors were furnishing live music for a square dance" in Watauga County, N.C., and they maintained a warm friendship for the remainder of Proffitt's life. Frank Proffitt's most famous contribution to popular music was "Tom Dula," which was transcribed by Frank Warner in 1938 and eventually "catapulted the Kingston Trio to fame in 1959" as the ballad of "Tom Dooley." See Cratis Williams. 1966. "Frank Proffitt." *Mountain Life and Work* XLII (1): 6–7.

3. The banjo is currently on loan to the W.L.Eury Appalachian Collection of Belk Library, Appalachian State University.

4. Cratis Williams told this tale to Carl Ross on the campus of Appalachian State University in 1981. Dr. Ross recorded it, and Charlotte Ross transcribed the tape, in consultation with Mona Whitt Williams.

5. A nationally known folklorist, Richard Chase collected stories throughout the southern and central Appalachians. For many years he lived in the Beech Creek community in Watauga County, North Carolina, where he came to know Cratis Williams. Among Chase's many books are *The Jack Tales* (1943) and *Grandfather Tales* (1948). Chase and Williams both participated for many years in Saturday summer folk festivals on the grounds of the Horn in the West outdoor theater in Boone. The Williams children recall story-telling sessions at Chase's Beech Creek cabin, and Chase was not an infrequent visitor in the Williams's home in Boone, with many of the conversations concerning not only the stories themselves but also the "proper" dialect in which to relate the stories in a more authentic manner.

Chapter Two ——————————————————————————

Growing Up in Sacred Wind

Starting Elementary School

The day before I was sent at the age of six to Middle Caines Creek School, my mother took us for a Sunday afternoon visit to the home of my grandfather David O. Williams, where she weighed all of us on Grandpa's scales. I weighed 35 pounds. That was the Sunday next after the fourth Saturday in July 1917, the weekend for the annual "sacrament meeting" of the local United Baptist Church. Bill Edwards, a photographer who lived on the creek, had been making pictures on the "meetin' house grounds." As he passed my grandfather's place, my mother had him make pictures of her three children and my aunt, who is four years younger than I. I have one of those pictures, which shows me as a thin, frail, and hollow-eyed child with an enormous wedge-shaped head too big for my slight body.

On the last Monday in July 1917, I enrolled in the one-room school (District 49) on the hillside across the valley from my father's home. The school, called Middle Caines Creek and Hillside, was in the Caines Creek United Baptist Church. About 75 children were enrolled in what was only a loosely graded school. Perhaps twenty, including my sister Mabel, were beginners.

My father had asked my Grampa Dave to buy a primer for each of us at Blaine the preceding Saturday. I recall that I went to my grandfather's to get the primers early on the day school opened. Because I had been impressed with the hymn singing at the church (the annual "sakermint" meeting) the day before, I was singing a primitive hymn as I passed the "high bank" on the old road, which paralleled the creek, down to my grandfather's home. My grandfather's family were eating breakfast in the "cook room" (summer kitchen) when I arrived. When Mabel and I arrived (before "books") at school,

84

Left–right: Mabel Williams, 5 years old; Cratis Williams, 6; Ralph Williams, 4; Aunt Elva Williams, half sister of Curt, daughter of David and Martelia, 3 years old, July 1917.

the teacher, Eugene Moore, called us to the rostrum and enrolled us in the record book. My mother had written in my primer "Cratis Dearl Williams, His Book." I did not know for 20 years that she had misspelled my middle name, which was written "Darl" on my birth certificate. I have only one vivid memory of my first day at school: the rays of golden sunshine that found their way through the beech trees surrounding the house and rested upon the teacher's face while he was writing our names in the record book.

My first teacher was Eugene Moore, who moved away soon after the school term ended. After about three months of my first year at school I developed tonsillitis and a bad cold. My parents did not send me back to school that year, for the term (6 months) was half gone. I had not quite finished my primer, but I knew the alphabet and could spell and write simple words on my slate. Only one incident of the year remains clear in my memory: Because of the crowded conditions in the school four or five other "primer scholars" and I sat on the short bench on the platform, the bench occupied by the preachers at church. Once I was drawing a tree on the blackboard (painted on the wall) which ran behind the bench when I noticed that the teacher, who was standing behind a student who was reading aloud, was looking directly at me. He had an ambiguous smile that puzzled and frightened me, for I expected reproval for wasting my time. The teacher spoke in a rather kind voice and told me to use my other hand. I had been drawing the tree with my left hand.

I recall that I started at the beginning when I returned to school the following year, one of fifteen beginners in a one-room school with an enrollment of 75, ranging from 5 to 18 years old. The school was held in the United Baptist Church building, which was constructed about 1885. My second teacher was Annie Young, who eloped to California with a man named Seagraves after teaching about three months. That year was completed by Harry Burton, later a successful merchant and banker at Blaine. My teacher for my third and fourth years in school was Randolph N. Boggs, a crippled man with a strong arm. He moved to Hitchens, Kentucky, after completing his second year of teaching at Middle Caines Creek. My teacher for the 1921-1922 term was Ulyssis S. Williams, my father's cousin. "Lyss" began the 1922-1923 term, but was shot and killed in November. Lucy Morris taught the school for the remainder of the year. She married Jesse Williams, Lyss's brother, and they went to Columbus, Ohio. My teacher the following year was Ora L. Boggs. During that year I took the county examination to determine whether I was eligible to go to high school. The examination lasted two days. I passed it at the age of twelve.

Not any of my teachers had graduated from high school. Most of them had attended teachers' institutes, held in one-room schools, to prepare for the county teacher examinations. One or two had spent a few weeks at a normal school or a normal institute.

The county superintendent usually visited the schools at least once a year. The superintendent in my first years at school was John Ekers, also a country lawyer and merchant from Fallsburg. The next county superintendent was Dock Jordan, who continued in office to 1934. The superintendent came to the school, hitched his horse to the "flying limb" of a nearby tree, walked proudly into the schoolhouse, greeted all loudly, and took a seat in the rear of the room. As soon as a natural change of order occurred in his plans for the day, the teacher invited the superintendent to speak to the school. The superintendent would commend the teacher, congratulate the children, relate how education had improved since he went to a three-month school, tell tales, recite poems, and point out that Abraham Lincoln, by hard-earned self-education, had prepared himself to become president, and that he himself would not be surprised if some bright-faced boy sitting there in front of him would one day become governor of Kentucky or president of the United States.

With Annie Young as my teacher, I began my second year of school still in a first reader. This year I was given a seat near the front of the room. I recall two or three "incidents" from my second year. Once my grandfather came lumbering through the doorway and interrupted with a "good mornin', m'um." He came to report that the teacher's brother had been killed in action and that his body was arriving for burial next day. School was dismissed. My grandfather walked beside the teacher to console her. I walked along by his side. When the grave was dug and ready, relatives were assembled, hymns sung, and preachers were on hand ... the teacher's dead brother walked into the crowd to attend his own funeral. He had sent the fateful telegram himself as a joke.

One incident was a source of embarrassment, both to my parents and to myself. I stole a small cut of a plug of tobacco from my mother and put it in a Prince Albert Smoking Tobacco tin I had found. After school I was chewing tobacco as I walked beside the teacher down the road. She asked me about it and how I came to have the tobacco. I told her that I had picked up a chew my mother had laid up and had put it in the tin box. My uncle, only a few years older than I and in school too, reported to my father what had taken place. My father, who had heard the report while visiting at my grandfather's after supper, and my mother woke me up with their conversation while they searched my clothing for evidence. As I opened my eyes, my father was inspecting the contents of the tin box and saying, "I'll ask him about it in the morning. I don't believe it, but he'll tell the truth. Cratis won't lie." I closed my eyes quickly, but I spent a restless night.

Uncle Wash

My Uncle Wash Boggs was a little man with a blunt beard, one that looked as if he had cropped it off straight across about four inches from his chin. Many old men in our community wore beards, but nobody had a chopped off one like Uncle Wash, whose shock of gray hair and old-looking eyes with heavy brows a little darker than his beard and hair gave him the appearance of the troll I had seen a picture of in my first reader, hiding under the bridge that the three billy goats trip-trapped across. Uncle Wash also had big tusk-like teeth, much stained with tobacco juice, that he would thrust out at children whom he wanted to frighten. He stuttered and sputtered when he talked, and his voice, though driven by considerable volume, was low-pitched like the growl of an angry bear dog.

He was a blacksmith. When children came into his shop and picked up his tools or disturbed the arrangement of his supplies, Uncle Wash would fix his ancient, hard eyes on them, flash his brown tusks, growl raspily, and stroke his broad beard as if he were thinking seriously of eating them up, bones and all. The children fell back in terror and fled as rapidly as possible, Uncle Wash chuckling in his throat but with his eyes looking hard like discs of gray steel. He thought frightening children by behaving like a boogerman was great fun. If their parents were in the shop at the time, Uncle Wash would laugh a growling laugh after the children fled.

Uncle Wash's wife, Aunt Rannie, was a short, fat woman. She had a low-pitched voice, too. When she and Uncle Wash carried on a normal conversation, it sounded like two dogs growling, but they rarely quarreled. People thought they got along very well together. They had raised twelve children, some of them tall and slender, some short and fat like Aunt Rannie, and some slight and wiry like Uncle Wash. Uncle Wash would sometimes walk with Aunt Rannie to church. They walked very slowly because Aunt Rannie was so fat. She would carry an umbrella to keep the sun off, for heat bothered her. She would turn red in the face, start smothering, and have to sit by the roadside to cool off when she walked too fast. Uncle Wash did not carry her umbrella for her. She was so fat that he could not stand close enough to her to keep the sun off. He would help her up the steps at church but would not go in himself. Instead, he would sit with loafers under a tree near the church house door.

Once when I was a very small boy, Uncle Wash and Aunt Rannie came to our house for Sunday dinner. Uncle Wash scared me that day by flashing his teeth at me when I kept pestering my father about wanting to do something my father did not want me to do. I ran away. Later, when I approached my father, Uncle Wash would flash his teeth. I stood some distance away and listened to Uncle Wash tell tales to my father. I think he did not want me to interrupt my father's attention to his tales and that was why he would show his teeth at me, like a dog about to bite.

One of the tales he told was about a chicken hawk that had been carrying off the biddies. Aunt Rannie would call him to shoot the hawk, but by the time he got his shotgun the hawk would have caught a biddy and flown away. But Aunt Rannie fixed that hawk. She was working in the kitchen, doing something, when the hawk swooped down right outside the kitchen door. Aunt Rannie heard the commotion, looked out, and saw the old hen flogging the hawk. She grabbed her broom, rushed out, and killed the hawk with the broom before it could get away. Uncle Wash laughed big and loud when he told it and slapped himself on his knees with both hands two or three times, making like Aunt Rannie striking the hawk with the broom. Papa did not laugh much. He just looked at Uncle Wash.

I was afraid of Uncle Wash after that for a long time. When I went with other children to see him work in his blacksmith shop I would stand just inside the door and watch him. The shop, made of logs, had no window. Smoke from the forge passed through a short chimney made of mud and field rocks and then wandered toward the eve of the blackened roof. The shop was always smoky. Uncle Wash would pull a pole attached to a big bellows shaped like a guitar body and the bellows would blow a stream of fresh air against the coals. They would become almost white with heat. You could see a horseshoe or a mattock change from black to a dull red and on to white hot as he pumped the bellows. Then he would take the object out with a pair of long tongs, hold it on the anvil, and beat it fast with a shop hammer, like he was making music. The white hot sparks would fly in all directions, but they would lose their glow by the time they struck anything. When Uncle Wash had the mattock as sharp as he wanted it, or the horseshoe corked just to suit his notion, he would souse it in a tub of water and hold it there for a few minutes to temper it. White steam would rise from the sizzling object and blow around Uncle Wash. He looked like what I thought the devil might have looked like with the coals glowing in the forge behind him and the steam streaming around him, except he didn't have a fishhook tail like the devil.

He would shoe horses in front of his shop, which had a roof that stuck several feet out toward the road. It was fun to watch him pare the horse's hoof down with a knife that had a crooked blade before he fitted the shoe. Then he drove nails through holes in the shoe and into the edge of the hoof until they came out an inch or two above the shoe. After all the nails were in, he would bend them down with pliers and strike them a time or two with a special hammer that had a ball on it instead of claws. He rasped the hoof with a big file to make it flush with the sides of the horseshoe. He seemed strong for such a little man as he held the horse's foot up with one hand and worked with the other. People rode from other creeks to get Uncle Wash to shoe their mules and horses. He would tell the people big windy stories as he worked, but he would not talk about his neighbors or tell things that would hurt other people. His stories were mostly about things he said he had done or that had happened to him.

He was a stubborn, strong-headed man and liked the way he was. He had always been that way, he said. He liked to tell about the time, when he was a little boy, that he disobeyed his father by crawling, against strict orders, back under the house through a narrow passage beside the chimney. His father had told him that he would get caught under the house and nobody could pull him out, but Uncle Wash crawled under anyway far enough to get his arms and shoulders wedged between the rocks, but his rump was still sticking out. When he discovered that he could not go on or back out, either, he began to squall in fright. His father found him caught there like a rat in a trap. But instead of trying to help him out of his predicament, his father picked up a board and whacked him across the rump until he pulled himself out. He was skinned up right tolerably, he said, but Great-Grandpa had no sympathy for him.

I liked to go to Uncle Wash's to play with his youngest son, Henry, only two or three years older than I, and with his grandsons who lived on the next farm, but I faded into the crowd when Uncle Wash turned his attention to us. I liked Aunt Rannie, who said little to us and went on doing her work around the kitchen or in her wash house just behind the kitchen. She paid so little attention to me, though, that I was not certain that she even knew my name. She had so many grandchildren, she might have thought I was one of them.

Uncle Wash was a careful worker and more fastidious about many things than his neighbors were. He kept his yard fence in good repair, the grass in his yard was always green and well cared for, and his house was neat and trim. His home was a double log house with a chimney between the log pens. It was said by some to have been built on another farm in 1822 by Uncle Wash's great-grandfather, the first Boggs to come from Lee County, Virginia, to live in the valley. Uncle Wash had bought it from a cousin and moved it, log by log, to its present site. Uncle Wash had weather-boarded it himself with carefully worked, smooth lumber which he kept painted with white paint. His house was trimmed in dark red. Mounted in the eaves were sections of wagon wheels, also painted red. His was the only house in the valley with wagon wheel sections in its eaves.

My father told about a spectacular display once of Uncle Wash's violent temper. Uncle Wash was as tenacious in his anger as a mud turtle, an animal said not to let go when it bites you until it thunders. Some young people, gathered at Uncle Wash's one Saturday night, were sitting around the fire after supper and listening to Uncle Wash tell windy tales. During a pause he heard a mouse gnawing behind the paper on the wall by the fireboard. He arose from his chair and held his ear close to the paper to determine the location of the mouse. Suddenly, he struck the paper with the sides of his hands on either side of the mouse, tore a hole in the paper with his forefinger, and forced the mouse out. When the mouse was half way out Uncle Wash grabbed it, and it bit him on the hand. He closed his hand around the mouse, squeezing it so tightly that its eyes began to pop out at him. Uncle Wash held the mouse before his face, looked at it for a moment, and said, in a rage, "B-B-By grabs, I'll make you b-b-bite me!" He snapped the mouse's head off with one chomp of his big teeth, spat it into the fireplace, and flung the remainder in after it. With mouse blood trickling down his beard, he said, as he took his seat, "I r-r-reckon, th' th' that'll be the last time he'll every try to bite *me*."

I became less afraid of Uncle Wash as I grew older, but not until a long time after the first day of my second year in school. Uncle Wash, the trustee of the school, appeared to present to us the new teacher, a seventeen-year-old girl who had never taught before. He sat on a bench near the door and waited for the children to find seats after someone had rung the big bell mounted in the attic above the door. When everyone was in place, Uncle Wash rose slowly and walked with dignity and deliberation to the front of the room, turning his head neither to the right nor to the left. He took a firm position in front of the children.

"Boys and girls," he said gravely, his voice very much like the low growl of a dog, "Annie Young has been hired to teach this school." His old-looking eyes began to harden into the steel-gray glint that I remembered. "She is young and not very big but she's got the learnin' she needs to teach you 'ens. I want you 'ens to pay attention to what she tells you and to mind her. If you 'ens d-d-don't," and his stutter reminded me of the rhythmical beat of his shop hammer on his anvil, "I hope she'll whup you 'ens as much as you 'ens need." His brown tusks dropped suddenly from under his mustache. "Tha's a plenty of beech switches a-growin' on the trees around here. If she needs help in tamin' any of you 'ens, I want her to call on me. I can make a switch cry 'meat' every lick." He glowered for a moment, his eyes as hard as gray stone marbles and the long tobacco stained tusks hanging prominently over his chin beard. The room was as quiet as a tomb as Uncle Wash walked toward the door with measured deliberation, plucked his battered hat from a peg, and left.

Elementary School Days

I recall rather vaguely a trial conducted by the local magistrate: The teacher was on trial for whipping the blood out of Jake Steele for "flipping" some of the students with a strip from an inner tube somebody had brought to school to use in making slingshots. I remember that my Uncle Wash Boggs, who was the trustee, was "defense" for Miss Young. My Aunt Marg, grandmother of Jake Steele, an orphan, described Jake's wounds. The teacher was acquitted, however, for older students offered evidence that the welt left by the beech switch the teacher had used was not significant and that Jake had been annoying and disobedient.

On another occasion the school was somewhat upset when the teacher's sister Lizzie, who had brought a horse for the teacher to ride to her home on Cherokee Creek, raided the teacher's dinner pail. It was about the middle of the afternoon. Lizzie, who was sitting on the preacher's bench on the rostrum, picked up the teacher's lunch pail, slipped it open, and took out a very large biscuit, a rough, rusty looking one. After examining it critically for a few minutes, she took a hatpin from her hat, ran it through the biscuit, and held the biscuit up for the school to see.

About Christmas time Annie eloped with a man named Seagraves and went to California, where she is still living. I have never seen her since, nor did I ever see Eugene Moore after he moved to Ohio following the close of my first year in school. After Annie Young left, Harry Burton came and completed the year. I recall nothing vividly about the months he was my teacher except that he removed his shoes to warm his feet by the pot-bellied stove in the middle of the room. Harry later became a successful merchant at Blaine. He was also a landowner and a banker. Many years later, while I was principal of Blaine High School, I attended his Sunday school class in the Blaine Christian Church.

In 1919 my teacher was Randolph N. Boggs (known as "Crippled Ran" because he had had polio and went on crutches). There continued to be about 75 children in the school. Ran remained in the room at recess and lunch time. Children played folk games and sang traditional songs under a spreading ash tree that grew by the side of the road. Big boys played tournaments of "big nickel" in a marble yard they had dug in the clay hillside. Big girls were spectators.

Ran encouraged me to read orally. I recall that he once invited the whole school to hear me read aloud the story about the dog and the cock that spent a night in the forest. The response of my "audience" to my cock-crowing was so gratifying to me that I began to aspire to skill in interpretation. I have considered this experience one of the most significant in my life. It sharpened my interest in school generally. Soon I was requesting permission to read history and geography with the "advanced" scholars. I was also attentive to recitations of classes ahead of me and at least once supplied the right answer to a question concerning a sentence diagram of the "advanced" class.

Ran also taught the school in 1920. Two incidents from that year remain in my memory, one most humiliating, the other most rewarding. A green-eyed, pale-faced little girl captured my fancy. I rushed to the recitation bench in order to sit beside her. I spent much time looking across the room at her during study time. At play time I sought to be her partner. One Sunday I wrote her a love note, which I addressed ornately and hid away in the bib pocket of my overalls. Alas, my note fell into the wrong hands next day and was carried to the teacher. Immediately after the mid-afternoon recess the teacher called everybody to attention, produced my note, and read it slowly and exaggeratedly aloud for all to hear. The laughter was loud and painful and I was filled with humiliation. Even the girl laughed. I was teased and tormented at school and at home. Although I refrained from saying anything either in my defense or against the girl, I studiously avoided the girl, but found myself being forced beside her on the recitation bench and as her partner in the games we played while the other children leered and grinned. Had it occurred to me, I am sure I would have declared that I would never forget that girl — but perhaps 25 years later I was in a hotel in Ashland, Kentucky. I had answered some Christmas greetings, which I discarded in the waste can, before I went out for breakfast. When I returned, the linen maid came from the linen room and addressed me as I was unlocking my door. She walked into my room and asked me if I remembered her. I looked carefully and it seemed that I had known those green eyes and that pale face before, but I could not recall when. She told me her name ... the name of my first sweetheart. She had quit school in 3rd grade and her life had been filled with hardships.

A more gratifying experience remembered from 1920 was my exhibit of models. Near my home was a bank of white clay ideal for modeling. During the late summer and early autumn my sister Mabel, my brother Ralph, and my aunt Elva, four years younger than I, spent many happy hours building and modeling with clay. We became quite accomplished, as critical abilities of the community saw it. I was so proud of a clay elephant and a clay man that I had made that I took them to school for Ran to see. He was immensely pleased and called the school to attention while he displayed my work and commented on it, observing in passing that the only criticism he would offer was that an elephant actually has one toe less on each foot than I had given mine. The admiration of the school for my exhibit was golden to me. However, one boy had apparently resented the whole affair, for when he went to the front of the room to ask the teacher to pronounce a word for him, he deliberately leaned on the table in such a way that he crushed my elephant to a heap of dust.

Ran moved away to a farm near Hitchens, Kentucky, after he closed the term. I visited him once, years later, while I was en route from the University of Kentucky to my home for the summer vacation. Although Ran had never attended high school, he was an effective teacher and had read considerably and intelligently. He was an agnostic, but he had the good sense not to discuss his beliefs with children in the school. I have marveled at the intellectual experience of this man whose schooling, except for a spring "institute" or two held in a one-room mountain school, was confined to what he had received from other mountain teachers of the same school I attended.

World War I on Caines Creek

World War I came closest to us in the restrictions then imposed that made it difficult for us to get sugar and flour at the stores. Turning six years old in April 1917, I was not yet a coffee drinker and do not remember specifically whether there was a shortage at the stores, but I do recall seeing my mother roasting barley to grind with coffee beans she had roasted herself.

Because of the sugar shortage my father grew a patch of sorghum cane to provide molasses both for home use and for the market. Instead of white cake and sugar cookies, we ate gingerbread, molasses cookies, and simple undecorated and unspiced cake that we called sweetbread. We sweetened stewed fruit with molasses, and my mother used molasses as "long sweetening" in pies and cobblers (which we called "sonkers"). Fortunately for us, there was a bumper crop of blackberries and fruits in 1918. As I recall, we picked 30 gallons of blackberries that summer. We canned about 12 gallons and my mother made jam and jelly of the remainder. I recall helping to stir jam boiling in a black pot over an open fire in the woodyard. My mother had put in too much molasses and we boiled the pot too long. The jam, almost as stiff as taffy, was hard to spread on corn cakes and biscuits. The jelly that year, both from berries and apples, was stiff and hard to spread.

Until autumn 1918, we had flour only occasionally. When my father was able to buy a bag at a store we would have a cake with icing on it, cookies flavored with vanilla, and biscuits for breakfast. The tough jam and jelly were so hard to spread that we preferred boiled molasses which we could dip from a bowl and pour over a biscuit already spread with butter. Apple butter and peach butter, both sweetened with molasses, were tough and rubbery and tended to roil up under our knives when we tried to use them.

On our way back from the store in the late summer either of 1917 or 1918 my brother and I found a brown paper bag of sugar, perhaps two pounds, on the bank by the roadside below the old church. The package was rectangular and wrapped and tied with twine string. It must have been lying there for a day or two before we found it, for it had hardened into a block. The paper had split beside the twine on the top side and ants were going in and out of the opening. Having no sugar at home at that time, we fancied the white cakes and cookies that Mama could make. We shouted our good fortune as soon as we entered the yard gate. But Mama would not have the sugar. Our speculation that the package had bounced from the basket of a horseback rider, perhaps Uncle Tom Rivers, on his way home from Blaine did not relieve her of her overpowering suspicion that some German, sympathetic with the Kaiser, had slipped back into the country and left poisoned sugar there to destroy all of us. She sniffed at the slit in the bag and thought the sugar had a strange odor. I was ordered to dig a deep hole in the sand by the creek and bury the sugar. The notion that Germans prowled about at night and left poison food lying around haunted us.

I prized biscuits for breakfast so highly that I would get up and peep at the breakfast table before deciding to come forth for the day. If I saw biscuits steaming on the table, I would wash my hands and face in cold water dipped from the bucket on the bench, comb my hair, and rush in to eat with my parents, even when I ran the risk of discipline for some indiscretion the previous day that my mother might have reported to my father. (No one ever dared to come to the table without having groomed himself for the occasion.) If I saw only corn cakes on the breakfast table, I slipped back to bed and waited for my father to leave for work.

My father grew a field of wheat in 1918. I remember seeing cradlers sitting beside their cradles in our yard while waiting for dew to dry so they could go into the field. There was excitement when the great red and gold threshing machine with its smokestack and rattling motor came to thresh the wheat. Many men came to help and my grandmother came to help my mother "cook for the work hands" that hot day. Some men gathered and hauled in on wagons the sheaves of wheat and others fed them into the thresher, which blew a pile of golden straw to one side and sent wheat, flowing like a little stream, into containers that were set on a sled. Not all the workmen could eat at the same table for dinner. Some, their faces sunburned and their foreheads white, sat on the porch and in the yard and fanned themselves with their hats while waiting for their turns at the table.

The great machine threshed all of our wheat in one day and moved on late that afternoon to the next farm. My father loaded his barrels of wheat on a wagon and took it to Webbville to be ground into flour. The mill kept some of the flour for toll. My father brought back one barrel and a stack of perhaps a dozen 24-pound bags of white flour, the paper bags gleaming, blooming blue blossoms of bag lining at one end, and decorated with colorful pictures of the Webbville Milling Company on the side. We had flour for gingerbread, stack cakes, molasses cookies, pies, and biscuits but we had little sugar for white cake and sugar cookies until after the war was over.

Once in the early days of the war the children sat together one evening on the porch and listened to the shouting and singing at the old church over on the hill, where people of the community had come together at a rally and a pie mite to give what they could to support the American Red Cross. We heard reports of starving children in Europe and heard stories about families so hungry that they cooked and ate their children as they died and of cruel German soldiers who strewed candy along hedgerows, waited for hungry children to reach through the hedges for the candy, and hacked their hands off with swords. We saw on posters at stores and in windows of homes, pictures of stern Uncle Sam, dressed in stars and stripes, inviting young men to enlist in the armed forces, of Woodrow Wilson framed with stars, and cartoons of the sinister and bloodcurdling Kaiser himself brooding over cruel plots to destroy America.

Early in the war we were deeply concerned that our father might be drafted. He was 27 years old at the time and in excellent health. We did not understand that his having a wife and three children might lessen his chances of being drafted. He received his call to report for examination. He and Harrison Edwards, who lived up the creek three miles above us, decided that they would ride horseback to Louisa to report. Harrison was to stop at our house for Papa to join him at 5 o'clock in the morning. I was awakened from deep sleep by yelling, the thumping of a club against the side of the house, and the barking of our dogs. This commotion continued for what seemed like a long time before my mother woke up and then woke up my father, who recognized Harrison's voice and leapt from the bed, amazed that he had been sleeping so soundly and was late. He had set the alarm on the clock but it had not gone off. After getting up, stirring up the fire, and lighting the lamp, he invited Harrison to come in and sit by the fire while Mama cooked breakfast and he fed the stock and milked. But when they looked at the clock, it was only 3:30. Harrison, who had an alarm clock, had set it incorrectly, risen at 1:30, and was an hour and a half ahead of time. Since he was up and about, though, my father got ready and he and Harrison rode away toward Louisa long before daylight.

My mother wept that day and we were all sad, thinking it possible that Harrison might come back that evening leading Papa's mule and report that he had been taken right on to fight Kaiser Bill. But they returned in late afternoon, both happy with whiskey they had bought. Neither was drafted, for the quotas for the county were met largely by volunteers and eligible unmarried men, some of whom were conscripted unwillingly.

Once before the war had ended, George Young, a deputy sheriff, came, hitched his horse to our gatepost, and called our father outside to talk confidentially with him. Papa sat on the step to our back door while George "sat on his heel" close by. I stood just inside the door to hear what they were talking about. A young soldier had been permitted to come home on leave and had not reported back for duty. The sheriff's deputy had come to search for him and wanted my father to tell him what he knew of the house in which the young soldier's widowed mother lived. My father described the house, reported what he knew about the barn and crib, and recalled as best he could the loft plan of the house itself, including a partitioned-off gable end in which sweet potatoes were stored for winter. The deputy got on his fine horse with a shining new saddle and rode away.

Late that afternoon the deputy passed down the road. The handcuffed soldier, dressed in uniform and hunching forward, was in the saddle, and the deputy, riding behind, was holding the spliced bridle rein that had been looped around the soldier, who did not turn his head toward the house. The deputy smiled broadly at us as they passed.

Once we saw a coffin being hauled on a wagon up the road with two or three soldiers following on horseback. We were told that the coffin contained the remains of a soldier named Frazier who had been killed in the war and whose body was being sent back for burial in the family graveyard. The Fraziers lived across the hill in Elliott County, too far away for us to go to the funeral. But we heard the chilling story of what followed: old Mr. Frazier found in the coffin when it was opened only a bag of bones; he opened the bag and examined the skull, which had upper teeth attached, and was convinced by what he remembered of his son's teeth that the bones were not those of his son.

Many young unmarried men from Caines Creek were drafted and some volunteered, but none of the many Williamses was at the right age or in the right condition to be drafted. My father, approaching 27 at the time the war began, and his cousins of similar age were married and had children. Their younger brothers did not become old enough for the draft before the war was over. But many of the Boggses, Griffiths, and Sparkses were drafted. I recall that my brother and sister and I were left with my grandmother while my father and mother attended a farewell dinner Heig and Lin Holbrook gave for their only son, Norman, a local teacher, the night before he left to join the army. The young medical doctor Henry Chilton Osborn at Blaine joined the Medical Corps.

During the hard winter of 1917-1918, when the canned fruit and vegetables froze in the boxes stored under our beds, I remember hearing our father, while looking at the deep snow in our yard as we hovered around the fire, expressing sympathy for the "soldier boys" in the trenches in Europe.

News came to us slowly. Occasionally someone would receive a letter from a soldier, or a farmer or a storekeeper would return from a trip by wagon or on horseback to Louisa, Paintsville, or Webbville and report the latest about the war, or a drummer at one of the local stores would dispense news.

Occasionally, a soldier would return on leave before shipping out for Europe. Children were awed by the khaki uniforms, but the snappy hats, tight jackets, jodhpurs, puttees, and tan leather goods the young men wore elevated the blood pressure and excited the fancy of many a young woman eligible for courtship. The unusual haircuts that soldiers had set the style even for boys as young as I, and almost every young fellow wore his hair clipped closely in a ring well above his ears and around his head almost to the crown and combed straight back in a pompadour. The soldiers liked to strut, especially if they had horses to ride, for they looked best on horseback and with big brass spurs shining on their carefully dressed tan shoes and with long overcoats rolled up and strapped across their saddles.

Then the war was over and the "boys" were back home. It was then that we heard fragments of songs popular during the war that we had not heard before — suggestive verses from "Parlez-Vous," wisps from "It's a Long Way to Tipperary," "Pack Up Your Troubles in Your Old Kit Bag," "Oh, Tell Me How Long," "Hello, Central, Give Me 609," but no one seemed prepared to sing any one of them all the way through. It was also the time when young men liked to flash gold teeth, wear dark glasses, exhibit charms on their watch chains, and let the tags on the yellow drawstrings of bags of Bull Durham smoking tobacco dangle from their shirt pockets.

Veterans continued to wear their uniforms for a long time after they returned. At church, pie mites, funerals, and memorial meetings they exhibited their snappiness and class with roving eyes and glad smiles, their brilliant style dulling considerably that of the younger fellows coming on dressed in their blue serge peg legs, uncreased and narrowed at the cuffs fully a hand span above their shoe tops. The vets charmed and bore away into marriage that generation of buxom girls, five to eight years younger than themselves, who wore their hair in puffs and dressed in shorter skirts, white blouses, and high button shoes. I had two aunts, only eight to ten years older than I, who were courted by and married veterans dressed in uniforms. I recall conversations in which the possibility of veterans' pensions and pensions for surviving widows were discussed in those days before social security benefits were available. Both aunts bore large families, outlived their spouses by many years, and received pensions as widows of veterans.

One of the veterans, "Little Plezzie" Boggs, a lively sprout who sang and danced, rode a fast horse, and provided merriment at gatherings, was among the last of them to marry, but Lutha Ward, the school teacher who walked from near Webbville on Sunday afternoon and back home after school Friday afternoon and who kept the hillsides ringing as she sang, charmed him and they married. She, too, was a widow for many years. She was the only person I ever heard sing:

> Good-bye, Ma! Good-bye, Pa!
> Good-bye, Jack, with your old hee-haw!
> I may not know what the war's all about,
> But you bet, by gosh I'll soon find out.

In the good times of the early 1920's people tended to forget the war. About the only reminders left were such things as army shirts, overcoats, and shoes that farmers would buy at secondhand army and navy stores in the towns and the kit bags that boys and girls bought to use as bookbags. My father bought a supply of dark woolen blankets that we used for years. Many of the articles of clothing the veterans brought back appeared again in the Depression years, when it was not uncommon to see poor men wearing army overcoats on cold days as they huddled around open fires on WPA projects.

The School Goes to a Funeral

Grancer Boggs had died of lockjaw. While helping Lawrence Sparks tear down a house that my grandfather had sold him, Grancer had stepped on a rusty nail sticking up from a board and driven it through his foot. That night he had lockjaw and suffered a painful death. His daughter, Lottie, was one of the "big girls" at school.

Our teacher, Ran Boggs, took us all to the funeral out of respect for our fellow student. Grancer's home was halfway up Kirby Branch and perhaps two-and-a-half miles from the school. The funeral was to be held from the front porch of the home.

It was a hot day in August. Perhaps fifty were at school that day. The school ate lunch early, and we ran home to have a snack and join the others as they passed our house. Many of the children of intermediate age raced ahead of the older students and the small ones, who held back to keep the teacher company. The teacher walked with crutches, but he had strong arms and could handle his crutches so well that he could keep up with an ordinary walker. We wanted to leave our snacks unfinished and join those who passed our house first, but Mama insisted that we take our time, for we did not have to be ahead of the teacher in the long line of children going to the funeral. She instructed us not to get out of sight of the teacher.

While Ran was crossing the bridge at the end of our lane, we joined the procession. Soon we moved ahead, but when we came to trees beside the road, we stopped to cool in the shade and wait for Ran to catch up with us. It must have taken us an hour to reach Grancer's house, which had been built at right angles to the road and facing down the valley. We could hear the chanting of ancient hymns as we approached the house, the rhythms rising and falling in a slow, plaintive melody. The yard was filled with people, some leaning against the fence, some squatting on their heels, and many young people sitting on the ground. Toddlers and dogs moved about freely in the crowd.

The corpse, dressed in a shroud of unbleached muslin, was laid out on a platform covered with a bed sheet. The black coffin, shaped like a big wedge, rested on the porch floor under the platform. The widow, weeping and red-eyed, was sitting in a cane-bottom chair at the head of the corpse and fanning away flies that kept wanting to light on the swollen face of the corpse. She had a weathered palm frond fan like those old women carry to church with them in the summer months. Members of the family and wailers sat in chairs on the porch and on the edge of the porch floor.

Singers, their little black songbooks open, stood together in the yard. After the school had arrived, the preacher rose from a chair near the door into the little house, made preliminary remarks, and read awkwardly an obituary. Then he dropped to his knees to pray. All who were members of the church knelt, too, but others only bowed their heads. The prayer, chanted in long strophes that ended in soughs that slid upward, carried a repetitive phrase that addressed God personally and entreated him to look down upon us today. Men reinforced the invocation with chants of "Amen," "Yes, Lord," "Grant it, Lord," "Mought it be so, Lord," "Bless us, dear Lord." Women wailed and chanted in high-pitched voices. The longer the prayer continued the more the faithful contributed, many at the same time but none in unison.

As the fervor mounted, the force of the preacher's voice increased. After ten or fifteen minutes, the preacher tuned his voice down and ended the prayer with a long "Amen," echoed by many of the faithful, but again, not in unison.

There was another long hymn. Then the preacher read from the New Testament about the tree that is cut down and chanted a long sermon with such force that he was wet with sweat when he finished. The preacher called on another to say a prayer, this time a brief, quiet prayer but pronounced in rolling rhetoric with a holy tone to it.

A communal song, "I Am Drinking from the Fountain," began. Everyone joined in. The pallbearers, singing as they fulfilled their offices, lifted the corpse from the platform, placed it in the coffin, and tacked the coffin lid on lightly.

Then six pallbearers, followed by six more to relieve them as they ascended the steep hill to a trail that led along a flat to the graveyard at the end of a sun-baked point, lifted the coffin to their shoulders and moved off with it. Members of the family followed the coffin. Then the preacher, the singers, and the wailing women trailed along, singing as they went. Other grownups and most of the school children scattered out, some taking short cuts, some finding alternative paths, and many running ahead of the corpse.

The trail along the flat was crossed by two rail fences. Men rushed ahead of the funeral procession, laid down the fences, and then laid them up again after the procession had passed.

After the coffin had been placed on a bier improvised by building two stacks of the boards prepared for covering the coffin after it was in the grave, the pallbearers fell back mopping their faces with their handkerchiefs and fanning themselves with their hats.

The preacher, red-faced and winded by the climb, removed his black hat and stood by the coffin while the crowd was assembling. One of the pallbearers drew the nails up from the long coffin lid with a claw hammer and slid it down the coffin about a third of its length. One of the women pulled back the corner of the shroud that had covered the face of the corpse and folded it behind the head.

The preacher invited those who wanted a last look at the "departed brother" to file by. In the meantime another song had begun and the women resumed their wailing. The face of the corpse, the sun beating down upon it, had begun to swell again. I could smell decaying human flesh and carbolic acid as I passed by the coffin.

After the crowd had passed by the coffin, the preacher dropped to his knees and prayed again. Then another song was chanted while a woman pulled the corner of the shroud over the face of the corpse and tucked it into the folds below. A pallbearer replaced the coffin lid and drove the nails down.

The preacher chanted in a low tone a commitment of the corpse to the earth, ending it with "ashes to ashes and dust to dust."

The pallbearers lowered the coffin into the grave with plow-lines. Each member of the family that cared to do so broke a sprig of greenery from a small cedar tree growing near the head of the grave of Grancer's father and threw it upon the coffin. Boards were then laid across the top of the box into which the coffin had been lowered and the gravehands broke the retaining wall of fence rails that held back the mound of earth beside the grave and began to fill it up. The coffin sounded empty when the first clods struck it.

The crowd began to disperse, but a few lingered to discuss the locations of graves of others of Grancer's family, for Grancer's folks had been too poor to buy tombstones. The graves were all marked only by field stones.

The teacher did not try to reassemble the school children. When we got back to the schoolhouse it would be time for school to let out.

We had had a lesson on dying and burying the dead. For a few nights after that, I would lie awake in the darkness and remember the corpse dressed in a shroud, the coffin with the long lid pulled down, the swollen face in the hot glare of an August afternoon sun, the odor of decaying flesh, and the hollow sound of the dirt tumbling upon the coffin in the grave.

Sometimes I dreamed about men carrying black coffins on their shoulders and once I was terrified by a dream in which I raced down from a hill top and came suddenly upon a grave that the pallbearers had forgotten to fill and in which Grancer was lying in an open coffin, his face muddy from the yellow water in which his body was floating. The corner of the shroud pulled over his face had floated loose and the nickels on his eyes were coated with mud. I wondered what he looked like now, after lying so long in a grave dug in the yellow clay at the end of a sun-baked point.

Appalachian Folkways: Death, Dying and Funeral Rituals

People living on Caines Creek during my boyhood days were almost obsessed with death. Many began preparing for it in their early maturity by laying aside articles of clothing in which they wished to be dressed for burial. Spots in the family graveyard were chosen. Instructions would sometimes include the choice of a preacher to preach the funeral. In one instance, the corpse of an old preacher was kept for three days in order to allow time for a fellow minister in his "faith and order" and a companion in his youth to ride horseback from Wise County, Virginia, to preach his funeral sermon. Hymns and chants were chosen for funerals and "funeral occasions" after the burial.

Coffin lumber, carefully selected and seasoned, was stored in barn lofts.

Occasionally one would have his coffin hardware and the cloth for lining and covering the coffin on hand when death occurred. An older person preparing for death might "speak to" the carpenter of his choice about making his coffin, to his favorite preacher about preaching his funeral sermon, and to a well-known singer of hymns about leading the singing at his funeral. Once in a while one would have his coffin prepared before he died, lie in it to get the feel of what death is like, and store it in an attic or a barnloft until needed.

Older people, sensing the approach of death, would call sons and daughters to their bedsides and give instructions relating to the disposition of personal possessions of significant sentimental value. Granny's candlemold, Grampappy's stout cane, the old sword that a pioneer ancestor had fetched out of Virginia, locks of hair snipped from the heads of relatives long deceased, ancient books with foxed papers and marbled linings for the covers that had lain for generations in corner cupboards—all articles that had been treasured by and well known to those who had grown up in the household were given away. Wills and testaments were not read until after the funeral, however.

Grandchildren were brought to the bedsides of older people to receive commendation and counsel while the grandparent let a hand rest on the grandchild's head or held it by the hand in solemn fashion. Sometimes a dying person would send for a neighbor with whom there had been a quarrel or who had been "miffed" by some remark or comment, in order to arrive at a peaceful understanding and harmony before death came.

Attitudes, traditions, and superstitions relating to death and dying were held in common by most of the people of the community. Death was considered to be the will of God, foreordained in the act of creation for all men. One "goes when his time comes." One's death is predestined by God for a given moment without regard for circumstances. Sometimes someone had "tokens" and premonitions of his own death and said things, changed his plans, and made arrangements that demonstrated to survivors that he was being guided by a "Power that was bigger than he was" toward death and preparation for it by "getting his business in order." Others were shown signs of the imminence of death in the household. A bird flew into the house, a child twirled a chair on one leg, a hen crowed from the barnyard fence, a mysterious light hovered over the family graveyard, someone in the family dreamed of losing a tooth, a kinsman met in some strange place the silent ghost of the one who was to die, or he appeared in unusual roles in the dreams of the members of his family. Any of these strange occurrences was considered a harbinger of the Dark Horseman on Caines Creek.

It was important that one have close by friends and relatives to comfort him while he lay dying. "Setting up" with the dying was a sacred duty of mountain folk. Close attention was directed to the "last moments" for signs to indicate whether the dying person might be among the elect. The last words spoken were remembered, interpreted, and sometimes "explicated" by the preacher who delivered the funeral sermon. The presence of a smile, a sound suggesting a blissful union of the spirit in eternal joy with the "angels," a quiet, peaceful exhalation of the last breath, the absence of struggle or apparent pain in a dying person held promises of salvation and were comforting to survivors, sure signs that the deceased had "made peace" with his maker. Painful struggles, or "hard" deaths, suggested that happy resolutions had not been reached.

Prior to the days of undertakers intimates and close relatives prepared the corpse for burial. Warm water and soap (preferably, neither had been used before or were subsequently) were brought for sponge-bathing the corpse. The body was then bathed with a weak solution of carbolic acid. If male, he was shaved and his face was braced with lotion and powdered. Hair was combed and arranged. The burial dress or suit (new when families could afford to purchase one) was put on. The preparations were made before rigor mortis whenever possible. When the corpse was "laid out," sometimes on a platform of boards across two sawhorses and covered with a clean bedsheet while a coffin was being built, the feet were bound together, a band was tied around the face to hold the mouth closed, eyelids were closed and held in place by coins (usually pennies), and arms were fixed in the position desired. (After rigor mortis, bands and coins were usually removed.) The corpse was then covered by a sheet and attended by friends who assembled for the wake ("settin' up with the dead"). New arrivals were treated to a solemn view of the deceased by an attendant who would turn down the sheet and replace it after the newcomer had "paid his respects." After the coffin was prepared, the body was then placed in it and it was set on the sawhorses or two kitchen chairs in the living room and left open for all to view the corpse at will.

Women gathered to cook, many bringing with them food from their own homes. Young people assembled for conversation, for wakes were social occasions. Often preachers came to pray and lead the singing of hymns in the evening of the wake. "Unregenerate" men brought whiskey which they hid in barns or the bushes by the roadside to share surreptitiously with their cronies. In the old days women wailed as the singers "hoisted" their death songs, preachers felt the "sperret," and those "happy in the Lord" shouted and chanted. In the meantime, young people of courting age engaged one another's attentions in the kitchen or a room across the hall or on the back porch, for life went on, even in the presence of death.

Conversations of those who sat with the corpse often turned upon the deceased. People exchanged stories and anecdotes that reviewed their experiences with the deceased, and his or her virtues were extolled. Often accounts of the illness and the death itself were told and re-told for those who arrived late, and particularly for relatives who came from a distance.

Funerals were commonly held in the home or, weather permitting, on a porch while those in attendance stood in the yard, leaned against the fence, or squatted on their heels at the edge of the crowd. Then the coffin was closed and the pallbearers carried it, sometimes on their shoulders, to the family graveyard usually on a point of the hill overlooking the ancestral home. At the graveyard the coffin was opened again, songs were sung, women wailed, men stood in rigid positions and with ashen faces and stony eyes, and preachers chanted and prayed, sometimes several at once. Occasionally bereaved women chanted hysterically accounts of their relationships with the deceased. Often they would faint and require the ministrations of older women skilled in the handling of such situations.

After the coffin was lowered into the grave, the box closed, and the crossboards placed in position, the members of the family began to leave the scene, for it was considered "bad luck" to watch the filling of the grave of a member of one's own family. Those who completed the filling of the grave liked to leave the graveyard in a group, for bad luck follows the last person to leave a graveyard after a burial.

The bereaved family returned home accompanied only by blood kin who might have come from a distance and would be staying a day or two before returning to their own homes. Personal possessions that held special significance for the deceased were buried with the body. Love letters were buried with the bodies of young people. Pocket knives or mementos of special significance were buried with the bodies of young men.

Sites of graveyards were chosen with reference to the rising sun and the dead were buried facing the east. Mountain folk believe in a resurrection of the body on the Judgment Day. Many mountain people who lost limbs in accidents or gun battles had the limbs buried in the family graveyard to facilitate the achievement of "wholeness" on the Judgment Day. Only older people planted yew trees and cedars in graveyards, for one who plants a yew tree or a cedar will die when the tree has become tall enough to shade his grave.

Ghosts of the dead return to haunt those with whom resolutions of misunderstandings had not been achieved or to communicate secrets that had not been revealed in life. Ghosts lead one to the hiding place of valuables or evidence needed for the solution of a mysterious problem. Ghosts of murdered people lead passersby to their remains or to the treasures they had hidden so skillfully that the murderer did not find them. Those who have died appear also in dreams and offer comfort and assurance to their survivors. After a ghost has managed to communicate his problem to a living person who has taken care of it, he rests comfortably with the dust in his grave. Very old graveyards, particularly those so old that nobody living remembers those buried there, have no ghosts, but a murdered person whose body was hidden in a cave or buried without ceremony in a shallow grave beside a trail through a gorge or along the stream through a dark and deeply wooded hollow might haunt passersby for generations.

Hymns sung at wakes, funerals, and at the graveside rites were not stereotyped. They tended to emphasize the promise of eternal bliss for the dead who had made their declarations of salvation, but for those who had not, hymns sung emphasized the need for "finding peace" before death arrived.

The memorial funeral a year following death and burial, formerly the only "real" funeral a deceased person might have, became a standard custom in time, even though the deceased might have been accorded full rites at the time of burial. The memorial funeral was held in late summer or early fall. Weeks of preparation preceded the event. The graveyard was cleaned off and "spruced up." Wild flowers and arrangements of old-fashioned flowers and "spargrass" (asparagus) from the yards of homes were placed on graves. Crude seating arrangements, often under canopies of freshly cut brush, were provided. A platform was constructed for the preachers. Roads leading to the graveyard were repaired. Buckets of water and dippers were brought and placed on the "preachers' stand." Food was prepared to feed the congregation. Pots of green beans, potato salad, coleslaw; piles of country ham, sausage, fried chicken; stacks of apple pies, cookies, and cakes; jars of sweet milk, buttermilk, cold coffee; baskets of biscuits and cornpone; stacks of muskmelons and watermelons, peaches, and apples were spread for the hungry crowds.

At memorial funerals bereaved family members sat in front of the preachers. If the widowed spouse had married again, the new mate sat with the family also and participated in grief with its members. Obituaries were read. Hymns tended to relate to "funeral occasions." A favorite in eastern Kentucky for the beginning of a funeral occasion was "A Twelvemonths More," the first hymn in *The Sweet Songster*. Hymns that glorified the union of the family in heaven were preferred, among them "The Parting Hand," "Beulah Land," "Will the Circle Be Unbroken." Others emphasized the "journey," among them "Poor Wayfaring Stranger," "Lonesome Valley," "Jesus Is Gone but He's Coming Back Again," "City of Four-Square." From the hilltops these modal songs, executed by people with leather lungs, rang down the dales and hollows like the voice of eternity itself.

In eastern Kentucky people who were resourceful considered it a solemn duty to "put away" their dead in a manner befitting their stations in life as solid citizens. Before it was possible to order gravestones from outside the region skilled monument makers prepared and inscribed stones selected from local quarries. Many of the oldest graveyards have in them locally prepared stones of excellent quality with still legible inscriptions at the graves of the patriarchs, some of whom came from Ireland prior to the American Revolution. Grave houses were common in my boyhood, and many may still be seen in the family graveyards. As population increased and poverty became more widespread, the quality of gravestones deteriorated. Rough, easily worked but rapidly deteriorating sandstone grave markers with rude inscriptions chiseled by semi-literate masons became common in the dark days following the Civil War. Still later, families became so poor and dispirited that they were unable to afford anything better than shaft-like field stones for grave markers for their dead.

By 1885 it was possible to purchase marble tombstones from dealers in county-seat towns, but many families were too poor to do so. Even the poorest of families, however, continued to take care of their humble graveyards and were able to maintain grave roofs, if not houses, over graves of the patriarchs until the coming of World War II when mass out-migrations left abandoned homesteads to grow up in bushes, scrub pine, and blackjacks and the graveyards to become hidden in masses of briars and sumac thickets with only a struggling cedar or yew tree to mark their location. Those who remain on the land now bury their dead in "memory gardens" near the villages and county-seat towns, no longer feeling the responsibility of earlier generations for the tending and care of their family graveyards.

Hugh and Hannah Boggs (Granny Hanner)

Hugh Boggs, son of John and Nancy Wells Boggs, was considered a prosperous man. He was a farmer and a timber man. A page is devoted to him in William Ely's *History of the Big Sandy Valley*. Mr. Ely implies that Hugh was imposed on by his less industrious sons. There is a story that Hugh's son Henderson bought all the land on the right fork of Caines Creek for a "ham of meat and a rifle-gun." Henderson's home, still standing and occupied at this time (1965) by his descendant Mrs. Opal Boggs Liming, is one of the better homes in that section. It is said that Hugh and his aged wife spent their last days with Henderson in that house. It is also said that Hugh's mother-in-law, Hannah Lyons Blevins, also lived with Henderson after she became a widow. She was over a hundred years old when she died and was one of the last widows of the American Revolution carried on the pension roll for Lawrence County. She was blind in her old age. There is an instance of a "judgment sent on" one of the old lady's descendants for laughing at her great-grandmother's infirmities: Phoebe Jane, daughter of Jim Goins and Matilda Lyons Boggs, laughed at her blind great-granny and "mocked" (imitated) her pigeon-toed walk. Phoebe Jane (always called Pet), who married Henry Hicks, became pigeon-toed and, later, blind, like "Granny Hanner."

An interesting story is also told of William Blevins ("Granny Hanner's" husband). He was the son of a "long hunter" from Wilkes County, North Carolina. His uncle by marriage also a long hunter, was named Walden. Old hunter Blevins, his sons, and his son-in-law took "long hunts" into eastern Kentucky before Daniel Boone ever visited Kentucky. The *Moravian Records* of North Carolina carry an item for 1751 reporting that Blevins and his sons brought to the trading post at old Salem more pelts than there was cash to pay for, but that they happily accepted goods in lieu of cash. Walden's Ridge is named for William Blevins' uncle. William (referred to locally as "Old Bill") was an unkind man to his family. He hung his meat in the rafters of his cabin, but would not permit his wife to use the hams, which he gave to a woman whom he kept on his land.

So many Boggses named their sons John, Jim, and Bill that it became necessary for people to assign them distinguishing nicknames. James Boggs, the son of Hugh and Hannah, was called Jim "Goin's" because he preferred to "traipse up and down the creek" when there was work to be done. He was "on the go" all the time. His brother John, who married Haley Griffith (pronounced "Griffy" on Caines Creek), was called John "Pune" because he was always complaining about his health — "punin' around," his neighbors said. In my own generation it was customary to distinguish persons with the same name by referring to the father of each: Clem's Jim, Jim Ran (the son of Randolph); by identifying them with the branch on which they lived: Ed Kirby (pronounced locally "Kyurby"); or by including a reference to a distinguishing physical or personality feature: Big Nelse, Little Hen, Thin Jim, Peh-hy Jim ("stammering" Jim). Women with identical names were identified by their husband's names: Hannah Jim, Marg Jarrett, Sally Ran, Mary Pleas, Mary Charley, etc.

My Great-grandparents:
John D. ("Hamey") Boggs and Nancy Griffith Boggs

My great-grandfather John D. ("Hamey") Boggs was born December 28, 1828, near the forks of Blaine in Lawrence County, Kentucky. His father, David Boggs, was the son of John and Nancy Wells Boggs, who came from Lee County, Virginia, to Caines Creek in 1821, and his mother was Sarah, daughter of Randolph and Hannah Whitley Holbrook, who came from near Traphill in Wilkes County, North Carolina, to Blaine about 1807. John Hamey Boggs's great-grandfather James L. Boggs, who had served in Captain Enoch Osborne's unit of militia at the Mouth of Wilson in Virginia during the latter days of the American Revolution, had followed his son John in 1825 from Three Forks of the Powell, now Big Stone Gap, Virginia. Randolph Holbrook was the son of John and Mary Hargis Hammon Holbrook, and a grandson of either Randal or John Holbrook, sons of Ralph and Elizabeth Holbrook,

Cratis's wife Elizabeth and daughter Sophie Williams in 1954 at the home of John Hamey and Nancy Griffith Boggs on Maple Branch of Caines Creek. Built about 1855, the house was subsequently occupied by Lou Boggs, daughter of John Hamey and Nancy, and Lou's husband Stephen Liming, then Lou's sister Mary Boggs and her husband (and first cousin) Pleasant Boggs, then by Phoebe Jane Parker and her husband Taylor Boggs.

who lived near the town of Chester, Cheshire, England. Randal and John had migrated to Virginia before Ralph Holbrook made his will in 1725.

John Hamey Boggs married Nancy Griffith, daughter of Robert and Margaret Caines Griffith, October 27, 1852. At first they lived in a cabin, where some of their children were born, on the south side of the left fork of Caines Creek and just above the forks at the mouth of the hollow behind what came to be called the "oil well bottom" on the farm later owned by my father, Curtis Williams. About 1858 they moved to a tract on Maple Branch a short distance away that they had bought from Nancy's father. (They might have moved their first cabin to this farm.) There they raised their nine children, and the home they built was still standing but in ruins in 1983.

John Hamey, a man of average height, had piercing eyes as hard as blue steel. He became bald in middle age and as an old man wore a white chin beard and mutton chop sideburns. A man with a volatile temper, he flew into a rage easily and was stubborn and unyielding.

Interested in learning, he bought and read books and kept medical reference works in the corner cabinet of his living room. He also loved birds and kept birdhouses and gourds on poles around the house for martins and bluebirds to use during the nesting season.

Industrious and resourceful, he planned well. He was prosperous for his time. He and his brother Randolph Boggs, who lived on an adjoining farm, grew apples for brandy making. They had large, well cared-for orchards. During the 1880's they ranked among the top five distillers in the county for taxes they paid on the whiskey they made.

John Hamey supported the Union during the Civil War. He enlisted in October 1861, as a private in Captain Walter O. Wood's Co. B., 14th Kentucky Infantry, and was discharged at Louisa in April 1863.

John Hamey's farm might well have exemplified subsistence farming at its best about the time housewives were beginning to use cookstoves for preparing food for their families and to barter at crossroads stores for gingham, calico, and muslin to replace the linsey-woolsey they had been producing on their looms. His rail fences were kept in good repair, his pastures were clean, his meadows were dotted with haystacks, his cribs were filled with corn and his barnlofts with fodder. He had horses and mules, herds of cattle, flocks of sheep, droves of pigs, and the place was lively with the cackling of hens, screaming of geese, and "padderwacking" of guinea fowls. He kept dogs and was especially fond of cats. He had "things hung up" in his smokehouse and was referred to as "a good liver."

John Hamey died about 1906 and was buried in the Boggs-Butler graveyard on the ridge between the heads of Maple Branch and Lick Fork of Cherokee. He gave his sons Washington and David each a farm. Robert, who never married, lived at the homeplace until his death in 1903. He gave the homeplace to his oldest daughter, Louisa, who married Stephen D. Liming. They had no children. They kept the place much as John Hamey had left it until Steve died in 1923.

My great-grandmother Nancy Boggs was born in 1833 on Dean's Branch of Caines Creek near Blaine, Kentucky, the daughter of Robert and Margaret (Peggy) Caines Griffith. Margaret Griffith was the daughter of Richard and Nancy Caines, the first white settlers on Caines Creek and for whom the creek was named. Richard and Nancy had migrated from Monroe County, Virginia (now West Virginia), prior to 1808, and possibly as early as 1796. Nancy Caines' maiden name is not known. Richard Caines, born in Ireland in 1753, was a private in the Virginia Line under Col. Buford in the Revolutionary War and was wounded at the Battle of the Waxhaws in the Carolinas in May 1780. He was placed on the pension roll of Kentucky in 1818 at $8 a month. He died in 1822 and was buried in the Caines Graveyard on Caines Creek. His widow spent her last days in the home of Robert and Margaret Griffith. Robert Griffith, born in Virginia, was the son of Abel Griffith. Robert Griffith's brother David married Margaret Caines' sister, Mary Jane.

John Hamey and Nancy Griffith Boggs's home; view from the back of the house.

Nancy Griffith married Hamey Boggs, four years her senior, and was the mother of nine children, all of whom lived to maturity: Louisa, Elisha Washington, David, Sarah, Elizabeth, Martha, Robert, Eliphus, and Mary. Robert never married, and Louisa and Eliphus had no children.

Nancy, slender, blue-eyed, with delicate features and of average height, was quiet and even-tempered. The fact that I never heard my father refer to her leads me to believe that she was retiring and undemonstrative, a home body who rarely left the branch on which she lived. It was said that she never in her whole life ventured as far from home as Louisa, the county-seat town, twenty-five miles away.

She was skilled in home crafts. She grew in her large and fertile garden patches of cotton and flax which she and her children processed. She enjoyed an enviable reputation as a weaver. The cloth she made was colored with natural dyes which she prepared herself. (I have one of her counterpanes, which was buried, along with other articles of value, for four years under the hearth during the Civil War. Except for some moisture damage and discoloration at the folds, it remains sturdy and the colors are still vivid.)

She was one of the first housewives on Caines Creek to preserve food by canning. I recall seeing on shelves rows of her stone jars which she sealed with paper and sealing wax. She had about her all of the equipment needed for ample and comfortable living: looms, spinning wheels, hackles, home coopered barrels for pickling, cider, and vinegar, crocks and jugs of heavy stoneware for storing lard, tallow, honey, and molasses, ash hoppers for lye for making soap, black iron pots swung over fire pits, candle molds, meat grinders, racks for drying fruits and vegetables. Her son Robert, who never married, was a skilled craftsman. He not only built for his mother a rotary churn which he patented, storage bins for flour and meal, fine tables, corner cabinets, shelves, and chairs, but he kept all of the buildings in good repair: the saddlebag house with wide porches along the two sides, the summer kitchen close by, two livestock barns, a sheep barn, pig pens, a chicken house, a sturdy smokehouse, two corn cribs, a coal house and woodshed, gums for stands of bees, boxes on poles for martins and bluebirds, a shop house, and a well of sweet water with a sturdy hollow-log gum and a giant well sweep. The homestead itself was a kind of village clus-

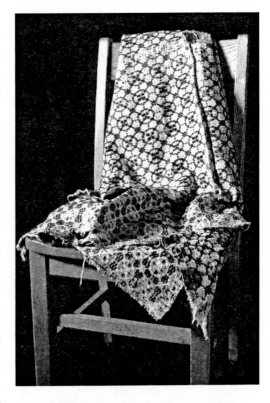

The counterpane woven by Nancy Griffith Boggs, buried under the hearth during the Civil War. A gift to Cratis from Phoebe Jane Parker and Taylor Boggs, who described it as "buried during the late hostilities."

tered around the dwelling house, which was set in the middle of a garden, along the paling fences of which grew a profusion of old fashioned flowers and shrubs and along the paths of which grew gooseberries, rhubarb, herbs for use in cooking and preserving, and rose bushes, "old man's beard," flowers for cutting, and "spar'grass" for decorating "flower pots."

When the Civil War began, Nancy was the mother of five children ranging in age from one to eight years. While John Hamey was away during the conflict, Nancy, with the help of Lou and Wash, took care of the livestock and grew a garden.

Neither Nancy nor John Hamey had any interest in church. Although Holbrooks and Boggses had been active members of the Blaine Baptist Church from its founding in 1819, only one Griffith, Sarah, second wife of Nancy's uncle Evan, had joined the Blaine church by 1860.

Smokehouse at John Hamey Boggs's home.

After the Civil War John Hamey and Nancy prospered. By 1883-1884, their apple orchards were so productive that John ranked among the top five in Lawrence County in the amount of taxes paid on apple brandy. With apples as a side cash crop, they had some "hard" money. No evidence survives to indicate that Nancy could read and write, but there was money to purchase a few books, which were kept in a corner cupboard and treasured by John Hamey and all of the children, who went to school and learned to read, write, and cypher.

Nancy died about 1902 and was buried in what was to become known as the Hamey Boggs Graveyard on the ridge between the head of Maple Branch and the head of the Lick Fork of Cherokee Creek. After her husband, who died about 1906, was buried beside her, a "soul" house, still in good condition in 1982, was built over their graves.

Uncle Jesse "Kirby" Boggs

Uncle Jesse "Kirby" Boggs, who died when I was nine years old, lived on the Kirby Branch of Caines Creek. I remember the double-log house in which he lived on the right side of the branch a few hundred yards above the home of Nathan O. and Ann Boggs Gambill. His house had beautiful chiseled stone chimneys built in the Williamsburg style. Uncle Jesse, the only "Rebel" veteran of the Civil War living on the creek, was very poor. Having divided his farm among his sons, Elijah, Ed, Grancer, and Clabe, he had worn out the land long before I was born.

I remember Uncle Jesse on two occasions: I saw him and one of his sons leading a jackass, loaded with bags of mayapple root, down the road to a country store. At another time I saw him riding a jackass past our house. His head was bandaged with a roll of white cloth. When my mother asked him what had happened to him, he replied in a treble, filled with self-pity, "Hey, dear-Lordie, me old mule fell down wi' me and come very near to a-killin' of me!"

Uncle Jesse died soon afterwards and is buried in a graveyard, in which the graves are marked only by field stones, located on a point overlooking the site of his home. In spite of the tales of his ferocity and cruel vengeance as a Rebel soldier, he was a gentle, almost childlike old man.

"The Old Sow Hant"

Uncle Plez had drunk more whiskey with the fellers at the dance at Stuttering Jim's house than he had been aware of. He did not run the sets himself. As he watched from his place against the wall the men and women hoeing 'er down as they "swung 'er on the garden gate" and ran away eight, he continued to exchange drinks, straight from the bottle, with other men who did not dance themselves but who liked to pick off the bouncing girls, their breasts a-flopping and their dress tails a-cracking, at the end of the sets and walk with them into the orchard while they cooled off.

Rose Ann, her auburn hair tumbling around her shoulders after a wild dance and with the beads of perspiration on her chin glistening in the light of the lamps from the tall mantel, was a plump one with tits that tumbled like two roosters a-fightin when she went into her clog as her partner "chased that pretty gal 'round the world." Uncle Plez liked to watch Rose Ann dance, but he noticed that she always went and stood by the fiddler between dances. Uncle Plez, while appraising Rose Ann as she ran the sets, noticed that the fiddler was eying him. Once, after he had caught Rose Ann's attention as she swirled by and drawn a broad smile from her, he glanced at the fiddler and saw rage flash from his eyes. Uncle Plez knew he would have to be careful. The fiddler was a fightin' man. He'd have trouble with him if he didn't work things right. Uncle Plez turned half away from the fiddler to listen to a tale about a hawk that had been catching his granny's chickens that Crippled Letch, propped against the wall and resting on his crutches, was telling to the little tads that had gathered around him. But Uncle Plez could see Rose Ann as she moved around the ring in the shoo-fly swing that would end that dance. Rose Ann had an eye for Uncle Plez. He could see that as plain as the nose on your face. He would have to figure out a way to get her to walk with him in the orchard. She'd be a plump little armful, he thought.

Stuttering Jim walked up. Uncle Plez gave Stuttering Jim his bottle and asked him to give the fiddler a dram when the dance was over. Stuttering Jim, taking a stout one from the bottle himself first, made his way around to the fireplace where the fiddler was standing. Stuttering Jim shook the bottle before the fiddler's face.

The dance ended. Rose Ann moved toward Uncle Plez while the fiddler was taking his dram. Uncle Plez and Rose Ann walked out through the gate and into the orchard. They were gone a long time. They could hear people laughing and talking at the house, but the music did not start again.

As Uncle Plez and Rose Ann were coming back through the gate, a rock struck one of the gate posts. The fiddler's voice rang out, "That for Plez! He can't steal my woman." A rock hit the other gate post. "That for Plez! He'd better make hisself sca'ce hyar if he knows what's good for his hide."

Uncle Plez did not go through the gate. Rose Ann returned to the house and Uncle Plez, not bothering to get his bottle back from Stuttering Jim, decided it was late and that he had better be a-moseyin' home.

Uncle Plez was pretty drunk. After being with Rose Ann he was right tired, too. He had not brought a lantern with him. The moon was down and a light rain was falling. It would be a long dark road home.

By the time he had reached the graveyard he could feel that he was getting wet between his shoulders. He would be dripping wet by the time he got home. Besides, he couldn't walk very fast in the pitch-black darkness.

He walked into the graveyard, crawled through the window into the little house over Granny Hanner's grave, and lay down on the coffin-like cover to wait for the rain to stop.

As he lay there, stretched out on the coffin-like grave cover, he could hear the rainwater dripping from the eaves of the little house. He was not really scared to be in a graveyard on a dark rainy night and it was dry in the little house. Maybe the rain would stop after a while and the stars would come out. It would be easier to walk then.

He was remembering Rose Ann and feeling lucky that the fiddler had decided to hit the gateposts with the rocks instead of himself, when he dropped off to sleep.

When he woke up at dawn he did not remember where he was. But he knew he had been awakened by the rumbling sound that came from the corner of the little house. It sounded like somebody rubbing a rock or something against the head of an empty barrel. The house shook. The timbers in it cracked and popped. Something was trying to push it in on him.

He looked out through the little window. White gravestones emerged out of the morning mist. He remembered that he was in the graveyard. He was lying on the cover of Granny Hanner's grave in the little white grave house with dark red trim. There stood gravestones with wisps of fog moving around them. He had been to the dance at Stuttering Jim's. He had been drunk, too, and gone into the orchard with the fiddler's woman. He had a bad headache, but the fiddler had thrown rocks at the gateposts, not him. That rubbing against the house was most queer, he thought.

Suddenly, he knew. He was about to stand at the Judgment Bar. The devil was after him. It was Old Satan thumping and rubbing against the corner of the house out there.

Uncle Plez sat up. The rubbing continued. The house was shaking. He leapt through the window and rushed toward the open gate in the graveyard fence. As he ran he heard a rushing noise behind him. The devil was after him for sure, he knew. The devil was grunting as he ran, but he could hear other things running, too. The devil had his imps with him, he was sure.

Beyond the gate he realized that whatever it was was no longer chasing him. He stopped and looked back. A big white sow with four or five spotted pigs beside her stood among the gravestones.

He had been hanted by an old sow.

The Nipperses

While we were sitting in our porch at dusk one summer evening, two men appeared at the paling fence around our yard. One of them issued the usual call, "Hello! Do your dogs bite?" Our dogs started up from their positions on the porch at the sound of the man's voice, but my father quieted them. "What 'd ye have?" my father asked.

They wanted to know what chances might be for them to "stay all night." They had traveled on foot all day, having walked from Magoffin County on their way to Webbville, where they would take a train and go on to Ohio to see the man's sister, who was dying. My father explained that we had eaten our suppers and that we did not have much room in our house for guests but that he did not like to turn tired strangers away. They would be pleased to have a piece of cornbread and a glass of milk and a chance to sleep, even if it were on a pallet on the floor, the man explained, but they had only enough money to buy train tickets and wanted us to know that they could not offer anything for staying with us.

My father invited them in, turning his attention at that moment to the dogs, who wanted to charge at them as they swung the gate open. The younger one, who had said nothing, paused at the gate and uttered a shrill whistle. From behind the henhouse marched in a row seven more ranging in size from a tall woman looking ghostly in a long light-colored dress to a child whose head was visible only through the slats of the paling. I think we were all so flabbergasted that no one said anything while the procession came trailing across the porch.

My mother invited them to come on into the living room, where a kerosene lamp on a stand table in the corner was lighted. We followed them into the room in wonderment. The children were drooping. Some sat on chairs, some on the side of a bed, and some on the floor near the hearth. Mama explained that she did not have enough cornbread left from supper to feed them but she thought there was an ample supply of milk and butter. If they could wait, she would build up the fire in the kitchen stove and bake more cornbread. They would wait.

Mama, the tired wispy woman, and the oldest daughter went into the kitchen. The man said their name was "Nippers" (Napier), that they had left Magoffin County early the preceding day, had eaten all of the food they had brought along with them, had slept in a schoolhouse the night before, and had eaten nothing all day except berries and fruit they had gathered by the roadside. He had money enough to buy railroad tickets for all of them, but they might not be able to eat again before they reached his sister's home. Soon the younger children lay backward on the bed or stretched out on the floor and went to sleep. Mr. Nippers told about his hard luck. He was a "rentee" in Magoffin County, and had to give a third of what he raised to the landlord. There had been sickness in the family. He himself was hardly able to work much of the time. His small children did not have shoes to wear on the long trip.

After a half-hour my mother called to say that the cornbread would be ready in a few minutes and that they might want to "wash up." She threw a clean sack towel across the water bench and asked my father whether he would draw a bucket of water from the well. Mr. Nippers began rousing the children from their slumber. They marched into the porch and washed their hands and faces and dried themselves with the sack towel and then filed into the dining room, where the cornbread, baked in an oblong tinware pan, was stacked in squares on a platter in the middle of the table. A bowl of white, fluffy butter was beside the pitchers of milk. Saucers, forks, and glasses had been placed for everybody. There was room at the table for only six chairs, but little ones stood beside older ones. We had followed to watch them eat, except our father who remained in the living room.

They ate ravenously, passing the butter around the table continuously. In fifteen or twenty minutes they had eaten all that was prepared. Then they filed back into the living room, each occupying the spot he had held before the rush to the dining room had begun.

My mother appeared after she had washed the dishes. Then sleeping arrangements were discussed. It was decided that the man and his wife would sleep in the bed in which my brother and I slept. My sister would sleep with my father and mother, surrendering her bed to the oldest daughter and two of her younger sisters. The four remaining Nipperses and my brother and I would sleep on pallets on the floor. Mama spread on the floor quilts and blankets, but there were no pillows. Since it was not very cold, and we could lie down with our clothes on, sheets would do for covers. The oldest son and a younger brother were given a pallet in the dining room. Doors were left open to permit needed ventilation.

My brother and I slept on one of our mother's aprons and had a spread for a couch as our cover. Soon everybody was asleep. Mr. Nippers snored loudly and called out in his sleep. His wife would whimper occasionally. The floor was so hard through the apron that I did not sleep much. To add to my discomfort, gnats came in through the open door and attacked me when I did not have my head covered. It was a miserable night.

We were up earlier than usual next morning. While my father did the chores at the barn and my mother prepared breakfast, the Nipperses washed and blubbered in the tin wash pan on the water bench. As they finished washing themselves, they came back into the living room and sat down.

Before long my mother announced that breakfast was ready. The Nipperses jumped to their feet at once and filed into the dining room. We followed, but Mama said we could wait, because the Nipperses had to be on the road if they were to get to Webbville in time to take the afternoon train. But we stood at the dining room door and watched.

A big bowl of gravy, a platter of steaming biscuits, and a plate of fried side meat were on the table. The old man and old woman had cups of scalding coffee, which they saucered and blew vigorously before lifting to their faces. The children had milk. They ate as gluttonously as they had the night before. After they had eaten everything that was prepared, they left the table. Mr. Nippers rounded them up and started them on the road to Webbville. His parting words were that they would have to be hurrying on, he guessed. If ever they should be passing through again, they would be sure to stop and see us. Several of the children had not said a word during the whole time they were with us.

After they were gone, Mama prepared breakfast for the family. Papa regretted that he had not sent our guests on their way when the seven additional ones had appeared from behind the chicken house, but then he wondered where those pitiful little "young 'ens" could have slept if we had not kept them. Mama added that they were all dripping with lice, she thought, and that she would have to wash and boil everything they had touched.

One evening about six weeks later, sometime in October, my father and my uncle, who had come over the hill after supper to visit with us, went down to Grampa Williams's to talk a while. We had gone to bed but were not yet asleep when the dogs began to bark excitedly. Then, from the gate someone called "Hello!" Mama got up, went to the door, cracked it open a few inches, and asked, "What 'd ye have?"

"This hyur's Mr. Nippers. We've walked from Webbville since 4 o'clock and want to stay all night with ye again."

Mama explained that her husband was not home and that she never kept travelers when he was away. Mr. Nippers was impatient. She knew them. They were all tired. The "young 'ens" were ready to drop. They had not eaten since they had left Ohio. They had asked to stay all night at houses along the road since it had begun to get dark, but nobody would keep them. They would all be willing to sleep on the floor for they didn't want to be no trouble to nobody.

No, Mama would not keep travelers when her husband was away from home. Well, could they come in and warm by the fire for a few minutes? The little young 'ens didn't have shoes, and none of them had coats, and it felt like there would be frost tonight. Mama replied that we had gone to bed and that they might be able to stay all night at the next house, or the next one, up the road and would have a better chance for getting to do so if they could get there before the people living there had gone to bed. They were hungry, Mr. Nippers explained. If they could just come in and warm by the fire for a few minutes and have a glass of milk and any leftovers from supper they would be chirked up and the little young 'ens would have better hearts for travel in the cold night.

Mama responded that she did not take in travelers when my father was away, closed the door, turned the latch in the lock and the big wooden button on the facing. Mr. Nippers began to curse and to call Mama bad names. Then rocks pelted the shake roof of our house and bounced and rolled along the top of the porch and the dining room and kitchen. The dogs set up a hullabaloo as they raced along the paling fence.

Mama took my father's pistol from its holster hanging on a peg behind the door, went to the back door, eased it open, and fired it once toward the sky. The dogs stopped their barking. There was no sound from beyond the fence. Mama listened by the front door for any rocks that might be thrown against the paling fence. All was quiet.

She then placed the pistol under her pillow and lay down again, but none of us went to sleep. We lay quietly, listening carefully for any noises beyond the fence or from the dogs trotting on the porch, and watched the coal fire, covered with ashes, glow between the bars of the grate in the fireplace.

Perhaps an hour later, the dogs began to walk on the porch, the latch of the gate clacked, we heard the gate open, and someone walked heavily across the porch and rapped loudly at the door. Mama brought the pistol from under the pillow, leapt from the bed, and took a position in front of the door. A tongue of flame flickered through the ashes on the fire in the grate, and we could see her there, her long hair hanging loosely down her back, glimmering in the dancing light. "What 'd ye have?" The response was a series of louder raps on the door. Mama said, "If you don't speak, I'm going to shoot through the door. I have the pistol pointed and my finger on the trigger." My father spoke, "W'y, what's wrong? It's just me."

Mama lowered the pistol, turned the button on the door facing, and flipped the latch. Papa and my uncle came in. They had thought it would be fun to give Mama a little scare but had not expected her to go crazy. Why was she swinging that loaded pistol around?

She recounted what had happened. Papa flew into a rage. That damned ornery son-of-a-bitch had left in the middle of the summer to sponge off his kinfolks in Ohio. Now, that he had wore his welcome out and it was too late for him to have to work with crops on the farm, he was dragging his poor woman and young 'ens back to Magoffin County to beg and steal all winter. Remembering that old Nippers had said back in the summer that his family had slept in a schoolhouse their first night out of Magoffin County, he wondered whether they might have gone over on the hill across the valley to spend the night in the church house there. He would go see, and if they were there he'd run them out.

He put on his pistol holster and my uncle took the shotgun from the rack above the door and they left for the church house. In about fifteen minutes we heard shots from the pistol and the shotgun, wild yells, and the screaming of children.

"Oh, Lordy mercy! Surely they have not gone over there and hurt them poor children!" Mama cried.

We could then hear Papa berating Mr. Nippers but could not understand what he was saying. We heard nothing from Nippers, and the children were no longer screaming. In a few minutes Papa shouted, "I said hit that road and be damned quick about it, you stinkin' son-of-a-bitch!" We heard no other sounds for a few minutes, and then there was a patter of muffled footsteps in double-quick rhythm as the poor Nipperses hurried silently across the bridge and on up the road past the house.

Papa and my uncle came in laughing. Papa was exultant. They had seen smoke rising from the chimney of the church and knew "in reason" the Nipperses were there. They slipped up to the church and listened, then peeped through a window. The stove door had been left open for a light so they could see how to arrange benches around the stove for warmth. A bucket full of coal was next to the stove and some big lumps were piled close by. The children were quarreling over who would sleep on the benches closest to the stove.

Mr. Nippers, stretched out on a bench in front of the stove, was scolding the children when Papa and my uncle let out with war whoops and fired their guns as they ran around and around the house. The double door had been barricaded, but they lunged against it with enough force to crack it four or five inches. Papa had told them who he was, that Mama had reported their behavior to him, and that he had come to drive them out of the church. He required them to remove the barricade and come out. Nippers had not said a word, but when all of them had got themselves together they began fumbling in the darkness down the hill, the family being herded along with Nippers behind. When they reached the foot of the hill, Papa had ordered them to "hit the road," and had been pleased with their response to his order.

"I'd be ashamed, driving them poor pitiful children out into the cold like that, if I was you," Mama said.

Next day, his cousin wanted to know why Papa had driven those poor people out of the church. They had asked to spend the night at three houses up the valley above us, but people just didn't have room for them. Under an oak tree about halfway up Kirby Knob they had built a fire and hovered around it all night.

Papa asked the cousin whether anybody had invited them in to have supper. No, it was so late when they came by.

"Well, we fed them and gave them places to sleep when they passed through here six weeks ago. It was damned poor thanks we got for our trouble. If you couldn't even feed 'em some cornbread and milk, you've got no right to pass judgments on me for driving them out of the church house, after the way they done Monnie."

Dow Boggs

Dow Boggs, son of William and Ann Johnson Boggs and a brother of Jesse, Clem, Hook Jim, Frank, Edmond, and others, became a legend. Stories about Dow would fill a fat volume. In my boyhood Dow had become what the community referred to as a "beggar," though his begging consisted of no more than staying in homes of relatives until he felt he was no longer welcome. He was blind, dressed in motley, and mentally affected, but he was a master storyteller with an exact memory. He was a victim of many pranks and, in his mental affection, extremely gullible. He liked to go where people assembled. Dow was present at church, funerals, memorial meetings, weddings, and wherever young people gathered for social activities. His family had cast him out.

I have three vivid memories of Dow. Once he came to my father's home when people had gathered there. He was wearing a shirt with no collar. The collar band, a bit tight for Dow, who had a neck like a bull, was held together with a brass collar button. Tied tightly around his neck about two inches above the collar band was an extremely bright-red tie that streamed over his front. He sat in a cane-bottomed chair tilted against the wall in our porch. He was bald. His spectacles were high on his forehead above his eyes. People were teasing him and he shouted his responses, bringing his heavy cane against the porch floor for emphasis from time to time. His sightless eyes, his square face with a wart-like mole on the lower part of his cheek, and his mustache growing straight down above a rather long mouth with a very wine-red lower lip that rolled outward above a square chin presented themselves in the plane bounded on the north with the dark glasses and on the south with the red necktie. Some of the big boys in the home in which he had visited had "gyarbed" him in a fancy "get up" becoming to one who proclaimed himself "presy-dint of these Newninty States of Amariky."

Dow was waiting for a letter from Molly Gould, the daughter of Jay Gould, to whom he had "given out" a letter, which one of the local pranksters had faithfully written down. While Dow was shouting about Molly Gould and his plans to call the Con-grass into session at Fallsburg, to which he was having the capital moved, one of the young men present came hurrying through the yard, addressed Dow as "Mr. President," and announced that he bore a letter which the postmistress had urged that he carry at once to L.D. Boggs, presy-dint. Dow asked that the letter be read, but not until he knew who had written it. The young man announced that the letter was from Molly Gould. He pretended to read a love letter, stating that Molly Gould was hopelessly in love with the presy-dint and had flown an airplane to Louisa, where she was waiting for him to meet her. Dow then asked that his reply be taken down and sent back at once to Molly Gould. I remember one sentence: "Tell her she can git me if she wants me." After the answer had been dictated, the young man pretended to discover written on the back of Molly Gould's letter a postscript giving an account of how Molly Gould's plane had wrecked and she had been flung "a straddle of a bobwire fence" and split open, but that the doctors in the hospital in Louisa had sewed her up and she was recovering, waiting anxiously for Dow's reply to her proposal. Upon hearing this news, Dow brought his chair against the floor with a thump and ordered that his answer be destroyed. He roared, "W'y, buddy, I hadn't got no use *fur* her, if she's been split open on a wire fence, Lord, God a'mighty!"

At another time I was eating Sunday dinner at the home of some cousins, the children of Will S. Williams. Dow was there. Will and grownups in the house were carrying Dow on "a mighty high horse." He was raging and waving his cane about. After the dinner was over, Dow made his way out of the house, across the yard to a cedar tree, and then, feeling along, all the way around the tree to within full view of those sitting near the window. He clapped his cane under one arm, lifted his glasses to his forehead, unbuttoned the fly of his pants, and urinated straight toward the house. At the end of urination, he caught a few drops in his hand and rubbed it vigorously into his blind eyes. Someone had told him that his sight would be restored if he bathed his eyes with urine.

Later Dow developed a bowel complaint. Unable to take care of his personal problems, he became a burden to people. His son was too poor to keep him. His one brother who could have kept him was dead. Some of the men on the creek decided that the best thing to do for him was to send him to the county poor farm. It is said that my great-uncle Jake Williams took him. Dow was told that the Con-grass and Sentant had met and were waiting for him. He was helped into a spring wagon and taken away. The keeper of the poor house was told of Dow's delusions of grandeur and advised to play the game with Dow, who had been a hard-working but very poor man before he lost his sight following a sunstroke. Once, when my father was taking me home from high school for the summer, we stopped at the poor house to see Dow. He was propped in a leaning chair against the wall beside the entrance to the building in which he stayed. His glasses were on his forehead. Just above the bridge of his nose was a dark brown spot about the size of a quarter. He explained that someone had told him his sight would be restored if he would put "ambyear" (tobacco juice) on his forehead. Other inmates were gathered about him. He was being treated as if he were president. I gave him a quarter with which to buy tobacco. When I turned at the gate for my last sight of L.D. Boggs, presy-dint, he was smiling benevolently while two aged women fought each other for the quarter I had given him.

I used to follow Dow on Sundays to hear him tell stories about the Civil War. He was too young to bear arms, but he had followed his older brothers. He was present when his brother Jesse killed John Sparks in Virginia because John, who had been a member of Jesse's company in the Confederate Army, had bushwhacked Jesse's cousins, who had been pro–Union. Dow knew every spring and trail from Blaine to Wise County, Virginia. Once he boasted, "I walked all the way from Wise County, Wes' Ole Fudginny, with my son Fyankie (Frank) on my hip and never put *de* (him, it) down but once, and *that* was to pee."

Dow was a gallant and courteous man in a quaint fashion. He would greet my mother, always shouting his felicitations: "Monnie, God bless your heart, honey, how do you come on this mornin, mum?" "Very well, Uncle Dow, how are you today?" "As good as God ever made a man, sisty, 'cept a little ail-mint on me insides." He would then sit and rest himself, with legs crossed and the suspended foot drawing up very slowly and releasing suddenly. He would call for a "glass o' buttermirk and a piece of cold wheat bread."

After a time he would say, "Hey, Lord, I reckon I'd better be a-mosin' on." "Where are you going, Uncle Dow?" "I'm a-goin' up to Kyurby's Ed's."

Dow understood human motives. He was wise in many ways, and many consulted him. His observations were quoted by people in the community. Once he was present when someone told of a widower in the community who had "sidled" up to a widow and asked whether she would like to marry "an old stag." Dow interrupted with his shout, "And what did she say!" "She told him 'no.'" "W'y, a course, the damned fool!" "What would you have said if you had been asking her to marry you, Dow?" "W'y, buddy, I'd a-looked 'er straight in the eye and a'said, 'Sisty, how'd you like to marry

Dow Boggs.

the rapidest bull that ever romped the woods?' and she'd a tuck *de* at a word. He hadn't got do sense he had de day he drapped from his manny's womb! Old stag!"

In his younger days Dow and his wife Regina, whom he called Jiney, lived in a cabin up a hollow (the Stillhouse Holler) on the farm on which I grew up. Across the branch from the cabin was a cave into which dry leaves drifted and remained all year. Jiney used to slip from her bed and meet men in the cave. Once the man she was to meet tired of waiting and stole down to the corner of the house to "eavesdrip." Dow was attempting to interest Jiney in sex relations. Jiney was being difficult. Finally, Dow roared out, "Now, look a hyar, damn you, as good I been to you and as much backy I give you, you simmer down as dough you dead." The eavesdropper reported that Jiney "simmered" and he returned home, mission unaccomplished.

At another time one of the men of the neighborhood called at Dow's cabin one Sunday morning, hoping to find Jiney at home alone. Dow was there. The caller finally decided that if they were to go "sarvice" hunting they might find an opportunity to slip away from Dow. They took a bed sheet and a basket and went into the woods. Soon they found a tree filled with ripe serviceberries. The visitor agreed to climb the tree and shake the limbs. Dow and Jiney spread the sheet below. Then they would roll the sheet toward each other and pour the berries into the basket. While Dow and Jiney were fumbling with the sheet between them, the man called down through the branches and accused Dow of engaging in sexual relations with Jiney. Dow protested his innocence. The caller said, "Well, Dow, you climb up and shake and see how it looks to you." Dow agreed to do so. While the caller and Jiney fumbled with the sheet they engaged in sex relations. The man said, "Now, what do you say, Dow?" Dow answered, "Well, buddy, hit do look that way to the man in the tree."

When Dow was old and unable to work he visited occasionally in the home of Preacher Clem, his brother, who was very poor. Once he was there during "plow time" when provisions were low. The supper was very meager, but Celia, Clem's wife, had fried a piece of country ham and laid it on Clem's plate, since he had to work so hard. Other members of the family were eating cornbread, meal gravy, and milk. When Clem finished asking the blessing, he looked at his plate and discovered that his meat was gone. Looking across the table, he saw Dow drawing the rind through his jaws. "Brother Dow, you got my meat, I see." "Well, Brother, the Bible, hit say to watch as well as pray."

After Dow was old and cast out by his children and living among his brothers and cousins, he liked particularly to be where young people of courting age assembled. Young men would rig crude pranks on him, encourage him to "make up to" young women, engage him in conversation for the delight of those present, and ask his advice about how to win the hearts of reticent maidens. Fond of relating his own experiences as a forceful and successful conqueror of maidenly scruples, Dow would wax eloquent in his shouted rhetoric and pungent speech. He advised forthright procedure and direct attack. Once I heard him give an account of his first experience at courting. When he was sixteen years old, he had "drawn up" to a young woman after church. Finding her willing to permit him to walk home with her, he "gathered her" and started. As soon as they were out of sight of the church crowd, Dow reported he grabbed her in a powerful hug and, as he pressed her to himself' said, "Lord, God, honey, you've got tiddies as big as Ma's old coffee biler!" An admitted lecher, he had at one time, by his account, led a half-willing woman to the brink of sex relations, but she protested that she was not clean. Dow told her to have no fears on that score, that if her "drawers are dirdy, sissy, you can pee and wash *de* (them) and fart and dry *de*."

Older women in the community were inclined to engage in brave and bantering speech with the license of the 18th century. They referred with a teasing frankness to private matters in bantering men at such semi-public places as country stores to which they brought baskets of eggs and braces of young roosters swung across their saddles, blacksmith shops to which they brought their gentle old nags to be shod, or mills to which they carried their "turns" of corn to be ground into meal or chop for their "biddies." Such banter was called "blackgyarbing" on Caines Creek. At one of these places a widow called Servanner (Savannah) appeared, her "comb" all red for pulling. Dow, in making conversation, said, "Servanner, you are the only datter [daughter] your daddy had, ain't you?" She responded, "Yes, *sir*! I'm the onliest one of my daddy's young 'ens but what had a prick." Dow bounced back with, "Sisty, you've got the purtiest place to put one that I've ever see-ed."

Perceiving that Dow was interested in a busty little armload of apple-cheeked tomboy in the home of one of his cousins, the girls' brothers and cousins decided to play a trick on Dow. One of the smaller cousins stuffed batten in two small bags and bound them on himself for breasts, selected a squash for a vagina, cut a hole in it, and glued horse hair on it around the hole, ran a rope horizontally through the squash and secured it in his crotch, stole one of the girl's dresses and slipped it on, and concealed himself in the washhouse near the kitchen door. The other boys lured Dow outside and into the garden behind the wash house and told him that the girl had said for him to wait there until she could slip away from the others, that she was "a-whettin' and a-honin' for it," and would be there as soon as she could manage. Dow was kept waiting in excitement while the boys, pretending to return to the house, concealed themselves in the darkness to observe Dow in the act of making love. When all was ready, the boy dressed as a girl slipped out of the wash house and into the garden. Dow assaulted at once, squeezing the rag breasts and fumbling at the skirts. Within a few minutes he had inserted with the primitive passion of a bull. As soon as he had, he shivered and said, "Oo-oo-n, honey, your guts am as cold as ice!" The hidden boys snorted, Dow realized suddenly that he had been tricked, and started backward, the boy pretending to be a girl jerked suddenly away, and Dow was left standing with the squash hanging on his penis.

Chapter Three ───────────────────────────────

Beyond the Big Sandy ...
and Home Again

Tenants in Ohio

One of the more memorable experiences of my childhood was our move to Selma, Ohio, in the spring of 1920, not long after we had recovered from influenza.

My father, unhappy with the arrangement with Grampa Williams about the division of the harvests with him and Grampa's unwillingness either to make him a deed for that part of the farm on which we lived or to sell it to him, decided that he might be able to do better as a tenant on an Ohio farm. Having made known his interest in moving to his aunt and uncle, Sarah Williams and William T. Boggs, who owned a farm on which they were prospering at South Charleston, Ohio, he had invited them to let him know whether a place for a tenant on a good farm close by should become available.

Soon a letter arrived written on stationery with a picture on it of a gate with stone posts, a gravel lane through a tree-covered yard, and a comfortable looking farmhouse visible at the end of the lane. The letter, from a farmer by the name of McDormin, said that a tenant was needed. An eight-room house, occupied formerly by the McDormin family, located on a gravel pike, and only a short distance from Selma, where there were stores, a school, and churches, was available. A washhouse was connected to the home. The homestead included also a good barn, a chicken house, a woodshed, and an excellent garden plot.

Mr. McDormin agreed to make the homestead and garden available rent free, to furnish a milk cow and feed for her free, to permit my father to own chickens and pigs, and to pay him $30.00 a month for five-and-a-half days a week of farm labor. In addition, he could have the use of a horse and buggy on weekends.

Papa was excited about the offer. He talked it over with Grampa, who agreed that it seemed to be a good offer. When my father expressed his preference for owning the farm on which we lived, Grampa made no comment. Hoping that Grampa would get around to offering to make a deed for or sell outright the farm on which we lived, my father did not answer Mr. McDormin's letter. One day in late fall while we small children were out for play period at school, we saw a red sports car with a tan top laid back cross the valley, rattle over the loose floor of the bridge, and stop on the bank above our house. Two slender men wearing strange caps with attached goggles got out, and my father came up to the road to greet them. They stood there for a few minutes and then went down the bank to the house. None of us had ever seen a red car before or caps and coats like those the men were wearing. Eight years old at that time, I felt proud that such a pretty car and such finely dressed men should be stopping at our home. Instead of waiting for the lunch hour at school to begin, my brother and sister and I rushed home at once.

The men and Papa were sitting in the porch. Papa was animated and doing all of the talking. No notice was taken of us. We hurried on to the kitchen. Mama, red faced and weeping, was trying to prepare extra food for the guests. We learned that the young visitor was Paul McDormin, the son of the farmer who had written the letter, and that the other man was someone who had grown up in our neighborhood and had come along to show young McDormin the way to our house. My mother was weeping out of shame for our poverty, our shabby house, its meager furnishings, and the coarse food she was preparing for dinner. She was distressed that Papa was doing so much of the talking, and so roaringly, that the other man did not have an opportunity to say anything.

We waited until the guests and Papa had eaten before we went to the table, but we examined the red car carefully, obeying our mother's strict orders not to touch it or get in it. The brass lights, the grill, the tool box on the running board, the tan cloth of the top folded back, the spare tire in a tan sheath attached to the rear, the glazed and hard-looking wood spokes of the wheels, and the new smell of gasoline, oil, and rubber filled us with wonder and excitement. While the men were retiring from the table, Mama came to the corner of the house and motioned for us to come for our lunch.

Later, we learned that Papa had signed a contract to move to the McDormin farm the following March. Mama was reluctant to move. The children, excited by the prospects of travel, living in a big house beside a pike and in a strange country, "as level as a floor," with railroad trains roaring through it and cars rushing up and down the pike, counted the weeks and the months before we would be moving.

In preparation for the trip Papa sold his mules and cattle, Mama most of her chickens. Papa spent much of his time preparing crates and gathering boxes for our furniture and belongings, including a crate for the dog and coops for a dozen hens and a rooster, all of which would be shipped by railroad from Webbville, the southern terminus of the E.K. Railroad eleven miles over the hills from where we lived.

Around the fire in the evenings Papa would tell about the fertile soil, the level land, the streams filled with fish, the long distances one could see, the gravel pikes, the railroad trains, and the general prosperity of the people in that part of Ohio to which we would be moving. In time, Mama, too, became enthusiastic about the plan to move. We asked questions about railroad trains, boats on the Ohio River, trolley cars, schools, forests, wild animals, to which Papa responded with glowing reports, for he had gone to our Uncle Willie's several times in the harvest season to work before he and Mama had married.

We would be boarding the train at Webbville on March 25. The last wagonload of furniture and the dog and chickens would be taken to Webbville the day before. We would spend the night of March 22nd at our Grandpa Whitt's, the night of March 23rd with our Aunt Lou, and our last night in Kentucky at Grampa Williams's. Grampa Williams would take us and our boxes and suitcases in his wagon to Webbville in time for us to catch the train that would leave about the middle of the morning.

The day before we left, Mama prepared a basket of food for us, fried chicken, ham biscuits, biscuits split open with jelly in them, gingerbread, cake without icing. That night we were sponge-bathed from a tin wash basin on the hearth before a warm fire in Grampa's living room and sent off to bed early.

We were rousted out long before day on March 25. After a big breakfast that included barley cakes with boiled sorghum molasses on them, we were loaded into the farm wagon. Mama and Grampa sat on the seat and the three children on a quilt spread on the floor between the seat and boxes and suitcases that had been tied to the sides so they would not slip up and down while we were crossing hills. Papa and my uncle walked in front, one carrying a lantern.

Instead of following the road to the Lick Fork of Cherokee, we took a trail past the graveyard. We huddled together quietly as we watched the gravestones dance in the dim light of the swinging lantern. My father and uncle laid down two or three rail fences across the trail before we reached the road at the gap between Deans Branch and Lick Creek. On a flat below the gap we were surprised to pass a chimney, stark and lonely in the dim light.

Curious, we were told that the chimney had been for the home of a family that had moved away many years before.

The road below the gap was steep and rocky. Grampa applied the brakes often as the wagon jolted and rocked from side to side. We were now traveling down Lick Fork, a road none of us children had ever traveled before. Soon after we reached the narrow valley we passed the ruins of a log cabin, overgrown with gray vines, standing among bare forest trees by the side of the road. Rube Parker, whom we knew, had lived there many years before but had moved away. The cabin, like the lonely chimney we had passed, was dark and ghostly in the dim light of the swinging lantern.

The road became level as we moved down Lick Fork. We huddled together on the wagon bed and pulled a quilt over our shoulders against the chill in the damp wind that had blown up. I dozed for a few minutes but was awakened by a chorus of roosters crowing. We were passing John Cooper's place and we could see lights through the windows of his white house on a low hill across the narrow valley. On her way from church once his wife had stopped to visit us and we had seen her at our Uncle Steve's store. As we traveled on, the crowing of the roosters seemed far away and I remembered a part of a verse from a song my father sang, while playing his banjo after supper, about Reuben, chickens on his back, bloodhounds on his track, and sixteen hundred miles away from home. There was a touch of homesickness in the memory, and the receding sound of the roosters' chorus had something of the loneliness of the tune about lost and hunted Reuben, who, if he died a railroad man, wanted to be buried in the sand and hear the whistle blow a hundred miles.

We arrived at the Hylton place at the mouth of Lick Fork just after a cool daybreak. The morning was generally cloudy, but a burst of light from down Cherokee Creek made it possible for us to see young fellows chasing mules in a barn lot while cows ate fodder scattered beside the fence. Crows were cawing, and two were idling in the breeze between us and the brightening sky down the valley. As our team slogged through a muddy lane crossing Cherokee valley, we saw an old man coming across the yard of his gray and weathered log house a few feet from the road. Water was standing in the ditch between the muddy road and the yard, which had swamp grass growing along the edge of it. Grampa greeted the old man as "Mr. Helton." In later years I was to learn that the old house, finally removed because the slow filling up of the bed of Cherokee Creek caused the bottoms to become swampy and the valley to flood easily, was the boyhood home of Jesse Stuart's maternal grandfather, whose family was buried in a graveyard on the top of a steep hill overlooking the old homesite and facing sunrise from down the valley.

After fording Cherokee Creek we turned immediately up the muddy road that ran along the creek. Soon we came to John Houck's store and post office.

The store was open and we could see smoke coming from the chimney. Papa asked that we go inside and warm ourselves for a few minutes by the stove. John Houck, a short, square-faced man with a jovial smile, was standing behind his counter. Posters on the wall included pictures of Democratic candidates for president, among them a familiar picture of Woodrow Wilson. Appeals for support of the American Red Cross and a picture of Uncle Sam inviting young fellows to fight Kaiser Bill attested to Mr. Houck's patriotism during the recent War. I do not recall that we bought any of the candy in the showcase, but we admired the fancy corner which served as the post office.

Perhaps two miles above the post office we passed a two-story white house with a double-deck porch with fancy banisters. This was the Jesse Young place, where our former teacher, Annie, had grown up, we were told. The road up the Cherokee Hill was muddy and winding. The children were permitted to walk up the hill but cautioned to follow the path beside the road to keep from getting our new shoes muddy. The walk helped us to keep warm.

The muddy wagon road down Dry Fork of Little Fork of Little Sandy River ran beside the creek much of the way. We passed houses more often as we approached Webbville. I remember noting and asking questions about two houses. Suddenly, we rounded a bend upon the largest home I had ever seen, a gothic house with gables and porches and elaborately worked trim and banisters for some of the porches. I learned that a family by the name of Glass lived there, a name I had not heard before. Just before reaching Webbville we passed a two-story white house of unusual length, the longest house I had ever seen. It was the Tom Boggs house.

And then we were in Webbville. There was the railroad, two ribbons of steel laid on wooden ties, that came to an end in the middle of a little bottom between the muddy road and a dark, unpainted depot. We had arrived before the train had come up from Willard. After unloading the wagon and saying goodbye to Grampa and our uncle, we filed into the depot, in which a few people were sitting on wooden benches arranged in reference to a heating stove in the middle of the room. We lined up for Papa to buy tickets from the congenial ticket agent, who smiled at us while asking our ages, a telegraph clicking away on a shelf beside him. The train was expected to arrive in about a half-hour.

I was dressed in overalls and a denim jacket, both of which my mother had made. My father had not found a suit in my size at Blaine when he had gone there to purchase clothes for us to wear on our trip. He thought we might have time to see whether a suit in my size was available at the store between the railroad track and the creek below the depot. Leaving the others in the depot, he took my hand and led me to the store. The merchant, a Webb, I believe, thought he might have a suit that I could wear. We went upstairs, where suits and overcoats hung on racks assembled in the middle of the room.

There were two suits that I might be able to wear, one brown the other blue serge. I chose the blue serge, and was asked to try it on. It was too big for me, but Papa said I would grow to it next year. It was a fancy one with shiny black buckles and straps for fastening the short pants at the knees and a big square buckle with black enamel on it for the coat belt. I liked it. Papa paid the merchant ten dollars. The merchant "threw in" a pair of galluses, and Papa buttoned them to the pants. He then removed the tags carefully. With my overalls and jacket in a paper poke under my arm, I walked proudly back to the depot. That was my first suit, which was big enough for me to continue wearing for three years.

The train arrived on time, a smoking monster with a bell ringing and a long lonesome whistle sounding as it came around a bend below the depot. It came in backwards, with one coach and an odd assortment of other cars, but not more than three or four altogether. There was hurrying about as workmen unloaded and loaded crates, boxes, and barrels, people, dressed up and carrying suitcases and boxes, got off the coach, and others gathered to get on. Officials wearing blue suits and caps with black patent leather bills dashed between the depot and the train, all looking important and attentive to their duties. Soon the conductor, who had stood by to help people as they descended the steps from the coach, took his position by the steps again and yelled "All aboard!" We were among the first to enter, the conductor holding our arms as we mounted the steps.

The coach was the finest compartment we had ever seen. There were rows of seats covered with red velvet, brightly polished brass lamps hanging from the ceiling, a strip of red carpet on the floor between the seats, and a polished stove with a blue-black pipe standing near the end. We were delighted that there was a window by each seat. The three children took a seat on the left side of the coach and our parents the one in front of us, Mama sitting upright with her basket on her lap. People kept coming down the aisle until the seats were all taken. Papa surrendered his place to an old woman and walked to the platform at the end of the coach where we could see him laughing and talking with two or three other men. As the conductor entered the coach we heard the whistle blowing again as the bell rang faster. The train started with a jerk and we were off, the whistle blowing long and lonely and the dark smoke streaming along outside the window as we went around the bend below the little village.

The conductor called "Tickets, please" and began accepting tickets, which he punched with a click and stuck under the hatbands of the men and on the seats in front of the women. I felt almost grown up when he punched my ticket and stuck it under the band of my black felt hat. The conductor, whose red face radiated geniality, muttered to himself as he collected tickets. When he accepted my wide-eyed sister's ticket he said, as if to himself, "I think it queer that a little girl like you must have a ticket, too." After he passed on down the aisle, my sister repeated what he had said, imitating his pronunciation and his facial expressions. We would have said, "Hain't it quare that a little young 'en like you hass to have a ticket, too."

Before he had finished collecting tickets, the conductor reached up and pulled a cord as he yelled "Bells Trace! Bells Trace! Bells Trace!" The train stopped. We looked out and saw a smiling boy sitting on a mule and holding another saddled mule by the bridle in the middle of a narrow road. A man walked over and was mounting the mule when the train started again, the whistle blowing and the bell ringing.

The morning was cloudy and dark. The tall bridges with broad flat looking iron frames through which the train rushed were stark and gray. We saw wide meadows with stubble still brown from winter and dotted with haystacks built around poles and cornfields with gray stalks marshaled in rows. Pasture fields on the hills were bare and trees along the ridges were dark etchings on slate skies. Houses, many of them imposing but with dirty paint, were located on little hillocks overlooking the valley, while dark barns with cattle standing at attention in the lots and facing the passing train were located by narrow roads that wound along beside the pasture fences.

We were fascinated by a lake contained within a wall of earth on which grass and bushes grew. The slate colored water was rippling in the March wind, and we envied two small boys with fishing poles standing on the far side where the water line hugged the foot of a hill. What a swimming hole this would be!

Before we had completely passed the lake the conductor came into the coach from somewhere in the front of the train and chanted "Willard! Willard! Willard!" The train slowed to an easy stop while crossing another of those frame-like bridges and passing a water tank on a stack of what looked like telephone poles. Stretching our necks to see to our right all of Willard we could, we marveled at the rows of houses, all looking very much alike and all with smoke streaming from their chimneys, that began only a little way from the railroad track. People were standing in the porches to see the train go by. Passengers on the right side of the coach were waving at the people, some of whom were returning the waves slowly and with puzzled looks as if they were trying to decide who it was on the train that knew them. Old people stood in bowed positions, grandmothers held toddlers by the hand, young mothers, with a hip flung out for support, held children in their arms, and all were looking as if they had come out to see a parade.

At Willard other people crowded into the coach and took positions in the aisle, resting their hands on the back of the seat near them. Conversations commingled into a fuzzy chorus that seemed to rise and fall with the rhythm of the clattering wheels of the coach and the chug-chug of the locomotive.

The coach was becoming warm. Soon the voice of the crowd and the rhythm of the train became a melody that accompanied the verses about Reuben, who must have been drunk to pawn his watch and trunk to get his low-down doney out of jail. As I repeated the verse, the melody and the rhythm came closer together.

The conductor appeared again and chanted "Hitchens! Hitchens! Hitchens!" We would get off here. The train crossed another railroad track on a long diagonal, and I could see to the right brick smokestacks all in a row. Mama said that was the brickyard and named two or three people from Caines Creek who had moved to Hitchens to work there. Looking ahead of the train, I could see two railroad tracks with a yellow station between them to which a sign was attached on which Hitchens appeared in big letters. The tracks were in a narrow valley with a steep wooded hill to the right and pasture fields to the left. There was a little town where the railroads crossed, but the depot seemed to be quite beyond it.

Most of the people on the coach got off with us at Hitchens, which seemed far from Caines Creek, although I learned later that it is only seventeen miles away. We had had our first ride on a train.

We waited a long time at Hitchens for the train from Lexington to Ashland. The depot was brighter and in better repair than the one at Webbville. We sat on benches with curved backs for a time. Then we crossed a court with packed gravel to a building only a short distance from the depot. People were sitting around eating things they had bought there. Mama had her basket of food with her. Papa bought milk for us and we ate fried chicken, ham biscuits, and jellied biscuits, feeling poor and ashamed as we watched others eat strange things they had bought at the concession at the end of the room. There was a sweet, hunger-stimulating odor in the room. Men who had eaten were smoking cigars. Some children were peeling bananas part way down and eating great mouthfuls at a time. Food was being cooked in an area beyond the counter of the concession stand. After we had eaten only half-heartedly, Papa asked whether we would like some "banannies." We had never seen "banannies" before, but we were most eager to eat some. I believe that they sold for a nickel apiece or six for a quarter. He bought six and we ate one each. Mama put the sixth one in her basket. The bananas were so good that we ate them as slowly as we could and still say that we were actually eating.

While we were waiting for the train, an extremely ugly woman with no nose but two large dark and hollow nose holes came into the depot. She knew Mama and entered into a lively conversation with her. The strange woman was the center of attention. Conversations stopped. People behind her hung their faces together and whispered, turning their chins at an angle to hear better the poor woman's conversation. Mama, glad to see the woman, was congenial and responsive but seemed amused privately at her account of her visit with relatives living near Hitchens, the wonderful places she had been to, and things she had seen. She was waiting for the afternoon train to Webb-ville, where some of her relatives were to meet her. She concluded her con-versation with the observation that "These hyur furrin places is nice but I am awful glad to be a-gittin back to the Newninety States again."

About the middle of the afternoon the train from Lexington arrived. We climbed into a crowded coach and were unable to get seats next to win-dows from which we could view the countryside. The conductor went through the same routines that the conductor on the E.K. had gone through, but soon after he had passed us a young man carrying a basket loaded with bananas, oranges, red apples and candies came through the coach hawking his goodies to the passengers. Our father did not offer to buy anything. The train stopped briefly at three little towns along the way before plunging through a tunnel shortly before we reached Ashland. We could see that we were passing build-ings but only their upper portions were visible to us. At Ashland it seemed that almost all of the passengers got off.

The station in Ashland was made of dull bricks, the first brick structure we had seen. It was a square, ugly building, but the bricks made it seem sub-stantial, permanent, and wonderful. We went into the waiting room to sit while Papa checked to see whether our furnishings were at the station and to inquire about directions to the boat dock on the Ohio River.

While we were waiting, my brother became interested in exploring the depot, which had a stairway going up to a balcony that ran along a second floor of the two-story waiting room with tall windows in it. While trying to restrain him and keep him close at hand, Mama noticed on a seat nearby a slight, heavily made up and beady-eyed young woman with a long thin nose and a snapping turtle mouth. The woman was smiling a twisted, ugly smile. Mama, thinking the woman was laughing at her and making fun of her poor attire, lashed out in a voice that reverberated through the station and brought the agent to his window at once, "You ugly, long-nosed bitch! You are laugh-ing at me. You fool with me, and I'll come over there and pull every hair out of your head." The poor woman, eager no doubt to be friendly and amused by the behavior of my brother, was astonished and cowered as she tried to explain that she was not making fun. "Oh yes you was!" Mama insisted. "Just for a little, I'll wring your neck and sweep this place out with you, you little painted whore!" At that moment Papa, a soldier in uniform beside him, entered. "What in the hell is going on here?" he demanded. As Mama began to recount in a loud voice what happened, the agent called out, "Calm down, madam, or I'll have to call the police and have you arrested for disturbing the peace." The ugly little woman burst into tears. Papa began to laugh at the situation. Mama's face flushed with anger as her eyes blazed malevolently at the weeping woman, who dared not lift her head.

As if nothing had happened, Papa said of the soldier beside him, "This is Harrison McDowell. He'll help us carry our baggage down to the boat."

"W'y, Harrison, I didn't know you," Mama said, her calm quite restored and the color receding from her face.

We gathered up our belongings and left the station. As we walked along on a wide sidewalk of concrete and hurried across paved streets, we were fascinated by the storefronts of buildings of brick and stone that rose even four or five stories. As we started to cross what must have been Winchester Avenue, Papa looked back to see that we were all together. Ralph, my brother, was missing. Our attention given in wonderment to all that was about us, we had not noticed that he had dropped behind. Papa rushed back to find him, and we turned to see whether he was in sight. About halfway up the block stood Ralph, his back bowed and his head down, peeing forcefully against a marble panel at the corner of a building. A stream was snaking its way from between his feet and across the sidewalk. People were passing, but nobody appeared to be noticing what the little boy was doing. We had not gone to a toilet all day and neither of our parents had told us that one was available.

Papa came leading Ralph by the hand and we all hurried across the avenue and on to the dock, where the boat was waiting. Four or five automobiles crawled slowly aboard. The drivers parked them in places designated by an attendant, who chocked them in position by placing triangular blocks behind the rear wheels. We were then invited aboard. Harrison McDowell took leave of us. We went aboard and sat on a deck bench against the walls. We could see that a large crowd was seated inside the cabin. Soon attendants untied the boat, the captain blew the whistle, a great motion from within shook the deck, and the boat began to move out, the muddy water lapping almost to the level of the floor.

Sitting across from us was a large, heavy-busted black woman in a starched white dress and wearing a white cap. She had a pleasant face and big smiling eyes. The first black person we had ever seen, she competed with the river and the tree-lined shore for our attention. My sister, leaning toward Mama's ear, said, "Mamy, look at that nigger." Mama shushed her and looked hurriedly at the woman to determine whether she had heard the remark. She smiled broadly, showing a row of fine white teeth as she surveyed us with a slow sweep of her wide eyes. Then she looked straight ahead as if she were not aware of our fascinated stares.

Sooner than we had expected, the boat reached the Ohio shore. The attendants tied it up, let down the gangplank, and invited us to disembark. Quite loaded down with our luggage, we made our way up a steep bank to a trolley car waiting at the end of the line in Coal Grove. We climbed aboard with the help of a conductor. The motorman sounded a dinga-ling-ling and the car moved out, sweeping down the track toward Ironton. The view from the windows of the trolley car was of the wide muddy river and the dark Kentucky hills undulating against a gray sky.

Papa told the conductor that we wanted to get off as close to the D.T. & I. depot as possible. After a while the conductor told us that we would be getting off at the next stop and that the depot was only a block away, as I recall. We got off, the conductor helping us to handle our luggage, and walked a short distance to the low, red brick station of the Detroit, Toledo, and Ironton Railroad. We found the station empty except for the master behind his window. The next train north would be the following morning. Papa bought tickets for us. No, people were not permitted to sit all night in the station.

Papa left us at the station while he went to find a hotel room for us. Soon he came back and reported that he had found a hotel around the corner that had only one room available and that the room had only one bed in it. He had taken the room, though they had charged him a fortune for it. Mama asked how much he had to pay, and he replied $2.00.

We went to the hotel, which was actually an old home that had been converted to a hotel. We climbed the stairs in a broad hallway and went to a front bedroom that had in it a double bed, a dresser, a movable clothes closet, and a chair or two. The bathroom was down the hall. Our father took us to the bathroom, the first trip all day for all of us except Ralph. He showed us how to flush the commode and to turn on water in the wash basin. There was a large white bathtub that stood on tall legs with feet shaped like the feet of a lion. We washed our hands and dried them on a clean sack towel. Then, with only a glass of water from the spigot to drink, we sat on the bed and ate our supper from Mama's basket, this time topping off the meal with sugar cake and gingerbread, which we called 'lasses bread.

The room had an electric light in it, a single, raw bulb screwed into a socket in the ceiling. There was a switch by the door for turning the light on and off. We took off our shoes and our coats and Mama and the three children slept crossways on the bed and Papa lay on the floor. Two dollars should have bought a lot of sleep for us, but we did not get our money's worth. We could hear the ting-a-ling and rush of the street car, the noises of the town, the long, lonesome sounds of freight train whistles, and the clacking and rumble of wheels on iron rails, all sounds that disturbed children for whom noises in the night had been the baying of dogs, the hooting of owls, and the rattle of loose boards as late travelers rode across the bridge at the end of the lane that led to our house.

We were up by daylight. We took turns in the hall bathroom, fascinated by the gadgetry and a bit frightened by the big bathtub that reminded me vaguely of a coffin, perhaps the ghost of a coffin. After we had washed and combed, we sat on the bed and ate from Mama's basket. Then we drank water from the glass we had found in the room. While we were eating we saw through the window the town coming alive. People were rushing along the sidewalk across the street from the hotel. Through a large window at the front of a one-story building directly across the street we could see three men standing in a row and moving at the same time as each turned a long roll of white dough on his low table. The men were dressed in white and wore tall white caps. They looked very much like the picture on the box that the big cookies came in that we had been allowed to buy a few times at Uncle Steve's store when there was a nickel due us after we had traded our eggs and chickens. Papa said the men were working in a bakery, rolling dough that would be baked into loaves of lightbread. He thought they were working in full view so people could see how clean and industrious they were. We had never eaten "light-bread."

At the depot we waited only a few minutes for the train. We rushed out to see it pull into the station. It was a prettier train than the two we had seen in Kentucky. The cars were red with yellow lettering on them. The D.T. & I. would take us all the way to South Charleston before dark. The three children took a seat across the aisle from Papa and Mama, but each wanted to sit next to the window. Papa told us we could take turns, allowing Mabel to sit there first.

The train wound through hills northwest of Ironton, stopping at little towns the names of which I had never heard. We went through a little town in which the houses were mostly log cabins similar to those which we had known on Caines Creek. Once I saw the locomotive far ahead of us on a curve and realized that the track at that point was halfway up the side of a wooded hill. The valley below was in forest as if we were going through a region in which nobody lived. I saw puffs of white steam coming from the locomotive and then heard the whistle blowing. I remembered standing on the hill by a big oak tree and seeing puffs of smoke come from the guns of quail hunters in the meadow below before hearing the reports of the guns.

The only town I remember along the way was Jackson, at which we stopped longer than usual. Beyond Jackson the countryside became more nearly level. We passed through rich looking farms with big barns with silos and fine houses, many of them of red brick and trimmed with green. One white farmhouse at the end of a paved walkway had brilliant red flowers showing through an upstairs window.

At lunchtime we ate again from Mama's basket and drank from tiny little paper cups that looked like envelopes that we could pull from a container beside the water fountain at the end of the coach. Young fellows wearing uniforms and caps came through the coach occasionally offering to sell fruit and food from baskets they carried with them. Our father did not offer to buy anything.

A quiet, well-dressed middle-aged couple sat in the seat ahead of us. The man produced a black case, which the woman opened on her knees. From it she took a dumpy looking black bottle, screwed the cap off, and poured coffee, still steaming, into the cap and a little tin cup. She then took smooth, puffy looking biscuits, broke them open and spread something on them. Then she took two big white handkerchiefs out of the case and spread one across her lap and the man spread the other over his knees. They began to eat the biscuits and drink coffee, occasionally picking up from the case small pieces of quite red looking meat and little squares of something that looked as if they had been trimmed from the center of a fried egg. There were also orange colored sticks and white sticks that looked slick which they ate with a chomping sound. Then they ate little squares of white cake with a hard icing on the top. We were so curious and so eager to see just what was going on that Mama had to ask us several times to sit back in our seats. After the couple had eaten the woman screwed the top back on the bottle and returned it to the case. Each folded carefully a white handkerchief and they were put in the case. Then she turned and, holding up three of the biscuits stuck together in a row, said, "Would you like to have these?" We looked at Mama for an answer. She said, "Take 'em if you want 'em." I accepted them but had to be told to thank the woman. Then I broke one off for Mabel and one for Ralph. They did not taste like any biscuits we had ever eaten, but we were too proud to ask questions. After the couple got off the train, we asked Mama what kind of good biscuits we had eaten. She could not rightly say, but 'lowed, mebbe, they might have been lightbread biscuits.

The day became brighter in the afternoon. The sun shone through the windows and the coach became warm, but we were too excited by the trip, too eager to see everything along the way, to feel drowsy. Once our father reprimanded us for turning our heads from side to side rhythmically while chanting an imitation of the chugging of the locomotive ahead. We noticed that many older people were sleeping in their seats, some of the men with their hats resting over their faces.

The train arrived in South Charleston in the late afternoon. Many people got off along with us, but rushed immediately to buggies and a few cars brought up to carry them home. We were the only ones to go into the little depot, which had the appearance of standing at the end of a street. We sat down while Papa asked the station master for help in calling by telephone the home of Uncle Willie and Aunt Sarah. He shouted into the telephone that we had arrived. In a moment, he turned to us and reported that Uncle Willie would drive his buggy up for us soon. While waiting, we stood by a window from which we could see level land stretching away as far as our eyes could travel, but woodlots on the farms gave us the impression that we were surrounded far out there by a forest. The sun, big and red and dull enough to be looked at directly without hurting the eyes, was hanging above the horizon along which dark blue scraps of clouds floated idly. Red sunshine rested on the wall across from the windows and we could see against it our dull shadows, bigger than life and oddly out of proportion.

We were at the window when Uncle Willie drove into sight, his horses pattering rhythmically against the courtyard. He stopped the team, tied the check lines to a standard, and climbed out, a fat man with a round face. When he saw us at the window, he made his bright blue eyes big, winked, and smiled. We were sure we would like him. He came in and helped us with our bags and boxes. We climbed into the buggy, Mama beside Uncle Willie, and Papa, with Ralph between his knees and Mabel and me beside him, in the back. Uncle Willie, sitting up very straight and with the check-lines drawn tightly, spoke to the horses, and away we went, the horses clattering in rhythm on the gravel road, as level as a floor and so straight that its sides came together in a line far ahead of us and the fences beside the road blended with it into the dark blue rim of the horizon at which sight stopped.

While we were passing a sturdy farmhouse set among trees, Uncle Willie slowed the horses to a walk, and Papa leapt from the buggy and opened a metal gate. We turned into the lane beside Uncle Willie's home, a pretty story-and-a-half house a stone's throw from the big home in the woodlot. Behind the house was a white barn with an electric bulb in the eave burning brightly. A pretty older woman, a younger woman, and a lovely little girl came into the side porch to greet us and help us with our things. They were Aunt Sarah, her daughter Gretta Mae, and her little granddaughter, Ruth Evelyn.

We helped to carry boxes from the buggy to the back porch. Papa went along with Uncle Willie to the barn, and we went into the kitchen, bright with light from an electric bulb in the ceiling, the great stove gleaming, and a sink at the end of which was a funny little short-handled pump with a spout that looked like a little trough. We then moved through a brightly lighted dining room. In it were a partly set table with a snow-white cloth and a cabinet, with glass doors through which we could see dishes glinting light, that stood against a wall covered with brightly colored paper.

The small sitting room was dominated by an elaborately wrought tall heating stove with isinglass panels in the door, through which firelight flickered. It was much like the pictures of such stoves, bounded by dark looking curlicues that twisted the imagination and tipped with handles and slides of bright metal from which dangled little twirls with swirling surfaces, that we had seen in Sears, Roebuck catalogs. A large lamp of milk glass with raised red roses painted on both the shade and the pot sat on a white doily on a "library table" of dark wood with thick curved legs. Most curious of all was a lounge with a raised headrest and covered with black leather drawn tightly into diamond shapes with black metal buttons at the corners of the diamonds. We had never seen one before, but there had been pictures of "sofas" like this one in the Sears catalog, too. It seemed so hard and inhospitable without back, headboard, and footboard. Besides, it was shaped like the corpse of an old man we had seen laid out on boards and covered with a sheet while the carpenter was making his coffin.

We sat on dark straight chairs with hard black seats, some placed in corners and some near the black stove with the glowing isinglass panels. If we sat back on the seats our feet stuck straight out, and if we sat on the edge, they dangled several inches above the floor, which was covered with a dark red rug with curious figures woven into it. We had seen pictures of rugs in the catalogs, too, but we had seen on the floors of the "fine" rooms of homes in Kentucky only round or oval rugs hooked from twists of old rags ripped from cast-off clothing.

Mama remained in the kitchen. We sat, solemn and quiet, in the midst of the finery in the clean sitting room so small that there was no place in it for a bed. Soon Uncle Willie and Papa came from the barn. Uncle Willie turned on the light, a bulb in the ceiling, opened the door of the stove and examined the fire, pulled some slides that created a clatter within the stove, adjusted the damper, and sat on the couch. He asked each of us our name and age and what "reader" we were in at school. He laughed a great deal, his bright blue eyes sparkling, as he asked questions and shifted himself on the couch, its springs groaning, the leather creaking, and the center sagging beneath his considerable weight.

Aunt Sarah announced from the kitchen that supper would soon be ready. We went to the back porch to "wash up," the three of us rubbing wet hands across the surface of a rounded cake of soap lying in a blue ceramic dish stamped with the image of a well-whiskered cat, and sudsing them in the pan of soft cold water on a bench between the posts of the porch. We dried our hands on a pretty towel on a rack, an innovation for us, for we had seen only drab sack towels hung from nails beside the kitchen door.

All of us sat together at the table, a curious arrangement for us. In Kentucky the grown-ups would have eaten first and we would have gone to the table after they had finished. I do not remember the main course of our "supper," but for the first time we ate fruit salad. It had in it slices of banana, orange, grapefruit, gratings of coconut, and dices of marshmallow. We had eaten banana only the day before at Hitchens. Once our grandfather had given us what he said was an orange but which we learned a long time afterward was really a tangerine. In that salad we tasted for the first time orange, grapefruit, fresh coconut, and marshmallow.

The experience was so vivid that our first taste of "lightbread," cut from a long loaf wrapped in a brightly decorated wax paper, was dulled, but the strawberry jam, our first, passed around near the end of the supper and which we spread on the crumbly lightbread, no doubt reinforced our memory of our first taste of yeasty loaf bread, which I remember as a dull white bread that crumbled easily, had a thin leathery crust, and shrank to tiny dough-like rolls in the mouth as it was masticated. How wonderful I thought it would be to be rich enough to afford lightbread as a replacement for the corn-bread and the big rough biscuits that we had been eating on the farm back in Kentucky.

We did not sit up long following supper. Soon after a passenger train with lights showing through the windows of the coaches in which people sat, looking straight ahead, swept eastward on the track across the road. Aunt Sarah explained sleeping arrangements for us. There were three bedrooms in the little house. We climbed up the stairs that were polished like furniture to our pretty bedroom with a fancy "coverlid" on the bed and a long bolster pillow with tassels dangling from the ends. Not able to come to a conclusion about whether we had enjoyed sleeping on a mattress in the hotel room in Ironton, we were in position to make a better judgment that night.

It seemed strange not to sink into a fluffy featherbed above a shuck mattress that rattled and whispered when we moved, but the linens smelled so good and the covers were so soft that we went to sleep very soon but without any consciousness of fatigue or weariness from the two-day trip so filled with new experiences. A long time afterwards, I woke up feeling too warm and smothered. I thought of faraway Caines Creek, the exciting trip, and what the morrow might hold as the rhythmical drone of snoring from elsewhere in the house lulled me back to sleep.

We got up early next morning, it seemed, but when we went into the porch to wash our faces and hands, we found that the sun was up ahead of us, a large ball of light beyond the bare limbs of the trees in the yard of the big house across the fence. We could see it behind us in the looking glass on the wall when we combed our hair. Washed and combed, we sat in the little living room and waited for breakfast until Uncle Willie and Papa came from the barn.

The breakfast was unlike any we had ever had. Little glasses filled with juice stood by each plate, along with larger glasses of milk. We sat at our places and drank the juice first, orange juice, bright yellow but sour. The empty glasses were taken away, and we passed our plates for Aunt Sarah to put food on them, a spoonful of oatmeal that had been sweetened with brown sugar, a fried egg looking white and clean around its yellow center, a piece of bacon fried crisp, and lightbread that had been heated in the oven until it was brown and on which dabs of butter had melted, leaving yellow places in the center of each piece. I had never eaten such a fine breakfast before. I recalled the big rough biscuits, fried potatoes, gravy, thick bacon or rusty ham, sorghum molasses, and milk still warm from the cow that we had usually had for breakfast back on Caines Creek. The strawberry jam that we had with our second piece of lightbread at Aunt Sarah's house was so good that we were pleased when she produced the loaf of bread in its bright waxpaper wrapper and cut off extra pieces of it for us to spread more of the good jam on. Aunt Sarah was pleased that we had liked the breakfast so well.

Soon after we had eaten, Papa and Uncle Willie left in a horse-drawn wagon to haul our furniture, chickens, the dog, and supplies from the freight depot to the house into which we would move. They would also take our bedticks to the straw stack and stuff them with wheat straw. By the end of the day they would return and take us to our new home.

We played in the small yard all day. Ruth Evelyn, perhaps not more than four years old, had a rocking horse and a tricycle that fascinated us. We were permitted to admire the rocking horse and to rock it with our hands but were not allowed to get on it because it was for little children. We could ride the tricycle though, if we would take turns and be careful. We bickered and quarreled so much about our turns and how long a turn was fair for each that our mother asked us not to ride it anymore. Ruth Evelyn, standing quietly by and watching with fascination our disagreement, had not herself asked for a turn to ride her tricycle.

We wanted to explore the barn and the woodlot across the fence but were not permitted to. We ventured from the yard to the lane to swing on the steel gate but were called back into the yard. When trains passed up and down the track across the gravel road in front of the house, we rushed to the fence to watch them go by. The few cars, mostly Model T's, that passed along the highway drew us to the fence. We pretended that we were cars and buzzed up and down the walk in the backyard, to which we were finally confined.

Late in the afternoon Papa and Uncle Willie returned. The house was ready for us, Papa said. He had driven over from McDormin's a buggy in which we would return. We hurried around to get everything together and climbed into the buggy. Papa sat straight and proud, Mama beside him. We three children sat in the floor behind the seat and craned our necks at the sights.

We passed a rambling farmhouse with many chimneys and painted green that Papa said his cousin Virgie and her husband, Granville Moore, lived in. We remembered their children, Inus and Opal, about our ages, from their visit to Kentucky a summer or two earlier. Papa said that we might visit the Moores some Saturday night and Sunday.

In the little town of Selma we saw the school which we would attend next year. The school year was not over at Selma, but we had gone to our school until it was out and it was too late for us to start at Selma this year, Papa explained. In the middle of the little town we turned directly west, but as we turned Papa pointed toward a big house we could see ahead and said that Mr. McDormin's brother lived there and that our Aunt Blanche, her husband Mason, and their children lived on that Mr. McDormin's farm. We would visit them, too, when we "got straightened out."

On our way out to where we would be living we passed a little square house with a tall green mound in the corner of the yard. Papa was at a loss to explain to us why anybody would have a tall mound of earth with green grass growing to the top of it in the corner of the yard. The mound was shaped like a huge sweet potato hill.

Not far from the village we passed a beautiful, large, well-kept house painted solid white. The trees and plants in the yard were "shaped" and the grass was rich looking. That was the home of the Custers, very rich people, Papa said. Our house would be the next one on that side of the road, for the Custers' woodlot extended to the back side of the garden that we would be tending. To our left directly across the road from the end of the Custer wood-lot was a dark log cabin with a mud-and-stick chimney sticking from the middle of its roof. Smoke was drifting lazily from the chimney. The Ganodes lived there, Papa said. The son-in-law had come and helped him and Uncle Willie set up our furniture.

And there, diagonally across the gravel-covered pike from the Ganode cabin, was the house in which we would live, a white house, the older part of which needed repainting. Smoke was drifting from the chimney in the middle of the older part. It had a front porch, the yard had a fence around it, and eight or ten honey locust trees stood in the yard.

Papa helped us down from the buggy and carried our boxes and the old suitcase into the house, warm from the fire he had built in a heating stove located in the middle of the living room. Our hickory bottom chairs stood about the living room and our old rocking chair had been placed near the heater. Papa had bought meal and flour that afternoon and had brought up some buttermilk and sweet milk from the McDormins, who lived on down the pike a few hundred yards. He built a fire in the cookstove in the kitchen dining room behind the living room. Mama could start supper while he took the buggy down to the McDormin barn and fed the horses.

Mama put a pan of corn batter in the oven to bake while she peeled and sliced potatoes, put on a pot of pickle beans, fried bacon, and made a pan of gravy. She had trouble with the stove. The wood did not burn well. The oven would not heat up enough to bake the bread properly. While she was struggling with the supper, darkness came almost suddenly. She went to light the kerosene lamp, which had been placed in the middle of the table, but it had no oil in it. She could not find the kerosene can.

Papa did not return from the McDormin barn for a long time. It was quite dark when he entered the house. He had been talking with one of the McDormins, whom he had seen at the barn, and darkness had slipped up on him. There was no kerosene, one of the things he "had not thought a breath of" while buying necessities that morning. He struck matches for light enough to find can lids, pieces of string, and lard to make grease lamps, which he set on the table and along the ledge of the stove. We had never seen grease lamps before. The fascination of the sputtering lights distracted our attention from our hunger while Mama struggled to finish cooking our supper. Papa found more wood for the stove, but it did not burn well either.

The supper was not very good. The cornbread was dry and had no crust, the bacon would not crisp, the potatoes were not quite done, but it was fun to eat in the flickering light of grease lamps, and the milk was good.

The sink in the kitchen had a pump with a trough spout like the one in Aunt Sarah's kitchen. After supper we wanted to take turns at operating the pump when Mama needed water. Papa continued to keep the grease lamps burning, replenishing the grease and preparing new string "wicks" as needed.

Back in the living room we sat around the warm stove with the door left open to give us light. The bright figures on the dark red wallpaper danced in the flickering light. We thought the wallpaper looked fine and rich, much prettier than the catalog leaves on the walls of our house in Kentucky. Mama was not happy with our new home. She sat in silence and wept while Papa talked about how fine it would be when we "got on our feet." He would bring the cow up from the McDormins' tomorrow. He had already released the chickens in our chicken house and fed them chop. Old Boss, the dog, was chained in the doghouse out back. Papa had fed him scraps from the dinner Aunt Sarah had prepared for him and Uncle Willie, but he ought to be fed again. Papa rose up and made his way into the kitchen, where he fumbled in the darkness until he found what was left of the cornbread. Then he went out back to feed it to the dog.

While Papa was gone something began to drip from the ceiling. It spattered on the bare floor and sprinkled us across the face. It was a slimy liquid that left our fingers sticky when we wiped it from our foreheads. It smelled sour and rotten. Mama had smelled something like it sometime, but she could not remember what it was. Drops that struck the heating stove sizzled and fried and then threw off a stench that was sickening.

When Papa came back, he wanted to know what that stink that smelled "worse 'n cyarn" was. We told him something was dripping from the ceiling. He struck a match and held it near the sagging paper overhead. Drops of the liquid were oozing through the sags. He punched one of them with his finger and the liquid came streaming through. Papa smelled it between his thumb and finger and moved close to the stove to sniff the drops sizzling there. He had smelled that odor before but could not remember what it was.

Taking the box of kitchen matches with him, he went into the new part of the house. We could hear him climbing the stairs and then walking around in the room above us. He was muttering to himself but we could distinguish only "damned son of a bitch," which ran through his monologue like a refrain.

When he came back, he ordered us to get ready for bed at once. He would have to put out the fire in the heating stove and remove any live coals from the cookstove and open the doors and windows. "Some son of a bitch" had stored a ton of pumpkins up there and moved off and left them. They had frozen. The heat from our stoves had begun to thaw them out. The juice would ruin everything we had if we didn't "get the damned things out of here as quick as we can." He would try to get up as soon as there was light and throw as many as he could out of the window before he had to go to work in the morning.

Mama stripped the bed in the living room in which she and Papa had meant to sleep and spread over the straw tick wrapping paper and an old quilt to catch the pumpkin juice. We crept in darkness to the room with two beds in it in the newer part of the house. Papa put the coals from the heating stove and the ashes from the cookstove in a coal bucket and took them into the washhouse and pumped water from the cistern into them. He opened the doors and windows, took sheets, quilts, and a pillow from the pile Mama had stripped from the bed, and said that he would sleep on a straw tick that had been placed on the floor in an upstairs bedroom in the newer part of the house. Mama and Mabel could sleep in one bed, Ralph and I in the other, in the downstairs room.

We did not have curtains for the windows in the house. After we were in bed for our first night in our new home, I could hear automobiles going up and down the pike and watch the light from their headlights pass along the white plastered wall of the room. Somewhere far behind the house railroad trains passed all night long, their lonesome whistles sounding far away and the rattle of their wheels on the tracks blending into a rumbling background to the pulsations of the soughing of the locomotives as they puffed their way toward some far off place. The bed was warm, though, and I could hear, in quiet moments, the whispering of the new straw in the tick under the feather bed. The door to the living room was closed. I could not smell the pumpkin juice, which had become less offensive after we had learned what it was.

Daylight came early in the flat country around Selma. We were awakened by the moving around of our father upstairs. Mama got up and dressed quietly for the day. We wanted to get up, too, but she asked us to stay in bed until she had a fire going in the kitchen, for there would not be one in the living room until the pumpkins had been thrown out. We lay quietly, but wide awake, listening to her rattle pans and dishes in the kitchen. When Old Boss charged barking from the lane onto the pike, I heard Papa scolding him. I rose up in bed and looked out. Boss was snapping at the heels of a tall Negro man hurrying down the pike as far on the other side of the road as he could get. He was swinging a black lunch pail in his hand and would look back occasionally as if he thought he might have to beat the dog off with the pail. When Papa had gone for a spade to lift the pumpkins with, he had unchained the dog for him to get some exercise and explore his surroundings. Papa restrained Boss and chained him up again.

Across the pike was a field that rose gently to a ridge beyond which leafless trees stood in a long line that joined woodlots on either end. Golden sunlight from a big pumpkin sun filtered through the limbs of the trees. In the field of brown stubble tipped with frost was a long dark straw stack with a bright patch on its side, the place where Papa and Uncle Willie had found the straw for our bed ticks, I thought. The top of the straw stack was sprinkled with gray frost.

Mama had left the bedroom door open. We could hear the scraping of the spade against the floor upstairs and the splat of bursting pumpkins on the frosty earth beyond the end of the house as Papa shoveled them through an open window.

Before Mama had finished cooking breakfast, Papa came into the living room with a pan and a fork in his hands. He punctured sagging places in the paper overhead, caught the streaming pumpkin juice in the pan, and poured it in the yard. After draining the heaviest sags, he cleaned the heating stove with a wet rag and built a fire in it. We got up and sat around the stove in the chilly air to wait for the stove to heat.

Mama had better success with the Ohio stove wood for cooking breakfast than she had had with supper. She had baked big biscuits, fried bacon, boiled molasses, and made a bowl of gravy. It was a Kentucky breakfast that we shivered over as we ate.

Papa had to be in the field with the team with which he would plow by 7 o'clock. He rushed away with two bacon and biscuit sandwiches, a biscuit and jelly sandwich, and a pint jar of milk packed into a paper sack for his lunch. He would not be back until about 6:30 that evening, he said, but he would bring with him a milk cow for us.

After he left, Mama had us sit by the heating stove in the living room while she washed dishes and became acquainted with her kitchen. It was a long time before she came in to sit in the rocking chair in front of the stove. By then the room was warm, but the smell of the drying pumpkin juice was strong. We noticed, though, that sags in the paper overhead were disappearing as the paper dried with brown borders around the spots through which the pumpkin juice had leaked.

After resting a while, Mama got up and made the beds. She then went up the stairs for the sheets, quilts, and pillow Papa had taken there, but she would not let us go along. We could explore later in the day when the house had warmed up. She made up again the bed in the living room and then brought a rag and a pan of warm water and cleaned pumpkin juice spots from the floor and the furniture in the living room and the dining room.

We looked out of the curtainless window of the living room at the yard fence, the honey locust trees, the grass, turning green, along the pike, the gray cabin of the Ganodes across the pike, and the dark leafless trees stretching away behind the Ganode cabin. At the back of the cabin, but detached from it, was a lime-washed board and batten house with a stove pipe sticking out of its top. Heavy smoke rose straight up from the pipe. A slender woman with a red cloth tied around her head rushed out of the white house and drew two buckets of water from a well with a pulley and chain hanging from a cross-bar. We could hear the chain screech against the pulley as she drew the water. With a heavy pail in each hand she disappeared into the little house.

We were permitted to look from the window in the dining room, too. The washhouse to our left cut off most of the view, but there was a garden between our backyard and the woods belonging to the Custer place. Peach trees grew near the fence on the far side of the garden, and we could see a privy with a worn path leading to it. We could not explore the rest of the house, though, until it warmed up, but we could look in a pantry at the end of the kitchen area. Here we found, besides canned stuff still in boxes that we had brought from Kentucky with us, some glass jars, curiously shaped bottles, a box of pieces of rolls of wallpaper, some like that on the walls of the living room and the kitchen, and folds of red and green crepe paper, the first we had ever seen.

The sun was warm. Soon the frost disappeared. The wind was not blowing. Mama decided that we could wrap up and explore the barn and chicken house, feed the chickens some of the chop, and see whether they had water, but we must not stay out long. Dressed in pullover caps and with sweaters under our denim jackets we ventured forth.

The lane between a field and the yard led alongside the washhouse straight into the big barn. Beside the lane was a doghouse, a pig house, a pile of loose bricks, a garbage pit, and a chicken house, in which our hens were clucking happily as they moved back and forth from the house itself into a sunny spot covered with woven wire and supplied with a container for water, into which Papa had put enough water for the day. Boss was so glad to see us that we released him so he could explore with us. The barn was empty except for the bag of chop Papa had bought for the chickens. The structure looked as if it had not been used for a long time.

We had centered our attention on the garbage pit when Mama called for us to return to the house. Bottles, jars, and tin cans left there still had labels on them. There were herring, sardine, mackerel, and salmon cans, split open in such a way that triangular pieces of metal rolled outward looked like flowers.

There were peanut butter jars and mustard jars. A ketchup bottle still had ketchup in it. There were blue bottles in which medicines had come, flat bottles for turpentine and castor oil, and long square-looking bottles in which food flavorings had come. When we removed the caps, many of the bottles continued to smell strongly of what had been in them. We wondered how long these bottles and cans had been collecting in that pit, down in which we could find ashes, bits of glass, and rusty cans beaten flat. We were so fascinated with the garbage that Mama had to call us a second time. We chained old Boss to his house and returned to the living room where we reported in our excitement all that we had found while we warmed ourselves by the stove.

We were eager to explore again, and Mama told us we might like to see what was in the washhouse, but cautioned us not to pump the water from the cistern. It was cold in the washhouse, so we could stay only a little while. The washhouse was a big room into which one entered from a little porch off the end of an empty room of the new part of the house. Near the center of the room was another of those short-handled pumps with a trough spout. A furnace for holding pots and tubs of heating water stuck out like a hearth from a chimney that went up among the rafters and extended through the roof. The chimney was made of rough brick daubed with earth. Low platforms for holding washtubs had been built between the pump and the furnace. The front part of the big room had a floor at the same level as the porch floor, but the back end of the room had an earth floor. The front part of the room had paneling, but the back part, where the earth floor was, had only the bare, unpainted weatherboarding showing between the rough uprights of the framing. Clotheslines had been stretched back and forth from wall to wall. One or two old wooden tubs had been left in the unfloored part of the room. On the floored part were pieces of worn furniture, including an ancient upholstered couch with curiously curved but upholstered arms, the thick upholstering of an elaborately flowered design held in place with blue-headed tacks. The couch had been placed against the wall and under a window. After we had satisfied our curiosities about the washhouse and tried the pump for the cistern, from which dark water with floating things in it came, we lined up on our knees on the couch and bounced up and down as we looked through the window at the Custer woods, in which we could see red hogs wandering, the garden with white skeletons of weeds and corn standing upright across it, the gray peach trees against the woven wire fence, and the weathered privy with a worn path to its half-open door.

Restricted to the house, yard, barnlot, and garden as our play area for several days, we explored every nook and corner of the place. We divided the wealth of bottles and jars from the garbage pit, built our own play houses of bricks from the pile near the chicken house, and played store and traded on bright days. In cold weather we romped in the empty upstairs rooms, including the smelly rooms in which the pumpkins had been stored. The little Ganode girl from the cabin across the pike came and played with us in the front yard on warm afternoons.

Two or three times we were permitted to cross the pike to play with the little girl in her yard. Once she took us inside the cabin to meet her aged grandfather, a white-haired man with smiling blue eyes and a goatee.

We were fascinated with the cabin, in the middle of which stood a massive fireplace made of mud and sticks and with a mud-and-stick chimney going through the shake roof. The cabin had no ceiling and only the area in front of the fireplace had a wooden floor. The beds and chests for storage in the back part of the cabin stood on an earth floor built up to the level of the wooden floor and beaten down hard and clean. The old grandfather sat in a comfortable rocking chair in front of a smoldering log fire, the low doors opposite each other open for ventilation and daylight in pleasant weather, for the cabin had no windows in it.

The little girl, whose name I have forgotten, lived with her parents in the board-and-batten house behind the cabin from the stovepipe of which we could see smoke rising straight up. We were never invited into her parents' home.

She played with us mostly on Saturdays and Sundays, for she went up to Selma to school during the week. One warm evening, when the moon was full, we played a chasing game around the honey locust trees in our yard, finding the game much more exciting with four persons playing it. When dandelions bloomed by the thousands in our yard and along the pike, she taught us how to wreath the flowers by roping them in twists of the green and red crepe paper we had found in the box in the pantry.

When our mother became more relaxed about permitting us to explore, we crossed the fence and explored the Custer woods. Once when the trees were leafing out we followed a path made by the red pigs that lived in the woods to a spring in a little hollow close enough to the Custer house for us to see through the trees upstairs windows of polished glass gleaming from the snow white gables. On another day we found a dead red pig, perhaps a year old, lying beside the path near the spring. We were tempted to go to the house and report what we had found, but our mother had told us we were never to go near the house.

We were never invited into the McDormin house. Once I was sent to the house for a dish of butter that Mrs. McDormin had told our father we might have. My mother would not permit me to walk down the pike. Instead, she sent me across the road and into the field, watching me to see that I got across safely. I walked up to the back porch of the fine house, where Mrs. McDormin met me and gave me the dish, which I carried carefully along a path inside the fence. I marveled at the barns and sheds scattered among the trees around the place but did not pause to examine anything.

On fair days we could see the railroad trains passing along on top of the river bank among the trees perhaps a mile away across the level fields behind our house. Once, when fish were biting, my father went fishing along the river. I think it must have been a Saturday afternoon. Just before dark he returned with a long string of fish, which we had for supper. They were mostly about a half-foot long and were so bony that we had to be careful not to become choked on fish bones.

One day a preacher woman, a Quaker, I believe, drove her buggy out from Selma to see my mother. While she was parking her buggy in the lane and hitching her horse to a post, my mother gave us careful instructions to stay out back and play while the woman was there, for we were "not cleaned up enough" for company.

Wanting very much to see what the woman looked like and to hear some of the conversation, we found a pole which we leaned against the wall just below an open window of the kitchen-dining room opposite the door into the living room, where the woman sat, her back toward us, facing my mother, who had a full view of the open window. With Mabel and Ralph's help, I shinnied up the pole to where I could see and listen. When Mama saw me, she signaled for me to get down. The woman, noting Mama's gestures, turned and saw me, too. She began to laugh and spoke to me, addressing me as "little man." Mama smiled wanly, for the woman's sake, I was sure, and in a controlled voice ordered me to get down from there and go play. I slid down the pole and we romped and yelled in the back yard.

Soon the woman, her long skirts swishing around her shoe tops, left the house. We followed as closely as we dared to watch her unhitch her horse and get into her buggy. She smiled at us, asked our names and what grade each of us had completed at school, and drove away. Mama switched all three of us for disobedience and rudeness, but not very hard. The woman, she said, was a kind of preacher woman and had invited us to come to her church. She lived in the little square house with the green mound, like a huge sweet potato hill, in her yard.

A man whom my father called Gib Beers also worked for the McDormins. After supper one evening he came by our house to pick Papa up in his buggy and take him up to Selma for an evening on the town. Papa shaved and changed clothes while Gib talked with us. A young, slender man, he told us about his wife, who did not have any children. They had been married only a short time. His wife had gone to visit her parents for a few days and he was "batching" in her absence, he said.

Just before he and Gib were to leave, Papa took from the dresser drawer his pearl-handled .32 Smith and Wesson revolver, of which he was proud, and showed it to Gib, who admired it while Papa extolled its qualities. Papa then slipped the gun into an underarm holster. Mama protested his taking the pistol with him. He did not need it, she insisted. But Papa said he was not going to "take anything off any smart aleck" and he might need his gun to protect himself. They left, old Boss barking and whining, for he wanted to go along, too.

Papa came back alone about midnight. He had walked from Selma. Gib had come into posses- sion of a pint of whiskey, which he had shared with Papa. They had gone into a little restaurant

Curt Williams's pearl-handled Smith and Wesson revolver.

in Selma where young people had gathered. Papa, fancying himself picked at by one of the young men, began a quarrel, cursing loudly and using obscene language as he threatened to beat the young fellow into a pulp if he fooled with him. The proprietor ordered Papa and Gib to leave. Gib went at once. Papa argued with the proprietor while boasting, as he patted his gun, that he had the "difference" if it was needed. The young people left the restaurant when they saw Papa threatening to pull a pistol. But Papa withdrew only to find, when he was outside, that the young people were gone and Gib had driven away and left him.

Mama upbraided my father for his foolhardiness while he railed against Gib for abandoning him.

Once after that Gib came by again, this time on foot and with a fine coon dog on a leash. Papa wanted to take Boss coon hunting with a trained dog, for there had been no coons on Caines Creek for a generation and Boss had never had an opportunity to hunt coons. Papa prepared his lantern, Boss becoming more and more excited about the prospects of a hunting trip as preparations were made. Again, Papa armed himself with his pistol, even though Gib explained that the game warden would arrest them if they should actually catch a coon or kill one at that time of year. But Papa protested that one needed to be able to protect himself when he went into the woods at night. Mama insisted that he did not need the gun and that if he should take it with him and the game warden should appear, he would make a fool of himself and get into trouble. She wept and Gib was embarrassed, but Papa took his pistol along anyway.

They found a coon in the woods beyond the Ganode cabin. We could hear the dogs barking, old Boss's bass completing a pleasant duet with the trained dog. Gib had a powerful flashlight by which they could see the coon's eyes shining from the top of a tree. But they leashed their dogs and went on until they found another trail. This time, Papa unleashed Boss, who soon treed the coon like a professional. The hunters then returned to the house, where they swapped hunting stories in low voices in the sitting room for an hour.

Although we lived on the McDormin place from March to near the end of May the weather never became as warm as we remembered that it had been at the same time of year in Kentucky. Except for the lush green grass and the carpet of dandelions there was little evidence of spring on April 5, my ninth birthday. Sometimes in Kentucky peach trees were blooming by then, "sarvice" trees had already shed their bloom, and the tender white blossoms of the puccoon were peeping from the dark earth in wood lots. It seemed that, except in spells of rainy weather, there was at least a light frost nearly every morning, even the morning of May 25, the day we left to come back to Kentucky.

But there were two or three frightening thunderstorms. During the first one we cowered together in the kitchen-dining room and watched the storm through the window. The storm, which came about 10 o'clock one morning, was the darkest one we had ever seen. Heavy clouds boiled and rolled, pressing themselves so close to the flat earth that the horizon gathered to within a hundred yards or so of the house, drawing down a curtain on the broad flat fields behind the barn and the tree-covered ridge beyond the river along which the railroad trains wailed at night. Only a corner of Custer's wood lot was left in our world. Then bolts of lightning raced down tree trunks and exploded in the earth only a few hundred feet away, shaking the house until the timbers groaned and the windows rattled. High winds twisted the trees until they tossed and roiled as if they were not grown into the earth at all. Following deafening claps of terrifying thunder, torrents of heavy rain beat against the windows and water rolled off the roof in sheets, overflowing the guttering. The assaults would continue for fifteen or twenty minutes before letting up, the horizon retreating as the rain became lighter. Then the wild dance was repeated. The storm lasted for two or three hours before subsiding into a quiet but heavy rain that fell straight down.

That storm, which occurred not long after my birthday, convinced all of us that one is helpless, at the mercy of the malevolent elements, and unprotected in flat country. We longed for the coziness of narrow valleys, for the snugness of sturdy hills gathered around, for the comforting assurance of a horizon beyond the hills and the fending off of dark clouds by rock-ribbed ridges.

Not permitted to go outside during the rest of the day on which the storm struck, we played in the washhouse. On my knees on the old couch and resting my elbows on the ledge of the open window, I watched the water drip from the eaves and plop in the leak. There was little sand and hardly any gravels at all in the dark soil being washed clean by the dripping water. While looking for gravels, I saw a vivid sky blue ball about the size of a marble lying in the leak directly under the window ledge. At first glance I thought it was a button, but it seemed to be perfectly spherical and I could not recall having seen a perfectly spherical button. When there was a lull in the rainfall, I raced outside and got it. It was a marble made of dazzling blue glass, deep within which was a swirling cloud of deeper blue. The first glass marble we had ever seen, it was a special treasure.

The following day was bright with sunshine and the world was quiet and clean. During the night buds on trees had burst and a thin haze of tender yellow, pink, and green leaves no bigger than the ears of mice shimmered across the Custer woods in which we could see near the spring a tall tree with a bright streak stripped from its side from top to bottom. Near it another tree knocked over by the storm was leaning uncertainly against its neighbors.

Spring came fitfully and slowly. Following the rains much of the landscape looked as if it were a series of shallow ponds, but after three or four bright days I could see dust trailing my father and other plowmen as they rode their plows across the long fields. But the time came when the Custer wood lot looked like a deep forest and blooming fruit trees turned the Ganode lot into a flower garden.

Our father never took us up to Selma or over to Clifton to a store, for he never borrowed the buggy to make a trip to a store himself. At least once he rode over to Clifton with Gib Beers one Saturday afternoon to purchase kerosene, sugar, meal, and flour. During our two-month stay we ate food we had brought with us from Kentucky, supplemented with milk from the cow the McDormins had assigned to us and eggs our own hens laid. Aunt Sarah and Uncle Willie did not visit us at all, as I recall, and our other Kentucky kinfolk, Aunt Blanche and her family and Papa's cousin Virgie Moore and her family each visited us once, but, as I remember, in both instances on Sunday afternoons.

We never went to church while we were there, but we visited Aunt Sarah and her family one Sunday, and spent two weekends at the Moores' and two Saturday nights at Aunt Blanche's.

Our first visit was to Aunt Sarah's about the third Sunday we were there. Papa went down to the McDormin barn for a horse and buggy while we were dressing ourselves in our best clothing. After he got back, he changed into his blue serge suit, and we climbed into the closed black carriage with a hard top and square lamps affixed to the door posts, a sedan, I believe. Papa and Mama sat on the seat and we sat on the floor. The horse clipped along at a lively pace, but it never found the smooth rhythm that Uncle Willie's horse had on the way from the depot in South Charleston to his house. Papa, seeming uncertain of himself as a carriage driver, scolded the horse considerably, which would lurch when he slapped the check-lines against its sides.

The carriage was so tall that we feared it might turn over when the right wheels dropped from the gravel bed of the narrow road. We did not meet anybody between our house and the intersection in Selma, but after we turned down the pike from Selma toward South Charleston we began to meet other carriages and a few automobiles. The road was so narrow that drivers slowed down and passed each other with care. When we were perhaps half way to Aunt Sarah's we pulled over to let some young people in a Model T pass us, but the driver of the car did not slow down. He passed so closely that the horse became frightened and left the road, jerking the carriage into the ditch. We were all flung together in a heap while the carriage rocked on its wheels. Certain it was going to turn over, Mama and Mabel screamed, but Papa struggled with the horse and got it back into the road, the carriage following with a lurch that pitched us against the dash board, Papa tangled up with us while trying to rein the horse. When we were in the road again, we looked back at the Model T hurrying on perhaps a half mile down the pike. The young driver had apparently not noticed that we had almost wrecked. From there onward and on the way back that afternoon, Papa pulled over and stopped when we met cars. The horse, he said, was skittish about cars, and didn't have any sense.

At Aunt Sarah's Papa talked a great deal about the fright we had had when the buggy almost wrecked. Uncle Willie invited us children to talk about it, too, and to tell how we felt. After dinner Papa and Uncle Willie went on a trip across the fields to the back side of the farm. Aunt Sarah, Mama, and Gretta Mae sat on the back porch and talked. We played inside the yard fence and watched cars go up and down the pike and trains pass on the track just beyond the pike.

Aunt Blanche and Uncle Mason were tenants on a farm that belonged to Mr. McDormin's brother. It was located immediately beyond Selma on the road toward Cedarville. On our first visit there we were wide-eyed with wonder at the imposing home in which these McDormins lived, a massive building with a wide porch reached by heavy stone steps and a circular driveway in front. We could see on a table beyond a broad window a fat electric lamp with a shade made of sections of glass, it seemed, each section a different color. The bulb was turned on and the lampshade had as many colors as a rainbow. More amazing was a pretty little longhaired girl, about our age, who was riding a Shetland pony around the yard in front of the porch. We never had an opportunity to talk with the little girl or ask permission to ride around on her pony, for we did not see her again. Our play area was restricted to Aunt Blanche's narrow yard, her garden, the barn, and the barnlot.

Aunt Blanche lived in a little house sided with green tarpaper roofing. It had a main room about 12 by 14 feet and a lean-to about 8 feet wide. There was no porch. Neither the front door nor the back had a stoop. The main room had been a milk house before Aunt Blanche and Mason moved into it when Mr. McDormin gave Mason a job paying him $20.00 a month, free housing, a garden, the use of a cow, and permission to grow chickens and a pig. After the children came, Mr. McDormin had added the lean-to to provide an extra room for cooking and eating and a bed for guests. Since his work was mostly the care and feeding of the livestock and milking and looking after cows, Uncle Mason was pleased to be living so close to his job, for the big barn with an earth ramp broad enough for hay wagons to be driven into the second story, was no more than a stone's throw from his back door.

Aunt Blanche, an excellent cook, had fish cakes for supper. The fish cakes, something we had never had, went especially well with pinto beans, cornbread, home-fried potatoes, and pickled beets. There was an abundance of milk. For sweetness, she had waxy cupcakes with

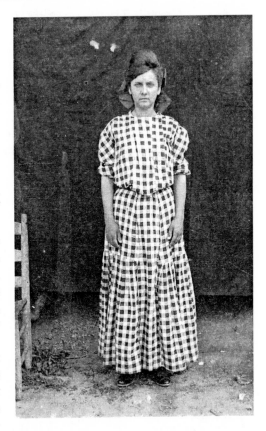

Blanche Williams Boggs, sister of Curt Williams.

a nutmeg flavor. While eating, we sat on a bench between her long table and the wall of her narrow but bright and cheerful kitchen-dining room with new blue paper tacked on the walls with big bright-headed tacks and gingham curtains at the windows. When time came for us to go to bed, Aunt Blanche prepared a pallet for the baby on the trunk at the foot of the bed in which she and Uncle Mason would sleep and set straight chairs with their backs against the trunk to prevent the child from falling off during the night. Her two towheaded little boys, Willie Curtis and Donald, would sleep in the bed next to hers. Mabel would sleep on a settee, Ralph and I on a pallet on the floor of the main room, and Papa and Mama in the bed in the lean-to. Preparations for bed were convivial and we felt warmth in our aunt's hospitality.

After Ralph and I lay down but before the adults were in bed, we heard in the distance a volley of shotgun blasts and some men yelling. Then shotguns were fired sporadically in several directions from the house and we could hear men yelling "Fire! Fire!" Uncle Mason, barefoot and holding his overalls half up, went to the window. "There's a barn afire across the fields there toward Cedarville," he said. He and Papa dressed themselves and went to the fire. We gathered at the window to watch.

As flames leapt high above the barn the fire, which might have been a half-mile away, seemed closer. We could hear men shouting and see their dark shadows rushing about. Then horses began to scream. Men were trying to pull them from the burning barn, but they were rearing, screaming, pawing wildly, breaking away, and racing back into their stables. The screams of the horses were terrifying. Then men began to shoot them, Aunt Blanche said, to kill them so they would not burn to death. There seemed no way to stop the fire, which mounted higher and higher in the dark sky. After a while there were no more screams from frightened horses, but we could see black outlines of men moving about. Then we could smell smoke from the fire, smoke laden with the odor of burning tar and hay at first and then of burning horse flesh. On our knees by the window we watched the flames subside and saw the blazing timbers falling, sending up new spurts of fire that shook out clouds of flaming particles that floated away in the darkness.

An hour or two later Papa and Uncle Mason returned. Someone had been smoking in the barn, it was thought. Tons of hay in the loft had burned. Only a few of the horses had been saved. They believed as many as fourteen horses had died in the fire.

We went to bed, but we could smell the fire all night. Next day smoke was still rising from the dark heap and the smell of burning horse meat was as plain as it had been the night before.

After a big breakfast that included a platter of fried eggs, Ralph and I went exploring down a lane beside the fence in front of Aunt Blanche's house. The lane, simply a haul road, was as straight as the fence, but beyond the barnlot it ran beside a little stream in which we looked for fish, but saw none. We found, though, a patch of what looked like "spargrass" planted in hills. Wondering why it was there, remote from a house, we plucked two or three of the young shoots, unfolding like green worms, and carried them back to the house. We learned that they were, indeed, spargrass shoots, and that the McDormins ate them as we did sallet. In Kentucky spargrass was used in flower pots and arrangements taken to the graveyards on Decoration Day. No one ever thought of eating it, but we knew there were people who would eat anything. Why, someone who had been to France during the war told that French people eat grasshoppers and snails. The very thought made our stomachs turn. We felt especially blessed that we had cornbread and soup beans instead of snails and grasshoppers and that we had plantain, poke, dandelion, whitetop, sorrel, and lamb's quarter for sallet instead of squirming spargrass.

Men and horses.

Later in the morning we sat on the bench behind the table in the narrow dining room and listened to Aunt Blanche and Mama talk as they prepared a big Sunday dinner. Papa and Uncle Mason, taking his towheaded, blue-eyed little boys, Willie Curtis and Donald, along, went for a stroll around that part of the McDormin farm that lay beyond the huge barn. After a while they returned, and we played in the narrow yard by the outside door of the main room while they sat in cane-bottom chairs they had brought outside. We could still see smoke rising from the heap of rubble where the barn had stood and smell the burning flesh of the horses. Men and boys dressed in Sunday clothes came to see the damage the fire had done, walked around the remains of the barn, and left.

Aunt Blanche had chicken and dumplings, canned green beans, big smooth biscuits, gravy, apple cobbler with sweet cream dip, and all of the milk we wanted for dinner. After dinner we sat in the yard again.

Some boys and young men gathered around the earth ramp to the second story of the McDormin barn. We could hear them laughing and talking. Ralph and I asked whether we might go over to the barn to be with the young fellows. Papa said no, at first, but Uncle Mason assured him that the young people were the McDormin boys and some of their friends and that they would be pleased to have us visit with them for a while. Papa then gave us permission to go but cautioned us to behave ourselves.

The boys were pleasant. They asked us about Kentucky and were especially interested in having us tell what hills were like, how cows and horses managed to stand up on them, and how farmers planted, cultivated, and harvested corn on steep hillsides. They wanted also to know what time of day

More men and horses.

the sun rose in the narrow valleys and when it set. They had heard of floods in the valleys and wanted to know where we built houses so they would not wash away. They laughed a great deal at our responses and seemed to enjoy us.

Then one of them took us on a tour of the great barn, through the cavernous hayloft with hay, both loose and in bales, stacked neatly. There was also a section in which horse-drawn farm machines rested. Then we went through the lower part, looking into stalls, harness rooms, and storerooms for chop and grain. There was one room furnished like a bedroom. Sometimes extra farm workers slept in this room, especially in harvest time when migrant corn cutters came through.

We then played hiding and chasing games in the hayloft for a while before sitting together again on the stone walls that bordered the earth ramp. If they found our speech peculiar they were too courteous to refer to it. If they thought we exaggerated our responses to questions they were gentle enough not to challenge us.

It was on this visit to Aunt Blanche's that we had our only opportunity to be with other boys while we were in Ohio. We recognized, I believe, that native Ohioans talked differently from us. The Ganode girl, Gib Beers, these boys talked much alike. Words were sharper and followed each other faster in their speech than in ours and they said "Ohio" instead of "Ohiuh," but generally we did not know just how it was that their speech was different. We noted, too, that the Moore girls, Inus and Opal, talked like Ohioans but that their father and mother talked like other Kentuckians. No one, however, made any comment about how we talked.

Papa's cousin Virgie, her husband, Granville Moore, and their daughters, Inus, Opal, and little Louise, perhaps two years old, were tenants in a rambling green farmhouse out on the road from Selma toward South Charleston. We visited them Saturday night and Sunday. One weekend the weather was dark with occasional showers and we were required to play inside. The house, which must have had twelve or fourteen rooms in it, was mostly unoccupied, and all of the doors that led from one upstairs room to the next and into closets from which doors exited into other rooms invited elaborate hiding and seeking games. We explored also the attic and descended into the basement, where we saw for the first time a house furnace, which was not being used then because the weather had warmed up with the showers. That evening we sat in a living room heated with a stove. Virgie, like Blanche, was a good cook. We had for dessert cake with layers of different colors and a hard icing. We had not eaten such a fancy cake before.

The other visit with the Moores must have been on our last weekend in Ohio, for we found a few small ripe strawberries in a strip beside the garden. The weather warmed up during the day and we played in a green yard that had been mowed. While we were there, a small airplane flew over, so low that we could see the man and woman in it and the bracing that held the upper and lower segments of the wings together. It looked very much like pictures of airplanes we had seen and associated with the Wright brothers. I believe it might have been the first airplane we had seen, certainly the first that was close enough for us to distinguish any of its features.

Papa went with Granville to a store while we were there. He brought back enough striped denim like that worn by workmen around a railroad train for Mama to make Ralph and me a pair of overalls and a blouse, which she did not make until after we had returned to Kentucky. He also bought for each of us caps at a secondhand store. Mine was like a railroad conductor's cap. It had a stiff and rigid crown and a remarkable shiny bill made of what Mama said was patent leather. Papa had paid a quarter for it. I put it on, rushed to a mirror to see how I looked, and strutted about proudly. It was too big for me, but after we got home Mama adjusted it to my head by stitching a band inside it. I liked it so well that I wore it wherever I went until it was quite worn out, the patent leather cracked and the bill broken down the middle.

Papa and Mama became unhappy. They talked in low voices late into

Curtis Williams and Mona Whitt Williams.

the night. We could hear their voices from their bed in the sitting room but not what they were saying as we wondered in uneasiness while watching the squares of light from the headlights of passing cars move around the wall in our uncurtained room. Sometimes Mama wept and Papa would leap from the bed in anger, climb the stairs to the room above us, and sleep on the straw mattress that lay on the floor there.

Then, one evening, he reported that he had told McDormin that he wanted $40.00 a month for his work. McDormin had been unwilling to increase his pay then but thought an increase might be possible the following year if crops did well. Papa became angry and gave notice that he would quit at the end of the month and go back to Kentucky.

We began to make preparations. Mama sold her setting hens and biddies to Aunt Sarah. We spent much time packing up our furniture again, and stuffing into boxes the clothing that we would not be wearing on our return trip. Papa and Mama quarreled a great deal, each, it seemed, pleased to be going back home but wanting to blame the other for the decision to return.

The Ganodes were sorry that we were leaving. The little girl's mother brought a cake to us the day before we left and stayed to help Mama. The little girl invited us over to play with her while things were being packed. The grandfather talked with us. He asked how we had liked living in Ohio. At the end of the conversation he told me that I would come back when I was a man and live in Ohio. That night after supper the Ganodes came and sat with Papa and Mama on the little porch while we played base in the yard. The honey locusts were in full leaf then.

The next morning Papa and Gib Beers loaded our furniture and belongings in a wagon and took them to the station. Then they returned and we climbed into the wagon to ride to Aunt Sarah's for our last night in Ohio. The Ganode cabin was snuggled darkly into a growth of fruit trees and shrubbery. We saw no one as we passed. The Custer house gleamed brightly in the morning sun, no occupant visible. In the Quaker woman's yard the little mound, green all the way to the top, was bathed with a heavy dew, but the door of her little square house was closed.

It was playtime when we passed the school in Selma. There must have been a hundred laughing and yelling children playing in the yard, with three or four young women dressed in long dark skirts and light blouses scattered among them, their teachers, Mama said. We watched the children at play and turned in the wagon and looked back at them after we had passed. No one seemed to take note of our passing, not even the teachers.

When we arrived at Aunt Sarah's, Papa and Gib unloaded what we would not be carrying with us back to Kentucky, a coop with setting hens in it, and a cardboard box with holes punched in it, in which there were twenty-five or thirty cheeping biddies which Aunt Sarah had agreed to buy along with their mothers. Then Gib bade us goodbye and drove back toward Selma. Papa walked across the fields to see how well Uncle Willie was coming along with his plowing.

Mama, who seemed tired and unhappy, sat on the little porch while Aunt Sarah and Gretta Mae worked in the kitchen, the door to the porch open so they could talk with Mama. We rode Ruth Evelyn's tricycle on the walk, romped in the yard, and played choo-choo train along the fence beside the grove of tall trees between Aunt Sarah's house and the Butcher place.

We were permitted to explore in the barnlot, since the spring winds had dried up the mud and the muck, but were forbidden to climb to the barn loft. Swinging the iron gate open and closing it again was so much fun that we made a game of it and were taking turns when Mama scolded us. Electric lights fascinated us. The lighted bulb in the eave of the barn roof, one of the first things about the barn to attract our attention two months earlier, was still burning. Aunt Sarah had said that it burned all the time, day and night. We wondered how such was possible.

That evening we sat and waited for supper to be ready in the little living room with the huge stove, now without a fire, the library table with the big legs, the unlighted fat lamp with the pretty globe, and the black sofa with the shiny tacks holding the upholstery. Uncle Willie, reclining on the sofa, which creaked when he moved, teased us and talked playfully to us while Papa sat in silence. After supper, Uncle Willie built in the big stove a small fire which flickered behind the isinglass panels. It was getting chilly outside, he said, and we might have a light frost again that night. After the passenger train to Columbus passed, we prepared for bed.

The next morning we rushed around to get ourselves ready for Uncle Willie to take us to the station in South Charleston. There was a light frost. As we turned from his lane down the pike we looked back at his newly painted little house bright in the sunlight, the white barn with its eave light still shining, the Butcher house through the leafy branches of the giant trees. I thought I might be seeing all of that again after I was a man.

The train to Ironton was crowded. Mama sat next to a window and held on her lap her basket, in which she carried some fruit and sandwiches made of light bread that Gretta Mae had fixed for us. Papa sat next to the aisle. We sat, three in a row, in the seat opposite them. After the conductor checked our tickets, Papa got up and went to another part of the train.

The trip was long and tiring. We went often to the water fountain, from which we drew water into little envelopes we could pull from a container, and we knew about toilets this time.

The little towns were half hidden by green trees fully leafed out. We could see men and boys working in fields and cattle grazing in green pastures. In the hills of southern Ohio the train passed through long stretches of dense forest and along a track that seemed much of the time halfway up the sides of hills that slanted into deep, forested valleys.

Mama wept silently much of the morning. Papa would return to his seat and sit in a sullen mood for a little while and then go to another part of the train. Once, when the train was going around a curve, I could see the last coach across the curve. Papa, his black Stetson hat pulled over his eyes, was standing with other men in the vestibule.

At Ironton we rushed from the station to the trolley line and caught a waiting car to Coalgrove. The tree-lined Ohio River was full and broad with rippling muddy water, and the green hills on the Kentucky side were bright with a sunlit sky beyond. A boat was waiting at the dock in Coalgrove. We went inside and sat near windows that would give us a good view of the Ohio shore. We were delighted by the waves that separated behind the boat as it made its way to the dock in Ashland.

Papa herded us along to the old railroad station in Ashland, expressing his hope, as he struggled with a suitcase and a pasteboard box, that we could make it to the station in time to get the late afternoon train to Hitchens. The train was loading when we arrived. Papa left us standing on the platform while he rushed into the depot to buy tickets for us. We were the last passengers to board the train, which pulled out with a jerk before we found seats, this time not all together but fairly close to one another.

The coach was warm. All windows were closed as we came through the tunnel west of Ashland. The sun, still high in the sky, was almost in front of us as the train rolled down the hollow below the mouth of the tunnel. Trees were in full leaf, growth along the little streams was lush, clumps of sumac rose in the pasture fields, blackberry vines were matted masses of green, and brilliant mayapple patches carpeted flats in the forest and the pasture fields. We were in Kentucky. Spring was more advanced here than it was at Selma.

Meadows were half-grown. Daisies by the thousands danced beside cow paths in pasture fields. Barnlots were overgrown with knee-high horse weeds so thick that each lot looked as if it were covered with a solid green carpet.

Every house we saw had close by a garden with patches of potatoes looking big enough to gravel, rows of onions standing at attention, pale pea vines hardly able to hold themselves upright, beds of leaf lettuce and mustard, corn hand high and waving like flags, bean vines dark and sturdy, a half-dozen or so rich and profuse rhubarb plants, and a patch of thorny gooseberry briars. Except that these lay on either side of the railroad track near Cannonsburg, Princess, and Denton, they could as easily have been scattered up and down Caines Creek.

Occasionally a housewife in tie-around apron and sunbonnet would stand by her hoe in her bean patch to watch the train pass. Cattle grazing in the pastures ignored the train but mules and horses hitched to wagons standing near stores would lift their ears straight up and watch us go by.

Soon the conductor came through and called "Hitchens! Hitchens!" We looked ahead and saw the row of smokestacks for the brick plant, the village where the E.K. Railroad crossed the C&O, and, far up the hollow beyond, the little station between the tracks. The train stopped briefly, the conductor hurrying everybody along. As many as ten or twelve left the train, three or four climbed aboard, the conductor waved to the engineer, and the train hurried on toward Lexington. We went into the little depot and stood while Papa asked about the E.K. schedule to Webbville. The afternoon train had already run. The next one would go at 8 o'clock the following morning.

We stood near the door while Papa talked with the ticket agent. Following the conversation, Papa asked us to sit and wait while he found a place for us to spend the night. We sat down on the long seats with curved backs. Others were sitting in the waiting room, apparently local residents who had come to see the train pass through. Some of those who sat with us had ridden on the train with us. Others who had dismounted were leaving with people who had come to meet them.

We could see people sitting in the little restaurant across the gravel court from the depot. Windows of both the depot and the restaurant were open, for the afternoon was warm, and we could hear animated conversation.

After fifteen or twenty minutes had passed, Papa returned to say that he had found room for us at the hotel at the foot of the bank directly across the railroad track from the depot. We crossed the track and walked down a steep path to the porch of the hotel, a two-story farmhouse that had been converted into a boarding-rooming house that the operators chose to call a hotel. Several people were sitting in chairs on the porch, among them Grampa's cousin, who had run away with his brother's "woman" before we left Kentucky but who was going back home without her. He had arrived earlier in the day on a train from Lexington. We did not ask about the woman.

We were shown where we would sleep on the second floor. Ralph and I would sleep on a cot in the hall and Papa and Mama and Mabel would sleep in a room with two beds in it, the other bed to be occupied by a middle-aged couple who would also be going to Webbville the following morning. We placed our things in the room and returned to the porch to sit with other guests until supper was ready.

We used an outside privy, washed for supper in basins on a bench near the dining room door, dried with sack towels, and combed our hair before a mirror on the wall. The hotel had no running water.

After a boarding-house supper, which people ate family style, similar to the dinners we had on Caines Creek, we sat on the porch again and grownups talked. Mabel, Ralph, and I, the only children at the hotel, were permitted to walk up the dirt road that went past the front of the hotel to the wholesale company in a building covered with new-looking metal siding that had been pressed to look like concrete blocks. The building was closed. Then we walked past the hotel in the other direction for a way, marveling at the wooden bridges leading from the road across the little stream, then dry, to the yards of the little houses that stood in a row between the stream and the railroad track. The little houses were well kept. Yards were smooth and green behind fences with gates at the ends of the bridges. Porches had painted floors, and some had banisters with flower boxes sitting on them. In the swing on one porch a man was bending over a ledger on his lap similar to ledgers in which merchants kept accounts. He did not look up at us. We saw no children.

Back on the porch of the hotel we listened to people talk, Papa participating in lively fashion and laughing a great deal. Mama sat silently in a cane-bottom chair near a porch post. Twilight came, bringing gnats and mosquitoes to plague us. When we began to nod, Mama went up to bed with us. The talking on the porch soon lulled me to sleep, but people coming up the stairs woke me with their talk in the hallway before they went to their own beds. Once, after a freight train roared through the little valley, I lay awake for a time and remembered Ohio while listening to noisy sleepers pick up again their deep snores like bumblebees in a jug.

We were up and dressed shortly after daylight, waiting turns shyly for our visit to the privy and using the wash basins on the bench two and three at a time. Breakfast consisted of thick bacon, big biscuits, creamed gravy, syrup, coffee for grownups, and milk for those who preferred it.

We were at the depot and waiting for the E.K. train before 8 o'clock, when it arrived. It had lost, by comparison, much of the grandeur we had seen in it two months earlier. The coach was not crowded, and no more than seven or eight boarded it at Hitchens.

Another view of the John Hamey Boggs and Nancy Griffith home, then the Steve and Lou Boggs Liming home. John and Nancy lived first in the upper cabin and then as the family grew they developed the rest of the property including the lower cabin, the wrap-around porch, the bedrooms on the ends of the porch, on this end a storage room for canned goods, and on the other end the loom room.

The track ran through meadows, plowed fields in which rows of new corn were pale green ribbons, and bottom lands with vivid green crops of young oats and wheat no more than knee high. From the bridges that looked like frames of flat steel as we approached them, we could see the clear water of low streams, meandering among sand bars, elder bushes with lush leaves sparkling with dew, slender willows with lacy leaves. Occasionally farm boys straightened up from their work to watch the train pass. But at Willard, where some of the passengers left the train, people stood on porches to see the train pass and a crowd had gathered at the depot. The engine was reversed on the turntable, received water from a huge tank mounted on poles, and backed the train on to Webbville, about three miles beyond Willard.

One of our uncles was waiting in Grampa's wagon at the depot. We did not go into the station. A part of our furniture had not yet arrived, but coops of hens and old Boss in his crate were there. Our cookstove and some other heavy pieces would not arrive for a few more days.

All of us climbed into the farm wagon. Papa, Mama, and my uncle sat on the seat and we sat in hay on the wagon bed. Along the road up Little Fork we saw families at work in their fields, some plowing, some hoeing, some

Detached kitchen at the home of Steve and Lou Boggs Liming. "[The home itself also] had a big kitchen on one end and a dining room on the other and porch along the front. During my boyhood there was a walk made of wood at the same elevation as the porch floors that connected the two houses"— Cratis Williams.

setting out plants. Vegetation was lush, even though the road was dry and hard and the streams were low.

We walked across Cherokee Hill, the road shaded with hickory and oak trees. The clay ruts were deep and rough, and the wagon bounced from side to side. At the foot of the hill we climbed into the wagon again and rode past places we remembered, the Jesse Young home, Sam Houck's Store, the Hylton home, John Cooper's white house on the hill, Sam Butler's, Uncle Dave Boggs's home among the pleasant shade trees. We met few people, for it was work season. Men were in the fields. Women in sunbonnets and wearing long-tailed tie-around aprons were bent over vegetables in prospering gardens.

At the foot of the Lick Creek Hill we left the wagon again and followed paths through the woods. We reached Uncle Steve's store long before the wagon did.

As we looked down from the top of the steep hill near the store, we could see Uncle Steve and Aunt Lou's place below us, the place where our grandmother was born and had grown up. The sight of the weathered and ancient buildings comforted us. The sheep barn, the hog barn, the dark log smokehouse near the well with a sweep, the old saddle-bags log house with long wide porches, the summer kitchen with its metal roof painted black, the rived paling fence around the big garden, the store building, the long barn beside the road with a log crib close by, and the profusion of apple, plum, and peach trees growing everywhere looked like prosperity to us.

We rushed ahead of Mama into the store. Two or three customers lounged about. Uncle Steve was behind his counter, his blue eyes twinkling and his red mustache twitching.

"And the very next day the cat came back," we sang. He laughed.

We had come back to Kentucky to stay.

Our Hardest Summer

The summer of 1920 was our hardest summer. After our return from Ohio we visited among relatives for a few days

Steve Liming and "Aunt Lou" Boggs Liming, January 3, 1921. (Aunt Lou was the daughter of John Hamey Boggs and sister of Martha Boggs Williams, first wife of David O. Williams, and mother of Curt Williams.)

while our furniture was being hauled from Webbville and set up again in our house, which had to be scrubbed and cleaned. Papa spent three or four days cutting the weeds that had grown in the yard, beside the lane, in the chicken lot, and around the barn and cribs. He carried in from the wood-lots poles which he cut into a pile of stove wood that would last us for a while.

Mama was unable to help with preparations. She and Papa quarreled much of the time. Before we had everything ready for moving into our house again, Papa decided that he would leave us to fend for ourselves while he found a job at "public works," for it was really too late to plant crops, he had no mules for plowing and not enough money to buy a team, and he was reluctant to borrow mules from Grampa, who seemed sullen and unhappy that we had returned from Ohio.

Some of our furniture, including our cook stove, had not been brought from Webbville when Papa left for Columbus, Ohio, to find work. Grampa agreed to send a team and wagon for the remainder of our furniture as soon as the corn was "out of the first weeds."

After Papa left, Mama, beginning to feel unwelcome at Grampa Williams's, went to visit with her father and mother until the rest of the furniture arrived. Feeling even less welcome in her parents' home, she decided to take us into our own house and cook in the fireplace until the stove arrived. But my uncles were able to go for the furniture and had set the stove up by the time we were in the house.

Papa had left some money with Mama, enough to buy meal and flour, sugar, and other absolute necessities. We had brought back from Ohio the salt-cured pork, dried beans, and home-canned fruit we had not used. Grampa Williams would let us have a gallon of milk a day, and we could have all of the potatoes he had planted in our garden, a flourishing patch that would soon have potatoes big enough to gravel. We had brought back a few hens and a rooster, but Mama decided that, except for the bran from meal and such kitchen scraps as the dog would not eat, the chickens could scratch for themselves.

Our house had become damp and musty during our absence, and many families of mice had moved in and were denning between the logs of our main room. The first night they would race behind the loose paper on the wall and then come out by the dozens to romp across the floor. At daylight Mama saw what she thought might have been as many as forty or fifty chasing one another in the middle of the floor. After we had eaten breakfast, she gave me fifteen cents and sent me to Uncle Steve's store for three mousetraps. That night we baited the traps with moist biscuit and set them, one near the hearth and the others in the front corners of the room. Soon after the kerosene lamp had been blown out, the traps began to spring. Mama would light the lamp again and I would empty and reset the traps. We had caught twelve or fifteen when we decided to go to sleep. By the end of the second day we had caught thirty-one mice and continued to catch a few each night for a week or two.

Mama was so afraid that someone might come in on us at night that she nailed all of the windows shut and kept the ax leaning against the wall by her bed. We left all of the doors open all day long, but the rooms became hot and stuffy after we went to bed.

Soon after we had moved in, Mama received a letter from Papa. He had a job as an ore loader at Buckeye Steel Corporation in Columbus, a hard pick-and-shovel job that paid 35 cents an hour. He worked ten hours a day, five-and-a-half days a week and could work all day Saturday and Sunday, too, whenever he wanted to. He might decide to do that later, after he had become toughened for the work. He had a companion on the job, a pleasant and hard-working "Hunkie" who couldn't talk our kind of talk very well. The Hunkie was trying to earn money to bring his wife and children from the "Old Country." Other workers teased the Hunkie and played pranks on him, but he seemed to like it. Papa was rooming and boarding at Milt and Rose Caudill's for $4.50 a week. He enjoyed rooming at the Caudill's place, but wished Rose would put a square of cornbread in his lunch bucket instead of the two thin slices of light bread.

Papa enclosed a five-dollar bill and advised that we spend as little money as possible. If he could hold up to do so, he would work four or five months, save all the money he could, and come back prepared to buy a team of mules, a cow, two pigs, and feed enough to last until he had made a crop the following year. He would then be ahead and in a position not to have to depend on anybody else or go into debt for anything. He pinned at the top of the letter a disc of skin from a blister on his hand and scribbled a note by it that calluses were growing where the blisters had been.

Mama wept when she read the note scribbled by the piece of skin. Thereafter she referred often to how hard Papa was working and became more and more careful about spending money.

Our diet was inadequate and monotonous. Breakfast each morning consisted of big biscuits, gravy, bacon, white syrup, and milk. For dinner we had cornbread and soup beans seasoned with side meat and fruit cobbler for dessert. Our supper was cornbread and milk. In a few days we began to have heartburn, for which we took bicarbonate of soda.

Mama, who had become fat and heavy, craved green things. Noticing a new growth of plantain in the yard beside the lane to the barn, she gave me a broken steel table knife and asked me to gather a dishpan full of the "sallet," which she washed carefully, seasoned with fatback, and cooked slowly. It was so good and added so much to our dinner that we continued to eat it each day until it grew so leathery and tough about the first of July that we could not chew it.

When the potatoes in the garden became big enough to gravel, we added boiled new potatoes and potato soup to our dinner. Mama sent me once to search for old field lettuce in the corners of a rail fence beside the meadow across the creek. What I was able to find she cut up and "killed" with hot bacon drippings. It was delicious with potato soup.

No one offered us anything from the gardens that were beginning to produce lettuce, green onions, and radishes. Our grandparents did not come to visit with us and bring things from their gardens. When we went in the late afternoon to Grampa Williams's for the gallon of milk Grandma had ready for us, we would raid the safe in her kitchen like hungry animals, but one day the kitchen door was locked and our two half-gallon jars of milk were waiting for us on the steps. Our aunt, who was churning in the yard, stared at the hillside across the valley while we shook the door a time or two to make doubly certain that it was locked. Fearing that we had done something wrong, we did not report to our mother that we had been locked out of the kitchen at Grampa's.

Trees were loaded with fruit. A "sarvice" tree across the creek by the pasture field was burdened with a heavy crop of luscious berries. The Gambill girls from the next farm came often to help us pick "services," which we ate as we picked until we were full. Then we would gather a quart can full for Mama. We had no cherry trees, but the Gambill girls invited us to come to their house and pick cherries from two trees in their yard.

One day in June the wife of one of my father's cousins, on her way home from the post office, stopped her horse by our gate to ask Mama how she was getting along. At the end of her conversation, she asked whether our green beans had "come on" yet. When Mama told her that we had moved back from Ohio too late to plant anything, she said she and her boys had picked a pile of the finest green beans she had ever grown and that Mama could have a mess of them if she would send one of us around for it in the morning.

We were so eager to have a mess of green beans that Mama gave my brother and me a pillowcase and sent us off as soon as we had eaten breakfast to get them so she would have time to cook them for dinner. She instructed us to be sure to ask how much she owed for the beans, just for manner's sake, but recalled that the woman had offered them as if she meant to give them to us. The cousin and his family lived in a log cabin up in a hollow. We arrived just as they were getting up. The bed in which one of the boys slept had the quilt pulled back across the foot so the sheet and straw mattress could dry, for he had all but washed the whole bed away. The stench, almost unbearable, was worse than that of a chamber pot. But resting on a paper on the hearth was a pile of beautiful green beans. We were invited to take a mess of them. After we had filled the pillow case about half full, I told the woman that Mama had said for us to ask what the price would be and that she would have the money ready for her when she passed our house again. The woman replied that 35 cents ought to be enough for them, she reckoned.

Mama was so angry when we told her the woman wanted 35 cents for the beans that she threatened to send them back to her. But when she opened the pillow case and saw the plump beans, all of a size, and smelled their appetizing odor, she decided they were worth 35 cents but added that it was shabby of the woman to pretend to be giving us a mess of beans and then charge us for them.

We sat together on the porch and helped Mama string and break the beans. She prepared them for dinner, along with boiled new potatoes, plantain, and cornbread. Hungry for green things, all of us stuffed ourselves. I ate so many beans that I foundered myself and was sick for two days. Even the thought of green beans for weeks afterwards made me retch, and I was not able to eat green beans again for nine or ten years.

Raspberries grew along fence rows and dewberries were abundant. I picked raspberries in a quart tin cup to have with cream and sugar and sharp dewberries for cobblers, which we sweetened with molasses in order to save sugar. But we were hungry much of the time. The hens, scratching for themselves, laid few eggs, and the only meat we had was salt pork for breakfast and seasoning.

Mama found time to make my brother and me new overalls and jackets from the striped denim Papa had bought before we left Ohio. With my conductor's cap with a patent leather bill and my engineer's overalls and jacket, I felt very much like a railroad man, but we needed new shirts. The ones we had were faded and worn, but Mama thought they would do for a while longer.

One day we noticed a pile of dried mayapple root at Uncle Steve's store. We asked Uncle Steve what it was, how much he paid a pound for it, and how it was prepared for the market. That year he was paying fifteen cents a pound in trade for it. We would need to wash it well and let it dry in the sun until it was hard and brittle. We reported to Mama that we could sell Uncle Steve mayapple root for cloth for new shirts.

Equipped with buckets, an "eye" hoe that kept wanting to turn on the handle, and a much worn and very dull gooseneck hoe, we dug mayapple root for days, washed it clean in the creek, and spread it on the shake roof of the coal house to dry, taking it in each night to protect it from the dew. We were disappointed that it was so much lighter after it had dried than it was when we dug it, but we were pleased that we had enough mayapple root in our first load delivered to the store to buy the cloth Mama needed to make each of us a shirt. We chose white percale with a pink stripe, which Mama made into shirts with collars that had vertical stripes, like those young men were wearing then.

Enjoying financial independence, my brother and I continued to dig all of the patches of mayapple we could find. Each of us bought a pocket knife with a celluloid handle, a jimmy hat with a shoestring for a band, red boxes of big gingerbread cookies with hard icing, candy, sugar for Mama to use in baking cakes, and an occasional can of salmon which Mama made into delicious fishcakes for breakfast.

One day about the middle of June Mama told us that Tabitha Ramey, one of the older daughters of Jim and Liz, who lived up the other fork of the branch on which Grandpa and Granny Whitt lived, was coming to stay with us for a while and help her with the cooking and housekeeping, for she had reached the place that she was not able to do much. Tabitha, a strong, healthy young woman, appeared, all dressed up in a white blouse and black skirt and carrying a little bundle under her arm. A quiet person with a pleasant smile, Byth, as we called her, set about at once to get things in order. She drew water from the well, cooked, washed dishes, made up beds, and swept the floors. One morning she put out a big washing, carrying water from the creek for the black pot over a firepit. Not wanting to use our stove wood for heating wash water, Mama had us gather driftwood along the creek and bring in dead limbs that had fallen off trees in the woodlots for Byth to break up with the ax. That afternoon Byth did the ironing. Another morning she heated water and scrubbed our floors with hot water and lye soap and then rinsed them clean with cold water from the well. My brother and I had scraped from a soft stone near the church house the white sand she sprinkled over the floor. Next morning she swept up the sand, leaving the wood white and smooth, and set pots of pennyrile, catnip, and horsemint on the hearth to make the house smell sweet and fresh.

One afternoon Mama sent us early to Grampa's for our milk and requested that we ask my uncle Estill, only four years older than I, to come back with us to spend the night. A happy, lively chap, Estill romped with us in the yard, while Mama sat in a chair in the shade and Byth prepared supper. We ate earlier than usual and went to bed early, Estill and I sleeping together in a bed in the "back room." Sometime after we were sound asleep, Byth, with a lighted lamp in her hand, came in and woke us up. She asked us to get up and go get Grandma and Aunt Emily as quickly as we could and to ask Grandma to call Dr. Gambill by telephone to come. Mama was sick.

Our heads heavy with sleep, Estill and I struck out down the dusty road to Grampa's house. The moon was shining and a heavy dew had moistened the dust, which was soft and cool to our bare feet. Estill told me that Mama was about to have a baby. I was shocked. Although I was nine years old and had learned much from older boys about what causes babies and where they come from and that doctors do not really bring them in their little black bags and they do not really arrive in the mail from Sears, Roebuck, it had not occurred to me that Mama's sickness, heavy breasts, and big belly meant that she was going to have a baby. Grandma responded at once to our call. She came to the door and told us she would call the doctor and Aunt Emily, change her clothes, and go on to be with Mama. We should hurry on through the corn to get Aunt Emily, who would be ready and waiting for us when we got there, and walk back with her. We could hear Grampa snoring.

The corn was knee high. When we touched the blades, the cold dew rolled off on our bare legs and overalls. By the time we arrived at Aunt Emily's we were quite wet and our feet were cold.

Aunt Emily, her bonnet in place, a shawl around her shoulders, and her tie-around white apron hanging to her toes, was waiting for us at the gate.

On the way back we walked in front through the corn to knock the dew off so Aunt Emily would not get wet. Aunt Emily, who held her dress and apron up in front of her, could not walk as fast as we did. It took a long time for us to get back home. Byth had built a fire in the kitchen stove and pots of water on it were beginning to boil. We stood with Aunt Emily by the stove to warm from the chill and to let our clothing dry while the boiling pots sang comfortingly.

Soon we heard the doctor's horse thundering across the bridge at the end of our lane. Grandma told Estill and me to go with the doctor to our barn, help him put his horse in a stable, and then go back to Grampa's to spend the rest of the night. But we returned with the doctor to the kitchen, where Byth was attending to the fire and the pots of boiling water. The doctor called for a pan of warm water, removed his coat, and soaped and washed his hands several times. When we started to go along with the doctor into the living room, where Grandma and Aunt Emily were taking care of Mama, Grandma stopped us and hurried us out of the house, ignoring Estill's protests that we were cold and wanted to wait until we had become warm before we left. We could hear Mama crying and moaning as we left the house.

The warm stove and steam from the boiling water had knocked off some of our chill. The cool night air and dampness soon penetrated our thin shirts and left us shivering. Estill said we would warm up soon if we should trot, so we ran a short distance when we reached the straight level stretch in the road beside the meadow across the creek from our house.

We crept so quietly into the bedroom beside the stairwell that we did not disturb Grampa, who continued to snore rhythmically. The bed was cold. Our teeth chattered, Estill hugged me to him, my cold back pressed closely against him. I could feel his warm breath on my shoulders. When I woke up later, I was beginning to perspire. I moved closer to the edge of the bed and we slept until Grandma woke us up for breakfast.

The doctor had brought a baby, Grandma told us. It was a little girl with black hair. Mama had named it Ruth Evelyn, for Aunt Sarah's little granddaughter whose tricycle we had ridden while we were in Ohio. The doctor was still there when Grandma had left to be home in time to milk and cook breakfast for Grandpa. Byth was getting breakfast for the doctor when she left.

We wanted to hurry home to see the baby and be there when the doctor left. Grandma told us we could go after the doctor had passed along. In the meantime we drove the cows across the creek to the pasture, carried the kitchen slop to the hogs in their dry pen beside the barnlot, and dipped up some water for them from a spring at the roots of a beech tree in the barnlot.

Aunt Emily had arrived by the time we got back to the house. She reported that Mama and the baby were asleep when she had left and that the doctor, who had said both were doing fine, was eating the good breakfast Byth had cooked for him. Aunt Emily hurried on, trippingly behind the hem of her long dress, which she held up in front of her as she walked. She needed to help the girls cook breakfast for Uncle Jake and the boys, who would be working in the corn, she said.

An hour later the doctor passed, his bay horse, arching its neck as its fine tail trailed behind, moving along smoothly in a comfortable running walk. Grandma told us we could go see the baby, but we must be quiet and wait if we should find that Mama and she were still sleeping. She told Estill to bring in and cut some firewood and split kindling for Byth and to carry water from the creek for her for the black wash pot, for she would need to put out a washing and had more to do than she could get done, unless she got some help.

We hurried on. The sun was shining, having burned away the morning mist and dried most of the dew. The birds were singing. We could hear in the distance voices of men shouting at their mules as they plowed corn. It was a beautiful day for having a little sister.

Mama, looking weak and tired, sat on the edge of her bed. She was eating potato soup into which Byth had crumbled a biscuit. Beside her lay the new baby asleep. No bigger than a doll, she had a dark red face and fine black hair that looked as if it had been washed in oil. I wanted to know the color of the baby's eyes, but Mama said she had not yet opened her eyes and might not open them for two or three days yet. A baby's eyes look blue at first, Mama said. It might be a week before we could tell the real color of her eyes.

Estill and I carried poles and driftwood which Estill hacked into lengths for the fire under the wash pot. We then dipped from the shallow creek water into buckets and filled the pot and a tub on a low platform. Estill then hurried home to help Grampa hoe corn.

Mama and the baby slept most of the time. We were urged to be very quiet and to play in the driveway between the cribs and at the barn. We could see Byth as she rubbed clothing on a washboard in the tub and hung it on the palings around the yard to dry in the sun and we could smell the smoke from the low-burning fire under the black pot. After all of the white things had been washed and hung out, Byth put the colored clothing in the black pot to soak while she prepared dinner.

When the dinner was ready, Byth walked out to the barn to tell us that Mama and the baby were sleeping and that we were to be very quiet while we ate. Byth ate with us the dinner of hot cornbread, warmed-over beans, canned apples, and milk. We whispered when we talked. Mama woke up before we had finished eating dinner. The baby slept on. While Mama sat on the side of the bed and ate milk and bread, we were permitted to come quietly to the bed and look at the sleeping baby with her dark red face and silken black hair.

We were herded back toward the barn while Byth cleared away the dishes and continued with the washing. Late that afternoon Mama sat a little while in the rocking chair and held the baby, like a little doll, in her arms. We were permitted to visit with her quietly. The baby had not yet opened its eyes.

Three or four days later Mama was up and doing some of the work. The baby had opened its eyes. They were a deep blue, but Mama told us that all babies have blue eyes at first and that we would not know for a few days whether the eyes would be blue or brown. By the time Byth was leaving a week after the baby's birth, Mama was able to do the cooking again and the baby's eyes were blue. We were permitted to hold her for a few minutes when we sat firmly in chairs. We crooned and talked baby talk but the baby ignored us. Once Mabel thought she was smiling, but when she began to cry Mama explained that

Mona Whitt Williams and daughter Ruth.

babies do not smile when they are very young, and that what appears to be a smile is almost certain to be a colic pain.

Mama wrote a letter to Papa as soon as she was able to do so. He responded immediately, and sent money for Mama to pay Dr. Gambill for his services. He was then working every other weekend, sometimes twelve hours a day. He planned to come home for four or five days in July and then return to work until frosts came. He planned to buy a milk cow for us when he came home, if he could find a good one.

The summer of 1920 was a heavy fruit summer. Limbs on the yellow cling peach tree by our chimney were bowed with delicious peaches. We had sliced peaches with sweetened cream over them, peach cobblers and pies, and Mama canned some of them and prepared a few jars of preserves. Apples lay in heaps under the trees. We had fried apples for breakfast and apple pies and cobblers after the peaches were gone. Mama canned apples, made apple butter and jelly, and dried some for stack cakes when winter came.

Papa came to visit us in July during the blackberry season. Our pastures were not being grazed that summer. Vines in the fields were loaded with plump juicy berries. Papa picked enough for Mama to can eighteen gallons. He then brought in loads of berries for jam, which was made in the black pot over the fire pit in the wood yard, but the jam, sweetened with sorghum molasses, was so stiff that we did not use much of it.

While he was home, Papa went squirrel hunting once or twice. We had our fill of squirrel and enjoyed squirrel gravy with biscuits for breakfast. While walking home from Webbville Papa had seen a beautiful little jersey cow that had come fresh in the spring. The owner said he was willing to sell the cow, which was giving about three gallons of rich milk a day. If we thought we could take care of her and Mama was willing to milk her, he would go back and buy her. She was as gentle as a pet, a tawny colored little cow with a black nose. Her name was Bess. He would buy chopped corn for us to feed her and we could tie her with a long rope to bushes at the end of the meadow and let her graze during the day. I would have to take her to the watering place each morning before I tied her to a bush and each evening before I brought her to the barn, he charged.

Bess was a lovely cow. She was a little creature with a clean, smooth coat, intelligent eyes, a soft black muzzle, and a moist nose. She smelled like fresh milk and her breath was sweet, like the odor of tender grass. She enjoyed being stroked and would accept wisps of grass from our hands. Taking care of her was fun.

Papa was especially fond of Ruth, by then old enough to smile and respond to attention. She would smile her appreciation when Papa sang little ditties to her as he held her in his arms. He found at the barn a packing box about a foot high, four or five feet long, and two feet wide that he smoothed and brought to the house for a crib. Later, he said, it would also be a good play-pen.

Papa did not visit much with neighbors and kinfolk while he was home. Our relatives did not come to see him. He had visited among relatives who had gone to live in Columbus only occasionally. Mama thought he had learned that his kinfolk did not think as much of him as he had thought they did before we had gone to Ohio to live and then returned to Kentucky. She had decided that her kinfolk did not think as much of her as she had thought they did before the Ohio experience. She had not wanted to ask any of her own family or Papa's to stay with her when Ruth was born, and she had been well pleased with Byth, whose quiet ways, industry, and dependability she had liked. Both Papa and Mama began saying that they wanted to be sufficiently independent not to need to call on kinfolks for help or ask for favors.

At mealtime and in the evenings Papa told us about the hard work he was doing and the relationships with his boss and fellow workers he was enjoying. He told many anecdotes about the likable Hunkie who worked with him and conversations he had with Milt and Rose Caudill, in whose home he lived. Papa was thin and tough. He liked to exhibit his hardened hands and point out the thick calluses he had developed in handling a shovel. If he should be able to work until the end of September he would have the money needed to buy a span of mules, a hog or two, some white-faced Herefords, grass seed for rebuilding the pastures, and wire for fencing, and there would be some left over for a bank account. He wanted to be able to pay for what we needed without having to go into debt or borrow. He would never ask any of his kinfolks or Mama's to sign a note for him, and he did not intend to sign notes for any of them.

Papa and Mama did not quarrel during the week he was home. He liked Ruth, who enjoyed having him hold her. He would sit in the kitchen with Ruth on his knee and sing little ditties to her while Mama cooked breakfast. Ruth would smile for him.

Before he returned to Columbus, Papa cut down some of the sycamores and willows that grew beside the creek and chopped them into stove wood. When he was ready to leave, we had a great pile of it in the wood yard, enough to last all winter, he said. My brother and I could find dry poles in the woods, bring them in on our backs, and hack and split them for kindling, for the new stove wood would not burn readily until it had seasoned. We would not be needing any coal for the fireplace before he would be back about the beginning of October. If there should be a few cool evenings in September we could burn enough stove wood in the grate to knock the chill off the air and keep the baby from taking a cold.

One day while he was at home Papa walked down to Blaine and deposited some of his money in the bank there, but he established his account in his name only. He came back with a new set of school books, a tablet, and a pencil for each of us. My sister and I were in the same grade and could have used the same books, but he thought we should have our own.

He got up early enough one morning to walk to Webbville, eleven miles away, in time to catch the morning train to Hitchens. We could hear Mama cooking breakfast and Papa crooning to Ruth, but he slipped away before we got up.

We had more to eat after Papa's visit than we had had before. Mama could buy more at the store. We had butter for our biscuits and cream to pour over fruit cobblers. There was more rich, creamy fresh milk than we could use. What soured we poured into a trough for the chickens.

The summer had been a hard one for us. We had not eaten well. There were few eggs and little meat. Cornbread, potatoes, and soup beans had been our staples, but we had milk to drink and all of the berries, peaches, and apples we wanted.

It had been a marvelous summer for playing. As there had been little work for us to do and Mama had kept us out of the house during the day so she and the baby could rest, we had had time to plan and develop many projects. We discovered a bank of clay that was almost as good as modeling clay. We made tiny bricks and built cities with them. We modeled menageries of farm animals and tiny people. We built railroads with locomotives modeled from clay that we could push along over them. We constructed flutter mills and built water systems with hollow reeds. Other children came to play with us on Saturdays and Sundays.

Mama dressed us in our best and took us to the annual sacrament meeting at the church on the last Sunday in July. She looked bright and happy as she held her pretty baby, no bigger than a doll, on her lap. Mabel's hair was plaited and dressed with ribbons. Ralph and I were proud of our new shirts with pink stripes and our new striped denim overalls.

School started next day. There might have been as many as 75 children in the school that year. Little children were sent out to play under the supervision of older girls when fourth grade classes began, and we had a long noon hour. By the end of the week we felt that summer was over. It had been a hard one for us, but we no longer felt poor, we were no longer hungry, and we were happy.

Appalachian Folkways: At Play

Throughout the years, as the weather permitted, there were opportunities to engage in adventure and explorations in the fields and forests and along the streams. We learned to whittle "figure 4" triggers for setting "deadfall" traps and trapped wild animals, catching more often than we wanted to rats and fodder mice instead of skunks and 'possums whose pelts we sold to our father. We tried our skills with rabbit boxes but caught more mice and ground squirrels than rabbits. Occasionally we would accompany our father on a 'possum hunt with dogs, lanterns, flashlights, and sacks. We went fishing with hooks and lines in the spring when the creek was full or with sledge hammer and mattock when the creek was frozen over in the winter. When we saw a fish under the ice, we struck the ice with the sledge hammer to kill the fish and picked a hole in the ice a few feet downstream to catch him as he floated down, his belly turned upward. We "gigged" bullfrogs in season and caught soft-shelled turtles all summer, the delicious white meat of which we "dressed" for our mother to cook. We went squirrel hunting and rabbit hunting with dogs and a single shot .22 rifle. When the dogs "holed" a rabbit or a groundhog, we twisted him out with a length of tough greenbrier that grew profusely in thickets and along fence rows, shaving away the barbs on one end with our pocketknives, which we kept razor sharp and well oiled, and which were as much a part of our being dressed as the very overalls we wore.

After the frosts came, our father began hunting 'possum and skunk with his dogs. He kept the animals in a room at the end of the chicken-house which had been strapped tightly and provided with a metal grill over the window. The animals had freedom to roam about within the room, which had in it roosting frames for the chickens that used it in the spring and summer months and nesting boxes attached to the walls. After school and on Saturdays my brother and I roamed over the hills in search of wild grapes, plums, and persimmons to feed the animals as a supplement to the mush that our father prepared for them each day and the meat scraps from the kitchen. Our adventures in the fields and woodlots in search of wild fruits led to exploration of cliffs and caves, abandoned "coal banks," hollow trees, and animal burrows under rocks. We found and stored heaps of chestnuts, hazelnuts, hickory nuts, butternuts, and black walnuts. Before the freezes came, we sampled haws, crab apples, wild, leathery skinned apples that grew on the trees that had come up from seeds scattered by the birds, trees that we identified as wild apple trees. In these ventures we scaled cliffs, climbed trees, and explored caves.

When cousins visited us, we invented games, often pairing off to fight Roman battles with "stickweeds," which we used as javelins, as we maneuvered our campaign over fields of broomsage and of hillside pastures dotted with thickets of sumac, which we called "shoemake," and sassafras, which we called "sassifac," and clumps of sawbriars intertwined with scrub oak and blackjack bushes.

Another battle game we played was "Colonials and Redcoats," which we played among cliffs in the forest, using for guns and rifles straight sticks gathered for the purpose. Since nobody wanted to be a Redcoat or a "Hayshunt" (Hessian), smaller and younger boys were usually manipulated into the British forces by trickery played in choosing up for "sides." Once the armies were established, the Colonials held their hands over their eyes while their general counted aloud to 100, during which time the Redcoats concealed themselves in groups of two or three among the bushes and behind rocks and trees. The Colonials then began their campaign for clearing the country of Redcoats. Shooting was done by aiming the "rifle" and shouting "bang," "pow," or "bum!" Those who "positioned" and shouted first won the engagement and took their antagonists as prisoners to prison areas established for that purpose. After all Redcoats were accounted for, the number of "prisoners" in each camp was determined and the side with the larger number was declared the victor. Being small and younger than many of my cousins, I was more often than not a Redcoat in these engagements but the Redcoats won many of the battles.

Chasing games were popular in late summer and early fall. Fox and hound, in which foxes were given time while someone counted aloud to disperse to the forests and thickets to hide, was a game that could continue for an hour or more. Hounds were required to bay as they searched for foxes, which could steal from tree to tree or cliff to cliff as they were pursued. When a hound saw a fox he increased the tempo of his baying as he broke into a chase of the fleeing fox. For a hound to "catch" a fox, it was necessary that he run faster than the fox and tag him on the shoulder in passing him. Skillful and sly foxes could leap aside, avoid being tagged, reverse positions, and "wind" the hound. At the end of the game, the number of foxes that had been caught was determined. If more had succeeded in evading the baying hounds than had been tagged, the foxes were declared the winners.

Adaptations of base were sometimes agreed upon and rotten apples, corncobs, dried horse manure, or snowballs were thrown in lieu of tagging, which was used when sisters and female cousins were included in the games.

Throwing contests were engaged in by both boys and girls. Throwing stones at posts, or over treetops, or at a circle inscribed on the face of a cliff or the side of a building developed accuracy and skill that enabled girls to compete successfully with boys. My sister Mabel was normally the winner of contests in throwing stones over treetops as well as "skipping" thin flat rocks across the surface of pools in the creek and ponds in the meadows, a contest which required that the flat rock be skipped completely across the body of water.

Mabel Williams, age 15.

In early spring when the grey lizards crawled upon fence posts along the pasture fields to sun themselves, we would go lizard hunting. Armed with pocket loads of small, rounded stones selected at the shallows in the creek, we would take turns throwing at lizards from a distance of ten or twelve feet. Again, my sister was most successful in these contests. In late summer, sleeping lizards were "snared" with green haystalks that had been made pliable and looped with a loose knot. Lizards sometimes slept with their heads above the tops of posts to which they clung. If one were quiet and adept at dropping the loop over the lizard's head, he could then jerk the haystraw suddenly and catch the lizard. More skill and patience were needed to get the loop behind the head of a lizard clinging to a post below the top.

We also made bows from hickory and ash limbs, which we strung with wire or cord, and arrows from sourwood and Indian arrowwood, which we tipped with points made by driving small nails through brass cartridge shells and winged with feathers selected from rooster wings and tails when chickens were killed for Sunday dinner. Although we shot arrows at lizards on posts, fish hovering lazily in sunbathed pools in the creek, occasionally at snakes lying on drifts along the streams, and rabbits hunched in meditation at the edge of a field, I do not recall that any arrow I ever shot struck its mark. We made crossbows occasionally, too, but they were even less accurate than our bows and arrows as hunting pieces. Later, we were permitted to make slingshots from forked sticks, rubber strips from innertubes (which we bartered for with boys fortunate enough to own such wealth), and tongues from old shoes. They were more reliable as hunting pieces than bows and crossbows.

Estill Boggs and Taylor Boggs.

Appalachian Folkways: Borning, Child Rearing and Family Life

The use of folk medicine, superstitious formulas, and elements of witchcraft has been especially pronounced in Appalachian culture with reference to childbearing and the care of infants and young children.

As soon as the young mother was aware of her pregnancy she began paying attention to those things that might in some way affect the child. Belief in "marking" babies was widespread. An expectant mother in a moment of great fright who smote her forehead with her hand was not surprised at the brown silhouette of a small hand on the forehead of her baby. Another, frightened by a red turtle flung into the path at her feet, fell backward with her hand on her forehead. Her son had a red turtle on his forehead. The mother who hungered for fresh strawberries understood why her newborn daughter had a cluster of pink strawberries plainly etched in the skin above her stomach. The mother who in midwinter had hungered maddeningly for a mess of sallet greens understood why the child born later could never seem to get his fill of "sallet" greens as long as he lived.

An expectant mother thought it important that she maintain a happy frame of mind during pregnancy to assure a happy baby. Distress and unhappiness would cause the baby to have colic, skin rashes, and a surly disposition. Thinking good thoughts, engaging in pleasant reveries, expressing highmindedness in conversation would assure a thoughtful, considerate child who might become a preacher or a teacher or a leader among his fellows. An expectant mother who kept herself occupied with artistic activities like piecing quilt blocks, or crocheting, or reading could assure an industrious child interested in school, or in perfecting artistic skills.

Shocks might cause a mother to lose her child. Witnessing a fight or being frightened by a dog or a snake or a stroke of lightning might affect the child if the mother carried it to birth. The child might quake in terror in the presence of anger, or retreat in fear before the most pleasant of dogs, or weave like a snake when he walked, or run and hide under a bed or in a closet at the approach of a thunderstorm.

In the Appalachian tradition gifts of baby things to a young mother were not offered. She prepared for the baby herself and tried to have ready ahead of time a little cap, which she often made herself, two or three long dresses, and a supply of diapers (called "didies" or "clouts" in Appalachia) which she often cut from the corners of worn-out sheets, tails of abandoned shirts, legs of overalls, or any other piece of cloth that had seen its best days.

Typically, the expectant mother continued to perform her share of work in the home until the pangs of labor began. Even in communities in which medical doctors lived many expectant mothers preferred the services of competent midwives, referred to generally as granny doctors, the medical doctor being called to the scene only if unanticipated problems developed. Helping the midwife was a capable older woman who had children of her own and who could, in emergencies, "catch" babies herself.

When the expectant mother felt the first pangs of labor, she dispatched men in her family to fetch the granny doctor and attendants, and children in the home were sent to live with grandparents or other relatives until the birthing party, referred to humorously by menfolk as the "granny racket," was over.

The granny doctor kept herself prepared for her vocation. Often with the help of grandsons, she would have gathered a store of herbs, roots, and barks considered useful, all washed clean, dried, and in "pokes" hanging along the wall of her smokehouse: boneset, wild ginger, golden seal (yellowroot), puccoon (bloodroot), ginseng, mullein, bark from the spruce, the elder, the cherry tree, the root of an elm, catnip, pennyrile, dog fennel, and other *materia medica* by which she set store.

An extra long white apron or two in her "reticule" and a clean meal poke filled with little bags of herbs swinging to her side saddle, she arrived as quickly as she could at the home to which she had been called, dismounted, put her old nag in the hands of the husband who had fetched her, and entered the home, bearing confidently her store of trusted herbs and remedies.

Other women who arrived ahead of her might have carried in loads of stove wood and buckets of water from the spring, built a roaring fire in the stove as well as the fireplace, and have pots of water steaming and waiting. Towels and rags might already have been boiled and dried carefully before the blazing fire by the time the midwife arrived.

The husband was sent away, sometimes to the corncrib or the barn to be close at hand if needed, or to the home of a relative living nearby.

The midwife washed and scrubbed her hands, covered her head with a clean cap, changed her apron, and began her ministrations.

She might have found that a sharp ax had already been placed under the bed of the expectant mother to cut the pain of childbirth and a Bible under the pillow to sustain faith during the agonies of labor.

Sometimes the midwife would consider such things as the phase of the moon or the signs of the zodiac in predicting how long labor might continue, but she set about at once to make the mother comfortable, to reassure her, and to prepare teas and concoctions that might be needed. If the mother suffered from gas pains in the stomach, she was given a bit of a ginseng root to chew. If she had a fever, a tea made by boiling dog fennel and pennyrile together was administered. Ginger tea was prepared for frequent consumption to ease the pains of childbirth. If it were feared that the blood had become thick because of dark and cold winter months, sassafras tea sweetened with a little honey was administered to thin the blood and bring blood pressure down, or if the mother bled easily or "wasted" at menstruation she was administered a tea brewed from elder bark and wild cherry bark to assure that she would not "waste" after childbirth. Peachtree bark tea was useful in checking either vomiting or diarrhea.

After the child was born those in attendance made certain that it looked first into the eyes of someone other than its mother, for the life of one who looks first into his mother's eyes is a trail of disaster. Occasionally, an infant is born with a veil over its head. This phenomenon portends greatness. Such a child, usually if not always a boy, is credited with depth of insight, extraordinary understanding, a gift of prophecy, exceptional leadership. Mothers may be especially proud of such sons.

After the child was born, it was spanked soundly to enable it to begin breathing. The umbilical cord was tied close to the abdomen in the Appalachian tradition and a band of clean cloth bound around the infant. Some midwives considered it important that hives be induced as quickly as possible to assure a clean, clear skin. A few drops of a tea brewed from nettles was administered to cause hives.

The midwife and attendants stayed as long as they thought they were needed. If not enough food was around for a midnight dinner or a good breakfast, the husband was called and asked to provide a chicken. Attendants would cook a pot of chicken and dumplings, bake a pan of biscuits, prepare a bowl of steaming gravy, and boil pots of strong black coffee for the feast they would enjoy after mother and baby were resting comfortably.

When mother and baby were resting comfortably, the father and children sent away from home were invited to return. Curious younger children who inquired about where the baby had come from were told that their mother had ordered it, or that the midwife had fetched it, or that it had been found in a hollow stump or tree. The stork that brings babies did not visit Appalachian families.

Babies in Appalachia were breast-fed unless it was discovered that the mother's milk produced colic or rashes or that not enough milk was produced for meeting the baby's needs. Sometimes a baby was given as a supplement to breast feeding a "sugar tit" of butter and sugar tied in a little white rag to suck while it was going to sleep.

Mothers breast-fed their babies wherever and whenever they became hungry. No shyness or shame was attached to exhibiting a breast for the baby to feed. At church, funeral meetings, public gatherings, family reunions, mothers sat around feeding their babies naturally and easily and without embarrassment. A baby continued to nurse at the breast until the next child was expected or up to the age of four or five sometimes if it was the last baby in the family. At church or other public gatherings a four- or five-year-old child would sometimes hurry in from play with other children and stand beside its seated mother to nurse.

After a few weeks of breast-feeding the infant the mother would introduce the child to other foods. In the days before commercially prepared baby foods were available, the mother chewed thoroughly the food she wanted to feed the baby and transferred it from her own mouth to that of the child, at the beginning with her fingers and later with a spoon. As the child developed skill in taking food from a spoon the father or an older sibling would feed it at mealtime soft foods like gravy, mashed potatoes, bean soup, pot liquor, canned apples or peaches.

The traditional Appalachian family was patriarchal in structure, but the mother more often than not made decisions for the father, whose responsibility was to administer and execute. Family life in Appalachia was determined largely by the influence of the predominantly Scotch-Irish character of the pioneer settlers. Among the Scotch-Irish, old-time Calvinists in their theology and view of the world, the husband and wife were of one flesh, one spirit, and one head, the husband's, but the long, long Celtic influence on the shaping of their lives left room for a high level of partnership and sense of equality between the sexes. Males were not chivalric in the middle-class sense. A mountain man did not demean himself or downgrade women by stooping to such customs as tipping the hat or removing it, rising upon the entrance of a woman into his presence, offering a woman of comparable age or younger his seat, helping a woman over a style or up steps, relieving a woman of a load she might be carrying, or offering to let her ride the horse while he walked. The mountain man and woman were equal in these aspects of life and the woman did not expect a man to behave toward her as if she were weak, physically inadequate, or inferior.

Theological views supported the concepts of children as a blessing and of a woman's having been "fated" or "predestined" to "have her number" of children. Children were accepted as the will of God. They were special blessings, and traditionally, economic assets. Even though children were often born in unsanitary circumstances and delivered by midwives whose ministrations included happy mixtures of myth, witchcraft, and herbal remedies, they were surprisingly healthy and the mortality rate, before mountain folk began to abandon the traditional foods produced on their own farms for cheap imported food, was amazingly low.

Mountain folk, who practiced severe restraints in the sharing of tender emotions, cultivated the habit of lavishing love, kindness, and attention on children, particularly infants, toddlers, and "yard young 'ens." They were cuddled, fondled, tossed about, and bounced on trotting knees and on happy feet of fathers, uncles, and grandfathers. Their needs and wants, even when whimsical, were met, often to the place that the infant became a tyrant in the household and rode the father's shoulders as he worked in the fields. Small children in mountain families enjoyed more love, attention, consideration, perquisites and prerogatives than did children in all of Christendom.

Mountain families were close. Although members often quarreled, fought, and even killed one another, they rose to one another's support against a common enemy. Moreover, they felt a keen sense of loyalty to and responsibility for one another. Children growing up in this atmosphere "experienced" family in a unique way. They belonged and were important. They were protected and looked out for by older members of their immediate family and by cousins and relatives when members of their own family were not present. Retarded children and incompetents, accepted as God's will and instruments for effecting His own plans, enjoyed the privileges of other children as far as their competencies would permit. They were ordinarily assigned to the supervision of another child, but they went where others went, played with normal children, and were loved and cared for at home. It was difficult to get mountain parents to agree to send children to institutions and hospitals for special care and treatment because they feared the children might not receive the love and consideration to which they were accustomed at home.

The illegitimate child in mountain society was not ordinarily discriminated against because of his illegitimacy. The widespread practice of polygamy in the mountains down to the beginning of the 20th century resulted in large numbers of illegitimate children who were normally provided for in the land divisions and wills of the father and supported by him while growing up. In case a mother died, her illegitimate children were accepted into the homes of their fathers where they grew up, equally and respected, along with the legitimate children. This interesting phase of our history reinforced the theological notion that man is in the image of God and is due respect solely on the basis of his worth of character. Until mountain culture began to be affected by the pious flummery and hypocrisy of Victorianism, the bastard in the mountains probably suffered less from social ostracism than the bastard in any other social group, including blacks in the South.

The infant, male or female, was normally referred to as "it." Until about 1920 infants and toddlers, both male and female, wore dresses until they were three or four years old. Even as late as 1890 mountain boys often wore long-tailed shirts but no pants until they were eight or ten years old. By the age of four or five sexual differentiations were made and girls began playing feminine roles and boys masculine roles in family life and in the division of labor. Boys began ordering their mothers and sisters about as their fathers did. Girls began working with household tasks that males did not perform. By this time they had progressed from infant, or "lap baby," to toddler, or "set along" child, to "little tad no taller than knee-high to a grasshopper," or "yard young 'en."

Families tended to be large and homes small. The smaller the home and the larger the family, the more dogs were kept. Travelers through the mountain country were impressed by yardfuls of towheaded, blue-eyed children romping with dogs around mountain cabins. Not only were children given their own dogs and cats, but often they owned individually chickens, pet pigs, calves, or animals brought in from the forest.

Women were responsible for the care of the house, the supervision of the children, growing the garden (though his high and exalted lordship, the father, plowed it), and gathering and preserving such foodstuffs as wild berries, grapes, and tree fruits. Both boys and girls helped with these tasks, especially with garden work. Men grew field crops, worked in the wood lots, built fences, made and repaired farm implements, hunted, and fished. When crops were ready for hoeing, all members of the family except the infants and toddlers, and an older one to care for them, worked in the fields. Six-year-olds, both male and female, carried their hoes into the fields and worked alongside their older siblings and parents all day long. The whole family working together made the task seem like fun.

The woman, traditionally, in Appalachia was busy most of the time. Before the coming of calico and gingham to the country stores, she prepared flax, wool, and cotton for spinning, wove beautiful and sturdy cloth, knitted, and sewed. She also gathered and dried food: beans, berries, pumpkin; or pickled it: sauerkraut, pickle beans, pickle corn, relishes; and made jams, jellies, and apple butter. As she grew older she became a matriarch, an influence that held the family together. She was a source of wisdom and practical knowledge, preserved the traditions, and generally sang the ballads. Although her old man was nominally the legal head of the household, she often developed a diplomacy by which she could get what she wanted without confrontation, for mountain folk, conditioned by a culture with a Calvinistic tinge, avoid confrontations when possible.

The mountain boy was disciplined by both father and mother to the age of 12, the year of "accountability." After that, he was advised and counseled with but not beaten as a matter of "principle," though occasionally a father in a rage would swat his son. A son accepted and forgot a swat from an angry father, but he rebelled against a beating on "principle." He was a free agent at the age of 12, privileged to set aside parental counsel as he wished. Thereafter, parents watched with loving concern and fierce loyalty their sons go on toward maturity, sow their "wild oats," make their mistakes, marry at the age of 20 or 21, and settle down to "becoming old married men."

The mountain girl, however, was not accorded the freedom of her brother. She was taught the routines of keeping house and preparing food, supervised when she went away from home, and accompanied by brothers when she was permitted to go to church, a play party, to the country store, or wherever young people might be meeting. By the age of 11 or 12 she was exhibiting signs of womanhood and attracting the attention of males. Often by this time some young man, perhaps 16 or 17 years old, had set his sights on her. If so, he visited the house often to talk with her older brothers or sit by the fireside and "chew the rag" with the father. He became her "protector" and fought off any young man who entered the lists for her favors.

She was not given a year of "accountability," and the father continued to beat her for misbehavior until she married. In the older days she could disqualify herself for marriage to a man of her own age or up to six or eight years older if she were sexually free or should "happen up with an accident" and become pregnant. If such were her misfortune, however, she was not irretrievably lost, for older widowers sought out and married younger women who had "made a mistake," taking into their own home as their own children any illegitimate children, who were accepted as members of the family in "full status." After her marriage, a woman's mistake tended to be forgotten by her family and friends.

As boys advanced toward maturity they learned "what men know" from their older brothers, uncles, and grandfathers. They mastered the four-letter words, roaring oaths, and resounding rhetoric that males use while learning also how to shoot guns and pistols, use tobacco, and drink whiskey. At the same time, they learned that man talk is not engaged in in the presence of women. Girls advancing through adolescence learned from older girls "woman talk," not essentially different from man talk, but also that such talk was not engaged in in the presence of men.

Grandparents and older relatives were important in the lives of mountain children. Although parents disciplined children and forbade them to do things, grandparents normally did not. The little boy visiting his grandfather learned stories of mountain life, historical matter relating to the family and the community, and skills that the father lacked time and patience to teach. Girls learned similar things from grandmothers. Grandparents were often trusted advisers and fountains of wisdom, warmth, and support for mountain children.

In the old days in the mountains child abuse was rare if we except the harsh Calvinistic discipline traditional in mountain families. Homes were small and crowded. Opportunities for sexual abuse of children by fathers were rare, and children were normally protected from older persons in the community by older persons in the family. Incest between siblings, though not unknown, perhaps was not as frequent in the mountains as in even middle-class homes elsewhere in America.

Following World War I, however, mountain folk began moving toward the "larger society" in their customs, practices, and attitudes. We have among us now the same problems that people operating in urban, industrialized society elsewhere in America have. But we are still close enough to the older values and the older ways that social and professional people who work with mountain folk might improve their effectiveness by becoming better acquainted with them.

Borning, living, and dying in Appalachia were intensely person-centered. The mother in childbirth was the center of a festival of joy. The midwife and her attendants, loaded with their herbs and teas and filled with rituals and reassuring formulas from superstition and lore, made the act of childbearing as comfortable and significant as possible. The infant, sweated and purged and accorded significant rituals, was the center of the family until it could fit itself, still an individual in its own right, into the structure of the family. The dying or the dead commanded in a supporting culture that attention and respect that mountain folk thought were the just deserts of one who had lived among them.

Chapter Four ————————————————————————————————

In the Family Spirit(s)

Grampa Jeff Gets Drunk (on my whiskey)

Once my father had stored in glass jars six gallons of peach whiskey of exceptionally fine quality. It had been aged in a charred keg and flavored and colored uniformly with burned brown sugar. He was saving the whiskey for future occasions and did not want it disturbed, but I slipped into the whiskey one summer afternoon when everyone except myself was gone from home and poured a small amount from each jar into a pitcher and thence into a Coca-Cola bottle until the bottle was filled. I then added brown sugar to increase the sweetness to suit my taste and hid the bottle under a broad leaf of burdock that grew beside the chicken house above the lane that led from the gate of our home to the road. From time to time I would steal to the burdock and take a small swig of the delicious whiskey.

One Sunday morning while I was swigging a taste from the bottle my Grandfather Jeff Whitt came by and discovered me. I offered him a drink from the bottle, which he accepted, helping himself somewhat generously, it seemed to me, but he did not ask about how I happened to have the whiskey. I returned the bottle to its place and Grandpa Jeff went on to church. Later that day, after church was over, I returned to the burdock for another taste of the whiskey, but the bottle was gone. Since only Grandpa knew my secret, I concluded that he had taken possession of my whiskey on his return from church and might turn it over to my father.

The following day my father was called from his work in the fields to report to the local justice of the peace to sign a peace bond for my grandfather, who, the preceding afternoon, had come to the house of the preacher, his next-door neighbor, in a state of intoxication, "raised a racket," in an argument

190

about the meaning of a scriptural passage, flashed an old pistol, and threatened to shoot the preacher, who had ridden to the home of the squire to "swear out" a peace warrant for Grandpa.

That night, chagrined and shame-faced and "a-lookin right chawed," Grandpa came over the hill to our house to try to make adequate explanation to my father, who was annoyed by having to leave his work to sign a peace bond and distressed that my grandfather, at his age, should have gone on such a tirade. The two of them were sitting in darkness on the porch and near enough to the open door of the room in which my brother and I slept for me to hear the conversation. My father was "lecturing" Grandpa and shaming him for what he had done. After hearing all of the lecture he could stand, Grandpa interrupted with "Pshaw, Crate gave me the whiskey." Incredulous, my father asked "What?" "Crate gave me the whiskey." There was an extremely long silence, it seemed to me, as I lay holding my breath and waiting for the response. At length, my father hissed a sibilant polysyllable, a common four-letter word, which was followed by an even longer silence. I lay quietly in bed but in mortal fear that my father would come and jerk me out of the bed and give me a "jack-up, Gentile, No. 1 good whuppin" that I would not be likely to soon forget. Instead, the conversation turned on other subjects and I soon went to sleep, but fearing the "lecture" which my father was almost sure to deliver at the breakfast table the following morning. The lecture never did come. My father never referred to my corruption, at the age of ten, of my grandfather, and my grandfather never mentioned my bottle of whiskey to me. I never let either of them know that I had overheard their conversation that night, willing as I was to let sleeping snakes lie.

A Bottle of Liquor at Each End of the Corn Row

I was 12 years old and my brother was 10. We had helped our father and mother hoe our twenty acres of corn in the Plez House bottoms out of the "first weeds." The rows in the upper bottom were so long that we could thin and hoe only one round apiece in a half-day, with time out for resting about fifteen minutes at the end of the first row. Papa kept four or five rows ahead of us with the double-shovel plow, and then he would hoe a row, too, beginning far behind us and overtaking us halfway down the field. That way, we could hoe sixteen rows a day. In the middle of the morning our older sister, who stayed at the house to be with our little sister and to cook the dinner, brought us a jug of fresh water from the well. We would hold the jug on our crooked right arms, raise it to our lips, and let the cool water from the stone jug gurgle into our mouths. It took skill and control to keep the jug steady.

If it jiggled on an unsteady arm, it could mash one's mouth, or chip a front tooth, or, even, maybe, break a tooth.

It took us two weeks to hoe twenty acres. We would hoe the field out of the "second weeds" about three weeks after we had begun the first hoeing. Grampa Williams had been late with his planting that year, but he was even later with his hoeing. He hired my brother and me to help him during our week between "weeds" for our own crop. He would pay each of us a dollar a day.

We reported for work Monday morning after we had done our chores at home. It was fun to work for Grampa. He was in the "nipping" stage at the beginning of one of his long periods of alcoholism, which were lasting about six weeks at a time then. He sauntered to his work and told stories as we worked side by side down the corn rows, or sang little ditties, some of them with naughty words in them. We worked silently at home, for Papa considered talk on the job a waste of time. We could not sing or whistle when we worked at home, and we were scolded if we had to go to the bushes for any reason. Besides, we could sit down to rest only once in the forenoon and once in the afternoon.

But it was different at Grampa's. Sometimes Grampa, who sweated a lot, would stop right in the middle of the field, take off his soft hat, wipe his face and forehead with a red bandana handkerchief, and then drape the handkerchief over his head to protect himself from sunburn, for instead of tanning he turned red. He would then announce that "she's a hot 'n, 67 degrees hotter than the middle kettle of hell, by God! Let's cool a minute." We would then all sit down to rest right there, our hoes standing like sentinels beside the last hill of corn we had hoed. Grampa would fan himself with his floppy hat, sometimes unbuttoning his shirt and fanning his hairy chest, down which streams of sweat trickled and leapt from hair to hair, rolled over his stomach, and disappeared in his jeans.

In the middle of the morning Grampa said we needed some fresh water and a spell of rest. We walked up to the yard, shaded by apple trees, and sat on benches and chairs while Grampa drew a fresh bucket of water from the well. We drank from a dipper that floated on top of the water. After we had all had a drink of the cool water, Grampa thought we might stand the heat better if we had a little nip of "sankum suly." He disappeared into the house for a few minutes and returned with two pint bottles of amber colored whiskey, which he said was "royal." He had made it last fall from dried peaches and it had been in a charred oak keg since then, hidden deeply in the hay in his barn loft. It was a hundred proof and as smooth and gentle as a baby's skin.

Each of us took a swig from one of the bottles that we passed among us, each smoothing off the top with the palm of his hand before passing it on.

Then we returned to the field. Grampa put one of the bottles in the weeds at the end of the field and stuck the other one in his hip pocket. After we had hoed our rows to the other end of the field, Grampa drew the bottle from his pocket and we all took another swig. Then he hid that bottle in the weeds beyond the corn rows, adding that as hot as it was, a feller needed some encouragement to get from one end of the field to the other.

Our uncle, only four years older than I, was plowing ahead of us. When he had finished plowing eight or ten rows, he would hitch the horse at the end of the field and help us hoe. Grampa's field was not as long as our upper Plez House bottom. We could hoe a round in his bottom in an hour. But he had another bottom across the creek that we would hoe after we had finished this one, and the rows in it were twice as long down the middle, but the bottom was beside a winding creek and most of it had short rows in the bends. The rows did seem shorter with a bottle at either end of them. We were near the far end of the field in our second round following our spell of rest in the yard when Gramma called us to dinner. Instead of having us finish hoeing the rows, as Papa would have had us do, Grampa sighed with relief as he stood his hoe in the ground and said we would go eat.

As we passed out of the field he retrieved the bottle from the weeds and slipped it into his pocket. We took turns washing our hands and faces in the cool water in the basin on the bench, dried on a coarse towel hanging on a nail, and combed our hair with a big-toothed comb that rested in a little rack below a spotted diamond shaped mirror in a wide unpainted wooden frame that hung from a nail on the wall of the "cook room."

Gramma's dinner smelled good. We looked at it steaming hot on the table. Grampa thought, as hot as the day was, that we ought to sit in the shade of the apple trees for a few minutes and let it cool. He produced the bottle, helped himself to several swallows, bubbles racing up the neck of the bottle as his Adam's apple moved up and down, and then passed it around. Grampa fanned himself with a big weathered palm frond fan that he had taken from a basket on a table that stood on the back porch, the kind of fan that old ladies attired in black dresses and black slat bonnets and wearing white aprons carried to church with them in the summertime. As Grampa fanned he unbuttoned his shirt all the way to the band of his heavy jeans and fanned his chest, and his belly too. He did not wear an undershirt in the summer, but we could see the band of his muslin drawers, which looked like pajama bottoms, I learned much later in life, and which Gramma made for him. We didn't talk much while we were letting the dinner cool.

After about ten minutes we went to the table, my brother and I and our little aunt, four years younger than I, sitting on a bench along the wall behind the table, Grampa in a broad cane-bottom chair at the head, and Gramma and our uncle in chairs opposite us. We had plenty of food: cornbread, butter,

Left: David O. Williams (Pa Dave), in 1930. Caught on a hot summer day at work when the itinerant photographer came through, David O. plucked a bouquet of flowers to spruce up his appearance. Right: Martelia Swann Williams, in 1930, same day.

fresh mustard with side meat cooked with it, new green peas, green onions, sliced potatoes cooked in milk, thick pieces of fried side meat, and cold milk fresh from the cooler. For our sweet tooth there was a plain spiced cake with honey to go over it. Grampa didn't like to wear his teeth, so Gramma fixed things he could eat without teeth. He drank his buttermilk from a pint-size tin cup with a handle on it and cut his meat into little cubes so he could swallow it without having to chew it first.

He was expansive at the table and told little stories about his boyhood and his days at school in the old log schoolhouse that still stood just above the well in his garden, the same schoolhouse that he put a partition in and lived in while his first wife, our real granny, was alive. My father and his two full sisters were born in that old schoolhouse, which became the property of the original owner of the land after the school was moved into the church house across the valley from where we lived. He had used the old schoolhouse for a ware room for his distillery after moving into his present home, and then it had been used for a "cook room" (summer kitchen) until he closed his store and began using the store building for a summer kitchen. The old schoolhouse was then being used as a storeroom and a smokehouse. Grampa thought it had been there since about 1855. There had been only one school-house in the valley before it, and it had been a little building made of round logs and with no chimney that had stood at the lower corner next to the creek of the field in which we had been hoeing corn that morning, the field called the vault bottom because our real Granny's tomb was located at the upper corner of the lower end of it.

Grampa remembered the little school building, which his brother-in-law had later used as the main stall for his barn when he lived in a little house on the bank across the creek from the older schoolhouse. Andy Woods had been the first teacher in the school. Grampa's mother and uncles and aunts had gone to school there. He thought the school might have been built nearly a hundred years before, probably about 1830. Before that, people had not gone to a schoolhouse, he thought, but sometimes someone in the community would hold school a few weeks in the early fall, when the weather was pretty, in his home, or in the yard of his house, or under a tree at the forks of a road. He thought there had been a school of some kind at Blaine from the time people first came into this country. Almost all of the old people could read and write and some of them were pretty good scholars.

He told about his first whipping at school. His cousin Polly Gambill, who later married Ike Edwards, was the teacher. She had sent him to the willow grove down by the creek to find a switch with which he was to be whipped. He had brought back one that was too small to suit his teacher. She sent him back for another, one about as long as his arm. We knew Polly, now an old woman. She had lost her mind; her husband had left her; her only son had gone away to live in West Virginia. Polly had spent a year or two in the insane asylum at Lexington, but she was then living with her sister Hannah down the road about two miles. Polly whooped, and staved, and shouted crazy things when she would come visiting. One could tease her a little and get her started. She carried in her "reticule" a picture of her son as a young man with curly hair combed back pompadour style. Polly would talk about his pretty hair that stood seven feet above the top of his head and chant loudly, as she danced and swirled about, a strange mixture of facts, gossip, and refrain lines from nursery rhymes and songs. When she came to see him, Grampa would tease her about the whipping she had given him. She would chant and dance in response but make no reference to the whipping.

Schools had already begun to change by the time Grampa started. His oldest sister had gone to the little log school at the lower side of the Vault Bottom. That had been a blab school. Everybody had studied out loud. When the children were practicing their spelling the old a, b, ab way and the teacher had swarped the top of his table with a stick and ordered them to "spell out" while somebody was passing along the road between the school and the creek, it had sounded like the Day of Pentecost. The louder they studied the better

David and Martha Boggs Williams.

people thought the teacher was. "W'y, sometimes you could hear a school half a mile away." But Grampa's sister was a "champeen" speller. He had studied the Blueback Speller, too, and the McGuffey readers, but he was not as good a speller as his sister. He was a pretty good "scribe," though, and Martha (my real Granny) was the best scribe in school, when she went.

After dinner we went to the shade of the apple trees in the yard to rest. Grampa sat in a cane-bottom chair with a wide seat, which he had made especially to accommodate his own broad bottom. Our uncle lay on his back on a bench and covered his face with his handkerchief so the flies and gnats couldn't bother him. My brother and I lay on the soft grass between Gramma's patch of "sparegrass" and her bed of tiger lilies. Soon our uncle was snoring, lying there on his back that way, and we were dozing. Grampa would nod in his chair, his head moving forward toward his chest. Then he would snort, swipe wildly at the flies that were racing across his face, straighten up in his chair and repeat it all.

After about an hour, Grampa snorted, swarped viciously at the flies, and fairly roared, "These God damned flies! They're worse than the plagues of Egypt, by God. Well, hitch up the horse. I guess we'd better hit the cornfield again."

We all rose stiffly from our positions, my brother and I picked up our straw jimmy hats with shoestrings for bands, and Grampa found his soft floppy hat on the end of the porch. We dragged ourselves to our hoes, still standing beside the last hills of corn we had hoed, their handles quite warm from the broiling sun. It took a few minutes for us to work up enough sweat to drive the sleep and the trifling feeling out of us, but by the time we had reached the ends of our rows we were in the swing of our work again.

Grampa remembered the bottle in the weeds. He took another drink and handed the bottle to us. I took only a taste. It seemed to me that I did not want a very big drink so soon after the rest period. My brother took a big one, though. Grampa returned the bottle to the weeds and we began working our way toward the upper end of the field. The rows seemed longer in the hot afternoon than they had seemed that morning. Grampa was not as talkative now and did not sing any songs or recite rhymes. I could not think of anything that I felt was worth saying, either. Moving backward as I had to because I could not hoe either-handed, the way Papa and Grampa could, I found myself concerned with what a short distance we had moved from the lower end of the field and how far it still was to the upper end.

But we finally got to the upper end. Grampa said it was "too damned hot" to hoe corn. His face was red and his shirt was wet with sweat. "Let's get us a drink of fresh water and blow a minute," he said, as we walked toward the shade of the apple trees. He emptied the water bucket in Granny's lily bed and brought a bucket of fresh, cool water. We drank a dipperful apiece and sat down to cool, Grampa fanning himself vigorously with the palm fan. After resting a half-hour, we drank more water and went back to the field, but Grampa thought we needed another nip before we hit the rows. He found the bottle he had hidden in the weeds on the way from lunch and each of us drank again, but mine was only a taste, for I did not seem to want much, as hot as it was. My brother, though, took another big one.

Thunderheads were rising beyond the ridge to the west, big white ones that boiled up, bold and dense. Soon one covered the sun and a cool breeze moved down the valley. Grampa stopped, removed his hat, opened his shirt, and enjoyed it. We were encouraged to strike faster licks with the breeze blowing at our backs, and when I bent over to thin a hill of corn, it caught in my overalls and I could feel the cool around my hips and on my back. The cloud moved on soon, but it was not as hot after that, and the corn blades rippled in the breeze.

At the end of the row Grampa found the bottle he had hidden in the weeds and each of us took another swig or two from it. This time it tasted pretty good and I treated myself more generously than I had at the other times we had taken drinks. My brother took two or three big swallows. Clouds continued to boil up, cover the sun for a few minutes, and then move with the wind.

With the cool breeze in our faces as we moved up the rows and on our backs as we moved down, we did not rest again, but we had a drink from the bottle at either end of the field each time we hoed a row. After a brief period of completely cloudy weather, in which flashes of lightning streaked across the sky and thunder cracked and rumbled among the hollows, the clouds moved on and the sun came out again, but there had been no rainfall. It was cool after that, though, and the corn blades rippled like ribbons in the breeze the rest of the afternoon. Grampa became happy again. I could feel the pleasant effects of the drinks and was happy too. Grampa's little fragments of songs and rhymes and his cheerful whistling made us laugh a lot. My brother laughed more than I did, though, laughing a long time at those things Grampa did or said that tickled him most.

Our uncle finished plowing the field about 4:30 and took the horse and the double-shovel plow toward the barn, pulling back on the plow so that it swung just a few inches above the ground as the horse rushed along with it. He had the checklines tied around his waist and he pulled back against the horse so he could hold the plow above the earth. When the horse slowed down, the plow would touch the earth; but then our uncle would yell and curse and the beast would speed up, the plow rising again a few inches as the horse surged forward. We watched him until he disappeared behind the corncrib. He never did come back to help us complete the hoeing, though.

We hoed on, the drinks from the bottles making us feel better and better. It did not seem that we were working, it was all so much fun. About 6 o'clock we hoed the last rows. Grampa stood leaning on his hoe while we finished. My brother, who had the bottom row, had more weeds and grass to scalp from the bank below it than we had in our rows, so I turned to meet him while Grampa stood and watched. When the last hill was hoed, Grampa let out a roar like a bull. It was sudden and so loud that we were startled for a moment before we realized that Grampa was simply celebrating the completion of the job, as we always did when we finished a field job. It was an expression of triumph over the weeds and grass that try to choke out young corn before it is big enough to outgrow them, an awesome kind of threat against the unwanted plants to let them know that you'll be back in two or three weeks to chop them to pieces again if they dare to continue growing.

Grampa then found the bottle in the weeds and slipped it into his pocket. As we came out of the field, our hoes on our shoulders, he found the other bottle. When we were in the yard again, he asked us to sit down for a few minutes while he drew fresh water, which he set on the ground by us. We then drank again from one of the bottles, my brother making bubbles run up the neck as Grampa had done. I was feeling pretty good already, so I took only a small swallow and drank a dipperful of water. Grampa was glad that he had one of his fields hoed and said we would start on the one across the creek in the morning if it didn't rain. It might take us two or three days to hoe that one.

Ralph and I started home, both pretty happy. We walked up the creek bed. The waterway was almost dry, with pools here and there in which we could see a few fish up to five or six inches long; but fish didn't bite very well that late in the spring. Later, we might seine the holes that had bigger fish in them and look for bullfrogs and turtles too. Soon Ralph began to sing, but his voice was so low-pitched and croaky that he had trouble managing the tune.

We remembered a patch of raspberries on a bank below the end of a meadow. We climbed out of the creek bed at that point and found the raspberries bountiful and ripe. Nobody had picked any of them. We picked and ate the sweet juicy berries, all covered with the grey powder that ripe raspberries have on them, yeast, our father said, that makes raspberries especially good for wine.

Ralph Williams, age 14.

After we had eaten all the berries we wanted, we hurried on. I went on to the pasture to drive the cows in and Ralph stopped at the house to do his share of our "jin jobs" (chores). I sang and was happy as I lowered the bars and let the cows out of the pasture. Punching them out of the bushes and weeds on the creek banks, among which they ran to rid themselves of flies and to eat tender horseweeds and bright green broadblade grass, was more fun than usual. I did not feel tired the way I did when I worked for Papa, and Grampa had stopped work at least an hour earlier than Papa did.

After I had driven the cows into their stalls and fastened them up, I came on out the lane to the house. Mama was standing in the corner of the yard and looking at Ralph, who was half sprawling and half sitting on the chopblock in the woodyard across the lane. He had an arm load of stovewood, the ends resting on the chopblock, which he was hugging tightly while muttering to himself as he struggled to rise to his feet. His face was pale. I had not noticed before that he had smeared the raspberries from ear to ear across his face.

"Something's wrong with that young 'en," Mama said.

"I reckon he might be drunk. Grampa had a bottle of whiskey at each end of the field, and I noticed that Ralph hit it pretty hard every time we finished a row."

"How are you feeling?"

"Oh, I feel fine. I didn't drink as much as Ralph did. I didn't know that he was getting drunk, but now that I remember back, he laughed a lot at Grampa's little songs and rhymes and croaked when he was trying to sing to himself while we were coming home."

Ralph had stopped trying to get up. He was sprawled against the chop-block hugging his load of wood, some of the sticks having slipped halfway out of it and resting against the side of the block. Mama tried to talk to him, but he seemed not to hear her. He mumbled and muttered, but we could not understand any of his words.

Papa arrived soon. When he saw Ralph in that condition and with the raspberry juice all across his face, he wanted to know what had happened to "that boy."

"He's drunk," Mama said.

"Damn a man that'd do that to a little boy, if he *is* my daddy," Papa swore. Turning to me, "How do you feel?"

"I feel good. I didn't drink as much as Ralph did."

Papa then walked over and broke Ralph's determined grip around the load of wood, which went sliding down either side of the chopblock. He pulled him to his feet, but Ralph could not stand up. Papa then got behind him, held him up in front of him, and walked him up and down the lane a few times. Ralph did not try to respond to any of Papa's questions. Papa then set him down against the woodpile. Ralph lurched forward with a heave and a retch and began to vomit, almost falling forward as the blue stream belched from him. Papa held his head. He choked and sputtered and vomited again, his dinner, streams of liquid, bile. He continued heaving and retching, even after nothing was left in him.

Papa picked him up and carried him into the yard. He was very pale and quiet. Papa set him on the walk and Mama brought a cup of cold butter-milk. She held it to his lips and urged him to drink. He made no effort to speak. At first, each drink of the buttermilk came back immediately, but after a while some stayed down for a few minutes before returning. Then he was able to drink a cupful. Papa laid him along the wall on the porch to sleep for a little while. Then he woke him up and had him drink a cup of cold water to restore his liquids. Ralph did not want any supper, but he slept well after we went to bed, though he was a little noisy.

A heavy rain fell that night. It was too wet to hoe corn the following day. Wednesday Ralph did not feel like hoeing corn. But I helped Grampa and Gramma and my uncle hoe the corn in the field across the creek. Ralph didn't work any more that week. I explained that he was sick, some kind of a summer sickness that made him puke a lot and left him weak, too weak to work.

The rows were much longer in the bottom across the creek. Except for Wednesday morning, when it was damp and the sun was shining so hot that the thousand-legs turned out by the double-shovel plow curled up and died, the weather was cool and a breeze was blowing. Like I said, Gramma helped us hoe that field. She told stories and sang in her thin, silvery voice fragments from ballads and hymns, and Grampa whistled and sang and recited rhymes. We had a bottle at each end of that field, too, but Gramma would not drink any of the whiskey. She preferred to chew tobacco for her encouragement, but Grampa and I both liked to work toward the bottles. I usually took only a sip or two, though, just enough to leave a good taste in my mouth and make me feel happy from one end of the field to the other. It was a lot more fun to work for Grampa than to work at home.

A Man Dies When His Time Comes

Grampa and Charlie Flanary had been friends for years. They visited each other and drank together. They decided that they would buy a tract of timber and saw it into lumber during a boom. Men of their word and honest in their dealings, they did not draw up a contract. After the job was finished, they met to make their settlement with each other only to find that they were not in agreement. Charlie was sure that Grampa owed him more money than Grampa was willing to pay. They quarreled and parted.

Late one afternoon a few days later Grampa was feeding his pigs in a lot with a ten-rail fence around it. Charlie Flanary approached the lot and announced that he had come to collect the money that was due him. Grampa protested that nothing was due him, that the settlement had been made according to their agreement. Tempers flared. Charlie pulled a pistol and emptied it at Grampa, who had pulled a rail from the fence and was advancing toward him. Every one of the six bullets fired struck a rail in the fence. Grampa leapt over the fence and rushed at Charlie, who turned and fled, the empty pistol dangling in his hand.

Grampa returned to the house, loaded his pistol, and hung it on a nail beside the door, just in case Charlie returned.

After the family had eaten supper, Grampa sat in front of the fire and thought about the agreement he and Charlie had made. He was sure he understood it correctly and knew that Charlie thought he also understood it correctly, but Charlie had tried to kill him. He would have to be prepared to protect himself if Charlie should come to his house again.

Lonnie Boggs (left) and Charlie Williams, son of David Williams, named after
Charlie Flanary. Charlie was later shot and wounded in a conflict with his father.

Soon the dogs began to bark. Grampa got up, took his pistol from the nail, and stationed himself at one side of the door.

Charlie called out from the gate, "Dave, I'm a-comin' in."

"No, you can't come in. You've tried to kill me. I don't want to have anything more to do with you."

"Yes, I'm a-comin' in," Charlie replied as he stepped upon the porch.

Grampa opened the door. Charlie, his hands hanging by him stood before the door. "I'm a-comin' in."

"If you take one more step, I'll kill you," Grampa said as he leveled his pistol at Charlie's head.

"We need to talk this thing out and I'm a-comin' in," Charlie said as he started toward the door.

Grampa pulled the trigger as Charlie stopped, erect and quiet before him. The pistol did not fire. Grampa pointed the pistol skyward and pulled the trigger again. The pistol discharged with a roar.

Charlie advanced a step and Grampa pulled the trigger again, but the pistol did not fire. Again, he aimed it at the sky, pulled the trigger again, and the pistol fired.

Grampa dropped the gun and took Charlie by the hand. As they shook hands warmly, Grampa said, "A man dies when his time comes. Come on in."

Charlie went in and sat by the fire. They reviewed their agreement. Each had understood it differently, but they reached a compromise and Grampa paid half of what Charlie had thought he should receive. Charlie sat with Grampa a long time while they talked of other things. When he left, they were friends again.

Grampa named his next son Charles.

The Whitts

The end of the summer of my thirteenth year marked the close of my childhood. Many childhood experiences not connected with school directly are vivid memories for me. I remember a visit that summer from my great-grandfather William Whitt, who was born about 1840 on Devil's Fork near Sandy Hook (then called Martinsburg) in a part of Morgan County, Kentucky, that was later included in Elliott County. He was a son of Moses Whitt and his wife, a Mauk, who were married July 17, 1834, in Morgan County, and a grandson of Richard and Lavisa Adkins Whitt, who migrated from Pike County, Kentucky, to Morgan County in the 1820's. We do not know the parentage of Richard Whitt. Lavisa may have been the daughter of Moses Adkins. Moses Whitt's wife might have been the daughter of Peter Mauk (1781–1859), who came to Blaine about 1823, and his first wife, Hannah Sparks. The

Whitts were a large family in Eastern Kentucky and, along with Adkinses, so numerous that others in Elliott County said the Whitts and Adkinses and the broomsage were taking the country. It was also said that the stream on which they lived was called Devil's Fork because the Whitts were as mean as the Devil his own self. Grampap Bill Whitt had one sister, Crildy (Corrilda), who married a Howard and lived rear Sandy Hook in Elliott County, and at least three brothers, Peter, Mitchell ("Boog"), and Mack (Mauk?).

Soon after the Civil War, Grampap Bill married Rosalind Adkins, possibly his first cousin. Rosalind's parentage is not known. Rosalind, called Babe within the family, was younger than her husband. She was born about 1850 in a part of Morgan County, Kentucky, that was included later in Elliott County. The date of her marriage to William ("Old Bill") Whitt was not remembered, but it was soon after the close of the Civil War. They lived for eight or ten years after their marriage in a cabin on Devil's Fork of the Licking River in Elliott County before coming to Blaine when their oldest son Jeff, my grandfather, was a small boy.

Granny Babe was the mother of nine children: Jefferson Davis (Jeff), Robert, Emma, Augustus (Gus), Grover Cleveland (Cleve), Annie, Mitchell, Nora, and Jay. Three of her children, Annie, Mitchell, and Jay, died young of tuberculosis. Her son Gus, unmarried, was cruelly murdered at the age of 17. Only two of her nine children, Jeff and Nora, had children to reach maturity.

Granny Babe was a frail slender woman with dark curly hair, which turned grey early. Like her husband, she kept her eyes closed much of the time in conversation, opening them only during pauses, and like him, she spoke very old-fashioned English. She helped her husband with work in the fields and she and the children raised the garden.

That summer Bill Whitt had come back from Ohio, where he was living with his son, Cleve (Grover Cleveland). He was then 78 years old (and lived 15 years longer), tall, slender, straight, and agile with a mass of black hair on his head and a thin, grey wisp of a goatee which he stroked slowly as he told stories in extremely old-fashioned English, including "thar," "s's he," and "s's I," as he sat with his small, keen, and hard blue eyes either closed completely or narrowed to slits. He kept his eyes closed while talking but opened them while listening to responses. A cold-natured man, he often wore an overcoat while hoeing corn. He smoked home-grown "twist-bud" tobacco in a foul-smelling pipe with a crooked stem, which he kept lighted with a live coal from the fireplace. Bill Whitt supported the Confederacy during the Civil War, but we believe he must have been a member of a guerilla band.

Grampap Bill told tales of the Tolliver–Martin feud,[1] about his murdering Craig Tolliver's father in bed, about the murder of his own son, Gus (Augustus), years later by, he was convinced, Cal Tolliver and others sympathetic with the Tollivers.

About 1875 while still living on Devil's Fork Grampap Bill had become involved in a dispute over the ownership of land, it was said with the father of Craig Tolliver, the leader of the Tollivers in the Tolliver–Martin feud. The dispute was taken to court. Tolliver won. Enraged, Grampap Bill went into Tolliver's home and shot him to death in bed. Craig, a boy in his teens, was standing by. Bill Whitt was arrested and lodged in the Morgan County jail at West Liberty. A time came while he was waiting for trial when he was the only prisoner in the jail and he began to plan his escape. He told Granny Babe his plan and instructed her to take their only child at the time, my grandfather Jeff (Jefferson Davis), to Lawrence County and wait for him there at the home of one of the relatives, where he would soon join her. Grampap Bill engaged the jailer in conversations each evening as long as he could. After a time the jailor had built up enough trust in him that he did not bother to arm himself when he went to deliver Grampap's supper. Grampap saved his fat meat for a week or two. One evening when the jailor arrived, Grampap, who had removed his shirt and greased himself with the fat meat, darted past the jailor when he opened the door. The jailor dropped the supper and grabbed him by the arm but could not hold him. Grampap rushed to the Licking River before the jailor could get his gun, sound the alarm, and pursue, and waded the river for several miles in case dogs should be used in a search for him. He traveled by night, sleeping in cliffs during the day, and made it to Lawrence County, where he met Granny Babe. Jeff was a small boy, and when Granny Babe walked from Devil's Fork to Blaine to meet her husband she carried my grandfather on her hip when he became tired.

They bought a small farm on Lower Laurel Creek about four miles west of Blaine, on which they struggled in poverty while trying to raise their nine children, many of whom, like their mother, suffered from tuberculosis. They lived in Lawrence County for about thirty years. No one ever came to capture Grampap to return him to jail or bring him to trial for the murder of Tolliver, but he felt that the murder of his son Gus, years after the Tolliver–Martin feud had ended with the gun battle in the streets of Morehead, had been Tolliver revenge.

Grampap, critical and quarrelsome, did not manage his affairs well. For Babe, afflicted with tuberculosis, life was a desperate struggle with extreme poverty and illness, a bickering family, and a quarrelsome husband.

After their son Gus, a lively young fellow, was cruelly murdered about 1900 at the age of 17 by unknown persons, Grampap and Granny tried to help identify the murderers. Grampap suspected that Cal Tolliver and a Manning had murdered his son in revenge for Grampap's murder of "Old Tolliver," but not enough evidence was produced to bring indictments against anyone and there was no hard evidence that Cal Tolliver had actually been involved. Grampap mortgaged his little farm for money needed for legal fees in an effort to convict Gus's murderers. He lost his farm and became a tenant farmer. After that, the Whitts, living from hand to mouth, were poor tenants for a few years on the farm on which I grew up on Caines Creek. About 1908 they moved to Pactollas, a few miles below Grayson in Carter County, where they were tenants living in a shack. Here Granny Babe and some of her children died of tuberculosis and were buried at the expense of the county in graves marked only by field stones in a Pactollas graveyard. After Granny's death, health authorities of Carter County ordered that the shack and its contents be burned to destroy tuberculosis germs. Grampap went to live with his son Cleveland, who had no children, in Cincinnati.

When he returned to Caines Creek to visit his kin, he was wiry and agile for his eighty years or so. He told us stories about his life, including an account of his "killing Old Tolliver." He then returned to Cincinnati, where he died at the age of 93 in 1933. He had willed his body to a hospital in return for needed medical attention in his last days.

One of the tenant houses in which Grampap had lived was on the farm on which I grew up. After Grampap moved away, the house was converted to a stillhouse in which my great uncle operated a licensed distillery for a time. After my father and mother came to the farm, my father tore the house down and used the lumber in it to make a chicken house, which still stands in the chicken lot beside the garden on our farm.

I remember also my only experience with Grampap's brother, Mitchell, whom people called Boog. Boog, a fiddler and dancer, had been married several times. Also a tenant farmer, he worked hard during the day to earn money and provisions for his family and would then go to play his fiddle, dance, and drink whiskey at neighborhood "play parties" in "waste" (unoccupied) cabins. After a wild night followed by a day of hard work, Boog suffered a paralytic stroke and fell in the doorway of his cabin just as he reached home. He was never able to work again. His family abandoned him and he was living alone in a miserable shack on Needmore Branch of the Dry Fork of Little Sandy River near Webbville when he decided he would come back to Caines Creek to visit his kinfolk. The first time I saw him was on the playground at the school. During the morning recess and while we were playing beside the road, an extremely ragged, muddy, and badly crippled old man appeared. He dragged a useless leg as he pulled himself painfully along with the help of a short crutch with a cross at the top. He planted the crutch firmly in front of him and, grasping the cross with both hands, lurched hoppingly after it with his good, drawing the game one even with himself. Some of the children knew who he was. Play stopped and the children gathered around him, many of them flinging cruel comments about his rags and the filthy pouch that he had swung over his shoulder. He had a beseeching face, bloodless and pallid, and he was clean shaven. His large, hollow-looking blue-gray eyes were almost without expression, but a playful, and half-fearful too, crinkle gathered at the corners of his eyes as he spoke to the children crowding in front of him and obstructing his way. He straightened himself up as far as he was able to and said, "Old folks, old folks, you'd better git to bed/Before you put meanness in the young folks' head." Then he yelled in a cracked old voice, "School butter! School butter! Ye'd better git out of my way!" and dragged himself onward. The children taunted him in response to "school butter" and threw mud at him. I did not understand at the time that he was my kinsman.

When I got home at lunchtime, the old man was sitting on the porch floor with his legs resting on the ground and in his "sockfeet," his socks quite worn out and his feet covered with grime. My father was attempting with a chip to gouge out the dirt packed into the gnarled and worn out old shoes. He would hand a shoe to Boog for him to examine. Boog would say, "See if you can gouge out a little more of that thair dirt jammed down in that thair toe." His old pouch was hanging on a nail driven into the porch wall. I went on into the kitchen and asked my mother who the old man was and why he was there. I then learned that he was her great-uncle, that he had been abandoned by his wife and children, who had gone off to Oklahoma and left him after his stroke, and that he was on his way to my grandfather's for a visit. At dinner Boog talked about how good the tomato dumplings were and promised my mother some of the tomato seeds he was carrying in his "boodget-poke" to my grandmother.

I never saw him again, but my grandmother told about his visit at her house. The weather turned bitterly cold that afternoon and the ground and the streams began to freeze before darkness came. Boog was sitting in front of a roaring log fire on the hearth as he began his preparations for bed. When he pulled off his disreputable old shoes, held on his feet by pieces of string drawn through the top eyes of each, and then peeled off his worn out and filth-stiffened socks, Grandpa said, "Pshaw, Boog, why don't you never warsh them stinkin' feet?" Uncle Boog replied, "Jeffy, I try to be awful good to them thair old feet. S'I, they have carried me over many a rough place in my life-time."

Boog slept in a bed in the fireplace room, but the fire went out during the night. Next morning Grandpa built a big fire and sat waiting for the room to become warm before asking Boog, who slept on, to get up and get himself ready for breakfast. As Grandpa was ready to wake Boog up, he noticed a sheet of ice on the floor by the bedside. He said, "What's that water doing thair on that thair floor? Pshaw, Boog, have you pissed on my floor?" Boog replied, "S'I, Jeffy, S'I, yes, I turned over thair along in the cold night and made a little water." It was as if one ought not to be held morally responsible for what happens in the night. But Grandpa told his uncle that he would not be able to keep him another night and that he would have to leave after breakfast.

Boog departed after breakfast. He made his way over the frozen earth to a home on the Lick Fork of Cherokee Creek where he stayed, making himself welcome until the weather began to moderate by playing a fiddle the people owned and singing his repertory of songs. When the weather was warm again, he dragged himself over the hills toward his shack on Needmore Branch, but along the slippery path above a cliff near his home he lost his footing and plunged over the cliff to his death on the rocks below. Several days later some hunters found his body, twisted and broken and frozen stiff. People living up and down the branch gathered in and buried him in an unmarked grave near his shack. He was the last old-time minstrel, fiddler, and dance caller whose career had begun before the Civil War. An old Rebel soldier, like Grampap Bill, he had not been eligible for a pension, there was no social security or old age pension system for his relief, and he had been too independent and proud to go to the county poorhouse after he found himself old, crippled, and abandoned. He had lived and died for his pride.

My grandfather Jeff was fond of telling two stories about himself that he could remember from his childhood days on Devil's Fork. When he was perhaps two years old his father and mother had tied him to a stake near the chimney of the cabin in which they lived and had spread a quilt upon the ground for him to play on while they hoed corn in a stumpy field close by. In the late afternoon Granny came to the house and prepared a cup of milk and crumbled cornbread for him and returned to the field. When his parents came home at the end of the day, Grandpa was ringed about with coiled rattlesnakes to which he was trying to feed bread and milk with his spoon. Granny screamed and the snakes darted into holes among the rocks and stumps in the yard. He remembered vividly the bright eyes of the rattlesnakes surrounding him in the sunshine of a late afternoon.

The only schooling Grandpa ever had was a three-month term on Devil's Fork. He wore a long-tailed linsey-woolsey shirt to school, as most small boys did in those days when all cloth was woven at home. He followed a path through the woods to school. One morning while crossing a log that lay in the path he discovered what he took to be four or five kittens playing by the log. He gathered them up in the tail of his shirt, carried them to the schoolhouse, and dumped them in the floor to show what he had found. They were baby skunks. The teacher and the other children fell back and the skunks sprayed Grandpa. The teacher sent him home for a good scrubbing and a change of shirts.

Grandpa did not return to school after the Whitts reached Lawrence County. During his three months in school in Elliott County he had learned to read and to "figure" but he could write only his name. Because Grampap was a "fugitive from justice," the Whitts did not return to Elliott County and Morgan County often to visit their kin. Grandpa knew very little about

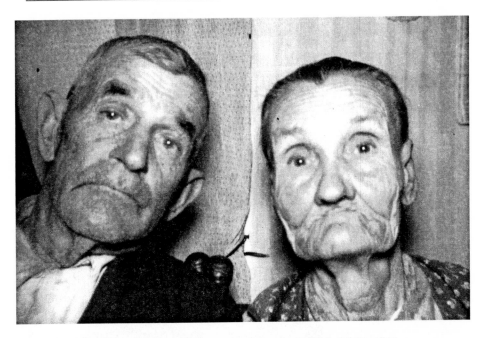

Grandpa Jeff Whitt and Grandma Mandy Griffith Whitt, 1954.

his kinfolk. If he knew that his ancestor Spencer Adkins had presided at the first "squire's court" ever held in the Big Sandy Valley, that his great-great-grandfather Robert Whitt had been with George Rogers Clark in the Northwest Territory campaign, that his great-grandfather had been a member of the Kentucky Legislature before the Civil War, that his grandfather and great uncles were the founders and early officials of Elliott County, he never referred to it. He always used the quaint, extremely old-fashioned English he had learned in his boyhood and gave the impression of belonging to an earlier age in speech and manner.

A small man who never weighed more than 120 pounds in his life, one whose father had moved into the community under inauspicious circumstances and finally left it in extreme poverty, who struggled for acceptance in a social setting that rewarded brawn and physical power, and whose quaint English set him apart, he was laughed at, taunted by rowdies, and teased by those who considered themselves better favored than he. But he read, found opportunities to discuss his reading, had a remarkable memory, understood finance, and was clever in many ways in the management of his affairs. More than any other of my kin he came closer to having an intellectual view of the world and how it operates. Systematic and logical in the development of an argument, he was a formidable antagonist in a theological discussion and sought opportunities in an almost completely unintellectual social setting to enhance his self-esteem by engaging in discussions of religion even at country stores and family gatherings.

A deeply frustrated man, Grandpa Jeff protected himself from the violence that was pent up within him by never owning a gun. Squelched and taunted by bullies, he recoiled in silence, but his anger would rise when he had a drink or two of whiskey, and he would become sharp-tongued, quarrelsome, and abusive. Agile and light-footed, he would avoid physical confrontation with a verbally gored antagonist, find three or four small stones, and maintain enough distance to throw them effectively when he needed to protect himself. He was so skillful as a "rock thrower" that he could bring back about as many squirrels from a hunt as the average man could kill with a rifle.

Unprepared physically to fight, he nevertheless enjoyed watching a good fight and thought one occasionally added zest to community life and went a long way in setting off a public gathering in style. With a thimbleful or two of whiskey in him, he found a wide gulf between the moral theory of his Calvinistic religion and the application in practice of its principles. He loved to set neighbors against each other, to stimulate verbal confrontations and fights, to become involved by "facing" an antagonist with what he had said about the aggrieved one whom Grandpa was sponsoring. On such occasions, he carried three or four carefully selected stones in his pockets as his arsenal of defense in case he needed to use it.

But his intellectual view of the world, shaped as it was by his fundamental religion, did not exclude superstition. He believed in "omens," signs, forewarnings, and supernaturalism, including ghosts and apparitions. He told an interesting story about his participation in a search for Swift's silver mines. It was believed that Swift's mines were among the caves of Laurel Creek. In fact, people living in the neighborhood believed they knew the very cave in which Swift had hidden a cache of silver bars, but their digging and exploration had never revealed any signs of the treasure.[2]

Sitting around a pot-bellied stove in Eck Berry's store, men from Blaine and the neighboring communities hatched a plan to see for themselves whether there was silver hidden in one of the caves.

Tom Lester, Grandpa's brother-in-law, was well acquainted with the cliffs and caves of the Laurels. He knew the cave said by many to be the one in which Swift and Spurlock had hidden their silver,[3] and he knew people who had gone there to wait for the ball of light that crept through the western opening of the cave at midnight to hover over the spot beneath which the bars of silver were said to have been buried, but always the gust of wind that ushered in the ball of light carried it into the earth below before it could settle above the hiding place.

Several men from the community had sought the help of a famous medium in Huntington, West Virginia, in locating lost items as well as in communicating with the dead. Dr. H. Chilton Osborn, a young physician in Blaine, agreed to consult the medium the next time he was in Huntington about the location of the cave and the procedure to follow in retrieving Swift's lost treasure. After Dr. Osborn announced that he was going to Huntington on a certain day and would see the medium if she were available, a party of men began to make preparations for the treasure hunt. Heig Holbrook agreed to furnish a gallon of whiskey. Tom Lester, Grandpa, and others would bring picks, mattocks, and shovels. Dr. Osborn himself would bring a special light by which they could see to dig.

Dr. Osborn returned with information the medium had communicated to him and a time was agreed upon for the search. In the briefing, Dr. Osborn reported that the medium had succeeded in communicating with Swift, who reported that his cache was hidden two feet down by a ledge that extended along the wall of the tunnel cave and that his ghost would appear at midnight through the western opening and descend through the earth to his treasure provided there was neither light nor noise in the cave. The spot could be marked and the men could dig there and find the silver.

The men met at the entrance to the appointed cave to wait for midnight. As Heig's jug was being passed among them, Dr. Osborn repeated his conversations with the medium while the men listened quietly around the fire they had built to hold back the darkness and reassure themselves with its light. At eleven o'clock by the doctor's watch they crept into the cave and ranged themselves, leaning rigidly on their tools, along the wall opposite the ledge to wait in perfect silence for the ghost to appear at midnight. Heig's whiskey had helped. The courage of each was reinforced by the companionship of the group but, at the same time, the imagination of each, fueled a modicum by Heig's firewater and confined by silence, became increasingly activated as the minutes passed. No one knew the time. Minutes seemed long in the tense silence of absolute darkness.

At what might have been midnight a sudden gust of wind roared through the western opening. Courage broke, and before the ball of light appeared all the men in the party fled as one man. Heig should have provided two gallons of whiskey. After the experience, no one in the group was ever willing to go into the cave again. Grandpa believed Swift's treasure awaited the man who had the courage to watch the light ball descend into the floor of the cave, mark the spot, and dig it out.

Once Grandpa felt impelled to go on a spree with some congenial and free-hearted companion who could be depended upon to furnish the whiskey they would need, for he was tight-fisted and stingy with his own money. Knowing that his friend Clabe Steele, who lived on Abb Creek, would respond to priming, Grandpa bought a half-pint of moonshine whiskey and walked over the hills to see Clabe. Producing his bottle, he offered Clabe a drink, but took only a sip himself. Soon he pulled the bottle again, but barely touched it to his own lips. After a while, the bottle was empty, but Clabe had merely had his thirst whetted. He suggested that they ride over to Wallowhole Creek in Elliott County and buy a gallon. Grandpa seemed reluctant to go along, but Clabe urged him to ride behind him on his horse, and away they went.

They were gone three days. Weary and heavy-headed with hangovers, they were making their way back to Clabe's house about 10 o'clock the third night, Grandpa riding behind and holding to the saddle. The night was clear but only a feather of a moon was shining. As they rode across the ford of Abb Creek on their way to the trail up the branch on which Clabe lived, the horse stopped to drink from the pool. Clumps of young willows growing on the bank of the creek drooped toward the surface of the water. Wisps of mist floated along the water course in the dim moonlight. As the horse finished drinking, Clabe reined in the bridle, but the horse became startled at some movement in the bushes and shied and skittered.

"Look, Jeff, thair's a hant!" Clabe said, pointing toward a wisp of fog floating by.

"Whur? Pshaw! I don't see nothin."

"Right thair. Hit's a tryin to git on the horse behind you."

"Pshaw! Don't get up hyur behind me! Git up thair in front of Clabe!" Grandpa said, flinging his arm wildly at the streamer of fog. "Thair's more room up thair."

Clabe delighted in telling the story of their "hanting" in Grandpa's presence. Grandpa would sit with his eyes closed and a smile playing around his mouth while he pulled at his nose slowly, but he would neither confirm nor deny Clabe's story.

Cal Tolliver

During my father's boyhood Cal Tolliver came occasionally to the distilleries on Caines Creek for whiskey. Everybody knew that Cal had been the little boy who had rushed across the yard in front of the hotel in Morehead, relieved his Uncle Craig of his gold watch after Craig had fallen in the feud battle, and escaped around the corner of the hotel while bullets were whizzing around him. Sometimes he would tell about the bullet that tore a hole in the seat of his pants but did not hit him when he bent over the body of his dead uncle, slumped on the steps of the hotel, to pull the watch and chain from his vest pocket.

Cal was a middle-aged man while he was coming to the distilleries for whiskey. He enjoyed his notoriety as the sole Tolliver survivor of the feud battle, and he liked to keep alive his reputation as a bad man. Sometimes, when he was feeling high from whiskey, he would do things to remind people that he was bad and dangerous.

Once, when he entered the liquor store after a drinking bout with his cronies, he noticed that all conversation stopped and that people were watching him closely and straining their ears to hear his conversation with the storekeeper. After he had purchased his package of whiskey, he was leaving the store when he saw a wide-eyed little girl leaning against the counter. He stopped suddenly in front of her, looked her straight in the face as she cowered before him, pulled the lower lid of one of his red eyes down, and said, "Did you ever see a Tolliver eye?"

The little girl was terrified, but she could not tear herself away from his stare. After a long moment, in which everybody was frozen with fright, Cal released his eyelid, looked around with a menacing grin, and left the store.

At another time he was purchasing a package of whiskey when a little boy came rushing into the store, laid a nickel on the counter, and asked the storekeeper for the worth of it in stick candy. The storekeeper, interrupting his negotiations with Cal, turned and waited on the boy.

When the little boy had his poke of candy in his hand, he looked up at Cal, whose eyes were withering him. The boy was transfixed.

"I wish I had a five-acre field full of little boys like you," Cal said.

"W'y, Mr. Tolliver, what would you do with that many boys?" the merchant asked.

"I'd like to shoot 'em and watch 'em die."

One day while my grandfather Williams was away from home Cal and a companion rode their horses into the yard of my grandfather's home and called. Granny walked into the porch to see what they wanted. They had come for whiskey. Granny called my father, then about fifteen years old, to get a package of whiskey for each of them. They paid for the whiskey, stored it in their saddlebags, mounted their horses, and started down the road. At the end of the yard, Cal pulled a big pistol and fired it toward the sky.

My father grabbed his rifle, left the house by the back door, rushed around the corner, and took a position behind an apple tree. He fired at Cal but missed him. Cal turned in his saddle and shot in the general direction of the house.

Papa advanced to another tree, took deliberate aim, and fired again. Cal's black hat bounced off his head in front of him, but he caught it. He turned and fired his pistol again at the house. Papa fired his rifle again.

When the bullet whizzed by Cal's ear he applied his spurs to his horse's flanks and sped away. He never returned to Grampa's distillery again.

Ye Offspring of Vipers[4]

Things had not been going well for the preacher right lately. He had reined his horse under the shelter of an oak tree on the knob to escape a sudden shower and lightning had struck the tree, splitting it from the top to the butt. He had been knocked from his horse, he thought by a falling limb, but quite addled by the incident he was not sure whether the lightning had knocked him from his horse or whether a limb had done it. When his senses came back to him he was lying on the ground, his hat beside him, there was a bruised swipe across his forehead with blood oozing from it, and his back hurt him, but God had been with him. No bones were broken. His horse had raced away, but when the preacher picked himself up and looked around, he saw the horse a few yards away against a rail fence. The saddle girt had broken and the saddle lay on the ground there beside the preacher, its blanket tumbled nearby and both saddle and blanket becoming soaked with rainwater.

By the time he had caught his horse, repaired the saddle girt, and was mounted again, the shower was over, but the preacher was soaking wet, and the saddle under him was wet and sticky. He made his way slowly down the trail toward Barkers', where he was going to visit for a while and discuss with Henry and Louella Barker a verse from Matthew, "Ye serpents, ye offspring of vipers, how shall ye escape the judgment of hell?" This verse, he thought, might bring down power if used as a text when he stood to preach the next monthly meeting of the Hardshells. He fancied it might bring the wrath of God down upon those who had been talking about him lately.

It was not that he had a clear understanding of what the traducers had been saying about him. So far as he had been able to make it out, the talk had to do with his spending so much time at the Barkers', especially when others were working in their crops. Someone on the porch at the store, where he had ridden one day while on his way home from the Barkers' to buy some salt and baking soda for his old woman, had teased him in a vague way about hanging around the Barkers' so much. Another had asked whether he helped Louella string beans while Henry chopped wood to cook supper with. When he noticed that one man winked at the other and both lifted their eyebrows at him, he did not offer to respond to their questions. As he was going past them into the store, he was sensitive to their watching him carefully, and all of them laughed loudly at a comment made by a third man in such a low voice that the preacher had not heard plainly all that was said, but he was sure he had heard "sassage grinder" in the comment. His old woman had reported that one of the neighbor's young 'ens had asked one of theirs why the preacher was spending so much of his time at the Barkers'. Little Eddie had not known what to say. The preacher knew there was talk going around. He'd better see whether the Lord had anything to say about it if the "Sparrit" should happen to come down to lift him up next time he stood to preach. Henry and Louella might be a heap of help to him as he wrestled with the problem.

The sun was out again and his clothes, though still wet, were steaming when he climbed off his horse at the Barkers' gate. He hitched the horse to a post for the picket fence and went into the porch, where Henry and Louella were sitting in cane-bottom chairs and waiting for the weeds and bushes to drip before returning to their field.

The preacher walked stiffly as he held his hand to the "small of his back."

"I see you got caught in the rain," Henry observed.

"Yes, I'm soakin' wet clean through and through. But that hain't the worst of it. I reckon I was struck by thunder and lightnin', too."

He related to them all that had happened, best he could remember. Henry took him into the bedroom and gave him a pair of his pants and a shirt to wear while his clothes dried in the sunshine from the top of the picket fence along which they were spread.

Henry's shirt would not button and the waistband of his pants did not meet on the preacher, but he was dry. He set his shoes in a sunny spot on the porch floor and stretched his socks out beside them to dry. Dragging up another cane-bottom chair, he sat near Henry and Louella there on the porch. He complained that the small of his back was sore and he had a pain in his belly. Louella fetched the camphor and liniment from the fireboard. The preacher stood up and lifted the tail of the shirt for her to rub his back with the medicines. The preacher felt relief from pain as she applied the aromatic ointments and rubbed vigorously.

He sat down and talked about the "tales that were a-goin' around." He thought the text about the offspring of vipers might please the Lord to put words into his mouth that would scorch the tale-bearers and please the righteous the next time he stood up to preach at the meeting house. Henry, Louella, and he tried to patch together from wisps of conversation the preacher had heard and their suspicions about what the tales might be. All thought the text about the offspring of the vipers would be an appropriate one for the preacher to use. Henry went to the corner cupboard and found the family Bible, a big book with hard covers. He sat down and spread the book across his knees. He searched in Matthew until he found the verses the preacher would want to use. He read them painfully aloud several times. The preacher thought he could remember them and could call other verses to mind, once he had hit his pace in his sermon. After a long discussion of the tales and much speculation about who was "a-naratin 'em around," Henry returned the Bible to its place and invited the preacher to "stay around" while he led the horse up to the stable for a few ears of corn and stopped by the back yard to hack up a few sticks of wood for Louella, for it was getting nigh on to supper time.

After Henry left, the preacher began to complain about the pains in his belly. Louella invited him to lie on his back at the edge of the porch and she would rub his belly with the camphor and liniment. The preacher lay down, pulled the shirt open, and moved the waistband of the pants to expose his belly. Louella stood on the ground, her back to the gate, and rubbed his belly with camphor and liniment. The preacher's pain was eased so pleasantly by the massaging that he permitted her to continue for a long time.

The gate was opened suddenly. When Louella turned around, she was surprised to see Maggie Campbell, a basket of eggs on her arm, and a strange smile on her face, advancing toward the porch. When the preacher lifted his head far enough to see Maggie, he pulled the shirt over himself and tugged at the pants.

"The preacher was struck by lightning," Louella said. "Both his back and his belly was hurt. I have been a-doctorin 'em with this here camphor and liniment."

"Laws o' mercy," said Maggie, "I reckon every man a-livin' on the waters of this creek would go out and get hisse'f struck by lightning if he thought he could get his neighbor's old woman to rub his belly with camphorated oil. Now, you take me, I wouldn't hardly do it for my man Jeff, much lessn the preacher."

Louella was stunned, but the preacher, sitting on the edge of the porch and pulling Henry's shirt as far across his chest as it would go, related again what had happened to him and his horse on the knob. Maggie stood by the stone step and listened, inserting, " 'Pon your honor!" in the breaks in the preacher's narrative. When the preacher had finished his story, Maggie, offering no comment, observed that it was a "vagerish hot day" and that she was famished for a drink of cold spring water. She stepped upon the porch and drank a dipperful of water from the cedar bucket on the shelf.

"Well, I'd best be moseyin' on to the store," and she left.

The preacher, Louella, and Henry all agreed that Maggie, long-tongued as she was, would be bound and beholden to try to make something out of what she had seen and would tell it at every house between there and the store and to everybody that might be at the store, too, stretchin' the tale a little more every time she told it, till a body would hardly be able to recognize it by the time she got through fixing it up a little more from first to last.

The preacher was deep in the mulligrubs by the time Louella had the supper on the table. He kept telling Henry over and over what Maggie had said and what he had said, in relating to her the account of what had happened on the knob. It was as if he thought some new word, some increment that he might have forgotten, some leap to another way of looking at what Maggie had seen when she opened the gate might lift him out of the fix he found himself in.

After supper he and Louella and Henry sat on the porch. The preacher called for Henry to fetch the Bible and read again the verses about the offspring of vipers. They chanted some hymns from the little black hymnal, the preacher following, for he was not able to read the fine print in the little book.

Then he began to speak, beginning with "O ye generation of vipers! Who hath warned ye to flee from the wrath to come?" The modified text was the refrain of his impassioned chant as he pranced about on the porch, his barefeet slapping the floor and the tails of Henry's shirt swirling upward as he twisted and turned and flung his arms about.

As he puffed and spewed, his face became red and perspiration trickled down his chest and ran into the open waistband of Henry's pants. Suddenly, he stopped, lifted a dipperful of water from the cedar bucket, and gulped it down. Then he slumped into a chair and allowed his knees to fall far apart. He was spent.

"What if Maggie tells some pack of startenated bare-faced lies to the members of the faith and order and you and Louella are brought up at the church?" Henry inquired.

"We'll make 'er out a l'ar," Louella snapped.

"Yes, we'll say she didn't see nothin' out of the ordinary," the preacher added.

"Ever'body knows she's a long-tongued tale-bearer," Louella continued. "We are two agin one. And you had just the minute before left to feed the horse and cut wood for the kitchen stove. Your testimony will help, too, if they try to church us."

They sat in silence for a few minutes. Then the preacher got up, gathered his shirt and pants from the picket fence and his shoes and socks from the edge of the porch, and went into the bedroom.

"I'd better get ready to go home."

Henry went to the stable and bridled and saddled the preacher's horse and led it to the gate. The preacher climbed on awkwardly.

"The Lord giveth and the Lord taketh away. Hit's time he giveth. I have faith that he'll send down the Holy Sparrit to lift me up when my turn comes to preach next Sunday." The preacher rode away.

Next Sunday morning my father and I were the only ones at home when we saw the preacher riding down the road beside our yard fence. Instead of going on across the bridge and to the church house, he turned out our lane, dismounted at the gate, hitched his horse to a post, and stepped into our porch.

"Curt," he said, "I've got a terrible sinkin' spell this morning. I want a drink of whiskey, if you've got any. I need to be lifted up to preach the sermon the Lord has called me to preach today."

"Well, I don't like to turn down a man in need," my father said. "I've got some of the best you ever tasted in a bottle at the barn. Set around and I'll go get it."

The preacher sat down. He stared straight in front of himself as if he might have been watching a worm crawl out of the ground out there in the yard a few feet from the edge of the porch. He completely ignored me as I tried to see what he might be looking at.

In a few minutes my father called from within the house. The preacher got up and went inside. I followed.

"This is the finest peach brandy I ever tasted," my father said as he handed the quart bottle about half-filled with amber-colored liquor to the preacher.

The preacher held it up between his eyes and the open door. He shook it slightly and watched the beads dance and snap themselves out along the rim of the brandy. He drew the cork from the bottle, held a finger to one nostril, and inhaled the fragrance of the liquor.

He looked at my father. "I've got to face a congregation that's got a lot of people in it that's rotten at the heart," he said. His voice began to rise, but there was a low hum like bees swarming behind and around his words as he continued. "They are a pack of wo'ves in sheep's clothes. They're l'ars and hippercrits! They've been a-traipsin' up and down this hyar creek a-talkin' about me."

He tilted his head backward and raised the bottle to his mouth. Bubbles raced up the neck of the bottle as his Adam's apple pumped several swallows of the whiskey into his stomach with a little grunt following each swallow.

"O ye generation of vipers! Who hath warned ye to flee from the wrath to come?" He chanted, holding the bottle poised for another drink.

"That's powerful liquor," my father said proudly. "It's 110 proof. It'll make the lion and the lamb lie down together, a rabbit spit in a bulldog's eyes, and a young man love his mother-in-law."

"Yes, by God, and a preacher lay his Bible down!" He turned the bottle up again and drank most of what was left.

"Preacher, you'll get so drunk you can't get on your horse if you drink any more of it. I don't begrudge you the whiskey. You're welcome to it. But I'd hate to see you get drunk."

"Get drunk, hell and Goddamnation! The sparrit is a-liftin me up. I'll preach the devil out of hell. Blue blazes'll be lickin' around every lyin' bitch and fornicatin' bastard in that den of vipers, that generation of l'ars and hippercrits before I get done with 'em."

He turned up the bottle and emptied it. As he lowered the bottle, my father reached for it. The preacher was dazed for a moment. He started again to say something, but his mouth wouldn't work right. Then he began to sing in a fuzzy voice "Down by the Riverside" but he trailed off into obscurity before he reached "Shout all over God's heaven." As he started to move he pitched forward, but my father caught him with one hand while handing the empty bottle to me with the other.

"Bring his horse out to the barn," my father said to me as he supported the preacher through the back door of the house.

My father helped the preacher to the shade of a poplar tree that stood beside the creek at the end of the meadow across from our barn. He stretched him out on a bed of broadblade grass near the trunk of the poplar. The preacher was mumbling "Jenny racer o' fipers" just before he passed out completely there on the ground. We let the horse drink at the waterhole and hitched him inside the driveway of the barn.

My father and I sat on the porch and watched people pass on their way to church. We saw Henry and Louella go across the bridge. Soon we could hear singing at the church house. Then we thought we heard Brother Cal Johnson's chant, but we thought only one preacher preached that day. The meeting did not last long. We sat in the porch and watched the church crowd go up the road.

After we had eaten the dinner Mama had prepared for us, my father went somewhere. About the middle of the afternoon some young people came and sat with me in the yard. While we were talking, the preacher, his back slumped into an arch, his chin hanging almost to the saddle horn, and the bridle swinging loosely in his hands, rode out the lane toward the bridge and on to the church house. He did not turn his head toward the house as he passed.

In about fifteen minutes he rode past our yard fence, but again he did not look toward the house.

My father and I never told anybody about the preacher's experience with the "sparrits" that dragged him into the patch of broadblade grass and kept him from delivering his sermon to the offspring of vipers. He and Louella were never "brought up in church." Maggie told everybody in the valley about having caught Louella rubbing the preacher's belly. They countered by bringing up Maggie for bearing false witness. With three against one, Maggie was excommunicated, but the "Sparrit" never saw fit to come down and lift the preacher up far enough for him to deliver his scorching sermon. It was not necessary. The vipers had been eliminated by strategy.

Preacher Lant Gets Drunk

Pa had thirty acres planted in corn that year, all hillside land. The season had been a good one. Enough rain had fallen at the right time for the corn to grow tall and the ears to fill out well. As a usual thing, Pa cut and shucked all of the corn himself, but cool weather came in early September and he feared

Curt Williams at his barn on Caines Creek, 1950s. "He never wasted anything. His farm looked like a park. The fences were straight as arrows and the wires were stretched tightly. Every year he gave time to cleaning the fence rows. He mowed his meadows clear to the water's edge and to the edge of the fence, and his haystacks were neat and his barn was clean"— Cratis Williams.

the first frost might ruin the fodder before he could finish the job. He would need a field hand to help cut the corn.

He walked over the hill and hired the preacher. Brother Lant Collier, moderator of the local Hardshell Baptist Church, was a desperately poor man who lived with his sickly wife and ten half-naked children on a worn-out rented farm in the head of the hollow across the hill from our place. He had grown only eight or ten acres of corn in the ribbons of bottomland that meandered with the branch on to better favored patches in the flats above the first steeps of the hills. He needed some cash money to buy shoes and sweaters and jackets for his young 'ens. His older sons could cut his corn while he worked for Pa for two dollars a day and his room and board. He agreed to come next morning and go to work.

Preacher Lant was a good worker and tall enough to handle the heavy corn easily. The only thing was that he did not have much to eat at home and he tired out pretty quickly during the first two days.

We had plenty to eat. Garden stuff was at its best, our hens were slamming out the store pay, the cows were giving gallons of rich milk, and we still

Curt Williams's barn as seen from the meadow.

had two middlings of bacon and a jowl or two, and several ham hocks hanging in the smokehouse. Ma cooked big meals for the preacher, whose appetite was hearty and who would drink a quart of milk with each meal besides a mug of hot strong coffee that he would pour into a saucer, blow lustily on, and draw with a slurping sound through the heavy black mustache that drooped straight across his mouth. After each swallow of the hot coffee he would exhale forcefully with a "ha-a-a-ah" that sent the little droplets of coffee clinging to the ends of the hairs in his mustache skittering across his saucer and bouncing off his plate. But he mended right smartly from eating the good food and had gained about as much strength as Pa had by Wednesday.

Pa had set sixty gallons of corn mash for making his supply of whiskey for the next year. It was hidden in two thirty-gallon barrels half-buried in the ground in a clump of bushes beside a spring in the cove at the head of the ravine in the hog field. He had not been to the barrels for three or four days and had thought that the mash would not have worked off and been ready for the still before Friday night. When he slipped away after work Wednesday to see how the mash was coming along, he found it ready to run. Few bubbles were rising in it. One big drink of it made a body's head buzz and his eyes whizz. The mash would begin losing its strength fast after another day.

At noon Thursday Pa told the preacher that the springs and water holes in the hog field and the pastures were getting low. They had filled up with sand

and mud during the rains and had to be cleaned out, now that the brutes were not getting enough water to drink. He would attend to the water holes and springs that afternoon and Preacher Lant could go on with the corn cutting.

Pa went to the cove and set up his still, built around it a furnace of rocks and mud, placed the barrel for a flake stand close by, secured the copper "worm" in the stand, and filled the barrel with cold spring water. He then filled with mash the twenty gallon still that he had engaged a coppersmith in Huntington to make for him years before, put the cap in place, and sealed connections with paste made of barley flour and water. A pile of wood near a spring in a shaded cove invites hunters, "sang" diggers, and prowling boys to search for mash, but a few dead limbs from trees, pine knots rich with resin, dry chunks wrested from rotting stumps, and old rails strewn casually along a wire fence can be for a still furnace a supply of wood that hardly anyone would notice. Pa had already gathered and carefully laid out enough wood, but if he needed more, the old rails along the wire fence were not far away. By starting the fire in the furnace before he had completed the setting up of his rig, he had going a low burning fire that would hold for at least two hours when he left the still in time to do the "jin jobs" around the barn.

After supper Pa complained of being tired. Preacher Lant had worked hard, too. He had taken only one short rest all afternoon. A man working alone is driven to work harder when he sees what little one man can do in a big field, he allowed. They were pleased to "hit the shucks" early. After the preacher lay down, Pa slipped out of the house and went back to the still. At daybreak he returned to do the early morning chores, eat breakfast with the preacher, and go into the field after the dew had dripped from the corn blades.

After supper that evening Pa said that he needed to go up the creek to see a man about a debt the man owed him. He did not know when he would get back. Preacher Lant could sit on the porch as long as he wanted to and "turn in" when he felt like it. Pa, unlighted lantern in hand, then left by the front gate, stopping to scold the dog that wanted to go along and to explain to him that he was not going possum hunting, just because he had a lantern in his hand. The dog, disappointed with Pa's refusal to let him go too, howled piteously and ran along the inside of the yard fence protesting.

Preacher Lant tried to comfort the dog with soft words, but old Boss, ignoring him, continued to howl and cry with Pa cursing him as he disappeared up the road. The dog, still refusing to respond to Preacher Lant, tried to jump over the yard fence, but he was getting old and fat and did not succeed. He barked in protest and lay down with a moan.

After about five minutes, Boss leapt to his feet and barked loudly as if he were ready to dash off after a rabbit that had unwarily ventured within range. With a great surge of energy he sprang to the top of the fence at the corner of the yard, succeeded in getting his paws across the top rail, struggled

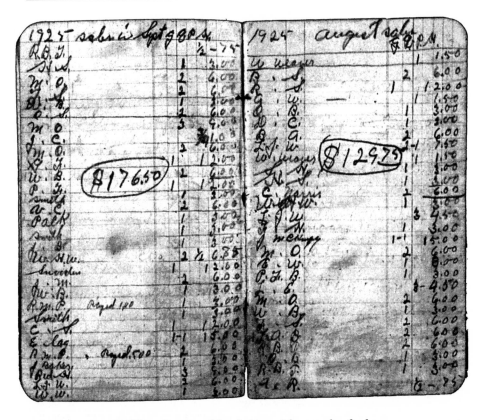

Curt Williams's moonshine ledger with records of sales.

for a moment, and then, by bracing his heavy body against one wall of the fence, propelled himself across.

Instead of going up the road and out of sight behind the chicken house, as Pa had done, Boss climbed the bluff toward the woven wire fence surrounding the hog field. He attempted to climb across the leaning fence, but he caught his hind feet in the sagging wire after he had his shoulders over the top. He struggled to free his hind feet, but the more he struggled the more the fence swayed down hill away from the posts. Unable to get over the fence or to free himself from it, he began to howl.

Preacher Lant went to help the poor dog. He crossed the fence and pulled the woven wire uphill, enabling the dog to shift his weight so that he was no longer hanging from the leaning fence. Preacher Lant placed a hand under the dog's haunches and pulled. The dog struggled for a moment before landing in the path above the fence and taking off up the hill before Preacher Lant could grab him by the collar.

Preacher Lant tried to coax the dog down the path to the gate, but Boss ignored him. Preacher Lant followed, but the dog soon disappeared in the bushes.

Pa, busily filling the still with the last twenty gallons of mash, was not surprised by the dog when he arrived, wagging his tail triumphantly but holding his head close to the earth while begging for acceptance. Pa spoke to Boss kindly and he lay down by one of the saplings from which a rope had been strung to hold the tarpaulin hung a few feet from the mouth of the still furnace to hide the light of the fire from anybody who might be prowling the hills. Pa continued with his work, built a fire that flamed brightly at first, capped the still, and sealed the connections. He then blew out the light in his lantern and sat down to watch the fire.

Pa had begun to doze when he was awakened by a snapping of dry sticks in the bushes off to his left. Boss, losing his hearing, did not respond to the sound. Pa picked up his long-handled shovel and hid behind a tree to wait. Soon sticks snapped again. Pa moved silently to the next tree in the direction from which the sound had come and waited. Sticks snapped again and he could hear the swish of leaves on limbs of bushes through which somebody was walking stealthily. Pa moved to another tree and waited. He heard the rasping sound of a sawbriar tugged from its anchorings by a walker. He moved to the next tree, beside which a pig path ran toward the upper side of the clump of bushes from which the sounds came.

While waiting, Pa was wrestling with his decision to knock the prowler on the head from behind with the shovel, burn his body in the still furnace, and bury his bones and buttons at the bottom of a post hole. It might be the informer who had spied and reported one of the Lyon boys to the deputies only a few weeks ago. If so, Pa would put him to sleep so gently and swiftly that he would lift up his eyes in hell in time for breakfast.

The glow from behind the tarpaulin gave barely enough light for one hidden behind a tree to see a human form, but it was important to stand in the shadow of the tree, to hide by its dark side. An intruder approaching from the clump of bushes would be walking into the glow against which the tarpaulin was outlined. He would not be able to see Pa standing in the shadow of a tree trunk.

The bushes parted. A tall man moved slowly and silently into the path. He stopped and was motionless as he faced the dark tarpaulin outlined only dimly against the glow. He wore dark clothes. His face and hands were blurred gray splotches, but he did not appear to be carrying a rifle. He came forward three or four cautious steps and stopped again, erect, silent, almost as if he were not even breathing. He was a broad-shouldered man with long arms and big hands. He was too big to be the informer who had turned in the Lyon boys. Maybe he was another informer or a deputy. He took four or five more steps, putting his feet down in an easy, searching way and flinging his arms for balance. He was not carrying a rifle, certainly. If he were a deputy, he was not wearing his badge, for there was enough light to reflect off a badge. He had to be an informer. He bent over slightly, as if he were trying to see around the end of the tarpaulin, and crept forward four or five more steps. Half-crouched and looking as if he were trying to see around the other end of the tarpaulin, he stopped directly in front of Pa and not more than six feet away.

Pa raised the shovel for the death blow. But the end of the shovel had touched a twig on a limb of the tree and made a slight whisking noise. The crouching form turned his head suddenly toward Pa but did not see him in the deep shadow. Pa checked his blow and looked at the profile, now made clear against the glow coming around the far end of the tarpaulin. There were the fine forehead, straight nose, drooping mustache, and strong chin of Preacher Lant's face.

Pa carefully lowered the shovel, stole behind the tree, and peeped around it. Not seeing anybody at the still, the Preacher went behind the tarpaulin. He called Pa's name softly, but Pa did not answer. Instead, he moved quietly to a tree from behind which he could see the preacher.

Preacher Lant studied the construction of the furnace, ran his hand lightly along the connection from the still cap to the worm, tested the temperature of the water in the flake stand with his finger, and bent over and smelled the singlings trickling into a half-gallon jar. He straightened up and called Pa's name again softly. Seeing the cartons of jars against the tarpaulin, he went over and opened one. He held his finger against one nostril and inhaled slowly the aroma of the whiskey. He tipped the jar to his face, took a taste, and smacked his mouth and licked his lips as he stood stiff and tall, holding the jar only a few inches from his chin.

Pa was watching carefully as the preacher lifted the jar to his head and drank rapidly several swallows of the fiery liquor, gulping with a little grunt after each swallow. He lowered the jar and sputtered and shivered as he wiped his mustache with the back of his hand. He screwed the cap on the jar and sat down on a stump, fixing his gaze on the low fire in the furnace and resting the jar between his knees. Soon he removed the cap, tilted the jar to his head again, and drank for a long time, maybe as much as five minutes. Pa could hear him gulp after each swallow.

Pa laid the shovel down quietly, crept through the woods in the direction of the wire fence, found two rails, and returned, crashing through the bushes as if he were unaware of the preacher's presence. He approached the site of the still with the preacher in full view. When the preacher heard the noise he screwed the cap on the jar hurriedly, returned it to the carton, slipped to the end of the tarpaulin and darted behind it just before Pa arrived. Boss, having become accustomed to the preacher's presence and being old and hard of hearing, slept on.

When Pa threw down the rails and peeped around the tarpaulin to look for the preacher, he could barely make out his form staggering along the pig path that ran above the thicket through which he had found his way to the still.

Ma heard the preacher slam the yard gate and stumble across the porch to his room. He did not light the kerosene lamp, but fumbled around in darkness in getting his heavy shoes off, each striking the floor with a thump amid what were at first indistinct mutterings. Having difficulty pulling the galluses of his overalls off his shoulders without unfastening them, he was addressing himself with mounting anger to the "confounded things" when he fell backward on the bed, the springs complaining against his weight. He pulled himself up on the bed fully dressed except for his shoes.

The mutterings and mumblings soon accommodated themselves to the tune of "That Beautiful City," which the preacher "heisted" with considerable skill and sang completely. He then began to pray as loudly as if the Lord were waiting on the top of Fork Ridge a half-mile away, the words of his prayer punctuated rhythmically with apostrophes to the Lord that trailed off with a sough and were terminated with a gasp. Having apparently engaged the Lord's ear, he moved from his prayer into a shouting routine that expressed his great happiness, his voice as strong as the bellow of a bull. He then lay still for a few minutes.

With a groan, he flung his feet on the floor with a heavy, dead thud that shook the house to the rafters, attempted to rise, but fell back to the bed, his weight crashing the springs. There was a moment of quiet. Then a long nasal hum preceded his lifting the tune of "This Is a World of Trouble," a slow-moving plaint about the sorrows and tribulations of this old world here below.

Halfway through the song Ma heard a horseback rider crossing the wooden bridge beyond the end of the lane. She requested the preacher to hush and go to sleep. People passing the big road would not know what was going on.

The preacher ignored her and finished the song. He then called out to Ma and asked whether she was under conviction for her sins. She did not reply. The preacher then raised his voice to a chant and began to preach, a garbled and disorganized sermon about the sins of the heart, the turning away from the call to salvation, the wickedness of pride and stubbornness against the invitation to "come unto me," for "I knock at the door."

Another late traveler crossed the wooden bridge. Ma yelled out to the preacher to be quiet and go to sleep.

"Quiet, hell and god-damnation!" bellowed the preacher. "Who's a-goin' to be quiet when Jesus comes?"

The preacher gulped and swallowed hard a few times as his sermon lost momentum. Then there was a groan followed by a heave that sent a stream of vomit spattering across the floor. Ma leapt from her bed, grabbed the slop jar in one hand and the lamp in the other, and hurried into the preacher's room.

He was sitting on the edge of the bed, fully dressed except for his shoes, which were on the floor between his feet and half-filled with vomit. Ma set the lamp on the dresser and placed the slop jar between the preacher's feet. He attempted to say something, but another mighty heave convulsed him and he vomited again, mostly into the slop jar. As he attempted to straighten himself, he took a deep breath and was seized by another heave. He leaned so low over the slop jar that Ma, fearing he was going to fall from the bed on his face, grabbed him by the hair of the head to hold him in place. He heaved and retched, but by now only gall trickled from the ends of his drooping mustache. Then the heaves were dry, though no less vigorous, as the preacher surged forward, Ma holding him tightly by the forelock, as if he were bent on puking up the very soles of his feet into the slop jar. After a while the heaving and retching gave way to hiccups.

He managed to ask whether he might have a glass of water. Thinking that he was probably able now to sit up, Ma took the lamp into the kitchen and returned with a glass of water. The preacher sipped at the water slowly taking only a few drops at a time. The hiccups subsided and he straightened himself out on top of the covers and went to sleep.

When Pa returned to the house next morning, he told Ma about seeing the preacher drinking the first-run singlings, that he had come within a "pee" of killing the preacher with the shovel but the preacher didn't know it, and that the preacher had never seen him at all. The way the preacher was wobbling and weaving as he staggered down the pig path, Pa was surprised that he had ever made it to the house at all. Ma gave an account of the preacher's "services" for her, followed by the puking and the mess that it would take a half-day and a quart of lye soap to clean up.

The preacher was later than usual to breakfast. He was shame-faced when he said, "Lord, I was a sick man last night. Something I ate didn't agree with me."

He looked at Ma for her response, his bloodshot eyes begging her to accept his story. Ma looked at him a moment and then at Pa, who nodded his head slowly.

"Yes, Preacher Lant, you were a mighty sick man last night," she said.

The preacher relaxed, but he did not have much appetite for his breakfast that morning.

Moonshining in My Family[5]

My Williams ancestors, the last of my pioneer ancestors to come into Kentucky, left Scott County, Virginia, in 1837 to come to Kentucky. Their

Old Hen Boggs's distillery, surrounded by neighbors and friends.

teams drew crude wagons loaded with the stills and brandy, while the children and women of the family walked along behind the wagons. Arriving in Blaine, Kentucky, my great-great-grandfather set up a saddle shop and a whiskey distillery. Up the valley he found a rock angled in a natural bowl shape; he chipped a little trench out of that rock, and he used it as a basin for driving the tar out of knotty pine trees that grew there. He used tar both in his tannery shop and his distillery. The creek that ran through there got the name of Tar Kiln.

My family had always said that the family line with the whiskey making tradition left Pennsylvania in 1794. That tradition has come down in my family to my own generation and I am the only one who has not been a distiller. The distillers were licensed. I was present when my grandfather's distillery was closed as I was his mascot when I was a little boy. My grandfather Williams was a tough-minded old fellow and held out to the very end, until he was officially closed down, giving him the dubious distinction of having been the last legal distiller in eastern Kentucky. Records of the whiskey taxes collected in Lawrence County in 1885 indicate that the two largest producers were my great-grandfather and his brother. The two competitors were their cousins who lived across the mountain. The fifth-ranking man was a very distant cousin who lived about eleven miles away. It looked as if it was members of my family in this county who carried on the whiskey tradition.

Those who paid their taxes were within the law. A government man would come by every now and again and check the stock and records. Later on the small licensed distiller had to have on his property a storekeeper and gauger who had qualified for that position by having taken an examination just as postmasters did. The job of the storekeeper-gauger was to see that the ingredients in a run of whiskey were correct, that the proof was acceptable, that it was placed in a barrel, aged, and the date stamped on a little lead pellet, and all of that was put on the barrel and the barrel was rolled into a warehouse and turned periodically, so the staves above would not crack and let it evaporate. After the prescribed time it was ready for market. Typically, this little licensed distiller could not sell whiskey himself in small dribs, but he could sell it in a five-gallon package. The result was that all the boys in the neighborhood who wanted from a half pint up would pool their resources and one person would go and buy a five-gallon package of whiskey from the manufacturer at the still itself.

An overwhelming number of Appalachian people did not conform with the law as their ancestors had apparently done. They felt the tax was unjust and they did not want to pay it. Their operations then became surreptitious. So they would find a place near a spring—it could be in a draw up near the head of a hollow where there would be a spring, or in a ravine near a creek, provided there were trees around. Anywhere it could be hidden would be suitable.

After the feud spirit had arisen in the mountains, people had to be careful of their neighbors who might report them, especially if they were enemies as a result of antagonisms that grew up during the Civil War. Making whiskey had to be secretive.

The moonshiner, contrary to popular opinion, was normally a respectable citizen in his community. He owned his land, he was a man of honor, and he took his obligations of citizenship seriously. Moreover, he was resourceful and skillful in planning and execution, for considerable care and preparation are involved in the making of whiskey. Managing the operation to avoid detection from snooping neighbors requires shrewdness. Planning a "run" of whiskey within the framework of secrecy and deception requires administrative skills and expert timing. Making contraband whiskey came to be called "moonshining" because it was made at night, particularly when the moon was bright.

To make whiskey the moonshiner needed a fine copper still. Sometimes it was inherited; sometimes he would make for himself what he would refer to as an "excellent rig"; sometimes it was two copper kettles riveted together with a copper bucket to make the cap and copper tubing. He would hide it in a hollow tree or a cave, then set his mash. Those who were making it the old-fashioned way did not add any sweetening. They could sprout and make their own malt, which required time, and the malt itself had a natural sugar

Williams Henderson Boggs, Old Hen, at age 92.

in it and that enhanced the productivity. A gallon to a gallon and a half from a bushel of grain was standard.

Later on when moonshining and bootlegging became profitable, moonshiners could triple the output by adding sugar or molasses. The old-timers resisted this compromise. They would bury their barrels partway into the ground so that they would be easy to hide, but in the wintertime they would build a rack around them and pack the rack with horse manure because horse manure maintained an even, warm temperature; if a cold snap came, they would build a fire and heat a load of iron objects, like plow points or anything else made of iron that they could string on a wire or a chain, and drop those heated objects in each barrel for a few minutes to keep the temperature up so that the fermentation process would continue. Then when it was time to distill, they would slip out at night and ring the place with wires or ropes on which they hung tarpaulins and quilts, so that the fire light couldn't shine through. A natural cover of foliage was desirable, as the smoke wouldn't be so obvious against green trees. They worked in secret. After the mash had been distilled (sour mash was called "beer"; the local pronunciation was "be-aar"), they would then clean the still carefully and double distill the run. The first run was almost pure alcohol, but the alcohol content diminishes, and they would keep running until a little bit would not flame when dashed into the fire. Then they knew that the alcohol was pretty well distilled. A little liquid was needed to cut it in order to maintain the proof, so they kept on hand a keg full of distilled water that had some of the flavor of the grain, so that they could mix the very powerful first run with the later, weak run, and maintain a hundred proof product. Without the hydrometer, they tested by pouring into a clear vessel — a little bottle or glass with a mid-line — a mixture of the weak and the strong. When shaken, and the bead floats along the line so that 50% is exactly above the line and 50% exactly below, it is 100 proof. The more above the line the bubble stands the higher the percentage of alcohol. Some moonshiners were skilled at timing the bursting of the bubbles, but this was not as accurate as use of the halfway line around the bottle.

Most moonshiners did not engage in moonshining for economic reasons. They liked to drink good whiskey and would pull off one run a year in the late fall for their own consumption. It was very carefully made, doubled and twisted and strained through a charcoal bag hung on the end of the worm to cut out what the mountaineers called "bardy grease" (verdigris), the poisonous, oily substance that comes out of the copper. They would age it in wood for a time and then transfer it to jugs and bottles, and would have enough good whiskey to last a year or two. They would hold some back for three years, for that would enhance the quality.

Moonshining became an economic activity largely after the 20th century began and it became very profitable during the Prohibition experiment. In my own valley, after my grandfather's still was closed and during Prohibition, those who had studied at the feet of the masters knew how to make moonshine. Some of the most productive moonshining in that whole section of eastern Kentucky took place in the neighborhood in which I grew up and in the valleys where the people shared my kinship ties. Those who wanted to profit from the sale of whiskey would go to a favorite moonshiner (one who would sell to a neighbor or somebody who needed a bottle for medicinal purposes) who had run out and wanted a jug; sometimes it would be on a swap basis. The man who made money for it normally was called a bootlegger. As those who made whiskey learned that the bootlegger was less and less particular about what he bought, they would give him a cheaper and cheaper product. He was called a bootlegger from the habit in the early days of concealing the whiskey in those big, loose, leather boots that were commonly worn during the last quarter of the 19th century. So, with the flat bottles hidden in those boots, one who wanted to sell whiskey would walk into town, where the fellows were trading horses at court day, and dispense his contraband, pulled from his boots, for a price.

Liquor from Wallowhole

One crisp October afternoon during my first year as principal of the high school at Blaine an agent for a company that sold class rings turned out to be a man a year or two older than I who had taken classes with me at the university and with whom I had become acquainted socially at campus

dances and sessions at the Paddock following library hours. I scheduled a
meeting of the seniors for him to show samples of his rings and quote his
prices.

After he had finished with his business, he told me that he was continuing to live in Lexington and that he would very much like to take back with
him to "share with his friends there" ten or twelve gallons of good moonshine
whiskey from the mountains and wanted to know whether I would be willing to introduce him to a trustworthy moonshiner who made safe whiskey.
I told him that I did not buy moonshine myself, but that my father knew a
moonshiner not far away in Elliott County whose whiskey was of excellent
quality. Perhaps my father could be persuaded to go with him and recommend
him as a safe customer. If he cared to wait until the school day was over, he
would be welcome to go home with me for supper and to spend the night if
he were willing to share my bed with me. I added that it might be necessary
that he ride a mule over the rough wagon road to Wallowhole Creek, if my
father wished to go along with him, for I did not believe he could drive his
car up and down the steep ridge that was the dividing line between Elliott
County and Lawrence County.

He was pleased to wait and go with me. After I had finished my work
for the day, he followed me over the five miles of rough and dusty road to
my father's home. My mother had not yet begun preparations for supper. I
took him to my room where he unpacked his overnight bag. He then went
along with me to drive the cows from the pasture, bring in wood and kindling
for the kitchen stove, feed the hogs, and draw water from the well. He talked
about having lived on a mountain farm in his boyhood himself and having
done similar chores.

We then went to the back porch and washed our hands and faces in the
tinware wash pan that rested near the water bucket on a shelf suspended
between two porch posts and returned to the front porch to visit while my
mother finished preparing supper and my father came in from the fields.

My father was willing to go with him. He wanted to buy at least ten gallons if the moonshine suited his taste and if the price was right. My father
thought it would be possible, if he were a careful driver and "used" to driving in the mountains, for him to get his car over the road. It was narrow
and gullied and steep but people did come over it in pickup trucks in dry
weather. The man might not have any whiskey at that time, or he might not
think it safe to sell a stranger whiskey, even if he could vouch for him as a
safe customer. If he could drive his car, I could go along, too, and that might
help in establishing the moonshiner's trust.

It was getting dark by the time my father had finished milking and we
had eaten the good dinner my mother had prepared. The coupe my friend was
driving had high rear wheels, but he drove very carefully, mostly in second

Curt Williams and his son Cratis Williams.

and low gear, over the rutted roads. By the time we had reached the top of the hill, it was pitch dark. The ruts and gullies in the steep road down the ridge appeared to be chasms of unknown depth at times, but riding his brakes he eased along in low gear and succeeded in holding the car wheels on the ridges between the ruts. The high rear wheels required that we brace ourselves against the dashboard while the car limped haltingly down the hill.

The road down Wallowhole Creek for about a mile and then up a branch for a quarter of a mile lay in the streambed much of the way, but there was no water in it then. When we came to the gate of the moonshiner's yard, from whose dark house of unpainted boards and battens lamplight streamed from windows and an open door, my father requested that we wait in the car while he went in and asked whether the man had any whiskey, what the price was, and whether he would be willing to sell to a man who had been my college friend and for whose safety I could vouch.

My father, outlined against the light, which caught along the sides of tall white oak trees in the yard, approached the house in the midst of a chorus of barking dogs that came down the path to meet him. A woman appeared, silhouetted in the doorway, and called off the dogs, addressing each by name. My father announced himself and asked whether her husband was home. While she was replying that he was up "to-wardge the barn somewhures," to come right on in and "pay the dogs no mind, they wouldn't bite you no way," that he would be in "in a little bit, " we saw a man hurrying from the house along a path in a stream of light that came from behind the house, possibly from the open door of a wing in which the kitchen and dining room were located.

In a few minutes the man came sauntering back toward the house through the column of lamplight. We could hear voices and occasional laughter but could not distinguish any words in the conversation.

Soon my father returned to the car and in a low voice told us that the moonshiner had in boxes twelve gallons of pure corn whiskey, 100 proof and aged in a charred whiteoak keg for twelve months, and that he had put it in one-half gallon mason jars only last week. He asked $15.00 a gallon for it, but would be willing to sell the total amount for $150.00. If my friend could take that much and found the price satisfactory, he could give my father the money, we could come in the house, where the woman would offer us a drink of it from a sample kept for that purpose, and that if my friend liked it, my father would then go looking for the man at the barn while we talked to his woman. When my father returned to the house, the whiskey would have been placed in the trunk of the car and we would be ready to leave.

While my friend was considering silently the price asked, my father added, "this man makes his whiskey in a pure copper rig and strains it through a bag of charcoal when he doubles it. I sampled what he has, and it's prime stuff." We could smell the odor of whiskey on his breath.

My friend took out his pocketbook, turned on the ceiling light of his car, and counted his money slowly. He then counted out seven twenty-dollar bills, pulled a ten from toward the front of his pocketbook, and handed the bills to my father, who counted the money slowly and slipped it into his hip pocket.

We got out of the car and started toward the house, the four or five dogs gathered around us and barking as my father talked to them while they darted in to sniff at our legs and touch our hands with their noses.

We entered the house through the open front door over which was a small stoop. A woman sat in a rocking chair by the fireplace, in which bright flames leapt from a newly made wood fire. Between her and the wall was a wooden box in which firewood had been placed. In the corner behind her was a stand table with a cloth hanging from it and on which stood a lighted kerosene lamp with a clean globe. The room, much larger than the usual living-bedroom in mountain homes, must have been sixteen by twenty feet. Lamps on two other tables in the room were lighted also.

My father introduced me as his son and presented our companion as a school friend of mine. No names were called. She invited us to find seats while we waited for her husband to come in. He had been gone "a right smart little bit" and would surely be in "shortly." We drew chairs toward the fireplace. My father then asked whether she would let me have a "dram" of that good whiskey he had sampled a while ago; it was the best he could remember having tasted in "many a moon." The woman smiled broadly as she leaned over and drew a quart jar from the woodbox. When she held it up, we could see beads dancing along the wavering rim of the amber-colored liquor. My father accepted the jar from her, removed the lid, and tilted the jar to his lips. He took only a small amount and smacked his mouth rapturously. Then he handed it to me. I tasted it. It was mellow and smooth but with a strength that gripped one after the smoothness had sweetened itself out on the tongue. I held the jar between myself and the light, jiggled it, and

Curt Williams, 1933.

watched the beads, resting well above their equators, race along the rim of the liquid. I observed that it must be above 100 proof. I then handed it to my friend, who closed one nostril with his forefinger and smelled it slowly and deeply. He then tilted the jar to his lips and tasted it lightly, looking straight ahead as he smacked his mouth and licked his lips. He looked at my father, whose intent face was fixed in expectancy as he stood before him. He turned the jar up and took two or three swallows as his highlighted Adam's apple moved up and down rapidly. Lowering the jar, he soughed air through his half-open mouth deeply two or three times and nodded his head affirmatively and emphatically. As he returned the jar to my father, he praised the whiskey for its smoothness, flavor, and fire and added that it certainly was pretty in the lamplight.

My father returned the cap to the jar and handed it to the woman, who held it upright in her lap and stroked it as if it were a baby for a few minutes before returning it to the woodbox. My father, explaining that we were "in a little bit of a hurry" and that he wanted to ask her "old man" about a timber deal they had discussed the last time they were together, said, "You boys wait for me here. I am going up to the barn to see whether he will talk with me while he pulls the cow's tits." The woman added, "I reckon you'll find him up there, or maybe at the hog pen. He likes to watch his shoats eat."

The woman, who had lived with the man as a "common law wife" for fifteen or twenty years but had borne him no children, did not get up from her rocking chair. I engaged her in conversations about how far along she was with her autumn work, how her beans had done, whether she had yet pickled any beans, or prepared leatherbritches, whether she had dried her apples yet. She was talkative and pleasant, her broad smile flashing and stray hairs from her top-knot bun glistening in the light that flickered from the lamp on the table behind her. She was plain, gaunt, and slabsided, but she was cleanly dressed in what appeared to be the cotton print used in the Depression years for making feed sacks. Her house was clean and well kept. The big room was lined with what we called building paper then, the bright discs through which tacks were driven to hold it to the walls and ceiling glittering in the lamplight like stars on a bright night.

After a while I heard the lid of the trunk of the car slam. My father entered through the back door soon afterwards. He had found the man at the hog lot, they had discussed their business, and we could go now. The woman asked whether we would like another drink from the jar. My father did, but my friend and I declined. My father invited the woman to come over and see us sometime and we left.

The trip back was a slow, cautious one. My friend crept up the steep hill in low gear, applying the brake gently when the rear wheels of the car began to slip into ruts and gullies. We stopped near an old cemetery on the top of the hill for the engine to cool. We got out and looked at the sky, bright with stars but with no moon. I asked my friend whether one still paid a dollar in Lexington for a short half-pint of moonshine. It was still the going price, but sometimes some of the students coming back from Pike County brought raw, white whiskey with them that they would sell for seventy-five cents.

As he inched the car carefully down the hill to Caines Creek, slipping it occasionally into reverse gear to let the brakes cool, I calculated his profit for the sale of his contraband. By cutting the whiskey with distilled water to about 80 proof, he would have about fifteen gallons of salable moonshine. At twenty-two short half-pints to the gallon at a dollar apiece, he would gross $330.00 for his load and his profit would be $180.00. My salary that year was $85.00 a month.

My father's conversation was animated. The moonshiner had not wanted to meet his customer. He sold only to close friends and relatives whom he had known all of their lives. By doing the way we had done it, the man was glad to sell. It had taken some time to carry the whiskey from its hiding place under the cornstalks and litter in the corner of an unused stall in the barn to the car. The moonshiner was "getting along in years." My father had carried both boxes down himself. Six gallons of whiskey is a pretty heavy load for a man who has worked hard all day.

When we were home, my friend opened the trunk of his car and looked into each box to see whether any of the jars might have been broken in the trip across the hill. Everything in order, he locked the trunk and we went to bed.

Because he was scheduled to visit three high schools the following day, my friend said he would need to leave as quickly as possible the following morning. I explained that my father and mother got up about 5 o'clock at that time of year and that breakfast was usually ready by 6 o'clock, but that I normally did not try to get on the road to school before 7 o'clock. He thought if he could get away by 6:30 he would have time to call on the three high schools he hoped to visit.

We were up, shaved, dressed, and ready when my mother invited us to the breakfast table about 6:15. My father, still animated and talkative, reassured our guest about the quality of the moonshine, the dependability of the moonshiner, and the bargain price he had been able to negotiate for him for the quality of liquor.

My friend took leave of us about 7:40. As we stood watching him back his car carefully out of the lane, my father said in a level voice toned down nearly an octave, "I came out all right on that deal. George only wanted $10.00 a gallon for the whiskey." I remembered quickly that I was making only $4.25 a day as a high school principal.

NOTES

1. The Tolliver–Martin feud in Rowan County, Kentucky, began at an election booth in August 1884, and ended in a 2½ hour gun battle in the streets of Morehead on June 22, 1887. It was estimated that more than 2,000 shots were fired, but nobody was ever brought to trial. Young Cal Tolliver, age 14 at the time of the shoot-out in Morehead, was reported to have stood in the open and fought throughout that battle.

2. The legend of Swift's silver mines is an enduring and widespread story with many, many variations. In a recent summary of the story, Brook and Barbara Elliott write, "According to the legend, John Swift, of Alexandria, Virginia, discovered several silver mines in the hills of eastern Kentucky. His first finds were in 1760, and there were several others. In addition to the mines themselves, there are, so it is said, caches of silver coins and ingots waiting to be found." It is said that Swift himself was unable in his old age to relocate the mines, but left a legacy of maps, markers, and stories which have inspired treasure hunters for over 200 years. None have succeeded in locating the treasure. The Spurlock family settled along the Cumberland Gap in Kentucky "specifically because of the lost mine" and were closely associated with the search for the lost treasure hoard. See Brook and Barbara Elliott, "Searching for Swift's Lost Silver Mines," *Kentucky Living*, April 2001.

3. Although the Spurlock family name is closely associated with the search for Swift's silver, none of the variants of the story which we discovered listed a Spurlock as one of Swift's co-miners or, according to some versions, fellow pirates who simply buried stolen Spanish silver in the mountains for safekeeping and invented the mine story as a cover for their wealth. The name most commonly appearing as a cohort of Swift is that of Munday (Monday, Monde).

4. Originally published in *Appalachian Heritage*, 1980, 8 (2): 32–37.

5. Adapted from "Moonshining and Feuding in Appalachia," a speech in the Appalachian Experience Series, Oak Ridge, Tennessee, April 26, 1979; audio tape transcription by Barbara K. Lingerfelt, See also Cratis D. Williams, 1967, "Moonshining in the Mountains," *North Carolina Folklore* xv (1): 11–17.

Chapter Five

A Day's Ride by Mule
to High School

In 1921 Ulyssis S. Williams, my father's first cousin, was my teacher. "Lyss" had been one of the "big scholars" in the school during my first two years, but he had taken the teachers' examination and been awarded a certificate. He had also attended a short winter "institute" before he began teaching on Catt Creek in 1920. After being away from the school on Caines Creek for only one year, he returned, at the age of 21, as the teacher, and he was a good one. Particularly interested in health and physical fitness, he began teaching playground activities, taking breaks for 10 minutes of drill in calisthenics, encouraging us to wash our teeth daily and to bathe at least once a week. He ordered samples of Colgate's tooth cream and distributed them among us. The school had a "pie mite," proceeds from which were spent for curtains for the windows of the old church and for tidying up the grounds. He gave "head marks" for achievement in spelling and promised rewards for the best spellers. He was an extremely strict disciplinarian, wielding the beech switch with a deft hand. Although many families had moved away following the shutdown of distilleries in the valley and because of "boom times" in northern cities, the attendance record of the fifty or sixty enrolled in the school was good, for Lyss also promised attendance awards to those who came on time every day.

I was janitor and built fires in cold weather. I received 5 cents for sweeping the floor and 5 cents for building the fire. I continued to read history, geography, health and physiology, civics, and agriculture with advanced students. Lyss "quickened" us with his enthusiasm, firmness, integrity, and concern for our achievement and improvement. He told us about books he was

reading and permitted us to borrow his books, for there was no library in the school. I remember that I received my only "whipping" in school that year — for talking to my seatmate without the teacher's permission. At the end of the year I received a perfect attendance award (50 cents) and a spelling award (25 cents). I ordered two books with my money: *Buffalo Bill* by William F. Cody and *Jesse James, My Father* by Jesse James, Jr., books which I read many times.

Lyss was elected also to teach the school in 1922. On Sunday, November 12, of that year he was shot and killed by Elbert Caldwell at church on Abb Creek, where Lyss had gone to meet

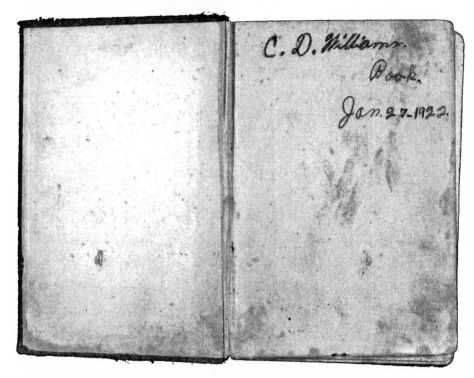

Top left and above: Cratis's book *Buffalo Bill*, and inscription.

Roberta Stafford, to whom he was engaged. Caldwell's motive for killing Lyss was never made clear. He was quite drunk, however, and had engaged in a quarrel with young men from Caines Creek before Lyss arrived at the church. Lyss was shot at such close range that his clothing caught fire. He died instantly, without speaking a single word. My mother and my brother and sisters were visiting at my aunt's home on Deans Branch that day. Our cousins and we were gathering chestnuts when Lyss's brother Jesse came racing his horse up the rocky road. There was no saddle on the horse. Jesse was dressed in work clothes, and he carried a shotgun balanced across the shoulder of the horse. He told us Lyss had been shot and killed and that he was going to search for the murderer. We left Aunt Eliza's soon, crossing the hill to my Uncle Jake's home to await the arrival of the corpse. Uncle Jake, one side of his face shaved and dried lather on the other, was drawing a bucket of water when we arrived. He did not have on a shirt, and only one of his overall suspenders was fastened. He had stopped midway in his shaving operations when the news of his son's death reached him. He had, however, fortified himself with several drinks of whiskey, for in our community it was considered a shame for a sober man to weep, but an intoxicated man could charge his tears to whiskey. The women present were wailing in piercing, primitive notes, as was customary at wakes and funerals in my community then. Lyss's body arrived after dark. It had been placed on a sled drawn by mules and brought over the hills. The yard gate was removed, a post pulled out, and a part of the fence laid back in order that the team might be driven as close to the door of the house as possible. Men stood about swinging lanterns while others worked at the gate and fence. Shadows danced eerily, women screamed, and men maintained a grim silence. Lyss's body lay long and stiff on the sled, a sheet draping away from the bridge of his high nose. As his body was being transferred to a bed in the "lower room," the Baptists raised a plaintive chant, their voices trailing upward at intervals in fading notes.

My father, his brothers, my grandfathers, cousins, and others from the valley were searching for the murderer. In fact, they searched day and night for two or three weeks before Caldwell, who was hidden between the sills under the floor of a smokehouse behind his father's home, became ill and was turned over secretly to officers. My mother and my brother and sister spent much time at Uncle Jake's during the wake and funeral. I held a lantern for the carpenters as they made a coffin for Lyss. He was not buried until Wednesday, for Uncle Jake wanted relatives living in other states to have an opportunity to attend the funeral. One whole day was required to travel the twenty-four miles from Louisa, the county seat, to my Uncle Jake's home. Although Lyss's body was bathed frequently with carbolic acid, decomposition was rapid in a heated room crowded with watchers and singing and praying Baptists.

Family members of Jacob Peters Williams gathered in front of his log house. Included (left–right, front row) are Jacob Peters Williams, Jr. (seated adult); Emily Swann Williams; David Oscar Williams (seated adult); and Martelia Swann Williams. Harrison Williams, son of David and Martelia, is standing behind Jacob P. Williams, Jr. Standing far right in back row is Ulyssis (Lyss) Williams. Lyss was shot and killed in 1922.

No one from my community had ever gone away to high school. I overheard a conversation between my father and mother one morning following my father's all-night search, along with dozens of Williams relatives, for the man who had killed Lyss. He told my mother that Lyss had been the only one of our family who was determined to "get an education" but that his murder "just looked like it wasn't meant that a Williams would ever be allowed to have one." With a mighty oath he swore that if one of his children wanted an education he would "work on his hands and knees for a dime a day, if need be, to see that he had a chance to get it." Only eleven years old at the time, I vowed secretly that I would challenge my father to the sacrifice that he declared he was prepared to make. During the remainder of that school year I advanced from third grade to the fifth and began in the sixth grade the following year, the year in which I took the county examinations and passed them.

A Williams family funeral, around 1924 or 1925. The Williams family cemetery lies in the background; Curt Williams, wearing the cowboy hat, stands above the hearse; Jacob Peters Williams, Jr., stands on the far right.

My father had many misgivings about whether I was yet old enough to take to school. He had talked the plan over with my grandfather Williams, who raised many doubts. It would be a costly venture, I was very young, the town was filled with temptations and evils, and, like most of the Williamses, I liked "my dram." He advised against the plan, but proudly admitted that I was "sharp for my age." My mother reassured my father, who wavered often, and talked separately with me about how I should behave, the temptations I should be prepared for, the importance of choosing friends who enjoyed studying and knew how to behave themselves, the dangers of wasting my time with foolish girls, and the necessity that I be willing "to mind" Simps and Nola Boggs, my father's cousins in whose home I was to stay.

For several weeks before the close of the school in February, my mother prepared clothing for me to wear to high school. I ordered a blue serge suit, a black felt hat, a sweater, three shirts, and a tie from Sears, Roebuck with money I had saved from selling mayapple root, black walnuts, and my pig. On February 10, 1924, before I was thirteen years old, my father loaded me and my belongings in the farm wagon, hitched the mules to it, and we started at 5:30 in the morning for Louisa, twenty-five miles away. We toiled our way over trails of mud on a wet, cold day with light snow lying on the weeds and rail fences and arrived in Louisa after nightfall. My first view of Louisa from the gap in Town Hill is unforgettable. There she lay, stretched from the foot of the hill to the bridge across the Big Sandy River and fading away toward the bluffs that ended abruptly at the river's edge to the north and the south, her hundreds of gas lights all glowing together in the cool breeze of a winter night and her leafless trees swaying like lace against the aura. And before we reached the foot of the hill, the lonesome whistle of a long and rattling freight train kept repeating itself as it streaked through the town, followed by the swaying clatter of perhaps a hundred coal cars clacking rhythmically on the rails long after the locomotive itself had passed.

At the foot of Town Hill, we turned immediately to our left and stopped the team in front of Davis Martin's livery barn, where my father found feed and quarters for the mules, Bec and Pearl. Then, with the battered old suitcase and a pasteboard box or two in our hands, we walked to the end of the short street to the home of W.S. ("Simps") Boggs and his wife, Nola, also a Boggs before she married Simps, where I was to board and room. The street was unpaved and muddy, but there was a paved sidewalk on which boys were riding red "coaster" wagons, the likes of which I had seen only in the Sears, Roebuck catalog.

At Simps' house I shared a room with his three sons and Nola's brother Ted, who had also come to town to go to school but who returned to Caines Creek before the semester ended. I slept in a bed with the two younger sons. The house was exciting to me. There were gas lights suspended on lead pipes from the ceilings, gas stoves in each room, and a sink with running water in the kitchen, but there was no bathroom in the house at that time. The house was a lively one, for visitors from out in the county came often for dinner or to spend the night, at which time there would be a doubling up for sleeping arrangements. My father left me in the care of Simps and Nola the following morning and departed for Caines Creek. As I recall, he agreed to pay $4.50 a week for my room, board, and laundry.

A snow fell on Sunday. Children of the neighborhood frolicked and tumbled in the snow. On Monday morning we walked along the snow-covered sidewalks in the bright and clear sunshine to the "college," the name of the building in which the 7th and 8th grades and the high school were housed. The building had been the home of the Kentucky Normal College, which had closed and sold its property in 1922 to the town.

I was presented to the superintendent of the Louisa public schools and the principal of the high school, S.B. Godby. I had come to go to high school, but after talking with me, Mr. Godby assigned me to the 7th grade, asked questions for my record, accepted my check in the amount of $3.00 for my tuition for a month, wrote me a receipt, and took me down the hall to the classroom of Miss Nell Burton Cox, who had come down from Wolfpen, in Pike County, to teach at Louisa. Miss Cox introduced me to the class of about thirty youngsters and assigned me to a double desk shared by Harlan Martin, the son of the man who operated the livery barn in which my father had quartered his mules. It appeared to me that I was the smallest boy in the room. As I looked around, the boys and girls were bright-eyed and smiling and the teacher was young and pretty with small, keen eyes and curly hair with a spit curl on her forehead. She was heavily made up with rouge on her cheeks and brilliantly red lips, the mode of the times as I was to observe later.

The texts for the class were mostly the same books I had used at the Middle Caines Creek School. We had assignments, study periods, and recitations. As I recall it, we had homework assignments only in arithmetic and composition. Soon after I arrived we took our six-week tests for the ten subjects we studied. There had been no grade reports in the one-room school I had attended. Apprehensive about the tests and the grade card I was to receive, I read all of the material that had been covered during the period to the time of my arrival on February 12. When I received my report card I was pleased to see 10 A's on it. Ted, who shared the room with me at Simps's, would not show me his card. My card, which I was to have Mrs. Boggs sign, disappeared. I was embarrassed to have to report to the teacher that my card had become lost, but she said she remembered my grades and would enter them on a new card for me at the end of the second six weeks. I recall that I had a feeling of homesickness about a week after I was in school, but it passed away rapidly and the semester was an exciting new adventure for me.

About the first of May Mr. Godby came by the classroom and announced that the best student in the room would receive a scholarship prize at the commencement exercises. The class was excited and questions began to fly as to who would receive the prize. Miss Cox was unwilling to suggest a candidate, but many of the students speculated that I would be the prizewinner. After two or three days a young fellow whose father was a member of the school board (chairman, I believe) raised a question as to whether it would be fair for one who had entered the class so late in the year to receive the prize. The students generally thought the prize should go to the best student and speculated that I was the best student. The following day the principal came by the room again, and without looking at the class, walked to the desk where the teacher was seated and told her in a low voice, but one loud enough for the hushed students to hear, that her nomination of her best student should be submitted soon and that only students who had been enrolled all year were eligible. He turned and left the room without looking at the students. The son of the school board member received the scholarship prize.

But Miss Cox told me that she wanted to give me a prize herself on the last day of school. However, she "forgot" to bring the prize and asked that I meet her afterwards at the entrance to the drug store up the street and she would give it to me then. I was waiting for her when she came hurrying by. When she saw me, she said, "Wait right here." She went into the drug store (operated by the school board member) and returned with a metal pencil in a box which she gave me. There was no card, no note, nothing written down. I still have the pencil. Miss Cox did not return the following year. I never saw her again. My grades for the semester were 27 A's and 3 B's.

When I showed my card to my father, he asked me to explain what the grades meant. I told him that A was the best grade a student could receive. He looked at the card intently, running his finger up and down the columns, and handed it back to me as he asked, "Well, what in the hell are these Bs doing on here, then?" He had given me 50 cents a week for spending money, paid $4.50 a week for my board and room, and paid 75 cents a week for my tuition. Money was hard to come by. He had sacrificed, and he expected perfect performance in return.

The semester in the 7th grade had been a significant experience for me. Even though most of the work had been repetition, I had learned that I could compete successfully with boys and girls who had come through a graded school in town and that my achievements as a student did not isolate me from my fellows. In fact, I felt that I was admired and respected by them, even though I was the smallest boy in the class. Once the 7th grade was asked to present the program for the weekly assembly attended by both the high school students and teachers and the 7th and 8th grades and their teachers. I was chosen to read a poem. My reading of Joaquin Miller's "Columbus" was my first presentation to an audience larger than a class. I had no stage fright and felt that I had communicated successfully with my audience when I received a round of enthusiastic applause. Back on Caines Creek at Friday afternoon "piece sayings" it had not been customary to applaud. There I had evaluated the effectiveness of my presentations on the basis of attentiveness and facial expression. A burst of applause was a more rewarding response. I have never been plagued by stage fright and have always enjoyed audiences.

Playing with the boys of the neighborhood in which I roomed gave me opportunities to know many of them intimately. We played sandlot baseball in the late afternoon in an open area near humble homes in which black families lived. Black boys played with us. On weekends, when the weather permitted, we played cowboys and Indians in Town Hollow and among the groves on Pine Hill overlooking the town. The Negro boys were "Indians" and the white boys were "cowboys." There was never a misunderstanding or a fight between the groups. Occasionally, on rainy or snowy evenings, we visited in the homes of the black boys or they visited us. We had no articulated feelings of superiority and the black boys were not deferential in their dealings with us. This experience in integration at so early an age I have considered a most fortunate aspect of my education, and the black boys whom I played with as a boy have been my friends for a lifetime.

Once a ball went over the paling fence and hit the vine-covered cottage in which a black family lived. I went in to retrieve the ball, which I threw back to the pitcher. At that moment the woman, a beautiful older mulatto, appeared at the door and "lectured" me about the danger of breaking her windows. I was not defensive and listened courteously. After the lecture, we talked of other things. She asked who I was and about my family, of whom she had heard. She then told me about herself, born in slavery and the daughter of the master and the housekeeper. She hated her white father. I liked her so well that I talked with her many times after that and she sometimes brought me cookies or gingerbread but never invited me into her house. She had no children. Her husband operated a barbershop in a wing of the cottage that opened directly on the street. I went to his shop for haircuts for two or three years. He charged 10 cents for cutting a boy's hair, and many of the white men who patronized him considered him the best barber in town.

When we had done well with our classwork in Miss Cox's room, she treated us to a chapter from *Tom Sawyer* until we had heard all of it and then to *Huckleberry Finn*, which we had perhaps half finished by the end of the semester. Excited by Huck's life as a "river rat," we were inspired to build rafts to float on Lick Creek, backed up much of the time when the Big Sandy River was up or when the dam was "in." Here we also set fishtraps, swam in the raw on warm Saturday afternoons, and explored the mysteries of the gorge through which the creek flowed. It was there that I learned to swim and along the banks of Lick Creek that I was first tricked into attempting to eat wild onions.

Hearing the story of Huckleberry Finn added mystery and romance to my experience with the Big Sandy River, which flowed by the school. The river was up much of the time during the semester, and when it was not up, the dam was raised so that it appeared to be a deep, slow-moving, muddy stream. Timber men were still bringing long rafts of logs down the river during the early 1920's. I was fascinated by the mat of earth near the front end of each raft and on which a campfire burned. The raftsmen had close at hand long poles which they used to keep the raft from coming too close to the river bank. I do not remember any tents or shelters on the rafts. I assume the raftsmen slept under tarpaulins on the earth mat and near the campfire. Occasionally small steamboats plied the river. At the sound of the whistle of a steamboat children rushed to the bank of the river to wave at the captain and the passengers standing about on the deck. One or two houseboats were anchored above the town.

One day Simps and Nola's youngest son, Lowell, and I were "exploring" the riverbank near the lock and dam at a time when the dam was down. We came upon a rowboat anchored to a stump. We decided we would take a short ride. I had never been in a rowboat before and was surprised that the two of us, rowing furiously and most awkwardly, could not get the boat to cross the river. Instead, it went rather rapidly downstream. Soon we found ourselves several feet from the bank and frightened. We began to try to get back to the bank, but before we were able to do so, we were perhaps a quarter of a mile below the stump to which the boat had been tied. Finding that we could not row the boat against the current in our efforts to return it to the stump, we got out, dragged it partly ashore, and tied it to a small willow tree growing on the bank. In a mysterious, Huck-like vow we promised each other that we would say nothing about our adventure. Above the line of willows along the bank we sat down, took off our sodden shoes and wet socks, and turned our shoes upside down to drain. We wrung the water from our socks, then cleaned the mud from the soles of our shoes, put socks and shoes back on, and slogged our way home. We were concerned that the owner of the boat might not find it, that somebody might have seen us in it, and that we might find ourselves in trouble for stealing a boat. We kept our secret, though, and never heard anything at all about a lost boat.

My semester in the 7th grade at the county-seat school, the broadening of my experiences at play with the boys and girls who lived in town, and my fascination with the few automobiles, the railroad trains, the boats and rafts on the river, the high bridge across the river to West Virginia, the gas lights along the streets, and the town itself had whetted my desire to return to high school in the fall, for I had received the report that I had passed the examination for admission to high school and the information that my tuition costs would be borne by the county board of education.

When the one-room school near my home opened on the last Monday in July, I returned to attend the 8th grade for five weeks before I would enroll in high school on September 1. The teacher of the Caines Creek School was Lucy Gay Sparks. A spelling tournament was scheduled for the last Friday in August at the Martha School, about four miles from my home and across a mountain in the next valley. In order to prepare for the competition, I took my spelling book along with me to spend the night with another boy who was also accounted a good speller. His father was "putting off a run" of moonshine whiskey that night. After supper we took our spellers and went along with him to the still, hidden snugly in a patch of tall horse weeds between a grove of sycamore, water birch, and willow trees and the creek. We lay on a tarpaulin in front of the still furnace and by the light of the furnace fire pronounced to each other all of the words in Jones' *Master Speller*, the ring of the whiskey sounding down the copper "worm" and tinkling from the charcoal-filled straining bag into glass jars, the air suffused with the sweet copper-tinged fumes of whiskey and the faint odor of wood smoke, and the katydids chorusing their nightsong of dying summer from the nearby trees. We finished our drill sometime after midnight and went to the house and to bed. The following morning I was home in time to get the mules curried and saddled for the trip over the mountains to the Martha School. We assembled at our own school and went as a group of riders, girls dressed in long riding skirts and the boys in their Sunday best, to the tournament.

The Martha School was a log building, but it was sealed with painted paneling and was all "spiced" up for the spellers and their teachers from perhaps three or four other one-room schools. A "pronouncer" was chosen from among visiting teachers and the judge was our host, Mr. Charley Sparks, brother-in-law of Mary Gambill Sparks who became editor of the *Big Sandy News* at Louisa later. The supreme irony of the match for me was that I was eliminated on the word "whiskey," which I spelled without the *e*. Although the judge consulted an unabridged dictionary, which rested on a wide window ledge, and discovered that "whisky" is an alternative spelling, it was decided that the word as listed by Jones would be considered the correct form and that I should be eliminated.

The Martha School building had been constructed on land that had been a part of the farm of my great-great-grandfather David Boggs whose sister, Elizabeth, was the ancestor of the Sparks family that owned and lived on the old Sparks farm. My ancestor and his wife, Sarah Holbrook Boggs, were buried in what became known as the Sparks Cemetery beside the road at Martha and near the site of the old school. There is a story that late in the 19th century a teacher at the Martha School who was preparing for his examinations in medical school decided he could learn Grey's *Anatomy* better if he taught it. His "big boys," many of whom had returned to the school year after year to repeat the upper grades because there was no high school available, were eager to have him teach them Grey's *Anatomy*. They learned so well that 14 of them became medical doctors later. Their influence on other members of their families was such that the Upper Blaine Community has produced more doctors per thousand of population than any other community in the United States.

One may find doctors and dentists bearing the names of Gambill, Holbrook, Skaggs, Sparks, Evans, Bailey, Lyon, and the like all over eastern Kentucky. These families have links with the Upper Blaine Community. According to legend, during the 1930's the Martha School building was given to Jean Thomas, the "Traipsin' Woman," who had it removed to Catlettsburg, and later to the grounds of the "Wee House in the Woods," as a McGuffey school.

High School: First Year

During the summer following my semester in seventh grade at Louisa in 1923-1924 I anticipated with happiness and day dreams entering high school in the fall. Louisa seemed far away. It had not been possible for me to go back, even for a brief visit, after my return to Caines Creek at the end of May, for a trip on horseback would have required two full days of travel. Having observed what other boys wore to school, though, I spent much time studying the mail order catalogs to find articles of clothing suitable for school.

My grandfather employed me to help with the hoeing of his corn after we had "dug our crop out of the first weeds," and paid me fifty cents a day. I worked for him seven or eight days that summer. There was a bumper crop of blackberries that year. My brother and I contracted with a moonshiner to pick blackberries for him for twenty-five cents a gallon. We made $7.50 each picking berries.

By the end of July I had saved enough money to order new clothes and my mother gave me enough to include also a pair of shoes. The new things arrived in time for me to wear them proudly to the monthly meeting of the church for August and to a memorial meeting at the Boggs–Butler graveyard on the ridge between Caines Creek and the head of the Lick Fork of Cherokee Creek. I felt finely dressed in my blue serge suit with a belt and shining black buckle for the coat and short pants with buckled knee straps, a new shirt with which I wore a flowing tie that I had bought in Louisa the preceding spring, a pair of long black stockings with sturdy ribbing, and new black "slippers" of dependable "gun metal" leather. Although Sundays in August were hot and I perspired freely, I was so proudly dressed that I did not remove my warmly lined coat, even while climbing the long hill to the graveyard.

It had not occurred to me that my father might be changing his mind about sending me to high school. I talked about my plans in his presence and told people I would be enrolling on September 1. I mentioned to my father that we should arrive in town in time for me to register by noon and buy my books. He did not talk about plans for making the trip. At the breakfast table on September 1 I asked whether he planned for us to go in the wagon or ride the mules. It was then that he told me he had decided not to send me to high school.

I was stunned and speechless and wanted most desperately to cry but felt it unmanly to do so in the presence of the family. After I was at the barn and releasing the cows to drive them to the pasture, I wept bitterly. The cool dew on the grass, the clear, fresh air, the birds singing, the bright sunlight streaming through the tops of the willows and sycamores that lined the dry creek bed up which I was driving the cows and the sand and gravel of which slipped under my bare feet, all seemed oddly at variance with me as my eyes burned, my hot tears flowed, my nose ran, and I choked with sobs. I felt completely crushed.

After the cows were in the pasture I dawdled and dragged along as slowly as I thought I could afford to do and returned to the house, for I did not want to show any evidence of my weeping, of my weakness, of my bitter disappointment. Having blown my nose several times, wiped my eyes dry, breathed deeply to clear away the sobs, I entered the kitchen. Only my mother was in there. She looked at me without betraying her recognition of my anguish and told me that she had talked with my father after I left, and that he had changed his mind about my going to school. He had gone down to my grandfather's to get my uncle Charley to take us to town in his new Chevrolet touring car, and said that I should get myself ready for the trip as quickly as I could. I bounced back with enthusiasm, poured warm water into the washpan for a quick sponge bath and washing my feet, and was ready for the road, radiant, happy, and smiling, when Charley drove up in his blue Chevrolet, the sand-colored top all laid back and the odor of gasoline floating through the morning air. Grandpa had decided to go along, too, but we would pick him up on the way back. The old battered suitcase was packed. As I waited for my father to change clothes, I was filled with excitement about riding in a car to Louisa.

We did not show tender emotions in our household. My mother did not weep when I was ready to get into the car. We did not kiss, or say goodbye or touch each other. She simply said, "Be a good boy. Write to us along and tell us how you are." She stood by the gate until the car started and then turned and went back into the house, for she considered it "bad luck" to watch anyone leave. I did not look back toward the house as we drove away, for it was considered bad luck to look back, too.

In those days the road down Caines Creek was located beside the creek from the Hannah post office to the Lower Caines Creek School. That section of the road was sandy and dusty in dry weather and an extended mud hole in the wintertime. I remember how the car wheels spun in the sand as we drove past Jim Ran Boggs's barn, beside which his buggy stood, dark and shadowed by the trees that grew along the edge of the road. The car kicked up a cloud of dust that drifted back upon us while its wheels were spinning. Then it would spurt forward in a weaving motion as Charley struggled to hold it in the road. At Blaine we stopped for gasoline, which my father paid for. As we approached the top of the Blaine hill we barely avoided a collision on a sharp curve in the narrow road with a car being driven by Port Dobbyns, who appeared to be "coasting" down the hill. We were in Louisa by 11 o'clock, having driven the twenty-five miles in about three hours, a trip that had taken all of a long day by wagon when my father took me to school in February and that would take less than an hour by the time I would be driving my own car ten years later. Instead of crossing Town Hill into Louisa,

Charley drove around the hill and down Lick Creek along the unpaved Mayo Trail, now U.S. 23, along which I could see the creek in which I had fished and gone swimming in the spring.

We parked by the courthouse square, and I walked up to the school in time to register before we were sent onto a trial of our schedules for the teachers to take rolls and give us the names of our textbooks. While waiting with 60 other freshmen in the study hall for the trial schedule to begin, I was observed by Mr. Godby, the superintendent of Louisa Public Schools and the principal of the High School. Speaking to two or three senior boys standing beside him, he said, "What's that little cricket doing in here?" The boys thereafter called me Cricket, my high school nickname and the name my high school classmates and friends still use after a half century in addressing me.

I was assigned four subjects: algebra, English, general science, and Latin. When I met the teachers in the classrooms, I learned that all of them were from outside the Kentucky mountain region. The mathematics teacher, Andrew F. Janovisky (later changed to Young), a graduate of Maryville College in Tennessee, came originally from Hungary. The English teacher, Helen Porter Roberts, was from Lexington and a graduate of the University of Kentucky. Nonus Quay Gilmer, the albino science teacher, was from Toccopola, Mississippi, and a graduate of Mississippi State University. Staunton B. Godby, the Latin teacher, was from central Kentucky and a graduate of Center College at Danville. While a sheet of paper was being passed around for us to sign our names, the teachers wrote on the blackboard the names of the text books we were to use, the prices we would pay for them at the drugstore uptown, and the pages we were to read as assignments for the following day.

On my way to meet my father on the courthouse square I stopped at a pair of scales on the sidewalk beside the entrance to one of the stores, dropped a penny in the slot, and read my weight and received my fortune on a strip of card. I have forgotten my fortune, but I weighed sixty-five pounds. The day before I had entered school at the age of six, I had weighed thirty-five pounds. My mother had said that at the age of two weeks I had weighed three and a half pounds. Certainly, I had grown more during the first six years of my life than I had grown during the last seven.

My father said he was in a hurry to get back home, so he gave me the money I would need to buy my books, paper, pencils, a ruler, and a compass and we drove out to Simps and Nola Boggs's home, where I was to stay. I arrived in time for lunch and my father, uncle, and grandfather left for Caines Creek, hoping to arrive in time to "do up the work before dark." They did not eat lunch, as was customary among country people who were in towns and villages at lunch time in those days.

I was in high school. I intended to be a successful student and hoped to excel. I had preferred Latin to history, which I could take the second year, because I hoped to be able to go to a law school after I had finished high school. After lunch I walked back to town and bought my books and supplies. That afternoon I sat in the porch and read the assignments for the following day.

Only fourteen of the sixty freshmen had signed up for the beginning class in Latin. The teacher requested that we stand at our seats to respond to questions. After talking for a few minutes about Romans and their language, he asked a question about why we have different languages, a question that had been answered in the pages assigned for reading. I stood up at my seat to indicate that I was prepared to answer the question, but became frightened when I looked about and discovered that I was the only one standing. As I was preparing to sit down, the teacher called my name and I answered the question. A wise man, the teacher then called on the whole class to follow in unison his pronunciation of simple Latin words in a paradigm included in the assignment, but I was pleased that I had been prepared and had had the courage to answer his question. I made A in Latin for that semester.

There were twenty-four students in my general science section. Mr. Gilmer, whose vision was impaired and who was afflicted with a slight palsy, assigned us alphabetically to numbered seats. When he consulted notes or a book, he held the material close to his face and read through a magnifying glass, his head shaking and his hands trembling meanwhile. After seating arrangements had been completed, he began discussing the pages in the text he had assigned for reading. After a bit he turned to questions, calling names of students as he looked from the sides of his eyes in the general direction of the student who should be located in that sector of the room. Students were better prepared to respond to questions in the science class than they had been in Mr. Godby's Latin class. Soon he asked for the common name of the molecule H_2O, deliberately and somewhat painfully passing the question in alphabetical order from one to another of perhaps ten or twelve who did not know. As students responded that they did not know, he would repeat his question and proceed to the next student. Wellman did not know. The question was repeated for me. When I responded "water" and Mr. Gilmer almost shouted "correct," the class applauded as if I had won a contest. I made A in general science for that semester.

In fact, Mr. Gilmer invited me soon to become one of his laboratory helpers, a service I performed for him for four years as I progressed with all A's through biology, chemistry, and physics, and learned from working with him in the evenings as he prepared for laboratory work the following day patience, love of work, accuracy, respect for truth, and professionalism. An extremely clean man whose fine hair was radiantly white at all times and whose pink face glowed joyfully despite his handicaps, Mr. Gilmer owned more suits, more well cared-for shoes, and more beautiful ties than any man I have ever known. Immaculate, organized, meticulous, even fastidious, professional, courteous, gentle, but also courageous and sharp-tongued when the occasion required it, he exercised an enormous influence on me. His Christmas greeting sent to me at Sacred Wind from faraway Toccopollo, Mississippi, every year I was in high school reminded me in the isolation of winter-locked Caines Creek that there was another world out there and that my teachers from that world remembered me when they returned to it.

My English class had more students in it than any of my other classes. Miss Roberts, who might have been a beginning teacher, did not seem to have her work well organized, but she tried hard. Her emphasis was upon improving the written and spoken word. We had a reader for the class, *Literature and Life*, Book 1, but we did not use it much. Miss Roberts, a small, unattractive woman, favored the daughters of the well-to-do families in the town. Most of us, especially those from the country, felt uncomfortable in her presence. She was disposed to see a great deal that was wrong with our writing and speaking and very little that she could praise and encourage us to build on, but she deferred to daughters of important families in the town and would wait for them to walk with her when she left the building at the lunch hour and at the end of the day.

Although my other teachers were also from outside the mountains, they spoke to me when I met them in the hallway or on the sidewalks, but Miss Roberts did not. She looked straight ahead as if only she were in the hall or on the sidewalk. She was what we called in the country "proud," one who thinks herself better than others. I found it difficult to like her, but I was determined to do all I could to meet her requirements and to please her.

Prepared and eager, I entered into discussions easily, but it seemed to me that Miss Roberts did not always understand clearly what she was saying. Her explanations were often parroted from Clippinger's book, which we were using as a text. When we discussed what we thought Clippinger meant, she would become confused and call upon one of the town girls as if she were a referee. After the town girl had spoken, Miss Roberts would smile as if she were "home safe" and move on to something else.

I had one of the most humiliating experiences of my life in Miss Roberts' class. We had submitted our first theme on "An Interesting Experience," for which I had received a grade of B–. There had been no notations of any kind on the paper itself, but below the grade on the back of the paper Miss Roberts had written "Paragraphing poor." My feeling of helplessness was mollified though when she called on me to read my paper aloud as one of the more interesting ones submitted. I had written about my having hidden my teacher's overshoes in the coal bucket back in the one-room school on Caines Creek and then finding them for her after she and the other students had searched for them for a while. The teacher had hugged me as if I had been a little knight in armor for rescuing her in distress. I had not been able to find the courage to admit that I had hidden her shoes in the coal bucket myself. The students in the English class enjoyed my paper and applauded me after I had read it.

We then turned to oral assignments in which we were to deal with the "spoken word." Feeling good about the acceptance of "An Interesting Experience," I was encouraged to think that I might improve my grade with "An Anecdote." Miss Roberts reviewed the *do's* and *don'ts* for anecdotes and called for volunteers. I volunteered first and was called to the front of the room, where I assumed the recommended posture for facing an audience, my feet planted side by side firmly on the floor, my body erect, my chest out, my chin up, my arms stiff by my sides, and my fingers pointed rigidly at my shoe tops. I was prepared to tell about Dave Prince's stuffing the overalls in the smoke-pipe of Granny Blythe's kitchen stove. Just as I was getting into my story, Miss Roberts interrupted me and requested that I repeat the sentence I had just spoken.

"Hit was a-gittin' 'way up in the day," I repeated.

The town girls restrained giggles.

"Say it again," Miss Roberts commanded.

"Hit was gett*ing* 'way up in the day," I repeated with more precision. The town girls, now unrestrained, laughed outright. I could feel my face flaming as Miss Roberts asked me to say it again.

"Hit was getting *a*way up in the day!" I almost shouted.

The town girls, now joined by some of the country children, laughed louder and longer.

"*It*, not *hit*," Miss Roberts corrected.

Then the country children laughed uproariously while the town girls merely smiled at Miss Roberts as she looked in their direction. I managed to complete the anecdote, but my heart was not in it. I had the feeling that neither Miss Roberts nor the class was listening, and I was so deeply injured myself that I did not really hear the anecdotes others told that morning.

The humiliation was so deep and painful that I resolved to learn spoken English so well that no one would be likely to laugh at me again. Many years and a Ph.D. in English were required to salve my wound completely. My spoken English improved rapidly as I moved through the freshman year, but I was never able to make an A for Miss Roberts.

Miss Roberts required that we read and prepare a 12- to 15-page written report on a novel each six-week period. We were asked to purchase at Atkins and Vaughan's the novels we were to read if we did not have copies at home. Everybody read and handed in reports on the same novel at the same time. After three or four days, the reports were returned to us and we spent a class period discussing the novels. I purchased for forty-five cents each copies of *Ivanhoe*, *The Last of the Mohicans*, and *Treasure Island*, published by Macmillan in the Pocket American and English Classics Series. These novels, which I still have, were the beginning of my personal library. Simps Boggs was glad to lend me his worn copy of *Oliver Twist*.

I recall struggling with *Ivanhoe* and *The Last of the Mohicans*, both of which I read at fifteen pages an hour by the gas light at the end of a lead pipe sticking from the ceiling above the dining room table of Simps and Nola Boggs's home. The stories I found interesting, but I did not own a dictionary and there was not one in the Boggs home. *Ivanhoe* inspired me to try my hand at retelling parts of it in ballad verse, but the strange long words in the static passages of *The Last of the Mohicans* I stumbled over like stones as I attempted to follow the adventures and misadventures of Alice and Cora on their dangerous trip through the wilderness. My reading speed had improved, though, by the time I read *Oliver Twist*, and I raced with excitement through *Treasure Island*.

Miss Roberts stayed only one year at Louisa. She returned to Lexington and married a psychology professor at the University of Kentucky. Many years later, in the late afternoon of the day on which I had submitted my M.A. thesis in English at the University of Kentucky, I met Miss Roberts walking alone on the campus and recognized her. She was looking straight ahead as if only she were walking on the sidewalk.

"Helen Porter Roberts!" I said.

She turned and looked at me for a moment.

"I was in your freshman English class at Louisa thirteen years ago," I explained.

"You are Cratis Williams," she said. "I have thought of you many times and have wondered whatever became of you. You were the *littlest* boy back then. Why don't we sit down here and visit for a few minutes?"

We sat on the steps of Frazee Hall and talked for a few minutes. She did not remember the incident in which she had crucified me with shame. As I strolled back to my room I remembered a story I had read once about Pontius Pilate in old age. When someone asked him about his part in the events leading to the crucifixion of Jesus Christ, he was puzzled and asked "Who?"

Mr. Janovisky, whom we called Jan, taught mathematics and coached football. (At that time we did not have basketball, for we had no gymnasium.) I remembered him as the kind man who the year before had given me the envelope from which he had drunk water at the pump for me to use while he operated the pump for me. It had not occurred to me that one could use a common letter envelope for such a purpose, and I had not wanted to use my composition paper for making paper cups, as others in my class did. Although I remembered him, he did not indicate in any way when he called my name in his class in algebra that he remembered me.

I thought Jan was a good teacher and a patient man with compassion for those of us who struggled with mathematics. I was not a good student in algebra, even though I attempted to complete faithfully the assignments he gave us each day. He did not call for papers. His method of teaching was simple. He sent the class to the blackboards stretched along three walls of the classroom and assigned us problems by numbers from the textbook. After two or three minutes he would spot those who were having trouble, go to them, and ask questions until they were able to solve their problems. When all problems assigned had been worked at the boards, we took our seats and were called on to explain our problems. Then he presented the assignment for the following day, working on a few examples with our participation. If there was time left, we began preparing the assignment. About once a week he gave us a short test but he returned papers only when he felt that re-teaching was needed before we could advance.

I made many errors in my board work, as did the quiet little girl with the pretty face who stood beside me. Jan would come and assist us in a low voice so carefully and tenderly that neither of us felt intimidated by him or humiliated in the presence of those of our fellow classmates who learned algebra more quickly than we. As hard as I struggled and with all the patience and compassion the teacher was able to give me, I barely made C's in algebra, but I did not hate the subject because I was only an average student in it or resent Jan because his efforts with me did not succeed in improving my understanding enough for me to become more than an average student. Jan gave me so much encouragement and hope that I might one day become an apt student of mathematics that I took three-and-a-half years of mathematics with him, but I made C's for him the first two years. The A's I received in plane geometry encouraged me to think that I had overcome some of my deficiencies. The only D I ever received as a course grade was in trigonometry at the end of the first semester of my senior year; that grade convinced me that I had advanced as far as I might ever be able to go in mathematics.

A surprising thing happened after we graduated. I read in the county paper an account of Jan's marriage to the quiet little girl who had stood beside me at the blackboard in his classes. By then he had had his name changed legally from Janovisky to Young.

After school had been in session three or four weeks my father rode his mule to town one Tuesday to see me and to attend the county fair, which was being held in a vacant lot behind Skagg's Garage and alongside the old abandoned Labaco plant. Bud Hawkins and his troupe had a tent for their shows set up behind the garage. My father enjoyed the plays and took me with him to see one each of the three nights he was there. He also bought for me a box of crackerjacks during the intermission each evening while a jazz band, composed of young fellows who must have been no more than teenagers themselves, played pieces that young people in the towns were singing and whistling at the time. I remember admiring particularly a bright-eyed young man with patent leather hair and wearing a bow tie who would rise up and make his saxophone whine to "Shake That Thing," an almost pornographic piece, I recognized years later upon recalling some of the lyrics that I learned. The band played the same pieces each evening. The young man, as if he were constructed of rubber, weaved and wriggled like an eel as his saxophone whined out the melody of the refrain.

Circuit court was in session at the time of the fair, too. One of the young men from Caines Creek was to be tried for discharging his pistol into a house, while riding around it and yelling like an Indian on the warpath, and injuring one of the young women who lived there when the bullet passed between her big and her second toe as she was lying on her back on a bed in the living room. Many of those involved in the case, including the widow into whose home the young man was accused of having discharged his pistol, the daughter who had been injured, the defendant in the case, and an attractive young woman prepared to swear that the defendant had spent the evening at her home and could not therefore have been the person who discharged the pistol, were staying in the home in which I was boarding, for all of them were relatives of the Boggses. The little house was crowded at night with three and four adults sharing the same bed and the children lying on pallets on the floor of the dining room and kitchen. The judge had recessed the court for some reason one afternoon during the trial, and all of those involved in the case had remained at the Boggs home after lunch. About the middle of the afternoon Mrs. Boggs left the porch on which most of the crowd sat and went into the house to attend to something cooking on the stove. While passing through the dining room, she noticed that a door to a bedroom off the dining room had been closed. When she opened it, she discovered the defendant in the court case and the attractive young woman engaging in sexual activity on one of the beds in the room. She raised a hullabaloo. The young man leapt up and left the house by the back door. The young woman sat on the edge of the bed and wept as she stuffed her purple bloomers into her bosom.

Mrs. Boggs, feeling some compassion for the weeping and confused young woman, permitted her to remain in shame in the room. The crowd on the porch, having heard enough to know what Mrs. Boggs had discovered, sat in silence as the young man hurried across the yard and on down the sidewalk. He did not return for supper.

The young woman would not eat at the table with the adults that evening. She remained hidden in the room until the children were eating. Then she came out, her nose and eyes red from weeping, and ate with the children. After we had eaten, Mrs. Boggs slipped me aside and asked me whether I would go with the young woman to the Bud Hawkins show. She wanted to get out of the house and would pay for my ticket if I would go with her.

We walked in silence, she clinging pathetically to my arm, the four or five blocks to the Bud Hawkins tent. I recall that she had an offensive body odor and that her breath was bad. At the entrance to the tent she gave me a dollar and asked that I buy the tickets. She stood aside while waiting for me to purchase the tickets, for which there was enough money to get one adult and one child ticket for the most remote part of the tent. But she did not enjoy the show. From time to time she would shudder, lean forward, lift the tail of her skirt to her face, and blow her nose. After the show we walked back as silently as we had come. I felt deep pity for her but was pleased to remember that I had seen none of my classmates in the section in which we had sat at the show.

Late one winter afternoon while we were sitting together in the little living room of the Boggs home someone rapped so loudly on the door that it rattled in the frame. We looked and saw a short, bulky figure in a heavy overcoat standing quite close to the glass. Mr. Boggs opened the door. Henry J. Pack, his slender little wife dressed primly in a tightly fitting black coat and a black hat with a black feather on it standing close by, began to jabber. He wanted to know whether Simps Boggs lived there. He had been a friend of Simps Boggs and had voted for him in his race for the office of circuit court clerk. He and his wife, Trinvillie, had come in the spring wagon, which we could see drawn along the yard fence beyond, from Blaine. The day had been cold and blustery, the roads had been muddy, and they were cold, tired, and hungry. He wanted to know what chances might be that they could spend the night.

Mr. Boggs explained that he did not follow turning any of his friends away so long as there was room in his house for them to lie down and he had a crumb to share with them. He invited them to come in. Mr. Pack said that his "wife Trinvillie, a mighty good woman she is, she is," would come in and warm by the fire while he returned the horse and wagon to the livery barn. He then rushed to the wagon and hurried back with a battered piece of canvas luggage that he called a "telescope" and handed it to Simps.

As Trinvillie came tripping with mincing steps through the door, we noticed that she had a clay pipe in her mouth. The pipe, quite dead, had either turned upside down on the stem or she had been holding it in her mouth upside down. She sat by the gas-burning fireplace and extended her hands, gloved in black, toward the flames that played up the asbestos backwall as she stared in fascination at them. The little clay pipe with an unstained reed stem stuck straight out in front of her face.

Henry and Trinvillie slept that night in the room that the three Boggs boys and I shared. The four of us slept in one bed that night, two at the head and two at the foot. A stand table on which we kept our books and school supplies was located by the window and between the beds. I did not sleep well, though. Henry suffered from some kind of bronchial infection. While Trin-villie snored in a pattern that included a high screech like that produced by a saw hitting a nail, Henry coughed, whooped, cleared his throat, and spat what he could cough up out onto the floor between the beds.

The following morning, when I went back into the room after break-fast to get my books, I found that Henry had spat on them, too. Without say-ing anything to the Boggses, I went to the bathroom, rolled off toilet paper, stuck it into my shirt, and slipped back to the room to clean my books. I then took them with me into the bathroom and wiped them with damp toi-let paper, but where gobs of phlegm had rested on them were faded spots that I could not wash away.

The Boggs boys decided to spend the Thanksgiving holidays with their great uncle Hugh Boggs, who lived up a branch that flowed into the Big Sandy River near Potter's Station four or five miles below Louisa. They invited me to go along. Uncle Hugh had one daughter, Alice, at home and two or three sons not far from our ages. The boys liked to hunt rabbits, and we could all go rabbit hunting. We walked the railroad tracks down to the mouth of the branch on which Uncle Hugh lived. The weather was pleasant, although recent frosts had left a chill in the air.

Uncle Hugh, a second cousin to both my grandfather and my grand-mother, had grown up on Caines Creek, married Hannah Church, a local girl, and left soon after his marriage to live "over on the River." I had heard of him before coming to town to school but had never met him until he came home with Simps one day for lunch. He had liked Simps's sons and me and had asked that we all come to see him and hunt rabbits and gather persim-mons with his boys.

Uncle Hugh lived in a large old-fashioned house, a part of which was of sturdy log construction. The living room had a big stone fireplace with logs burning in it around which we lounged. Aunt Hannah and Alice cooked an abundance of food and especially good creamed gravy for our potatoes and big biscuits. Simps's brother Nelson was staying at Uncle Hugh's place at the time. I thought he was what we called then "sweet on" Alice, who kept herself neatly dressed and smiling as she worked around the house. She sat beside Nelson when we all gathered around the fireplace to talk in the eve-nings, and Nelson would slip his arm around her occasionally and hug her toward him. Aunt Hannah was not very talkative, but Uncle Hugh, Nelson, and the boys, one of whose names was Russell, kept a lively conversation go-ing.

We went rabbit hunting twice. I had no gun, but I went along and enjoyed finding persimmons and cracking walnuts and hickory nuts with rocks and eating the kernels. We roamed over much of the countryside, traveling as far up the ridge as Five Forks and dropping down a branch that flowed into

Blaine Creek near Fallsburg. The second day we hunted was cloudy and damp and we would get cold if we stopped very long in one place. As I remember, the boys killed two or three rabbits each day, which we cleaned for Aunt Hannah to cook.

One thing disturbed me for a time. I kept hearing a moan and chatter followed by high-pitched laughter from somewhere in the house. Nobody said anything about it, and the Boggses talked on as if they heard nothing. During the first night I was there I could hear this curious moaning and high-pitched laughter from time to time all through the night. It seemed to be coming from beyond the wall of the bedroom in which most of us boys were sleeping. But there were no windows in the wall from behind which the sounds came. I had the feeling that there was no room on that side of the wall, for the big bedroom appeared to be an extension of the living room, from which a door led to an ell that was the kitchen and dining room, which had a porch along the side of it.

After we had finished eating breakfast the first morning we were there and had returned to the fireside, Aunt Hannah came to the door and asked that someone bring Hettie to be fed and to warm by the fire. Two of the boys disappeared. In a few minutes they returned carrying a high chair in which was strapped a badly deformed little girl with a misshapen face. Her head was not much bigger than a grapefruit and she drooled at the mouth. Her hair was fine and thin, and her little arms and legs were useless, but her eyes were as bright as a mouse's eyes and about the same color. She would not have weighed more than thirty pounds and was no larger than a three-year-old child.

The boys placed her chair in front of the fire. Hettie was obviously delighted. She cooed and rocked back and forth against the straps that held her in her chair. Alice brought a pan of warm water and a washcloth and washed Hettie's face and hands and feet while Nelson cooed, made faces, and prattled, to which Hettie responded with bursts of high-pitched laughter, her wrinkled little face contorted as her eyes sparkled. Then Nelson fed her soft food from a white bowl. Hettie would open her mouth like a baby bird and lean forward to meet the spoon. Much of her food dropped from her mouth as she smacked and drooled. After she had eaten and Alice had cleaned her face, the boys took turns cooing at her and responding to her laughter with high-pitched laughs like hers.

I felt it inappropriate to ask what might be wrong with Hettie and whether she was one of the Boggs children, but after she had visited with us and been returned to the little room that had been built against the wall of the bedroom and had only an outside door, one of Simps's boys asked about her.

A year or two prior to our visit Uncle Hugh had gone rabbit hunting. While passing a little house near the edge of the woods he noticed that the curtains for the windows had been removed and the house looked as if it were empty. There was no smoke coming from the chimney, and there were no dogs, or cats, or chickens in the yard. He had not heard that the family living there had moved away, though. He was almost past the house when he heard the pitiful mourning of one of the deformed children. He turned and peeped through one of the curtainless windows. There on the floor of an empty room lay the children. One had died and the other was very weak.

He hurried on to a neighbor's house and reported what he had seen. The neighbor, who knew that the family had moved away, "gone out West," they had said, nearly a week before, went with him back to the house. They forced the door open and Uncle Hugh took Hettie home with him while the neighbor rode up to Louisa to report to officials what they had found.

Hettie's father and mother, who were first cousins, had died, leaving the two deformed children in the care of an older daughter and her husband, to whom the home and farm had been deeded. The daughter and her husband had sold the little farm for cash to someone in town. They had abandoned the children and left the county. No one knew where they had gone.

The court had left Hettie with Uncle Hugh and Aunt Hannah, who were being paid by the county for taking care of her. Hettie was twenty-eight years old, according to the records in the courthouse.

After Simps's boys and I returned home, we reported to Mrs. Boggs what we had learned about Hettie. Thereafter, we teased Ruby, Simps and Nola's little daughter, by cooing at her like Hettie and breaking off the coos with hyena laughter.

As winter moved in after Thanksgiving, we restricted our play activities to the vacant lot behind Johns' barbershop on fair afternoons, but on clear Saturday mornings we played in the hollow behind the town and among the pines that grew close together on Pine Hill. Boys from all over town joined us in the afternoon to play ballgames and on Saturday to play cowboys and Indians in the forest. Our trips down town to the Garden Theatre every Friday night to see serials and cowboy movies provided us with models for good-guy and bad-guy roles as we reworked our scenarios from week to week. We were ardent admirers of William S. Hart and picked up some of the stunts of Charlie Chaplin and Ben Turpin.

In the evenings local boys came to visit us occasionally, among them Nick McGuire, Robert Estep, and Normal Skaggs, all of whom lived in the neighborhood. Aunt Fannie Pigg, whose husband, Uncle Tom Pigg, a Civil War veteran I had seen out walking on fair days the preceding spring, had died during the summer, came in the evenings to talk with Simps Boggs about legal matters. She liked children and would stay on and tell us stories. She knew many of the legends about Swift's silver mines and told stories about mysterious murders, ghosts that walked in graveyards at night, and haunted houses. We hovered around her to listen. She had a bright smile and almost white hair that caught the glint of the gaslight in a kind of halo as she told in a throaty voice, low-pitched for a woman, of strange things that had happened in olden times. At climactic moments she would pause, look at us intently, and laugh low in her throat before reciting the chilling punch line. Then she would study our faces while waiting for a comment or a question.

After the excitement of preparations in town for Christmas, little Christmas exchanges in our class meetings at the school, and an assembly at which we sang Christmas songs and teachers told what they planned to do during the holidays, we broke for a two-week holiday season. My father rode one mule and led another in from Caines Creek on Friday and we rode back on Saturday, a cold, cloudy day.

I was already saddle-galled and sore by the time we reached Adams, where we stopped at Monroe Adams' store and post office to feed the mules and to eat Vienna sausage and crackers while warming by the potbellied stove. The road up Little Blaine Creek in those days was beside the creek. It was already an extended mudhole. A pond of muddy water in the road in front of the store looked lower from the keg on which I was sitting than the clear water in the creek beyond.

Old Pearl, the mule I was riding, would lag behind. I wore no spurs, as my father did, but attempted to keep Old Pearl moving by striking her with a switch my father had cut for me. She paid little attention to my switching and as I grew tired she moved more slowly. My father would stop his mule, Old Bec, and wait for me to catch up with him. Then he would slap Old Pearl on the rump with his hand, shout indignities, and swear at her. She would take off in a long lope but soon fall behind again. While we were stopped to let the mules drink at a ford on Rich Creek, I became aware of mental fatigue from having the melody of "Shake That Thing" running through my mind so constantly. It seemed that the rhythm of Old Pearl's gait was that of the tune the saxophone player with the patent-leather hair had whined out at the Bud Hawkins shows in the fall.

We arrived home in the late afternoon. I slid off Old Pearl by the yard gate and my father handed down to me the old suitcase that he had kept balanced across the saddlehorn for twenty-five miles. I was so sore that I walked spraddle-legged across the porch to the front door. My mother and my brother and sisters came to greet me and returned to their chores, except my little sister, Ruth, only four years old at the time. She sat on my lap as I warmed myself by the fire and asked more questions than I was prepared to answer.

The Christmas season in 1924 was cloudy and cold. I resumed my share of chores on the farm but spent most of the cloudy days by the fireside where I played games with my little sister or read *Oliver Twist*, which I had brought home with me with the hope that I might find time to finish it before return-

Ruth Williams, Cratis Williams's sister, at nine years old in 1929.

ing to school. I found it more interesting than either *Ivanhoe* or *The Last of the Mohicans* and was able to read more pages an hour in it than I had been able to read in the other books.

Mr. Gilmer's pretty greeting card, sent from faraway Mississippi, arrived a day or two before Christmas. With my brother and sisters, I hung up my stocking for Santa Claus to fill with the usual assortment of candies and red apples taken from the mound in the garden the first time the hole had been opened the day before. Christmas Day was bright and warm, a summer contrast with the dreary days that had preceded it and the blustery days that followed it. I walked alone across the steep hill to see my grandmother on Christmas Day and to eat dinner with her. On the way I stopped to rest by a tall pine near the top of the hill and looked at the brilliant glint of Trap Branch flowing like a stream of silver between the high rail fences far below my grandfather's barn. Grandma had baked a huckleberry cobbler for dinner.

One Friday afternoon I went to the one-room school I had attended the year before. Enrollment had dropped, and only a few of the little children who lived up the branches and toward the head of the creek were able to get there because of the muddy roads and cold weather. Some of the families had moved away, for it was reported that "public works" were good and workers were being "taken on."

Few people visited during that season. The only time I dressed up in my blue serge suit with short pants and a vented coat with a shining black buckle on the belt was to go with my brother and sisters to have the postmistress, who had a box camera, to take a group picture of us. The road was so muddy that day that we walked through the meadows, scaling the fences as we came to them, to get to the post office.

Although my little sister was a lively companion, I felt lonely much of the time and longed for the day when my father would take me back to school. High school had been so different from the seventh grade the year before and

I had made many new friends. I liked my teachers, too, though I had some reservations about Miss Roberts, but even she had been more kindly disposed toward me in recent weeks. I enjoyed telling my brother and older sister and other children how high school was different from grade school and how one rushed from one class to another when the big bell in the tower was rung, I especially enjoyed telling about how hard high school was and the long hours students had to study, read books, and write papers in preparing for their classes. My high school teachers, from faraway places, had ridden the train down Big Sandy River to reach their homes or visit friends, one to Mississippi, one to Tennessee, one to Lexington. Most likely even Mr. Godby had taken his family by train out to Danville beyond Lexington. My accounts were listened to with wonder, it seemed to me. I must have been accounted a world traveler at age 13 by my former schoolmates.

Our trip back to Louisa was made on another cold day but the sun shone part of the day. Grampa Williams went along with us. But this time, instead of riding down Brushy Creek and across the hill to Rich Creek as we had done before, we rode up Brushy Creek, crossed a ridge, and came down Little Blaine Creek. Grampa thought this road was only a little longer than the other, had the advantage of one less mountain to cross, and would be easier on our mules. I remember sitting on the mule beside a white picket fence around the yard of Milt Burgess's home while Grampa engaged in conversation with Milt, whom I had never seen before. As we were riding away, Grampa explained that Milt's wife, the heavy woman who came out to the porch to greet Grampa, had been Lyda Morris, Charley's sister, but I could not remember that I had ever met Charley Morris. Lyda was Aunt Rannie's niece he explained. Aunt Rannie had married my grandmother's brother Wash. Lyda was a first cousin to Uncle Wash's children, Cora Han, Bamy and Marylee Griffith, Maude Maddox, Myrtle McGuire; Troy, John, Will, and Charley; Henry and Harry. It seemed strange to me that Milt Burgess had come so far over the hills to court Lyda Morris, but Grampa explained that he and my Uncle Jake had ridden all the way to the head of Brushy to court my step-granny and Aunt Emily. But Uncle Wash's children had married people who lived close to them, most of them from Caines Creek. Lyda seemed to be so much better off than Uncle Wash's children were.

Along the road up Brushy Creek and down Little Blaine Creek, Grampa knew many of the men working around their barns or chopping wood in the "chip yards," or visiting with passersby on horses who had reined up by their yard gates to pass the time of day with them. Grampa would address them heartily with his booming voice and so loudly that sometimes women and children would appear at the windows of the living rooms or come out into the porches to see who was passing. Grampa would sometimes tease one of the children in his loud voice while the mother hunched in the cool air and wrapped her apron around her arms to keep them warm.

Grampa was right. This road was an easier one to travel by horseback than the other. The gap at the head of the branch through which the road passed to Little Blaine was so low that it did not seem like much of a hill.

We passed Monroe Adams's store before it was time to eat lunch. The horses splashed through the dark pond in the road in front of the store and the clear creek beside the road rippled along over sand shoals as if the bed of the stream were higher than the muddy road. The sky was beginning to be cloudy. It looked as if we might have rain or snow before we could get to Louisa. White stalks of horseweed and ox-eye daisy marshaled along the creek banks stood out as the day grew darker. Broomsage in the meadows and hillside pastures rippled and waved like the surface of a pond after someone skitters a rock across it.

As we approached the Twin Bridges at the Forks of Little Blaine, we could see to our left ahead of us the Devil's Salt Stand, a table-like rock formation on the top of a low ridge beyond a schoolhouse.

Fearing that we might get wet, and since I did not have a rain coat, Papa said we had better hurry along and we could stop at Bussey's Store at Busseyville for a "bite to eat" if the weather didn't look too threatening when we got there. Beyond the Twin Bridges the road had been built along the foot of the hill across the valley from the creek. There were mudholes in the clay road, but there were long stretches between them and we could ride three abreast at a faster pace. We rode silently, the creaking of the leather in our saddles responding to the rhythm of hoof beats.

We dismounted at Bussey's Store, hitched our horses to the rack, and went in. It was later than lunchtime. Mr. Bussey was not there. The store was being kept by his son Randall, a senior at the high school whose younger sister, Regania, was in my class. One customer, who had already done his trading, was sitting by the stove, his basket beside him. An old man, apparently Randall's grandfather, was sitting away from the stove. The old man, dressed in heavy clothes, his face quite red, appeared not to be interested in what was going on. I thought he was probably hard of hearing. Although Grampa shouted at him, his responses did not indicate that he understood Grampa, who was trying to tell the old man that he was a cousin of one of his daughters-in-law.

Grampa ordered a slice of tub cheese, Papa a can of "Vyeenie" sausage, and I a can of sardines. Randall tore off three pieces of slick wrapping paper from a roll on the counter, spread them on the counter, and laid a horseshoe nail on two of them. He placed a slice of the rat cheese on the other and then a handful of soda crackers from a barrel on each. He opened the can of Vienna sausage with a hatchet blade, prying the segments back so that the top of the can looked like a flower, and set it out for Papa. He took from his pocket a heavy knife with several blades, one of which he opened, a short, heavy hawk-billed one, and ran it around the edge of the top of the sardine can. He curled the lid back and set it out for me. He then asked whether we wanted anything to drink. Papa and Grampa did not like pop, but I ordered an Orange Crush. He picked it out of a wooden box, pried off the top with a heavy bottle opener, and set it out for me, the warm liquid spewing up and running down the outside of the bottle.

We stood at the counter and ate. Grampa, who had no teeth, gummed his way into the piece of cheese, making a half-moon with the points moving toward his ears. He would stop from time to time, break up a cracker, and toss the crumbs into his mouth. When he munched, his jaws moved fast like a sheep's jaws. Papa carefully extracted the sausages with the horseshoe nail and ate each in small bites directly from the nail, alternating with bites of cracker. I lifted each sardine from the can with my horseshoe nail, laid it carefully on a cracker, and bit off pieces of the cracker. The crackers were tough, but occasionally one would break and spill the sardine on the paper. I would then pick it up with my horseshoe nail and put it directly into my mouth. The Orange Crush would bubble over when I lifted it to my mouth. I could feel the soda rushing into my nose from the back side when I took a big swallow of it. We ate ceremoniously, no one saying anything. Randall sat in a chair near the stove and talked with the customer who had remained for a visit after he had done his trading. I thought I observed a half-amused, half-quizzical look on his face as he glanced from time to time at Grampa as he ate his way into the slice of rubbery cheese and munched his cracker crumbs like a sheep.

Papa paid for our lunch. We climbed on our horses and hurried on toward town. At the top of Wallace Hill we came into a mist. The road was wet. The hooves of our horses sank more deeply into the clay road. We whipped up our horses in order to try to get to town before the mist became rain. From the top of Town Hill we saw Louisa half-hidden in fog with dark treetops, church steeples, the big flourmill, and the top of the bridge across the river to Ft. Gay swimming in it. Light rain began to fall.

We stopped at Davis Martin's livery stable to leave our horses for the night. Several loafers had gathered at the stable to swap yarns. Davis stayed long enough to hear the ending of a story before he came out, laughing, to take care of our horses.

Papa and Grampa walked with me to the Boggs home and went in to speak to Simps and Nola. Simps was not at home, but they visited with Nola for a few minutes. They would stay at Wallace Jordan's boarding house, they said, and if Wallace did not have room for them they would go to Vess and Nan's boarding house.

I was saddle-sore and worn down from the twenty-five mile ride. After unpacking my suitcase and pushing it under my bed, I sat by the gas fire in the living room to dry my damp clothing. But I was glad to be back at school, eager to see again my teachers after their holidays in far-off places, Lexington, Danville, Tennessee, sunny Mississippi.

There was excitement among the students the first day back. Many were sporting new jackets, sweaters, caps, and shoes. Conversations were lively about things they had done during the holidays, parties they had attended, visitors they had had in their homes, exciting adventures they had experienced. Teachers told what they had done, cities they had visited. But each teacher became somber before the class ended and called our attention to final examinations coming up the following week. Having nothing exciting to report about my own holidays, I welcomed the attention called to final examinations.

I reviewed hard for the examinations, reading again all of Caldwell and Eikenberry's *General Science* that we had covered, reviewing Clippenger's *Written and Spoken English*, practicing the drill's in Smith's *Beginning Latin*, and working again representative problems in the algebra textbook. My confidence grew as the time for examinations approached. Feeling uncertain of my skills in "spotting" what teachers would be likely to ask on examinations, I did not know what they might consider important or unimportant. My fellow students, giving much attention to what teachers might ask, exchanged opinions and sought out students to supply them with answers to hypothetical questions. My ego was flattered when many of them consulted me, especially in science and Latin. Most of the teachers, aware of the concern of their students, took time to review in classes what they considered most important. These reviews, which appeared to spark uneasiness in most students, bolstered my confidence, except for algebra.

When report cards were distributed, I was disappointed with the C I had received in algebra but A's in science and Latin and B in English made me eligible for the honor roll. As I inquired around among my friends I found only one who had made better grades than I had made. I had established myself as a successful high school student, and my fellow students were recognizing me as a kind of a "resource" when they needed answers to questions for which they did not want to search their texts to find. Having achieved this status, I found it fulfilling to maintain it for the remainder of my time in high school. The smallest and the youngest boy in the class, I could be a better student than the largest or the oldest.

A few weeks after the Christmas holidays a boy in the eighth grade asked me one day whether I would be interested in taking over his route for the *Grit*, which he delivered every Saturday morning. He received thirty copies, of which he delivered twenty-one to homes and tried to sell nine on the streets. Sometimes he was unable to sell all of the nine copies, but when that happened the carrier could tear off the title and date for the first pages of copies not sold and return them along with the money he would send to the company and not have to pay for them. *Grit* sold for a nickel a copy, of which two cents went to the carrier. I could earn prizes by increasing the circulation of the paper. He showed me a bright dollar watch with a fancy fob which he had won for increasing circulation by ten subscribers, I believe it was. He handed the watch to me to examine. I looked at it, studied the second hand as it jerked its way around the circle, held it to my ear to listen to the loud ticking of its works, slipped it into the watch pocket of my knee pants and smoothed the fob down. It would be nice to have a watch of my own, I thought. I considered the offer. All he would want for the route, he said, was forty-five cents that people owed him because they did not have money at hand when he delivered their papers. He had a list of them. They had said they would pay him the next time he came around. One woman owed him fifteen cents. She would receive money from one of her children who lived in Columbus, Ohio, in a few days, she had been saying, and would pay him. She asked him to keep an account of it.

He then showed me a little notebook in which he had the names of his regular customers (but not streets on which they lived). Following some of the names he had written in pencil "owes five cents." He would give me the little book. When I explained that I did not know where the people lived, he said I could get one of the Boggs boys to go with me. I thought they would not know either and might not want to go with me unless I paid them. Sensing a reluctance to deal with him, he offered to go along with me on the first trip and allow me to earn the money. That way, he said, maybe he could collect what people owed him. We could cover the route in about three hours. If we were lucky, we could sell the nine extra copies on the streets as we covered the route. Sometimes he was able to sell them nearly all by crying them off along the platform at the depot when the down train went through at 10:30 in the morning.

I was turning his proposition over in my mind while looking at the watch and holding it to my ear to hear it tick. He picked the papers up at the post office about 9 o'clock, he said, and usually had them all delivered by noon. Sometimes he would have to go down around the drug store and the courthouse Saturday afternoon to sell the extra copies, but not often. Usually, he said, when he was not able to sell all of the extras was on rainy days when there were not many people in town.

Sixty cents for three hours of work was pretty good pay, I thought. If I could increase the circulation to fifty I could earn a dollar in three hours, as much as my father paid hands to work for him on the farm for a full ten-hour day. I agreed to take the route.

Saturday morning he met me at the post office, where he introduced me to the postmaster and told him I was taking over the *Grit* route and that he would ask that the bundle be addressed to me thereafter. The postmaster produced the bundle of papers, I put them in the canvas bag with "GRIT" in big bright red letters on it, and we started. I was in business.

We started down the main street, along which men were already beginning to gather in little clumps to talk and swap stories. He held in his hand a copy of the paper and cried "*Grit*, just five cents!" as we passed the men or met people. Occasionally, someone would buy a copy. He would hand me the nickel and take another paper. After a trip around the courthouse yard, where people sat on benches, and through the hall, along which people stood talking outside office doors, we set out on the route. We had sold five of the extra copies.

As we met people on the streets, he would hold up a copy and ask, "Do you want a *Grit*?" Most of those whom we met ignored us and looked straight ahead as if they did not see us. A middle-aged woman with a basket on her arm stopped and bought a copy. "We can probably sell the other three at the down train," he said.

Our first delivery was to Mr. Waldeck, who operated the cleaning and pressing shop. I was introduced. Mr. Waldeck wanted to know whose boy I was and where my parents lived. He knew my grandfather, he said. Our next stop was at Dr. Bussey's office. Dr. Bussey, an aged man with whiskers, was leaning back in his chair by a window and reading a western magazine. I was introduced, but Dr. Bussey only looked at me as he straightened out in his chair and drew from his pocket a long leather purse from which he dug a nickel with his bony fingers, which he handed to us in exchange for the paper. He did not speak, but spat a stream of tobacco juice into a crusted brass spittoon beside his chair before returning to his magazine. We then climbed three flights of steep stairs to Dr. Bromley's office. Dr. Bromley was talking to a patient. When he saw us, he produced a nickel and exchanged it for the paper without stopping his conversation to speak to us. Dr. Bromley was a tall, handsome man with sharp eyes. He was well dressed, and his office was being kept better than Dr. Bussey's which seemed unclean and had stacks of papers and magazines on the floor along one wall.

We then started out in town. We did not stop at many of the fine homes. Instead, we climbed stairs to rooms and apartments in which mostly old people lived, some of whom would leave us standing at the door while they went inside to find the nickel. Each time, I was introduced, but most of our customers seemed to pay little attention to me as they accepted their papers and returned to their rooms.

We went to shabby homes down unpaved streets, into alleys, along the railroad track, and to the unpainted board and batten houses around the northern edge of the town. One aged man with dirty ears and scabs and scales on his face lived alone in a small one-room house that might have been a smokehouse before it became a residence. Another large, rawboned old man wearing a ragged black felt hat, a crusty blue serge coat, faded bib overalls, and heavy rawhide shoes came from a little weathered two-room boxed house perched on stilts against a hillside to meet us at the top of steep wooden steps. The nickels many of them gave us looked yellow and felt waxy from having shared a pocket with a piece of plug chewing tobacco.

We hurried to meet the down train. Teenagers, representing restaurants and sandwich shops, or mothers who wanted to earn a little cash of their own, rushed along outside the cars crying "sandwiches," which they carried in oblong baskets, dry unwrapped sandwiches, cheese, bologna, boiled ham. Windows of the cars flew open and people stuck their heads out, looked into the baskets, picked out the sandwiches they wanted, and handed the money down for them. We mingled with the sandwich criers to offer *Grit*, holding up copies so people might be able to read headlines.

After we had sold three copies, we returned to the route, the southern sector of the town. Our subscribers here were mostly gray-haired women living in comfortable looking but old homes. It was they who sometimes did not have handy the nickel needed to pay for the paper, but all paid up except the one who owed fifteen cents. She had not yet heard from her son and didn't have a penny in the house, she said, but she was sure she would hear from him soon. It was a good thing, she said, that Mr. Bromley gave her credit at his grocery store, or she might go hungry sometimes. We extended credit to her for another copy of *Grit*.

We finished the route a little before 12 o'clock by the pocket watch and sat on the steps of the old Masonic Hall to settle our business. He would have to send in the money for the papers we had sold that morning, so he needed ninety cents for that and fifteen cents for what the woman who had no money owed him. I had 40 cents and a 20-cent debt to collect for my morning's work. I was flushed with excitement and thought of possibilities for increasing the circulation of *Grit*, for I certainly wanted one of those prize nickel-plated pocket watches with a fancy leather fob. I rushed to the Boggs home in time for dinner, my empty bag with GRIT in big red letters on it flapping against my side and hanging almost to my knees. Being the *Grit* boy helped me to learn the town. I experimented with my rounds in order to reduce the time needed for delivering the papers. Then I began knocking at doors and asking housewives whether they would like to become "regular customers." Many agreed to let me leave the *Grit* every Saturday, whether they were home or not, and to pay me when I found them home. This required that I develop a more sophisticated record-keeping system. After two or three weeks, I had no copies left to cry in the streets, so I requested that ten additional copies be sent. Before long I had increased circulation enough to earn the pocket watch, which I was extremely proud to own and carry.

By about the beginning of March I requested another increase in my allocation of copies, with which I received promotional material, lithographs, suitable for framing, of animals and birds as gifts to new subscribers. I became more aggressive as a crier on the streets and at the railroad station and requested more copies for sale.

As the number of copies I could sell increased, I decided to go across the river to Fort Gay, West Virginia, to cry off papers at the windows of a Norfolk and Western train that stopped there briefly. Bridge toll each way for pedestrians was three cents. I would have to sell at least three copies of *Grit* just to recover travel expenses. My one venture across the river convinced me that there was not much fleece to be plucked there. I went early enough to meet the train, sold a copy of *Grit* to one or two or three persons waiting to board it, ran desperately along the platform crying "Grit," but nobody opened a window of any of the cars, and then rushed back to the station and sold a copy to the only person to get off the train, an ample woman with a pleasant smile who would be waiting for someone from the country to pick her up at the depot. The station master was not interested in reading *Grit*. He said it had the biggest lies and the tallest tales in it he had ever read in any paper.

Across the railroad tracks and upon the hill a way were some little houses. I walked up there to do some door-to-door selling, but only one housewife bought a copy. Having recovered my expenses for bridge toll, I had started back toward Louisa when three boys about my age came running up a lane from between the depot and the river. As they approached, they began yelling obscenities at me and requesting that I wait right there.

I stopped and waited. Although they were making a lot of noise, I saw that they were not really angry. They arranged themselves in front of me in a semi-circle. For a moment they were silent. Then the largest of them, in a quiet voice, asked who I was and when I had moved to town. When I responded that I was from Louisa, the least one yelled, "Louisa! Boys, let's put him back across the river!" The middle one jumped at me as if he were ready to attack me, but I did not retreat or offer to defend myself. I added that I was not really from Louisa but from Blaine and was staying in Louisa to go to high school. The largest one said, "You are in high school? Boy, how old are you?" We then settled into a conversation. They were rancorous because a gang of Louisa boys had thrown rocks at one of them and chased him out of Louisa and across the bridge a day or two before. He thought he knew the names of the boys who had done it, but I had never heard of any of them and assured them that I certainly held no grudge against Fort Gay boys and would not throw rocks at people. I glanced at the depot and saw the woman standing at a window and looking at us. I then referred to Fort Gay boys and girls in my high school class, all of whom I considered friends. They knew some of the persons whom I had named.

They walked along with me to the end of the bridge and allowed me to depart in peace. I did not look back, for I thought they might attack me if I showed any evidence that I was afraid of them. When I stopped halfway across the bridge to pay my toll, I looked to one side enough to see that they were no longer in sight. The toll collector, an aged man with a mustache, bought a *Grit* from me. As I walked on, I congratulated myself on having talked my way out of a fight without being cowardly, but I did not try a second time to extend my business operation to Fort Gay.

At the dinner table at Boggs's I reported that I had gone to Fort Gay to see whether I might sell copies of *Grit* but had had little success and that three boys were about to attack me but that I had talked my way out of a fight. Mr. Boggs advised me that it was dangerous for a young fellow to go to Fort Gay alone. Fights between Louisa boys and Fort Gay boys had gone on for years. Before Kentucky Normal College had closed one of the students there had gone to Fort Gay one night and a gang killed him. Feeling had not yet died down between Louisa boys and Fort Gay boys. I might get hurt over there, he said. His account frightened me. The fear that I had not felt while talking with the boys at the depot welled up within me and chilled me. For a few weeks my dreams were troubled from time to time by the sudden appearance from a familiar alley of three boys who tried to surround me as I attempted to race away but found myself handicapped by my bag of papers and unable to call out because my words had no sound.

Thinking that more shopkeepers in Louisa might be interested in *Grit*, I called on many of them — Mr. Workman at the shoe shop, Mr. Ferguson at the men's store, Mr. Wells at the sales store, Mr. Jake Isralsky at the department store, the druggists— but only three or four became subscribers. When I called on Mr. Crutcher at the grocery store, where I had bought bananas and oranges a few times, he gave me a tongue-lashing. He had been selling *Grit* at his store for years. Recently, he had not sold his quota. Boys like me would sell for a few weeks and then quit. People who always read *Grit* would switch to a delivery boy and then, when the boy quit, they would want to buy from him again. It was an annoyance for him to have to keep changing his order. There was little money in it for him, but he liked to accommodate his customers. Crestfallen, I retreated from his store and relaxed my efforts with shopkeepers.

Instead, I concentrated on finding new subscribers among housewives. When I turned my route over at the end of May to Charles Lowe, a tall young fellow in the sixth or seventh grade, I had forty-three regular customers and was selling seven copies of the paper on the streets for a total of fifty copies. I was earning the dollar every Saturday morning that I had set as my goal.

After I had been delivering *Grit* about three weeks, Normal Skaggs, whose parents lived a few doors from the Boggses, asked me whether I might be interested in taking over his *Cincinnati Post* route. Older than I but behind me a grade or two in school, Normal was thinking of quitting school and getting a full-time job. If he succeeded in finding another job, he would not have time to deliver the *Post*, copies of which arrived in Louisa about 7 o'clock in the morning, for that would be the time at which he would go to work if he found a job. He received 86 copies of the *Post* six mornings a week and delivered 81 to regular customers on the route and sold up to five on the streets. When papers arrived promptly, he could cover his route by school time. If the papers arrived late, he finished the route at the lunch hour. He collected every Friday afternoon.

The *Post* sold at three cents a copy. The delivery boy received seven-eights of a cent for each copy sold, except that he could keep the difference between what he had to report for the paper and the nickel that people usually gave him when he sold one on the street.

I was not sure at first that I would be interested in taking the route. I asked for time to think the matter over. We got up about 6 o'clock at the Boggs home and usually had breakfast by 6:30, for Mr. Boggs liked to get to his office in the courthouse by 7 o'clock. If I could eat breakfast and be at the post office by 7 o'clock, I would be able to deliver the papers by school time, but I had been using that hour for study. I thought about the proposition for a day or two. By increasing the circulation to 100 I could earn $5.25 a week. That and my earnings from the *Grit* route would bring me $6.00 or a little more a week for ten or twelve hours of work, counting the time needed for collecting from my customers Friday afternoon.

Six dollars a week, I thought, was a lot of money. I could dress myself in fine stylish clothes and still have money to buy a soft drink or an ice cream cone at the drugstore occasionally, and I could go to the picture shows whenever I wanted to and even ask a girl to go with me and have enough money to buy her ticket, treat her to a box of popcorn, and take her by the drugstore for a soft drink and ice cream afterwards. I was approaching the age of 14 and had noticed that many boys and girls in my class came to see the moving pictures together, and I could see them afterwards sitting at the little round tables in the drugstore and sipping soft drinks through straws while laughing and talking like the grown-up folks, including some of the high school teachers, who sat at other little tables and ate ice cream with chocolate on it from dishes or tall glasses with little spoons as they talked and laughed. The drugstore smelled good and was well lighted with soft lights hidden away so that the counters and glass shelves on which cosmetics of all kinds were kept seemed to glow. I had sat a few times on one of the round stools at the counter for an ice cream cone or a Coca-Cola spurted from a fountain into a twinkling glass with crushed ice in it while admiring all the while the clerk in a snow-white jacket, with his hair parted in the middle and curling in waves toward his ears and fixed in place with pomade, filled orders deftly with his soft hands, but I had not yet sat at one of the little tables. There were some girls in my class, not those whom the larger boys in the class and some from the classes ahead of us rushed, who smiled at me and teased with me. Perhaps one of them would like to go with me, but they were older than I and taller and usually much larger, too, for I did not yet weigh 70 pounds. If I should never be able to stew up enough courage to ask one for a date, I could always drop back to the eighth grade, or the seventh grade, or even the sixth grade in which there were attractive, bright-eyed girls about my own age and size who were already using rouge, painting their pretty lips to look like Cupid bows, rolling their stockings, and wearing shoes with high heels.

Having noted already that older boys at school, especially those who lived in town, were beginning to wear bell-bottom pants and jackets with box backs, wide lapels that, when matched by buttoning the two buttons on the coat, looked like huge arrowheads split down the middle, and hidden pockets with flaps, both pants and coat made of soft blue-gray flannel, I had begun to think that it would be nice to have a new suit with my first long pants for my birthday, but I had not thought such a dream could come true while I was still a freshman. Perhaps I could earn money enough during the summer to have one by the time I returned to school as a sophomore the following year, I had thought. I could feel as stylish as any of the boys in school if I had one of those tightly fitting jackets, a pair of pants that would fit so snugly in the rump that I would look as if I had been melted and poured into it and that would begin flaring at the knees into a bell so big in diameter that the toes of my shoes would wink when I walked. I would want light blue shirts, like those most of the boys in style were wearing, and a bright red bowtie and red socks of the same shade. A snappy blue-gray hat with a striped band would complete my attire.

With six dollars a week coming in I might be able to outfit myself completely, even including a new pair of shoes, by my birthday. I decided to accept the paper route and to work as much as time would permit at increasing the circulation.

I told Normal that I would accept the route. He wanted me to take it over as quickly as possible, the following week if I could. He came to my room that night to explain to me how to make out reports. I would be sending in a check at the beginning of the following week for what I owed the publisher. I would need to set up a bank account, he said, but I had already done that in order to handle the *Grit* account without having to pay money order fees. Then he showed me his account book, which had the street address below the name of each subscriber. There were five squares behind each name to check for each week during the month the customer had paid his bill. Some had not paid for several weeks, but he said that I could have whatever I could collect after he had turned the route over to me. I could go along with him Friday and Saturday mornings to learn where the customers lived.

One thing I would have to do before I could accept the route was to find someone to sign a bond for me. He produced a copy of the bond that the publisher had sent him to give to his successor after he had notified the publisher that he would soon be turning the route over to someone else. The bond would have to be signed and sent in to the publisher in time for it to arrive by next Monday, he said. Mr. Boggs might be willing to sign it for me, he thought.

I accepted the bond, made out, as I recall, for $50.00. I knew Mr. Boggs would sign it for me if I should ask him to do so, but I felt that I would be imposing on his generous nature to ask him. That night I went over in my mind the men who, among those who bought *Grit* from me, might be willing to go on my bond. Dr. Bromley had taken time, when he was not seeing a patient, to talk with me and was interested in my progress at school. He seemed to like me and to believe that I was going to succeed. I liked him. I would go to his office tomorrow and ask him first. If he should decline, then I would see Mr. Waldeck. If Mr. Waldeck should turn me down, I would then ask Mr. Boggs.

The possibility of having money of my own with which to buy clothes and other things I might want excited me. I remained awake a long time after I had gone to bed fancying myself all dressed up and being admired for my sharpness by my teachers and the students in my class.

After school the following day I called on Dr. Bromley. There were no patients in his office at the time. Dr. Bromley, his back to a window through which bright sunlight streamed, was sitting on a high stool and working on account books spread on a "secretary" with a slanted top. "What can I do for you, young man?" he asked, his fine looking fountain pen poised above a ledger sheet. It occurred to me that perhaps most people would have addressed me as "sonny" instead of "young man." I was feeling like a young man as I told him that I wanted to accept the *Cincinnati Post* route and that I needed a bondsman who was acquainted with me and willing to state that I was truthful, honest, and trustworthy. I knew he did not know me very well, but I had thought of him first because he had seemed to me to know me well for the short time we had been acquainted.

"How much is the bond for?" he asked as I handed the paper to him.

"Fifty dollars," I replied.

Without asking me to be seated, he adjusted his glasses and read the paper. With a flourish of his big fountain pen with the gold clip glinting in the sunlight he signed his name in bold black ink, picked up a blotter and stamped it with a thump over his signature, and handed the paper back to me.

"You will do well," he said. "Everybody will get a paper on time, rain or shine, you will keep careful records, and you will send in the money you owe on time. I am glad to help you out."

He clapped me on the shoulder with a strong hand and I departed, feeling proud of myself and determined to take care of every business detail connected with delivering the *Post* exactly as I was supposed to.

I descended the three flights of steep stairs and emerged directly on the sidewalk, along which people were clustered in conversational groups. As I passed the drugstore I saw young fellows wearing tight jackets, bow ties, and bell-bottom pants leaning against the building, one foot, with a loud sock screaming, propped against the wall. Painted young women in cloche hats, soft colored coats with fur collars extending down the fronts and pulled tightly around them, bare knees flashing above rolled stockings, sauntered up and down the sidewalks, clacking high heels against the concrete as they waggled from side to side as far as they could without falling. The young women looked straight ahead, like tin soldiers, but the young men all turned their heads slowly as one and watched them pass, studying their "brave vibrations, each way free," speculatively. The Jazz Age had arrived.

I went by the post office and mailed the bond to the publisher of the *Cincinnati Post* in the envelope that had been provided for the purpose.

Thursday morning I rushed to the post office by 7 o'clock to meet Normal, who was late, but the mail cart from Fort Gay had not arrived yet. About the time Normal arrived we saw an aged man shuffling along behind a big wooden box with two wheels attached to it. He was coming off the wooden floor of the bridge when we saw him, and we could hear the hollow rumble of his crude cart. Normal said he would let us pick up our papers from him, so we dashed to meet him. He stopped the cart and gave us our papers.

Normal hurriedly cut the seagrass strings that bound them, handed me a half dozen, and stuffed the others into a dirty bag that had "CINCINNATI POST" in black letters stamped on it. He gave me also the little route book in which names and addresses of his customers were written. We raced down Front Street, Normal calling out to everybody we met "*Cincinnati Post!*" and flashing the streamer across the front page. A few reached into their pockets for change as we approached them and handed me three pennies or a nickel in exchange for the paper. Only one waited for change after he had handed me a nickel. We had sold the five copies before we reached the corner at the bank.

We hurried on almost at a lope, Normal folding papers as he went and flinging them against the front doors of homes as he called out "*Cincinnati Post!*" He would tell me the name of the person who lived there as we approached each house. I would look at the name and address in the little book to help place customer and home in my mind.

We raced along uneven sidewalks down unpaved streets near the river and then back to Lock Avenue, north, crisscrossing the avenue and dashing down side streets as we needed to. The pavement stopped at the end of Lock Avenue, but we had four or five customers living in the muddy lanes without sidewalks beyond Lock Avenue. We then turned up the railroad track that ran parallel to Lock Avenue about a block away until we passed the big mill. There we turned westward and delivered in the section of town called "Italy," where mostly poor people lived in little houses along unpaved streets and lanes.

In about fifty minutes we had covered the route and were back home in time to pick up our books for school as the big bell in the tower at the "college," now the high school building, was ringing the first time, ten minutes before classes started. We were able to get to school on time, but I knew it would take almost perfect timing and a lot of rushing around to be able to cover the route and be at school by 8 o'clock. In rainy weather or in snowstorms one might not make it and have to finish delivering at the noon hour.

The following morning I was able to remember most of the houses at which we were to deliver papers, and by the third morning I knew the route. By then, too, I had developed the pace, a kind of jog, that was needed in order to cover the route in the time available to us. I had noted that most of the papers were being delivered to rather humble homes and less pretentious business establishments. A few black families took the *Post*. I asked Normal about this. Most of the well-to-do families read the *Ashland Daily Independent*, which produced a Sunday paper and cost more. Emmanuel Sargent delivered it on a bicycle each evening after the up train came through. Normal thought Emmanuel, an upperclassman and an outstanding debater at the high school, probably had as many as 200 customers. He had increased his subscription and won a bicycle, Normal had heard. The *Cincinnati Enquirer* was also delivered in town by Mr. Murray, whom we had seen a time or two, an old man with rheumy eyes and a scraggly beard, dressed shabbily in a ragged coat, dirty canvas leggings, and coarse work shoes. Normal thought that Mr. Murray probably did not deliver as many *Enquirers* as he did *Posts*.

Normal turned his route book over to me Sunday. He had been able to collect almost all that was due him, but had made several trips to some of the homes. One old lady, who owed him for several weeks, had looked at him through a front window but would not come to the door the last two times he had called. I could have what she owed if I could collect it.

The route was all mine next week. I rushed down to the end of the bridge to meet the shuffling old man with the mail cart, grabbed my papers, stuffed them into the dirty bag, and took off down front street, yelling with vigor "*Cincinnati Post* here! Read all about _____! *Post*, mister?" and then ran on, the full bag of papers bouncing me from side to side. By the end of the week I decided that I could sell five more copies on the street. As I collected on Friday afternoon I stopped at two restaurants, a secondhand clothing store, a sewing machine repair shop, and a garage. The proprietors all subscribed. I requested that my allocation be increased ten copies. I had difficulty, though, selling ten copies on the streets every morning, but instead of returning the front page titles and headlines to be debited against my account, I would rush into a place of business, slap a paper down, and call out "A free *Cincinnati Post*, compliments of the delivery boy. Read it to see whether you would like to have it delivered six mornings a week for only fifteen cents." Many of the owners of these places subscribed.

Then Floyd Collins became trapped in the sandstone cave. Daily papers carried full accounts of his situation and pictures relating to efforts to rescue him, pictures of derricks and drilling equipment, of professors Funkhouser and Webb of the University of Kentucky at the scene. Each morning I would read two or three paragraphs of the lead story to be able to report just enough about changes in Collins' situation to whet reader interest and bark it out with a closing comment, "Read all about it in the *Cincinnati Post*! Right here. *Post*, mister?" I also used the Collins story as I called on people living near those who were already taking the *Post* to induce them to subscribe. I did not want to extend the route into new territory because I feared I could not get it covered in time to be at the school by 8 o'clock. As the sensational Floyd Collins story dragged on, people began to rush out of their houses and hail me, holding nickels out toward me. "Here, boy! Give me a *Post*." When I would ask "Would you like for me to deliver you one every morning?" many became subscribers. Within a month I had raised my subscription to 100. My account at the Louisa National Bank was growing. I had not yet bought any new clothes and had spent only a little of my money for picture shows, soda pop, as fond as I was of Nehi, and vanilla ice cream.

One bright morning just before the lunch hour Professor Godby at the school released students in the study hall to play in the sunshine beside the building. I do not recall why we were released but believe that carpenters might have been doing some alteration in connection with the reserve book area at the front of the room. I was tossing a ball with someone when I heard my name called. Standing at one of the windows of the study hall were Professor Godby and a tall slender man with busy hair, a pink complexion, and small, almost sky blue eyes. The tall man, well dressed in a gray suit, was smiling at me as if he had known me sometime in the past and was glad to see me again.

"Cratis, this is Mr. W_____, the field representative of the *Cincinnati Post* for the Big Sandy Valley," Professor Godby said. Mr. W_____ reached a spidery arm down to shake my hand, which he squeezed firmly with long soft fingers that met around it, while he smiled, his sleepy looking eyes never quite making contact with mine.

"Mr. W_____ says that you have increased the circulation of the *Post* about twenty-five per cent in the few weeks you have been delivering it here. He has asked that I give you a half-holiday to be with him. He wants to take you to lunch and to the picture show this afternoon. You may go with him if you wish."

Immensely pleased that I had so distinguished myself as a carrier that I was to be treated by the field representative himself and honored with a half-holiday, I asked for a few minutes to get my books and supplies together to leave with George Sweatnam, our friendly building custodian, who had permitted me several times, against the rules of the school, to enter the building and sit in the study hall before the doors of the school were unlocked in the morning.

I met Mr. W_____ in Mr. Godby's office. We started toward town, he with his rubbery arm resting lightly around my shoulders and his long soft fingers hanging beside the right lapel of my coat. He walked slowly, for I was taking two steps to his one and we were not falling into rhythm very well. He was so effusive in his high praise of my achievements, which had not occurred to me as particularly praiseworthy, and so filled with compliments about what a clean and bright looking chap I appeared to be that I began to feel ill at ease. His arm about my shoulders and the long fingers dangling down my chest made me uncomfortable.

He had engaged a room at the Brunswick Hotel, he said. It was too early for lunch, but we could sit on a bench between two trees beside the street in front of the hotel and enjoy the sunshine until it was time to wash for lunch. Then we would go up to his room and get ourselves ready to eat at my favorite place. I felt uncomfortable again, for I had no favorite place. I had not yet eaten in a restaurant.

As we sat on the bench he wanted to know what I had done to increase the circulation of the *Post* so much in such a short time. He would interrupt frequently with complimentary comments and philosophical observations. There was something unusual about the way he would look at me. His small eyes would narrow to slits as they darted about, never quite making contact with my own. The smile that he wore, almost constantly and even when he narrowed his eyes, seemed so shy and self-conscious that I decided he was really just "somebody that stayed plagued all the time." When I said something that pleased him particularly well he would touch me in some way, sometimes by clapping his long hand on mine, or nudging me lightly with his elbow, or pressing his long leg against mine for a second or two. It made me uncomfortable, for I was not accustomed to coming into physical contact with men. It occurred to me that he was not really very much interested in what I was telling him, for he would make observations that indicated that he had not been paying close attention to my account, particularly his philosophical and moralistic interludes which I had difficulty in relating to what I had been saying. We went to his room. He handed me a towel and told me where the washroom was. I could tidy up first, he said. When I returned he was stretched out on the bed, but he hopped up, grabbed his traveling kit, and left to tidy himself up. He smelled fresh with mint when he returned and he had dressed his hair with a tonic that smelled like a barbershop.

"Well, where shall we eat?" he asked.

I could not find the courage to say that I had never eaten in a restaurant. "John Garred's restaurant is a good one," I told him. John Garred, half-colored, and his family operated a restaurant down the street toward Crutcher's grocery store then. I had looked in several times in passing. People sat at tables with white cloths on them, used white cloth napkins, and were served by the attractive red-haired and blue-eyed daughters, their golden complexion looking vibrant as they rushed about in white uniforms and smiled like sunshine. It seemed to me that there might not be a better restaurant in town from what I had observed through windows.

Several of the tables were occupied. We stood for a moment, and Mr. Garred himself came from behind his cash register, showed us to a table near the front, and placed a menu before each of us. I studied the menu, the first I had ever seen. Lunches were 35 cents. One could choose from among three or four meats and two vegetables from among four or five. Peach cobbler came with lunch. The drink, coffee or milk, was included. I thought eating in a restaurant was an expensive proposition that only quite well-to-do people could afford. Mr. W_____ was certainly generous to treat me to this experience, and to a moving picture show and possibly a box of popcorn and a soft drink afterwards. Why, he was willing to spend 50 or 55 cents to treat me. That was more than half as much as I earned each morning for delivering the paper.

Soon one of the smiling red-headed girls came to take our orders. Mr. W_____ asked me to go ahead. I ordered breaded pork chops, mashed potatoes, green peas, and milk, foods with which I was familiar, except that I did not know precisely what breaded pork chops were. The girl hurried away and returned with the food on a big round tray, which she carried balanced on an uplifted hand and lowered so carefully to the edge of the table that I marveled at her skill. She placed the steaming food before us, set separate little dishes with peach cobbler in them a little to the left of the spoon, and stood a glass of milk beyond the end of my fork and knife all so carefully that I decided that these matters were always taken care of in this fashion. The breaded pork chops were light brown, the heap of mashed potatoes had a small pool of melted butter in the top, the peas looked as if they might have been cooked in thin gravy, and the two tiny biscuits looked like little cakes. The food was unusually good. I had never tasted better food, I thought.

Noting that Mr. W_____ was eating very slowly, I slowed down from the sprinting pace at which I had begun. He had an interesting way of crooking his arm and approaching his mouth in such a way that the end of his fork was pointed straight at his face. I could not recall having seen anybody eat like that before. He had ordered beef. I thought it must have been tough (the middle of it looked red as if it had not yet got done), for instead of bearing down with his fork to tear a bite loose, he proceeded fastidiously to cut each bite off with his knife, while holding the piece down with his fork, then lay his knife down, transfer his fork to his right hand, and lift the bite to his mouth, approaching it in a head-on manner. He had such funny long spidery arms, maybe this was the way he had to eat, I thought.

We talked as we ate, Mr. W_____'s eyes hopping at mine occasionally like a brace of fleas making an attack. He was interested in the subjects I was studying at school, wanted to know the ones I liked best, and discussed scientific topics with me. He then asked about my teachers, the ones I liked best, and why I liked them. He had graduated from an academy in Tennessee, where he had grown up, but had not gone to college. He liked science, too, but he read a great deal and was interested also in good literature. One could learn a great deal about mankind by reading literature, he assured me, but reading popular fiction he declared a waste of time.

Although Mr. W_____ had not finished eating all of the food on his plate, as I had done, he stopped just about the time I was considering how I should eat the peach cobbler. I had not yet used the spoon, so I assumed that one ate cobbler properly with a spoon. Always before, I had taken cobbler from a big bowl directly into my plate. Was I supposed to rake the cobbler from the little dish onto my plate? If not, was I supposed to set the little dish in my plate and then eat the cobbler from the little dish? While I was pondering these matters, Mr. W_____ set his plate, with a small piece of raw looking beef, a biscuit, and a bite or two of each vegetable left uneaten, back toward the center of the table, picked up the little dish of cobbler, set it where his plate had been, and poured over the cobbler some cream from a little pitcher already on the table when we sat down. Then he picked up his spoon and began to eat the cobbler, a little line of the yellow cream showing between his lips as he turned the cobbler over slowly, his mouth closed primly.

I could feel myself blushing as it occurred to me that Mr. W_____ might have perceived my problem and stopped eating what was on his plate in order to show me how I was supposed to eat my cobbler. I looked at him but his face did not betray anything to indicate that such had been the case. Between bites he continued his account of what it was like to go to an academy, at which students lived in a dormitory, kept study hours at night, and were supervised by teachers who lived in the dormitory with them. Subjects one studied at an academy were mostly the same as those studied in public high schools except that almost all academy students took more Latin and mathematics than students in public high schools usually took nowadays.

After eating the cobbler, we continued to sit at the table for a while. The waitress came, took away our dishes, and poured more coffee in Mr. W_____'s cup. I sipped water from a glass that had been brought with the meal while he very slowly drank his coffee, into which he had poured a little cream that he stirred around with an extra spoon the waitress had brought for him. After a while the waitress returned and asked if we cared for anything more. Then she placed on the table two little pieces of paper, which Mr. W_____ picked up and looked at for a moment. He moved his chair back from the table, reached into his pocket, drew out some change, and placed a dime by his plate. I wondered why he was doing *that*.

We got up from the table then, and Mr. W_____ placed his chair against the table. I did the same. He stopped by the cash register and laid the little pieces of paper before Mr. Garred, who looked at them and said "Seventy cents." Mr. W_____ counted out the money. Mr. Garred said, "I hope you enjoyed your lunch," as he put the money in the cash register, which rang like little bells when he opened the drawer.

As we walked back toward the hotel, Mr. W_____ looked at his watch and said we had more than an hour before the moving picture show would open. We sat for a few minutes on the bench by the street. Mr. W_____ asked about my family, what my father did for a living, how many brothers and sisters I had. He thought it admirable that my parents were willing to send me to town to go to high school. Then he said he liked to lie down and stretch out on his back for a few minutes after the noonday meal. We would go up to his room where he could rest. I could lie down, too, if I cared to.

I explained that I never lay down in the daytime unless I was sick, but that I would sit quietly while he took a little nap. If he should drop off to sleep, I could read something, he explained, for he always carried with him a good magazine or two.

When we were in his room, he removed his coat and hung it on a peg in a strip of wood fastened to the wall, loosened his tie and unbuttoned his shirt, and lay on his back on the bed, his head propped up on the two pillows. I sat in the chair between his bed and the window. After a minute or two he requested that I bring the chair to the other side of the bed so he would not be looking into the light coming through the window when he talked to me. After my chair was in position, he looked at me a long time, it seemed to me, this time his eyes fully in contact with mine. "You are a pretty boy," he said. "I bet the girls fall over one another for your attention. Do you have a little sweetheart?"

I explained that I had no sweetheart, that girls were friendly with me, especially girls in the seventh and eighth grades, and that the big girls in my own class teased me, but that none of them would want to go out with a little fellow like me. I was the youngest and least boy in my class.

Then he asked whether I had ever "been with a girl." When I began explaining that I was with girls all the time, he interrupted to say that he meant had I ever known a girl sexually. I had not. Had one ever offered herself to me? No. Then he moralized. I was fortunate, he said. Many young fellows lose their sense of direction because they know women sexually too soon in their lives. Men sell themselves down the river for just a few seconds of sexual joy occasionally with a woman. A man runs the risk of either getting her into trouble and then paying for her mistake or catching a disease from her that will cripple him, or make him go blind, or destroy his mind. He paused a long time to wait for the horror of such an eventuality to sink in.

I explained that I had wondered what a sex experience would be like. He did not answer my question but emphasized again the brevity of the period of joy. "That's all there is to it," he said. "It's not worth the importance that men place upon it." He looked at me a long time, the smile gone from his face and his eyes, though slitted, boring into mine so intensely that I looked away.

I asked him about his family. He had been married, he said, but he and his wife were divorced. There were children that she kept. He paid her a part of his salary every month. His life with her had not been happy. Sex experiences are all very much alike and reach climaxes that are always the same thing. A man pays a high price for such short moments of joy, and they get to be boring before long, besides.

He was quiet for a while, but I could feel his eyes stabbing at me as he lay there with them half-closed as if he were ready to drop off to sleep. But he never did go to sleep. I sat quietly, for he had not provided me with the magazine to which he had referred.

He opened his eyes after ten or fifteen minutes and said again, "You are a pretty boy. The girls will be after you before long, and offering themselves to you. Keep your pants buttoned and you will be all right." Then he half closed his eyes and was quiet.

I was then sorry for him. He was unhappy, a bitter and deeply disappointed man. He was not asleep, but his face was relaxed. He was a handsome man with hair that was partly curly and stood up, his nose was straight and thin, and his face was balanced. I could not then see his tiny eyes, but he had heavy sunbleached eyebrows that clung to the very edges of his brows. I had noticed that they moved about considerably, as if they were fastened on with loose hinges, when he squinted his eyes. One of his arms lay beside him, his soft-looking hand curled up so that I could see his fingernails, which were long, neatly trimmed, and showed almost white half-moons where he kept the skin pushed back.

Suddenly he sat up and looked at the gold watch he drew from a vest pocket. He got up and adjusted his collar and tie before the mirror on the wall above the washstand with a blue pitcher in a blue bowl on it. "We will have time for a soft drink before we go to the picture show," he said. He put on his coat.

At the door he flung his arm around me, drew me in front of him, and hugged me to him. I resisted, but he was strong. The top of my head reached to his stomach. He tilted my face toward his and said, "You are a fine, pretty boy!" Then he released me.

We stopped at Dr. Skaggs's drugstore for drinks. I ordered a bottle of Orange Crush, but he did not want a drink, he said. We came outside and stood at the edge of the sidewalk next to the street, where I drank my drink. It was still too early for school children to be coming to the afternoon show. People passing were grownups, some of whom I knew. When they spoke to me I did not feel as proud to be seen with Mr. W_____ as I had been while sitting on the bench earlier in the day or at John Garred's Restaurant. I felt guilty and demeaned by having been hugged, like a sweetheart, by a full-grown man, but I did not understand why I felt that way.

Sometime after I had finished drinking my Orange Crush and deposited the bottle in a rack at the edge of the sidewalk, Mrs. Tillman, who bought both *Grit* and *Post* from me, took her seat in the ticket booth at the Garden Theatre. Mr. W_____ was among the first to purchase tickets. We were among the first four or five to enter the theatre. He invited me to find a seat I liked. He followed and sat beside me, his tall knees reaching almost to the top of the seat in front of him. Soon the theatre was almost filled up with yelling schoolchildren, mostly of grade school age. Then Edith Adams appeared at the piano resting on the floor and to the left of the stage. She played music popular at the time and some of the children sang the lyrics as they remembered them but not all sang the same lyrics at the same time. "I loved her in the springtime/I loved her in the fall/But last night on the back porch/I loved her best of all" was popular then. Some of the children had bought hot popcorn from Mr. Kirk, who lived in a wheelchair that he whirled deftly around his popcorn stand at the entrance. Mr. W_____ asked me whether I would like popcorn, but the bottle of pop had filled me up and I did not want any. He did not buy any for himself. When Mr. Cains, the owner and operator of Garden Theatre, located in the Cains Building right in the middle of Front Street and directly across from the entrance to the courthouse, had decided the crowd was in, he signaled to Ed Tillman, the projector operator, to begin the moving picture. I do not remember the picture.

Mr. W_____ sat beside me bolt upright. The children thrilled to the picture, some struggling to read the conversations flashed on the screen on bars below the panels and sometimes continued on spotted panels between pictures, but Mr. W_____ gave no indication that he was responding to the show at all. When the screen went blank between the changing of reels, conversations of the children mounted to a bedlam. When Mr. Tillman had problems threading the projector or repairing broken film, Mr. Cains would turn on the lights and Edith Adams would play the piano again. At those times Mr. W_____ would crane his neck and look around but he did not attempt conversation. He did not touch me or lay his arm along the back of my seat during the show.

After the show was over and we were on the street again, I asked Mr. W_____ what time it was. It was late enough in the afternoon for me to take leave following a brief conversation on the bench in front of the hotel, for I needed to pick up my books from George, the custodian of the high school building, before he closed it for the day. Mr. W_____ was glad I could be with him for a pleasant half day. I thanked him shyly for the lunch, the drinks, and the show, for I felt uneasy in thanking people. It seemed that I had difficulty finding appropriate things to say. He repeated his congratulations on my having built up circulation for the *Post* and promised to be back in a month to see me again. I was not completely happy with the prospect of another visit, but told him that I would see what I could do to get more customers for the paper.

Professor Godby, who had not yet left the building, saw me through the open door to his office getting my books from George's "office." He came out to ask me whether I had enjoyed my half-holiday. I gave an enthusiastic account of dinner at the restaurant, the soft drinks, the moving picture show, but did not feel that I should say that I found Mr. W_____ a peculiar man. Mr. Godby congratulated me on my success with the paper route.

At the supper table at Boggs's I gave also a glowing report of the treat Mr. W_____ had given me for my success with the paper route and that I had not come home for lunch because he wanted to buy me a lunch at a restaurant. The Boggs boys were especially impressed by the report. I did not refer to Mr. W_____ as an odd fellow, because I did not want to introduce a negative note into what had been a day of new experiences for me.

I continued to find new subscribers to the *Post* and, as the Floyd Collins affair dragged on, was able to sell more papers on the street.

Just before my birthday I decided it was time for me to look around for a new suit with long pants, new shirts, red socks, a red bow tie, and, if I had enough money, a new hat and shoes. I went to all of the stores and looked at what was available. There were no suits with long pants for boys of my size, but at "Jake-the-Jew's" store there was in my size a blue-gray flannel suit with a light pencil stripe that I liked. It had a box-back coat with flaps and hidden pockets like those the older high school boys were wearing. It was the only boy's suit without a belted coat that I found in my size. There was also a pair of long pants that would fit me, pearl gray corduroy with bell-bottoms. I tried them on with the coat and admired myself in front of the mirror. A woman who worked for Jake assisted me. She would cut the pants off to my length if I decided to buy them.

I found also two light blue shirts with soft collars attached. I had been wearing to school collar band shirts with starched collars held on with bright golden looking collar buttons with mother-of-pearl bottoms. These collars were high but not as high as the celluloid collars that most of the men teachers wore, collars that were so high that they looked like white pipes reaching to the ears of men with slender necks, like Mr. Roberts, whose collar seemed to stick as much as three or four inches above his coat collar. I was glad to be giving up the collar band shirts. Some of the bigger fellows, especially older ones from the country, continued to wear them, but they were still wearing short pants, too, though some of them were as tall as full-grown men, but only one or two of the men teachers wore shirts with soft collars. Mr. Vaughan, the new teacher, wore some striped shirts with soft collars, and Jan, the mathematics teacher and coach, wore white shirts with soft collars. Styles were changing, I guessed, especially for young men. Mr. Vaughan and Jan, both unmarried, were responding to changes in styles.

I bought the suit, corduroy pants, and shirts at Jake's, proud to present him with a check against my own account at the bank, but Jake did not have red socks and bow ties that suited me and his hats with striped bands did not fit me. I wanted to look for shoes last, for I might not have enough money to buy everything I wanted, and I could get by for a while if I had to.

I found a gray hat with a striped band at the Bargain Store, but Mr. Wells had no red bow ties and red socks. My suit, long pants, and shirts in one bag and my hat in another, I walked proudly to G.J. Carter's, where I found a bright red bow tie, already tied and fixed on an adjustable band, and two pairs of red socks of the same hue as the tie.

When I got to Boggs's I went into my room and dressed myself in my new finery, adjusting the bow tie like a garter until it would stay fixed directly above the button of my shirt collar. Then I put on the hat, turned the brim down at a rakish angle, studied my appearance in the mirror, and walked into the living room for all to see me. After receiving compliments, I went back to my room and changed from the short pants to the long corduroys and returned to model them for the Boggses. The older daughter, Pearl, perhaps two years older than I, teased me about becoming a "little man" in the long pants, but all thought I looked "nice" in my new finery, which I said I would wear first to Sunday school and church that weekend. I had not bought new shoes, though, and did not think I had enough money to do that yet.

My father came to town to see me for my birthday. He took a room at Wallace and Genoa Jordan's boarding house and then came by Boggs's for a brief visit and to get me to go to town with him. I did not tell him that I had bought new clothes. When he asked whether I needed anything, I told him that I needed a new pair of shoes. He looked critically at the shoes I was wearing, which were run down at the heels and turned over at the sides considerably, though they were polished and clean. The uppers were still good, he said, but they needed half-soling. We stopped at Workman's shoe shop for me to have new half-soles and heels put on them. Mr. Workman "threw in" a new pair of laces to replace the broken and knotted back together laces he had to cut away in order to fit the shoes on the last.

We walked on downtown. I could hear the leather of Papa's underarm pistol holster creaking as we strolled along, for he never left home unarmed. While passing Dr. Skaggs' drugstore, we met someone whom my father knew. We stopped and engaged in conversation. After a few minutes had passed, Papa reached into his pocket and produced a dime for me to go in and buy me some ice cream with. He did not eat ice cream or drink soda pop himself. When I returned he was standing alone at the edge of the sidewalk and facing the entrance to the drugstore. Loafers leaning against the walls and the telephone poles looked at us as I joined him and we moved on. I thought Papa felt uncomfortable and I was vaguely uncomfortable. Then, I looked at him in a kind of comparative way. He was dressed in his best, but his clothing was old-fashioned. He never bought cheap clothing for himself, and his suits were always tailor made and his hats Stetson's best, but his coat was long, his pants were pegged, his neatly brushed black hat had a wide brim and a band not much wider than a shoe string, his white shirt was buttoned at the collar, and he wore no tie. I thought the loafers were snickering at us. When I heard laughter, I glanced back at them and they were all looking at us. My father did not look back.

We stopped at the Bargain Store, where Papa wanted to look at shoes. He needed a new pair of Sunday shoes, he said. Mr. Wells was helpful. Papa tried on several pairs of shoes, checking carefully the workmanship of each and asking the price. But the styles did not suit him. Then Mr. Wells produced a pair that looked very much like the pair Papa was wearing, blunt, high-toed shoes with heels higher than were stylish that season. He tried them on. They were a perfect fit. He took them off, bent them in his hand, inspected the insoles, pressed the spur pieces firmly, felt the leather, checked to see that the tongues were stitched in strongly. He asked the price. They were cheaper than any of the other pairs he had tried on. He bought them, pleased that the best shoes in his size in the store were the cheapest.

Mr. Wells looked at me. "Don't you need a pair of new shoes, too, young man?" he asked. I looked at my newly repaired shoes and replied that they would do me for a while longer.

Papa then said that maybe I ought to have a new pair for Sunday. Mr. Wells asked me to remove my shoes. He measured my foot and brought several pairs in my size. I rejected some of them without trying them on, those with blunt, high toes and high heels. After I tried on each pair, my father would ask the price and then examine the shoes for the quality of the workmanship. I chose a pair of black shoes with low heels and slender toes, but not peaked. The price was $3.50, robbery, my father said, for a pair of young 'ens' shoes, but since it was my birthday and I liked them, he would buy them for me.

Mr. Wells asked whether I would like to wear the new shoes and carry my old ones in the box. I could be breaking the new pair in that way, he said. I looked at my father for a moment, but he was waiting with no expression of approval or disapproval on his face. I decided to wear the new shoes. Mr. Wells went over to a table on which socks and stockings were kept and brought back a pair of black ribbed stockings. He was "throwing them in," he said, for a young fellow ought to break in a new pair of shoes with new stockings. While I was changing stockings and shoes, Mr. Wells and Papa talked about the weather and the condition of the roads, Mr. Wells laughing a great deal at Papa's responses, which did not seem to be especially funny to me. The tones of their voices had changed, too, now that the trading was over. Mr. Wells had seemed uncomfortable while Papa was complaining about the high price of young 'ens' shoes. It occurred to me that he had thrown in the pair of black stockings to make Papa feel better. When I was ready to go, Mr. Wells dropped the box with my old shoes and stockings in it into a paper bag and handed it to me. As we left, he invited us to come back again. "We have a sale every day here," he said.

Instead of walking back past the drugstore to the Boggs home, we went up to the railroad track and followed unpaved Jefferson Street between Dr. H.S. Young's eyeglasses store and the passenger depot. I could hear the leather in my new shoes and Papa's underarm holster creaking rhythmically as we walked along in silence.

Papa stopped off at Jordan's Boarding House. He would come by Boggs's after supper for a short visit with Simps and Nola and we would then go back to the depot and watch the train pass through and maybe on downtown and stand around for a while.

After supper Papa came for a brief visit. He "settled up" with Simps and Nola for my board, room, and laundry for the rest of the year. He would leave soon after breakfast the following morning and would not try to see any of us that early in the day. Papa was at ease in Simps and Nola's home.

He laughed a great deal and teased Pearl, who had developed rapidly into womanhood and was wanting to date a handsome young man who rode a spirited horse in from Smoky Valley. Her parents, thinking that age 15 was too young for her to begin dating, discouraged her. My father's teasing included a reference to a possible interest of young men in her. To her mother's comment that Pearl was not old enough to be courting, Pearl responded that if she was not old enough she certainly was big enough. Everybody laughed heartily at her clever response, for Pearl did, indeed, appear to be much older than 15.

Papa and I walked to the depot by way of Davis Martin's livery stable, at which we stopped for me to see Old Bec, the mule he had ridden in from Caines Creek. I rubbed her nose by the light of a lantern and talked to her, but she did not indicate in any way that she knew me. As we left the stable, though, Bec nickered. Papa thought the nicker meant that she had recognized me and was saying goodbye to me.

April 5 had been a bright, warm day. That night was pleasant and calm. There was little evidence of spring, though. Between gaslights glowing steadily at street corners we could look up through the still bare branches of the elms at the stars. We could hear the far-off rumble of railroad cars clacking along the tracks, the puffing whisper of locomotives, and occasional long, lonesome wails of the whistles echoing in the valleys. Against the rumble of moving trains we could hear animated and happy conversations from gas-lighted homes with windows and doors open to let in the warm fresh air. Children were playing on porches and in yards.

A large crowd had gathered outside the depot to watch the down train come through, happy laughing people, many of them holding children by the hands as they stood about and exchanged pleasantries with neighbors. Papa and I found a place against the corner of the depot and watched. Nobody knew Papa and only two or three of the older high school boys from the county and living in boarding houses near the Boggs home spoke to me. We waited a long time for the train. While waiting Papa remembered that his great aunt, who had married Dr. Hamilton Swetnam, and moved to town with him, had lived in a house, no longer there, directly across the track from the depot. She had become addicted to drugs in old age, Papa said. Men used to stand on the platform at the station and watch her through her bedroom window lift her skirts and shoot drugs into her hip with a needle. He had never met the great aunt himself and had learned that her nephews and nieces from the country did not visit in her home when they came to town. She had become too fine and proud and they did not feel welcome in her house, Papa thought.

When the train arrived, boys representing restaurants and sandwich shops in town raced up and down under the open windows of the coaches and hawked their wares. Many people, bags in their hands, and helped down the steps by the important looking conductor, rushed into the arms of people who had come to meet them. Others, after saying hurried goodbyes to those who had come to the depot with them, crowded one another at the steps when the conductor yelled "All Aboard!"

As the train pulled out people left the station in all directions. Soon no one but Papa and me were left. We looked inside the waiting room, where we saw a plain-looking and shabbily dressed young woman sitting on a bench. Two sun-tanned younger men wearing black hats, shirts buttoned at the collar but with no ties, dark red coat sweaters, blue serge pants with narrow legs, and high-toed shoes were trying to engage the attention of the woman, whose eyes brightened in the glow of the gaslight as she giggled and studied them up and down speculatively. A third man, somewhat older, and wearing new overalls with the legs rolled up above his shoes, stood in front of the young woman. He watched, his shoulders hunched, as he made a cigarette adeptly, closing the little tobacco bag by inserting the tag on the yellow drawstring between his teeth and giving it a quick jerk with his left hand. He rolled the cigarette with his right hand, licked the side of it, twisted one end of it, and stuck it in his mouth. He straightened up and returned the bag to the pocket on the bib of his overalls, fastidiously displaying the tag with a picture of a bull on it that dangled from his pocket. He then reached into his side pocket, drew out a long wooden match, lifted up his leg, and ripped the match along his thigh until it burst into flame. Although there was no breeze blowing, he cupped the match with both hands as he held it to his cigarette, looking straight at the woman meanwhile. When he caught her glance, he tossed his hand toward the door. She got up and they went out together.

Papa and I walked on down to Front Street. Along the way we saw young people turn the corner toward us, walk as far as Jeems' livery stable, stop for an awkward moment, and then walk back the way they had come. Front Street itself was lively. Young people by twos and threes walked past the brightly lighted drugstore, the Garden Theatre, Ferguson's men's store, Atkins and Vaughan's, Page's barber shop, and under the clock above the entrance to the bank. They would disappear around the corner for a few minutes and then return. Young men leaned against the walls; older men clustered between the sidewalk and the street; old-timers of the town, their wives with them, sat on the benches outside the Brunswick Hotel. We could hear peals of laughter from country people gathered about the entrance to the courthouse. Children, many of them ragamuffins from the back alleys of the town and along the river bank, chased one another over the courthouse grounds, some stopping occasionally to drink water from the noisy pump. Everybody was responding to the feeling of spring, the warm calm of an early April evening, a lovely time for a birthday.

Papa and I stopped in front of the drugstore. We stood for a few minutes between the sidewalk and the street, our backs toward the courthouse. People walked past us as if they were in a hurry to get to their destination, but in a few minutes they walked past just as fast in the other direction. Young fellows leaned silently against the wall and turned their heads in unison as they watched attractive girls disappear in the crowd. Near us and smoking his pipe slowly stood a big man with his back toward the crowd. I noted that he was looking at us, but he did not speak. Papa reached in his pocket, drew out another dime, and handed it to me as he told me I could go in and buy myself a cone of ice cream. When I returned, he and the big man were talking. The big man was talking as if he was annoyed. He was obviously laughing at my father, who was relieved that I had returned.

Papa said in closing the conversation, "Well, I just thought you were somebody I had seen at the Union Camps."

The man, his voice different, said, "Is that your boy?"

Papa explained that I was his oldest child and was in high school.

"What class are you in?" he asked.

I told him I was a freshman.

"My daughter, Evelyn Burney, is a sophomore."

"I know Evelyn." I said.

"Well, son, let's go," Papa said.

Evelyn Burney, the pretty girl with blonde hair who wore a dark blue skirt with cream colored gores, had been especially nice to me. I had thought she might like to go to a movie with me some Friday night but had feared because she was older and a sophomore that she would decline my invitation.

As we walked on toward the bank at the corner, Papa said, "If that son-of-a-bitch fools with me, I'll put a streak of daylight through him." Papa had asked the man his name, where he lived, and what kind of work he did. Mr. Burney, who had come to Louisa from a central Kentucky town, did not understand yet the ways of mountain folk.

We walked on past the Savoy Hotel, crossed the paved street, and went down the unpaved road in front of Compton's shop. We turned west in front of the house in which Mae Farley, one of my classmates lived. "That is the house that Uncle Dave Boggs lived in while he was County Judge," Papa said. I could barely remember Uncle Dave, who had died in office while I was in first grade. Our school was dismissed for his funeral, but I did not attend it. Uncle Dave was my grandmother's brother. Someone had pointed out to me his picture hanging on the wall of the courtroom.

Papa and I turned west at the Farley home and wandered over by the big flour mill where I had played among the bins, barrels, and stacks of bags of flour and meal with the Boggs boys and Kay and Jay Moore, twin sons of the operator of the mill. From the mill we walked back along unpaved Jefferson Street toward the passenger depot. The road was dark. A light breeze was blowing, but the stars were bright. We trudged along in silence, my new shoes creaking rhythmically along with Papa's underarm holster like a new saddle, as I looked at the stars and picked out some of the constellations that I had learned about in general science. Space was limitless, some of the stars I was seeing were millions of miles away, the world was small but wonderful, and I was fourteen years old that day and ready, I thought, to become a young man soon. I thought of my new clothes.

Except for the office in which Mr. Wellman, a green shade above his eyes, worked at the telegraph, the passenger depot was dark. We saw through the windows three or four people sitting on benches in the waiting room, their cigarettes glowing in the dark. As we turned the corner at the depot we met the town policeman hurrying along. He spoke as if he knew us but did not address us by name.

On the way back to the boarding house we met no one. Lights were on in only a few houses. We heard only the far-off rumble of railroad trains and the echoes of our hard leather heels striking the sidewalk. At the gate at Jordan's Boarding House Papa pulled out his pocketbook, removed a dollar bill, and handed it to me. "You might need this to buy paper and pencils," he said. "Be a good boy. Write to us along. Let me know when I am to come for you at the close of school." He turned into the boarding house.

The Boggses had gone to bed. I usually took my weekly bath on Saturday night from a big washpan used for that purpose. The Boggs home had an indoor toilet and a wash basin but no bathtub. Water was heated in a teakettle on the gas stove, poured into the washpan, and carried into the toilet room, where it was tempered with tap water. Thinking I might disturb the family if I prepared for a bath, I decided to take it in the bedroom after breakfast next morning.

The house pulsated with the rhythms of sleep. By the gas light always left burning in the dining room I undressed and slipped into bed with Lowell, the youngest of the sons. I lay awake a long time thinking about my birthday and my father, who had ridden his mule 25 miles to help me celebrate it and would ride back home the following day. I knew that the new shoes, the dimes he had given me to buy ice cream, the dollar bill he had handed to me at the gate, and the money he had paid to settle up for my board, room, and laundry for the remainder of the year represented a real sacrifice for him. I wondered whether I should have told him that, by selling *Grit* and delivering the *Cincinnati Post*, I was earning six dollars a week and had bought what he would have called "a new rig of finery."

Next morning I put on my old clothes for breakfast. Then I prepared water for my bath, which I took in the bedroom, applied rose pomade to my hair and combed it slicked down and parted in the middle, and dressed myself completely in new clothes, choosing for Sunday school and church the short pants rather than the corduroy trousers. With my red bow tie riding my Adam's apple, my box coat with flap pockets, and my new hat cocked at a jaunty angle I felt that I was as well dressed as it was possible for me to be as I surveyed myself in the dresser mirror. The Boggs boys and I trotted off to Sunday school, arriving early and in time to stand around outside the church with other boys before Sunday school began. I was aware of attention to my new clothes, but no one mentioned them to me.

After the general meeting in the church, we went off to our Sunday school rooms, the boys of my age to Mr. Lafe Wellman's class. Mr. Wellman, who loved to sing and who was a supporter of baseball, gave special recognition to boys who could bring others to Sunday school with them. It was said that his was the largest boys' Sunday school class in town. Even the ragged boys who lived in the alleys and along the river bank and who played hooky from school during the week came to his Sunday school class, many of them boys whose parents did not go to church at all. Mr. Wellman, who owned a hardware store across the street from the courthouse and near the old boat dock, knew the poor boys from the river bank and encouraged them to play baseball and come out to his Sunday school class. Sometimes he would hire some of them to do odd jobs for him around the store. Mr. Wellman, who had a long, thin face and did not laugh very much and who was brusque in his conversation, was a hero for the boys because he understood them and knew how to make them feel proud of their achievements.

The Boggs boys did not stay for church after Sunday school. I sat proudly among some of my high school classmates at church and enjoyed participating in the congregational singing.

After Sunday dinner at the Boggses, I walked down to Thomas Luther's photography shop at the end of a short street that stopped near the J.T. Justice Lumber Company to have my picture made. Mr. Luther was one of my *Post* subscribers and bought *Grit*, too. We had already become good friends. He had explained to me the processes of photography, shown me many of the pictures he had taken at reunions, celebrations, political speakings, and special occasions like the arrival of a boat at the dock, and had recited humorous poems and stories for me. I believe he did not normally do business on Sunday, though, but he invited me in and took plenty of time and special care in making my picture, a formal pose on a special bench with a romantic background painted on a screen. After the sitting, Mr. Luther talked with me for a long time in his reception room, a well-lighted place with bright April sunshine flooding it. Mr. Luther's wife, whom I never saw, was an invalid for whom he had arranged peep holes through which she could see him in conversation with people in his reception room, shuffling about in soft house shoes as he worked. She knew who I was, he said, and liked for me to come into the shop to leave *Grit* and to talk with him. When I went for my pictures a few days later, I was pleased to see that Mr. Luther had mounted one of them in his exhibit of recent photographs he had taken. I thought he must have been proud of his success in taking a picture of me.

I walked from the photography shop down Lock Avenue to the home of John and Dova Boggs, both distant relatives, where my uncle Estill, who had come into town to enter high school at the beginning of the second semester, was staying. Estill was there. His roommate, George Burchette, had gone home for the weekend, but another high school student, Violet Rice, who was also rooming at the Boggs home, was there, too. I visited with Estill in his room for a while. He admired my new clothes. I told him about the long pants I had bought and planned to wear

Cratis Williams in clothes he received for his fourteenth birthday, April 1925.

to school. He asked whether I had shaved yet. I had not. He looked closely at my upper lip and observed that some of the fuzz was beginning to look dark. It would not be long, he said, before I would need to shave. He opened a dresser drawer, produced an Eveready safety razor with a blade in it, and handed it to me. It had been a prize in a Cracker Jacks box. He had a razor and did not need the Eveready. The single-edge blade would last a long time, he said, and if it became dull, I could sharpen it by honing it on a newspaper. After it wore out I could buy another blade at the 10-cent store. I slipped the razor into my coat pocket, for I did not yet want anyone to think that I might need to begin shaving soon. I used the razor from a Cracker Jacks box for ten years before deciding that double-edged blades might be more economical, but I did not begin using it until I was fifteen, and then only to shave my upper lip about once a month.

Estill and I came down to the living room and visited with the Boggses and Violet Rice for a while. Violet suggested that we walk down to the lock and dam to enjoy the April sunshine and see the river.

The picture of me that Mr. Luther took that day was a reminder through

Cratis Williams in clothes he received for his fourteenth birthday, April 1925.

the years of my turning fourteen, my new clothes, my father's fifty-mile muleback ride to be with me on my birthday, my first razor, and the fullness of expectation at the threshold of adolescence.

The new clothes boosted my ego considerably during the following weeks, for I felt of age all dressed up in the box coat, the long pants, red bow tie and red socks, and the jaunty hat with a striped band. Girls, I thought, took a new interest in me. As spring moved down the valley everybody began to shed winter clothes and dress for the new season. The quality of social life changed. Groups began to plan parties and outings.

Mae Farley, who lived in the house in which my father had said my Uncle David Boggs had lived while he was judge, invited me to her birthday party. Mae, perhaps 16 at the time, had included me among her guests, even though I was a year or two younger than most of them. It was the first time I had been sent a written invitation to a birthday party. I was not sure of just how I should respond, but we had studied invitations in Miss Roberts' English class. In the text I found model invitations and model responses. I bought a box of note paper, responded in my finest handwriting, and sent an acceptance through the mail, glad that I had the money needed for the purchase of the paper and for the postage. When I shared my joy with the Boggses, Pearl pointed out that I would be expected to bring a birthday present. I was puzzled by what might be appropriate and the amount of money I should spend on the present, but Pearl suggested that a box of candy wrapped in pretty paper, tied with a ribbon, and bearing a birthday card would be appropriate. Girls liked candy, she said, and candy was always appreciated.

I bought for fifty cents a pound of chocolate covered cherries in a pretty box with a picture of a bunch of red cherries on it. I found a birthday card that was small enough to go with the box. Pearl helped me wrap the box and tie a narrow red ribbon around it, sharing with me, I thought, the excitement of the occasion. I signed the birthday card with my full name and addressed it to Miss Mae Farley. My gift, ready in all of its formal trappings, was stored in the dresser drawer to await the night of the party.

Dressed in my finest and with my hair parted in the middle and smoothed down with rose pomade, I arrived at the Farley home at the same time as Leon Wetzel, an eighth grade boy perhaps a year older than I. Except for two or three girls who lived close by, Leon and I were the first guests to arrive, a bit early, we discovered. He, too, had a present. We knocked at the door. Mrs. Farley appeared. We did not introduce ourselves, but she led us into the living room, each clinging to his present with one hand and holding his hat in the other. Mae had not yet appeared but one of her friends, Minnie Miller, was there. Minnie introduced us to Mrs. Farley, who relieved us of our hats and invited us to place our gifts on a little table on which an elegant but unlighted lamp stood. The room was lighted by a double gas lamp at the end of a lead pipe that came down from the ceiling. Chairs were arranged in a row along the walls, leaving space in the middle of the room to play games. Leon and I were invited to sit down. We sat side by side in dining room chairs near the door, each stiff and upright and holding rigidly to the seat of his chair as if he feared that he might fall off any moment if he did not hold on for dear life.

Soon others arrived, all of them boys and girls I knew and many of them from my class at school. All were dressed in their finest, the boys wearing ties and with their shoes shined to a gloss. But most of us were stiff and quiet while we waited. When the chairs were almost all occupied, Mae came through the door, her hair curled and wearing a new rust-colored dress with a long waist and a short skirt, a dress like big girls were wearing that year. She was radiant and excited. Behind her was her sister, Helen, who might have been four or five years older than Mae.

Helen supervised party games, one of the more active of which was "spin the plate." Included were games like "heavy, heavy hangs over your head," "thimble," and "going out west." As the games progressed, we became more relaxed, laughed more, and teased one another.

Once through a door that was opened briefly I saw Mr. Farley, his hair combed neatly and wearing a white shirt under his overalls, in the act of sitting down in a rocking chair near a fireplace. After the party was under way, Mrs. Farley went to sit with her husband.

About 9:30 Helen, Minnie Miller, and another girl, Mae's visiting cousin, I believe, left the room and returned with a small table on which rested a birthday cake decorated with tiny lighted candles, a tray bearing teacups, small plates, forks, and napkins, and a steaming pitcher of hot chocolate. There was considerable excitement among the guests, and Mae radiated happiness. Never having seen the likes myself, I tried to be sufficiently calm and at ease to hide my ignorance of such arrangements. Everything in order and with Mae standing behind the lighted cake, her eyes dazzling with the dancing lights of the tiny candles, Helen invited us to sing "Happy Birthday," a song I had never heard before and which I did not know. I was somewhat comforted by the feeling that others present did not know the song either as we stumbled through it. Helen, no doubt sensing that many of us were attending a birthday party for the first time, invited us to sing it again, louder this time. We repeated the song with so much gusto and assurance and Helen beamed her appreciation so joyfully that we applauded ourselves.

Mae took a deep breath, leaned to bring her pursed mouth even with the lighted candles, and blew hard, extinguishing all of the candles but three. With a grimace of disappointment fixed on her face, she watched the lights on the three candles straighten up again while the narrow columns of smoke from the extinguished candles stood at attention. The guests were quiet for a moment.

Then some of the girls began to chant, "Three more years! Three more years!" I did not understand the meaning of the ritual. Helen said, "Mae will not get married for three more years." Mae then inhaled, extinguished the three remaining candles, and cut the cake.

We filed by for a piece of the cake and a cup of chocolate, which we held on our knees. One of the young men knocked against the elbow of the young woman sitting next to him and caused her to spill her chocolate on her party dress. He was more embarrassed than the young woman as Helen attempted to clean away the chocolate with a napkin, explaining for the relief of the young man that accidents will happen.

After cake and chocolate, Mae took a seat beside the table on which the birthday presents were stacked. Helen brought a pair of scissors and Mae opened her presents, reading the card attached to each, exhibiting the gift, and thanking the donor as she smiled brightly at each. Most of the boys had brought candy, so my gift was not distinguished for the imagination and creativity of its donor. Girls gave compacts, lipsticks, powder, handkerchiefs, boxes of stationery. Mae then thanked us all for coming to her party.

Mrs. Farley appeared and took a position near the door. She told us where we might find our hats and wraps. We filed by Mae, now standing beside her gifts and with the wrappings in a loose pile on the floor beside her, and wished her many more happy birthdays. We shook Mrs. Farley's hand and told her we had had a nice time, some of us shy and bumbling as we did so.

Following the party I felt a new dimension of friendship with Mae and Minnie Miller and with the other young people who had been there. Sometimes I would pause for a brief conversation with Mrs. Farley or Helen when

I found them sitting on the porch of their home as I was making my rounds to collect for the Cincinnati *Post* each week. I was glad to have learned about parties and how one conducts himself at them.

Other occasions that brought boys and girls together as spring advanced included a Sunday afternoon walk during apple blossom time along the railroad track to Wallbridge perhaps three miles up the river above Louisa and two walks on the tracks to Fullers Station four or five miles down the river. Those going on these excursions, arranged by Pearl and friends of her age, were the young people who lived near the Boggses or stayed in boarding houses close by. The trips down the tracks to Fullers were especially exciting to us. We started about three o'clock and amused ourselves by stepping from tie to tie as long as we could stand to take the short steps, stepping to every other tie as long as we could stand to take the long steps, and then walking with our feet at angles on the rails themselves in contests to see who could walk the farthest without slipping off the rails. We arrived at Fullers in time to have peanuts, cookies, and soft drinks at a store near the railroad station before the up train arrived. Having bought our tickets at the little station, we rode the train back to Louisa and dismounted like veteran travelers into the crowds that gathered to see the train "go through," each having spent about 25 cents for his excursion.

I was continuing to build the circulation of the *Cincinnati Post*. By the beginning of May I had won the pocket watch and fob I had coveted and was displaying the fob proudly from the watch pocket of my pants. Near the end of class periods, I liked to consult my watch and enjoyed having students around me crane their necks to see what time it was, for not many students owned watches.

While we were still having frost on the ground occasionally, Mr. Gilmer announced that we would be dissecting birds in our general science laboratory the following week. Since the science department did not have specimens in stock, each of us would be responsible for furnishing his own bird. This assignment, he said, would provide us with an opportunity to try our skills with nets, snares, bird boxes, sling shots, or rifles. The assignment gave many of the students, especially the girls, much concern. I had no rifle and was not a good marksman, and I had no slingshot. As to nets, snares, and boxes, I had none and did not know how I might come into the possession of one.

That afternoon my uncle Estill, Bill Ball and one or two of his friends came by my room to invite me to hunt birds with them. They had rifles. I could either borrow a rifle and kill a bird myself, or one of them would kill an extra one for me.

We walked up the road across Town Hill to find birds. We saw many birds, but they were either in the air or perched on trees and posts too far away for us to shoot them. Although several shots were fired, even at birds in the air, no one killed one. The boys decided to seek the permission of some farmer to hunt birds in his barn at night. Armed with flashlights, poles, and nets, they thought it possible to capture some birds. But I was not able for some reason to go with them.

When Monday morning came, I did not have my bird. I liked to be prepared, so I was unhappy. The ground and the roofs of houses were covered with a heavy frost but the weather was changing. A dark bank of clouds hid the sunrise. Smoke from chimneys was rising straight up and feeding into a pall of smoke hanging low over the town. The papers had arrived late that morning, and I was having to hustle to get them delivered before the big bell at the "college" rang ten minutes before classes began. To add to my anxiety, a long freight train tore through town just as I was ready to cross the track to deliver papers to two or three families on the other side. I had to wait five minutes or so for the train to pass, the thick billow of steam and smoke from the locomotive spreading out in a low layer along the track.

After the red caboose passed, I hopped over the rail in a hurry, and there between the tracks and frightened by my sudden appearance was a fluttering sparrow that could not fly. It had been scalded by the steam from the locomotive, been swept under the cars between rushing wheels, and fallen upon the ties, where it had lain quietly until the train had passed over it. It was not difficult to capture for its eyes had apparently been damaged, too. I wrapped it in my handkerchief and put it in my coat pocket, feeling that I had been the recipient of a special dispensation. Only four of us had birds for dissection that morning, three boys who walked in from farms out toward Busseyville and myself. Only I had a live bird, but mine was expiring fast and had died by the time Mr. Gilmer had completed regrouping us so that six students were assigned to each bird. I did not tell Mr. Gilmer or the class how I had come by my bird; but my own group, which found my account incredible, thought the bird had been delivered to me miraculously.

High School: Second Year

In 1925–1926 I lived in the home of Ambrose L. and Fannie Skaggs, the parents of Roy and Darcy Skaggs, both of whom were high school students. Mrs. Skaggs was herself a high school senior that year. At mid-year, Mrs. Skaggs's brother, Ernest, who had just finished teaching a one-room country school at Terryville, came to live with us and finish his high school program. Fred Adams came in from Irish Creek to begin high school the second semester. In order to ease her load of increased domestic responsibilities, Mrs. Skaggs brought from Upper Blaine an attractive, neatly dressed young woman, Goldie Stinson, to clean, do the laundry, and cook.

My teachers were Mr. Janovisky for second-year algebra first semester and arithmetic second, Mr. Gilmer for biology, Mr. Rollins, a recent graduate of Asbury College at Wilmore, Kentucky, for English, and Helen Hughes, a local girl who had graduated only recently from the University of Kentucky, for history. Mr. Godby, who became the superintendent of Boyd County schools, had been replaced as superintendent of the Louisa public schools and principal of the high school by a local boy, a graduate of Georgetown College, William H. Vaughan. High school enrollment had increased, too, as more students from the county had come to live in boarding houses and the homes of relatives in town and go to high school.

The new Louisa High School, to graduate at the end of 1926-1927 its first freshman class, had already grown to the capacity of the old Kentucky Normal College building. It had been necessary to build for the seventh and eighth grades a two-room frame structure behind the old building in order to provide space for a science laboratory and an additional science classroom. The old science classroom, originally the kitchen of the Byington family, who had lived in the building while Mr. Byington was the president of the college, had been converted into a storeroom for laboratory equipment and supplies. At the southern end of the white frame "junior high" building were indoor toilets with outside entrances to replace the privies and the old Byington barn beside a ravine that cut deeply into the high bank of the Big Sandy River. At the privies and barn we had used old newspapers, magazines, and catalogs stacked over the years in the loft of the barn by the Byington family, but the new facilities were supplied with rolls of toilet paper. However, we continued to drink from paper cups we made ourselves of folded notebook paper, the water drawn by an old fashioned hand-operated pump from a deep well outside the main building. As I recall, fountains inside the building had not been installed when I was graduated in 1928.

When I first went to the school the "library" was a locked cabinet with glass doors that stood against the wall in the hall and near the principal's office, although a tattered dictionary on a stand was available to students in the study hall. I believe it was at the beginning of 1925-1926 that the library was moved to a "cage" at the end of the study hall and that a few open shelves of books that one might pick up and look at were provided. However, there was no librarian. The study hall keeper made a record of books borrowed and scratched the record when they were returned. The collection of books grew, largely, I believe, from donations of townspeople, while I was attending high school, but the library remained in the cage at the end of the study hall and there was no librarian.

Miss Lyon, the music teacher who had come up from central Kentucky, had been replaced by Betsy Burgess, a local girl and daughter of a medical doctor who was also a member of the board of education. Miss Burgess, who might by this time have already become Mrs. Elswick, wife of a promising young attorney, also directed plays. Mrs. Alverson, a teacher of business subjects and who had come from outside the region, had gone. Her department had been closed and the rooms it had occupied were converted to the use of the growing music department. Mrs. Rollins, wife of the new English teacher, was a part-time teacher who gave individual instruction in elocution.

I became 15 that year. Conditions for study in the Skaggs home, a ten-room new house, were better than they had been in the crowded much smaller home in which I had lived the previous year and a half. Except for Mr. Skaggs, a carpenter and farmer who commuted to the farm the family owned at Busseyville about six miles from town, and for Goldie, whose efficiency, engaging smile, and happy disposition helped to make our living more pleasant and orderly, we were all students. Mrs. Skaggs subscribed to several good magazines and had a daily paper delivered at the house. She also had a shelf of books for reference and leisurely reading. Much of our conversation at meal time (all of us came home for lunch, too) was about subjects related to our school work or things we had read in the magazines or the daily paper. Friends who came to visit us were usually students, but we enjoyed also visits from kinfolk and former neighbors of the family who had moved to town or who came occasionally from the Upper Blaine communities to Louisa to see relatives and neighbors who had moved there.

On Saturdays during a splendid autumn I went along with Roy and Darcy and their father to the farm at Busseyville and helped to gather bushels of apples, dig potatoes, pick beans, and cut cabbage. The farmhouse, nestled comfortably against the southern slope of a gently rolling hill and guarded by two magnificent white oak trees near either corner of the front yard, was not occupied at the time. Much of our harvest was spread on the floor in the house to wait there until it was needed at the home in Louisa. On our trips to the farm we also gathered bags of satiny chestnuts from the ground under giant trees that grew along the line fence up the face of the long hill, and we picked up pocketfuls of tawny hickory nuts nearly as big as walnuts and plucked hazelnuts from clumps of bushes growing along the sides of springs and streams in the pasture fields sprinkled with pungent horsemint and blooming with the lazy bee blossom that fitfully completes its life between the light frosts of October. Back home in Louisa Mr. Skaggs played "hull gull" with us as we conned one another's stores of chestnuts, hazelnuts, and hickory nuts.

A widowed great aunt of the Skaggs boys, Aunt Mary Hamilton, had moved to town. Having no children of her own, she was lavishing her generous love on an intelligent tan and white dog named Ted and a fat and bright-eyed black and white cat that slept between Ted's forelegs or snuggled closely against his warm flanks. We enjoyed visiting Aunt Mary, who encouraged us to play games in her house and yard as we romped with Ted. She baked

"Louisa High School building (1902–1950), distinguished by its bell tower, was the home for about twenty years of the Kentucky Normal College, which closed its doors in 1922 and sold its plant to the Louisa Public Schools. I attended high school in this building, 1924–1928. While I was a student there, the school had a maximum enrollment (9–12) of 225 and a teaching staff of 11. Ten years after graduation from the school I returned as principal. By then, this building was being used for junior high school classes (grades 7–9). Senior high school students used a newer building, occupied first about 1933 and still standing, next door to this one. My office (1938–1941) was in the newer building"— Cratis Williams exceptionally good sugar cookies, gingersnaps, stack cakes, and fruit pies, which she served with spiced apple juice before we were to go home. Two boys living close by and sons of families related to both Aunt Mary and the Skaggs boys, Sherrill Phillips and Elmer Lyon, sometimes came to play with us. Later in the year we were privileged to attend Aunt Mary's wedding when she married a gentle, kind old man, Uncle Nelson Sparks, a widower who came from his farm in Upper Blaine to live with her in her comfortable little house on a grassy knoll overlooking the street and to share with Ted and the cat her love and kind ministrations. When we called on the old couple on Sunday afternoon following the wedding, Aunt Mary had cut out donkeys and tails for us to use in a game of blind man's bluff called "pinning the tail on the donkey." Not very communicative, Uncle Nelson sat and watched with animated light blue eyes as we pinned the tail on the donkey in the wrong places.

Although I never owned a bicycle myself, I learned to ride Darcy's small bicycle that year. All the boys in the neighborhood who were outgrowing coaster wagons were buying bicycles which they learned to ride in the lot of the cavalry barn near the Skaggs home. It was while I was learning to ride the bicycle that I scratched an insect bite on my temple. Streams of perspiration, laden with dust wheeled up from the horse lot, had washed over the bite, and it became infected. It developed into an ugly boil that plagued me for the next four years. Having learned to ride the bicycle, I went along with "bicycle gangs" from time to time as they pedaled along the few newly paved streets that led to the courthouse square and the business section of town. The new highway then being built up the Big Sandy Valley had not yet been paved, so our gang riding was confined to the town streets not yet crowded with automobiles.

The winter of 1925-1926 was cold. The town reservoir, which had been improvised by lining Fort Bishop, the Civil War fort on top of the hill overlooking the town, with concrete walls, froze over that winter. We did not own ice skates, but we went in parties to skate on the flinty ice in the reservoir, frozen so deeply that the town's supply of raw river water, often muddy after freshets and floods upstream, was cut off for several days.

Most of the houses in the town had only faucets by the kitchen sink for "town" water. Those who drank it boiled it and filtered it, but the sewer system was not adequate for disposing of the sewage of the town. The Skaggs home did not have a bathroom. We heated pots of water and bathed from washpans in our rooms. The two-hole privy was located over a pit at the back side of the lot. We drew our drinking water in buckets from a well on the back porch of a boarding house half a block away.

One night I became dimly aware of much activity elsewhere in the house as abdominal pains woke me up. The pains, passing like waves, mounted in intensity, and, before I was fully prepared to admit that a trip out back through the darkness was a necessity, I found that unless I hurried I might not be able to make it to the privy in time to head off an accident. Pulling on my pants and slipping my feet into my shoes without taking precious time to tie the laces, I rushed headlong down the stairs and in a half-bent posture on toward the back door, half-embarrassed to see all the members of the household up and scattered along the way through the dining room, kitchen, and laundry room, all with the gas lamps on, highlighting my hegira through the ranks of smiling but nonetheless puzzled faces. As I fumbled hurriedly with the lock on the back door, Ernest called out that it was a good thing for me that I had appeared. Perplexed by the remark but without time or inclination to determine its significance, I dashed toward the privy, my shoe laces whipping at my legs and my shoes playing loosely on my feet. Halfway there I flung one of my shoes, which I decided not to bother to find just at that time. The rowling pain was so severe and the need for relief so intense that I thought I had waited perhaps two seconds too long as I released my pants and thumped myself down on the bench. An explosion was followed by a mad rush outward of everything in me, like the crashing of wild waters down a valley after a dam has been dynamited. But the relief did not meet my Gulliver-like need for satisfaction. The pain continued. Other floods, driven by the growling anger of my bowels, followed in rapid succession. After what seemed eight or ten minutes, I realized that, even though the pain continued, I was thoroughly, completely, and absolutely purged but that had my tonsils given away my entire intestinal tract would have turned itself inside out and fluttered behind me in comfort on the night breeze like the tail of a comet.

Not much improved in posture, I took time to find my shoe in the dead grass beside the path but decided not to bother to put it on. Entering the house in a low stoop, my shoe dangling at the end of the laces, I found the other members of the household in conference around the dining room table. It was then that I learned that since I was sleeping through the hour of animated wakefulness shared by the others, a conclusion had been reached that I had obviously put croton oil in the drinking water to play a prank on them. They were prepared, at the moment of my dramatic appearance, to pull me out of bed and spank my bare tail with magazines as Ernest dragged me by the scruff of the neck up and down the line. My affliction, painful as it had been, was also at one and the same time my salvation.

We reviewed carefully our dinner, each making a judgment on what he had or had not eaten and drunk. At length we decided that the drinking water, of which I had taken only a small amount, must indeed have been the cause of our agony. Ernest then decided to take a walk through the neighborhood to see whether lights were on in homes of people who obtained their drinking water from Mrs. Jordan's well. We waited. He returned soon with the report that lights were on in some of the bedrooms of the boarding house and in two or three other homes. Next day we learned that people in other houses had suffered from the same complaint, but nobody ever knew who had poured the croton oil in Mrs. Jordan's well. Before God, I was not the one who did it!

An epidemic of measles struck the students that year. I was out of school and in bed most of the time for nearly three weeks with the debilitating disease. I recall that my skin had begun to peel and my hair to fall out by my fifteenth birthday, which I spent in bed, and that my eyes were still so weak that the window blinds had to be closed. Mrs. Skaggs and Goldie prepared hot teas and lemonade for me to drink to "break out the measles," a prescription that I much preferred to the sheep dung tea that was still being used in the community in which I grew up. In spite of her own school work and her obligations at home, Mrs. Skaggs took time to care for my needs and Goldie checked on me periodically to see that I was as comfortable as it was possible for me to be. After the high fever that provoked terrifying dreams and delirium had subsided, Mrs. Skaggs would lead me to a cot in the upstairs sitting room where I lay with a folded towel over my eyes to hear her read aloud to me the novel on which I was to write a report that month. Roy and Darcy sat by to hear the novel, too. Then she or one of her sons would read chapters from my biology and history texts to keep me up to date with my class at school. After a few days I lost completely both my sense of smell and my sense of taste except for a measles taste that remained with me for two or three weeks, a taste that has recurred ever since during the early stages of a bad cold. Eating tasteless food in my feverish condition sometimes led to vomiting. I lost weight and came out of the illness with new pink skin and a hairline that had receded fully an inch. My hope that the hair on my forehead would grow back was never fulfilled, but the other hair came back wavy and darker than the hair I had lost.

My father rode his mule in from Caines Creek to be with me two or three days during the period of high fever. When the fever subsided and the peeling began, he went back home.

A relative of the Skaggs family, Uncle Daniel Skaggs, a widower with a fleece of white beard, had come to town recently, married a widowed Mrs. Huff, a neighbor of Aunt Mary Hamilton, and moved in with her. I had heard of Uncle Daniel, who was Sherrill Phillips's grandfather, but had never seen him. While I was at the height of my fever one afternoon and either sleeping or carried off in a delirium, I was brought suddenly back to wakefulness by a delightfully cold sensation of a weight on my forehead. I opened my eyes and looked up at the edge of a huge bony hand and a great fleece of white beard above which I could see the sharp features of an old man looking intently at Mrs. Skaggs through steel-rimmed spectacles. There were black hairs growing out of his ears, his eyebrows were black, and occasional black hairs grew from weather-tanned cheeks, but the fleece of beard and his full head of hair were as white as new snow. He was saying to Mrs. Skaggs that he believed my fever was ready to break. He and his new bride sat down for a few minutes. Goldie brought glasses of hot spiced apple juice for them to drink. I could hold my eyes only half open for a few moments at a time, but I noted that his new wife was plump and comfortable looking and that Uncle Daniel raised his heavy white mustache with the index finger of his left hand when he lifted the glass of apple juice to his lips. A part of the conversation concerned the marriage of another old widower who had ridden in from Blaine to another widow, Mrs. Johns, who was also a neighbor of Mrs. Huff and Aunt Mary Hamilton. Uncle Daniel allowed that Mrs. Johns had "driv her ducks to a pore market" when she had married him. He was right. Mrs. Johns sent him back to Blaine in a few weeks.

Cratis Williams age 16.

The bout with measles ended my childhood. My voice had not yet changed, I had grown no pubic hair, and there had been no growth of beard on my upper lips but troubled dreams and frightful nightmares had done something to me. The curtain had fallen at the end of the first act. I was now troubled with self-doubts that had not been present before. I doubted my self-worth. I realized the poverty in which my family lived and felt ashamed of myself and my kin. I was beset by anxieties that were to remain with me for fully ten years and by feelings of inadequacy and low self-esteem that I was to struggle with as an adolescent attempting to establish boy-girl relationships and a desirable social life.

Grampa Takes Me to School

Grampa Dave said he was going to Louisa on Sunday to take some beans, corn, tomatoes, and cabbage to my uncle, who was newly married, going to school, and not earning very much in the part-time job he had. He would have room in his wagon for me and would like to have me go along with him. My father decided that I should return to high school with Grampa because it was a busy time for him, as he wanted to finish cutting the willows and sycamores along the creek for the winter supply of stove wood, put in new posts for one of the pasture fences, and grub the bushes on the top steep of the old orchard field before corn was ready to cut. If I could go back to school with Grampa it would save him a whole work day.

Grampa had begun to "tip the bottle" the week before. No one could say yet that he was on one of his periodic drunks, but everybody except Grampa himself knew that he was working toward it. Papa thought it might be another week before Grampa would actually become drunk. He was in his happy stage then, and it would be safe for me to ride with him and I would enjoy being with him.

I took a bath in the washtub in the smokehouse shed, dressed for the trip, and packed the old suitcase and a box before an early dinner. Grampa did not want to drive his wagon up to our house for me. He would be glad to have me go with him if I could have everything I wanted to take along at his place and in his wagon and be ready to leave when he was. He thought he would start on the trip just after dinner.

My brother and I ate our dinners hurriedly and he helped me carry my load down the dry creek bed to Grampa's house. Grampa was finishing his dinner when we arrived. He had already curried and geared his horses, and hitched them to the wagon, all packed and waiting in the lane beside the coal house. The spring seat on which we would sit was in place. We set the suitcase and the box in the wagon and waited for Grampa to complete last-minute arrangements.

Grampa untied a corner of the tarpaulin over the load on the wagon, slid my suitcase and box under it, and tied the corner securely to the side of the wagon bed. We climbed aboard. Grampa slapped the check lines against the rumps of the horses and ordered them to "get up." The horses surged forward, Grampa upright on the spring seat and with the check lines drawn tightly. When the dog darted from behind the coal house to go along, too, Grampa turned on the seat, flinging his heavy leg against me, and withered the poor cur with such a stream of compound oaths that she slunk into the tiger lilies, her tail clamped tightly in humiliation. Grampa's stream of blazing fury did not run out until after the dog had completely hidden herself from his fiery wrath.

Grampa, returning then to his upright position, cracked his long whip twice above the rumps of the horses so it popped like a Stevens .22 and the horses took off at a fast clip. As we left the lane he shouted at Grandma, standing quietly by the garden fence, that he would be back Tuesday. His voice, not yet pulled back from the elevation it had reached during his apostrophe to the dog, boomed as if Granny had been standing on the far side of the meadow instead of six or eight feet from the wagon. She nodded her head affirmatively, watched us drive beyond the cribs, and then disappeared around the house.

By the time we had reached the road, Grampa had calmed down. He was in a happy mood, all dressed up in clean clothes, his big shoes oiled and his new tan broadbrim hat with a narrow band cocked jauntily over his right eye. As the horses struck their pace along the dusty road, Grampa began to sing fragments of little songs that ran through his mind, interrupting himself to cluck at the horses when they seemed inclined to slow their pace. When we were about ready to go down an incline, Grampa would pull a rope harnessed to himself that applied the brake shoe to the rear wagon wheel to check its speed so it would not force the horses to go downhill faster than they should.

We did not meet many people in our valley, but as we passed houses at which people had gathered on the porches or in the shade of trees in the yards, Grampa would call out jovially without stopping to hear what any of them had to say in return. After we had gone about three miles and come to a shady stretch of road in a dusty sandbar that ran alongside the creek, he reined the team to one side and stopped beside a sycamore tree. The horses needed "to blow a minute," he explained. He then invited me to feel in the corner of a pasteboard box filled with green beans, hidden under the upper end of the tarpaulin, for a pint bottle of "sankum suly" he had concealed there.

I felt about under the tarp and drew out the bottle, filled to the neck with light amber colored whiskey and corked securely with a red corncob stopper long enough for one to pull with ease, and handed it to him. The stopper popped when he pulled it from the bottle. He asked me whether I wanted a drink. I did. He handed the bottle to me. I wiped the top of it with the palm of my hand and took a swallow. It was good corn malt whiskey that he had made the preceding fall and aged in a charred oak keg. It went down smoothly and left a flavorsome smoky taste in my mouth afterwards, its sweetness and gentleness obscuring its high proof. I handed the bottle back to him as I felt the warmth of the drink spreading from my stomach.

Grampa took a sip from the bottle, held it between his knees for a minute or two, and then took a small swallow of it. He offered it to me again, but I declined. Then he started to stopper it but decided to have another swallow before doing so, this time a bigger one. He inserted the stopper, pounded it once with the heel of his big hand, and gave it to me to return to the bean box. I thought he was determined that he would not get drunk but was responding in spite of himself to the temptation of the excellent whiskey.

He drove on, sitting quite upright on the wagon seat and urging his horses onward at a faster pace as we passed the Big Hickory Tree in the wide bottom at the mouth of Deans Branch, where a Sunday afternoon baseball game was in progress and several young people, all dressed up in their Sunday best, sat on their horses lined up along the fence and watched the game and talked among themselves. Grampa did not speak and they merely glanced at us as the wagon wheeled by.

Before turning into the Blaine road at the mouth of Caines Creek, Grampa stopped the horses again for them to "blow a little." Allowing that I might like another "little dram," he called for the bottle again. I found it and offered it to him. He insisted that I have a drink first. I uncorked the bottle, took a sip from it, and passed it to him. This time he drank three or four swallows quickly, returned the stopper to the bottle, and handed it back for me to hide in the beans.

We drove on, the horses striking a smooth gait on the sandy Blaine road. We saw only three or four loafers sitting on the edge of the porch to Eck Berry's store as we passed through the village of Blaine. They stared at us curiously, but Grampa, his hat cocked jauntily and holding the checklines taut, drove on without speaking. We drove through Burton town and up the old road that circled the hill past Punkin Knob to the top of the ridge. It was necessary that he stop three or four times to let the horses rest a minute or two, but he did not call for the bottle again while we were climbing the hill.

The horses had begun to sweat by the time we had reached the top of the hill. Grampa pulled to the side of the road and let the horses cool in the shade of an oak tree that stood on the ridge. He let them rest a long time. He sat upright on the wagon seat and dozed for a few minutes. Noting that the sides of the horses were no longer heaving when they breathed, he turned and asked whether I wanted another "little nip." I produced the bottle, uncorked it, and barely tipped it to my lips before handing it to him. He held it up and looked at it as if he were determining how much we had already drunk. Then he turned it to his head and took several deep swallows from it. I noticed that the bottle was only half-full as I returned it to the bean box.

Grampa kept the brakes applied most of the way down the steep side of Brushy Hill. We did not meet anybody, for this "old road" to Brushy Creek, too steep, even, for Model T Fords, was not being used much by 1926. The new road, circling around points and in and out of hollows and draws, was a mile longer than this road, which had washed out considerably and on which the wagon rocked and twisted and shook until our load shifted as far from side to side and back to front as the tightly tied tarp would let it move. Grampa, pulling at the brake and sliding on the seat as the wagon sidled along slanting places, jerked the checklines, pulled his heavy weight back to his end of the spring seat, and shouted oaths and obscenities at the horses with such a force that he might have been heard for miles, his booming voice echoing from hillside to hillside.

Traveling was easier after we turned into the road down Brushy Creek, but the horses, not used to motor vehicles, became excited when we met cars, their trails of dust fogging behind them and settling on the bushes and horseweeds that lined the roadsides. As a car approached, Grampa would rein the horses toward the trees that grew along the creek so the blinds on their bridles would keep the horses from thinking the cars were moving straight toward him.

Once while the wagon was rolling along smoothly I heard a car horn blowing behind us. I looked back and saw a man in a shining new sedan close behind us. I told Grampa a man in a car behind us wanted us to pull over so he could pass. Grampa ignored me and did not look back. As we approached to our right the mouth of a lane that led under the trees and across the creek, the man sounded his horn again for Grampa, who was driving in the middle of the narrow road, to pull over. I told Grampa the man wanted us to pull over.

Without turning his head, Grampa roared out, "I pay my taxes and own as much of this road as that damned son-of-a bitch does. There's room over there for him to get around me. Let the bastard do it if he wants to. I'm not going to drive my team off the road just to please him, by Thee, damn. I bet you a dollar he don't pay a goddamned cent of taxes, the big-feelin' son-of-a-bitch."

The man tooted his horn again. I looked around at him. He was laughing. I motioned for him to pass us on the right at the intersection. He seemed to be stopping the car as he fumbled with the gear shifts. Then the car bounded forward, its motor roaring and the horn blowing. He passed us at great speed, cutting back into the road so sharply that the car barely missed the horse on the gee side.

The horses, frightened by the car, reared in their harness as they lurched to the left and then tried to leave the road. Grampa leapt to his feet and struggled with the checklines. The left wheels went into the ditch as the wagon tilted and the boxes thumped against the floor of the wagon bed. But Grampa brought the horses under control and reined them back into the road.

The driver of the car stuck his arm from the window and waved as he sped on. A woman wearing a tight black hat beside him turned her head and stared sternly at us, her bright red mouth pursed primly. I looked up at Grampa, who was standing in the wagon bed. He was bareheaded. "Son, jump out and hand me my hat. If I'd brought my gun along, I'd a busted every tire on that car," he said, as the car disappeared around the bend, trailing a cloud of gray dust.

I climbed out of the wagon and picked up Grampa's hat. It had bounced off his head on to the tarp and then into the dust-covered weeds above the road. I dusted it off, climbed aboard, and handed it to him.

The horses were nervous when we met other cars along the way. After that, when I told Grampa a car was behind us, he would look around, throw his hand up at the driver, and choose a place to pull over to let it pass. The cars passed us slowly and carefully and the horses did not try to rear in the harness again.

When we passed Mr. Evans' place far down on Brushy Creek, Mr. Evans, members of his family, and guests were sitting on the porch and in the shade of trees in the yard. Grampa threw up his hand and waved as he boomed out greetings.

Mr. Evans walked out toward the road as he hailed us. Grampa reined his team over to the mailbox and stopped. After exchanging pleasantries with us, Mr. Evans asked whether we might make room in the wagon for an old lady, Aunt Bamy Giles, to ride into town with us. She had walked across the hill from her brother's place that morning with the hope that she might catch a ride with someone. She did not want to ride in a car because the smell of gasoline and the motion made her sick. She wanted to get back to the home of her son with whom she had lived ever since her old man had died.

As we were talking with Mr. Evans, Aunt Bamy came tottering along the walk toward us, her white hair gleaming below a red bandana tied around her head. She was carrying a bundle of clothes in a white poke. Grampa looked at me quizzically. Then his expression changed as cunning narrowed his eyes.

"W'y, yes. We'd be glad to have her ride with us. Crate here can ride in the wagon bed and Aunt Bamy can sit here beside me on the seat."

"No, I don't want to take the child's seat. I can sit in the wagon bed," Aunt Bamy said.

"The wagon will jolt you all to pieces," Grampa countered. "Crate is young and limber. He won't mind riding back there. You sit up here with me on the spring seat."

I climbed out of the wagon and Mr. Evans assisted Aunt Bamy, Grampa holding her hand, as she struggled to climb over the side of the wagon box. I walked to the rear, stepped upon the coupling pole and across the end gate, and sat down on the floor of the wagon bed. We went on.

Grampa and Aunt Bamy entered into a lively conversation, both talking loudly and at the same time, for neither of them heard well. When we came to a sandy stretch of road shaded by tall trees growing along the bank of Blaine Creek, Grampa reined the horses to one side for them to blow again. Aunt Bamy's pink skin was covered with perspiration and her light blue eyes, looking weak under white brows and against her thin, pink skin, blinked as if they were not focused as she talked and laughed at Grampa's quips and observations. She did not have a fan. Grampa, observing that she looked hot, gave her his broad brim hat to use as a fan.

While we were cooling ourselves, Grampa said, "Aunt Bamy, I've got some good whiskey in the wagon. It's mighty hot, and we must soon tackle that hill. A little drink of whiskey would help us stand the heat better."

Aunt Bamy, fanning herself faster for a moment, allowed that it might. Grampa asked me to produce the bottle. He popped the stopper out of it and handed it to Aunt Bamy. Aunt Bamy squinted at it, smelled it for a moment, fumed the bottle to her head, and took several swallows while Grampa, upright and stiff on the wagon seat, watched silently. Aunt Bamy, smacking her toothless mouth and licking her thin lips, pronounced the whiskey "mighty fine truck" as she returned the bottle to Grampa, who barely touched his lips with it and did not offer it to me at all before replacing the stopper. Instead of asking me to return the bottle to the box of beans, he slipped it into his hip pocket.

When we were halfway up the Rich Creek Hill, Grampa thought the horses were getting too hot. I asked whether it might help if I walked up the hill. He thought it might. While the horses were cooling above a sharp bend in the road, Grampa produced the bottle again. Explaining that I would wait at the top of the hill, I walked on.

Grampa let the horses rest a long time. I could hear him talking loudly and Aunt Bamy laughing longer than she had been at funny things he was saying. I had almost reached the top of the hill before Grampa started the team again. He was now laughing himself at the things he was saying and singing little fragments of "Old Granny Hobblegobble, She Come Home" between his shouts at the horses.

I was waiting at the top of the hill. Grampa stopped the wagon to let the horses rest again. He produced the bottle and handed it to Aunt Bamy, who thought she ought not to drink any more, for she was buzzing from what she had drunk already. Grampa assured her that the whiskey was good protection against the heat of the day and that it would take much more of it than she had drunk to make her sick. She laughed and took several swallows from the bottle before handing it back to him. He held it up, looked at it a moment, and returned the stopper without taking a drink himself.

I climbed back into the wagon and we drove on. Grampa considered taking the Chock Alley Trail across Dry Ridge, but decided that there might be more cars on that road than on the road past Thomps Berry's store. The Thomps Berry Road was steeper in places, but it was a pretty good road and shorter than the Chock Alley Trail, which wound around and around to get a grade that cars could run on.

After mounting a steep near the foot of the hill, we came to a long straight stretch of road along a flat that had never been cleared. Where the road left the flat at the end of a point, the trees were thin and stunted. Many shrubs and bushes, including huckleberry and wild gooseberry, grew along the profile of the point. Grampa stopped his wagon at the bend of the road and asked me to hold the team for him, while he went into the bushes to see whether huckleberries were growing there as they used to. He had stopped there once and found so many huckleberries that he gathered enough in his hat to make a pie. Aunt Bamy thought huckleberry season was past but Grampa thought they grew until frost.

Aunt Bamy and I sat in silence in the wagon while Grampa was making his trip into the bushes. When he returned, he reported that he had found no huckleberries, but he believed that the big patch he had been to once was farther up the hill. Maybe I would like to go look for it while the horses cooled and rested.

As I started up the path, Grampa lumbered into the seat beside Aunt Bamy and produced the bottle again. I looked back and saw her holding her head far back with the bottle sticking straight up from her mouth. Grampa was leaning away from her and watching intently.

I knew there were no huckleberries, but I wanted to get far enough away from the wagon for Grampa and Aunt Bamy to feel that they could be confidential. Although I climbed all the way to the top of the ridge and saw green gooseberries, wild grapes, sumacs turning red, and berries on dogwood bushes, the huckleberry bushes were quite bare and their leaves were turning brown. But I never got out of the sound of Grampa's and Aunt Bamy's voices, though I could not understand everything they said.

Aunt Bamy was happy. She laughed a lot and giggled sometimes like her ribs were being tickled. Then there was a little while in which I could not hear either of them. The silence was broken when Aunt Bamy shouted out, "Don't, Mr. Williams, don't, now!" After a moment, she said in a normal voice, "Mr. Williams, I'm dirdy."

As I started back down the hill, Grampa called out as if I might have been on the ridge across the valley, "Crate, are you ready?"

"I'm coming, Grampa. I can't find any huckleberries up here. The birds must have eaten them."

I climbed into the wagon bed and sat on the floor behind the tarpaulin. Grampa started the team. Neither he nor Aunt Bamy said anything while we were traveling around the hill.

As we approached Thomps Berry's store near the gap, Grampa asked whether we wanted anything to eat. It was getting along in the afternoon and it would take three or four more hours to get to Louisa. I looked at my fob watch, the one I had won for increasing my sales of *Grit* two years before. It was 4:30. Aunt Bamy had eaten a big dinner at Mr. Evans's and thought she did not want anything. I thought I might like crackers and a can of sardines.

We stopped at the store, which was located above the road and had a porch along the front. Mr. Berry and a neighbor sat on the porch. Grampa tied the checklines to the brake pole and we got out of the wagon. Aunt Bamy, insisting that she did not want anything to eat, remained in the wagon.

Mr. Berry, whom Grampa had known for a long time and whose wife was his distant cousin, inquired about people he knew at Blaine. Grampa boomed answers. Mr. Berry opened the cans of sardines we ordered, set them on the counter, handed each of us a horseshoe nail, and placed a handful of crackers on a piece of wrapping paper spread on the counter between us. We stood by the counter, speared the sardines on the crackers, and ate, Grampa munching fast like a sheep as he wallowed the crackers in his mouth, for he would not wear his false teeth.

Mr. Berry asked whether the old lady in the wagon was Grampa's wife. When Grampa explained that she was Aunt Bamy Giles, who had been staying a few days at her brother's place on Blaine and was returning to Louisa, where she lived with her son, Mr. Berry remembered her from earlier years.

Aunt Bamy sat quietly on the wagon seat, her pink face gleaming, her white hair tumbling from under the red bandana tied around her head, and her pale blue eyes staring blankly straight ahead. She held the white poke of clothes on her lap.

I finished eating my sardines and crackers ahead of Grampa, who talked a lot while he was eating and who could not crunch his crackers with his gums. After he had finished, he tilted a corner of his sardine tin to his mouth and drank the oil. Perceiving that I did not want the oil in my can, he also drank it.

While Grampa was paying the dime we owed for the sardines, I studied the stick candy on display in the glass showcase on the counter. There were soft sticks of peppermint, which we called sugar candy to distinguish it from the brittle hard candy, for a penny a stick. I bought three sticks, which Mr. Berry put in a paper poke for me.

Back in the wagon, I gave Aunt Bamy and Grampa each a stick of my candy. Grampa whipped up the team and we started again. From my position at the end of the wagon, I could see Grampa looking straight ahead and Aunt Bamy, now as far from Grampa as she could get on the spring seat, doddering her head a little as she put bits of the sugar candy in her mouth and wallowed them around, her chin moving up and down quickly as she turned the piece of candy quickly between her toothless gums. There was no more conversation. After we had eaten our candy, Aunt Bamy's head would nod as she dozed while the wagon moved over straight and smooth stretches of road. When the wagon jolted, she would straighten up again and then settle into another nodding doze. Grampa did not notice that she was napping.

Grampa did not seem to be in much of a hurry after we were on the Little Blaine Road. The horses idled along while Grampa's shoulders were drooping and the checklines were sagging. The sun was not as hot as it had been and shadows were beginning to stretch out from cattle in pasture fields and posts beside the road. Grampa had calmed down so much that he would now pull over to the side of the road to make room for cars to pass us without even clucking at the horses. Aunt Bamy sat quietly far over on the other end of the seat from Grampa, her head nodding like her neck had become limber. So much of her white hair had worked itself from beneath the red bandana that it was beginning to fall around her shoulders.

By the time we had passed the Devil's Salt Stand on the hill before we reached the Twin Bridges across Little Blaine, we were seeing men and boys around barns and blue smoke rising from kitchen chimneys. It was getting late, but the sun would not be going down for a long time. The road was smooth now, the horses cropping over it at their own rate.

Grampa roused from his lazy spell, though, as we went through Busseyville, but Aunt Bamy continued to nod. So much of her hair had shaken loose that the bandana became skewed. She took it off, still tied in the shape of her head, and held it with the poke in her lap. Then all of her hair was hanging around her shoulders and falling before her face when she nodded. She seemed much older with her hair hanging loose.

At the top of the Wallace Hill Grampa let the horses rest. The hill was not very steep, but the horses were beginning to get tired. He sat on the seat and looked at Aunt Bamy, nodding as if the wagon were still in motion.

"Well," Grampa announced loudly, "we're almost to Louisa."

"Where are we?" Aunt Bamy asked.

"On the Wallace Hill."

"What time is it a-gittin' to be? Hit seems like a long time since we left Breshy, 'pear like."

"Oh, it's time to drive the cows in." Turning his whole body toward me at the back of the wagon, Grampa asked, "What time is it, Crate?"

I looked at my fob watch.

"Half past 6:00," I replied.

"Is your son expecting you?" Grampa asked of Aunt Bamy, who seemed not to hear him. "I said is your son expecting you?" he shouted.

"No, he does not know I am coming back home." Then she dozed again.

Grampa started the horses, slapping at them with the checklines. The wagon was rolling along smoothly over the dusty clay road, but Grampa thought we should be going faster. He cracked his blacksnake whip once at the horses and they broke into a brisk trot which they kept up until we started up Town Hill.

From the top of the hill Louisa stretched lazily among the trees, the late afternoon sun bathing in long rays the Big Mill, the spire on the Evans House, and the dull gray tower of the Baptist church. Smoke from a train that had passed through town and was whistling long and lonesome as it turned the bend down the river was spreading itself in a long thin layer above the tree-tops.

Grampa stopped the wagon in front of the boarding house, lumbered awkwardly out of it, and handed me my suitcase and box.

"Be a good boy and study hard," he said. "I'll be back in town for circuit court. I might bring you a bottle of something to cherk up your spirits."

Aunt Bamy, not nodding so much now, was wiping her hair back behind her ears. Grampa climbed back in the wagon and drove on to deliver Aunt Bamy at her son's house. They were sitting closer together on the spring seat, Grampa upright and his hat cocked at a rakish angle as he held the checklines taut.

Levi J. Webb

One of the persons outside the family who exerted a strong influence on me while I was growing up was Levi J. Webb, one of the last of the colorful old-time horseback drummers in eastern Kentucky.

We called few people "Mr." We addressed our teachers at the one-room school by their first names and referred to the county superintendents, who rode horseback up the valley once a year to visit the school, by their full names without prefixing "Mr." Even the preachers were both addressed and referred to by their full names without prefixing "Preacher." But all of us called Levi J. Webb "Mr. Webb."

Mr. Webb was an imposing man. Inclined toward corpulence, erect, red-faced, clean-shaven, well groomed in his white shirt, string tie, tough clothes, gaiters that came to his knees, strong shoes, and stylish canvas cap in winter and panama hat in summer, Mr. Webb represented to us sartorial splendor in the older traveling man.

Mr. Webb spent one Monday night a month in our home for thirteen years. We did not keep a country store, and most of the time on his monthly rounds he spent his nights in the homes of the country merchants on whom he called. But I knew him and enjoyed seeing him at our Uncle Steve's store for four or five years before he began spending in our home his first night out from Webbville, where he had grown up and from which spot he began his itinerary each month. At Uncle Steve's store he leaned against a counter and took the order for hardware and notions that his company, located in Ironton, Ohio, sold.

He emanated efficiency with a style that was no doubt calculated to impress both those who saw him in action and the merchants whose confidence he sought. He would take off his jacket, in the breast pocket of which he carried a bracket of cigars, and lay it carefully across the counter beside him.

Then, with a fine cigar in his mouth, which he would puff lightly as a kind of punctuation to an item as he entered it on the order form, he would adjust the stiff celluloid collar hugging his pink neck, straighten the string tie, pull the cuffs of the sleeves of his white shirt, with gold links gleaming, up his arms, adjust the ornate armbands above his elbows, and with a heavy, most substantial looking fountain pen selected from a row of pens and pencils clipped securely in his shirt pocket, fill out the order form for what the merchant thought he could sell before Mr. Webb came again the following month.

After taking the order, Mr. Webb would then tell about other items that might appeal to farmers and their wives … new decorations for harness, leather goods, strong pliers, well chains, pokers with nickel-plated handles, new lines of tea kettles, cookware, crockery. If the merchant was interested, Mr. Webb would consult the index of a big catalog with a flexible but substantial black cover that he carried in his polished saddlebags, open the catalog to a picture of the item, and extol its virtues in a precise voice that had flowing behind it a melody of nasalization that gave his speech, studded with colorful expressions and clever euphemisms, a quality of distinction and an air both of significance and good humor. His grammar, while not labored and scholastic, was nonetheless close enough to that of important people who came out from towns to convey the impression that he was an educated man who knew his way around in fine society beyond the hills. People liked him so well that they gathered at the store when it was too wet to plow and hoe or harvest or too cold to work outside to wait for his coming on the first Monday afternoon of each month.

In no hurry after he had transacted his business, Mr. Webb would answer questions for news about events in the towns, or the progress of farmers with their crops as he observed them from horseback while riding through the country. He was especially pleased to respond to questions asked about equipment for farming or tools and gadgets that might come in handy for farm folk. Often he would open up his big catalog and show pictures and read aloud what was written in the catalog. Occasionally a farmer would request Uncle Steve to place an order for something he decided he wanted. Each month Mr. Webb brought a new anecdote or two for the amusement of those who liked to swap yarns from their perches around the potbellied stove in cold weather or, in more tolerable weather, from their positions on the edge of the porch that ran along the front of the store.

In those days Mr. Webb spent the night at Uncle Steve's. Not long after Uncle Steve's death the store was closed and Aunt Lou, who had no children, invited Aunt Mary and her family to live with her. But Mr. Webb continued to spend the first night out from Webbville there. Things were not the same, though. It became necessary to move Mr. Webb from the large guest room, now occupied by Aunt Mary and her husband, to a tiny bedroom at the end of the porch. The room had a window that would not open and the old-fashioned corded bedstead with a shuck mattress and featherbed was not comfortable. It was necessary to keep the door open at night for air and there was no screen. When another country store at the mouth of the branch beyond the high hill that he crossed to get to Aunt Lou's closed, Mr. Webb found himself going out of his way to stay at Aunt Lou's, but he had stayed there so long that he was reluctant to try to find another place.

An embarrassing incident led to his decision to change his route and to stop at our house. One summer on a quiet, humid, and hot night when gnats and mosquitoes moved in from the garden that grew next to the house, Mr. Webb, unable to sleep, slipped from his bed, closed the door, and lay on a bench along the wall of the porch. A thunderstorm followed by heavy rainfall cooled the air, beat down the insects, and brought fresh breezes across the porch. Mr. Webb sat up to watch the rain, hear the water drip from the roof of the porch to the "leak" along the edge, and inhale the refreshing air. While he was sitting there, Aunt Lou came from her room, rushed past him to the edge of the porch, squatted on the top step, and urinated. When she turned to go back into her room, she saw Mr. Webb sitting there. Mr. Webb, recognizing that he had been discovered, spoke in his precise, courteous manner, "Well, Mrs. Liming, we have had a nice shower." Aunt Lou hurried on into her room without responding. It was she who reported the incident to Aunt Mary and her children after Mr. Webb left next day, and it was her nephews and nieces who told everybody about it. Aunt Lou dismissed the incident with a scoff. "Nice shower, indeed! The old fool!"

But Mr. Webb stopped and asked whether he might spend his first night out at our house the next time he came around. He did not mind sleeping in the extra bed in the room in which my brother and I slept. Our house was a convenient location for him. There was also a stall in our barn for his horse and we had plenty of corn and hay. Most importantly, he liked good whiskey. Uncle Steve had always been able to provide him with a quart while he was living, but Aunt Mary's sons sometimes forgot to have a quart ready for him. He understood that my father kept some of the best on hand at all times. He liked better than anything two or three snorts of good whiskey before he ate his supper and another substantial drink before he lay down at night.

We were pleased to have him as a monthly guest. He would come riding his sleek, well-curried bay horse out of the lane, and call out convivial greetings to us as he passed on toward the barn. Singing and whistling while he prepared the horse for the stable, he led him to drink at the pool in the creek close by, fetched the ears of gleaming corn from the crib and pitched down hay for him to eat, and found hidden in the grain bin in the saddleroom the quart jar of whiskey placed there for him.

With his carefully cared-for saddlebags over his shoulder and a newly lighted cigar in his mouth, a delicious kind of topping for the two or three drinks of whiskey taken straight from the jar before he left the saddleroom, he would come sailing across the porch to our room, where he deposited his saddlebags, removed his collar and tie and his gaiters, put his jacket on a hanger, and found his shaving kit. He would then join us in the porch or sitting room and talk jovially with us about things that we had "been into" since he had called last. One of us would bring a pan of warm water, soap, and a towel and a shaving mirror. He would wash his red face, apply lather, and shave rapidly with a safety razor, talking all the while and laughing easily at our responses to his questions. When my father came in from the fields, Mr. Webb would sing out greetings followed by his favorite euphemistic oath, "By shots!" All of our neighbors called my father "Curt," but Mr. Webb, who had cultivated a semi-formal mode of address, called him "Curtis" and my mother "Mrs. Williams."

Mama enjoyed having Mr. Webb. She set before him the finest food we had to offer. He was gracious and never failed to make clever compliments about special dishes that he knew had been prepared because he was a guest. If she offered apologies for some food that had not turned out well, he would reassure her. Sometimes he would talk about the poor quality of food and the shabby accommodations he found in some of the homes of the merchants in the "upper counties" where he stayed. He never referred to these places by name, but he would observe that the appearance of homes often had little to do with the quality of cooking within them or the comfort of the beds offered guests. One place he referred to through the years as "a boar's nest if I ever saw one, by shots."

Once he found only my sister at home when he arrived. My mother had come to the field to help us hoe. When my sister explained that we were all working in the corn field and that she was preparing the supper, he observed, "By shots! It's a poor house that can't afford at least one lady."

Mr. Webb enjoyed playing setback. Occasionally Grampa Whitt would come to visit after supper and we would play, Mr. Webb responding to the plays with his clever remarks and good humor. Once he and Grampa discussed kinship, for Mr. Webb was descended from Whitts. They believed they were second cousins, but Mr. Webb continued to address Grampa as "Mr. Whitt," never Jeff, as others did, or "Cousin Jeff."

When Mr. Webb learned that I was to go away to school, he took a special interest in me and would engage me in conversation about history and current events. He told me that I could subscribe to *Pathfinder* for a quarter a year and gave me a quarter and the address I would need. He rarely found people who could discuss current events with him on his rounds. He would enjoy talking with me about what was happening in the world. I subscribed to *Pathfinder* and continued to receive it until it was discontinued. He told me about *Grit* and I subscribed to it. During the summer months while I was at home and sometimes the first Monday in January while I was home for the winter holidays we would talk about current events and national news.

Mr. Webb lived in Louisa. Once or twice a month he was able to leave his horse in a livery stable and take a train to Louisa to spend a weekend at home. While I was in high school there I saw him on the street once but he appeared not to recognize me. During my freshman year in high school when I carted the *Cincinnati Post* and delivered *Grit* on Saturday, his wife took both. Once on a Saturday morning he came to the door, but when he saw that I was only the *Grit* carrier he called to his wife and turned away without recognizing me. I never referred to these brief encounters with him when he came to our home thereafter, nor did I

Cratis Williams age 16.

ever let him know that I delivered the *Post* and *Grit* to his wife, knew his beautiful daughter who, along with her husband, operated the movie theatre in town, and who permitted me to pay only a dime for a ticket to the movie until I was fully sixteen, nor did I ever refer to his granddaughter, a petite, lovely girl whose charms set the hearts of all the boys in town to throbbing. Mr. Webb, the drummer, belonged to the country. His family in town was something else.

The Bad Man at the Boarding House

One evening after the down train had passed through town a middle-aged couple arrived at the boarding house. The man was carrying a heavy suitcase strapped with belts and a battered boxlike case similar to that carried by tobacco salesmen and the woman a ragged cardboard suitcase with loops of cord tied into the rings to replace the handle. They had walked up from the passenger depot.

When they arrived, Aunt Nan was alone in the little sitting room that doubled as the bedroom for her and Uncle Vess. Uncle Vess had not yet come down from the livery barn. Aunt Nan was cordial when she invited the new arrivals to come in following a rap on the door, but she was bewildered when they walked into full view under the gas light at the end of the lead pipe that stuck down a foot or more from the ceiling.

I looked up from my book at the dining-room table. I had not seen these people before. The man, a black hat shading much of his face, stood with his baggage in his hands. He was a big man, better dressed than men who came on horseback or in wagons from back in the county when court was in session. He wore a blue serge suit but no vest and tie. His coat was not buttoned. His solid gray flannel shirt with the collar buttoned under his clean-shaven and red chin fit him tightly across the stomach. A black mustache that started up in the shadow of his hat brim drooped past the ends of his mouth and curled toward his ears. He was a handsome man, but he looked awkward and uncomfortable standing there so straight and tall under the light and at the foot of the bed in the little room. He bowed his head slightly toward Aunt Nan, her great bulk caught in the rocking chair beside her bed and her huge legs crossed at the ankles as they stretched toward the little fireplace. The man's presence intimidated her. There was something sinister and threatening about the man, although he had not spoken yet.

His companion, though obviously dressed in her best, was quite plain. She wore no makeup, but her hair, barely visible below a tightly fitting black hat, was bobbed. Her face was tanned and weathered like the faces of country women who came to town with their husbands to trade at the stores or hear trials at the court. But she must have thought of herself as a young woman, and she was daring to have her hair bobbed at her age.

"Nan, I'm Vessie," she said, "and this here is my new man, Griff Blevins."

"I knowed who you was as soon as I see'd you. Pleased to meet you," she added, looking toward Griff.

"The same, mum," he replied in a light voice like that of a timid boy.

"We have rode down on the train from Beaver Creek," Vessie said. "Griff here got in a little trouble back up there yesterday. They claim he killed a man. The law is lookin' fer him. We thought we'd come down and stay a few days with you and Pa while things simmer down a little back in Floyd County. Later, if the wind blows enough to dry up the muddy roads, we will get somebody to take us out to the mouth of Brushy for a few days, or Pa might let us know about somebody from out that way that would have room fer us in his wagon when he goes back home."

"Vess hain't come in yet. He' s still at the livery barn."

There was a long period of silence. Aunt Nan looked at Vessie, whose face was fixed in an anxious smile. Griff had set his suitcase down and was holding his black hat in his hand. His thick gray hair contrasted strangely with the sinister aspect of the black mustache drooping below his mouth and curling toward his ears. His small baby blue eyes had quizzical crinkles at the corners. He was studying Aunt Nan almost as if he were prepared to spring upon her if she should make a false move.

Aunt Nan, who looked at Vessie, mostly, was so slow in responding that I was expecting her to say that she had no room for them, which was her usual response to people who asked for a room and whom she did not want to keep. I could feel the tension as the three of them held their positions as if they were posing for a photographer to take their pictures. Aunt Nan turned her head slowly to steal a glance at Griff but cowered suddenly when her eyes met his.

"Well, you can stay, I reckon. Vess wouldn't want me to turn his own daughter away from our door."

"We're obliged to you, mum. We'll be as little trouble to you 'ns as possible," Griff said in the light, soft voice that one did not expect from such a brawny man and one who had killed someone on Beaver Creek only yesterday. "After things have blowed over up the river, I aim to go back home and turn myself in to the high sheriff."

Aunt Nan drew her heavy legs into a sitting position and pushed against the arms of the rocking chair to free herself from it as she rose, grunting.

"I'll show you where you'll sleep," she said, as she lumbered past them toward the door of her "fine" room, which joined her sitting room and had a little fireplace with a gas grate, a mantel over it, and a mirror above the mantel reflecting what was in the sitting room.

With her hand on the door knob, she turned. "Have you 'ns had your suppers?"

"We eat a san'rich apiece that we bought from one of them there boys that was a-cryin off san'riches and things when we got off'n the train down at the passenger depot. 'Tweren't much to it. Jist two pieces of lightbread with a thin slice of cheese slapped betwixt 'em. They was awful dry and choky."

"Vess's supper is a-warmin for him in the oven. I'll have Sylvia put on coffee to bile and fry you some aigs and sassages." She raised her voice and called toward the back of the house, "Hey, Syl! Fry four aigs and some sassages. Bile a new pot of coffee. Warm over the biscuits. Two people will be a-eatin with Vess everwhen he gits here."

Sylvia, immaculate in a white starched dress, red lisle stockings, and clean red shoes, appeared immediately, lighted the gas lamp in the kitchen, and began to prepare the supper. I could hear Aunt Nan and Vessie talking in low voices in the guest room.

I picked up my book and papers and went into my own little room off the kitchen. I could hear Sylvia humming as she worked at the stove.

Before I could become interested in my book again, I heard Griff ask Sylvia for the flashlight. He then tramped through the kitchen on his way out back and slammed the screen door as he left.

Uncle Vess arrived before Griff returned. I could hear him and Vessie and Aunt Nan talking at the dining room table, but I could pick up only wisps of the conversation.

Aunt Nan, her voice raised in concern, said, "We don't want to get in no trouble. We cain't let him keep whiskey in the house. The shurves might find out he is here and come with a search warrant. We'd be in trouble, then."

Vessie's voice had an urgency in it that topped Aunt Nan's concern. "He's a good man but he's also a dangerous one. I hear tell that the one he killed yesterday was his seventh. I don't aim to contrary him none."

Uncle Vess was slow and deliberate in his response but I could not understand what he said. I could just make out a few words, but I heard him say, "Brushy," "Pard Martin," "Arb Thompson."

The screen door slammed after Griff as he entered the kitchen. Uncle Vess, his voice raised, said hurriedly, "Somebody will be a-comin in from out that way in two or three days, maybe."

At breakfast the following morning I found myself sitting across the table from Griff and Vessie. Two men and a boy, teamsters from the oilfield beyond Blaine who had slept in the big bedroom, were at the table with us. Uncle Vess sat at the head of the table and saw that the platters and bowls of food were passed along. Conversation among him, the two older teamsters, and Vessie was lively, but Griff, the boy, and I ate in silence.

Griff had taken a drink of strong whiskey before coming from his room. I could smell it on him all the way across the table. His face was red. But his pale blue eyes, the crinkles relaxed now, below the full head of gray hair had a touch of gentleness in them. He lifted his big mustache with his left index finger as he put sausage and egg into his mouth. While chewing his food he looked directly across the table at me with fleeting merriment in the pale eyes as if he were half-ready to invite me to play a game with him. I half smiled in response, remembering that I was looking straight into the eyes of one who only two days before had killed his seventh man. It occurred to me that he sensed my fascination with his skill in getting his food in his mouth without smearing egg and gravy on his mustache. His eyes crinkled and he appeared to be smiling as he looked at me straight in the eyes. I smiled back and his smile completed itself. He lifted his coffee cup to his face, paused for a moment as he looked at me, lifted his mustache again, and took several swallows of the steaming coffee. When he set the cup in the saucer, he smiled again quite plainly.

In the meantime conversation had been lively, but I had heard little that was said.

After breakfast, I returned to my room and read my book until 7:30. Then I drew a glass of water from the tap and went into the back yard, where I brushed my teeth.

While I was assembling my books and supplies in preparation for my departure for school at 7:45, there was a knock at my door. It was Aunt Nan.

"Griff Blevins has a gallon of whiskey with him. He's in trouble back up in one of them there upper counties. Vess and me are afeard that the shurves'll come a-lookin' for him and find it and we'd be in trouble."

She paused, tilted her head on her fat short neck and studied my face for a moment.

"Me and Vess thought you might not mind if we hid the whiskey in your room. If the shurves come, they'll be searchin' his room, I think. If they search the whole house and find it in your room, you'll be gone to school."

I thought for a moment while I looked around the room and considered where might be the best place to hide Griff's whiskey. Beside my little dresser was a shoeshine box I had bought for a dime from one of my friends who had decided that he would go out of the shoeshining business and liquidate his assets. The stand was a dried peach box, now painted red, that had one end slanted to hold the foot of one whose shoes were being shined. The back side of the box, in which I kept shoe polish, brushes, and shining rags, was open.

"Reckon it might go in this shoeshine box," I said. "We could drape a shine rag from the top and a sheriff would never in the time of man think to look in it for whiskey," I allowed.

Aunt Nan looked at the box. "I believe it'd go in the box, all right," she said.

That afternoon when I returned from school, I found two half-gallon jars of white whiskey in my shoeshine box, but one of the jars was not much more than half-full. Griff and Vessie were in their room. I thought Griff had probably poured enough whiskey from the jar into a bottle to do him till next morning.

We ate supper at 6 o'clock. There were no extra boarders that night, so I sat at the table with only Aunt Nan, Vessie, and Griff. Conversation was mostly between Vessie and me, but Griff took a lively interest in what was being said and smiled into my face frequently. I felt that he was a basically good and kind man. He had little to say about subjects introduced for conversation and when Vessie asked for his opinion he would reply in his light, soft voice and almost purringly that he had "never thought about it much." Vessie would then hurry on. When she expressed an opinion of her own and turned to Griff for comment, he would deliberate for a moment, his baby blue eyes coming into sharp focus as the crinkles gathered, and respond slowly and softly, "You may be right, Vessie."

After supper Griff and Vessie, neither of whom had ventured from the house all day, decided to walk down to the passenger depot to see the train go through town. It was a warm evening in March and nobody would be likely to recognize Griff. I was about to return to the school to help Mr. Gilmer unpack laboratory equipment and supplies that had arrived that day. Aunt Nan thought I might not mind walking with them as far as the depot. A little boy with them might "keep down suspicion," she said, and everybody in town knew me.

As we walked along Vessie kept a conversation going, mostly with me. Griff offered only brief comments, like "Could be," "Maybe so," "I hadn't never heared of it," "I don't rightly know." He smelled strong of whiskey, and I could hear the sloshing of whiskey in the flat bottle in his inside coat pocket and the creaking of the leather of his underarm holster.

We did not meet anybody on the sidewalks between the boardinghouse and the depot. A crowd had gathered there, though the train would not arrive for nearly an hour yet, even if it was on time. Griff walked with a deliberate, even stride, his right forearm held closely against his chest as if he were trying to steady the bottle in his coat pocket so its contents would not slosh. As we approached the crowd, Griff slowed his pace and took me by the hand as if I were his son.

We walked into the shadow of the depot and stood close to the walk parallel to the cross street, our backs to the wall and with me nearest the window, through which I could see students who rode the train sitting on benches and trying to read books by the dim light. Dick Cyrus, the town policeman, whom I knew, came in a long stride from around the corner, his badge glinting in the light and his pistol holster flapping at his side. Griff gripped my hand slightly, but the policeman spoke to me and hurried on without casting a glance at Griff in his dark suit and big black hat standing there in the shadows. Griff relaxed his grip and in a moment released my hand. I took leave of Griff and Vessie and hurried on, hoping that nobody in the crowd would recognize Griff but wondering just what might have happened had the policeman spoken to him instead of me.

Griff and Vessie slept late the following morning. As I was getting ready to leave for school, Aunt Nan called me to her chair and whispered that Griff and Vessie would be leaving that afternoon. Uncle Vess had spoken to a man from the mouth of Cherokee who would let them ride out with him to the mouth of Brushy, where they would stay a few days, till things settled down up on Beaver Creek, and Griff could go back home.

"Don't say nothin' about the whiskey to a livin' soul," she cautioned. "Looks like Vessie could find her a man that hain't allus a-gettin' in trouble. Her other men was allus a-drinkin' and a-swarpin' and a-fightin' and a-shootin'."

I never saw Griff again and do not know what became of him. I was unable to reconcile his baby blue eyes, crinkling smile, soft voice, and gentle manners with his reputation as a desperado with seven notches on his gun.

I never would have thought of him as a dangerous man, just from talking with him and exchanging smiles with him.

Finishing High School with William H. Vaughan[1]

I remember the first time I saw Bill Vaughan. As a high school freshman I was assigned to a study hall which he was keeping for a day or two while Mr. Godby, the principal, was working out teaching assignments to accommodate an unexpected increase in enrollment. Mr. Vaughan, dressed in a brown suit with pinstripes and a light tan shirt with pencil stripes and a soft collar of the same material, was standing by the door. I remembered that my father also had a brown suit with pinstripes, perhaps of the same material as Mr. Vaughan's suit but much more old-fashioned in cut. Other men teachers at the school were still wearing high celluloid collars and suits of solid colors, mostly blue and black. Mr. Vaughan, I learned, was a local man who had graduated from college only recently. To me he did not look like a teacher as he stood there, somewhat awkwardly dressed in brown pinstripes and rocking on his toes as his head doddered slightly as if he might have had a palsy. With his straight nose and dressed in his brown pinstripe suit and soft-collared striped shirt he looked a bit like my father, I thought. Some of the seniors who knew him were talking with him in a half-bantering manner. He was smiling uncertainly and returning the banter but almost as if he were half-fearful that he might not be accepted. Students generally were ignoring him as they scrambled for seats of their choice and behaved as if they were unsupervised. Mr. Vaughan, I thought, was probably a weak teacher for whom students held little or no respect.

I was either moved out of that study hall or Mr. Vaughan was assigned a class that met at the same time as the study hall. I saw him only occasionally during the year, usually in the hall or at the assembly every Friday, but I do not recall that I ever had a conversation with him and think it possible that he might not have known me at all. Later, I began to hear that he was a good teacher, that his classes were exciting, and that students liked him very much.

Something happened in the spring of 1924-25 that might have contributed to a decision of the board of education to release Mr. Godby as the superintendent of the Louisa public schools and principal of Louisa High School and to elect Mr. Vaughan as his successor. One of the teachers, Mr. O.O. Roberts, a tall man with a small head perched on a slender neck cased by the highest celluloid collar I ever saw, slapped Julia Jane Burgess following a quarrel with her in one of his classes. Mr. Vaughan's brother Edgar, a member of the class, sprang to his feet and struck Mr. Roberts in the face with his fist, bloodying his nose. A melee followed. At the chapel soon afterwards I saw Mr. Roberts, a handkerchief to his bleeding nose and tears in his eyes, come into the auditorium flanked by one or two of the other teachers and some of the senior boys. Edgar and other young fellows were disposed to drive Mr. Roberts from the room but were being restrained by fellow students. Other students in that sector of the auditorium, where the seniors sat, were milling about in confusion. Mr. Gilmer, the near-sighted albino science teacher, sensing the mounting of a mob spirit, walked among the crowd ordering people to be seated and pinching the arms of those standing within his reach as he threatened to "flunk them for the semester." Almost single-handedly he restored order. As feeling mounted against Mr. Roberts for "striking a girl," Edgar's reputation as a defender of the honor of a lady grew. Students in the lower classes considered him something of a hero. Julia Jane's father, Dr. Burgess, was a member of the board of trustees. We never knew what transpired in board meetings, but neither Edgar nor Julia Jane was penalized, Mr. Godby and Mr. Roberts were not re-elected, and Mr. Vaughan was chosen as Mr. Godby's successor.

The following year I began to become acquainted with Mr. Vaughan, who found opportunities to talk with me occasionally because I was on the honor roll. Near the end of the year he included me among the honor students whom he invited to a wiener roast on the grounds of the tabernacle at Smoky Valley, about five miles west of Louisa. He also arranged transportation for us and encouraged us to bring our dates. I recall that he and upperclassmen smiled approvingly at me, then only 15, when I escorted Virginia Graham, a lovely gray-eyed eighth grade girl with dark curly hair, to the picnic, for most of the sophomore girls were a year or two older and much more mature physically than I. Mr. Vaughan himself was the master of ceremonies. We sat on the ground around the fire and told stories and sang after we had eaten wieners and roasted marshmallows. Before leaving for home, those of us who cared to told humorous stories. Mr. Vaughan told a Pat and Mike story with a trick line in it:

> The happiest days of my life
> Were spent in the arms
> Of another man's wife —
> My mother.

Later, I learned that Mr. Vaughan loved a good story and was skilled at telling jokes, which he liked to exchange with both his peers and his students.

I was a student in Mr. Vaughan's American history class during my junior year and he was my Sunday school teacher at the Baptist church. These associations with him led to a special kind of friendship. Once early in the year when he found me late one afternoon loafing near the drugstore he invited me to have a banana split with him. I did not admit to him that I had never eaten a banana split before, but I felt that he knew. We sat at the counter and watched the clerk prepare the splits and then ate them slowly, neither saying anything. He often invited me into his office after classes were over and talked with me. I do not recall that I ever presented myself at his office. I was busy with club activities after school and Mr. Vaughan would meet me in the hall or call to me as I passed his office door and invite me in for a visit.

He was especially interested in my background and encouraged me to tell him about my great-grandfather, who had been a prosperous farmer, merchant, distiller, and miller. He knew the family of my great-grandfather's sister, Mary Jane Swetnam, who had become "town folks" long ago. He wanted to know about going to a one-room school and asked many questions about my teacher (and my father's cousin) who had been shot to death at a country church in 1922. He was interested in the stories I knew about my mother's family and encouraged me to tell about my great-grandfather's participation in a feud, his escape from the Morgan County jail, and his coming to Blaine. He enjoyed especially well the anecdotes about old-timers, most of them my blood kin, that I liked to tell, and drew me out when I told stories about the Civil War that I had heard the old soldiers tell. He relished my accounts of hard-shell Baptist church services, funerals at which women wailed, funeralizings at family graveyards in August and September. He liked to hear accounts of 'possum hunting, ginsenging, berry picking, bean stringings, corn shellings, shuck tearings, and the like. And he would return from time to time to the subject of moonshining and liked to have me describe the processes involved in that secret occupation. From time to time he would congratulate me on my progress in rising above my background, for though he was keenly interested in all I told about myself, my family, and my community, he was convinced that my objective should be preparation for a successful life in middle-class society, of which he saw himself as a representative in its finer aspects, for he did not use tobacco, drink alcoholic beverages, or speak profanely.

It was during my junior year that I learned what a great teacher Mr. Vaughan was. Early in the year he let us know that he was interested in having us read, ask questions, discuss, and read some more. As I understood it, high school history teachers typically spent much time dictating study questions geared to a text, assigned a few pages of the text for reading and finding answers to the questions, and then called on students individually next day to respond to the questions that had been dictated the previous day. Mr. Vaughan did none of that. In fact, he made no page or chapter assignments from the text at all.

He moved from one "big" question to the next, the questions somewhat parallel to the presentation of material in the text, as an approach to American history. I think only nine big questions were dealt with during the entire year. The first question had to do with the settlement period. He began his class by calling for questions. At first, there were none. He then asked questions, directing the same question to many persons in turn without indicating whether he accepted or rejected responses. Soon students began asking questions for clarification, but Mr. Vaughan referred the questions to other students. Lively discussions were generated in which Mr. Vaughan himself played the role of moderator.

From time to time he would become animated and ask, "Where did you learn that?" If he felt the student might become fired up, he would ask, "Have you consulted _____ ?" After two or three days, he would then ask us to write in 10 or 15 minutes our answer to a question, to provide an opportunity for us to organize such factual information as we might have at hand, including notes and the text, and draw a conclusion. He took up the papers which he never returned to us. We continued to discuss the big question for two or three additional days. Without telling us when we might expect to be called upon to do so, he would ask us again to write for 10 or 15 minutes in response to the same question that we had answered before, but he still did not return the papers. Then, one day, he would lecture for a half-hour on the big question. Students were asked if they had questions. The following day he moved on to another big question.

Soon we knew that he was watching the growth and depth levels of our understanding of our history. When he felt that we understood one big question, he proceeded to the next.

He called for no term papers, no book reports, no notebooks. At midterm we wrote for a period, using any materials we had with us, in response to a kind of developmental question or two. These papers he read carefully and returned with grades on them. At the end of the semester we responded to one or two other questions in a similar fashion. I was only 15 years old when I enrolled in American history. By the end of the year I had read widely and freely and developed skill in organizing and synthesizing material, a skill that I found most useful in college and in graduate seminars later.

Mr. Vaughan's class was always lively, and the material was exciting. I was sure I had learned history and understood why we had a North, a South, a West, a Civil War, and a new nation. And yet, Mr. Vaughan had never seemed harried and overworked as a teacher. He had not spent weekends going through term papers and notebooks, or nights writing out study questions to dictate next day or scoring test papers on which students had responded with names, dates, places, and "three reasons why...." He had given us no opportunities at all to substitute busy work for learning.

Mr. Vaughan's Sunday school class at the Baptist church for young men of high school age, which must have been the largest Sunday school class in town, was conducted in similar fashion. We had quarterlies, but we were never catechized on the contents of a lesson and then offered an orthodox platitude as a synthesis of it. Instead, Mr. Vaughan came prepared to ask us a big question relating to the implications of the lesson for a young man who had reached the place in his life that he was doubting, raising questions, testing rules of conduct, feeling guilty, or attempting to seal off his religious attitudes from the problems he had to deal with in relating to his parents and his peers. Again, Mr. Vaughan seemed not to know answers himself but referred questions first to one and then another. Toward the end of the half-hour Mr. Vaughan

Cratis Williams age 17.

would respond for three to five minutes to the discussion, sometimes with an account of an experience of his own, or the story of some young man who had dealt with such questions acceptably, or with a Biblical story, or one of the parables of Jesus. One left Mr. Vaughan's class with his ethical dimensions extended but with little or no thought of whether the experience had made him a better Baptist, or, for that matter, even a better Christian. He simply knew that his values had been clarified for him and that he felt increased moral strength.

During my senior year I was the editor of the *Louisian*, the high school paper published every other week. Since there was not a room in the building for use as a newspaper office, Mr. Vaughan permitted me to use a few cubicles in his big roll-top desk for filing, a corner of the conference table in his office for a dilapidated typewriter and a work space, and a shelf in the closet under the stairs for storing materials and the old typewriter when I was not using it. He gave me a key to the outside door of his office and one to his roll-top desk. Thus, I could work in his office in the afternoons and come back at night for meetings at the conference table with my staff and for work sessions. He rarely came back in the evenings, but often we sat together in the afternoons, he working at his desk or talking with teachers and students.

I understood that I was not to impose on his time or obtrude myself into his conversations with people who had come to talk with him. Like the three monkeys, I appeared to see not, hear not, and speak not, but I learned during the year many confidences which I was not privileged to reveal. Occasionally, Mr. Vaughan would discuss with me troublesome discipline cases that gave him special concern. It pleased me to observe that he always left room for offenders to save their self-esteem, keep their integrity intact, and think of themselves as essentially good people who had either made mistakes or been victimized. Careful not to confront one with an accusation or to attempt to refute what patently was untrue, he needled and probed with little questions that chipped at the base of the problem. Sometimes he would say that he would talk with others and then discuss the matter further with the offender the following day, or two or three days later. At the conclusion of the meetings, Mr. Vaughan usually had something good to say, preferring when such was available, to pass along some compliment or commendation from a teacher or a student leader. The effect seemed to be, usually, that the student in trouble left the office with the feeling that Mr. Vaughan was his friend and wanted to support him as far as circumstances would permit and that others thought better of him than he had suspected. It did not occur to me at the time that I was serving a useful internship in the handling of discipline in high school, simply by being present but behaving as if I were not there.

Then he would discuss the school paper with me occasionally, praising what he liked especially well and offering suggestions for improvement in writing, layout, and balance. Sometimes he would prepare me for writing editorials and reviews of the cultural events, which I wrote myself, and he would suggest the names of students in the junior and sophomore classes for me to meet and invite to write human interest stories, poetry, and short stories. A day or two before the Glee Club was to give its annual program, he handed me a copy of Walt Whitman's "I Heard America Singing" and suggested that I might like to use it as a model for writing an editorial about the program. I wrote "I Heard Louisa Singing" and endeared myself not only to the director but to the happy girls in the club as well. He knew how to make me feel so good about the paper that I never felt his suggestions for improving it were adverse criticism or that he had the slightest doubt about my capabilities as an editor.

The occasional conversations, some of them for two or three hours, we had during the year helped me with decisions I had to make as a high school senior. Once he explained to me what was involved in earning a master's degree, and after that, a Ph.D. degree. He took me by his home one afternoon to let me read his M.A. diploma and told me about his own plans for a Ph.D. He talked with me at length about possible resources available to me for a college education and assured me that he would keep me in mind should there be opportunities for academic scholarships, "workships," or student loans.

Then one day he turned in the swivel chair at the roll-top and handed me, unfolded, a letter from James L. Creech, president, Cumberland College, and asked me to read it. The letter promised a tuition scholarship, a work-ship with a value equivalent to the cost of room and board, and limited loan funds for the salutatorian or valedictorian whom he could recommend as a young person likely to succeed academically at the college and to the sound-ness of whose moral character he could attest. It had not occurred to me before that I might be either the valedictorian or the salutatorian, but he told me he had been checking senior records and that I had a very good chance of being one or the other. I asked for explanations of scholarships and what might be involved in workships in maintenance and care of the grounds. I would receive no money in hand for either, he explained, but my tuition would be free and the value of my work as perhaps a janitor for two or three hours a day and cutting grass or trimming hedges on Saturday mornings would be credited to my expenses for room and board. I would need some money of my own for books and supplies, clothing, pocket change, travel to and from the col-lege, perhaps a hundred dollars, he thought. I was not certain that my father would be able to help me, but since I felt that I might be able to borrow that much from my grandfather, I told him I would like to apply for admission to the school and to have him recommend me. He told me what I should say in my letter of application. He would read it and have me revise it if I needed to and send it along with his recommendation.

Cumberland College was a junior college, he said. I did not know what that meant. He explained that it was a two-year college at which one could complete the freshman and sophomore years and then transfer to a "senior" college, like Georgetown or the University of Kentucky, and complete his col-lege program. Cumberland College also had an academy which offered high school work, and both college and academy students lived in dormitories on the campus. I could qualify to teach by graduating from Cumberland, teach a while, save my salary, pay back what I owed Grandpa, and go on to the uni-versity if I chose to go there. And it was a good college with an excellent fac-ulty, he had heard. One of his classmates at Georgetown College, a Baptist preacher and teacher by the name of Buell Kazee, taught music at Cumber-land and enjoyed working there, he understood.

I took the materials and studied them carefully. Two or three days later I had prepared on a page of theme paper tentative answers to questions and written a letter of application. I had indicated that I might be able to bring with me to Cumberland College as much as $100 which I hoped to borrow from my grandfather. Mr. Vaughan went over the material carefully with me, offering suggestions for a few minor changes. After discussing with me work possibilities for the summer, my father's financial situation, my grand-father's potential as a financial resource, and my needs for clothing, he advised that I indicate that I might be able to supply as much as $200 toward meeting my total expenses, but might also need to borrow up to $50 from the college loan fund. I prepared the final copy of my application materials and gave them to Mr. Vaughan, who wrote a letter of endorsement for me and sent the materials on to President Creech.

A few days later, I received a letter of acceptance at Cumberland and a copy of the college catalog. I showed these to Mr. Vaughan, whose happiness for me supplied me with confidence, for I had not yet let my father know that I was applying for admission to college. Not long afterwards Mr. Vaughan told me that the faculty and the board of education had approved a plan for selecting an honor graduate to receive at the commencement exercises an 18-inch silver loving cup. The name of the recipient was not to be announced until commencement night. A committee of seniors was being appointed to develop guidelines for selecting nominations for the award. He invited me to be the chairman of the committee. We were to develop a list of qualifications for the honor graduate, get it approved by the entire senior class, and submit it to him. He would then invite the faculty to nominate at least three graduating seniors whose scholarship, character, school citizenship, and record of participation in extracurricular activities might qualify them for the award, which was to be a significant recognition of the person who most nearly exemplified the ideal student at the high school. The board of education would then select one of the three nominees for the award.

The committee and I met two or three times and developed a list of qualifications for the ideal graduate. We then met with the entire class for discussion, modification, and approval. Since our list included both musical accomplishment and participation in athletics, I felt that I was not likely to be one of the nominees for the award.

Mr. Vaughan accepted the list, studied it carefully, helped with rewriting it, and then asked that I publish it in the *Louisian*. Faculty members found occasion to refer in class to the selection of an honor graduate for commencement. Seniors, becoming interested, began to speculate as to who among us might best exemplify the ideal graduate. Names mentioned were of students with high scholarship records who had not only participated in the social activities of the school but were also good athletes or accomplished in music. No one included my name as one who might qualify. I did not feel excluded by the omission of my name, for it seemed to me that I did not qualify for the honor.

One day Mr. Vaughan asked me who in my opinion might best exemplify the ideal student. I mentioned Ward and Bill Patton, both good students, excellent athletes, and exemplary school citizens, who had walked in from the country to go to school, and Shirley DeBoard, whose name was always on the scholarship honor roll, who participated in musical activities, and who would almost certainly be the valedictorian at commencement. Since I had not included my own name, Mr. Vaughan asked why I did not consider myself eligible. I explained that I had not participated in athletics and music activities and felt that I was not eligible, but when he observed that I had been a good student, a leader in many important school activities, and a successful editor of the school paper, and that it would be difficult to find a student who met all of the qualifications, I began to think that I might not only be one of the nominees but also the recipient of the honor award.

Nothing more was said to me about the possibility of my being among the nominees. As discussion of the award became livelier among the seniors, and parents in town heard more about it, names of barely average students who had participated in school activities began to be mentioned as possible recipients. Two or three of these students had clusters of supporters who promoted their candidacy in discussions with teachers and other students. Sometimes Mr. Vaughan would ask me what I was hearing among students about the award. When I mentioned names to him, he would summarize briefly the special qualifications of each but declined to rule anybody out as a candidate on the basis of deficiencies.

Then one day Mr. Vaughan told me the faculty had met and selected the nominees, the board of education had selected the honor graduate, and the silver cup with appropriate lettering had been ordered, but no one would know who the recipient would be until the award was bestowed on commencement night.

When the seniors learned that the honor student had been selected, interest intensified. Teachers were questioned closely to see whether they might reveal who the nominees had been. Parents of aspirants quizzed board members, one or two finding enough encouragement to speculate among friends and kinfolk that they were fairly certain who the recipient was to be. Mr. Vaughan and the members of the faculty kept straight faces and tight upper lips, but when Mr. Vaughan bore in on me rather intensely a week before commencement about the progress I was making in preparing my salutatory — for Shirley DeBoard had indeed become the valedictorian — and expressed a special interest in whether my parents and my sister might be able to come from Caines Creek, 25 miles away, to attend commencement exercises, I began to entertain the possibility that I had been selected.

Two days before commencement Mrs. Marcella Wilson, in whose home I shared a room with her son Garland, a member of the graduating class, called me aside for a confidential conversation in her porch swing. She had found out from a friend who had talked confidentially with a member of the board of education that I had been selected as the honor graduate. It was a deep, dark secret that I was to keep. She had not told anyone except me and did not intend to reveal the secret to another living soul. I was stunned. I did not doubt the truth of what Mrs. Wilson said, whose great joy, she declared, was that she could be the first to let me know, but I felt that the knowledge was a burden of guilt to me. I was grateful to her, but wished also that she had kept her secret. Now the honor could not come as the surprise it was meant to be. Not privileged to reveal Mrs. Wilson's secret, I was now constrained to act as if all that was to happen was a surprise. I was bound to practice duplicity, to pretend, to polish my skills in hypocrisy. I was to cultivate an appearance of stony-faced innocence in the presence of those who would speculate as to who the recipient of the award was to be. Bitterest of all, I could not let Mr. Vaughan know that I knew or let a shift in my glance, a faltering of my voice, a pause in my discourse raise the slightest suspicion that I had learned the secret.

Deeply pained and shocked, I did not sleep well, but I kept the secret while talking with Mr. Vaughan and watching him enjoy what he considered a triumph in the confidence and faith that led to an overwhelming surprise. He was pleased that my salutatory address was well prepared and that my father would be present to see me graduate.

The loving cup, awarded to Cratis Williams as honor student of his high school graduating class.

When time came in the commencement program to present the honor student award, the overflowing crowd was hushed and expectant as Mr. Vaughan took his position at the podium, beside which the gleaming cup on an ebony base rested on a small table covered with black velvet. Mr. Vaughan talked of school spirit, loyalty, sound character, scholarship, citizenship, dependability, leadership, and of how the ideal student would exemplify all of these qualities. He reviewed the procedures followed for selecting the honor student. Then he began to identify the characteristics of the recipient, broad generalizations at first but becoming more specific as he proceeded. Before the time that he was ready to conclude his presentation with the announcement of my name, I was aware of his reviewing my own credentials and began to observe the looks of recognition in the faces of the hundreds present. That was the moment of crisis for me, for it was then, I thought, that I should appear to be most surprised and uncontrollably happy. I was happy, indeed, and filled with emotion but there was also the taint of deception in my behavior. I wished so much that I had not been "tipped off" by Mrs. Wilson, who was my good friend whom I loved and whose smiling but tearful eyes stabbed at me as she listened intently to what Mr. Vaughan was saying.

With the announcement of my name, a great round of applause filled the auditorium, punctuated here and there with shrill whistles of some of my admirers. As I proceeded from my seat on the stage to the podium to receive the award, I noted that Mr. Vaughan was rocking on his feet and that his head doddered slightly from side to side as I had observed the first time I ever saw him before the students in the confused study hall my first day in high school nearly four years earlier. His eyes were moist and his handshake was firm. After I had accepted the beautiful trophy, he hugged me as the crowd sent up another round of applause. As I became somewhat ashamed of my flood of tears, I was comforted by noting that the women teachers and the senior girls were also weeping. While returning to my seat, I felt that Mr. Vaughan's regard for me was deeper than that of a teacher for his student, that he loved me as a father loves a son.

"Why a Mountain Boy Should Be Proud"[2]
by Cratis Williams, Editor
The Louisian (Louisa High School)
December 1927

In the Kentucky mountains, there lingers, even in these days of the twentieth century, folklore and customs dating and pointing to the Elizabethan days as the period of their origin.

It is the nature of the mountaineer to sing of the deeds of one of his fellow men; to be sincere in the strongest meaning of the word; and to retain the patriarchal type of family life–not because he is backward or non-progressive but because he is not polluted with the blood of a hundred nationalities and because there is preserved in his veins the nature of his ancestors— the Celts and the Anglo-Saxons.

Only in the rustic simpleness of the mountaineer's home is the strong faith of the Puritan preserved and the equality basis of mankind observed in its full meaning. The unit society of the mountaineer is the strongest form of equality and democracy. Only in the mountains do the fortunate think themselves equal to the unfortunate–only in the mountains is there a total absence of class distinction–only in the mountains does the wealthier man's son feel himself justified in taking his mother's hired maid-servant for a bride! In the mountaineer's life hypocrisy finds no place–he is either an honest-to-the-people sinner or in strong adherence to the Word of Truth.

In the purity of the mountain type rests the true American family life. In the mountaineer's lowly hut, home life is the sweetest and brotherly affections are strongest. Mountaineer parents are more devoted to their children than any parents. It is not the desire of the mountaineer to scale the heights of popularity but his life is wrapped up in his children that they may make the best in life.

The mother of the mountain boy takes more pride in her muscular, stalwart son than the mother of any other boy. She coaches him to be noble, brave, sincere, loving, and humble in her singing of some folk ballad or sweet old religious hymn scorned by outsiders. But why need we care for their scorn? Do we not get that dialect nobly? Yes, it was handed to us by Shakespeare, Bunyan, and King James' Bible students. Is that not a loftier origin than the African Negro or the trashy immigrant?

Now, that the mountain boy sees the nobility of the mountaineer, that he sees the purity of his race, and the beauty and wonder of his heritage may he take advantage of his disposition and sing, with pride, patriotism and democracy of the mountains.

Salutatorian Address
Louisa High School Commencement
May 25, 1928[3]

It is my great pleasure and privilege, tonight, as the salutatorian of my class, to welcome you to the celebration of the commencement of our lives in the world.

We are commencing that part of life that follows high school life. School life is closed with some of us while Life's school is ushered in to all of us. We are now prepared to persue [sic] the career allotted to us by Divinity. We are stepping out upon the great stage of life as inexperienced actors— yes, upon the stage trodden by the myriad-minded Shakespeare, the poetic Spenser, the "Rare Ben Johnson [sic]," the phylosophical [sic] Socrates, the oratorical Demosthenes and Webster, the scientific Edison, the historical Alexander, Alfred, Washington, and Bonaparte, the daring Christopher Columbus and Charles A. Lindbergh.

As we face the inevitable hour when we must step forth upon the Great

Stage of Life prepared for the drama that each of us is to present, it is natural that we should look back over the great drama that has already been presented and wonder just what sort of a part has been designed for our attention. And as we cast our glances backward, we are appalled by the magestic [*sic*] splendor of the scenes that have been presented. Indeed, of all the masterpieces of comedy and tragedy that the pens of all the great world dramatists ever put on paper, was there ever anything more thrilling than the histories of great nations and their leaders as they came on the stage of action, played their parts and then "went the way of all humanity" leaving the stage clear for the next players— the Senior class of 1928.

From the beginning of all true thought, the providence of God has been the most beautiful and the most sublime of all life's mysteries. The

Cratis Williams, 1929, at 18 years old.

scholarship of the world has fathomed great depths of knowledge; the philosophers of the ages have handed down to us many grand and deep thoughts; poets have touched the chords of our hearts with their songs of mystic power and revaling [*sic*] truth; but no human mind has ever yet been able to form any adequate conception of the marvelous dispensations of the divine control.

Providence has indeed been grateful to us, that He has bestowed upon us the privilege of attending a high school like ours which has induced us to delve into the treasures of history and search out the good in decayed civilizations, in literature, religion, scientific theories, and wars that we may adopt the good and profit from the bad that we find in them. We are intoxicated with pride in that we are numbered in the privileged few who have taken advantage of the opportunities offered them and who have reached the top of high school on the road to knowledge and fame.

With us thus far, life has been a rose-strewn pathway, a gently flowing Afton, as compared with the great life which we are taking up tonight. We realize that we have persued [*sic*] our course diligently thus far because the

Cratis Williams at 18, in 1929.

occasion of the night designates that end. We also have a full realization that nothing is attained without work.

We bitterly lament that the current of Life will not flow so smoothly with us in the world as it has in our high school days. Is there a picture anywhere more pleasing and more consoling to us than one of high school life? A picture of youthful innocence, or admirable companionship? A picture of a place where smooth-cheeked boys gaze into the laughing eyes of pure and innocent young ladies; where careing [sic] teachers greet you with a tender smile and where we prepare ourselves for future life. Had I the painter's touch of Michael Angelo [sic] and Rapheal [sic], the silver tongue of Demosthenes and Webster, the literary ability of Homer and Shakespeare, I could not present a picture more consoling than a picture of innocent school life! We bitterly lament that we have to give up these pleasures, yet our cup bubbles over with delight in that we have chosen the right course.

Doubtless all of us have also eaten the bitter fruit of ignorance and toil and manuel [sic] labor, otherwise we would not have chosen the course we have followed. We are aware of the fact that from time to time the world has frowned on us and that we have had no little difference in climbing this far on the road to success.

But there are many times in every lifetime when everything seems dark and disheartening. Even as young as we are, we have had our glimpses of this universal experience of mankind in our existence. Even in our preparatory days we have learned the meaning of disappointment and sorrow — to some degree, at least — from the human standpoint, and have seen times when it was hard for us to look up to the stars in the melancholic solitude of eventide and feel perfectly sure that "all's right with the world."

But understanding that this is an inevitable function of human life, we are indeed glad to feel that we are a necessary part of the divine plan of creation, that everyone of us, no matter how humble of origin or meek of spirit, is placed upon this earth in our own particular spheres for a definite purpose with an individual mission that no one but ourselves can perform — that the Great Omnipotent holds our destinies in the hollow of his hands, and shapes our paths according to his own all-wise, all-powerful conception. When we once grasp the magnitude of this great truth we will understand how true it is that no matter what comes to us as individuals, as a class, as a school, as a community, or as a nation, still the magnificent glory of God triumphs on High.

Be ready then, dear friends, to applaud our worthy efforts and encourage us on to each approaching climax, as we welcome you to the celebration of the commencement of our lives. Again I welcome you, and yet not I, but the class of 1928 who is speaking through me.

NOTES

1. Adapted from Cratis Williams, 1985. *William H. Vaughan: A Better Man Than I Ever Wanted to Be.* Appalachian Development Center, Morehead State University, Morehead, Ky. Second Edition, 15–27. Used by permission.

2. This is the first evidence of Cratis Williams's development of the theme of the Celtic ancestry of Appalachian mountain people, a theme that he would pursue for the rest of his life. He was writing during a time of considerable xenophobia and debate concerning immigration; that xenophobia is reflected in this essay, but it was a view which he soon abandoned.

3. The *Big Sandy News* did not publish the speeches given on commencement night, May 25, 1928, but Cratis Williams kept a newsprint clipping of his salutatorian address from that night. The clipping was probably from the *Louisian*, but the issue could not be located, thus, the source of the clipping cannot be confirmed. There is little doubt, however, about the authenticity of the speech itself.

Chapter Six

Moving on to College
and the "Big World" …
and Beginning to Look Back

Through the help of William H. Vaughan, I was awarded a tuition scholarship and a "workship" by Cumberland College at Williamsburg, Kentucky,
which I attended for my first year of college in 1928-1929. During this year,
I took courses needed to qualify at the end of the year for a certificate to
teach in elementary schools. My father asked Arb Gambill, the local trustee
of the Boggs School on Caines Creek, whether he would recommend me to
teach the school for 1929-1930. Arb, even though recognizing that I was only
eighteen years old and small for my age, agreed to recommend me. Ora Boggs,
who had taught the school for three years, did not want to continue. My father
wrote to tell me that I had a school for the next year.

Knowing that I had a job for the following year stimulated my interest
in the education courses that I had been permitted to include as an extra load
to add up a total of 36 semester hours for the year. Professor A.R. Evans' course
in classroom management, geared specifically to the needs of one-room
teachers in the mountains, became one of my most exciting courses. Even
Mr. Creech's course in arithmetic and how to teach it generated so much
enthusiasm that I overcame my feeling of inadequacy in mathematics and
made an A in the course.

After a year at Cumberland, I became a one-room school teacher at the
Boggs School on Caines Creek in 1929. It was possible for me to teach the
school, which would begin the last Monday in July and end the first week in
February, and return to college for the second semester and the first summer

term. I continued my college education in this manner at the University of Kentucky, receiving the A.B. degree in June 1933.[1]

Taking Thanksgiving at Big Creek

During my year at Cumberland College, one of my friends, Herbert Marcum, Jr., invited me to go home with him for the Thanksgiving break. We sat together in the afternoon study hall, and when we found Miss Bess Rose, the supervisor, engrossed in student themes she read during that hour, we engaged in whispered conversations about the plans for the visit and some of the things we might do if the weather was favorable.

Herbert lived near Big Creek in Clay County. Big Creek was a little mountain village on the Red Bird River near where Horse Creek flowed into it. Herbert Marcum's home was on a low point at the mouth of Horse Creek, but his grandfather, Grover Cleveland Marcum, lived in the little town itself about a mile away. We would visit his home. The only thing discouraging about visiting Big Creek was that it was cut off and had only mud roads and trails leading into it. We would have to ride horses from Garrard, where we would get off the train that went on to Manchester, across the mountain and down Horse Creek to his father's home. If I would agree to go, he would write home and ask that an extra horse be brought by whoever was to meet us at Garrard. It would take all night for us to get to Garrard by railroad train, but on the way back we could make good connections and arrive in Williamsburg Sunday night.

The only thing, it might rain, and if that should happen, we might have to spend the whole holiday season at his father's home at the mouth of Horse Creek. I should take my yellow slicker along, as well as my overcoat. Whoever would meet us with horses would bring oilskin riding coats if it looked rainy. We would not have any trouble getting from Garrard to his father's home, even if it rained every step of the way, but if the Red Bird River should happen to rise we could not get to Big Creek at all, for the only way to cross the river when it was up was by a swinging bridge for walkers and that was no help when the valley flooded. One could not get to the bridge, even, when it flooded.

But we would still have fun. His mother, who had gone to Sue Bennett Academy in London, where she had studied art and learned how to paint pretty pictures, was one of the finest cooks around. There was also a houseful of brothers and sisters who were a lot of fun. Sometimes they capped popcorn as they sat around the fireplace in the dining room on cold nights, or made popcorn balls, or boiled taffy. His father and mother also had a hired girl and a hired man to help with the work around the house and barn. They liked to pick banjos and guitars and sing love songs in the kitchen after supper, when all of the dishes and pots and pans had been washed and put away and the kitchen tidied up.

I decided to accept Herbert's invitation and wrote to my parents that I would be going home with one of my classmates for the Thanksgiving holidays. He wrote to inform his mother that he would be bringing home a guest and that an extra horse should be sent to the station at Garrard, where we would arrive on the morning train on Thanksgiving Day.

At the college we had our Thanksgiving program in the dining hall on Tuesday night because most of the students would be leaving as soon as their classes were over on Wednesday. Herbert and I went carefully into the details of our travel plans. Since we would be traveling on horseback, we decided that traveling bags would be troublesome and that we should take nothing along except what we could carry in the pockets of our coats. Also, we would be walking a great deal and might even want to go rabbit hunting, so I should wear old shoes and old pants. He could find old clothes at home, but if we should decide to go into the fields and woods I could wear over my pants an old pair of overalls that could be found at his father's home, though I might have to roll the legs up considerably.

After classes Wednesday I hurried to the dormitory where I changed shoes and pants and put an extra pair of socks, extra handkerchiefs, and a toothbrush and a small tube of toothpaste in my raincoat pocket, bundled the raincoat and tied a cord around it. I was ready to go.

We walked down to the bus station and bought tickets to Corbin. The bus was crowded with students, many of whom lived along Highway 25 and commuted to the college daily, but we found seats. When the bus stopped along the way, I watched students walk toward their homes and tried to remember who they were. Mary Jones got off at Rockholds, as did my desk partner in the chemistry laboratory, Maude Creekmore.

The railroad depot in Corbin was next door to the bus station. We went in and checked schedules and bought tickets to Barbourville for the latest train that night, for the train to Manchester would not leave Barbourville until the following morning. Then we explored the town, walking as far north as the campus of a Catholic school that stood on a hill. We looked into shop windows, walked down side streets, explored lumber yards near the railroad tracks, wandered back to the bus station, and finally ate a hamburger and a piece of pie at a little restaurant nearby. We sat in the bus station for a while and then went to the railroad station and sat. Some quiet college girls whose faces we recognized were sitting in the station, but we did not know them very well and did not seek conversations with them. Herbert was shy in the presence of girls, anyway, and I did not suggest that we cultivate their acquaintance.

It must have been 9:30 or 10:00 o'clock before we boarded the train to Barbourville. The coach was not crowded, but a few mountain men dressed in clean overalls and shirts and wearing blue serge coats and black hats were already seated, some of them relaxed in their seats and smelling of moonshine whiskey. They were sitting quietly and seemed not inclined to engage in conversations with one another. The girls who had been waiting in the station also came into the coach and sat silently together. Apparently they were country girls or daughters of miners who lived in little camp towns on up the river in Bell County or Harlan. Herbert and I found seats together and sat silently as the train moved out of the station.

After the conductor came through and collected tickets, lights were turned off and many of the mountain men went to sleep. We watched the rows of street lights describe circles as the train moved around curves and into the darkness. The trip to Barbourville seemed to take a long time, although we might have arrived by 11 o'clock.

Several passengers, including some of the men in blue serge coats and black hats and two or three of the college girls, got off at Barbourville with us. Many of them went into the depot, where people were sitting in the half-lighted waiting room and nodding in their seats. We found seats next to each other, slumped down in them, and tried to sleep, but we merely napped occasionally.

When morning came we found a little restaurant and had egg sandwiches and coffee for breakfast. It might have been 7:30 when we boarded the little two-coach train to Manchester. The coach was crowded at first and we stood up in the aisle, but people got off at little stations scattered along the wide valley of Goose Creek, and we were able at first to get seats separately and finally together. There was much conversation at first, and then a strange quiet again with only a few conversations in low voices. People had immobile, unanimated faces, and the men in black hats and blue coats, still smelling of moonshine whiskey, were slumped together at the back end of the car. Herbert told me in a low voice, and almost whispering at times, that a battle between the Bakers and Howards, of Manchester, who had feuded for many years, had broken out in that coach only a short time before. He called my attention to several bullet holes in the walls of the coach.

From time to time I looked out the windows at the farmhouses in the valley and the humble little homes strung along the lower sides of hills. Once, when the train stopped near the foot of a steep hill, I saw a little weathered house at the end of a steep road up to it. The porch was already filled with men and boys sitting in cane-bottom chairs and on the floor, their feet dangling off the high porch and swinging rhythmically as they peered at the train. Dogs lay on the porch among the boys and looked at the train, too, their heads postured in quiet dignity. A stooped older woman with a bucket in each hand was climbing the hill. The buckets seemed from her bent position to be full of water. She must have preferred going to the spring for water herself to asking one of her sons to fetch it for her. Smoke rose in dark billows from the two chimneys of the little house. I fancied that one might have smelled the side meat frying on the kitchen stove if the windows of the coach had been open.

The little train started again, but it stopped briefly at many whistle stops, where people got off and others got on, before we arrived about 8:30 at Garrard, a little village on the bank of a small river that had tall trees beside it, many of them shedding leaves that morning. We went into a general store with a high front porch below which a muddy road hugged the steep bank of the river, moving sluggishly, its dark water covered with fleets of cupping sycamore leaves sailing slowly downstream.

The general store, which had a clean oiled floor, was warm and comfortable with the usual pot-bellied stove in the center and a few kegs and wooden boxes scattered about for the accommodation of those who might want to sit and swap yarns. Only the merchant was there, though. Herbert asked whether any of his relatives from Big Creek had been in yet. The merchant did not remember that anybody from outside the local community had been in that morning. Herbert explained that some of his relatives were to meet us there with horses, and we sat on boxes near the stove to wait. The merchant took little notice of us. Only two or three children came for purchases while we waited, Herbert jumping up from time to time and looking up the road to see whether some of his relatives were in sight.

About 9 o'clock, as he stood in the door, his face brightened as he announced that he saw them coming, Grandpa and his little brother. Grandpa was leading a horse, all saddled and ready, for me. Herbert would ride the other horse and the little brother would ride behind him on the blanket that had already been spread for him. Soon they rode up, dismounted, and hitched the horses to the rack, even though Herbert and I were on the porch and ready to depart.

I was presented to them. Grandpa Cleve Marcum was a big man, given to corpulence, with a fine face and a huge black mustache with ends that came down past his mouth. He wore a well-blocked black hat with a narrow band and a broad brim, a dark coat unbuttoned and open, a white shirt that hugged the expanse of his ample belly, and a little black string bow tie like southern planters and Kentucky colonels wore. His sturdy jeans were stuffed into leather boots on which spurs were fastened. Herbert's little brother, with an open, frank smile and some tufts of hair curling above the edge of his cap, was dressed in clean overalls and a denim jacket.

I shook hands with them ceremoniously and they were glad that I had come for a visit. Then they turned their attention to Herbert, of whom the grandfather was proud, because he was going to college, and whom the little brother admired because he was the big boy in the family, had been out in the world already, and was back home for a visit.

Mr. Marcum then went for a brief exchange of conversation with the merchant, while we admired the horses. When he came out of the store, I was invited to mount the horse that had been led. The stirrups hung too low for me. Mr. Marcum adjusted the straps so I could rest my feet in the stirrups comfortably. Everybody mounted, we started.

The road to Horse Creek, which turned off the muddy road along the river bank perhaps a half-mile from the store, was little more than a rutted and rocky trail that rose steeply along the face of a hill and then wound toward a gap in the mountains. Our horses struggled up the point but were able to strike gaits as we reached the level stretches around the mountain and toward the gap. It was a cloudy day, but the clouds were light and high and did not promise rain right away. Visibility was clear, but the gray hills covered with patches of broomsage in the brown pastures and dark forests that clung to the steeps and ran down the ridge lines were depressing. One could see little houses, many of them made of gray and weathered boards and battens and others of dark logs chinked with red mud and all with black shake roofs, strung along up hollows and ravines and in flats near the heads of hollows.

Smoke was rising from the chimneys of the houses, mostly blue wood smoke. I could imagine that something special was being prepared for Thanksgiving dinner in many of them, a rabbit hunted down in a broomsage patch, a 'possum caught the night before and now roasting behind a bank of sweet potatoes, a chicken that had been favored at feeding time for the last two or three weeks. Some had no doubt butchered a hog early in order to feast on spareribs and tenderloin balanced with soup beans and kraut but complemented with biscuits and gravy made rich with the drippings from fried fresh pork. Persimmon pies, apple cobblers, cakes layered with crab apple jelly, gingerbread, thick and waxy with sorghum molasses, no doubt waited in many a corner safe as surprises for those who might save room for them at the end of the feast. From the gap in the mountain we could see from one side far down the valley up which the little train had come the prosperous looking farms with white houses and big barns. Manchester lay only a few miles to our left. We could see smoke lying along the hilltops in that direction. Before us was the valley of Horse Creek, the narrow little trail to it lying partly in the rocky bed of a branch ahead of us with rail fences snaking along on either side of it. Two or three miles ahead the valley curved out of sight, but far beyond rose a gray ridge which Herbert said was on the other side of the Red River probably seven miles away. He lived this side of the river at the foot of that ridge, and Grandpa Marcum lived just beyond the left end of it on the other side of the river.

The horses moved slowly down the steep trail, their hooves making suck-ing sounds as they pulled them from wet yellow clay or knocking sounds as they struck the flint-like boulders that lay in the bed of the stream. As the horses stalked along cautiously, our saddles moved toward their shoulders and we braced ourselves against the saddle horns to keep from pitching for-ward.

As soon as we reached the foot of the hill we began to see little, long, win-dowless cabins made of round poles and chinked with mud. Very few had porches. Some had chimneys between the two rooms, some a fieldstone and mud chimney at either end, and most a fieldstone chimney at one end only. Doors of the cabins were open, and people stood in doorways or sat on crude benches against the walls while children and dogs romped about the litter-strewn yards, some with paling fences made from weathered slats that had been riven from cuts from knotless sections of pine trees, but most with no pretense of an enclosure. Little patches of gardens, enclosed with slat paling fences, had mounds from which the roots of buried cabbages protruded and hillocks in which potatoes and apples were buried. Well gums with sweeps from which poles with cedar buckets dangling at the end swung or with pul-ley wheels hanging from arches above them stood in most yards, but people living in the little houses in the flats up the mountainsides carried their water from springs in the draws close by, some of which were covered with little log houses looking much like those in which people lived. A woodpile or a heap of coal stood near each cabin. Few had coal houses or woodsheds.

As we rode down the valley it appeared to become more heavily popu-lated, but the quality of the housing was consistent, except for one lime-washed house, made of boards and battens, covered with a metal roof, equipped with an outside chimney of squared stones, and having glass windows with green frames. It stood at the fork of a creek and appeared to have been there longer than the log cabins.

The valley belonged to a timber company that had taken out the valu-able trees several years earlier. Those who lived in the little cabins were squatters, many of whom had come to work in the timber and had stayed on after the timber was gone.

Horse Creek was a valley of very poor people. Occasionally we met peo-ple along the trail. They did not look hungry, but they were poorly dressed and their faces were streaked with dirt and soot. Many were wearing odd assortments of clothing, including articles worn by soldiers in World War I, Norfolk jackets of tweed, tuxedo jackets worn with patched overalls, stiff with grime, swallowtail coats, and the like. The articles of clothing had been bought at secondhand stores or from hucksters who drove wagons up the valley in good weather from Big Creek. Some families received free clothing from mission schools in the region.

I do not recall having seen either a church or a school in the valley, but people appeared to be social. At the end of a little cabin in a flat above the trail several men were butchering a hog, which had been scraped and was swinging headless from a derrick as we passed. Women sat on the benches against the wall of the cabin and children of all ages were playing in the yard. They were all occupied with one another and took little or no note of our passing.

The road down Horse Creek continued in the creek bed until we reached a place at which the creek appeared to be entering a gorge. At that point, it climbed in a rutted red clay bed toward a low gap. After we had gained elevation, the road wound around a low hill that was covered with broomsage and on toward the black roof of a white farmhouse, to the right of which was a cluster of farm buildings. Herbert said that we were almost home.

Soon we were there. Grandpa Marcum insisted that we come down to see him before we returned to college on Sunday. We climbed down from our horses, which Mr. Marcum and the little brother took toward the barn. The Marcum home, though an old-time house, was a proud one that stood on a hill overlooking the Red Bird River Valley, although it faced the trail through Horse Creek valley.

When we went into the house, Herbert's mother and three or four younger brothers and sisters came to meet us in the unheated "front room," which doubled as a reception room and a guest bedroom, but there was a fireplace in it with a finely worked mantel above which was one of his mother's paintings and before which there was a screen with her decorations on it.

We all went into the large dining room reached by descending three or four steps from the front room. A cozy fire flickered on the hearth. A long table with chairs by it stood near a window. Cane-bottom straight chairs and rocking chairs with cushions and doilies hanging over the backs were arranged about the fireplace. The room had a high ceiling. More of Mrs. Marcum's paintings decorated the walls. Hunger-rousing odors came from the kitchen where the hired girl was rattling pots and pans. We sat by the hearth while Mrs. Marcum, who had not shown emotions or offered herself to be embraced by her son, inquired about his health and his progress at college. The younger brothers and sisters were smiling and attentive. Herbert gave glowing reports of his progress academically and of the friendships he had made among the boys in Felix Hall, but expressed his disappointment in the quality and quantity of food served in the dining hall at college.

Mrs. Marcum explained that the "big dinner" for Thanksgiving would be served in the evening because her husband, Herbert, Sr., was on a trip and would not be back until suppertime. We should "wash up" and get ready, for the hired girl would soon have something ready for us to eat.

We walked through the kitchen, warm and steamy and filled with good odors, to the back porch to wash our hands and face in the basin that sat on a bench between two porch posts. Herbert took the basin into the kitchen and brought it back with steaming water in it, which he tempered with cold water from the bucket sitting on the bench.

While preparations were being made, I noticed that a big garden stretched along the top of the low ridge below the porch and that there were grapevines on racks, fruit trees, and walnut trees growing in the space between the edge of the porch and the garden itself. Chickens were pecking about in the grape arbor. To the right, white shoats were standing near a feeding trough.

What appeared to be ancient roads around the hillside beyond the garden were covered with short green grass that looked like bluegrass. Herbert explained that the place had been a slave farm before the Civil War and that slave cabins had once stood on either side of the grassy road. Some of them had been preserved at the other end, now in the barn lot, for use. One was a wool house, another a storage room for tools, another for odds and ends. The slaves had been raised there and taken down the river to New Orleans to the market when they were big enough to bring a good price, but following the war freed Negroes had left the mountains. He did not know where they had gone. There had also been salt springs not far away at which people had boiled water for salt since pioneer days. The springs had been very important during the Civil War.

The view from the porch swept across a bend in the Red River. The hollow place in the mountains a mile down the river was where Big Creek joined it. The trail on the other side of it to our right led a few miles upstream to Beverly, where the Red Bird Settlement School was located. We could not see it from there, but just out of sight to the right was one of the stations of the Mary Breckenridge Nursing Service. If the weather was good, we might walk up there on our way to his grandfather's home in Big Creek. It would not be far out of our way.

We wet our hands and soaped them with an oval cake of soap that lay in a dish on the bench. We then washed and dried on a sack towel with twin red stripes down either edge of it, combed our hair before a mirror on the wall, and went back to the dining room. Soon the hired man, whose first name was Shirley, came in from the barn lot. He went into the porch, washed and combed, and came back to sit with us. The pleasant hired girl, flushed by the heat from the cook stove and her eyes beaming at Shirley, came in with bowls of food, a pane of steaming cornbread, and pitchers of milk, which she placed on the table, already set for guests. We found places and ate a "light meal" of side meat, fried potatoes, leatherbritchy beans, cornbread, and tumblers of cold milk, followed by apple pie.

After the meal, we sat by the fireplace again, Shirley along with us, for a half-hour. Then we went on a tour of the grounds. The road went through the barnlot. Bars lay beside posts for easy use when it was necessary to close the barnlot for retaining cattle that might be left to roam in the lot rather than confined to their stalls. The barn was built against a hillside, and part of the loft had not been boxed in, the opening left for ventilation and for ease in pitching down hay and fodder for scattering on the ground in the wintertime. The loft was filled with hay and much of the corn fodder had already been brought in. The saddle room below had an assortment of harnesses, bridles, saddles, and riding equipment in it.

Among the field machines parked here and there in the lot were a rusting mower, an ancient hay rake, a disc harrow, and a tooth harrow. A farm wagon stood in a special shed, and wheels and abandoned parts leaned against the wall. Plows were arranged along the wall beyond the wagon.

In addition to the big barn there were little buildings for special purposes: a hog house, a sheep barn, a chicken house, a corncrib with strap walls through which piles of corn gleamed.

But there were not many animals around. Two or three fat hogs were in the house, oblivious of their destiny as they grunted for attention. Shoats roamed freely in the lot. Chickens stood around in little flocks, shepherded by proud high-headed roosters that looked at us with quick jerks of their heads as their wattles shook. The hens busied themselves with their exploration for food on the ground around them, stopping from time to time to scratch the earth vigorously, and then searching carefully for any nuggets they might have turned up. After we had passed a flock, the rooster would crow triumphantly, lower his wing, and cluck lovingly as he circled the hen that engaged his interest most appealingly at the moment. Other hens, taking no note of their lord and master and exhibiting no signs of jealousy as he engaged in his love dance, concentrated their energy and attention on their search for food in the litter-strewn earth.

The younger brothers had special things they wanted to do. After a while Herbert and I were touring alone. He invited me to climb with him to the top of the hill behind the barn. After we were in the woods, he produced a pistol and a small box of cartridges. His mother and father did not know he owned the pistol, which he had bought at a bargain price from one of the fellows back at college for $5.00 because he needed money. We could try it out, and then, if I didn't mind, he would like for me to carry it until we were ready to go back to Williamsburg on Sunday. If any questions were asked, he would say that I had a pistol.

Herbert carved a small circle on the trunk of a white oak tree. We stepped back ten paces and took turns shooting one round of cartridges, walking up to measure our success after each shot. Neither of us was a marksman. The dogs, which had ignored us as we had made our tour of the barnlot, came to us after hearing the discharges of the pistol. Herbert then gave me the empty pistol, which I concealed in my inside coat pocket. It was the second and last time I have ever carried a concealed weapon. We then went on to the top of the steep hill, from which we could see in the valley and across the river the pretty little Swiss-like cabin that was used as the station by the Breckenridge Nursing Service.

The clouds were getting dark and the landscape began to look gray and depressing, punctuated here and there with scrub pines. We made our way back to the house, arriving only a short time before a light rain began to fall. We lounged on the porch for a while and watched the chickens go for shelter, a sign, we thought that the shower might not last long. The rain brought cool air. Soon we went to the dining room and sat before the low fire that smoldered lazily on the hearth. The sisters were already there, but the little brothers had found something at the barn that engaged their attention. Mrs. Marcum and the hired girl were preparing the Thanksgiving dinner in the kitchen.

Herbert, Sr., arrived about 6 o'clock. He was wearing a heavy gray overcoat and a battered gray hat with a caved in crown and a broad brim. He had not taken an oilskin riding coat with him, so he was damp. Herbert presented me to his father, who merely acknowledged me as he punched up the fire with a poker, and took a chair close to the hearth. I thought I smelled moonshine whiskey on him. He sat looking into the fire as he spread himself to dry his damp pants before it. He said very little and took no notice of what was going on around him or of the conversation, which proceeded as if he were not present.

Soon we were invited to prepare for supper. Plates were already set and dishes of relishes, pickled cucumbers and beets, and bowls of jelly and jam were in place. After washing our hands and faces and arranging our hair, we took seats at the long table. The little daughters helped to bring the food from the kitchen: chicken and dumplings, gravy, mashed potatoes, baked sweet potatoes, green beans seasoned with side meat, boiled cabbage, pickled corn, a platter of biscuits, pitchers of milk. Herbert sat at the head of the table and his mother at the end near the kitchen. All of us, including the hired girl and the hired man, found places at the table.

No blessing was asked. Food was passed from person to person around the table. Conversation was lively, but Mr. Marcum ate in silence, although he was attentive to what was being said. Mrs. Marcum urged that we have more of this and that and asked that we pass our glasses up for more milk. After a while, she advised that we save room for the cobbler and when she thought we were ready, the hired girl brought in a white bowl of huckleberry cobbler, which was passed around, each dipping from it and putting on the plate from which he had eaten as much as he wanted. Then a pitcher of dip was passed and each poured from it enough to cover his portion of cobbler. After a time, people began to leave the table without ceremony and find seats around the fireplace. We had eaten a sumptuous Thanksgiving dinner of the kind that was traditional in the mountains. Except that my mother and sisters would have stood to serve, the dinner was essentially what I might have had in my own home had I been there.

Talk around the fire following the supper was desultory. The big meal, the loss of sleep the night before, a warm fire, and the cold rain falling outside made Herbert and me sleepy. Mr. Marcum began soon to nod in his rocking chair. He roused from a snore once and took off his boots. Then, leaning back in his chair and with the bottoms of his feet turned toward the fire, he went to sleep. The smaller brothers and Shirley stared at the flames dancing on the logs. In the meantime, Mrs. Marcum, the hired girl, and the daughters were working in the kitchen, laughing and rattling dishes, cutlery, and pots and pans.

The dishes cleared away and the kitchen readied for the next day, Mrs. Marcum returned to the dining room. Seeing us drowsy and lazy, she suggested that since we had not slept much the night before we might like to go to bed soon. I would sleep in the guest room. She would put an extra quilt at the foot of the bed in case it should turn cold during the night. The girls came and sat for a while, but they, too, became quiet and lazy. By 8:30 or 9 o'clock we began to get up and leave for bed. Nobody said good night, simply, "I'm going to bed."

Herbert and I went into the guest room, where a lighted kerosene lamp stood among pictures of relatives in upright frames on a standtable. A chair was placed for me to lay my clothing on. Then we went outside for a few minutes. If it should become necessary for me to get up during the night, I could step around the corner of the house to the outside chimney. The temperature had dropped several degrees since we had been outside before supper. The wind had come up and the light rain was blowing into the porch. Herbert took leave of me and went to another part of the house to sleep in the bed that had been his since he could remember.

The guest room was cold. I shivered as I removed my clothing down to my BVD's and laid it piece by piece in the chair. I blew out the light and climbed between the cold sheets, which bore the sour odor of homemade soap. My teeth chattered while I waited for enough warmth to become collected for me to straighten out into a comfortable position on the fat featherbed. Having pulled the covers up to my chin, I was soon lulled to sleep by the sound of the guitar that one of the hired hands was playing beside the kitchen stove two doors away. Occasionally I was aware of indistinct conversation and Shirley's low singing in a mournful mood of the "Prisoner's Song." A soulful handling of "I'm Tired of Living Alone" was followed by the hired girl's low laughter. But I slept well and did not need to get up to go to the chimney corner all night long.

I was awakened after daylight Friday morning by the rattle of the fire-shovel against the bucket as Shirley removed ashes from the fireplace in the dining room. Between dozes I could hear the wood popping in the fire he had made and was aware of increasing activity in the house as people clomped on the steps that descended from the hallway directly into the dining room. Continuing to doze intermittently amid the increasing clatter from the kitchen and the morning sounds from the barn, I dreaded the chill in the room and drew the covers tightly under my chin as I luxuriated in the warmth of the featherbed, dropping easily from wakefulness back into dozes filled with dreams that melted into childhood experiences on my father's farm.

Herbert came in from the dining room. Breakfast was almost ready. It was time to get up. Herbert had slept well, too. His familiar bed had made him feel at home. He remained with me while I dressed as fast as I could in the chilling air. We went to the chimney corner together.

By the time we had washed our hands and faces from the same basin of warm water on the bench, others were at the table eating breakfast. We took the same places we had occupied at dinner and helped ourselves to fried eggs from a platter, thick bacon fried crisp, fried potatoes, steaming biscuits nearly as big as a saucer, gravy from a white bowl, boiled molasses made frothy with baking soda, and white butter from a dish, and passed our cups for strong black coffee hot enough to scald the hair off a butchered hog.

Everybody was lively and alert. The girls teased and the little brothers made saucy remarks. Mrs. Marcum, pleasant and efficient, had the pitcher of milk and the big granite-ware coffee pot beside her plate at the end of the table and filled up again the glasses and cups as they were passed to her. Mr. Marcum, his face more animated than it had been the evening before and directing more of his attention to those who were talking, said little himself. With our uncommonly good appetites, one would hardly have suspected that we had fed so well at our Thanksgiving dinner the evening before.

The weather had cleared before daylight and a light frost had formed. Overhead the sky was blue, but banks of cloud, rising like mountains them-selves, lay beyond the ridge on the far side of Red Bird River and obstructed the sunrise. Smoke from chimneys down the river had collected in an amber-colored cloud suspended below the top of the mountains and hovering quietly over the valley. Shirley, expecting the sun to climb above the clouds in an hour or two, thought we would have a fair but cold day. It had not rained much, enough to make the roads muddy perhaps, but not enough to raise the water level in the river. If Herbert and I would wait for about an hour after the sun came out, the roads would probably be dry again and we could walk down to Grandpa Marcum's without getting our shoes very muddy.

We sat around the fire while the dishes were being washed. After a lazy hour or two by the hearth, during which the brothers slipped away to do things that interested them, Herbert proposed that we walk out to the barn-lot to enjoy the morning sun. Mr. Marcum had already gotten up quietly and disappeared.

In the barnlot Mr. Marcum, his overcoat buttoned and his hat pulled down over his ears, was sitting on a pile of posts, an old man with a straw of broomsage in his hand was squatted on his heels before him, and the two boys were standing by. The old man, dressed in motley, picked his teeth with the straw as he talked. He lived upon Horse Creek and had stopped for a visit while on his way to Big Creek to see a "feller down there." When he rose from his heels to go, his frock coat with a velvet collar seemed strangely at odds with his rough mud-caked shoes, stiff bib overalls, and battered hat that had lost its band. He wore no collar with his collarband shirt, which was open at the throat because there was no collar button. But he was clean-shaven with little flecks of dried blood on his face where he had nicked himself with the razor. Tobacco juice had dried into little cakes at the corners of his mouth. When he smiled, his thin upper lip stretched across an expanse of gum above his stained teeth. He allowed that he "had better be a-moseyin' on" and departed, his frock-tailed coat slapping against the backs of his legs as he made his way down the trail through the barnlot.

We sat in the warm morning sun for a time, nobody saying anything. The boys left after a while and disappeared behind the barn. Herbert invited me to go with him up the hill behind the clump of briars and wild grapevines in a thicket to watch for rabbits. He called to the dogs, but they did not come. We left Mr. Marcum sitting quietly and motionless on the pile of posts, his back turned toward the sun.

As we approached the thicket we picked up rocks and threw them into it to scare up any rabbits that might be hiding there. We walked around the thicket and threw rocks into it from above, but no rabbits ran out. When we looked back toward the barnlot, we could see Mr. Marcum sitting in the sun.

As we walked around the hill just below the woods that covered the top, we threw rocks into every thicket we passed, but we never did scare up a rabbit. Out of sight of the house and barn, we entered the woods and walked along the ridge of the hill for a while. Occasionally we could catch through bare trees glimpses of the Red Bird River valley stretching toward the south-west. We never scared up any rabbits, though, and the wild grapes we found on a vine that had grown from a thicket to the lower limb of a tree at the edge of the forest had dried so hard following the frosts that we could not eat them.

Stopping under a chestnut tree that towered above other trees, we turned over burs in search of chestnuts that might have been missed by squirrels. The few we found were worm-eaten and rotten. Herbert cut a mark on the trunk of the tree with his knife and asked for the pistol, which he loaded with cartridges he had been carrying loose in his pocket. We stepped away ten paces and took turns shooting at the mark, but our marksmanship had not improved since the day before. Thick-shelled hickory nuts under a scaly-bark hickory tree not far away were hard to crack with stones, but the kernels, dried to black threads, were bitter. The only thing we found that we could eat was mealy black hews with frosty skins growing on a thorny bush below the trees, and they had no real flavor to them. Not even a skin of a persimmon was left under a tall persimmon tree beside the remains of a rail fence at the end of an old pasture.

We made our way back to the house, noticing as we came near the barnlot that Mr. Marcum had gone, even though the sun was shining and the clouds that had boiled above the ridge beyond the river had disappeared. So we could be on our way to Big Creek, Mrs. Marcum prepared for us a snack consisting of biscuits and bacon left from breakfast, beans taken from the pot warming in the fireplace, milk, and dried apple stack cake from the safe in the corner of the kitchen.

There were no clouds in the sky. The haze that dimmed the ridge beyond the river meant that we might expect rain late in the day or the following night, Mrs. Marcum told us. We decided not to carry raincoats with us.

The trail below the barnlot descended to the bank of Horse Creek, along which we walked for a short distance before crossing the creek on an elevated footlog just above the point at which the creek flowed into Red Bird River. On the other side of the river a muddy but more traveled road with field stones beaten into it in low places hugged the stream as it wound toward Beverly where the Red Bird Settlement School was located.

While we were on the footlog a woman in sophisticated riding pants and boots passed up the road, her well-groomed horse glistening in the midday sun as the leather in the fine saddle creaked and the big tan saddlebags flapped in rhythm with the spirited gait of the horse. The woman smiled and greeted us as she hurried on. Herbert explained that she was one of the Breckenridge nurses and pointed out the station, a neat Swisslike cabin with a well-kept yard, that stood on a little flat above the road a short distance up the valley. He thought she might have been returning either from the post office at Big Creek or a birthing party for one of the poor mountain women down the valley.

The pathway along the edge of a bottom led to a swinging footbridge across the river not far from the mouth of Big Creek. We climbed up steps to get to the bridge, a flimsy contraption with runs of two boards nailed to cross pieces secured to two cables and with a third cable stretched about waist high and slightly to one side for one to hold to keep from falling off while the bridge was swinging. I had never crossed a swinging foot bridge before. Herbert thought it better that he cross first, explaining that one could maintain better balance when dealing with only the swinging rhythms of his own footsteps. He trotted across the bridge without having to use the guide cable, but his swaying back and forth as he hurried across, perhaps ten feet above the rushing, turgid water, made me afraid.

He turned at the other end of the bridge to watch me. Too frightened to attempt to walk without holding to the guide cable, I began inching along, dragging my feet on the boards rather than stepping. The more I depended upon the guide cable the more the bridge rocked with me, and I began to fear that the cable would stretch so far away from the bridge halfway across the river that I could not hold to it and keep my feet on the bridge, too. Herbert advised that I not bear weight on the cable but simply touch it with my hand to balance myself on the bridge, but that if I should lose my balance to grab the cable and hold to it until the bridge balanced itself again. I stood quite still on the bridge until it felt secure enough for me to relax my grip on the cable, and then I tottered across, gaining speed beyond the halfway point. My legs were trembling when I reached Herbert, but I did not want him to know that I was as frightened as I really was.

He had never fallen from the bridge, he explained, and so far as he knew people never did, unless a dog started across while they were partly over it. The bridge would bounce up and down in response to a dog trot and sometimes the dog would try to pass one on the bridge and knock him off before he could accommodate to the rhythm the dog created. It was always safer to let the dog cross first.

The main road down Red Bird River seemed very old. The bed, worn down in places almost level with the river, had bushes, ferns, and moss growing along the banks beside it. The field stones beaten into low places did not keep it from being muddy, and it was necessary occasionally to climb the bank to get around a mud hole or a pool of stagnant water. The air along the shaded stretches of the road was dank and smelled of earth, decaying wood, and wet leaves. Where the sun was shining on it, the road had a sour odor tinged slightly with the smell of a wet barnlot or a swamp in a meadow. Herbert believed the road had been there since pioneer days and that it had been an Indian trail before that. Indians had lived in the valley. In fact, the river had been named for a friendly chief called Red Bird, he had heard.

It was a healthy valley and good crops grew in the sandy loam of its bottoms, but the stream bed had filled up considerably after the timber had been cut. There was a time when people had boats and canoes along the river and fished a great deal but it was too shallow and had too many shoals for boats now, and there were not many fish left. In early days people had built their homes on the bank of the stream and there were a few old graveyards close to the river that were flooded now when the river got up. He knew of one old graveyard right down next to the river in which there was a stone for one of the first settlers who had died at the age of 113, according to dates on the stone.

Some of the early settlers were born across the ocean. His ancestor Marcum was German, he thought, and he had heard that he was the son of a count and had spelled his name a different way, probably Merkhem, or something like that.

Big Creek was a little village with a store or two, a small post office on stilts above the road, ten or twelve houses with outbuildings and sheds around them, and a square two-story schoolhouse built of locally baked pale red bricks. Three or four narrow cross streets connected the road that went on up the creek toward Bear Branch and Leslie County with a parallel road along the foot of the hill across the creek. People had collected at the stores and boys were playing in the school yard, where there was an outdoor basketball court. Big Creek High School had produced some good basketball teams, but they had never made the name for themselves that the Carr Creek High School team over in Knott County had done, and Carr Creek, which had won the national championship, had only an outdoor court, too.

We walked up to the high school first. Herbert knew some of the boys playing on the grounds. He talked proudly of his success at college and assured the boys that they would like it at Cumberland. He had not gone out for the team at Cumberland, but Cumberland was going to have a fine team. Two or three of the Carr Creek stars had won scholarships to Cumberland.

We then walked to Grandpa Marcum's home, a large two-story house with a double-deck porch and a sunroom, located at the lower end of the parallel road across the creek. The house was weathered but in good repair. The grounds, about which were scattered shrubs and clumps of barberry bushes and rose briars, were neatly kept. We went into a pleasant living room with a big fireplace at the end of it. The windows had what appeared to be pongee curtains that let in soft light from the outside. Grandpa Marcum wasn't at home, but his wife, a step-grandmother for Herbert, as I recall, was pleasant and gracious and invited us to sit and visit with her. A hired woman working in the kitchen came to meet us, too, and Mrs. Marcum asked that she bring us some of the layer cake with white filling and a hard icing and a glass of apple juice each.

On the way back home we walked up to the nurses' station to get a good view of it from the front. It was a neatly made log structure with an overhanging roof and bright windows through which were visible pretty curtains and half-pulled shades. The grass in the yard was even and green and close by was an attractive little barn for the horses. The place looked like a model for the native mountain folk to follow in the construction and care of their own log cabins, but the architectural pattern of the cabin differed from the traditional oblong of the mountain cabin in that it seemed to be square, the chimney was located in the middle of the structure, and the porch was across the end of it instead of along the side. It was painted dark green and the chinking between the logs was smooth and white like plaster instead of cracked and red like the mud chinking usually seen between the gray logs of cabins.

The swinging bridge was not as difficult to cross on the way back. Less fearful than before, I was able to balance myself more easily by looking ahead as I walked and depending less for assurance on the guide cable.

Shirley and the hired girl, sitting together in the dining room, were entertaining themselves with the guitar. The girl sang "Barbara Allen" in a high lonesome voice. We sat and listened. The ballad was almost the same as the variant my grandmother sang, but the girl sang with less effort and did not use as many pauses and slides in her voice as Grandma used, but Grandma, who sang the ballad while working was not forced to adapt her melody to the requirements of an accompanying instrument. She had more freedom to decorate her singing with grace notes and pauses. I noted that the hired girl had said of the rose and the briar that they grew to the top of the old church wall "twill" they could grow no higher. Afterwards, I observed that both she and Shirley used "twill" instead of "until" in their speech, which seemed more old-fashioned than my grandmother's speech in that they used such expressions as "it were" and "s' I be," which appeared to mean "it's if I be."

Following supper that night the hired girl and the daughter made taffy from molasses boiled slowly in a black skillet on the stove while Shirley popped corn in another skillet and poured it into a large dishpan. After the taffy was pulled and laid out to harden before being broken into sticks by striking it sharply with a butcher knife, another skillet of molasses was boiled and poured over the popcorn. The girls giggled and teased as they worked the popcorn into balls and stacked them on a platter. We sat around the fireplace, in which a slow fire smoldered, as we ate popcorn and taffy and told riddles, most of which I had heard around the hearth while I was growing up. Instead of responding directly to a riddle, each said "I know" after he had solved it. The one asking the riddle would repeat it for anyone having difficulty solving it and stress significantly the word that was the key to its solution.

My riddle, which the older ones knew, was:

Twelve pears a-hangin' high,
Twelve men a-ridin' by;
Each rech up and took a pear
And left eleven a-hangin' there.

For the daughter who "gave up," I explained that only one man, whose name was Each, had taken a pear.

Many of the riddles were introduced with a reference to what "I" saw while "a-goin' past the church house door," or "a-ridin' through yonder gap," or "a-comin' down the high-cut road," or "a-crossin' over the church house style." Others were rhyming similes and metaphors that sometimes suggested the bawdy, like:

> Four legs up,
> Four legs down,
> Soft in the middle,
> Hard all around. [Bed]

Or,

> Round as a biscuit,
> Busy as a bee,
> The purtiest little thing
> You ever did see. [Watch]

After riddles, we played "William, William, Tremblety Toe" for such penalties as getting our hair pulled, our ears pinched, or our noses tweaked for being the first to speak, smile, or show our teeth. Grimacing, crossing our eyes, or twitching our noses, we concentrated on one another until we broke into smiles and paid our penalties.

Rain fell during the night. Saturday morning was cloudy and dark, but no more rain fell. We sat around the fire and talked. Occasionally, someone from up on Horse Creek came by, stopped for a drink of water at the well, and talked for a few minutes. As he departed, he announced where he was going and invited Mrs. Marcum to "come up sometime." She responded that she would when she could, and for him to stop again when passing.

That afternoon Herbert decided that we would go back down to Big Creek to see Grampa and to wait for the mail carrier, who usually arrived about 5 o'clock. We found the trail and the road muddy, the pools of water in the main road wider than they had been the day before, and Red Bird River swollen and silty.

More people were gathered at the stores Saturday afternoon than Friday. We stood around for a while listening to the men seated on kegs and boxes swap stories and laugh. Men clustered at hitching posts or gathered around tree trunks listened intently to a yarn spinner and then laughed uproariously, slapping their thighs and doubling in merriment in response to punch lines. Occasionally, someone would call out, "Hey, come hyar! I want to talk with you about a little business matter." The two would then retreat to a ravine, or behind a clump of bushes on the bank of the creek, or to a stable behind one of the houses and be gone for a while. As they returned, they would stroke their mustaches with the backs of their hands and smack their mouths, the guest sometimes winking significantly at one of his cronies as if to say, "Al hyar has got a bottle of 'shine that you'd like a dram from, Charlie." Soon Al would invite Charlie to retire to talk over a little business matter with him, too.

Big boys appeared from time to time, made small purchases, stopped for the completion of some tale, and then hurried to the school yard, from which came voices of boys playing. Only occasionally did a woman appear, usually an older woman wearing a crisp gingham bonnet, a long–sleeved blouse, and riding skirts, and mounted on a family nag or mule. She would hand down her basket of eggs to some man to hold for her. He would hold her mount by the bridle close to the bits for her while she dismounted, hand her the basket, and hitch her "brute" to a post or the flying limb of a tree. When she entered a store, she spoke ceremoniously to everybody without looking at anyone, walked up to the counter, and deposited on it her basket of eggs. While she "traded," the men sat silently on their perches and listened to the exchange between her and the grave merchant, who had taken his position with dignity behind his counter. After the woman had traded and gone, the men would resume their tale telling.

Grampa Marcum was not at home, but he had left word that one of Herbert's little brothers could come down Sunday morning and get his horses for us to ride over to Garrard to catch the train back to Barbourville. We declined the invitation to come in and have a snack and went up to the schoolyard, where two teams were having a practice game of basketball, even though the court was still wet and the ball was heavy and without much bounce in it. Girls of high school age stood around the court and cheered when one of the mud-spattered players made a basket. Some of the girls had short hair, but many of them were still wearing plaits and pigtails. Their freshly washed dresses of gingham and calico, most of them belted with bows behind, hung unevenly with hems slightly above the tops of coarse shoes in order to reveal spans of tan lisle stockings. Herbert spoke to some of the older ones and introduced me. They were shy and barely recognized me as they continued their conversations with Herbert and referred to persons whom they had known that had gone to Cumberland.

About 5 o'clock we returned to the post office to wait for the mail carrier. The little room with a cage for the office in the corner and a stove in the middle was already filled with people, mostly older and middle-aged men. No women were present. We were barely able to squeeze inside the room, which was becoming warm from the mass of bodies packed inside it. The men were engaged in animated conversations that created a babble of voices that pulsated in a rhythm similar to that of frogs in the springtime or a flock of cackling hens. The postmaster stood silently behind the counter of his cage, on which a lighted kerosene lamp stood, the only light in the little room.

Darkness came early. As we waited, the tempo of the rhythms increased, and much laughter rattled across the patterns and died away. We were aware at first of such distinct odors as bad breath, woodsmoke settled in serge coats, oily hair, unclean bodies, scalded feet cased in muddy rubber boots, strong tobacco, and moonshine whiskey, but all of these became blended together as the temperature of the room rose from body heat. Becoming drowsy, we wormed our way to the open door and leaned against the jambs, noting that a light rain was falling.

About 6 o'clock the mail boy rode up to the little platform, dismounted, hitched his horse, and stepped through the door. People fell back to make room for him. He slapped the pockets on the counter and took from his pouch a packet of letters that he had gathered along the way. Laying the packet of letters to be stamped aside, the postmaster opened the pockets with a little key.

The crowd became silent as the postmaster began to call out the names of persons who had received mail. One whose name was called would raise his hand and yell "Hyur!" The postmaster would start the piece of mail in his direction, all heads turning to watch the letter move toward its destination as it was handed from one to another above the tilted noses of the crowd. When the postmaster called out the name on the next piece of mail, all faces swung around to attention again, watching the letter move from hand to hand toward its fortunate recipient. As many as ten or twelve pieces of mail were passed out, when the postmaster announced, "That's all," and turned to stamp the letters in the packet.

Conversations began again. One man, explaining that he had left his "specs" at home, called on Herbert to read his letter aloud to him. It was a circular from a mail order house in Chicago that offered premiums for orders taken for kitchenware and small household articles. The man was excited by the prospects but was puzzled as to how that feller away off out there had ever heard tell of him, for he had never heard that man's name mentioned before in all of his borned days. Another made his way to the counter and held his letter close to the lamp but at arm's length as he spelled aloud laboriously the words in a short letter from his wife's sister who had gone away and married a man in Ohio. Those around him listened attentively as he relayed the news and told things he knew about the "quare" man his sister-in-law had married and who had come down to Big Creek for a visit four or five years ago. Another, disappointed that he had not received a letter, walked up to the cage and asked the postmaster whether he was "shore" there had not been a letter for him. As he asked his question, he pronounced his name, assigning himself initials as if he were a businessman in Manchester or Hyden. He then explained that he had "give out" a letter to his daughter "more 'n a week ago" to a man up in Cincinnati about wanting to trap and buy fur that winter and wanted a price "sheddle." The man had had plenty of time to "ancher," he 'lowed.

There was no mail for the Marcums. We left the office in a drizzle of cold rain, and we had not brought raincoats with us. By the time we reached the swinging bridge we were trudging along in pitch darkness, for we not brought a lantern along either. Herbert preceded me across the bridge, I stubbed my toe on an uneven riser and fell toward the bridge, but caught the top of it in time to prevent myself from smashing my face against the end of it. As I attempted to pull myself upright, I became aware of the rushing water and was paralyzed with fear. Instead of trying to stand up and walk, I crawled across on my hands and knees, the bridge swinging and jiggling uneasily under me as I inched my way along.

I was humiliated by the experience and fully expected Herbert to tease me about it or to tell about it when we got home, but he made no comment about it at all, either as we splurged through the puddles and mud holes in the darkness or sat by the fire washing and drying our feet after we had eaten our supper.

The family had already eaten, and the dishes had been washed, but the hired girl had set our suppers in the warming closet of the stove. We took off our wet coats and hung them on the backs of chairs near the fire to dry while we ate. By the time we had washed our hands and face, our suppers had been set for us on the dining room table. The hired girl, dressed in her best clothes, her hair arranged in puffs over her ears, her cheeks and lips rouged, and her eyes shining, looked tidy in a little white apron with ruffles around it that reached only to her knees. Shirley, newly shaved and in a clean shirt and new overalls, sat by the fireplace as he chorded the guitar. The Marcum family was elsewhere in the house. The dining room was turned over to Shirley and the hired girl as a place for them to court on Saturday nights.

After we had eaten, we brought pans of warm water to the hearth, washed our feet, placed our shoes bottoms up against the jambs of the fireplace for them to dry out by morning, hung our wet sox on chair rungs to dry, and went into the guest room. I put on a pair of sox that I had worn the day before and Herbert sat barefoot. After sneezing two or three times, I slipped on my overcoat and Herbert found an old sweater that he had worn to high school.

We talked a long time, but our interest by then had turned back toward Cumberland. We discussed our teachers, Dr. Wood, Mr. Evans, P.R. Jones, Gorman Jones, Miss Anderson. I ventured a comment in admiration of an attractive and popular young woman who lived in town, but Herbert thought she "looked like something the cats had drug in" to him. A handsome young man from Barbourville, who dressed stylishly, was a favorite of the more sophisticated coeds, and rated well enough with the professors for them to direct comments to him in class, made Herbert's "ass want a chew of 'backer." If he'd had a chance, he would have "slipped it out behind the house and a-give it a chew." But we were in full agreement in our estimates of young men who lived near us in Felix Hall. Both of us admired a trio of delightful cutups from Corbin, Arliss Taylor, Jerome Rogers, and Steeley Terrell, and we liked the solid character and quiet confidence of staunch Milton Walker, who had a shock of stubborn red hair and whose workship duties included carrying slops from the kitchen to the hogs kept in a pen beyond the tennis courts beside Felix Hall. The hogs would soon be butchered, we thought, but no doubt President Creech would find pigs to replace them, for he did not like for anything to go to waste, not even kitchen slop.

We also admired red-headed Claude Acuff from Knoxville who was so clever at the piano in the reception room at Felix and whose repertory of hillbilly songs brought us delight almost every evening before we had to be in our rooms at 7 o'clock. Claude playing fast numbers and diminutive Park Howard dancing were a good show team. Park had put on a real show at the fall party when he danced to Buell Kazee's playing of "Sourwood Mountain," and Buell had thrilled all of us with his singing of "Ramona." Most of the guys at Cumberland were good fellows, we concluded, and they were interested in making good grades, too. Why, sixty of the ninety freshmen (whom we called "juniors") had been valedictorians or salutatorians of their high school classes.

Cumberland College seemed far away and wonderful to us. Students there, some of whom had come from New York, New Jersey, Ohio, Indiana, Virginia, Georgia, Tennessee, and places outside the mountains of Kentucky, represented the big world to us. Isolated Big Creek, where we had been crowded into the little post office with laughing mountain men, unclean, unshaven, tobacco juice caked at the corners of their mouths, and many of them smelling sour from moonshining whiskey, was a long way culturally from Cumberland, where one crossed the ravine dividing the campus on a slender viaduct arching toward the sky instead of a narrow swinging bridge with boards on it that were slippery when it rained, and where one sat down in classrooms with painted walls and among young people with clean bodies and fresh clothes and smelling of perfumes and cologne and scented pomades on carefully groomed hair to hear professors who wore a fresh shirt and a different tie every day and who talked as if they had traveled the world up and down and were prepared to give us the counsel we needed to enter into it successfully. Tomorrow we would be returning to Cumberland.

Herbert left for his room. I tiptoed to the chimney corner, noticing that the rain had stopped and a few stars were visible between the clouds that were beginning to pull apart. I undressed, blew out the light, and crawled between the cold sheets, smelling of homemade soap. The plunking of the guitar, the soft singing, and the low laughter of Shirley and his girl by the fireplace in the dining room soon lulled me to sleep.

The sun was shining Sunday morning and the landscape was clean and fresh, more like early spring than late autumn. Breakfast was late. No one was hurrying. Nothing was said about attending church, but the girls had on fresh dresses and the boys clean shirts and overalls. Only the hired girl looked less dressed up than she had been the evening before.

After breakfast we went to the barnlot to sit in the bright sunshine. Herbert's brother curried and saddled a horse to ride down to Grampa Marcum's, where he would curry and saddle Grampa's horse and lead it back for me to ride to Garrard. He would ride behind Herbert and bring the horses back from the railroad station.

People passing through the barnlot on their way to visit relatives down along the river were wearing as their Sunday clothes clean shirts and overalls that they would wear all week. Older men wore battered black hats, with narrow bands and broad brims, cocked jauntily on their heads, young men tweed caps with bills that were limp and flopping, and boys pullover caps rolled above their ears and stretched tightly across the tops of their heads. No women or girls passed, for mothers stayed home to cook for the broods of children and girls stayed to take care of them. The passersby spoke courteously but did not stop for conversations, their dogs hurrying along beside them and shying away from us as they went by.

After the brother returned from Big Creek, we went back to the house to pack our things. Mrs. Marcum prepared a box of food for Herbert to take back to college with him and put it in a white sack for ease in carrying it on a horse. She insisted that he share the food with me.

We ate lunch ahead of the family, the horses were led up to the gate, and we departed with little ceremony. Mrs. Marcum was glad I had come home with Herbert and invited me to come again, anytime. Mr. Marcum had not returned from his Saturday trip. Shirley and the hired girl remained in the kitchen. The sisters stood about solemnly and made no comment. As Herbert swung into his saddle, his mother asked that he write and tell them how he was getting along. After we had reined our horses into the trail, I looked back at the house and Mrs. Marcum and the girls had already gone inside. I wondered whether they feared that watching one of the family depart might bring bad luck to the traveler. Herbert did not look back.

Women and children at the shacks along the trail and spaced on the flats up the sides of the mountains were outside, women sitting on the benches against the log walls of the little houses and children playing in the yards.

We met many young folk along the trail. Boys who had come together at trees beside the trail lounged about or squatted on their heels in semicircles by the side of the trail. Girls, traveling by twos and threes, were dressed for Sunday in their clean but poorly made dresses of calico or gingham. They wore their hair in puffs over their ears, their lips were painted a brilliant red, and their cheeks were rouged. There was an air of gaiety about everybody we saw from the mothers who sat on the benches along the walls of the cabins to the little children who played in the yards.

As we climbed the mountain toward the gap at the head of Horse Creek, I looked back down the valley at the sharply visible little houses, the trees cleanly outlined against the landscape, and the great ridge, looking quite close, beyond Red Bird River. The sky was blue and the bright sun ran along the top of the mountain to our left. Birds sang from leafless trees and lone hawks soared above.

Topping the gap, we could see far down Goose Creek. The white farmhouses gleamed in the afternoon sunshine, the broad meadows were green following the rain, and the big gray barns were sharply outlined in the clear air. Humble homes and dark cabins up the hollows and in the coves and along the flats to our right looked close at hand, and we could see women sitting on benches by the walls and children romping about the yards in Sunday play.

At the railroad station we dismounted and I held Herbert's bundle and bag of food while he threw the stirrups across the saddle of the horse I had ridden. His brother adjusted the stirrups on the saddle of the horse he and Herbert had ridden, climbed on, and departed, leading the horse I had ridden.

Several people were waiting for the little train. Only one or two got off when it pulled alongside the station, whistling saucily and blowing out steam. We crowded aboard and stood in the aisle, recognizing two or three Cumberland College students sitting quietly by windows in the car.

Connections with trains in Barbourville and Corbin were on schedule, but cars were crowded, and we recognized more Cumberland students, looking happy and glad to be returning to college.

We arrived in Williamsburg on time. We hurried to our dormitory, where I gave Herbert the pistol I had carried in my inside coat pocket; we deposited our bundles in our rooms, and washed for dinner. The dinner bell rang, and we rushed to the dining room in Johnson Hall. Students were lively and talkative after their holiday trips, but many others would arrive on later trains.

That night I prepared to meet my Monday classes, but as I read my assignments, my mind kept wandering back to Big Creek, the swinging bridge, the crowd gathered in the little post office, the poor people who squatted in squalid cabins on the abandoned land along Horse Creek. I had taken one of the most deeply impressive trips I was ever to take in my life.

Fifty years later, while driving along the Daniel Boone Parkway, which was built through the little village of Big Creek, I noted that the highway appears to have been built over the site of the square brick structure that was Big Creek High School. Grampa Marcum's house, now abandoned and weathered but still looking remarkably sturdy, had been isolated by the parkway. I was not able to see from the highway the house in which Herbert's family lived, but I thought I caught a fleeting glimpse of the low hill at the mouth of Horse Creek on which it had stood. Perhaps it burned, or had been torn down. A little house on stilts but now with a porch across the front of it looked remarkably like the post office into which the men crowded to wait for the mail boy to arrive. I wondered where all of the poor people on Horse Creek went, and what became of Herbert, whom I never saw again after I left Cumberland College, and whether Shirley won the hired girl's heart, married her, and went away to live in a hillbilly ghetto in Dayton or Middletown.

Appalachian Folkways: Holidays

While I was growing up on Caines Creek holidays were observed but not often celebrated. Heirs of the Reformation, my relatives took little or no note of Easter and Christmas as religious holidays. The few times when the monthly meeting of the United Baptist church fell on Easter Sunday or Christmas Eve or Christmas Day, no reference to the holidays themselves was made in the services. These holidays were secular, not religious.

Loosely, we observed New Year's Day, Easter Sunday, Decoration Day, Independence Day, Thanksgiving, and Christmas, but the annual sacrament meeting at the church, the memorial meetings at family graveyards in late summer or early autumn, and election days had more of the holiday mood around them than did the national holidays. People normally did not work in their fields on New Year's Day, Thanksgiving Day, Christmas Eve, or Christmas Day, but they did on Decoration Day and Independence Day if crops needed attention.

Holidays were times for visiting for children and young people. If weather was favorable, children would visit cousins on New Year's Day and celebrate by playing games in the barns or fields or shooting firecrackers or discharging such crude explosive devices as tin cans with a few grains of carbide in them, or touch guns loaded with black powder. Young people of courting age met for taffy pullings and making popcorn balls. Middle-aged men would sometimes have shooting matches, at which they would exchange drinks from their bottles or jars of whiskey.

Sometimes young men would get together to welcome the new year by shooting guns at midnight or discharging blasts of blackpowder. Courting couples, when they did not go to parties on New Year's Eve, would have dates for watching in the new year, often with the young woman's entire family ranged about the fireplace with them. It was customary to write the new year as quickly as one could after the stroke of midnight. One might write the date on the hearth with a charcoal or in the soot on the backwall of the fireplace with a poker. There was no crying in of the new year or singing.

New Year's dinner (at midday) included the simplest of foods, for it was believed that a simple dinner assured prosperity and health for the ensuing year. Hog's jowl, cornpone, leatherbritchy beans, stewed pumpkin, hominy, boiled cabbage or canned mustard, stewed fruit with gingerbread or an undecorated cake, and sweet milk or buttermilk constituted a more or less typical New Year's dinner.

New Year's Day normally marked the end of the solstice festivities, which, in Appalachia retained more of the Roman than of the traditional Christian holiday. However, the twelve days of Christmas continued through Old Christmas, noted as a sober time by all and observed by some families as the true Christmas.

Old Christmas, which occurred on the 6th of January, represented an unwillingness of conservative folk to accept the Gregorian calendar adopted in 1752. A few families in my community were still observing Old Christmas during my boyhood on Caines Creek. Santa Claus came to children in these families on Old Christmas Eve and left gifts in and around their shoes placed inside the front door of the house. Stories were still being told about Old Christmas in many homes. The elder was supposed to leaf and bloom at midnight for a brief moment, at which time cattle in the barns faced Bethlehem, dropped to their knees, and lowed. But these marvels did not transpire for one who stayed up to watch. People occasionally could hear cattle lowing, sheep bleating, horses nickering, and roosters crowing at midnight and stories were told of travelers who had been amazed at the brief sight of bloom-covered elder bushes along the streams, but one who stayed up to spy on these mysteries invited bad luck for a whole year. Believers in Old Christmas stayed home on January 6 and ate simple foods. It was a solemn day.

The long winter from the Christmas season to Easter was unrelieved by holidays. The last day of the one-room school term on the first Friday in February sometimes brought parents and grandparents to the school for the teacher's treat of stick candy distributed among the children and for such awards and honors as he might have decided to bestow on those who had perfect attendance records, or had led their classes in spelling and arithmetic. On such occasions, however, only the teacher bestowed gifts.

Attention was called in some homes to Lincoln's and Washington's birthdays. I am sure I had never heard of St. Valentine's Day before I entered the school at Louisa. In my own home, though, we knew about St. Patrick's Day, which was my mother's birthday. My mother knew an Irish song or two, which she sometimes sang on her birthday. We knew that one wore green on St. Patrick's Day, and we were told that St. Patrick had driven the snakes out of Ireland, but we did not know he was Catholic. We knew jokes about Pat and Mike, the Irishmen, but we had never seen a real Irishman.

The Easter season was plainly a celebration of fertility. If weather permitted, gardens and flowers in the yard were planted on Good Friday. Easter Sunday itself, having no special religious significance for us, celebrated the egg. Children would steal eggs from the nests of the hens for days and hide them in the barn to wait for Easter morning. Then the eggs were all produced and prepared for breakfast. One ate as many eggs as he could for Easter breakfast. Except eggs for breakfast, no special food was associated with Easter, though by this time "creasy greens" (watercress) and "sallet," a mixture of tender wild greens cooked together, would be appearing on tables at dinner time in most Appalachian homes. Sulphur and molasses, and sassafras tea, and spring bitters for cleansing the blood and toning up the system had been taken by Easter and young people were prepared to indulge their taste for fried eggs to the point of surfeit.

No special visits because of Easter occurred among grownups, but children visited one another and played in the forest, just beginning to show signs of spring, or in fields covered with tender new-green grass, or along the streams where they watched fish spawning in nests near the shoals, or frogs mating in eddies and ponds. Often boys, especially, took along eggs, leftover biscuits, a little salt folded in a page ripped from a Sears, Roebuck catalog, a pot slipped out of the kitchen when nobody was looking, and a handful of kitchen matches for a dinner of boiled eggs in the hills. Doing things when nobody was looking was an accepted part of the Easter tradition.

We did not boil and paint eggs for Easter. There were no egg rollings. We never heard of the Easter Bunny, for rabbits were not associated with Easter for us. Baby chicks held no significance for us. We did not eat jelly beans, colored gum drops, or other candies at Easter time. All of these things, I learned later, are a part of Easter for children who are taught that Easter is a religious holiday and who often come together in Sunday school picnics for egg rollings. Easter in Appalachia celebrated creation, birth, beginnings.

In my early childhood Decoration Day was being observed by many families on Caines Creek, especially those in which soldiers in the Civil War had died, though many old veterans continued to live down to about 1920. Debris was cleared from the graveyards, stones were straightened, and graves were decorated with roses, just coming into bloom on May 30. Memorial services were held occasionally, but by about 1930 Decoration Day had come to mean little more than the day on which families cleaned off their graveyards and deposited roses at the headstones of graves.

Independence Day was never celebrated in any special way while I was growing up on Caines Creek. Unless it fell on Saturday or Sunday, people worked in their fields on Independence Day. We talked of Independence Day and knew its significance, but no special foods were eaten or customs observed. If Independence Day fell on Saturday or Sunday, though, young people would get together and shoot firecrackers and discharge guns, and daring young men would drink more whiskey than usual and discharge their pistols along the roads. We knew that Independence Day was celebrated "away off" with brass bands, soldiers marching, patriotic speakers, and people in summer clothing drinking lemonade and eating ice cream cones at stands set up in courthouse yards. So far as I knew no one from Caines Creek ever went to Louisa, the county-seat town, to "take in the 4th." But during the oil boom across the hill at Martha we could sometimes hear lone horseback riders crossing the wooden bridge late at night. My father said they were oil well workers returning from trips home to celebrate the 4th of July, for we did not use "Independence Day" in our speech.

We knew nothing about Labor Day. One-room schools, which opened the last Monday in July, did not observe Labor Day. But we did not miss national holidays in late summer and early fall, for that was the time for family reunions, funeralizings at the graveyards, association meetings of rural Baptist church congregations, and shooting matches. It was also the season for bean-stringings, molasses-makings, apple-peelings, and workings, which were attended by young and old, both male and female.

We did not know about Halloween with its ghosts and goblins. I went to my first Halloween party after I was in high school.

Thanksgiving Day was observed throughout Appalachia, but like Christmas, New Year's Day, and Easter, it had little or no religious significance. Unless weather conditions were right for butchering hogs, no work other than caring for the farm animals was done on Thanksgiving Day. Sometimes men and boys would go rabbit hunting, but the emphasis of Thanksgiving was upon the dinner. People visited on Thanksgiving Day, especially young people, and ate the midday dinner wherever they happened to be.

Turkey was not served for Thanksgiving Day on Caines Creek. A few farmers in my early boyhood grew turkeys for the market but not for their own tables. I remember seeing drovers struggling with flocks of turkeys along the trails. Once, when I was perhaps eight years old, I assisted drovers in getting their turkeys together again after they refused to cross the wooden bridge near our home and escaped into the bushes along the creek.

Instead of turkey, we ate fresh pork when hogs had been killed, or chicken and dumplings, or rabbit. Sometimes a woodchuck (groundhog) or a 'possum was parboiled and baked, banked with sweet potatoes, for Thanksgiving dinner. Tables were heaped with cornbread, biscuits, bowls of fall beans, pickled beans, sauerkraut, pickled corn, sweet potatoes, mashed potatoes, white butter, turnip greens, mustard, gravy, relishes and pickles, and stewed fruit. Always, there were stacks of pumpkin pies, which, more than any other food symbolized Thanksgiving for us. We drank apple juice, grape juice, sweet milk, and buttermilk. That was also the time when my father drew for the first time blackberry or grape wine he had made that season, a glass of which was offered to each of us who cared to have it before we were called to the table.

Thanksgiving Day was a time for enjoying the bounty of the land and the fruits of our industry in a spirit of good fellowship. We had no special games or customs apart from the dinner itself associated with Thanksgiving. When the time for doing the evening chores came, Thanksgiving was over.

Country schools were dismissed for Thanksgiving but opened again next day. We did not have a Thanksgiving weekend.

Thanksgiving Day marked the end of autumn for us. After that, one found in the woods no more grapes worth gathering. Kernels in most nuts had frozen by then and were not fit to eat. Though a few pink-sided horseapples might still be clinging to high limbs in trees, they were rarely fit to eat after Thanksgiving. Persimmons had ripened, plopped to the earth, and been consumed by 'possums and other "critters," wild plums had dried into tasteless blue prunes on the limbs, and crab apples had fallen in heaps after the first heavy frosts. Only haws, still clinging to the limbs, were edible, but they were tedious to eat.

Roads that had been beds of dust almost to Thanksgiving Day became by the middle of December rivers of mud, frozen hard as a billy goat's horns one day and bottomless pits of muck the next. People were housebound by Christmas. Children were wearing long underwear, wool socks, heavy stiff shoes, and extra layers of clothing and hovering around roaring fires to keep warm. Boys wore the shabbiest of their Sunday pants under their overalls, two shirts, and a denim blouse. Children did not wear overcoats, but many had sheepskin coats or coat sweaters to slip into when they needed to go outside.

Christmas came just in time to head off the restlessness and bad temper that develop among children crowded together in uncomfortable chairs and on stools around a fireplace, competing for the warmest spots and bicking over such crude play things as their imaginations might have led them to create. But usually there was little special planning for Christmas. People did not send gifts ahead, or exchange gifts on Christmas morning. I think I must have been in high school before I saw a Christmas greeting.

But there was a sense of Christmas in the air. People geared up for it emotionally, not as a religious holiday but as a winter celebration. It was a time for grownups to put on their best clothing and visit; for men to drink whiskey with their cronies and shoot their pistols; for big boys to shoot firecrackers, fire blasting powder, and make noise; for children to anticipate what goodies they might find in their stockings, hung carefully on chair rungs, on Christmas morning; and for women and older daughters to make pans of cookies, apple stack cakes, cakes covered with meringue and decorated with bright red cinnamon drops, fruit pot pies, called "sonkers" on Caines Creek, and a spicy "dip" or sauce to pour over them.

At the approach of Christmas and continuing to Old Christmas young people of courting age had "get-togethers," sometimes in homes, sometimes at crossroads, sometimes in abandoned houses (called "waste houses" on Caines Creek). The party was sometimes a taffy-pulling, sometimes a gathering to hear music makers, sometimes a chicken-cooking in a waste house following a lively "play-party" (euphemism for "square dance"). Parties generally had the appearance of "just happening" and were always incidental and open to all who cared to attend. Certainly, they required no elaborate preparation and generally cost little in resources and nothing in money. Young people dressed in their best to attend these functions, courting, as the saying went, "up a storm" the whole time.

At the same time middle-aged people and "old married folks" (all married people, regardless of age, were referred to as "old") might meet, not by plan but incidentally in homes and play cards, the most popular of the card games on Caines Creek being "setback." (After a span of a half-century I can still hear voices filled with triumph and fired with victory shouting, "High, low, jick, jack, and the game.") Sometimes the games would continue far into the night, but if the weather was "lowering" and threatening, people might play in the afternoons, too. Some winters the preferences for games on dark and cold afternoons were checkers and fox and goose, in which the pawns were red and white grains of corn. Old people paid little attention to the approach of Christmas, but on Christmas days grandpas and grannies, wrapped and buttoned up to keep warm, would visit among their children, retrieving from deep pockets fruit, candy, or some "pretty" (toy) for the least of the grandchildren. A granny might have a little poke of cookies in one apron pocket and a carefully washed blue salve bottle in the other, for children were pleased to have bottles, jars, and colorful boxes and cartons as toys. Grandparents expected no gifts for Christmas.

I recall that our grampa and granny came to visit one dark and cold Christmas afternoon when we were quite small. Granny, who had a "little poke of brown sugar cookies" in one pocket of her long tie-around gingham apron and two or three carefully washed small bottles in the other, dispensed her goodies as soon as she entered the house, and went on into the kitchen to visit with our mother. Grampa sat before the fire a long time while watching us divide among ourselves and eat the cookies. Then he reared back in his chair and drew from his pocket a piece of yellow fruit, which he said was an orange. He gave it to me and told me to peel it, pull it apart, and divide it with my brother and sister. It was the first orange we had ever seen, and I believe we might not have seen another for a few years after that, when I learned that what Grampa had given us was not really an orange after all but a tangerine someone at Blaine had given him.

On Christmas Eve children were more animated and created more confusion around the fireside than usual. More often than not fathers who had gone to crossroads stores or villages not far away to "find Christmas" and swap tall tales with neighbors around potbellied stoves arrived home late Christmas Eve and ate alone suppers that had been kept warm for them in the warming closets or ovens of the kitchen stoves. Mothers not completely worn down and exasperated would sometimes placate the young 'ens by "capping" popcorn in the fireplace, or singing, or telling folk tales, or reciting accounts of Christmas in their own girlhood. Soon after the father joined his family by the fire, where he might remove his shoes and toast his feet by the coals while reporting news learned at the store or making predictions about the weather if the fire should happen "to spit snow," the children were sent off to bed with strict instructions to go to sleep soon, for if Santa Claus should happen to come by and find somebody awake in the house he would not stop and just might not have time to get back to that house all night, he was so busy. The foolhardy young 'en who was so thoughtless as to play in the fire by punching it with the poker or lighting the end of a stick of kindling and making "fire rings" with it was reprimanded severely, for he would either wet the bed or have to get up, possibly at the very moment Santa Claus, having parked his sleigh on the roof, was ready to come down the chimney.

The father, left alone by the fireplace, sat quietly and stared into the fire until all were asleep. Then Santa Claus came. He stuffed apples dug from the "hole" in the garden earlier that day into the toes of stockings left hanging from chair rungs, packed in bundles of mixed candies (gum drops, chocolates, jelly beans, hard balls that one could hold in his mouth a long time, and curious animal shapes in marshmallow) all done up in pages ripped from an old Sears, Roebuck catalog, stuck in the top of each stocking an assortment of five or six sticks of hard candy wrapped in catalog leaves, and poked in just far enough for it to show anything special he might have brought, like a "French harp," or a knife with a celluloid handle, or a pair of gloves with a yellow fringe on the cuffs, or a red or yellow nickel pencil. On the chair beside each stocking he would sometimes leave a nickel tablet of lined paper or a new slate. Toys were not normally given, though occasionally a little girl might find a stuffed doll with a plaster head in her stocking. Cap pistols had not yet arrived for little boys.

Children were not permitted to rise on Christmas morning before the fire was roaring in the hearth, the father had gone to the barn to "feed the brutes" and milk, and the mother was ready to go into the kitchen to prepare breakfast. Then the children came bounding in, their bare feet slapping the cold floor, the seats of their long underwear bagging to their knees, and their breeches or dresses trailing along on the floor. Each rushed to his stocking, cast his clothing on the floor, and "glommed in," crying out each goody as he found it. It was not until after each gift had been examined, the pieces of candy had been counted, and comparisons of Santa's bounties had been made that they put on their clothing, sometimes in confusion, the least ones getting their shoes on the wrong feet and the larger ones their underpants on backward.

Children prepared no gifts for one another, parents, or grandparents, nor did adults exchange gifts. There was no notion connected with Santa Claus that he brought gifts only to good children and punished naughty ones by passing them by. He was equally good to all. As to "crafted toys," children did not expect to find them in their stockings but made their own or enlisted the skill of a grandfather in making what they could not make themselves. Larger boys would sometimes make for smaller members of the family such whittled toys as tops from wooden spools on which sewing thread had come. Called a "jimmy dancer," such a top, when well balanced, might spin for a long time when skillfully flipped. Jointed monkeys were cut from abandoned wooden "shakes" or shingles from old roofs and rigged with thread on sticks so they could climb. Jointed dancers cut from the wood and strung on sticks could be made to dance by thumping a thin board on which their jointed feet were permitted to rest. A corn cob with a crude head carved on it could be dressed as a doll for little girls.

There was no Christmas music, and we sang no Christmas songs or carols, though my mother when young, had attended a community "Christmas Tree" a time or two at Blaine, where there was from 1885 to 1916 a little normal school, and had learned "Once Upon a Midnight Clear" and a few verses of "Jingle Bells," which she would sometimes sing while working in the kitchen at Christmas time. She could also recite a part of "The Night Before Christmas," which she had heard at the "Christmas Tree" in Blaine once when she was a girl, and she could recite a few lines of "Backward, Turn Backward, O Time, in Your Flight," heard at one of the programs.

Christmas trees, which were introduced into Appalachia as early as the late 1880's by the teachers in the church-supported boarding schools, brought with them the religious significance of Christmas, which had been ignored or carefully suppressed by the hard-line Calvinistic churches of the region. Christmas carols and songs, pageants based on the nativity, reading the story of the birth of Jesus, reciting poems about Christmas, and the exchange of gifts were a part of the institutional Christmas tree programs. Moving finally into such public buildings as courthouses or Masonic halls, Christmas tree programs as community celebrations had become fairly well accepted at some one-room schools by the late 1920's, but in most of rural Appalachia few homes had Christmas trees prior to the 1930's.

Children remained at home Christmas morning and enjoyed what Santa Claus had brought. Sometimes grandparents arrived to share Christmas dinner at midday, a meal not much different from a Sunday dinner except for the traditional stack cakes filled with dried apples, berry sonkers with rich cream dip flavored with spices, and white cake decorated with brilliant red cinnamon hearts. After the dinner, children were permitted to visit other children in the community and parents would sometimes go calling, their pockets filled with candy, fruit, and sometimes a bottle of whiskey or homemade wine.

When one met a neighbor on the road, he shouted "Christmas gift!" as soon as he could. The one who shouted first was treated by the other before he pulled from his pockets or "reticule" his own treat, both exchanging felicitations and sharing good fellowship as they treated each other.

Noise making was also traditional at Christmas time. Boys of intermediate age liked to get together on Christmas afternoons and shoot firecrackers, young men of courting age would shoot their pistols along the roads and trails, and men engaged in shooting matches. For children of school age, Christmas was a day out of school, but since school terms continued for only six weeks, few children received gifts of clothing for Christmas, for sweaters, pullover caps, wool stockings, and winter shoes, all to last all winter, had been provided in late October or November.

The Double Murder at the Sledges'[2]

People were not sure where Old Bill Sledge came from. Some said Old Virginia, others North Carolina. As folks became better acquainted with him they thought it most likely that he had come in here because he was in some kind of trouble back where he came from. He seemed mean enough to have killed somebody, or to have robbed a store, or to have burned one of his neighbors out, but there was no telling what.

He bought the farm with the wide bottom on it at the mouth of the creek. Some of his apple trees stood on the knoll a long time after his house had burned and he had sold his farm and moved up to Trap Branch.

Old Bill had been married before and brought with him some of the children by the first marriage. But he had his second woman with him when he came, a woman much younger than he. She had a child before she took up with Old Bill. Nobody ever asked whether she had been married before, or whether the pretty little girl with raven hair and flashing eyes was base-born, the result of an accident that her mother had "happened up against" before she ever knew Old Bill, or whether her mother was actually married to Old Bill.

As the girl developed, Old Bill began taking her around with him. She would ride astride the horse behind him and cling to the saddle as Old Bill rode up and down the valley or to the stores at the Mouth of Hood. Later, he would take her into the woods with him when he went squirrel hunting, "sanging," or to cut firewood with a crosscut saw. People could hear her screaming in the woods, but nobody felt compelled to go into the woods to see what was happening.

When she was fourteen she bore a child, a pretty little boy with black curly hair and flashing eyes. She called her son Ben. When Ben was a year old and she had weaned him, she ran away, leaving her child behind for her mother to raise. Nobody knew where she went, but folks thought maybe her mother had scrimped and saved enough money to send her back to her people in Old Virginia or North Carolina or wherever it was they had come from. Nobody ever heard tell of her again after she left the Mouth of Hood in a hack bound for the county seat.

Ben grew up with his half-brothers and -sisters. Being as his mother was a half-sister to his own half-brothers and -sisters, that made all of them his uncles and aunts, too, and in a way, I reckon, he was his own half-brother, but he didn't look like the rest of them. They were blue-eyed towheads. He favored his mother. Nobody outside the family ever mentioned to Ben the circumstances surrounding his birth, but he knew that Old Bill was his daddy and Bill's woman was his grandmother.

As I was saying, after Old Bill's house burned, he sold his farm and bought a little hillside farm on Trap Branch. His new farm had on it only a one-room cabin with a lean-to and barely enough bottom land for a garden. His big family lived there. The Sledges were dirt poor after they moved to Trap Branch. Every now and then Old Bill would work a day or two for another farmer for jowl and bacon to furnish enough grease to season the beans, cabbage, and turnip greens, and to fry meal for water gravy to have with cornbread and boiled potatoes. Even the coffee was made by boiling parched barley.

Old Bill's boys were not good workers. They mostly lay around the cabin quarreling, fighting one another, and drinking moonshine whiskey that they made in the deep wooded hollow behind the cabin. His girls were lazy and vicious. They had young 'ens, some thought by their own brothers, that they laid to young men up and down the creek who would go there on Saturday night. But the Sledges were good-looking people, wore clean clothes when they went visiting, and rode gaited horses with the flair of fine folks. The girls finally took up with widowers and took their illegitimate broods with them into their new homes.

Ben was a better worker than the older Sledges. When he was about 20 years old, he married the striking daughter of a man who had come to the creek to live a short time before from one of the counties up the river, maybe Magoffin. Ben went across the hill to Jobes Creek to live on a little branch-water farm like the one on which he had grown up. He became skilled in many lines of work: farmer, sawmill worker, carpenter, coffin maker, blacksmith, and moonshiner.

Not many people lived near him on Jobes Creek. He did not try to make up to neighbors. When he went visiting, he rode across the hill to be with his kinfolk, but he worked at sawmills, helped to build barns, reportedly made coffins for people who had died, and helped out at moonshine stills when he was up with his own work. His wife was industrious and saving. Ben was considered a "good liver," a man that kept his fences fixed, the bushes cut in his pastures, his house and out-buildings in good repair. He was prompt and fair in his business dealings and paid every penny he owed.

A tall, spare, and handsome man with a heavy black mustache and a shock of curly hair, Ben took pride in his personal appearance. His clothing clean, his fine black Stetson hat brushed, and his boots greased when he rode proudly out of his hollow in a creaking new saddle on a sleek, all-gaited black horse, Ben was an important looking man. But no one felt close to him. In crowds, he smiled a half-grudging smile below a forehead seamed by arched wrinkles, and he listened but said little himself. Yet, he was a frequent visitor among his kin and people whom he considered to be his friends.

He came to church but remained outside the building. He attended funerals and memorial meetings but moved only at the edge of crowds. He would even ride his black horse to the county seat during court and stand inside the courtroom to watch proceedings and listen to the lawyers when he was not himself involved in trials that were in progress. He rode to the jockey grounds of Baptist associations and watched horsetraders ride their plugs but hardly ever did any trading himself.

People thought well of Ben Sledge as a worker and generally as a neighbor and a familiar person at public places, but they did not try to get close to him. Women called him handsome and he was careful in observing courtesies usually accorded women, but they recoiled from him.

Things were whispered about him. His wife hardly ever left the branch on which they lived, it was said because he beat her and because of the shame she felt from having each of her three daughters bear an illegitimate child by their own father. It was also said that Ben visited whorehouses in the county seat town and had carried back to his wife a bad disease that she had suffered from for years and that he would not let her go to a doctor nor bring medicine to her. Two of his daughters had laid their children to young men to whom they had made themselves available after Ben knew about their pregnancy. In each case, a meeting had been arranged for the father to be able to appear to have just happened on the scene during intercourse. But the youngest daughter was feeble-minded. Ben's efforts to help her arrange a meeting with a young man, himself feeble-minded, failed. This daughter bore an illegitimate son, also feeble-minded, and continued to live with her parents.

Ben's older sons, both skilled like their father, married and left home. The youngest son, whose responsibility would include taking care of his father and mother in their old age and his feeble-minded sister and her child, was destined to inherit the home place. He married and moved into a little house he built around the point of the hill below his father's barn. His industrious wife, Noly, and their two small sons visited Ben's home each day and all helped out with stringing beans, chopping kraut, peeling apples for apple butter and drying, and other seasonal jobs that require all hands available for completion.

But there was trouble on the Sledge farm. The youngest son, Martin, had grown up resenting his father for his cruelty to his mother. Both father and son, aware of the depth of the resentment, avoided references to parental relationships in their conversations. When phrases dropped in unguarded moments reflected Ben's hatred of his wife, Martin's eyes flashed anger as he grew pale and rigid. Ben considered his son a dangerous enemy and knew that he always carried a pistol. They feared each other.

While the grandsons were playing in the barnlot and the retarded daughter and her child were picking beans or gathering apples, Ben's wife, Cely, who liked her daughter-in-law, reported to her much of the trouble she and her husband were having. For the previous five or six years Cely had refused to let Ben touch her because he had brought home the bad disease. He would beat her sometimes, or she would slip out of the house and hide behind trees or foddershocks or dodge behind outbuildings while he searched for her in the darkness. A few times he had fired his pistol at her when he had seen her rushing through the night from one hiding place to another. He was usually drunk when he behaved like this. Cely would sleep in the barn or the smokehouse loft or the corncrib. Next morning she would slip into the house and prepare breakfast, which Ben would eat in silence while she worked around the kitchen stove. They ate together at the same table only when other members of the family were present and they hardly ever talked to each other, even in the presence of other members of the family.

Ben and Martin had finished their annual run of apple brandy and reset the pummies for sour mash. They had been drinking heavily from their new supply of brandy. Ben, who had been drunk for nearly a week, became careless in his talk and infuriated Martin, also drunk at the time, with unkind references to Cely. Martin reached for his pistol to kill his father, but Ben, unarmed himself, fled. After that, Ben kept his pistol in his pocket but was careful not to refer to his troubles with Cely.

The following Sunday morning Martin and Noly, who had taken their sons to spend Saturday night with Noly's parents, went up to Ben's house to help Cely get her morning's work completed so she could go with them to a memorial meeting at the Butler graveyard on the ridge above Jobes Creek. They found Cely slumped in a chair at the table and weeping. Ben, wild from a week's drunk, had driven her from the house the night before and stumbled through the darkness nearly all night trying to find her. He had finally gone back to the house shortly before daylight. He had never seemed so dangerous before.

Noly poured a cup of coffee for each of them, including the retarded daughter and her son. They were sitting at the table sipping coffee and talking when Ben entered the room.

Ben, usually clean and well groomed, looked like a wild man. His hair was disheveled, he had not shaved, he was barefoot, and he had pulled his overalls on over his long-handled underwear without bothering to put on a shirt. His eyes flashed flames when he saw his weeping wife sitting at the table. Martin, rigid and pale-faced, watched.

Without speaking, Ben whipped out his pistol and fired it at his wife. Cely, screaming, fell to the floor as the bullet whizzed over her head. Noly dived under the table screaming as she saw Martin half rise from his chair while pulling his pistol from his pocket. Seeing that his son was drawing his pistol, Ben turned and fired at him but only grazed his left shoulder as Martin dodged. Martin fired at his father, who was advancing toward him, but he fired too soon and his bullet struck Hettie, the feeble-minded girl, in the hip as she was trying to rush from the room. Then, in the same moment, Ben fired at Martin's heart and Martin at his father's head and both of them dropped to the floor dead. Hettie lay screaming by the door, her son hovering over her.

Cely and Noly, wailing in anguish, clung to each other as they looked in horror at the scene before them. They could do nothing for a few minutes. Then Cely approached Ben's body, leaned over it, and laid her hand on his still chest above his heart. He was quite dead, his dark eyes growing darker in the mask of seamed wrinkles in his forehead, the deep lines that grooved their way from the sides of his nose into his heavy mustache. There was a bullet hole with a blue sponge in it in the middle of his forehead, between two of the seamed wrinkles. His pistol lay on the floor just below his right hand, the fingers curled upward as if he were asleep.

Noly felt for the pulse beat on Martin's limp wrist. He was dead, his blue eyes beaming darker even as she looked at him. She sat beside him and lifted his head into her lap as she wailed. Cely came and touched him, but she did not weep again.

Her face bloodless and her eyes big and hollow, Cely turned to Hettie, who lay writhing in pain by the door, her son trying to hold her still. Blood was oozing through the back of Hettie's dress. Cely lifted the dress to examine the wound. The bullet had gone into her hip at an angle, struck the bone, and torn an ugly hole in the flesh as it had come out. She looked at the door facing and saw the bullet half-buried in the soft poplar.

Cely thought Hettie might recover with no more than a limp. She sent the boy down the road to the store at the mouth of the branch to ask Mr. Slack to call the doctor for Hettie and to fetch Sim Butler, the local squire, and to bring neighbors for an inquest. She then brought a pan of warm water, a bottle of turpentine, and some clean cloths and dressed Hettie's wound, leaving her on the floor until enough people would gather in to carry her to a bed without hurting her. Noly went across the hill to report the killings to her father and ask her brothers and sisters to spread the news among neighbors.

Soon people gathered at the house, some bringing the food with them that they had prepared for the funeralizing at the Butler graveyard. Squire Butler arrived and held an inquest. The bodies were placed on beds and men dressed them for burial while two carpenters made coffins in the driveway between the corncribs and young men dug graves on the top of the point above the barn.

Late that afternoon just after I had arrived home from a visit with friends in another valley and heard the news of the double murder, an aged bareheaded woman with gray hair and a gray face appeared at the gate and asked to see my father. I did not know her, but I called my father. I asked her to come in, but she said she wanted to talk with my father confidentially and she would just wait there. Her eyes were large and hollow-looking, and the lavender shawl she wore around her shoulders gave her gray hair and face an ashen tint. She stood quietly by the gate, her long, gray hand resting on a post.

My father appeared, addressed her as "Aunt Cely," and invited her to come in, but she asked him to come to her, that she wanted to talk with him confidentially. He walked to the gate and they talked in low voices. My mother came and looked through the door. "That's Cely Sledge," she said. "I have not seen her since before your daddy and me married. She was pretty when she was young and is still a good-looking woman in spite of all the trouble she's had. I wonder what she has come across that long hill all by herself to talk about, after what's happened over there."

Suddenly, Cely screeched, "That's where it is! I want you to go over there and tear it out of there! Cut it up!"

She turned on her heels and ran back toward Jobes Creek.

As she had thought all day about the killings, she had decided that the root of all the trouble was the moonshine still. Besides, the men who had gathered in to sit up with the dead had found it. They were already drunk on the mash and maybe the whiskey they had found hidden around. Some of them were acting up. She was afraid there would be more trouble. The sheriff's deputies would probably find the still, and she did not know what might happen after that.

Papa had told her that he would come over after supper and get some of the fellows to help him tear the still out and hide it in a cliff somewhere till the trouble blew over. Then she could decide what to do with it. Papa saw no use in destroying it right away. A good still is worth something.

When Papa arrived he found the preacher and a few of the faithful in the hardshell church already there singing plaintive hymns while women wailed. Sounds of sawing and hammering came from the corncrib, where the coffins were being made. Most of the men were drunk. Out in the darkness beyond the reach of the lamplight through the doors and windows of the house and the lantern light at the crib they hunkered on their heels in little clumps, telling tales, laughing loud, and whooping at the punch lines of jokes and accounts of rustles they had pulled as they passed around jars of moonshine and sour mash.

Children squatted beside their wailing mothers. Young people had gathered in the kitchen and dining room, where they plucked food from platters and bowls and ate, talked, and laughed. Cely, hollow-eyed, tearless, ashen-faced, sat erect and silent on the edge of the bed in which Hettie lay, her wound probed and dressed by the doctor, who had come and gone.

Ben's face looked dark in the dim light from the lamp on the stand table between the two beds. The band holding his chin in place while he was becoming stiff had been removed, but the nickels holding his eyelids down had been left. It was decided that his face needed shaving, that maybe his heavy beard had actually grown some after his death. Hair, beard, and fingernails continue to grow for a little while on a healthy man who dies suddenly. Most of the men were unwilling to try to shave him, but all agreed that he should be shaved. A half-drunk neighbor, admitting that he had never shaved anybody's face except his own, and that not very often, volunteered to shave Ben if someone would hold the light for him.

Ben's shaving mug, brush, straight razor, bay lotion, and talcum were brought, along with a pan of warm water, a cake of hand soap and a towel. The fumbling volunteer prepared Ben's face for the razor and then began shaving upward against the wiry beard. Soon black blood began to ooze from the slits, but the volunteer shaved on, simply wiping away the blood with the towel. When someone protested that he was cutting the man's face all to pieces, he observed, "W'y, brother, he can't feel it. He's dead, ye know," and continued. When he had finished shaving the sides of the face, he called for a drink of moonshine before tackling the chin and throat. "His beard is as tough as bobwire," he said. Slitting the throat even more than the sides of the face, he finished the job, wiped away the blood, applied the bay lotion, and caked the face with talcum powder. Then he removed the nickels from the eyes of the corpse and dropped them into his pocket as he said, "Well, sir, I'll just charge you a dime for the last shave you'll ever get here in this old world."

Papa asked one of the older sons of the Sledge family where Ben kept his still hidden when he was not running it. Then he asked two young fellows to help him dismantle it. They destroyed the furnace, poured out the mash, and rolled the barrels into the barn, where they turned them upside down in a dry stall. Papa hid the still, worm, and connections in the hollow oak that was a marker between the Sledge farm and the Bentley tract, where Ben's older son would find it after the trouble died down.

The burial took place Monday afternoon. Ben and Martin in their black coffins rested on kitchen chairs on the front porch of the house while the funeral was being held. Cely, dry-eyed and ashen-faced, weeping Noly, Ben's wailing daughters, and sober-faced sons sat in cane-bottom chairs behind the coffins. People stood around in the yard, or leaned against the fence, or squatted on their heels while chewing grass blades at the edge of the lane. The hardshells sang funeral plaints, women wailed, and babies cried. Then the little preacher with a lame leg asked that they kneel while he prayed. His long cadenced prayer, rising to heights that echoed among the hilltops, asked for blessings on the quick and the dead and salvation for those deep in sin. Women shouted and wailed with fervor. Then he preached a sermon about the sower that cast his seed, some on stony ground. There was more singing while those who had not viewed the corpses filed by the open coffins, then a short prayer in a more subdued style asking for guidance and safekeeping in the faith. Ben's oldest son put the full-length lids on the coffins and drove down the nails that would hold them in place.

The broiling sun beat down upon the crowd as it zigzagged its way up the steep hillside to the graveyard at the top of the point. Pallbearers sweated in the August heat and "spelled" one another often as they struggled with their burdens up the hill. As the entourage drew close to the graveyard, the lame-legged preacher thought there should be a song appropriate to the occasion, but did not suggest one.

Before further consideration could be given to a song, a young woman with a loud voice and who had not been winded in the least by the steep climb to the graveyard began "You've Got to Reap Just What You Sow," two or three joining her for a few lines and then dropping out. She finished the song as a solo, apparently without thinking that it was, maybe, too appropriate for the occasion, even for the strict hardshells' taste.

My Tonsillectomy

I had suffered from tonsillitis from time to time since I could remember. Sometimes infections from the throat spread also into my ears and I would have earache accompanied by fever and then the bursting of pustules within and the draining of blood and pus onto my pillow at night. To relieve the pain from the ear infection during the period of fever, my mother provided me with a spoon with a bent handle. I would warm it by the fire, pee a few drops into it and pour the urine into my ear, and then stuff in a wad of quilt batting to hold it there. I kept the spoon hidden behind the mantel. As I recall, the warm urine sealed in with the quilt batting brought relief from pain and I could go back to sleep.

When pustules appeared on my tonsils, my father prepared for me a gargle consisting of table salt, alum, vinegar, and yellow root (golden seal) dissolved in warm water, sweetened with rock candy, and tempered with whiskey. The gargle not only cleaned away the pustules on my tonsils but also removed the white coating from my tongue. The tongue and the whole inside of my mouth would smart from the presence of the salt and draw and pucker in response to the alum. Then a second mouthful would wash away what the first one had drawn off and I could taste for a long time the blended bitterness of the yellow root, the sourness of the vinegar, and the sweetness of the candy and whiskey. My mouth then felt clean and the pain in my throat would be relieved.

Between the Christmas and New Year's Eve of 1928, while I was home from Cumberland College, I developed tonsillitis and earache. The infection made me feel bad and kept me hovering close to the fireplace for warmth against the chills of the fever. I went with my brother and sister to a party at the house on the joining farm, but my ear seemed to be stopped up, my throat was sore, and I did not enjoy participating in the party activities as much as I usually did.

The following morning my throat was swollen and I had swelling below my left ear. My father administered his remedy and advised that I stay close to the fire for a day or two. When the swelling went down, he said, he would take me to Dr. Gambill at Blaine to have my tonsils removed. He thought it would not delay my return to college, for he understood that people just sat down, had their tonsils cut out, got up, and went on about their business and that the soreness lasted only three or four days.

The swelling under my ear started to go down in a day or two and no new pustules had appeared on my tonsils, though one of them was still enlarged. The first day we set for the trip to Blaine was wet and cold with snow blowing in the air. My father thought it might not be good for me to be exposed to weather like that after my tonsils had been removed, so we waited for a better day. I sat close to the fire that day and held a warm wet cloth against my neck to help the swelling go down.

The weather changed that night. The following morning was bright and clear but there was frost on the ground and blowing in the air. My father saddled the mules while my mother found overalls for me to wear over my suit, two pullover wool caps, and a warm scarf to wrap around my neck. All bundled up and with an overcoat on over everything else, I climbed on Old Pearl, the tall pearl-nosed mule, to ride the five miles from our home to Blaine.

Dr. John Gambill did not know we were coming. He was not in his office when we arrived. I waited in the bank, cozy and warm from a gas heater that hissed at me as I hovered over it, while my father walked up to the doctor's home. Soon I saw my father and the doctor coming down the walk and went out to meet them at the door of the office.

Dr. Gambill placed me on a stool by a window and peered into my throat as he pressed my tongue down with one little wooden paddle and the sides of my throat back with another. There were no pustules visible, he said, but one of the tonsils was swollen. He thought it might bleed considerably if it were removed then. It might be better if I were to wait until the swelling had gone down before having it removed. I expressed anxiety about being late to college following the holidays and wondered whether he was willing to remove the swollen tonsil anyway.

He looked at my father for a moment, but my father said nothing and looked as if the problem were to be settled between me and the doctor. Dr. Gambill then asked me about college, whether I was liking it, how long it took me to get from Blaine to Williamsburg, and what I expected to become after I finished college. Then he picked up two little paddles and repeated the examination. The swollen tonsil would probably bleed a great deal, he repeated.

He poured some water into a flat pan over a gas burner, lighted the gas, and placed some instruments of shiny metal in the pan to sterilize them. He then washed his hands at a sink, put on some tightly fitting gloves, spread a white towel across my chest, pulled a stand with a basin on it close beside me, and swabbed my throat and tonsils with alcohol. The swabbing made me gag a time or two and I thought I might vomit but did not.

Then with a pair of little tongs he picked an instrument from the steaming flat pan. After it cooled for a moment, he took it in his hands and manipulated it to see that it was working well. It seemed to be a metal tube about eight inches long with a thin double wire run through it that could be pushed out to a loop and then pulled with a little handle back into the tube. He laid it carefully on a white cloth on a little table close by. Then from the steaming pan he plucked a thin little rod that was bent slightly at one end and laid it on the white cloth to cool. Another tube and another rod remained in the pan.

Standing between me and the window, he inserted the tube, extended the fine wire loop, and worked it around my less swollen tonsil with the little bent rod. He laid the rod down and pulled the wire firmly with great force. I could hear the wire cutting the tonsil from its stem and feel the pull against my throat, but there was not much pain. The tonsil came rolling across my tongue and I spat it into the basin on the stand beside me. The blood began to gush from the stub where the tonsil had been. The doctor allowed me to spit the blood into the basin and then asked that I gargle something for a minute or two.

He had difficulty getting the wire loop behind the swollen tonsil. When the blood from the stub for the other tonsil began to strangle me, he permitted me to spit it out, had me gargle again, and then tried a second time to work the loop behind the swollen tonsil. I was strangling again, but he kept on working. I managed to swallow the blood that was collecting in my throat. He laid the little rod down and pulled the wire to cut the swollen tonsil. Again, I could hear the wire cutting the flesh but my throat felt as if he were pulling it out along with the tonsil. This time, only about two thirds of the tonsil came out, followed by a gush of blood. I held my open mouth over the basin and let the blood flow into it.

After the tonsil had bled for a few minutes, the doctor swabbed it with something that tasted a bit like vinegar. Then he worked the wire loop behind what was left of the swollen tonsil and pulled again. Again, I had the feeling that my throat was being pulled out. A disc, perhaps a half inch thick, of tonsil flipped from my throat. The doctor looked disappointed.

He explained that a part of the tonsil was left but that it would not be possible for him to remove it with the instrument. It would heal and would probably give me no trouble, but it would take longer to heal than the stub for the other tonsil.

The tonsil continued to bleed, though. I would hold my head over and the blood would run out of my mouth into the basin. Soon both sides of my neck below my ears began to pain sharply and some of the blood was collecting in my throat so that I had to swallow it.

Dr. Gambill thought I ought not to ride back to Gaines Creek with my throat bleeding like that. The liquid that he had me gargle from time to time did not stop the bleeding. After half an hour, he told my father that I could stay in his house for as long as I needed to and that his niece, Louise, could look after me until the bleeding stopped and it seemed all right for me to ride a mule back home.

My father assisted me up the flights of steps that led to the Gambill home on the low hill across the road from the old Methodist church. When the two Gambill women and Louise met us at the door, he apologized for the shabby paint-covered overalls I was wearing and asked the doctor when he should

return to take me home. The doctor thought I might be able to go home the
following afternoon if it was a fair day.

Louise assisted me upstairs to a bedroom, prepared the bed for me, placed
a basin on a table beside it for me to spit blood into, and left me. I undressed
down to my shirt and long underwear and climbed into the bed. I was not
able to sleep for the bleeding, and it seemed that I was having to swallow
much of the blood.

At lunch time Louise brought a tray on which were a cup of chicken soup,
a glass of milk, and a glass of bright red apple juice. I sat on the side of the
bed and drank the liquids very slowly, for each time I swallowed I felt as if
I were pulling a heavy load of pain out of my throat and letting it drop back
suddenly with a noisy splash. But my throat was not bleeding as much as it
had been.

By the middle of the afternoon I could sleep a few minutes at a time by
lying on my left side. By supper time the bleeding was reduced to a trickle
that collected in my throat and had to be swallowed. I dressed and ate supper
with the family but only liquids had been prepared for me. Some time after
I returned to my room Dr. Gambill came in, checked my pulse, took my temperature, looked at my throat, and gave me a mild liquid laxative to com-
bat the constipation that he said would result from my having swallowed so
much blood. If bleeding did not begin again and I did not take a cold or develop
a fever, I ought to be able to go home the following afternoon, he said.

I slept well for a time, lying on my left side. I was aware of intermit-
tent bleeding in my throat, but only a few drops of blood flowed at a time.
Finding that clearing my throat increased the blood flow, I lay in such a way
that the blood trickled into my mouth. Deep into the night I woke up completely, aware that I had been having bad dreams, one of which was about
my trying to respond to my mother from a hilltop on our farm when she
appeared between the chimney of our house and the garden fence and called
for me to come to dinner. I was unable to sound my voice. When I tried to
answer, only a hiss came from a pained throat. After I woke up, I groaned
enough to assure myself that I had not lost my voice and I found that my
throat was extremely sore but that it was no longer bleeding. I lay awake a
long time in the quiet darkness and wondered whether I would be able to
return to college on time. Sleep in the latter part of the night was deep and
untroubled. I was becoming only dimly aware of the stirrings in the Gambill
household when there was a knock on the door.

When I said "come in," heavy sore lumps moved in my throat and my
voice was feeble and thin. Louise entered with a glass of warm salt water for
me to gargle and a glass of warm red apple juice for me to drink before I
reported for breakfast. After gargling and drinking, I dressed myself before
going to the bathroom to wash my face and hands and comb my hair.

Dressed and arranged, I joined the Gambills for breakfast. The Gambill women had cooked oatmeal and poached an egg for me. Dr. Gambill said I should eat soft foods only for at least three days and should avoid cold drinks and hot drinks. The women had warmed a cup of milk for me. Breakfast table conversation was lively, but I did not attempt to participate in it. Before the breakfast was over, the telephone rang for Dr. Harry. He finished his breakfast hurriedly, excused himself, and went to change his clothes for a horseback trip to a home over the hills from Blaine. About the time we were finishing breakfast, Dr. Harry, wearing rubber boots into which the bottoms of heavy wool pants had been stuffed, a flannel shirt, a long overcoat, and a leather cap, left to saddle his horse and respond to the call to visit a sick child. Dr. John looked into my mouth, checked my pulse, and laid his hand on my head to determine whether I had fever. Since the day was clear, even though frost was heavy on the grass in the Gambill yard, he thought I would be able to go home when my father came for me, but I should not return to college for at least five days. He then left for his office down in the little town.

I sat with Charley in the living room and listened to the radio while waiting for my father. Charley and I could not engage in conversation, for talking hurt my throat.

Although the doctor had said that I might be able to go home in the afternoon, my father arrived about 10 o'clock. Not wanting me to strain to mount the mule, he helped me into the saddle. We rode slowly up Caines Creek, for my father thought a cantering, trotting, or loping pace of my mule might cause my throat to hemorrhage. There was no wind that day. The sunshine was bright, and the frozen roadbed was melting into puddles of thin black mud that spattered when the hooves of the mules struck it. We rode so slowly that it took us nearly an hour to cover the five miles from Blaine to our home. But the frozen earth had melted so fast that we were spattered from head to foot with black mud.

My mother warmed milk and crumbled into it cornbread from which the crust had been removed for the main dish for my lunch. I had also a soft egg, a cup of bean soup, and a dish of stewed apples. Then I took off my shoes and lay down, fully dressed but with a comforter over me, for an hour or two. (We thought it unmanly to undress and go to bed in the daytime unless we were very sick.)

After my nap, I wrote a letter to President Creech at Cumberland College telling him that I had had my tonsils taken out, that there had been considerable bleeding, and that the doctor had said I should not attempt to ride horseback to the railroad station for at least five days. I would be three days late after the holidays, and he might want to get somebody for the first week following the holidays to sweep and clean the classroom for which I was responsible, since breathing dust from the floor and the erasers might be hard on my throat before it had completely healed. I wrote also to Dean Reuben Lawson explaining my situation and asking him to have the Yates boy deliver the mail for me until I returned.

The next three days were cloudy and dark with occasional rain and soft snow blowing. But the earth had not frozen again. I sat in a rocking chair between the window and the fireplace during the day and read books I had brought home with me from college. The soreness on the right side of my throat and neck was almost gone, but the stub of the left tonsil was swollen and sore. A hard sore pane of swelling extended from my ear to the base of my neck. When I looked into my throat in the looking glass my father used while shaving, I could see the raw stub with a whorl of ridges and hollows in it like a wilted red rose. Bits of soft food and yellow pustules were scattered across it.

My father prepared a gargle for me to use to clear away the food and the pustules, but I found it necessary to dislodge some of the food particles with the end of my fountain pen. Dislodging the food did not hurt much, for the ridge-like surface of the stub did not have much feeling in it. The soreness was mostly behind and around the rim of the ugly stub.

The sun was shining on the day that my father took me to Webbville, but the road was muddy. The hooves of the mules sank into the wet clay and made sucking sounds when they were pulled out. We could not ride very fast.

Not many people were traveling on the trains that day. The coach of the "Blue Goose" on the old E.K. Railroad from Webbville to Riverton had only a few passengers in it. I was the only passenger waiting in the depot at Hitchens for the west-bound train to Winchester. I sat near the stove in the little depot and read.

The only person to come in during the long wait was a tall man with dark hair, a high nose, and small black eyes and wearing a long light gray alpaca coat. He sat on a bench for a short time and left. Because I had admired his coat, I remembered that I had seen him come into the station for a few minutes and then leave while I was waiting for my train on my way home from college. I saw that same man wearing his fine coat come into the depot, sit for a few minutes, and then get up and hurry away every time I was in the Hitchens depot for the next three years. In all of those encounters, though, I never saw him looking at me or at anybody else. I wondered what his story was, why he came, in his fine coat, to sit in the station for a few minutes near train time, why he was not working, whether he might have been some kind of railroad detective or watchman, one of whose charges was to check passengers, or whether he was looking for someone who had left Hitchens and might return some time, a wife, a sweetheart, an enemy. He never spoke to the station master. The station master apparently took no note of his presence.

The train to Winchester had only a few passengers on it. People sat alone in seats for two and read, or looked out the windows, or slept with hats pulled down over their faces. I had a long wait between trains at Winchester. Since the sun was still shining and it was not very cold, I walked a few blocks through the business section and then returned for supper to a little restaurant in a shabby building across the railroad tracks, where I had soup, milk, and a piece of apple pie. Only four or five people were eating at the little restaurant.

Long after dark I boarded the L. and N. train for Williamsburg. Again, not many passengers were traveling. Soon after the train started the lights in the coach were turned off and people leaned back in their seats and slept. I removed my shoes and lay down in two seats, lifting my knees to fit into the space. I sat up to look out the windows at the towns through which we passed and recalled again, as the train passed through Berea, the night I spent sleeping on newspapers on the floor of the railroad station there.

It must have been 1 o'clock in the morning or later when I got off the train in Williamsburg, the only passenger to dismount there. Only the station master, the baggage man, and a taxicab driver were at the station. I retrieved my bag and engaged the taxicab. When the driver let me out at the end of the long walk leading to Felix Hall I paid him a quarter.

As I walked toward the dormitory, shifting my heavy bag from hand to hand, I could see frost dancing in the air between me and the glaring lights fastened to the gables of the building more than three stories up. The building seemed taller than I remembered, no lights shone from any of the windows, and my footsteps echoed across the lawn. Remembering that lights had been out since 10 o'clock, I felt guilty about coming into the building at 2 o'clock in the morning.

The front door was locked. I considered whether I should tap at Dean Lawson's window and decided that, before doing so, I would see whether a back door that opened into a courtyard between the wings of the building might have been left unlocked. There was no walk around the east side of the building. Trees and bushes at the edge of a forest grew up to the wall, but the raw bulbs high up in the eaves provided enough light as I stumbled uncertainly along with my heavy load, the frost bloom crunching under my feet.

The door was unlocked, but the light bulb in the narrow stairwell had burned out. I lugged my suitcase up the steep, dark stairs to my room, located on the second floor, in the corner of the building across from the exit to the stairway. Once inside my room and looking again at the familiar furnishings, I found it hard to believe that I had been gone three weeks. Except for the vivid memories of my tonsillectomy and what happened afterwards, my holiday season was something apart from me now, something that belonged to the past.

My tonsil stub was still sore. It did not heal for a long time. Particles of food would lodge in the crevices and holes in the stub, sometimes causing infections that I would break by punching the pustules with the end of my fountain pen. I would then gargle Listerine to wash away the pus and blood. For many years I continued to have tonsillitis on the stub, but finally the whorl contracted and withered to a ragged scar in which fragments of food would sometimes lodge and I would have to punch them out with the end of my fountain pen.

Appalachian Folkways: Illnesses, Accidents, Healing and Curing

Home remedies were used for the treatment of minor illnesses, ailments, and injuries. My father, who, as a boy, had gone along with his grandmother, an herb doctor and skilled midwife ("granny-woman"), to tote the "yarbs" she gathered annually, knew the properties and uses of medicinal plants, barks, and berries. He had also inherited from his maternal grandfather a substantially bound copy of Dr. King's *The Family Physician,* published in 1874, to which he referred for herbal treatment of illnesses. When we became ill, or behaved in a "pindly and droopy" fashion, or developed sores, boils, or rashes, or injured ourselves, he would examine us gravely and prepare a treatment.

Skunk oil ("polecat grease") was administered when we developed croup. Perhaps the worst medicine I ever took for an illness was rancid polecat grease. I was forcefully held and required to gargle with it when I developed croup one winter when I was perhaps four or five years old, though my retching and vomiting and the heightened anxiety of my father and mother might have intensified and made permanent my memory of an experience from my second or third year. A hot poultice of fried onions was applied to the upper part of the chest when we developed a cold that was accompanied by fever. My father determined whether we had fever by checking our pulse, looking at our tongues, and laying his hand on our foreheads to make a judgment about our temperature. For a persistent cold accompanied by a barking cough, we drank hot catnip tea, sweetened with sorghum molasses or honey, inhaled the fumes from a mentholated salve dropped in boiling water in a pot, hooded by a large towel the edge of which we would lift above our noses while inhaling, and wore on our chests ("breasts") woolen cloths soaked in turpentine, creosote, liniment, and kerosene. Thus treated and poulticed, we bathed our feet in a pan of water as hot as we could stand, "baked" them dry by the fire, and rushed off to bed. The woolen poultice caused us to itch and the concoction produced blisters, both of which were considered desirable. The colds usually broke under this treatment, the coughs became productive, and breathing was improved, but we were required to wear the poultices pinned inside our "long handles" until the cold was declared cured.

For an upset stomach, both catnip and ginseng tea was used. Children who were restless at night or suffered from bad dreams were also administered catnip tea. If the child had difficulty urinating, a tea made from crushed watermelon seeds was administered. If he wet the bed or urinated too easily a few drops of ratsbane tea at night was considered helpful. Among the more superstitious mountain folk, children were required to wear suspended from a string around their necks small bags of asafoetida to ward off colds and a lead pellet to protect them from witches and demons that tormented them with nightmares. The less superstitious had children sleep with dirty socks over their noses to stave off nightmares.

For a sore throat we gargled a bitter and puckering liquid strained from yellow root and alum boiled together, fortified with whiskey, and made tolerable by dissolving rock candy into it. The "medicine" stripped the white coats from our tongues and the infection from our throats, disinfecting both by the alcohol it contained. The remedy was also used as a treatment for tonsillitis, with which I was plagued every winter until I had my tonsils removed.

Occasionally we caught the itch. We were required to take a spoonful of sulphur in molasses before breakfast, bathe at night in water as hot as we could stand and on the hearth in front of a roaring fire, anoint ourselves liberally and vigorously with a salve made of lard and sulphur, and wear the same clothes until we were cured. In preparation for a treatment for itch, we selected clothing and bed linen that could be abandoned after the cure. I caught itch (called "the seven-year eech" in my community) at least twice while in grade school, once in college, and once while teaching in high school. The odor of sulphur rises from one's skin for several days after the treatment for itch is over. Others are able to smell it and know that one has had itch. An alternative but extremely painful remedy is the liquor from pokeroot, one application of which is effective and leaves no tell-tale odor.

For ridding ourselves of head lice, common in crowded schoolrooms, we anointed our heads with oil (castor oil, kerosene, lard) and combed our hair with fine-tooth combs, examining the combs carefully after each stroke for lice or nits which we "cracked" between our thumbnails. By the time I was in fourth or fifth grade it was possible to buy at the country stores a powder called red percipitate ("red passipity") for ridding one's self of nits and lice. People who habitually had itch or lice were considered "onery and lowdown." Self-respecting folk not only rid themselves of both as quietly and rapidly as possible but did the same with chinches ("bed bugs") as well. Since people did not admit readily that they were afflicted by any of these plagues, teachers found it difficult to deal with the problems when they arose at school.

Along with my frequent attacks of tonsillitis I suffered also from ear infections. Occasionally, infections would break and blood and pus would flow from my ears. Before the infection had reached the breaking point I suffered intense pain, the area around my ears would swell, and I would develop a fever. Treatment included bathing the swollen area with a strong liniment and applying hot wet cloths and even pouring warm urine into the ear and stopping the ear with wool or cotton batting. Sometimes tobacco smoke was blown into an aching ear.

In early summer we were "wormed." If we became lazy, restless and fretful, and did not sleep well, our father would look for light rings around our mouths just at the outer edge of our lips. The presence of a ring around any of our mouths was the harbinger of worming time. On the day set for the ordeal we did not eat breakfast. Instead, we drank in cold coffee either a vermifuge tea produced from the steeping of the leaves of the vermifuge plants that grew in the corner of the garden or a white powder obtained from the country doctor. A half-hour later we took liberal doses of castor oil in cold coffee. We were instructed to "go" on a sandy beach behind the willow trees near the barn, to count the number of worms on the sand each time we went, and to report the number to our mother, who kept score for the competition. I remember that my brother, of darker complexion than my sister and I and around whose mouth the light ring usually appeared first, won the competition one summer with a score of 37. It was sometimes necessary that we be wormed several times each summer. Our father insisted that eating green apples, which we often picked up from the ground in the chicken lot where apple trees grew, caused the worms. He would often preface the announcement of the worming day with the accusation that he saw we could not "leave them green apples alone." The problem of worms in the children of the community was general. Stories were told about children who had died from worms and from whose mouths and "hind ends" worms had crawled soon after their death. Once at school one of our playmates, who began to choke at his seat, rose up beside his seat, reached back into his throat with his fingers, pulled out a long white worm, and tossed it on the floor. The episode was so frightening that no one laughed.

Insect bites and stings often became infected and developed into open sores or, at times, boils. A bee sting could be treated with a raw onion, a poultice of salt, soda, and water, or three leaves, each from different plants of any kind, crushed together and applied directly to the sting, but the standard treatment of a sting of a bee, wasp, or hornet was the application of a chew of tobacco. I remember one humiliating encounter I had with a hornet. When I was in the early grades in school and before there were screen doors and windows, I was wallowing on the bed one morning in late summer while my mother combed and braided my protesting sister's hair in preparation for our leaving for school. The weather was warm and flies were everywhere in spite of all the "tanglefoot" pads scattered about on tables and cabinets. Since hornets devour flies, my parents were pleased to have them build nests in the eaves of the buildings and they were welcome guests on the porch and in the house, even though they required respect on their own terms. While wallowing about, I rolled over on a hornet that stung me hard in the fleshy part of my rump. I yelped like a dog as I sprang to my feet. The hornet had responded to the invasion of his rights with such fury that he found it difficult to disengage himself from the seat of my overalls. My mother came running to see what was the matter and brushed the hornet away. I was required to take off my "britches" and lie on the bed for her to examine the sting, already swollen to the size of a half walnut and sending through me waves of severe pain. She sent my sister for baking soda, took a pinch of it, wet it in her mouth, and rubbed it on the place. Knowing that I was particularly sensitive to bee stings, she wished that there were tobacco to apply to my injury, but there was none. She advised that I lie still while she waited for the "big school young 'ens" from up the creek to come along. Soon a young woman, perhaps 17 or 18 years old and so advanced in her studies that she was called on to continue with the classes when it was necessary for the teacher to be absent from the schoolroom, came along the road. My mother asked her whether she had any chewing tobacco. Fortunately, she had just "wet through" the sizeable chew of home-grown she had in her mouth at the time. She came in and she and my mother together applied the chew to my sting, she holding it flatly and firmly against the sting while Mama continued to braid my sister's hair. The humiliation of my having to reveal my nakedness to the young woman made me shy in her presence for a while, but she was sufficiently insightful and considerate never to refer to the incident or to betray by glance or smile that she even remembered it.

In the late dry afternoons tiny black gnats attacked us. After rains, mosquitoes came. To discourage them my mother filled vases and "flowerpots" with "pennyrile," a pungent mint-like plant that grew along the face of the poor and sun-baked hillside above our hog lot. Slapping at gnats and mosquitoes was a regular part of communication as we sat on the porch following the evening meal. We were advised not to scratch but to rub insect bites with the ball of the hand. At night, though, we reverted to the instinctive mode of dealing with itching and often "dug ourselves raw." We applied liniment to painful bites, but such relief from distress as we enjoyed probably came more from the rubbing than from any curative properties the liniment might have had.

Running barefoot through wet weeds and grass brought infection to raw sores from insect bites, and impetigo (summer sores) was common among all of the children at the school. The standard treatment was either a salve made of sulfur and lard or a carbolic salve which every household kept. This salve could be bought from traveling medicine men who sold other salves, ointments, liniments, cordials, laxatives, women's tonics, and other remedies as well as cake flavorings and spices. Those were days before adhesive plasters were available. It was not uncommon to see children striped out like zebra with bandages around arms and legs and sometimes necks and heads and with "finger pokes" and "toe pokes" for infected extremities. For "drawing out pizen" from boils, infected bruises on the feet, or splinters and briars embedded in the flesh we used several applications noted for their drawing power. Stone bruises responded to poultices made of the boiled bark of the root of the slippery elm. Boils could be brought to a head by applying fat bacon, the lining of an egg shell, a slippery elm poultice with alum in it, a jimson weed poultice, or a "drawing" salve. Splinters and briars could be drawn from infected spots with an application of a powerful drawing salve consisting of one portion each of mutton tallow, resin, and beeswax melted together over slow heat.

To dry up poison ivy, juice from either the jewel weed (waterweed, or touch-me-not) or slippery elm was used. A sprained ankle was bound in brown paper soaked in vinegar. A stone bruise, like a boil, could be brought to a head with an application of a slippery elm-alum poultice.

To protect ourselves from chiggers when we went berry-picking in late summer or helped to put up hay, we greased ourselves with a meatskin. Thusly greased, we sweated freely, the drops of sweat standing out like beads and rolling along on the slippery surface of the skin. Even so, the perspiration, would sometimes wash away the salty lard, particularly under the arms, in the crotch, and wherever clothing rubbed the body. Chiggers would attack these areas. After we returned home, we used strong lye soap when we bathed and rubbed kerosene under our arms, around our bodies where the "wesbans" of our clothing bound us, and in our crotches. Once a chigger had lodged himself, even removing him with kerosene would not prevent the intense itching produced by the bite. Chigger bites under the arm became infected easily and required generous applications of drawing salve to prevent serious boils.

For cuts, abrasions, and punctures turpentine was used extensively. If one cut his hand, the standard treatment was to clean the cut with hydrogen peroxide, wash it in warm water, rub turpentine in it, and bind it up. Once I was playing with the cider mill in my grandfather's distillery. Grampa had removed the handle to discourage us from playing with the mill, but I was turning the wheel by the spokes when the end of my middle finger became caught in the cogs and was ground almost off before I could stop the wheel.

Although I was not sensitive to the pain, I was surprised to see first the end of the finger chewed up and the nail flopping crazily at the side of it and then frightened at the blood that rushed out. I ran to my grandmother for help. She had me grip my finger tightly with my left hand while she prepared from a piece of white muslin, a finger stall with streamers to be tied around my wrist. She then poured hydrogen peroxide on the finger, washed it in warm water, and pushed it down into the poke, into which she had poured perhaps a tablespoon full of crushed rock salt. When the salt came in contact with the mangled flesh I danced a jig of excruciating pain and anguish. But the bleeding stopped soon and the finger appeared to lose its sense of feeling as the pain subsided. When I took the finger out of the poke next morning the mangled flesh was a pink, clean-looking mass, the bleached nail dropped away, and the end of the bone was visible. My mother washed it in warm water, applied carbolic salve, wrapped a clean cloth around it, and inserted it in the stall Granny had prepared. The flesh finally grew back over the end of the bone and a curved nail, shaped like the top third of a marble, ultimately grew in place, for the root of the nail had not been destroyed. Although five medical doctors were practicing within five miles of our home, my parents were so pleased with Granny's ministrations that they did not think it necessary to take me to a doctor.

Measles was broken out by administering hot toddies of various kinds, some including ginger, some catnip, some horehound. I was pleased that I had measles while I was away attending high school, for I escaped the ordeal of having to drink the sheep dung tea prescribed in my community for "breaking out the measles."

We escaped some of the illnesses that came to other children in our valley. We did not get typhoid, which raged along the valley one summer and led to recommendations of attending physicians that we build screen doors and windows for our homes and sprinkle quicklime in the pits of our privies. Nor did we suffer from the bloody flux from which two of our playmates in one family died on the same day, or cholera morbus, which took some of the older residents one summer, or scarlet fever which struck some of the families.

The influenza epidemic of 1918 did not reach our valley, but all of us in the family were down at the same time with influenza in the winter of 1919-1920. Having heard that so many in the county-seat town had died so close together from the disease during the epidemic that it had been necessary to bury many of them wrapped in blankets instead of in coffins, we were afraid that some or all of us would die. Approaching the age of nine years at the time, I was the last to succumb and the first to recover. I cut kindling, carried in coal, kept the fires going, carried out ashes, drew water from the well and boiled water for two or three days. I also carried out, emptied, and washed chamber pots and spittoons and did other chores that needed to be done. My grandmother cooked for us, Grampa would bring the food in a basket to the edge of the porch, and I would bring it into the house and serve it to those who were able to sit on the side of the bed and eat it. My uncles came and attended to the livestock. After I came down with the disease, my father's cousin who had had flu earlier in the year came and stayed with us until I was up again. My father and my brother were extremely ill; both suffered from high fever, and my brother was delirious. All had nightmares and were plagued with distressing coughs. We came through the terrifying experience with only one call by the doctor, who had left an ample supply of pills and powders for the entire family and instructed us concerning our diet while the fever was in us.

A wealth of folklore relating to ailments and physiological conditions existed in the community. Suckling babies often developed "thrash," especially but not always in the hot summer months. One treatment was to wash the baby's mouth with a brew made from boiling the bark from the root of a yellow oak, but more often than not mothers preferred the ministrations of people who were "charmed" by some magical condition. The seventh son of a seventh son or a man born after the death of his father would be invited to blow his breath into the mouth of an infected baby. If I recall correctly, only men possessed this magical power. Sometimes a distressed mother would carry her "young 'en with the thrash" on her hip over mountain trails to visit a charmer. Men who possessed the "power to cure thrash" offered their services freely, performed with gravity and a certain air of mystery, and did not accept pay, for they accounted their power a gift, not an achievement.

The removal of warts was accomplished by the use of an especially wide variety of nostrums and charms. Warts could be removed for firm believers by wart witches who, like fire witches, passed their hands lightly over the warts while reciting in a mumble incantations that no one could understand. An old person with the power to remove warts had usually learned the arcane art from an even older person willing to relinquish his or her own claim to dark power, for having passed along the secret one was no longer able to remove warts. My great aunt Lou had the power to remove warts. Once my brother and I went to see her to have our warts charmed away. Her first requirement was that we believe in her power. Both of us said that we did, but I held the secret reservation that I would believe fully only after my wart had disappeared. Aunt Lou took my brother by the hand, went into some kind of a trance, her deep blue eyes appearing to see us only incidentally as they became fixed on something through and far beyond us, began to rub his warts lightly with the tips of her fingers, and muttered in a hollow voice some incantation that we could not understand. Then she repeated the mysterious formula as she rubbed my wart. We were instructed to forget about the charm and promised that within a few days we would find that our warts were gone, if we had faith. A week later my brother's warts had disappeared, but it was necessary that I have a physician burn mine off after I was in college. Even though it had been bitten off later by an antagonist in a family fight, it had grown back much improved from the experience. My brother never doubted the efficacy of our Aunt Lou's magical powers. Lacking faith, I had to resort to science.

One might also "cause his warts to go away" by practicing the black arts on his own. He could prick the wart, rub the blood on a white grain of corn, and feed the corn to a black hen, and the wart would mysteriously transfer itself from his hand to the inside of the hen's craw; or, he could "sell" his warts by rubbing a penny over them, placing the penny conspicuously beside the road at a fork in it, and letting some person pick up the coin. One's wart would go away and reappear on the hands of the one who had picked up the penny. One could also steal a soiled dishrag, rub his wart with it, and bury the dishrag in the "leak" of the house. As the dishrag rotted, the wart would disappear. One overly scrupulous about petty thievery might prefer to bathe his wart secretly at sun-up in spunkwater from a decaying stump and say nothing about what he had done while the wart was disappearing.

There were also effective but less magical ways of removing warts. Tying a string tightly around a wart and tightening the string a little each day would cause the wart to dry up and drop off. Rubbing a wart daily with concentrated liquor derived from boiling oak chips would cause it to peel off. Touching a wart each day with canned lye would burn it away. Anointing a wart with oil obtained from earthworms ("redworms") placed in a bottle and left to broil in the sun would remove it. The same treatment was used for bleaching moles and freckles and for relief from rheumatism and aching joints. A less painful treatment was to rub iron rust on the wart daily until it went away.

Certain people were said to possess the power for drawing the fire from flesh burns. Like wart charmers, their powers were secret and were passed along to successors. They, too, muttered incantations, thought to be verses from the Bible, as they passed their hands lightly over burns. They did not accept pay for their services. A less magical treatment for burns was to bathe them in cold water for a while, rub baking soda over them, and bind them up with a clean, white cloth. Sometimes burns were treated with applications of fresh cow manure.

A plaque of lead suspended on a string around a child's neck warded off colds and kept witches away while the child was sleeping. Children plagued by nightmares could wear these lead charms to assure themselves of sweet sleep and pleasant dreams, for nightmares were caused by witches and evil creatures that could not operate in the presence of lead. Adults given to snoring and nightmares sought relief by smelling a dirty sock as they went to sleep.

No one in my family was bitten by a poisonous snake, though copperheads were found from time to time on the farm. We heard accounts of how persons who had been bitten had been treated. Applying the entrails of a chicken to the bitten place was said to "draw the pizen out." It was said that one could see the poison passing into a bottle of whiskey pressed tightly against a snake bite. We were instructed never to pick up a snake that we thought we had killed, for though a snake might be chopped into several pieces with a hoe it will not actually die until it thunders or the sun goes down. Experienced snake-killers, in fact, would hang dead snakes on fences to induce thunder and rainfall in dry, hot weather. We believed, too, that it was necessary to be especially careful in watching out for snakes where dragon flies "used," for dragon flies, which we called "snakefeeders," were said to gather food for water moccasins. We did not actually have water moccasins in my valley, but all watersnakes were referred to as moccasins.

We heard terrifying tales about snakes we should "watch out for." The glass snake, which glistened in the sunlight like a string of beads, could pursue one with almost lightning speed. If one were so fortunate as to escape from a glass snake and strike it with a club, it would break itself up and disappear in the grass and weeds; the parts would then reassemble, and it would resume its pursuit. The dreadful hoopsnake was even more dangerous, for it, too, pursued people, taking its tail in its mouth and rolling along like a hoop. When it was within striking distance, it would straighten itself out and shoot itself like an arrow at the person attacked. It had a hard stinger at the tip of its tail. Its poison was so powerful that one stricken by it dropped dead on the spot. If it should happen to miss its aim and drive itself into a tree, even the leaves on the tree would be wilting by the time one could look up. Though less formidable than either the glass snake or the hoopsnake, the blowing viper was to be given a wide berth, for he could rise on his tail and dance through the grass toward one with incredible speed. Within reach, he would flatten his head and blow his poison breath in your face, and you would die immediately. In windy weather, children needed to be doubly cautious about blowing vipers, because their treacherous songs sounded very much like the wind blowing through ripe, dry grass.

Blue racers, though they did not bite, were dangerous snakes. They were able to charm victims, including cattle and people, and would conceal themselves along the lower limbs of trees on hot days and wait for a colt, a calf, or a child to come to rest under the limb. Then they anchored themselves to the limb, lashed themselves with lightning speed around the neck of their prey, and choked it to death. If the prey started to flee and the snake was able to look it in the eye, the prey became transfixed or "charmed" and the racer choked it to death by drawing it tightly toward the limb. The blue racer fed on birds. While robbing a nest, it would lie quietly while waiting for the mother bird to return. Then it "charmed" her and ate her too. It was the same snake that would race you to the foot of the hill if you should happen upon it while picking berries, or gathering nuts, or hunting for the cows. It wouldn't bite you, but if it could catch up with you it might choke you to death, particularly if it could catch your eye and charm you before it commenced.

Sometimes snakes came into the house. Once the sill of my Grandpa's house began to decay and the wall and floor separated, leaving a crack an inch or two wide. One night my aunt, before she married, was fixing her bed. When she pulled down the cover, there lay a big snake coiled comfortably in the middle of her bed. She screamed and the snake raced off the bed but became confused about where to find the crack. When Granny understood that there was a snake in the house, she grabbed from the top of the kitchen stove a pot of scalding water, rushed into the room, and dashed the water on the snake, which, by then, was just ready to dart into the crack. The snake was able to make it to the crack, but not before several of its little white feet became visible as it dragged itself into the crack. Granny declared that she had never seen a snake with feet before or since. My aunt "snaked" her bed thereafter each night until a new sill was placed under the house after the crops were "laid by."

My father prepared each spring a "batch of bitters" for toning up our bodies after the long winters during which our food consisted mostly of staples, dried and pickled vegetables, dried and canned fruit, molasses, and milk and butter. We needed to have our blood cleaned, our bowels opened up, our skin cleared, and our nerves settled.

After the sap had risen in the trees and tender young plants had shot up from the floors of the woodlots, he would take an axe, a mattock, and a sack into the woods one morning and gather barks and roots needed for making bitters. A few times I went along with him to help carry the tools.

I do not remember all of the ingredients. If I recall correctly, they were not always the same from year to year and the proportions varied according to my father's judgment on what medication needs were greatest considering the rigor of the winter and the nature of our complaints and ailments. He dug roots of the slippery elm, the wild cherry, the red oak, the yellow willow, the poplar, and the sassafras. He peeled the tender bark from the spicewood bush, the sweet birch, and the ironwood bush. He included roots of a few blackberry bushes. We found wild ginger, the rattlesnake weed, mayapple, and yellow root. We then gathered dandelion, wild lettuce, sheep sorrel, and ladyslipper.

The afternoon was spent washing the materials and shaving bark from the roots. When it was cleaned and ready, it was dumped into a black cast-iron kettle, covered with water, and placed on the back of the cookstove, to simmer when the stove was hot and to steep and blend between heatings. After two or three days the red liquid, which my father called "ooze," was strained through layers of white cloth into a churn and allowed to settle for another day. Then he would carefully dip out the ooze and fill jars half-full with it. He dumped a handful of rock candy into each jar and finished filling it with 110 proof white whiskey. All of the jars were sealed and set in a row under the safe in the dining room to wait for the rock candy to dissolve. It seems to me that a week or ten days was required for the candy to dissolve. In the meantime the whiskey had blended evenly with the ooze, producing a ruby red liquid, the color determined largely by the amount of cherry bark that had been included in the mixture, my father said.

After the rock candy had dissolved, the bitters were strained through a white cloth again into earthen jugs, corked, and allowed to age for a few days. The concoction was ready for consumption by the middle of May. At dinnertime my father would produce the jug and pour for each of us a shot of bitters, which he dumped into a juice glass. We sipped the bittersweet and heady drink before eating. Its high alcohol content made us happy and improved our appetites and we developed a taste for the blend of bitter, flavorsome, and sweet oozes subsumed by the powerful whiskey and made gentle by the rock candy. His bitters were our spring tonic. I do not know whether it possessed all of the medicinal properties he claimed for it, but as an appetizer it brought us much joy at dinnertime.

We usually drank sassafras tea at breakfast time for a week or two each spring. The tea was made by boiling shavings from the roots of the red sassafras in water and sweetened with molasses. The light red liquid, taken steaming hot from teacups, was thought to be good for our bowels and our blood. As I recall, we drank sassafras tea at the same time in the spring that we each took a teaspoonful of sulphur and molasses before breakfast to build our blood, prevent boils, and brighten our skin. None of us ever had acne or pimples on our faces as we grew through adolescence.

It was considered most important that we take something periodically to move our bowels. When we were small children we were given castor oil from a spoon and a few sips of cold coffee to wash it down and to improve the taste in our mouths. Our mother preferred black draught and our father Epsom salts, both bartered for at the country store. As we grew older each chose the laxative that suited him best. Taking a laxative, the first important step in curing almost every ailment that befell us, was considered also an important preventative for colds and fevers, headaches, heartburns, acidulous stomachs, constipation, sleeplessness, and general listlessness. It was not until after I had graduated from college that I learned how to keep my bowels regular by choosing the foods I ate.

The child in Appalachia had a remarkably strong will to live. The mortality rate was surprisingly low, except for those instances in the 1880's and 1890's, when diphtheria, bloody flux, and scarlet fever swept across the land, wiping out even whole families within a week. Whether folk remedies were really effective or children survived because they were of a hardy race subsisting on the nutritious food produced from Appalachian soil must remain a moot question.

My First Hitchhiking Trip

I had never taken a hitchhiking trip. George Buckner, who had transferred to Cumberland College from Stuart-Robinson, invited me to hitchhike with him to Berea, where he had a girl friend enrolled in the academy there. I knew many students from my section of Lawrence County who were enrolled there, including Betty and Pauline Morris, whose party I had attended two or three weeks before I left for college. Betty and I had exchanged letters since that time.

I agreed to be George's companion if he could wait for me to complete my four hours of work obligation on Saturday morning. He had a date with his girl friend Saturday night and felt that we would have no trouble getting to Berea in time for him to meet his date if we could leave by 1:30. It was easier, he explained, for two nicely dressed college boys to hitch a ride than for one traveling alone to do so. He had been fairly successful at hitching rides, especially when he had a companion.

The job for the work crew on Saturday morning, October 20, 1928, was to move an old tool house from its location near the gray brick administration building to a site behind Roburn Hall, where it was to be used as a garage. I was assigned to a group to carry rocks on their backs from behind the gymnasium to the new location; the rocks were for use as corner stones. We carried them over the viaduct that connected the two parts of the campus. Although it was a cool, but bright and pleasant day, we were all covered with dust, perspiring, and tired when we were released at noon.

Following lunch in the dining hall in the basement of Johnson Hall, I hurried on to Felix Hall, took a shower and shaved, and dressed myself in collegiate clothes. George was waiting for me.

We had walked through town, across the bridge, and a mile beyond when a Mr. Steeley picked us up. He let us out in Corbin. We then walked through Corbin and about two miles beyond. A salesman picked us up and took us to within three miles of London. We stood at a bend in the road and flung our thumbs for a while, but no one stopped for us. George explained that most of those in the passing cars probably lived in London and, recognizing us as collegians, did not want to interfere with any opportunities we might have for longer rides.

With this discouraging thought in mind, we began walking again. As we walked through London we were impressed by the liveliness of the town on Saturday afternoon, the lovely homes set back from the streets and surrounded by fine oak trees, many of which still held wine colored leaves, and Sue Bennett College lying along a low ridge to the left of town. We continued walking for about three miles beyond the town before a farmer in a battered car picked us up and took us five miles up the road. We asked how far it was on to Livingston. He did not know for sure, but it was eight miles to the bridge across Rockcastle River.

The sun was low and riding in a bank of purple clouds along the hilltops to the west when the farmer let us out of his car. We started on. Fewer and fewer cars passed us. After it became so dark that we found it necessary to walk in the middle of the narrow road to keep from stumbling, the occasional driver who came by seemed to speed up at the sight of us. We could see kerosene lamps in the windows of homes, most of which were at the mouths of ravines across the river from the road. Dogs barked from far away and the river sang as its low water hurried over rapids. The gravel in the road rattled behind us as we trudged wearily along, now past conversation and each occupied with his own thoughts and memories.

We crossed the bridge about 9 o'clock and at 9:30 came to a little filling station that was still open. We went in. A woman holding a baby, two teenage girls, and a man who had driven up just before we arrived were in the station. The lively conversation and laughing we had heard as we approached the station stopped altogether as we entered. Addressing ourselves to the man, we explained that we were hitchhiking but that no one had been willing to pick us up after dark came. We thought we had walked a total of perhaps twenty miles since leaving the college campus. We were tired and would love to stay overnight somewhere close by if he could recommend a place. We hoped he might offer to keep us, but he explained that the nearest place to spend the night was the hotel in Livingston six miles away.

We asked him whether he would be willing to drive us into Livingston, and told him that we had money to pay him. He was afraid to undertake the trip in his car, because his radiator leaked pretty badly. Very hungry and thirsty, we bought soft drinks and a box of cookies and ate them. Conversation began again, but it was guarded and lacked the conviviality we had noted as we approached the station. After we finished our drinks and returned the bottles to the rack, we started on.

We had walked only a few yards away when the man called and told us to wait a few minutes and he would try to take us into Livingston. We stopped by the roadside. Following conversation that we could not hear, he brought a bucket of water and filled up his radiator, although most of the water from the bucket must have missed the spout, for we could hear it splashing and spattering on the ground.

After we were in the car he told us that the girls had urged him to take us to town because, they had said, we were not bums but college boys out on an adventure. We showed him our wide belt buckles on which Cumberland College had been inscribed. When he let us out at the hotel in Livingston each of us gave him fifty cents, the first money we had spent for travel on our trip.

We went directly to the railroad station, which, if I recall correctly, was behind the hotel, and bought tickets to Berea. The next northbound train was due at about 1:45 a.m. Still hungry, we went to a little restaurant where each of us ate a hamburger and drank a cup of coffee. Then we lay on benches in the waiting room at the station and slept until the train arrived. We were the only passengers to board the train at Livingston and no one got off there. Our coach was dark. There were not many passengers in it, and those few, mostly men, were sleeping with their faces covered with their hats. We found seats across the aisle from each other and went to sleep.

We arrived in Berea at 2:50. The station was open and the master was on duty in his office. Lights in the waiting room had been turned off, but enough light from the office came into the room for us to see that there were many people lying on the benches; a family group, perhaps five or six including small children, lay on newspapers spread on the floor in a corner of the room. George found a bench, but only seats were left for me. I looked around and found a newspaper in the wastebasket. I spread it on the floor beside George's bench and lay down on my hard bed. George slept soundly, but I was wakeful and uncomfortable. Many of the sleepers snored loudly, a small child in the corner whimpered occasionally while the mother tried to comfort it in a low voice, and freight trains roared past, it seemed, every time I was getting into a sound sleep.

We got up about 6 o'clock, in time to see a glorious sunrise over the distant hills. We washed our faces at the tap in the untidy washroom and left. We walked up and down the streets, through the college campus, and beyond to what appeared to be a second business section. I was amazed at the size of the campus— it was a much larger school than I had imagined. I was also impressed by the property and the industries the college owned. We wandered over the campus, back and forth, a long time before students began coming out of dormitories on their way to breakfast.

George and I went into a little restaurant that belonged to the college. While eating a breakfast consisting of a cup of coffee and an egg sandwich, I saw Douglas Sparks, a young man from Blaine, pass the window. I rushed out and hailed him. He pointed out his dormitory and invited me to come to see him after he had returned from breakfast. I went back into the restaurant and finished eating my breakfast. We then went to the dormitory, where we found Eulas Dobbyns, Howard Moore, Claude West, whom I knew, and others from Lawrence County whom I had not met. We washed our faces again, arranged our hair, adjusted our bow ties, and went along with the group to chapel; attendance was required of everyone.

The auditorium was filled to capacity. Claude West thought there must have been three thousand persons present. We were seated in the balcony. I could see Betty and Pauline Morris and Blanche Williams seated in the balcony at the end of the auditorium but was never able to attract their attention and never did get to speak to them while I was on the campus. A large orchestra with many instruments played unusually well, it seemed to me. There was also a religious service, and President Hutchins spoke, but I do not remember the nature of the service or what President Hutchins talked about.

Following the chapel exercises we went with Eulas Dobbyns to his room, where we cracked walnuts he and his friends had gathered. Claude West took us on a tour of some of the buildings, including a barnlike gymnasium with walls of upright boards and battens. On the tour we passed two boys engaged in a quarrel. One of them was Chinese, the first Oriental I had ever seen. He was greatly agitated and speaking in rapid-fire broken English that I could not understand.

My friends invited us to stay for lunch at the college, but thinking that we might not have enough time to make our way back to the railroad depot for the early afternoon train, we left before lunch. George had not been able to talk with his girl friend, but we would have to take that early afternoon train, we decided.

On the way to the station, we stopped and rested on a rock wall in front of one of the buildings on campus. While we were sitting there, a car passed in which we recognized some young men whom we had hailed for a ride the preceding day. Recognizing us, they stuck their heads from the windows, called us bums, cursed us, and told us to "get for home." Our pride was hurt so deeply that we merely looked at each other perplexedly and said nothing.

At the station we discovered that we did not have enough money between us to buy tickets to Williamsburg, or even to Corbin, so we bought tickets to London for $1.48 each, which left me with only a quarter in my pocket and Buckner with nothing. When we got off the train at London we started walking the thirty-one miles to Williamsburg.

About two miles below London we came upon a car wreck. We stopped and heard one of the victims of the wreck relate pathetically his account of what had happened. Before he had finished, a well-dressed man in a shining new car stopped to learn the particulars of the accident. After the victim, repeating what he had told us, completed his story, we asked the man whether he would give us a ride to Corbin. He studied our appearance for a few seconds. We decided later that he was impressed by our being dressed up and looking clean but that he also probably thought we were in some way involved in the wreck. He took us and let us out on the north side of Corbin.

We walked through the town and along the edge of the highway, crowded with Sunday afternoon traffic, for perhaps a half mile before two young men picked us up and let us out on the campus at 5:40. I hurried to my room, brushed my teeth, grabbed my B.Y.P.U. quarterly, and rushed to the church, where I was the captain of the group that led discussion in the program for the meeting. At the church my self-esteem began to be restored and fleeting memories of the hitchhiking trip were more pleasant than I had thought they might be.

After the meeting I walked down to the Sweet Shoppe and spent my quarter for a light but inadequate supper, the only food I had eaten since the black walnut kernels I had cracked for myself in Eulas Dobbyns' room that morning.

I had a date with a little blonde-haired girl by the name of Adkins who lived on the mountain across the river from town and attended the Holiness church, but I was too tired for the date. I was to meet her at the church and walk home with her. I went to the church, where the services had already begun and fervor was mounting as the brethren shouted amen to the preacher, upon whom the spirit had descended. I slipped inside the door and stood against the wall of the crowded little church until I picked out my date, who was sitting near the end of a bench opposite a window. I took a notepad from my pocket, wrote her a note telling her that I would not be able to keep my date, slipped out of the house, and handed it through the window to a young woman sitting near her. I waited until she had read it and recognized me at the window.

Back in the dormitory I met James Bowling, who invited me to his room to eat Vienna sausage and crackers. Following this feast, I went to my room to study, but I was too tired. I fell into bed and slept hard until my alarm clock woke me at 4 A.M. I then prepared for my classes, but the day was a dull one. I wrote in my diary at the end of the day that I thought I would not be taking another hitchhiking trip soon, for "the reaction is more unpleasant than the action is pleasant."

"The Person and the Big World"
Commencement Address, Cumberland College,
May 8, 1982[3]

I came to Cumberland College in 1928 when I was seventeen years old, one of ninety freshmen, fifty of whom were valedictorians or salutatorians of their high school graduating class. That was a critical year in the molding of my future and I have no doubt that Cumberland made a profound difference in my life. In the area of values, it was not long before the values of the teachers began to become my values, too, and the competitive environment emphasized, nourished, encouraged, and even made exciting the pursuit of excellence in scholarship, but, perhaps, most importantly, my pleasant interactions with teachers and serious-minded students nurtured a personal but somewhat muted confidence in myself that I could succeed at other institutions, bigger, tougher, less caring places like the University of Kentucky, and that I could succeed professionally after I was through school.

Cratis Williams in Lexington, Kentucky, during his days at the University of Kentucky.

It was important that I arrive at that conclusion at the age of seventeen. Cumberland College has helped thousands of insecure teenagers, up to eighty percent of them even more insecure because they were, like myself, from so-called deprived Appalachia, to gain the self-confidence needed for success. Cumberland has prepared many an individual to go as one person into the big, big world beyond the campus, that real world of cutthroat competition, struggle for fortune and power, and political duplicity.

You graduates are this day stepping out of an age of innocence. With confidence and self-esteem each of you is to contend in a world that might not show any signs of significant improvement since you arrived at this pleasant wooded retreat four years ago. You are essentially alone as you develop your own position. Soon you will run head-on into those who must be dealt with but whose position is "This and only this is the truth. I hold this truth to be sacred and incontestable. I am therefore absolutely and incontrovertibly right." You see the gap between stated values and performance in your leaders, your bosses, your colleagues. You see charismatic charlatans and self-seekers exploiting on every hand the timid, the fearful, those with shaky self-confidence and frail self-esteem. But with your own knowledge, wisdom, confidence, you deal with your interpersonal and social problems not with steely eyed cynicism but with a healthy skepticism sustained by compassion and respect for those who would mobilize you for their truths, their positions, their schemes for self-promotion. But certainly your own success as a liberally educated person will be assured by your own ability to remain an individual prepared to assess, consider, and choose those positions consonant with your own concept of truth and your own vision of justice and make those decisions that are right and comfortable for you.

You are now perhaps twenty-two or twenty-three years old, the age at which one thinks he has attained maturity. Maturity has been touted as a desired stage in the life process. I remain at least teasingly skeptical about that. Maturity too often is a flat, dull, half-dying, and unyielding surrender to mediocrity, sometimes a mediocrity propped up and held in place by threatening posturing and intimidating affectation. I am myself mature, even at my age, only in tightly structured and formal situations over which I exert no control, like weddings, funerals, dedications, somber occasions at which the bishop or the governor speaks, graduation exercises, and the like. Otherwise, I am mostly my real self, not much different from the curious, playful, teasing, happy boy who at the age of 13 rode his father's farm wagon out of an Appalachian hollow to school. Without regard for how I might look to you young people with vitality in your smooth skin, hair on your head, and color in your hair, I am young, too, have always been, and hope to remain so. Recently I came upon this revealing passage in a book by Tom Robbins called *Still Life with Woodpecker:*

> Humans have evolved to their relatively high state by retaining the immature characteristics of their ancestors. Humans are the most advanced of mammals—although a case could be made for the dolphins—because they seldom grow up. Behavioral traits such as curiosity about the world, flexibility of response, and playfulness are common to practically all young mammals but are usually rapidly lost with the onset of maturity in all but humans. Humanity has advanced, when it has advanced, not because it has been sober, responsible, and cautious, but because it has been playful, rebellious, and immature.

What a gem to find in the writings of Tom Robbins!

And then there is the matter of happiness. Alas, it, too, I fear, is something one has all the time and carries with him out into the big world. He does not find it out there. In the first place, it appears to be more an attribute than a discreet quality anyway. It is not so much a thing as it is a condition. One does not so much expect another to bring him happiness as he hopes to share his happiness with her. Love plaints, repeated ad infinitum, from Nashville wail out the miseries of the forlorn lover who depended upon another for happiness. When can we learn that happiness is self-generated!

Socrates, that incurably youthful octogenarian condemned to die for debasing the gods and corrupting the youth (that is, for challenging unexamined assumptions about religion and subverting prejudices that posed as truth), said to his students, "Know thyself." It took a long time for it to happen, but ultimately two whole new fields of knowledge, psychology and psychiatry, rose in response to Socrates' imperative. Knowing the world is really extending oneself. What is needed, then, is a multitude of good and just men and women to extend themselves to encompass the world. But the first challenge is to know oneself, the most difficult of subjects to master.

The second challenge is to be creative. In accepting this challenge, be prepared for the self-sacrifice that is often required of the person who is innovative, creative, and out front. One who discovers himself knows that he does not exist for the sake of any other and that no other person exists for him. He knows the injury of subservience and the insult of using others. He stands alone and is not against others. His vision is his own. But he does not condemn others for their vision, for he knows every one who has vision has a unique vision. His happiness rises out of the depths of his own personality. Secondhanders, imitators, incomplete persons, depending almost solely on others for their uncertain status and their weak well-being, are more jealous of happiness in others than they are of wealth, position, or power. They are servile in the presence of wealth, especially, but they are belligerent in the presence of happiness, the one attribute that they are unable to tolerate in another.

The happy inventor, discoverer, articulator of truth may be required by the mob or those whose power base is threatened to offer blood sacrifice for his creation. The unsubmissive one whose creation runs counter to the dogma supporting institutions or creeds is vulnerable. Prometheus, accused of stealing fire from the gods, was chained to a rock and torn by vultures. Adam, who ate the fruit of the tree of knowledge, was driven from Paradise. Socrates, for raising uncomfortable questions, was condemned to drink hemlock tea. Jesus, whose message to mankind threatened both the established church and the state, was crucified. Lincoln, who would save mankind, was assassinated for his pains. Men have always crucified their saviors.

Civilization has been a progression from one crushed truth to the next, each new civilization moving a bit closer, as Ayn Rand said in *The Fountainhead* "toward a society of privacy." Becoming one's self is moving toward the independence that is the prized possession of the private person. A great society provides room for its citizens to be private. Of all the mammals, only man has the ability to laugh and to blush. Mark Twain once observed that "only man blushes, or needs to." Oddly enough, man finds it easier to laugh at others and blush for himself. The challenge is to learn how to laugh at yourself and dissipate blushing altogether. One who can laugh at himself has learned how to put himself in perspective, to see himself as he really is. Laughter at self cleanses and purifies as tensions are released. But laughter directed at others is cruel and unforgivable. The stereotype of the stern, unsmiling Puritan captures the notion of our Puritan forebears that laughter is evil, sinful and has no place in a Christian society, but Puritans enjoyed private humor and were amused as individuals at discrepancies between theory and practice. Even stern old Cotton Mather could smile at himself occasionally. Humor and happiness are congenial companions. Learn to laugh, and happiness sits beside you.

In closing, I congratulate each of you on your achievements, urge you to gratitude to Cumberland College and its splendid faculty and to those back home whose confidence and support contributed to your being here, and advise that your education, which has just begun, continue as you progress toward self-discovery while becoming more and more that ever youthful person with vision who seeks truth and justice and the independence that can enable you to stand alone creatively but with the leavening of humor to sustain you as a mentally healthy person. You may be a martyr, you may be a leader, or you may be a nincompoop, but in any case, be yourself as you know yourself to be out there in that big crazy world.

NOTES

1. The complete account of teaching in the one-room Boggs School on Caines Creek is published as Cratis Williams, 1995. *I Become a Teacher: A Memoir of One-Room School Life in Eastern Kentucky.* Ed. James M. Gifford. Ashland, Ky.: The Jesse Stuart Foundation.

2. "When I gave you an account of a double murder that took place near my home a week before I left for college in the fall of 1929, you urged me to write down the story I told. Since some of the descendants of the old man involved in the murder have become successful professional and business people, I have assigned fictitious names to the characters in order to save the family from possible embarrassment if the account should ever be made public"— Cratis Williams to Jerry Williamson and Patricia Beaver, August 31, 1978.

3. Cratis Williams delivered this commencement address at Cumberland College in 1982; in May of 1984, he received an honorary doctorate from Cumberland.

Family Expressions
and Comments[1]

"Turn Off for Hell at Henry Creech's"

Some men had gathered around our well one hot Saturday afternoon to drink the cool, sweet water and rest from the heat. The moderator of the local hardshell church, so drunk he could barely manage to stay in his saddle, rode up, slid off his black nag, and drew a bucket of cold water. While he was drinking long and deeply from the dipper, one of the men teased him about a woman in his flock about whom there had been some "whispering." The preacher straightened up and proclaimed in what approached the holy tone, "W'y, I think she's the sweetest thing that ever stepped in shoe leather and the purtiest woman that ever pissed on the ground."

The men roared with laughter. Stunned for a moment, the preacher realized that he had bared more of his soul than he had meant to do. He leapt on his old nag, drove his spurs into her flanks, and took off across the wooden bridge. At the fork of the road across the valley, he turned up the creek and disappeared past the church, of which he was the moderator, at breakneck speed.

A day or two later Norman Blevins reported that his father was sitting on his porch when the preacher went racing past his yard on Blaine Trace, perhaps five miles from our home. The poor horse was wet with sweat and looking as if it were ready to drop in the middle of the big road.

Mr. Blevins had called out, "Where are you going in such a hurry, preacher?"

"I'm a-goin' to hell, by God."

"You've gone too far, " Mr. Blevins said. "If you want to go to hell, you ought to have turned off back up here at Henry Creech's."

The preacher wheeled his poor horse suddenly in the middle of the road and went charging back toward Henry Creech's.

In our family a euphemism for "go to hell" was "turn off at Henry Creech's."

"Virgie and the Young 'ens Like to Hear You"

Joe Johnson, after sampling moonshine from the jars of several cronies waiting in the bushes for the shouting at the meeting to begin, staggered into the hardshell church to sit with his wife and daughters back in the sinner section. After stumbling noisily over the feet of several people, he made it to a seat beside his wife. In his "best behavior" posture he sat upright and listened intently at the preacher, but the warmth around him soon made him sleepy. He began to nod and to come out of his catnaps with low grumbling, which his wife quieted by nudging him gently with her elbow.

After a while Joe slumped and his head drooped forward. Soon he began to snore. His wife nudged him gently again, but he did not respond. Just as the preacher dropped from his chant to a conversational tone, Joe's wife stuck her elbow in his side with force. Joe sat upright and listened, all attention.

The preacher declared that he had "held forth a long time" and would now "give way to one of the other brethern."

Joe, thinking his wife had struck him with her elbow to summon him to do something about the preacher's decision to "give way," commanded for all to hear, "Why, just preach right on, brother. Virgie and the young 'ens like to hear you."

One of our sayings, when one of us offered a distracting irrelevant remark, was "Preach right on, Brother. Virgie and the young 'ens like to hear you."

"Me a Pint, Jay a Pint, and Bal a Pint"

A poor widow lived with her two small grandsons on our creek. She tried her best to make ends meet from one year to the next by growing a good garden, a few small truck patches, and an acre or two of corn for her bread, preparing the soil and cultivating with her hoe. In late winter her cow died.

Hearing that Big Nelse Boggs, a prosperous farmer and storekeeper, had a cow to sell, she trudged with a basket of eggs for barter on her arm to his store one cold day, her head wrapped with a dark "fascinator" under her deep black poke bonnet. After she had traded, she stood for a moment at the counter, before asking in her deep, slow voice, "Mr. Boggs, have you got ary milk cow you would sell?"

"Yes, I have a young cow that came fresh last spring that I would like to sell."

"How much air ye a-astin' fer 'er?"

"Thirty-five dollars."

"How much milk does she give?"

"Oh, I don't know for sure. About a gallon, I reckon."

The old lady was thoughtful for a few moments. "Well, I don't want her, I guess. I don't want a cow that gives that much milk. I want a cow that will give me a pint, Jay a pint, and Bal a pint."

When we wanted to be sure not to buy more of anything than we needed, we would say, "I just want me a pint, Jay a pint, and Bal a pint."

"The Mare Might Kick You"

Uncle Ad Conway drove the mail wagon from Webbville, Kentucky, to the Sacred Wind post office at the head of the Left Fork of Caines Creek. Uncle Ad, also a Primitive Baptist elder, was a slow-spoken, creaking old fellow on his feet and was fond of moralizing in his conversations with people along his route who came out to the road to receive their mail from him. Even when he spoke gravely and gallantly to old ladies who were expecting no mail but sat on their porches or their steps while stringing beans or peeling potatoes, he would add beatific observations like, "It's a glorious day the Lord has provided for us," or, "Sister, the Lord is blessing us with this bounty of much-needed rain." Schoolchildren along the way, knowing Uncle Ad as a patient and good man but somewhat perplexed by his moralizing and his all-positive view of the world and all that lay therein, enjoyed pestering him.

Once, while he had stopped to put mail in our box, an eight or ten year old schoolboy on his way home from school, was climbing astride the coupling pole for his wagon to snitch a short ride. When he was ready to resume his journey, Uncle Ad turned and said to the boy gently and tenderly, "Don't, son, don't. The mare might kick you, and your parents would always blame me for it."

The likelihood of Uncle Ad's poor flea-bitten mare's kicking the little boy on the pole extending from the end of the wagon seemed next to impossible to us. When we wanted someone to stop what he was doing but could think of no logical reason why we were making the request, we would quote Uncle Ad, "Don't, son, don't. The mare might kick you."

"Will Your Bull Come for Calling?"

Uncle Lewis Sparks, when he was old and suffering from hardening of the arteries, brought his cow one Saturday afternoon to Arbie Gambill's farm for service. My brother Ralph was visiting with Ora Gambill, his high school classmate, at the time.

Mrs. Gambill asked Ora and Ralph to go with Uncle Lewis to the pasture in which the bull was kept. They saw the bull grazing contentedly on the flat above the second steep of the bush-grown field. It was decided that it would be easier to lead the muzzled cow to the bull than to drive the bull off the hill.

Ora and Ralph took charge of the cow and Uncle Lewis, a stout stick in his hand, followed. When they had led the cow to the flat above the first steep, they stopped to give Uncle Lewis, who was puffing, time to catch up.

When he was up with them, Uncle Lewis straightened up while clinging to his stick, and said without pause, "My old heart just goes pitty-pat, pitty-pat, pitty-pat! Do you know Willie Cordle's boys [his grandsons] that go down there to that high school? Will your bull come for callin'! Sook, sook, sook, sook, sook!"

When one of us talked in many directions at once, we would respond, "Will your bull come for callin'? Sook, sook, sook, sook, sook!"

"Thirty Cents and a Turkey Hen"

Men in our community would sometimes meet on rainy days to visit with one another and swap stories on the porches of country stores. At one of those meetings they got around to swapping accounts of how they had been able to get ahead in the world. The last to tell his story, an unlearned stutterer, had been able, after working hard and managing his affairs well, to buy his own farm. He had built new fences, bought a span of young mules, developed pastures for several head of fat cattle, and improved the buildings. He began his account with "F-f-f-fer, w'y now, you know, fellers, I -s-s-started out, dis w'y now, you know, wif f-f-f-furty cents and a turrrkey hen."

His story impressed his listeners so much that a saying in the community for accounting for the success of one who had begun from scratch was that he had started out with thirty cents and a turkey hen.

"A Bull's Pedigree"

One of the farmers in our valley took his cow to a neighbor's farm to be serviced by a young registered bull. The neighbor was not at home but his wife went along with the farmer to the lot in which the bull was kept. To make conversation while the bull was preparing to mount the cow, the farmer asked, "How far back does your beast's pedigree go?" The wife, puzzled for a moment, looked at the pawing bull and responded, "Well, I don't know how far back it goes, but you can see for yourself how far down it comes."

An observation we would make in response to an illogical statement was, "Well, you can see for yourself how far down it comes."

"Like a Sow Coon in Mishiggan"

Aunt Lou, our grandmother's sister, liked to read a monthly news magazine while she was churning. She read slowly, for she had not gone far in school. Spelling words to herself in a low voice, she would sometimes read aloud, and haltingly, items that she found interesting. Once my brother and I stopped on a lazy summer afternoon to visit with her. She was churning in her yard.

Her poke bonnet pulled forward to shade her eyes, Aunt Lou was bending over the magazine on her lap while pumping the churn dasher with her left hand. She did not hear us as we walked into her yard.

We could hear her mumbling to herself as she spelled words and then backed up to repeat what the sentence had said. When she looked up and saw us, she said, without greeting us, "This paper says here that a great sow coon passed over Mishiggan last month and done a lot of damage."

Thereafter we often referred to windstorms as worse than the sow coon that passed over Mishiggan.

"Good Am She, Pa?"

My father told of being at our Uncle Steve's store one rainy day when many men, unable to work in their corn fields, had gathered to swap yarns and while away an idle day. One of the men bought a can of peaches, opened it with the blade of a hatchet, and was eating the peaches with a spoon Uncle Steve kept for people to use when they bought canned fruit. He was eating ginger cookies along with the peaches when his son, eight or nine years old, arrived with a basket of eggs to barter for items his mother had sent for. After the boy had traded, he stood, mouth watering, and watched his father eat the last of the cookies. He asked "Good am she, Pa?"

His father, after swallowing the last bite and crunching the last cookie, answered, "Yes, good am she, Pa."

One of the sayings in our family, when one of us was eating something good as a snack without offering to share it was, "Good am she, Pa?"

"Moving the Well"

My mother's cousin, who had worn out his farm, decided he would move to the Ousley farm on Dean's Branch and let his land lie idle for two or three years. After the "house plunder" had been piled on the wagon and the family was ready to leave, his little son said, "I don't like the water at the Ousley place. Let's take our well around there, too."

In our family a metaphor for achieving the impossible was "moving the well."

"Smoking a Rabbit Out of a Haystack"

On his way to his fields one frosty morning my father met his neighbor's two small sons hurrying along toward our house. Excited, they asked my father whether he had any matches in his pocket. "W'y, what do you need matches for?" my father asked. Both talking at once, they explained that their dog had holed a rabbit under our haystack. They had tried to twist it out with a long sawbriar, had actually hooked the briar into it once, but it had pulled away. They had stopped up the tunnel under the stack at both ends with rocks and were going to our house to borrow matches to make a fire in the hole and smoke the rabbit out. My father, exploding in a temper fit, called them "damned little edients," and sent them home.

Smoking a rabbit out of a haystack was for us a metaphor for destroying a big thing in order to have a little one.

"Many a Young 'en Would've A-Left It A-Stickin' There"

My mother used to tell us a story of when she was a little girl on Ramey Branch of Hood's Fork. She had gone with her cousins to play with some children in a home not far away. One of the children, severely retarded, was unable to talk but was permitted to play outside with the others. It was in March, when winds were beginning to stiffen the mud in the mudholes in the roads. In attempting to cross the road the retarded child became stuck up in the mud. Others helped him out, but one of his shoes slipped off in the mud. He retrieved the shoe, and with stiff yellow mud stringing from it, carried it into the house to his mother.

His mother accepted the shoe while the child babbled incomprehensibly. Looking at the child with warm compassion, she said, "Now, hain't it sweet? Hit picked up its shoe and brought it in the house. Many a young 'en would've come off and a-left it a-stickin' there."

While we were growing up we would say, by way of a compliment when we thought one of us had done a clever thing, "W'y, many a young 'en would've come off and a-left it a-stickin' there."

"As Slow as John Blythe"

John Blythe's wife was giving birth under the ministrations of a midwife and neighbor women who had gathered for the birthing party. When the wife developed problems that the midwife was unable to handle, she called for John Blythe, who was waiting in the corn crib in case he might be needed, and asked him to hurry down to Blaine and fetch a doctor as quickly as he could, for his wife was in great pain and likely to die unless a doctor could save her.

John started on foot to Blaine, six or seven miles away, but he stopped at every house on the way to report that his wife was having a hard delivery and he was on his way to get a doctor for her. Three hours after he had left home, he reached the doctor's office and reported that the midwife was calling for help with the delivery of his wife's baby. The doctor saddled his horse and hurried to John's home, but the wife had died before he arrived, but not before she had given birth to a little girl.

Thereafter people in the valley would say of one who seemed not to be doing a job fast enough to avert a crisis that he was "as slow as John Blythe."

"I Know Her When I Taste Her, Sar!"

An old man in our valley was summoned as a witness to federal court at Catlettsburg. An old-fashioned gentleman with quaint manners, he found himself in a saloon with several young whippersnappers from our valley who thought they might have some fun at the old fellow's expense. One of them offered to buy him a drink. Permitting himself to be persuaded, he was uncertain as to what he should order. While the bartender waited in front of him for his order, the one offering to treat him suggested that he might like a shot of apple brandy. He leaned forward, narrowed an eye, and jutted his chin across the bar.

"Mr. Bartender, sar," he began, "do you have any of the distilled essence of the juice of the fruit that Adam ate, sar?"

The bartender, bewildered, looked at the old man and then glanced at his companion, who winked and jerked his head toward the old man. Smiling, the bartender turned away and poured a shot of dreadfully mean popskull whiskey and handed it to the old man.

He lifted the glass, jiggled it, and watched the beads wink. Holding one nostril and then another, he sniffed the contents, one eye narrowed and the other opening wide. Then he tasted the drink.

Smacking his lips like a professional taster, he declared, "Mr. Bartender, she am the stuff! I know her when I taste her, sar!"

When passing judgment with uncertainty within the family, we often quoted the old man's, "She am the stuff! I know her when I taste her, sar!" maintaining the trick in mountain speech of using "am" in third person for dramatic effect.

"Like As If You Was A-Hoeing Corn"

"Pappy" Pleasant McCoy, who moved to Blaine from Pike County to get away from the feud between his brother Randall and the Hatfields, was a Primitive Baptist. Since there was no Primitive Baptist church in the Blaine Community, Pappy McCoy used to have a service once a year at his home, to which he invited his neighbors to hear Uncle Ad Conway, a Primitive Baptist elder from near Webbville, preach.

Uncle Ad liked to preach a long time. One warm Sunday in August Uncle Ad had just about worn his congregation down when he indicated that it was about time, he reckoned, that he come to a close.

Pappy, who had been attentive and supportive, felt that, as the host, he should offer an encouraging remark.

"Why, preach right on, Brother Ad, just like as if you was a-hoeing corn, don't you know."

We used to say, when one of us had beaten a subject to death in a long discourse, "Why, preach right on, like as if you was a-hoeing corn."

"By Crackies, Virgie Writ That Granville Has Lost His Job"

Uncle Jake liked to be the only one to tell his own secrets. He would stop at the houses up and down the creek, tell his secret, and bind his listeners to secrecy.

One evening after supper Uncle Jake, returning from the Sacred Wind post office, stopped, hitched his horse at our gate, and came into the dining room. He had a letter from his daughter Virgie, he said, but there had not been light enough for him to read it when he picked it up at the post office.

He took the letter from the envelope, unfolded it, and squinted at it by the kerosene lamp in the middle of the table, moving the letter at arm's length from his eyes. Unable to make out what was written, he folded the letter, laid it on the table, and set the lamp on top of the pie safe. Then, his back to the wall, he held the letter at arm's length again and began to read, spelling words aloud slowly, and then pronouncing them.

Virgie's folks had not been very well, he told us, letting his left hand fall, the letter clutched in it, while he offered comments. Virgie "writ" that they were having a hard time, he reported, after struggling further with the written word. Later, he paused to announce that Virgie writ that they are having hard times in Columbus. At length, he again let his left hand fall, crooked the forefinger of his right hand across the hook of his scythe-like nose, and looked intently at each of us.

"By crackies, don't you breathe a word of this to a living soul," he said, "but Virgie writ that Granville has lost his job."

Thereafter, in response to an invitation to say nothing about what appeared to be inconsequential, or not really a secret, we would hook a finger across our nose and say, "By crackies, Virgie writ that Granville has lost his job."

"Hurt, Helt's Far and Goddamnation!"

Uncle Kennis Sparks's grandson returned in a secondhand Model T from a job he had held for a few weeks "over in the state of Ohiuh." He offered to take his parents and grandparents to church on a bright Sunday morning. Proud to be riding in a car, they were "all rared back" and looking their finest when the grandson, unable to negotiate a rather narrow and sharp curve, on which he met one of the Dobbyns boys, whizzing along in his new Chevrolet, left the road, turned his car on its side, and spilled his kinfolk down a bank.

The Dobbyns boy stopped and rushed back to help. No one had been seriously injured, it seemed. When all hands were to coordinate their efforts to get the car on its wheels again, suddenly Uncle Kennis took off across the meadow and toward the creek. The Dobbyns boy called out, "Are you hurt, Uncle Kennis?"

"Hurt, helt's far and goddamnation! I air kilt."

When nothing serious was wrong with us but we wanted to make the most of what had happened, in responding to a question, we liked to quote Uncle Kennis: "Hurt, helt's far and goddamnation!"

"Scare Me Again, John Blythe"

A story was told in the valley of how John Blythe and his wife became engaged to be married. John had called on the young woman only a few times when he "popped the question." Confused and frightened, the young woman did not respond.

Realizing that his proposal had scared the young woman, John did not ask the question again the next time he was with her. In the meantime, though, she had been thinking the matter over and was prepared to say yes when he got around to asking it again. On the third date a logical time for John to ask the question again arrived, but he did not ask it. Instead, he looked at her hungrily and remained silent. At length, she said to him, "Scare me again, John Blythe." He did, she accepted, and they were married.

It became customary for one who was willing to comply to encourage a person who was finding it difficult to ask a favor by saying, "Scare me again, John Blythe."

NOTES

1. The expressions and comments included in this volume come from a "collection of family and local anecdotes that, generally, ... members of the family and persons in the community would use as commentary in response to situations. So far as I know, no folklorist has ever done anything like this"—Cratis Williams to Loyal Jones, February 18, 1985.

My Schoolmates at Middle Caines Creek School (District 49), 1917–1924

From 1917 to 1924 the following were in attendance at one time or another at the Middle Caines Creek School (District 49) in Lawrence County, Kentucky. The school met during those years in the Caines Creek United Baptist Church building. The teachers were Eugene Moore, 1917–1918; Annie Young, until Christmas, 1918; Harry Burton, remainder of 1918–1919; Randolph Boggs, 1919–1920, 1920–1921; Ulysses Williams, 1921–1922, until November 10, 1922; Lucy Morris, remainder of 1922–1923; Ora Lee Boggs, 1923–1924.

The district began with the Jake Williams farm, included Maple Branch and the Jesse (Kirby) Boggs Branch, extended up the Left Fork of Caines Creek through the Peter Sparks farm, and included all of the Right Fork and its tributaries of Caines Creek.

Curt and Burt Blankenship, twin sons of John Blankenship, widower, who lived on Riggs Fork.

Reuben (Bud), Dorothy and Myrtle Boggs, children of Ed Boggs, widower, who lived on Kirby Branch.

Otis, Roscoe, and Hazel Boggs, children of Calborne and Matilda Boggs Boggs, who lived on Kirby Branch.

Clara, Nelson, and Fred Boggs, children of Charles (Jarrett's Charley) and Minerva Moore Boggs, who lived on the Left Fork.

Harry and Henry Boggs, sons of Elisha Washington and Miranda Edwards Boggs, who lived on Maple Branch.

Osha and Ova Church Boggs, in the household of Charles (Wash's Charley) and Cosby Church Boggs, who lived on Maple Branch.

Leona, Delbert, Ova, Goldie, and Ernest Boggs, children of Han and Cora Boggs Boggs, who lived on Maple Branch.

Curtis and Lillie Boggs, children of Pleasant and Mary Boggs Boggs, who lived on Maple Branch.

John Sherman Boggs, son of Jay and Lillie Creech Boggs, who live on the Right Fork.

Ora Lee and Thomas Boggs, sons of Jason and Mariah Johnson Boggs, who live on the Right Fork.

Opal and Myrtle Boggs, daughters of Lonnie E. and Minnie Boggs Boggs, who lived on the Right Fork.

Ova, Herbert, Russell, Opal (?), and Olive Boggs, children of Henderson (Little Henry) and Mollie Blevins Bogs, who lived on Briar Fork.

Beatrice and James M. Boggs, children of Charles (Jim's Charley) and Mary Gambill Boggs, who lived on the Right Fork.

Martha Boggs, orphan and daughter of Levi and Ethel Steele Boggs, who lived with her great aunt Ella Boggs Evans on the Left Fork.

Ruby Evans, daughter of Henry and Ella Boggs Evans, who lived on the Left Fork.

Dosha, Irene, Dova, and Pauline Gambill, daughters of Lonnie C. and Mae Holbrook Gambill, who lived at the Sacred Wind post office on the Left Fork.

Opal, Olga, Ora, and Ottie Mae Gambill, children of Arbie and Cynthia Sparks Gambill, who lived on the Left Fork.

Cula Gambill, daughter of Nathan O. and Ann Boggs Gambill, who lived on the Left Fork.

Tennie, _____, and Audie Griffith, daughters of George W. (Wash) and Hester Steele Griffith, who lived on the Right Fork.

Roma Jackson, daughter of Mary Jackson, who lived on Riggs Fork.

Thomas, Homer, Arnold, and Beatrice Johnson, children of Elisha F. and Arrena Gambill Johnson, who lived on Briar Fork.

Estill, Everette, Leonard, Opal, and Lillie Hardy, children of Jim and _____ Tillson Hardy, who lived on Briar Fork.

Curtis, Con, Herbert, and Kiotis Liming, sons of Elizabeth (Bess) Boggs and Jarrett Liming, who lived on the Right Fork.

Dewey Lyon, son of Estill Lyon, who lived on Briar Fork.

Fred Miller, who lived with his aunt and uncle Ora L. and Thelma Ison Boggs on the Right Fork.

Frank Pennington, who lived at the head of Right Fork.

Virgil, Clyde, Goldie, Emmet, Gladys, and Esta Riggs, children of Wilfred and Fannie Tillson Riggs, who lived on Riggs Fork.

James and Nelson Riley, sons of Moses (Mose) Riley and _____ who lived
on Hurricane Creek in Elliott County; came to the school a part of one
year.

Amanda and Mary Sparks, daughters of Peter and Margaret Glenn Sparks,
who lived on the Left Fork.

Noah and Jake Steele, orphans, lived with their grandparents, Jarrett and
Margaret Williams Boggs on the Left Fork.

Mamie and Percy Sturgill, children of Dick and Phoebe Stephens Sturgill,
who lived on the Right Fork.

Otis Wellman, son of Elisha and Margaret (Peggy) Boggs Wellman, who lived
on Riggs Fork.

Charles Wells, son of Benjamin and Rebecca Brainard Wells, who lived on
the Right Fork.

_____, _____, Bennie, and Margaret Wells, children of Nelson and Mahala
Nicely Wells, who lived on the Right Fork.

Myrtle Whiteley, orphan, lived with her aunt and uncle Benjamin and
Rebecca Wells, who lived on the Right Fork.

Ulyssis, Ashby, Jesse, Pearl, William J. (Bill), Luther, Helen, and Mary Williams, children of Jacob P., Jr., and Emily Swann Williams, who lived
on the "main waters" of Caines Creek.

Felicia (Felse), Charles, Estill, and Elva Williams, children of David O. and
Martelia Swann Williams, who lived on the main waters of Caines
Creek.

Cratis, Mabel, and Ralph Williams, children of Curtis and Mona Whitt Williams, who lived at the Forks of Caines Creek.

Delbert, Virgil, Arnold, Lonnie, and Opal Williams, children of William S.
and Rena Boggs Williams, who lived on the Right Fork.

Carrie Wheeler, orphan, who lived in the home of her aunt and uncle Elijah
and Kate Boggs Boggs on Kirby Branch.

Coming to school occasionally were Dorothy Shepherd, daughter of Scott
Shepherd, who lived in the home of Harrison and Alma Wells Williams; Mae
(?) Campbell, who lived in the home of Lonnie and Mae Gambill; and two
girls by the name of Creech, half sisters of Lillie Creech Boggs, who spent
summer months in the home of Jay and Lillie Boggs. One summer a boy with
an Italian name and a grandson of Henry and Phoebe (Pet) Boggs Hicks
came for a few weeks. If I recall correctly, he was staying in the home of Lonnie and Minnie Boggs.

Three of the children died before completing school. Carrie Wheeler
died of jaundice ("yaller janders") in August 1919. The whole school attended
her funeral. Early one summer Tommy and Beatrice Johnson died on the
same day of dysentery ("bloody flux").

Ulyssis Williams and Ora Lee Boggs, advanced students at the time I began in 1917, became teachers of the school later. Ulyssis Williams was shot and killed while attending church on Abb Creek on November 12, 1922. All of the teachers were deceased by 1979 except Annie Young Seagraves, who was living in California. At least 41 of the 115 who attended the school in those years had died by 1979.

In 1929, after one year at Cumberland College, I returned to teach the Middle Caines Creek School, which had been moved the preceding year from the United Baptist Church building to a new building about a half mile farther up the Right Fork. While housed in the church building, the school had also been called Hillside School. In the new building it was called Boggs School. I taught the school three years. Thirty-three students were enrolled the first year, but the enrollment had declined to sixteen by the end of the third year, 1931-1932. Among those who attended the school during those years were the following:

Lillie Boggs, daughter of Pleasant and Mary Boggs Boggs, who lived on Maple Branch.

Hazel Boggs, daughter of Claborne and Matilda Boggs, who lived on the Left Fork.

Martha Boggs, orphan, who lived with her great aunt, Ella Boggs Evans.

John Sherman and Sarah Edda Boggs, children of Jay and Lillie Creech Boggs, who lived on the Right Fork.

Myrtle Boggs, daughter of Lonnie E. and Minnie Boggs Boggs, who lived on the Right Fork.

James M., Ann, and Fred Boggs, children of Charles (Jim's Charley) and Mary Gambill Boggs, who lived on the Right Fork.

Ellis Blevins, son of Dewey and Cula Gambill Blevins, who lived on Briar Fork.

Ruby Evans, daughter of Henry and Ella Boggs Evans, who lived on Left Fork.

Ora, Ottie Mae, Lorraine, June Gambill, children of Arbie and Cynthia Sparks Gambill, who lived on the Left Fork.

Sarah, Martha, and Ruby Jackson, daughters of Willie and Fariba Wells Jackson, who lived on the Right Fork.

_____ Lohman, son of an oil driller who lived for a few months on Briar Fork.

Esta Riggs, daughter of Wilfred and Fannie Tillson Riggs, who lived on Riggs Fork.

Turner and _____ Riggs, sons of Henry Riggs, who lived on Riggs Fork.

Opal, Otis, and Charles Wells, children of Lonnie and Grace Cooper Wells, who lived on Briar Fork.

Bennie, Margaret, and Rebecca Wells, children of Nelson and Mahala Nicely Wells, who lived on the Right Fork.

Myrtle Whitely, orphan, who lived in the home of her uncle and aunt Ben and Rebecca Brainard Wells.

Mary Williams, daughter of Jacob P., Jr., and Emily Swann Williams, who lived on the main waters of Caines Creek.

Elva Williams, daughter of David O. and Martelia Swann Williams, who lived on the main waters of Caines Creek.

Ralph and Ruth Williams, children of Curtis and Mona Whitt Williams, who lived at the Forks of Caines Creek.

Opal and Ray Williams, children of William S. and Rena Boggs Williams, who lived on the Right Fork.

Ulyssis (Lyss) Williams, son of Harrison and Alma Wells Williams, who lived on the Right Fork.

During the five years that I had been gone from the school, many families had moved away. Others had moved out of the branches to places along the main waters of Caines Creek. Only one student remained on Maple Branch, none on Kirby Branch, five on Briar Fork, and three on Riggs Fork. Of the forty students who attended the school from 1929 to the end of 1931–1932, six had died by 1979.

At the University of Kentucky[1]

I entered the University of Kentucky at the beginning of the second semester in February 1930. It had been possible for me to complete my reports at the close of my first year as a teacher at the Boggs School on Caines Creek and get to Lexington in time to register before classes began for the second semester. I walked from my father's home on Caines Creek to Webbville, eleven miles away, and rode railroad trains from there.

Not yet provided with adequate luggage for travel, I carried my new valise in my hand and sent old suitcases and boxes by the man who drove the mail wagon from Sacred Wind to Webbville. At Webbville I checked the luggage to Lexington.

I had never been to Lexington before, but having subscribed to the Lexington *Herald* for use in my correspondence course in newspaper reporting, I felt as if I knew a great deal about the city, the Bluegrass region, and the history of central Kentucky. Going to the university was an especially exciting prospect for me. I considered it one of the finest universities in the South and felt that I was about to attend an elite institution.

At the railroad station in downtown Lexington I engaged a taxicab to deliver me to Bradley Hall, where a room had been assigned to me. I had a roommate, an older student by the name of Graybeal who had returned to the university to complete courses required for a superintendent's certificate, for he had been elected superintendent of his home county schools beginning the following school year. Mr. Graybeal, a serious, sober type, did not invite me to go eat with him or offer to show me around campus. He wanted also to go to bed early and took many naps when he hurried back from his classes during the day. At the end of my first day I wandered down many a wrong road in my search for University Commons on the top floor of new McVey Hall.

Registration the following day occurred mostly in the Administration Building, through which we filed several times, first on one floor and then the next. But we also went to other buildings for admission to class sections. When registration was complete, I had been permitted to sign up for seven courses, or 19.3 semester hours, including English, French, newspaper reporting and editing, political science, general psychology, sociology, and military science. My teachers were L.L. Dantzler, English; Miss Horsefield, French; Marjorie McLaughlin, journalism; Roy Owsley, political science; Mr. Graham, psychology; Mr. Shannon, sociology; and Captain Gallagher, military science. Three of my classes, English, journalism, and sociology, met in McVey Hall. Political science met in the Administration Building, psychology in the Psychology Building, French in Science Hall, and military science mostly on the marching field before the Administration Building.

NOTES

1. This was the last memoir that Cratis Williams began before his death in 1985. For more discussion of his years at the University of Kentucky, see David Cratis Williams and Patricia D. Beaver, "Introduction," in Cratis Williams 1999. *The Cratis Williams Chronicles: I Come to Boone.* Boone, NC: Appalachian Consortium Press, i–xli.

Some of Cratis Williams's Kin

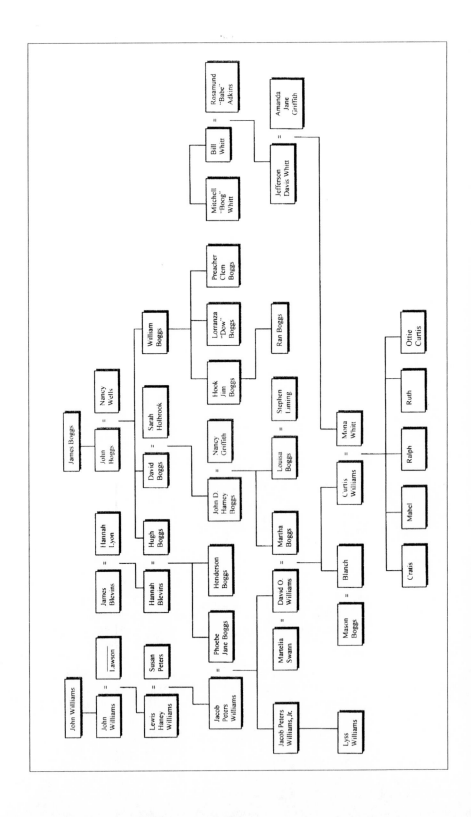

Index

Numbers in italics refer to pages with photographs